The Rise of the Federal Colossus

THE RISE OF THE FEDERAL COLOSSUS

The Growth of Federal Power from Lincoln to F.D.R.

Peter Zavodnyik

Praeger Series on American Political Culture
Jon L. Wakelyn and Michael J. Connolly, Series Editors

AN IMPRINT OF ABC-CLIO, LLC
Santa Barbara, California • Denver, Colorado • Oxford, England

Library of Congress Cataloging-in-Publication Data

Zavodnyik, Peter, 1969–
The rise of the federal colossus : the growth of federal power from Lincoln to F.D.R. / Peter Zavodnyik.
p. cm. — (Praeger series on American political culture)
Includes bibliographical references and index.
ISBN 978–0–313–39293–1 (hard copy : alk. paper) — ISBN 978–0–313–39294–8 (ebook)
1. United States—Politics and government—1865-1933. 2. Federal government—United States—History. 3. Constitutional history—United States. I. Title.
JK246.Z38 2011
320.473′04909034—dc22 2010037859

ISBN: 978–0–313–39293–1
EISBN: 978–0–313–39294–8

15 14 13 12 11 1 2 3 4 5

This book is also available on the World Wide Web as an eBook.
Visit www.abc-clio.com for details.

Praeger
An Imprint of ABC-CLIO, LLC

ABC-CLIO, LLC
130 Cremona Drive, P.O. Box 1911
Santa Barbara, California 93116-1911

This book is printed on acid-free paper ∞

Manufactured in the United States of America

To my mother and father

CONTENTS

SERIES FOREWORD

In describing the development of American literature from colonial settlement to the early twentieth century, Harvard professor Barrett Wendell noted that Britain and America began as one, particularly in shared language. "A common language, one grows to feel, is a closer bond than common blood," he wrote in *The Temper of the Seventeenth Century in English Literature* from 1904. "For at heart the truest community which men can know is community of ideals; and inextricably interwoven with the structure of any language—with its words, with its idioms, with its syntax, and nowadays even with its very orthography—are ideals which, recognized or not, have animated and shall animate to the end those who instinctively phrase their earthly experience in its terms." But after initial seventeenth-century settlement, the two diverged, leading ultimately to the eighteenth-century American Revolution. That divergence came from a lack of shared experience. While Britain rolled through the turbulence of urban growth, economic distress, and political revolution, America experienced "a period of almost stationary national temper" and retained its seventeenth-century idealism (what Wendell termed a delicate balance of common-law rights with a sense of Biblical Right) long after Britain's had passed. Thus, one common language came to be spoken in two entirely different nations. This divergence marked the creation not only of American literature, which emerged in full flower in the nineteenth century, but also a uniquely American political culture, a culture that Wendell could still see operating in the United States of William McKinley, Theodore Roosevelt, and Woodrow Wilson. This task, of understanding just what constitutes American political culture, what makes it unique from other nations as well as similar, and how that affects our current understanding of national development continues to fascinate American historians.

American political culture itself is a diverse concept, but at its base marks the boundaries, constructed over 400 years, of our political discourse and understanding. We understand political change through a particular, historically developed, American lens, unique from other nations and their collective experience. How we learn political culture is also multifaceted: from friends and family, schools and universities, media sources, religious leaders and texts, or the community institutions that shape our daily experiences of life. Daniel Walker Howe, in his seminal *Political Culture of the American Whigs* (1979), defined political culture as "an evolving system of beliefs, attitudes, and techniques for solving problems, transmitted from generation to generation and finding expression in the innumerable activities that people learn; religion, child-rearing customs, the arts and professions, and, of course, politics." Jean Baker in her *Affairs of Party: The Political Culture of Northern Democrats in the Mid-Nineteenth Century* (1983) likewise noted that "Political Culture assumes that the attitudes, sentiments, and cognitions that inform and govern politics are not random arrangements, but represent (if only we could see them as an anthropologist does the tribal rites of Tikopia) coherent patterns that together form a meaningful whole." This collection of impressions and attitudes we call "American political culture," distinct from other national traditions, is framed by the intellectual debates, party clashes, partisan disputes, religious difficulties, and economic stresses experienced since the eighteenth century and earlier. Put differently, Alexander Hamilton and Thomas Jefferson have been dead since the early nineteenth century, yet we still maneuver in the intellectual arena of political culture they constructed. American political culture, worthy of study in its own right, also helps frame contemporary policy disputes that rankle us in the twenty-first century. No debate over health care, environmental issues, foreign affairs, or economic policy occurs in a vacuum divorced from precedent, but is framed by developed and developing structures of political culture with roots stretching back hundreds of years.

The guiding theme of the Praeger Series in American Political Culture is explaining how cultural factors (education, family, community, etc.) and economic change (technological innovation, depression, prosperity, market alterations, etc.) intersect with political methods (elections, strategies, laws, policies, institutions, etc.) to shape human actions throughout

American history. While the series exhibits a theme, it is understood broadly to encourage a wide array of new projects and scholars from many disciplines—history, politics, law, and philosophy, for example. We welcome diversity in approach to historical topics, such as biography, institutional history, history of ideas, policy history, and the development of political structures, among others, but this series works within the discipline of history, not political science. We deal with political culture from a strictly historical perspective.

Peter Zavodnyik's history of expanding federal power sheds light on an understudied era of national government growth and contributes to our understanding of American political culture between the 1860s and the 1930s. With a keen eye for overlooked details, he meticulously narrates this era's laws, legislation, court cases, elections, and policies, giving readers a thorough political and policy narrative of America from Abraham Lincoln to Herbert Hoover. Scholars such as Morton Keller have seen federal growth in the Civil War years but posit it receded again after 1877 and the collapse of Reconstruction. Zavodnyik, on the other hand, portrays the post–Civil War period as a catalyst for continued federal government growth, and while other scholars stop at 1877 or 1896, he sees continuity down to the Great Depression—in debates over Civil War pensions, agriculture and conservation policies, tariff and taxation battles, civil service reform and growth, railroad regulations, workplace safety, and hundreds of other legislative dustups, bureaucratic proclamations, and Supreme Court cases. Most importantly, he challenges the traditional interpretation of government expansion throughout American history—that government growth comes in spurts and starts, or as economist Robert Higgs has suggested in *Crisis and Leviathan*, that growth increases dramatically during economic and military emergencies. Instead, Zavodnyik suggests that federal government growth came gradually and inexorably in the late nineteenth and early twentieth centuries as the economy changed, and judges and politicians of both parties read the Constitution in creative ways to support that growth. In other words, the 1930s New Deal was no sudden detour from traditional American political culture, but a logical extension of patterns rooted in the previous century.

This interpretation builds on his earlier work, *The Age of Strict Construction: A History of the Growth of Federal Power, 1789–1861* (Catholic University of America Press, 2007), which showed that centralized power grew in the pre–Civil War years through expansion of the federal patronage system, an ironic twist considering the most effective advocates of the spoils system were antebellum Democrats traditionally hostile to an assertive federal government. Those who hated central government hastened its arrival. Zavodnyik's *The Rise of the Federal Colossus* adds to our knowledge of American federal government institutions, especially in the understudied decades between 1870 and 1900, and how public demand calling for increased regulation of emerging corporations stimulated government expansion and contributed to the development of American political culture in the 70 years after civil war.

—Jon L. Wakelyn and Michael J. Connolly, Series Editors

INTRODUCTION

For the first 70 years of the Constitution's existence, Article I, Section 8's enumeration of the powers of Congress served as its most important feature. The meaning of its terms received lengthy examinations in Congress, the courts, and the newspapers. In contrast, the provisions of the Bill of Rights were rarely debated or litigated, and the separation of powers—the assignment of responsibilities to one or more of the three branches of the federal government—was embraced without incident. The enumerated powers of Congress remained the subject of discussion for many years in part because of divisions over how they should be interpreted. The states ratified the Constitution on the understanding that they ceded to the national government only those powers found in the Constitution. The Tenth Amendment enshrined this view of the federal government's authority: "The powers not delegated to the United States by the Constitution, nor prohibited by it to the States, are reserved to the States respectively, or to the people."

During the Constitution's early years, two schools of thought developed with respect to the powers of Congress. One group led by Alexander Hamilton, John Marshall, Henry Clay, and Daniel Webster gave them a broad reading in support of programs designed to promote economic development. A second group was represented by Thomas Jefferson, James Madison, and James Polk. Eager to limit federal activity and protect the rights of the states, it held that Congress must adhere to the constrained understanding of the powers of Article I, Section 8 revealed during ratification. The latter school—those who advocated a "strict construction" of the powers of the national government—prevailed during the antebellum period. By the 1850s, even advocates of a vigorous exercise of national authority refused to defend the notion that the general welfare clause bestowed a broad spending power, and the claim that the commerce power was exclusive—that the states could not regulate interstate commerce even in the absence of conflicting federal statutes—had been discarded.

Yet if the dam remained, cracks had begun to appear by 1861. Advocates of a broad construction of federal authority had become adept at finding precedents in early federal legislation for measures they favored, even if the cited examples were not always on point. They emphasized the words of the enumerated powers at the expense of historical context, so that hopelessly broad phrases such as the authority to "regulate commerce" served as the basis for novel legislation. Exercises of federal authority of disputed legality led Americans to investigate how they should respond to the assumption of powers by the federal government that had originally been reserved to the states. A great many Americans saw the national government as merely an agent of the states who created it, and within this group, some believed the states could renounce the Union in response to violations of the constitutional contract despite the fact that the Constitution contained nothing that implied a right of secession. The conviction of southerners that the Union was nothing more than a confederation of sovereign entities provided what they saw as legal authority for the secession of 11 states in the first months of 1861.

Differences over constitutional interpretation and the scope of federal authority did not serve as the primary causes of the secession of southern states; nor did highly publicized disputes over the power of Congress to ban slavery in the territories and the extent of the states' obligation to comply with the terms of the fugitive slave acts. Southern politicians were most alarmed by the prospect of a Republican-controlled national government wielding its prodigious pecuniary influence in their states. An elaborate network involving federal patronage—the "spoils system"—had developed in the years between 1829 and 1861 that enabled officials in Washington to influence political activity and commentary at the state level in a way that was wholly at odds with the federative nature of American government. The customhouses, post offices, and other federal entities provided scores of jobs and enabled those who controlled them to wield a degree of influence that dwarfed the power of those who presided over small state bureaucracies. During the antebellum period, caucuses and conventions determined party nominations. With the ability to vote in these gatherings available to anyone who appeared at them, a postmaster or customhouse official could send platoons of federal employees to these meetings and thereby decide who received nominations. An elaborate system of newspaper patronage also appeared during the antebellum period; state department contracts for printing federal laws went to newspapers in each state and hundreds of newspaper editors received places in the executive branch. The appearance of a vast network of patronage built on federal largesse contradicted the predictions of the advocates of the Constitution, who assured the country that the states would have more places to offer and wield more influence than the federal government.[1]

During the 1850s, two proslavery Democratic administrations deployed federal offices and contracts in a futile attempt to stamp out antislavery sentiment among Democratic politicians and newspapers in the northern states. It was the existence of this system that led many southerners to fear the election of a Republican president in 1860. Armed with federal offices and contracts, men such as Abraham Lincoln or William Seward could inject antislavery sentiment into the southern states. Southern politicians such as John Slidell were acutely aware of the potential of federal patronage as a political tool, as they had been at the forefront of the effort during the Pierce and Buchanan administrations to eradicate antislavery sentiment within Democratic Party organizations and newspapers in the northern states. As slavery was viewed in the South as well as in the North as a fragile institution, southerners feared that the introduction of antislavery sentiment in their states would pose a mortal threat to the institution. If the non-slaveholding whites of the South were convinced that it undermined their own fortunes, they would seek to abolish it. Southerners had labored for three decades to keep antislavery literature from entering their section, going so far as to require that federal postmasters in their states confiscate it as a matter of course when it arrived in their post offices. Thus the secession of the southern states in the weeks before Abraham Lincoln took the oath of office on March 4, 1861—they did not wish to risk having a president who had proclaimed the need to set slavery on a course for its "ultimate extinction" deploy hordes of antislavery zealots in their states. While neither Lincoln nor any other northern politician had ever claimed the federal government possessed the right to ban slavery in the states (at least in peacetime), southerners suspected that a Republican administration armed with federal contacts and jobs would wage a war of propaganda on it and produce its demise. In sum, while the federal government continued to adhere to a restrained conception of its lawful powers in 1861, the multiplication of federal offices and contracts rendered it a formidable and often destructive institution—at least in a political context—by the time of the secession crisis. Men as varied in their views as Daniel Webster and John C. Calhoun had spoken out against the use of federal offices to centralize the party system and eradicate dissent, but their warnings were ignored.

The Civil War itself promoted centralization, albeit in a more nuanced and indirect fashion than is normally acknowledged. With southern lawmakers absent, Congress provided funds for endeavors previously left to the states, and it used its tax power to reach subjects beyond the authorities listed in Article I, Section 8. It also issued money that was not redeemable in gold—a novelty that struck many as odd as the government's only relevant power was that of issuing coin—gold or silver money. Congress used its commerce power to bring banks within its purview despite the fact that reserve requirements had thus far fallen within the domain of the states. Following the war Congress relied on the Constitution's requirement that the states maintain republican governments as legal authority for the abolition of governments in the southern states in favor of temporary military rule. The Reconstruction amendments also proved subject to abuse. An amendment designed to protect former slaves was ripped from its original moorings and deployed in the cause of preventing the states from regulating certain economic activities. By 1910, federal judges had broadened the scope of this amendment to the point that it served as the basis for an effective judicial veto power over state regulations of business.

As recent works by Brian Balogh, Richard Franklin Bensel, and Kimberley S. Johnson have demonstrated, federal authority was exercised vigorously and for a wide variety of purposes during the period between the Civil War and the 1930s.[2] Consequently, the New Deal was not as radical a departure as has been often alleged.[3] Only a broad interpretation of the enumerated powers of Congress made the expansion of the federal sphere possible. In the years immediately following Appomattox, large Republican majorities ensured that the Hamiltonian view of the Constitution met only modest resistance. The Jeffersonian, "states' rights" approach suffered even after Democrats won back the House in 1874. Southerners themselves embraced a broader view of federal authority than they had before the war; surveying the destruction of transportation facilities in their section, they sought federal aid for projects they had once opposed as unconstitutional. Other groups once hostile to a vigorous exercise of federal authority also embraced national power. Farmers had formed the backbone of the states' rights, strict constructionist Democratic party during the antebellum period; by the end of the century they had obtained federal regulation of railroad rates—an unprecedented use of the federal commerce power. Some farmers wanted Washington to provide them with loans at artificially low rates and warehouses where they could store their crops while waiting for prices to rise—a venture that would have amazed even the most generous-minded broad constructionists of the 1850s. Farmers achieved these goals during World War I. Labor had not been enthusiastic about Henry Clay's American system, which it viewed as taking money from impoverished taxpayers for the benefit of contractors and manufacturers, but it looked on the national government in a new light during the years after the Civil War. When labor strife on the railroads resulted in the interruption of traffic on the major lines, the federal government responded first by deploying troops and later by supervising labor relations in that critical industry. The extension of the commerce power to issues such as workplace safety and wages on the railroads constituted a revolutionary innovation, and one that tied the fortunes of workers in the nation's largest industry to the wishes of congressional majorities in Washington.

Congress enacted novel legislation in a variety of areas during the Gilded Age and the Progressive Era, injecting the federal government into matters as varied as education, public health, and the reclamation of arid lands. The commerce power was deployed in the cause of food safety as early as the 1890s, and the tax power was used to deter activities, some of which were harmless, that met with the hostility of congressional majorities. Congress exercised its postal power for the purpose of enacting morals legislation, and the importation of books by famous authors was banned by customs officials on the grounds that they were obscene. While a program to aid primary schools with federal grants did not become law, a bill for that purpose passed one house of Congress or the other on multiple occasions during the 1870s and 1880s.

The number of Americans over whom the federal government exercised a pecuniary influence underwent staggering growth during the late nineteenth century, albeit due to policies that fell, for the most part, within the powers of Congress. Still, the fact that the fortunes of so many Americans turned on policies established in Washington conflicted sharply with the expectations of the founding generation—they believed the states would wield far more influence than the national government—and it did much to erode the decentralized nature of the federal system. The power to raise an army endowed the national government with authority to compensate soldiers. Republicans exploited this authority to the fullest during the period between 1880 and 1910, when they ran for office on promises to expand benefits for those who had served in the Union army during the Civil War. Pension Bureau agents visited northern states on the eve of elections to promise voters that their monthly benefits would be increased, effectively bribing them to support Republican candidates. These tactics proved enormously effective in helping Republicans overcome the increasing dissatisfaction of farmers and win critical swing states such as Indiana. Protective tariffs dated from early in the nineteenth century and the authority of Congress to impose them was no longer subject to dispute. As the percentage of American workers who toiled in mills and factories increased after the Civil War, the political potential of protection increased exponentially. Industrial wages in Europe trailed those in America, and workers as well as their employers accepted the argument that high tariff rates must be maintained to protect the country's manufacturing sector. That protection was affecting a massive transfer of wealth from consumers to large industrial concerns became evident by the 1880s and the unwillingness of Republicans to lower rates helped Democrats win both houses of Congress as well as the presidency in 1912.

The pace of centralization accelerated during the Progressive Era. Alexander Hamilton's claim of a broad spending power via the general welfare clause rose from the dead to authorize federal grants for vocational schools and maternal health. During World War I, the national government effectively set wages and prices in a variety of industries and determined the distribution of scarce resources, forcing some businesses to stop functioning altogether. It also encouraged the formation of surveillance networks, distributed propaganda to schools, and incarcerated women viewed as a threat to the health of enlisted men at nearby army bases. Federal oversight of economic activities without a direct relationship to interstate commerce ceased for the most part at the end of World War I, but innovations continued during the 1920s. Federal officials produced something of a bubble when they maintained artificially low interest rates and provided loans to banks and, in turn, stock speculators while reducing the reserve requirements of national banks. Regulatory agencies obtained control over critical industries such as the radio business and used it to bar from the airwaves speech they deemed injurious to the public interest. Farmers became the first interest group to obtain direct aid from the national government. In 1929, federal officials began spending millions of dollars buying cotton, wheat, and corn in the hope of elevating farm incomes; the effort was in vain. It served as a useful precedent when urban politicians sought aid for their impoverished electorates as the economy failed during the early 1930s. The national government responded to the downturn by providing the states with grants to aid the unemployed; it also loaned money to failing banks. The Supreme Court also expanded its authority by fiat. By 1930 the justices were on their way to acquiring a veto power over all types of state laws. This stemmed from a discovery made during the 1920s: The Fourteenth Amendment applied at least a portion of the Bill of the Rights to the states. This realization had eluded the justices for 60 years, in part because it eluded the country when the amendment was submitted to the states for their approval. In time this discovery would enable the federal judiciary to oversee every aspect of state activity, from the framework of courts to social welfare systems and schools.

No constitutional amendment expanding the federal government's spending and regulatory powers was enacted during the 70 years from the Civil War to the Great Depression. Yet federal power grew dramatically—mostly by construction—in ways that were both helpful and destructive. Small increments followed each other, and ground taken in the process of centralization was not abandoned. By the time the New Deal arrived all of the precedents necessary for the establishment of an all-powerful central government were available—Franklin D. Roosevelt and Congress merely enlarged the portion of the population that benefited from federal aid. The regulatory framework put in place during the 1930s seemed revolutionary at the time, but the regulations imposed on the industrial and financial sectors were not far removed from those already established for railroads and national banks. The labor laws of the 1930s built upon previous legislation that protected railroad employees. In sum, the revolutionary phase in the development of American federalism was not the New Deal and the period that followed it, but the preceding 72 years when national government began regulating banks, overseeing labor relations in critical industries, and providing aid to the downtrodden. The period between 1861 and 1933 also saw Congress abuse its authority for the purpose of giving certain industries and individuals a competitive advantage. Lawmakers in Washington also initiated the practice of routing public money into the pockets of voters for the purpose of manipulating them. While these practices would not reach epidemic proportions until the end of the twentieth century, their roots go back much further in American history than is normally acknowledged. These legacies of centralization came to life during the war that confirmed the national government's supremacy and matured during the following years, when its influence and power grew exponentially.

Chapter 1

FEDERALISM AND WAR, 1861–1865

THE ASSEMBLING OF ARMIES

The Civil War strained the federal system and accelerated the process of centralization. It also revealed that the government formed in 1789 was equal to the gravest challenge a nation can face. The war began with the bombardment of Fort Sumter by South Carolina troops on April 12, 1861. Major Robert Anderson surrendered the fort the following afternoon. A Confederate government purporting to represent the states of the Deep South had already proclaimed its existence at Montgomery, Alabama. On April 15, President Lincoln declared that "combinations too powerful to be suppressed by the ordinary course of judicial proceedings" existed in the states of South Carolina, Georgia, Florida, Alabama, Mississippi, Louisiana, and Texas. Pursuant to the authority vested in him by a law of February 28, 1795, the president called forth 75,000 members of the state militias to suppress said combinations "and to cause the laws to be duly executed."[1] The men were inducted into volunteer units of the Union army—the militias themselves were not deployed in the field. On April 19 and 27, Lincoln ordered the navy to impose a blockade on the ports of states in rebellion.[2] On May 3, the president called for 42,000 volunteers to serve for three years in the army and navy.[3] Offended by the president's actions, the states of Virginia, North Carolina, and Arkansas seceded and joined the Confederate States of America before the end of May. The Confederate Congress voted to move the capital to Richmond, Virginia. Tennessee declared its independence and entered into an alliance with the Confederacy, while other border states quaked with discord but did not secede. Kentucky declared its neutrality but remained within the

Union. Missourians, divided bitterly over the state's future, proceeded to wage a brand of internecine warfare on each other that was far worse than anything they had inflicted on Kansas. Governor Claiborne Jackson refused to act on the president's request for troops; instead he called out the state militia and some feared he would use it in support of the Confederacy. Union troops responded by arresting members of the militia. Leaders of the state government as well as members of the legislature fled to Arkansas. The latter enacted an ordinance of secession and joined the Confederacy despite having less than a quorum. Back in Missouri, a state constitutional convention that had rejected secession reassembled. It ruled the state until early 1865.[4]

To bring the rebel states to heel while inflicting a minimum of damage, General-in-Chief Winfield Scott proposed to use the navy to shut down the Confederate coast and an army of 85,000 men to take control of the Mississippi River. While the northern press grew impatient over Scott's reluctance to invade the South, even the Anaconda Plan required an armed force beyond the immediate means of the federal government. In the spring of 1861 it lacked the resources to house the soldiers it had called into service, much less send them into hostile territory. The administration worsened its difficulties when it decided to allow the states to organize volunteer regiments instead of establishing a national army devoid of state units. For the balance of the war, men identified themselves by their state regiment, i.e., the 2nd Iowa or 5th New York. This decision left soldiers under the command of their respective states until they were deployed in the field.[5] The War Department relied on the states to raise, equip, and organize volunteer regiments during the early months of the war, though the legislatures were free to ask the War Department to indemnify them for the expenses incurred. Regimental officers were appointed by governors or elected by the men who served under them. Some governors operated for a time under the mistaken impression that they retained authority over state units even after they had been integrated into the Union army; the attorney general found it necessary to issue an opinion holding that their authority ceased when volunteers were called for national service by the War Department.[6]

Congress allowed this situation to remain in effect when it convened in July 1861, in no small part because northern citizens identified so strongly with their home states.[7] The acquiescence of lawmakers also stemmed from the national government's limited administrative capacities.[8] Fortunately the Union was blessed with several governors who proved equal to the task of military organization, including Edwin Morgan of New York and Oliver Morton of Indiana. These men, along with other governors and the state legislatures, found themselves doing the bulk of the work in the early months of the war; they had to cajole and beg the national government to accept more troops. Before the end of April, Wisconsin appropriated $100,000 for the war.[9] Massachusetts would spend over $29 million on the war effort.[10] As late as 1865, New York State devoted half of its $12 million budget to the war.[11] The line that separated state and federal responsibilities in outfitting and equipping troops remained unclear. In late 1862 the *New York Evening Post* reported that the worst-equipped soldiers were those of Connecticut—they had not been paid in six months and many lacked blankets and winter overcoats. The state's legislature was mortified; it responded promptly with appropriations for the necessary supplies.[12] Union casualties at Bull Run were increased by the willingness of the War Department to allow state volunteer units to wear uniforms of varying colors—the confusion resulted in several accidental deaths. Shortly thereafter the states began complying with U.S. Army standards in the design of uniforms for their troops.

Before the war the federal government and the states neglected their military establishments, leaving them ill-prepared in the spring of 1861. Northern armories still contained flintlock muskets. Iowa had so few of these relics (1,700) that members of the state militia had to post a bond before using them in prewar parades.[13] The War Department had nearly 500,000 rifles; most of them were outdated. Federal officials provided some states with weapons, but many were in such poor shape they could not be used. Nor was ammunition readily available in the necessary quantities; Indiana had to build its own factory to manufacture it.[14] State and federal officials as well as Confederate agents raced to Europe to buy guns, where they proceeded to bid against each other and push up prices. As the war progressed, one northern state after another ceded purchasing authority to the War Department, though some officials resisted out of fear that supplies would no longer be purchased in their states.[15]

Nowhere was the chaos and disorganization of the northern war effort more evident than in Washington, DC. In the days following Lincoln's call for troops in mid-April, capital residents feared Confederates would occupy the city—the campfires of the rebel army could be seen across the Potomac River, flickering in the night. A southern clergyman preparing for a short journey to the South left his cat in the cellar of his Washington house with only three days' provisions—so confident was he that he would return promptly after Confederates occupied the city.[16] After mobs in Baltimore attacked Massachusetts soldiers on their way to the capital (April 19), Maryland officials ordered or at least acquiesced in the disabling of railroad bridges on the lines to Philadelphia and Harrisburg. They asked the president to route troops around Maryland and he complied for a brief period. Southern sympathizers destroyed telegraph lines, thus cutting off communication between Washington, DC, and Baltimore and in turn the rest of the North. Among capital residents, a lack of information from the outside world begat fear and paranoia. In time a full-blown panic set in—rumor had it that Confederate troops were approaching and civilians began evacuating the city. The approaches to major buildings such as the Capitol were adorned with artillery pieces. The executive square was to be the last refuge of the federal government. When all else was lost, senior officials would retreat to the treasury building where the entrances were barricaded and 2,000 barrels of flour were stored in the basement. The scare did not end until a train containing the 7th New York Regiment arrived on April 25.

When fear subsided, disorganization again ruled the day as the War Department's resources proved unequal to the task of properly feeding and housing the thousands of soldiers pouring into the city. Some had to be housed in the Capitol. A soldier of the 7th New York thought the décor reminiscent of a "southwestern steamboat saloon." He rejoiced in the open roof as it provided badly needed ventilation. (The dome was not yet finished.)[17] The 6th Massachusetts made its home in the Senate chamber; the commanding officer occupied the vice-presidential chair and the regimental colors adorned the gallery, the seats of which were prized for sleeping as they had abundant cushioning.[18] As summer neared, the capital's railroad and telegraph connections to the North were reestablished. Federal troops occupied Baltimore and imposed martial law. When Congress met later that summer, it provided funds for the establishment of a federal police force in Baltimore to relieve Union soldiers of the need to walk the streets of that volatile city.[19]

Slowly but surely, the war converted the modest capital of antebellum America into a bustling metropolis, part boomtown and part military camp. Overnight it was covered in a maze of telegraph wires, and the War Department ran lines out to some 40 forts that appeared on the outskirts of the capital. The War Department brought employees of the Pennsylvania Railroad including Andrew Carnegie into the city so they could operate the telegraph network as well as the railroads. As artillery shells could already travel three to four miles, Union Army officers realized that the Virginia bank opposite the city would have to be taken, and it was. Union troops occupied Alexandria; otherwise it would have threatened northern shipping as well as the capital. Freight and soldiers poured into Washington, and cows needed to sustain the army were deposited on the mall until one fell into a canal.[20]

During the first weeks of the conflict, the federal government tottered between ineptitude and the sort of heavy-handed conduct that the world had learned to expect from governments at war. The president ordered U.S. marshals to enter telegraph offices in the North and seize copies of all telegrams sent or received during the previous 12 months. The order was executed across the country by marshals acting in unison during the afternoon of April 20.[21] The federal government took possession of all telegraph lines radiating from Washington and censored dispatches sent north by newspaper correspondents.[22] Federal authorities took over the flour mills of Georgetown to feed the soldiers pouring into the capital, and the president spent millions of dollars on the war without congressional authorization.[23] When Congress finally met in July, the Republican majorities that remained after the exodus of southern members gave the president the power and money he needed. On July 13, Congress appropriated $5.76 million to pay volunteers.[24] It sought to raise $80 million by taxation. As increases in duties on coffee, tea, and sugar would not suffice, it also provided for the first direct taxes on land levied in a generation: a law of August 5, 1861, imposed a direct tax on the states and provided quotas each one would have to meet. New York received a bill for $2.6 million. The states were left the choice of paying the levy themselves or allowing federal assessors to value and tax real property within their borders. To placate farmers irritated over the land tax, the measure also imposed a tax on incomes over $800. On July 17, Congress authorized the secretary of the treasury to borrow up to $250 million and issue $50 million in non-interest-bearing treasury notes. A law of July 22 authorized the calling of 500,000 volunteers. It provided that governors would commission the field, staff, and company officers of each regiment. A measure of July 29 gave Lincoln authority to call out the army and navy as well as the state militias. On July 13, Congress authorized the president to ban all intercourse between the rebel states and the rest of the nation, and he did so on August 16, 1861.[25] Congress added a rider to an appropriation for the army that gave legal sanction to the president's proclamations and orders issued during the spring that concerned the army, navy, militia, and volunteers of the United States. Said acts "are hereby approved and in all respects legalized and made valid" to the same extent as if "they had been issued and done under the previous express authority and direction of Congress."[26]

On August 6 Congress subjected to confiscation all property used to aid the insurrection and authorized U.S. attorneys to initiate condemnation proceedings.[27] The law would have provided for the confiscation of all property of persons aiding the rebellion but the president refused to go along with a measure that would have had the effect of emancipating—at least in theory—a great many slaves. During the rest of the war, the extent of the national government's power to confiscate property in the South would serve as a source of intense debate. Radical Republicans wished to distribute the lands of rebel planters among former slaves; moderate Republicans and Democrats believed such a course would violate Article III,

Section 3 of the Constitution: "no Attainder of Treason shall work Corruption of Blood, or Forfeiture except during the Life of the Person attainted." They interpreted this provision as providing that while the national government could remove land from its rebel owners, the right of the heirs of those persons to that land could not be impaired.[28]

After George McClellan took over the Army of the Potomac in the fall of 1861, he spent months drilling the men under his command. He ignored the demands of Northerners to move on Richmond. While northern Virginia remained quiet, frictions in the Border States elicited a more aggressive response from the national government and the armies that spoke for it. After guerrilla war broke out in Missouri, General John C. Fremont imposed martial law in St. Louis on August 14 and extended it to the entirety of the state on August 30. When he declared that all property of persons aiding the rebellion would be confiscated and their slaves set free, he received a prompt rebuke from the president, who directed him to confiscate only property actually used in aid of rebel forces as provided by the Confiscation Act. The president proved more aggressive in responding to events in Maryland. With secessionists determined to sever the state's ties with the Union, the legislature met on September 17. Union soldiers arrested nine lawmakers. Two Baltimore editors as well as the mayor and a congressman also found themselves in military custody. Northerners were appalled, especially after the president refused to disclose the grounds for the arrests. The War Department later explained that the detainees had given "aid and comfort to the enemy."[29]

The year 1862 presented the Union with painful failures, dramatic victories, and ample evidence of the cost of modern war. Under the threat of removal, McClellan moved the Army of the Potomac via transports to the peninsula between the York and James Rivers in Virginia. After reaching the outskirts of Richmond and causing the Confederate government to make plans for evacuating the capital, the general responded to clashes with the enemy by withdrawing to a coastal plateau and demanding that Washington send him more troops. Although the Army of the Potomac vastly exceeded the Confederate Army of Northern Virginia in size, it was eventually called back to the outskirts of Washington. Robert E. Lee led Confederates in an invasion of Maryland that summer; the incursion ended with a Union victory at Antietam, where 4,800 men died and 20,000 were wounded. In the west, Union troops captured Fort Henry on the Tennessee River and Fort Donelson on the Cumberland River. In March 1862, Union troops landed below the bluffs of the Tennessee near Corinth, Mississippi, and prepared to sever the Memphis & Charleston Railroad, a critical east-west link. They sustained a withering attack by Confederates. The rebels appeared on the verge of a great victory in what became known as the Battle of Shiloh until reinforcements enabled Union troops to withstand a charge on the morning of the second day and turn defeat into victory. Memphis fell in June and New Orleans did so shortly thereafter. Late in the year Ambrose Burnside led the Army of the Potomac in an attempt to take Fredericksburg, Virginia. The effort failed when six uncoordinated charges produced nothing more than 12,500 Union casualties. While the Union effort on land had a mixed record during 1862, a blockade of southern ports reduced cotton exports to almost nothing and crippled the Confederate economy. It also produced severe inflation—a development that would eventually contribute greatly to breaking the will of the South.

FEDERAL RULE IN WARTIME

If the northern war effort had produced only mixed results in the field by the beginning of 1863, it had already wrought great changes on the home front. Under the necessity of war, a government of enumerated powers reached into every home in the North to extract men or money or both. In the process it altered the notions of Americans about the proper role of their national government. The power of the presidency expanded dramatically. Lincoln exercised "a wider authority than any British ruler between Cromwell and Churchill."[30] There was certainly no precedent for his administration in American history. The Illinois lawyer at the helm of the nation followed a course that fell within the law most of the time, with a handful of notable exceptions.

The president had to find his way in the dark. Faced with a war only weeks into his term, he had to act without the assistance of Congress or the numerous federal officials from the South who resigned when their states seceded. Almost immediately the executive branch started moving money among the departments and spending it without statutory authorization. By July 1, War Department spending had pushed the national debt to $91 million—it had been only $65 million the year before—and still not a single appropriation for the war had been made by Congress.[31] The May 3, 1861, proclamation seeking volunteers constituted an intrusion into the congressional sphere, as the power to raise an army is among the enumerated powers of Congress. The existence of a blockade for several months prior to specific authorization also appeared problematic, and in the *Prize Cases*, the Supreme Court came within a single vote of holding that the president exceeded his authority in that regard.[32] In his opinion for the majority, Justice Robert Grier concluded that April 1861 proclamations imposing the blockade fell within the scope of the authority of the president. He cited the onset of hostilities, international law, the Militia Acts of 1795 and 1807, and the August 1861 law ratifying the president's acts during the previous five months.[33] That the steps taken by Lincoln in the spring of 1861 were of indisputable necessity regardless of the law seems beyond doubt; still, he exacerbated the problem when he set the special session of Congress for July 4, 1861, instead of an earlier date.

Martial law was established in Washington, DC, and Baltimore as well as in Fort Leavenworth, Kansas, and large parts of Kentucky and Missouri. At one point Union army General Thomas Ewing Jr. ordered the evacuation of four Missouri counties in an attempt to stem the violence that plagued them. During Lee's 1863 invasion of Pennsylvania, martial law was established in parts of that state as well as in nearby counties of Maryland and Delaware—much to relief of citizens, some of whom requested it. Martial law proved an immense benefit in New Orleans. During the years prior to the war, the city government had already established a reputation for neglect and corruption. The city's commanding officer, Union general Ben Butler, though an accomplished thief himself—he earned the nickname "spoons" for stealing silverware from the homes of residents of New Orleans—put an end to the rule of street gangs and enforced sanitation measures that prevented the yellow fever outbreaks that had been an annual event.[34]

While the country did not protest the establishment of military rule in areas subjected to the chaos of war, the president's decision to suspend the writ of habeas corpus in areas at peace without congressional authorization produced intense debate. On April 27, 1861, he authorized General Winfield Scott to suspend the writ along the military line of transportation being established between Philadelphia and Washington.[35] On July 2, 1861, Lincoln issued a similar order with respect to the military line between Philadelphia and New York City.[36] Section 9 of Article I provided for the suspension of the writ of habeas corpus when "Cases of Rebellion or Invasion the public Safety may require it," but it was not clear whether this authority had been bestowed on Congress or the president. Many believed the power was vested in Congress alone. Lincoln defended his actions in a message of July 4, 1861: "As the provision was plainly made for a dangerous emergency, it cannot be believed the framers of the instrument intended that in every case the danger should run its course until Congress could be called together, the very assembling of which might be prevented, as was intended in this case, by the rebellion."[37]

Suspension of the writ was followed by the arrest of noncombatants by military authorities, even in parts of the North that were at peace. This practice received a profoundly negative response from Chief Justice Roger Brooke Taney. In May 1861, John Merryman, a lieutenant in the Maryland militia who had helped burn a railroad bridge outside of Baltimore—possibly the at the order of the governor—was arrested at his home by army officers and held in custody at Fort McHenry on charges of aiding the enemy. Merryman's lawyer sought a writ of habeas corpus from Chief Justice Taney, who was then at his home in Baltimore while on circuit. Taney granted the request; he issued a writ requiring General George Cadwallader to appear before him and to bring Merryman. Cadwallader responded by writing Taney a letter explaining the charges against Merryman; he cited the president's suspension of the writ of habeas corpus in Maryland and declared that he would not comply with the order. A U.S. marshal appeared at Fort McHenry with an order of attachment for General Cadwallader only to be denied entry.[38] When the marshal informed Taney in a crowded courtroom that he had been denied entry to the fort, Taney noted that the marshal could call a posse comitatus, but he admitted that it "would face a superior force." The Chief Justice concluded that "the Court has no power under the law" to execute its will.[39] Taney issued an opinion holding that the president had violated the Constitution and ordering him to produce Merryman in federal court; he arranged for a copy to be delivered to the executive mansion. In his opinion Taney noted that the power to suspend the writ is included in the ninth section of Article I, which "is devoted to the legislative department of the United States (Congress), and has not the slightest reference to the executive department."[40] Article II details the president's duties and powers; it says nothing regarding the writ of habeas corpus.[41] Taney's claim that Section 9, Article I applied to Congress alone was not accurate. Section 9 included a host of prohibitions that applied to the president as well as Congress, e.g., the provision barring the withdrawal of money from the treasury except on statutory authorization.

Lincoln did not comply with the order, thus setting himself at odds with a tradition of presidents complying with orders of federal courts. Taney may have lacked authority to issue the writ as his jurisdiction arguably did not extend to federal military installations.[42] As for the question of whether the president had the power to suspend the writ without congressional authority, Attorney General Edward Bates answered it in the affirmative. In an opinion of July 5, 1861, Bates pointed out that the duties of the office "comprehend all the executive powers of the nation, which are expressly vested in the president by the Constitution."[43] Therefore it is "the plain duty of the president to preserve the Constitution and execute the laws all over the nation; and it is plainly impossible for him to perform this duty without putting down rebellion, and unlawful combinations." In the event of such circumstances, "the president must, of necessity, be the sole judge, both of the exigency which requires him to act, and of the manner in which it is most prudent for him to employ the powers entrusted to him, to enable him to discharge his constitutional and legal duty—that is, to suppress the insurrection and execute the laws." Bates pointed to the Constitution's silence on the question of who may suspend the writ of habeas corpus and asserted that the president "has lawful power to suspend the privilege of persons arrested under such circumstances." For he is "especially charged by the Constitution with the 'public safety,' and he is the sole judge of the emergency which requires his prompt action." The alternative would be to require the president, when "he has fought and captured the insurgent army, and has seized their secret spies and emissaries . . . to bring their bodies before any judge who may send him a writ." Bates denied that the president would be obligated to obey such a writ.[44]

Section 1 of Article II of the Constitution provides that "the executive Power shall be vested in a President." That phrase alone did not authorize the president to suspend the writ of habeas corpus any more than the duty of a sheriff to execute the ordinances of a village bestowed a right to incarcerate residents without trial. Yet the emergency was of a proportion to eat the government alive if it did not meet it quickly, and it may not have been met at all if the country had been forced to wait until Congress assembled and authorized the suspension of the writ. What the Founders intended is hard to fathom. In Great Britain, the power of the crown to suspend the writ was recognized for centuries until Parliament enacted a law in 1679 reserving that power to itself. While most Republican lawmakers in Washington believed Congress alone had authority to suspend the writ, at least some legal scholars sided with the president.[45]

On the floor of the Senate, James Bayard of Delaware spoke approvingly of Taney's opinion. He pointed out that Baltimore was at peace when the writ was suspended and that the federal courts were open at the time.[46] Speaking in the Senate on May 2, 1862, Jacob Collamer of Vermont expressed his belief that the Constitution's language regarding habeas corpus "implies a large measure of executive power." In his view, "the exercise of this executive power in a time of war is almost without limitation as against the enemy; it is the creature of circumstance as they arise; it is in a great measure the law of retaliation; it changes with circumstances, and with changing circumstances is almost without limit." In Collamer's view, Congress could not impede or subtract from the executive power of the president with statutes—it could not, for example, order the president to burn down a city in the course of a military campaign, though the president could order that it be burned by the army if its destruction appeared to be a military necessity.[47] John S. Carlile of Virginia complained that the rebellion had been cited as an event necessitating the suspension of habeas corpus in regions where no rebellion existed. "Will it be contended that there is a single loyal State in this Union where the process of law cannot be administered through the judiciary?"[48]

In early 1863 Congress took up a bill authorizing the president to suspend the writ of habeas corpus anywhere during the course of rebellion when in his judgment the public safety required it. Wisconsin Republican James Doolittle objected because the bill did not state that Congress was bestowing this authority. He feared it might be interpreted as merely recognizing the president's inherent authority to suspend the writ.[49] When the bill became law in March 1863, it included precisely the language to which Doolittle objected.[50] It also required the State and War Departments to provide federal judges with lists of the persons residing in their districts who had been incarcerated "as state or political prisoners, or otherwise, than as prisoners of war." Said persons were to be released if grand juries failed to indict them. The State and War Departments submitted partial lists; they did not include the names of prisoners subject to military trial.[51]

On September 15, 1863, the president suspended the writ of habeas corpus throughout the United States, albeit only in cases involving persons being held by the military as spies, "aiders or abettors of the enemy," members of the armed forces of the United States, deserters or persons "otherwise amenable to military law or the rules and articles of war or the rules or regulations prescribed for the military or naval services." He cited the March 3, 1863, habeas corpus law without stating that the suspension was an exercise of power granted by it.[52] Civilians across the North found themselves subject to arrest and incarceration by military personnel or State Department officials. Persons accused of violating the laws of war were subject to trial by military courts regardless of whether they were alleged to have done so upon the field of battle or in areas far removed from it. At least 13,535 Northerners were arrested by federal authorities before the end of the war; most were released after brief incarcerations.[53] Early in the conflict these arrests were preceded by a telegram to Secretary of State William Seward describing the activities of the accused and requesting authority for detention; his reply was invariably in the affirmative: "arrest him."[54] Many of those arrested displayed sympathy for the rebel cause or passed information to the enemy regarding the movement of armies; others called for resistance to what they perceived as federal excesses, such as the draft. A network formed under the auspices of the State Department made thousands of arrests.[55] State Department officials did not bother accumulating evidence of wrongdoing by those they incarcerated.[56] Excesses led to the transfer of authority over political prisoners from the State Department to the War Department in February 1862. Secretary of War Edwin M. Stanton now possessed authority to arrest and detain indefinitely all persons he saw as posing a danger to the public safety. Stanton at first took a moderate turn; he declared that all political prisoners except spies would be released once they took an oath.[57] Most were released that spring. In time Stanton imposed order on the process, reserving to commanders of military districts the power to determine if civilians accused of wrongdoing should be detained. Provost marshals were appointed in each state. Arrests continued during 1862 despite the fact that Democrats made them an issue in the election campaign that fall.[58]

Even more appalling than the mass arrests was Ulysses Grant's reaction to the activities of profiteers in the Mississippi Valley. He became deeply frustrated with the penchant of traders for giving Southerners badly needed gold or silver in exchange for cotton in violation of laws that prohibited trading with the enemy. Receipts from illegal cotton sales enabled the Confederacy to feed its armies and may well have prolonged the war.[59] As he believed many of the traders were Jewish, Grant issued an order in late 1862 providing for the removal of all Jews from the Department of the Tennessee—large portions of the states of Kentucky and Tennessee. Thousand of Jewish families had to leave their homes.[60] Lincoln reversed the order's application to civilians in early 1863—though Jewish traders were barred from the Department of the Tennessee for the duration of the war.

The press, though often scurrilous and irresponsible, was harassed beyond reason. A boy selling newspapers on the Naugatuck Railroad was jailed for selling copies of the *New York Daily News*, which the administration viewed as disloyal.[61] Military officials suspended publication of the *Chicago Times*, the *Louisville Courier*, and the *Philadelphia Evening Journal*.[62] In June 1863, Federal Judge Thomas Drummond issued a temporary injunction barring soldiers from invading the premises of the building housing the *Chicago Times*; a few hours after the order was issued, soldiers entered it and destroyed copies of the newspaper at the order of General Ambrose Burnside, commander of the Department of the Ohio. After the mayor of Chicago led a demonstration, the president reversed the order. The state legislature passed a resolution calling the suspension an "infringement of popular rights and an invasion of the sovereignty of the state of Illinois."[63] The *Chicago Daily Tribune* defended the order as constitutional and castigated Drummond. It claimed civil courts have no jurisdiction over military officials or executive branch officers aiding the president in the exercise of his war powers and asserted that the judge's order was appropriately ignored.[64]

On May 18, 1864, the president ordered Major General John A. Dix to arrest and imprison the editors and publishers of the *New York World* and the *New York Journal of Commerce* for publishing a proclamation they falsely claimed had been signed by the president.[65] At the request of the

War Department, the Post Office stopped delivering certain newspapers in large parts of the North. Military tribunals tried the editors of the *Newark Evening Journal, Bangor Republican Journal,* and the *New York Metropolitan Record* for criticizing the draft. Two Iowa editors were removed to Washington, DC, by military authorities and placed in the Old Capitol Prison. The federal government suppressed approximately 300 newspapers in the North during the war. Even a congressman found himself arrested for criticizing the president.[66] Compared to these excesses, the army's willingness to suppress information regarding setbacks in the field, such as the Fredericksburg debacle of late 1862, seemed innocuous.

While most persons arrested by federal officials or military officers were released after a short time, some were tried by military commissions. This practice extended beyond the theaters of war to areas where civil courts were operating. A military commission in Washington, DC, tried William T. Smithson, a prominent banker in the capital, for corresponding with Confederates, and he was sentenced to five years in prison.[67] The most famous victim of the federal government's exuberance was Clement Vallandigham, Democratic Congressman of Ohio and a fiery critic of the administration's violation of the civil liberties of Americans. When General Ambrose Burnside, commander of the Military District of the Ohio, issued his famous general order number 38, prohibiting seditious speech as "implied treason"—a doctrine not recognized by law—Vallandigham took the bait. He gave a speech in which he complained of a "wicked, cruel, unnecessary war" waged by a tyrannical government for the purpose of effecting abolition. Army captains in plainclothes observed the speech and reported it to General Burnside. Three days later a company of soldiers arrested Vallandigham at his home in Dayton for expressing sympathy for the enemy and uttering disloyal statements.[68] Violent protests erupted among Vallandigham's supporters. A hastily called military commission tried the congressman in Cincinnati in the spring of 1863. After refusing to enter a plea, as he did not believe the commission had authority over him—southern Ohio was at peace—Vallandigham was convicted and sentenced to imprisonment at Fort Warren in Boston Harbor for the duration of the war. He sought a writ of habeas corpus only to be informed by a federal judge that the writ had been suspended. Vallandigham appealed to the Supreme Court; it refused to rule on the case due to a lack of jurisdiction. Justice James Wayne explained that Section 14 of the Judiciary Act of 1789 listed the types of cases that could be appealed to the Supreme Court; it said nothing regarding the rulings of military commissions.[69]

Lincoln commuted the sentence and banished Vallandigham to the Confederacy. The president defended the arrest on the grounds that the congressman sought to prevent the raising of troops and encourage desertions—if the government could shoot deserters, surely it could prosecute those who induced desertion.[70] Safely behind southern lines, Vallandigham assured his hosts that the Confederacy would prevail if it lasted another year—Lincoln would be denied reelection and the Democrats would reach an accommodation with the Confederacy. Vallandigham eventually reached Windsor, Canada, from which he ran for governor of Ohio. Before the war was over he returned to the North and continued to denounce the administration. He called on his own state of Ohio to secede if the Union did not allow the Confederacy to go in peace.

While Vallandigham's views were extreme, many Americans were frustrated with the Administration's excesses. Their sentiments were expressed by Pennsylvania Democrat John L. Dawson in the House of Representatives during the spring of 1864. He complained that "if any Democrat objects to an act of the administration, [the Republican Party] raises the cry of disloyalty, and insists that we should employ our time solely in denouncing secession. If we see the money of the nation squandered, the Constitution trampled upon, the laws disregarded, public liberty endangered, the right of suffrage taken away, the freedom of speech and of the press restricted and punished, the Union for which we are bleeding laughed at as a thing of the past, we must, according to my colleague's code of political morals, find no fault with those who do these wrongs, ask for no reform, seek no change."[71]

Perhaps the most novel use of the government's war powers was the emancipation of slaves. In November 1861 the president discussed with Congressman George P. Fisher the possibility of paying the slave owners of Delaware to part with their chattel, in part because such a program seemed most feasible in that state, as it had only 587 slaves at the time of the 1860 census. The president defended the measure as one that would help shorten the war despite the fact that Delaware had not seceded and was devoid of conflict. Fisher drafted a bill for the Delaware legislature designed to carry the proposal into effect but it succumbed to bitter opposition both within and outside of the state.[72] In his first annual message, Lincoln called on Congress to purchase slaves if necessary to secure their emancipation—at that point it could free them and colonize them outside of the United States. As for the question of authority, the president asked whether "the expediency amounted to absolute necessity—that without which the Government itself cannot be perpetuated?"[73]

In a message to Congress of March 6, 1862, Lincoln urged it to adopt a joint resolution offering to provide financial aid to any state that effected abolition. Somewhat disingenuously, he insisted that "such a proposition on the part of the General Government sets up no claim of a right by Federal authority to interfere with slavery within State limits, referring, as it does, the absolute control of the subject in each case to the State and its people immediately interested. It is proposed as a matter of perfectly free choice with them."[74] Congress embraced the suggestion and passed a joint resolution on April 10.[75] That the program was based on any authority listed in the Constitution seems doubtful at best; it was hard to see how compensated emancipation in the border states would have any effect whatsoever on the South or the Union war effort.[76] The administration sought the establishment of a program of compensated emancipation in the border states during the summer of 1862 but it received a poor reception, even when the president warned that the war would likely result in emancipation without compensation.[77] In his annual message of December 1862, Lincoln proposed an amendment authorizing federal grants of money to states if they agreed to abolish slavery prior to 1900.[78] In early 1863 both houses passed bills promising aid to Missouri in exchange for emancipation, but the two measures were not reconciled before the session ended.[79]

In the spring of 1862 the federal government began to clean its own house. Up until that time, Washington, DC, Marshal Ward Hill Lamon enforced the Fugitive Slave Act and municipal laws regarding involuntary servitude in the capital with unseemly vigor. He required slaves to carry a pass when they left the homes of their owners.[80] The actions of Lamon—a political appointee who had spent time in Illinois and was a friend of the president—did not endear him or his benefactor to radicals in Congress. In contrast, the military governor of the District of Columbia, General James Wadsworth, provided runaways with sustenance and shelter. He went so far as to forcibly liberate a slave woman who had been taken into custody by constables serving under Lamon.[81] An emancipation law applicable to the District of April 16, 1862, provided compensation to owners, with a maximum payment of $300 a slave.[82] Freedom was gained by 3,185 persons under the law.[83] The fugitive slave acts remained on the books and they were enforced in Washington when Maryland slaves flooded the District despite the fact that the fugitive slave clause appeared to apply only to states.[84] The acts were finally repealed in June 1864.[85] Lincoln himself undermined the faith of antislavery elements when he disavowed an order of General David Hunter of May 9, 1862, purporting to free the slaves of Georgia, Florida, and South Carolina. The president insisted that it was for him alone to make the decision as to whether slaves in any theater of war should be freed.[86] Radicals took heart from the decision of Congress to ban slavery in the territories via an act of June 19, 1862.[87] Although overlooked at the time, the law constituted a direct blow to the notion that the Supreme Court's decisions bind the other branches. Five years earlier in *Dred Scott*, the Court ruled that Congress did not have authority to ban slavery in the territories and held the Missouri Compromise void.[88] After it was issued, Republican lawmakers dismissed Chief Justice Taney's comments in his majority opinion regarding the Missouri Compromise as mere dictum and not binding on the other branches. In June 1857, Abraham Lincoln suggested the decision could only be violated if officials gave Dred Scott his freedom. He believed the opinion constituted a weak precedent, as it rested on faulty historical assumptions and had been issued by a divided court.[89] While the 1862 law was not tested in court before the Thirteenth Amendment was ratified, contempt for the reasoning in Chief Justice Taney's opinion was so pervasive that is highly doubtful that the law would have been invalidated even it had been.

The tide turned, finally and irrevocably, on September 17, 1862, when the president issued a proclamation declaring that slaves within states still in rebellion on January 1, 1863, "shall be then, thenceforward, and forever free." The U.S. military would "recognize and maintain the freedom of such persons."[90] The president insisted that the war remained an enterprise whose end was the preservation of the Union, but the fat was in the fire. The right of the government to effect emancipation in the theater of war had already been exercised in the Confiscation Acts, and except for a handful of naysayers, it was generally recognized.[91] While serving in the House of Representatives in 1836, John Quincy Adams had claimed such a power as an incident of war, though as secretary of state, Adams insisted that the laws of war did not permit confiscation of slaves or other private property (1820).[92] The proclamation was born of multiple considerations. There was a need to establish a uniform policy to be followed by all Union armies, and so lessen the temptation of politically minded generals to gain notoriety by acting the part of liberator in their locales. Lincoln also saw a need to head off Congress; he feared it might use the power of appropriation to hold the war hostage to the cause of emancipation.[93] The continuing machinations of pro-Confederacy elements in France and Britain, and the possibility of those countries demanding mediation between the two sides—which would have led to permanent separation—also played a role. The powers of Europe might intervene to restore their supplies of cotton and valued customers in the South, but it would be difficult for them to frustrate the purposes of the United States if doing so had the effect of preserving one of the last bastions of slavery in the Northern Hemisphere. Most important of all, the measure promised to deplete the southern labor force, inflict injury on its economy, and undermine the Confederacy's ability to wage war. Lincoln knew that the loss of their slaves would leave many Confederate officers with the choice of returning home to tend their fields or allowing their families to suffer through a winter of want and deprivation.

The Emancipation Proclamation of January 1, 1863, listed counties and states "wherein the people thereof, respectively, are this day in rebellion against the United States" and stated that all persons held as slaves within those regions "are and henceforward shall be free, and that the executive government of the United States, including the military and naval authorities thereof, will recognize and maintain the freedom of said persons."[94] As Union forces advanced during 1863, masters removed their slaves to interior locations.[95] The proclamation was not immediately carried out everywhere it might have been. General Ben Butler, commanding officer in Union-occupied New Orleans, insisted he could not free the slaves of that city as doing so would trigger a bloodbath, as racial frictions had reached dangerous levels. Slaves decided the matter for themselves when they could, escaping to Union lines where some were put to work for the Union army.[96]

The Proclamation received varying reactions. The *New York Times* approved, though it would have preferred to see it issued as a military order to avoid any confusion regarding its constitutionality, as in his civil authority, the president "has not the faintest shadow of authority to decree the emancipation of a single slave."[97] Former Justice Benjamin R. Curtis, whose lucid and powerful dissent in *Dred Scott* made him a hero to many, issued a pamphlet attacking the proclamation as beyond the war powers of the president. He saw it as targeting the slaves of loyal persons in the South, as the slaves of those aiding the rebellion had already been freed, at least in theory, by the Confiscation Acts. Curtis denied that the president had authority to free the slaves of loyal persons, as they were not fighting against the Union army or aiding the Confederacy.[98] That these persons were producing income with the help of slaves, which enabled them to contribute tax revenues to the Confederate government, seemed to undermine the arguments of Curtis. Within the Union army, most viewed the measure positively, though many soldiers did not take kindly to a move that threatened to convert the war's purpose from the preservation of the Union to the emancipation of slaves.[99]

President Lincoln disputed the charge that the war was being waged to free the slaves. As he stated in an August 1862 letter to Horace Greeley, he would save the Union without freeing a slave if such a thing was possible. "What I do about slavery and the colored race, I do because I believe it helps save the Union; and what I forbear, I forbear because I do not believe it would help save the Union."[100] In Congress vituperation as well as applause greeted the proclamation. Democrat Daniel W. Voorhees of Indiana let forth in February 1863 on the floor of the House. He bitterly recalled the president's numerous assurances that the war's only purpose was the preservation of the Union. Yet he has "gone vigorously to work, taking advantage of our national distress, to carry out every abolitionist measure ever dreamed of by the wildest and most enthusiastic zealots of the abolition faith."[101] Later that fall, after the president—evolving along with many others in his view of the war and the meaning of emancipation—spoke at

Gettysburg of a "new birth of freedom," the *Chicago Times* complained he had defamed the motives of the soldiers who were slain at Gettysburg. They "gave their lives to maintain the old government, and the only Constitution and Union."[102]

If emancipation was the most novel exercise of the government's war powers, the draft was the most critical to the war effort, even though it met with only partial success. It brought the war into every home in the North and constituted the most forceful and exacting use of federal authority in the nation's history. Proponents of the draft naturally claimed it qualified as necessary to the exercise of the power to raise an army.[103] Senator James Bayard of Delaware complained that it destroyed the militias that the Founders intended to serve as checks on the power of the national government.[104] A law of July 17, 1862, held a direct federal draft in abeyance in the hope it would cause the states to meet the quotas set for them in raising troops; it labeled each man between 17 and 45 a member of the militia.[105] Under the authority of that law, the War Department issued an order on August 4, 1862, providing for a draft of up to 300,000 members of the militia to fulfill any shortages remaining after the states conducted their own levies. Persons eligible for the draft were barred from leaving their counties of residence until the draft was completed. An August 8 order of the Secretary of War deprived those arrested for violating this provision of the right to seek a writ of habeas corpus.[106]

The exercise revealed the inefficiencies involved in acting through the states—not enough men were obtained, in part because the states exempted men in a variety of occupations from the obligation to serve.[107] A continuing shortage of men led Congress to enact the first strictly federal draft. A law of March 3, 1863, provided that able-bodied males between 18 and 45 constituted the national forces and were "liable to perform military duty in the service of the United States when called out by the president for that purpose."[108] Federal officers assigned to enrollment districts processed draftees and arrested those who deserted or resisted the draft. Men could pay $300 or provide a substitute to avoid service. Federal enrolling officers conducted house-to-house canvasses to locate and identify eligible males.[109] The *New York Times* applauded the law's passage. It denounced the state-based system that it replaced as "probably the worst plan the wit of man ever devised for keeping a large army in the field in full force and efficiency."[110] The *Times* dismissed suggestions that the law depleted the state militias and thereby violated the Constitution; men would be drafted "as citizens and not as [member of] a military organization."[111]

A total of four drafts were held before the end of the war; of the 776,000 persons called into service, only 46,000 eventually served in the Union army as draftees.[112] The 1863 draft law did serve to stimulate volunteering, causing the Union army to swell in size from 556,000 at the beginning of 1863 to over 918,000 by the end of the year.[113] Even as the military apparatus fell swiftly on those who frustrated the purpose of the draft, federal judges issued writs of habeas corpus for drafted men. Lincoln was so annoyed he spoke of arresting certain federal judges and sending them to the Confederacy.[114] Instead he issued an order in September 1863 that suspended the writ of habeas corpus in cases involving draftees.[115] The most notorious episode of resistance to the federal draft occurred in New York City. The metropolis had been sympathetic to the Confederacy and its laboring population—many of whom were immigrants—had no use for emancipation, which it feared would cause a glut in the labor supply and drive down wages. After the newspapers carried lists of draftees in their July 12, 1863, editions, rioters assembled in lower Manhattan and moved uptown, banging copper pans and closing businesses. They fought the police, ransacked the homes of the rich, removed rifles from the armory, and placed federal facilities under siege. Blacks were tortured and lynched in broad daylight. Federal troops moved in and imposed their will; they used a howitzer to clear Second Avenue. 119 persons died in the worst riot thus far in American history.[116]

REPUBLICAN INNOVATIONS

It would be inaccurate to say that measures such as emancipation, the draft, or the suspension of habeas corpus qualified as expansions of federal authority beyond the parameters established in 1787–1788; rather they constituted exercises of the government's war powers, which it had always possessed. That these powers had always existed did not lessen the shock of their deployment. Some of the most notable and novel exercises of federal power during the Civil War took place far from the conflict; the connection between some of these acts and the enumerated powers or the war was not always self-evident. Some of the most important novelties occurred in connection with the powers of taxation and appropriation. If mustering adequate manpower to put down the rebellion qualified as the national government's most critical challenge during the war, raising the necessary funds ranked a close second. Tariffs were raised four times, beginning with the Morrill Tariff of March 1861.[117] Under that law, necessaries were taxed at the lowest rate—10 percent, with items of lesser necessity taxed at 20 percent. Luxuries carried a 30 percent tax.[118] A tariff enacted on August 5, 1861, brought back duties on sugar, tea, and coffee—all necessaries, yet the federal government needed the revenue.[119] The tariff of July 14, 1862, imposed high duties for manufacturers to compensate them for the high rates imposed on imported raw materials. The average rate reached 37 percent.[120] The law produced increased prices as well as additional revenue.[121]

A law of June 30, 1864, pushed the average rate up to 47 percent.[122] During the war tariffs on imported salt were increased three times; the hikes enabled a New York company to double the price of its salt.[123] Burdens were all the greater because importers had to pay the impost in gold. While the increase in consumer prices arose out of an overheated economy and greenbacks as well as tariff hikes, Northerners suspected that the situation was being exploited for the benefit of a select few—those who turned out products or commodities that received protection. Proponents of high rates justified them on the grounds that they would last only as long as the war.[124]

The tariff's ability to warp the economy, its power to cause the flow of capital to run down channels it otherwise would have avoided and to seek investments made worthwhile only by the graces of the government, was not missed by lawmakers. Speaking in April 1864, Representative Alexander H. Rice of Massachusetts objected to yet another hike in the duty on wool—domestic production amounted to only 80 million pounds annually, while 135 million pounds was necessary to keep American mills running. More expensive wool—which was sure to follow an increase in the rate on imported wool—would mean reduced output by the mills and a loss of jobs. Onerous duties on raw materials, he complained, ran "contrary to the policy of every manufacturing nation on earth." S. S. Cox of Ohio responded that the manufacturers of New England were doing well—they were becoming the "nabobs of this country," yet they complained when farmers "ask for a little protection."[125] On June 2, Cox spoke of the duties on textiles that benefited those same manufacturers. He complained that a yard of calico that sold for 10 or 12 cents a yard before the war now cost 25 cents and the price of a yard of muslin had increased from 10 to 45 cents. He insisted that the rise in prices stemmed from increased duties. The Ohio Congressman claimed American manufacturers had already made $300 million in additional profits due to the price hikes they were able to impose since the enactment of the Tariff of 1862. The protective system, he complained, "makes the rich richer and the poor poorer."[126]

While tariffs served to transfer wealth from consumers to manufacturers, they did not meet the government's revenue needs. In 1862 Congress spent $500 million to fight the war; in 1864, over a billion.[127] Before the conflict was over, annual federal spending would grow from 2 to 15 percent of the gross national product.[128] Yet the government collected only $700 million in taxes during the war.[129] The balance was made up through bonds and greenbacks. Salmon P. Chase, secretary of the Treasury until late 1864, oversaw the effort to raise an adequate revenue. In early 1862 Congress gave the Treasury Department authority to issue

$500 million of 6 percent bonds redeemable by the government in five years. When early sales were disappointing, Chase turned to Jay Cooke. The financier sold bonds in denominations small enough to make them accessible to the burgeoning middle class of the North. He covered the country with subscription agents, advertised widely, and paid editors (via advertising) to preach the virtues of the issue. The campaign proved wildly successful; sales rose above $100,000 a day for a time.[130]

The task of raising funds was complicated by the inability of the Treasury Department to maintain an adequate currency. Its difficulties stemmed from Article I, Section 8—the only relevant power that it granted to Congress was the right to coin money. The national government did not have the means to coin silver and gold in the quantities that would have been necessary to enable the economy to rely on specie alone. State bank notes had long served as the most common circulating medium. The notes were supposedly redeemable in gold or silver; they were rarely worth their face value and Americans had to consult financial reports to determine the actual value of this depreciated paper before accepting it. State bank notes may well have constituted impermissible bills of credit, but the Supreme Court held to the contrary in 1837.[131] Shortly after the onset of hostilities, government demand for gold drove it out of circulation—though speculation in it remained rampant. Non-interest-bearing treasury notes as well as bonds served as substitutes in some areas.[132] City governments as well as banks and private businesses printed their own notes as the paper issued by the federal government remained in short supply, and the country remained awash in depreciating and often worthless state bank notes.

Desperate for a more reliable circulating medium, Chase convinced Congress to make postage stamps legal tender. The idea worked until the stamps disintegrated into inky, crumpled wads. Chase responded by issuing small denomination notes without congressional authorization. Congress eventually gave its blessing to these federal "shinplasters" that were issued in denominations as low as three cents. Chase also sought authority to issue $450 million in greenbacks or "fiat money" that was not redeemable in specie (gold or silver). Chase made the move reluctantly, but by early 1862, the prospect of an empty treasury left him with no real alternatives. Tired of having their gold reserves drained by the national government, the eastern banks embraced the measure.[133] Some lawmakers complained of their inability to find a power to issue paper money in the Constitution. Congress had issued paper money—bills of credit—during the War of 1812; the question was whether it could make these bills legal tender—obligating all to accept them as payment of debts—even though they were not redeemable in specie. Some believed the issuance of paper money fell within the enumerated powers if the notes were redeemable in gold or silver, on the theory that Congress can issue coin and paper could be made representative of coin.[134] Congressman Hendrick Wright of Pennsylvania was not of this view. He quoted Daniel Webster (1836) for the proposition that Congress "clearly has no power to substitute paper, or anything else, for coin, as a tender in payment of debts and in discharge of contracts."[135] William Kellogg of Illinois thought Congress possessed authority to "make currency for commerce" without elaborating on how far the creative power might be extended. Congress could pledge the "entire property of the country" for the redemption of said notes.[136] Timothy Howe of Wisconsin justified the issuing of greenbacks by claiming that the alternative—financing the war through yet more loans—would deprive the economy of capital and depress business activity.[137]

Financial difficulties forced the federal government to suspend specie payments on the last day of 1861. During the following weeks, government accounts ran dangerously low—soldiers and contractors went unpaid and the treasury was thought to be a month away from running out of money.[138] Congress authorized the issuance of greenbacks in February 1862; the notes were made legal tender for all debts except payment of interest on bonds and customs duties.[139] They were not redeemable in gold or silver. The issuing of greenbacks increased the government's financial resources for a time—it paid its debts with the notes as soon as they were printed. The notes ensured the overheating northern economy an adequate quantity of money.[140] Most important of all, greenbacks enabled the government to sell its bonds at reasonable rates and avoid ruinous inflation (prices did go up 80% during the war).[141] A March 1863 law authorized the issuance of $400 million in bonds and $150 million in greenbacks.[142] Greenbacks hit a low of 39 cents per gold dollar in the summer of 1864, before rising to 74 cents following Appomattox.[143]

Doubts regarding the power of the national government to make paper money legal tender lingered beyond the war and the Supreme Court ruled on the issue, for the first but not the last time, in 1870. Salmon Chase had been appointed Chief Justice in 1864. In an extraordinary bit of sangfroid, Chase wrote the majority opinion holding the legal tender acts of 1862 and 1863 unconstitutional with respect to debts assumed prior to the passage of those acts.[144] Chase denied that the war powers authorized the laws—they were not "appropriate and plainly adopted means for the execution of the power to declare and carry on a war."[145] As soon as the ruling was issued, interested parties went to work preparing appeals that would enable the Supreme Court to reverse itself. Prospects for a reversal were thought to improve with the appointment of two new justices, and relief was widespread when it became known that the Court would hear two appeals regarding the tender acts.[146] Sure enough, the Supreme Court reversed itself in *The Legal Tender Cases.*[147] Speaking for the majority, Justice William Strong noted that Congress had long acted under a broad view of its powers. "Under the power to establish post offices and post roads Congress has provided for carrying the mails, punishing the theft of letters, and even for transporting the mails to foreign countries. Under the power to regulate commerce, provision has been made by law for the improvement of harbors, the establishment of observatories, the erection of lighthouses, breakwaters, and buoys, the registry, enrollment and construction of ships, and a code has been enacted for the government of seamen."[148] Strong recalled that the legal tender law had been enacted at a time when the government had exhausted its financial resources but faced the necessity of paying soldiers in the field as well as those who sold supplies to the government.[149] As for the claim that the clause empowering Congress to coin money implicitly barred it from issuing paper money, Strong suggested that a power "over a particular subject may be exercised as an auxiliary to an express power (the power to make war), though there is another express power (the power to coin money) related to the same subject, less comprehensive."[150] In 1884 the Supreme Court held that Congress could make paper notes legal tender even in peacetime.[151] In his opinion for the Court, Justice Horace Gray explained that its authority to do so derived from the enumerated power to borrow as well as the power to coin money.[152]

Difficulties in the sale of bonds and the desire to supplement greenbacks with a second form of national currency led the administration to recommend the establishment of a network of national banks.[153] A lack of adequate depositories added momentum to the cause. Federal law barred state banks from holding federal funds; instead, treasury department officials deposited revenue in the handful of sub-treasuries located on the east coast.[154] Jacob Collamer, senator of Vermont, denounced a provision of the bank bill that would have imposed a burdensome tax on state bank notes. After listening to other lawmakers talk of using the tax power to eradicate state bank notes—and possibly even state banks themselves—he warned his colleagues that the use of the tax power to destroy state entities that met with the wrath of the national government could be deployed against different targets in the future. Collamer also objected to the federal government's establishment of corporations in the states—these entities would be impervious to state authority. He complained that the bill would make the United States the guarantor of the debts of the national banks. The treasury secretary's power to inspect the books of these institutions and close them down could be used by an unscrupulous official for political purposes, such as exacting campaign contributions.[155] The absence of southerners again proved critical—for decades most southern lawmakers had opposed a national bank as beyond the powers of Congress. Many had memorized the arguments heard at the time Andrew Jackson (1832) and John Tyler (1841) vetoed national bank bills, as well as the comments offered by Thomas Jefferson and Alexander Hamilton at the time Congress established the first Bank of the United States in 1791. The cause of a national bank had been hampered by the inability of advocates to settle on the clause of the Constitution that authorized the endeavor. Thus the charge of Henry Clay of 1811: the "vagrant power to establish a bank" had "wondered throughout the whole Constitution in quest of some congenial spot on which to fasten."[156]

With southerners absent from the capital, Secretary of the Treasury Salmon Chase's assertion that measure derived authority from the powers to tax, borrow, and regulate commerce and coinage elicited little protest.[157] While the bank bill did not encounter resistance on constitutional grounds, the large banks of the east bitterly opposed it. Lawmakers from New York and New England voted against it while westerners voted for it.[158] The National Bank Act of 1863 provided that associations of five persons or more could join the system once they deposited with the treasury at least $50,000 in U.S. bonds equal in value to one-third or more of the bank's capital stock. The banks would receive circulating notes worth up to 90 percent of the bonds. Said notes would be accepted at par as payment for all debts except customs duties. Failure of a member bank to redeem its notes in lawful money would result in forfeiture of its bonds and the sale of its assets by a receiver. Treasury officials were authorized to deposit federal revenues in national banks. Each member of the national bank system had to maintain cash reserves in an amount at least equal to 25 percent of their notes in circulation and deposits. Shareholders were personally liable for an amount equal to twice the value of their shares. Finally, the law authorized national banks to make loans and charge interest "at the established rate."[159] In practice, this provision allowed states to set the maximum rate of interest that could be charged by national banks within their borders.[160]

The law proved unworkable. The prospect of the financial markets barring the notes of the national banks led Congress to revise it with the National Bank Act of 1864. Among the provisions of the law was one barring the states from taxing the national banks.[161] The leading banks of New York City refused to join the national system. Among their objections was the provision requiring them to maintain their notes in a fixed ratio to the total value of the government bonds the law required them to buy. They would have to purchase more bonds whenever they dropped in value, as often occurred when the Union army met with adversity on the battlefield.[162] Under pressure from Jay Cooke—who threatened to set up his own institution in Manhattan that would alone have the privilege of accepting federal deposits—the banks relented and joined a system that routed money from smaller banks all over the country into their vaults.[163]

Congress established the national bank system in part to aid the sale of bonds—banks had to buy them to deposit them with the treasury in exchange for notes—but difficulties continued. Shortly before his resignation in 1864, Chase had to withdraw an issue of five-twenty bonds as the market was saturated. Only the discovery of gold in Colorado and Nevada saved the national government from the necessity of resorting to exorbitant bond rates to raise money (the gold stimulated the economy and improved tax revenues). At one point the national government attempted to claim ownership of the gold mines, as titles to western lands were not sold with mineral rights attached. Officials dropped the idea when they realized they could not spare the troops that would have been necessary to put the edict into effect. Even with the infusion of gold, Chase's successor, William Pitt Fessenden, had to resort to the skills of Jay Cooke to move a new bond issue in early 1865—the national banks proved inadequate to the task—despite the fact that Cooke was by then among the most unpopular men in the country, as he was thought to have taken too large of a cut from previous bond sales.[164]

The National Bank Act of 1863 imposed a tax of 1 percent on the circulating notes of national banks and 2 percent on the entire capital of state banks.[165] A law of March 3, 1865, levied a tax on state bank notes issued for circulation of 10 percent, a level that was considered prohibitory (effective July 1, 1866).[166] Congress enacted the measure in the hope that it would cause state banks to join the national system to retain the privilege of issuing notes. The idea of Congress using its tax power to achieve what it lacked authority to do directly with a prohibitory statute—the banning of state bank notes—was not embraced by all. Tennessee Senator Andrew Johnson struck at the heart of the issue in 1864. In his view, "the tax power is . . . given exclusively for raising revenue, except so far as it relates to the use which may be made of the power (to impose tariffs) for the protection of domestic manufacturers; and even as to that, as the Senate is aware, there has existed, and still exists, very contradictory opinions." He acknowledged that the motives of Congress in passing a law "cannot be inquired into in any judicial proceeding," yet he insisted that it did not have authority to ban state bank notes via prohibitory taxes.[167] Speaking on the matter in the spring of 1865, Senator Thomas Hendricks of Indiana complained that lawmakers favored the tax in the hope it would "clear the field" for the national banks.[168] John Sherman of Ohio thought that the state bank notes were themselves unconstitutional—states were explicitly barred from issuing bills of credit, so institutions of their creation—state banks—could not either.[169] Speaking in May 1864, he estimated there were

$400 million in U.S. notes and $167 million in state banks notes in circulation—far too much. The need to reduce this amount warranted the eradication of state bank notes.[170] The Supreme Court weighed in five years later in *Veazie Bank v. Fenno*, when it held that the prohibitory tax on state bank notes was a constitutional exercise by Congress of its power to establish a national currency.[171]

Income was taxed for the first time pursuant to a law of August 5, 1861 (3% on incomes over $800).[172] Before the war was over, approximately 10 percent of all households in the North found themselves paying federal income taxes.[173] The highest tax was eventually raised to 10 percent and deductions were allowed for state and local taxes, as well as rental expenses.[174] To allow deductions for certain activities was to subsidize them, at least indirectly; the practice had the same potential as a tool for reaching subjects beyond the enumerated powers as the imposition of prohibitory taxes on certain activities. In 1864 officials estimated that deductions for rental expenses claimed by residents of New York City alone cost the government $2 million.[175] The deduction itself likely contributed to a steep rise in rents, as it made people more willing to spend large amounts on rental expenses—doing so lowered their tax liability. Revenues suffered due to the abuse of deductions and the filing of false returns by many Americans. Their willingness to do so does not seem to have been appreciably affected by the fact that the newspapers routinely published returns until the Treasury Department stopped making them public in 1870. Between 1862 and 1872, the income tax produced about one fifth of the federal government's internal revenues—$376 million—despite the fact that less than 300,000 Americans earned enough to be subject to it. The tax was widely supported in vast areas where few persons earned enough income to incur any tax liability under its provisions.[176]

The July 1, 1862, Revenue Act imposed a tax of three quarters of 1 percent on the portion of all estates exceeding $1,000.[177] It also established a license tax for every conceivable occupation, thus requiring everyone from jugglers to lawyers to innkeepers to buy a federal license in exchange for the right to pursue their chosen vocation. The law established the Bureau of Internal Revenue and set up a network of assessors and collectors. Taxes were also imposed on the gross receipts of businesses. Thirty cents for every head of slaughtered cattle went to the federal assessor, as did one half of 1 percent of the gross receipts of railroads, steamboats, and ferry companies. The law set specific rates for items such as cigars, whiskey, playing cards, jewelry, and billiard tables and yachts; it imposed a 3 percent sales tax on the sale of all other manufactured goods.[178] Taxes on many products increased exponentially as the war progressed. The excise on whiskey grew from 22 cents to two dollars a gallon.[179] Higher taxes helped produce higher prices; pure alcohol—also heavily taxed—went from 34 cents a gallon to $4.25 in 1865, causing people to find substitutes for the alcohol-based burning fluid used for illumination in homes.[180]

Harper's Weekly acknowledged that there would be evasions of the new taxes, but it insisted that the tax on manufacturers and the income tax—the "two great taxes"—would be collected. It predicted that the increased burden on Northerners would make a people heretofore indifferent to public waste and devoted to expensive living aware of the need for economy in government as well as in their own lives.[181] Northerners were no doubt grateful for the education. Senator James McDougall of California saw in the internal revenue system the birth of an inefficient, overbearing bureaucracy that would accomplish little more than providing more offices for party managers to distribute among their legions. "Put this bill, in force, appoint your collectors, your inspectors, and your assessors, put them in the field, and they will be an army strong enough to take Richmond, or this capital if you please. I hold the greatest evil of republican institutions to be the multitude of offices permitted, and the multitude of men seeking office." He objected "to the army of officers (who will be appointed) to carry on this great machine and the country will object to it."[182]

Some did not bother complying with the revenue laws. Wholesale businesses were required to buy a new license whenever their gross sales exceeded a particular amount; many failed to do so and took out only one new license each year. Some issued false information regarding their sales to avoid the need to buy additional licenses. The *Chicago Daily Tribune* responded by announcing it would stop publishing information regarding wholesale receipts, as it "did not care to have the real business of the city officially belittled through (the) negligence of those who have failed to comply with it (the law)."[183] Ungainly as it was, the internal revenue system assured purchasers of bonds that the government would have the revenue necessary to meet its obligations—bond sales increased sharply once the internal revenue system began operating.[184] By early 1863, it was clear that if the war effort failed, it would be due to stumbling generals and not a depleted treasury.

An expansion of the revenue-collecting apparatus in time of war was unavoidable, but the license tax, above the other measures used to raise money, injected the federal government into areas that had formerly been left to the states. It was true that the law imposing license taxes specifically provided that said licenses would authorize no acts barred by state laws. Yet it was also true that lawmakers were acutely aware of the tax code's potential to stimulate activity they approved of, and to discourage activity they disliked. James F. Simmons of Rhode Island wanted to impose progressively steep license taxes on auctioneers—up to $1,000 in the larger cities—as his constituents were increasingly being victimized by what he called mock or "Jew auctions" in which associates of the seller bid up the price of an article to defraud innocent buyers. He explained that he wanted to put the auctioneering business into the hands of "responsible men."[185] James McDougall of California objected to a provision requiring two licenses of auctioneers—one for operating as a merchant and another for operating as an auctioneer. He was at a loss as to why auctions should serve as prey for the tax code. "What should be the reason for a law against auctioneers? I had thought that they were men who most promptly transacted the business of the country. In San Francisco nearly all the trade sales are conducted by auctioneers. . . . That is the way much of our wholesale business is done."[186] McDougall was also troubled by the proposal to require a federal license for every conceivable occupation. "There is hardly a subject of license in this bill that is not (already) made the subject of state license, many of town license; and now a person who wants to engage in an occupation has to go to the president of the town council, to the comptroller of the state, and to the agent of the United States; and when he has got these three licenses, he may go to work." In lieu of a broad, complicated, and invasive tax system and the bureaucracy necessary to administer it, McDougall suggested imposing a simple 1 percent tax on sales as well as a modest inheritance tax.[187]

McDougall was ignored and Congress plunged into the regulation of occupations via its tax power. A March 3, 1863, law imposed an extraordinary and burdensome requirement on auctioneers—they had to purchase a new federal license in every district they wished to work. The law exempted physicians, surgeons, dentists, and lawyers—occupations that also required travel—from this requirement.[188] Ambitions for the system outran its capacities almost immediately; officials failed to distribute licenses quickly enough to meet the deadlines for compliance. In October 1862 lawyers in Chicago found themselves facing the prospect of practicing law without a federal license when the required certificates did not arrive from the Treasury Department. When asked in court about the problem, U.S. District Judge Thomas Drummond indicated he would make no inquiries on the subject, but he warned that if the matter was raised in court, he would have to rule that any lawyer who appeared before him without a federal license was not a practicing attorney. He suggested members of the bar deposit payment for the license fees with the assessor and obtain the related paperwork, rather than wait for the federal government to deliver the licenses it required all to have.[189]

Congress continued to nibble away at the limits on its power of appropriation during the war. The prevailing view before the conflict held that Congress could only fund subjects directly related to one of the enumerated powers—Alexander Hamilton's claim that it could spend money on any subject conducive to the general welfare had fallen into disrepute.[190] During the 1820s, lawmakers offered the novel theory that the commerce clause bestowed a right to facilitate trade as well as regulate it in support of the legality of appropriations for the dredging of rivers and harbors. Advocates saw a precedent for these expenditures in the laws providing funds for navigational aids along the east coast such as lighthouses, beacons, buoys, and piers that had been made as early as 1789.[191] Others suggested that coastal improvements constituted exercises of the power to establish a navy. The forces seeking to broaden the spending power also relied on the language of the territories clause—it provided that Congress "shall have Power to dispose of and make all needful Rules and Regulations" regarding federal lands and property. They claimed that Congress could "dispose of" the territories or revenue derived from land sales in any manner it saw fit. The Distribution Act of 1841 gave western states 10 percent of the proceeds from the sale of land within their borders; the balance of revenues from said lands was turned over to the eastern states.[192] During the 1850s, Congress passed bills giving land sale revenues to insane asylums and agricultural colleges only to see them vetoed by Democratic presidents on constitutional grounds.

The Republican Party, new to the national scene in 1860, was composed largely of former Whigs who embraced a more generous view of federal power than their opponents. Following the exodus of southern Democrats from Washington in early 1861, Republicans found themselves in control of both houses of Congress as well as the presidency. They made the most of the opportunity presented to them. In the spring of 1863, Senator Ben Wade of Ohio introduced a bill donating lands in the West to the states for agricultural colleges similar to one that James Buchanan had vetoed in 1859. The Committee on Public Lands reported negatively on the proposal.[193] The reluctance of westerners to go along with the "land grab" was overcome with eastern votes for a homestead law and the land grant college bill became law on July 2, 1862.[194] The measure donated lands to the states for the benefit of the mechanical and agricultural arts, with the proceeds from the sale of the lands to be invested in bonds of the United States "or some safe stocks." The law required that the interest be "inviolably appropriated" by each state for the endowment and support of schools devoted to the above-mentioned subjects. Said funds were not to be used for the construction or maintenance of school buildings—thus requiring the states to spend their own money. They also had to submit annual reports to Congress regarding the progress of each college. States in rebellion were barred from participating in the program (they were made eligible for the program after the war).[195] Several state universities, including those of California, Minnesota, Wisconsin, and Illinois, were established with land sale revenues provided under the Morrill Land Grant College Act. The progress of the colleges in the years after the war was hampered for a time by the refusal of states to spend adequate sums on the schools—many were saddled with war debts that took decades to pay.[196]

A May 1862 law established a Department of Agriculture despite the fact that the subject did not appear among the enumerated powers of Congress. Nor was there much of a demand for such an agency among farmers.[197] The Department of Agriculture was authorized to "acquire and to diffuse among the people of the United States useful information on subjects connected with agriculture" and to distribute "among the people new and valuable seeds and plants."[198] The Patent Office had provided members of Congress with seeds to distribute among their constituents since the 1850s, thus the failure of lawmakers to explore the question of constitutional authority when they discussed the bill—they viewed it as merely transferring activities of the Patent Office to the new department. By 1864, the Department's activities included the publication of monthly crop bulletins and the operation of modest scientific facilities as well as seed distribution.[199]

The Homestead Act of May 20, 1862, authorized persons who were 21 or over, the head of a household, and either a citizen of the United States or a veteran to file a preemption claim for quarter sections (160 acres) of un-appropriated federal lands. Ownership would vest after the applicant occupied and improved the land for five years—one year if they served in the Union army.[200] The program was derided as an exchange of land for votes, though persons applying for the grants still had to pay a $10 fee. Enactment of the law was seen as a great victory by self-appointed tribunes such as Andrew Johnson who had been pushing homestead bills for years, yet it made little practical difference in a country where land was cheap and plentiful. Many of those who obtained grants took out mortgages to take advantage of rising crop prices only to default on their obligations when the inevitable bad crop arrived.[201] Others took up farming in the Plains states, where 160 acres was inadequate. Still, the law proved a boon to farming; it enabled struggling farmers to give up their eternal battles with the rocky soil of New England for more fertile areas, such as Iowa and Minnesota.[202]

The homestead law's progress was made easier by the fact that the Interior Department was already selling land for nominal sums; land had also been given away to veterans and railroads. In 1850 Congress turned land over to Illinois, Alabama, and Mississippi on the condition that proceeds from the sale of said lands be used to finance the construction of railroad lines from the Midwest to the Gulf of Mexico.[203] During the next seven years, Congress donated seven million acres in the Mississippi Valley to the states for railroad construction.[204] The Pacific Railroad Act of July 1, 1862, provided aid for construction of a railroad and telegraph line to the Pacific Ocean "and to secure to the Government the use of same for postal, military and other purposes."[205] As the statute itself implied, most conceded the right of Congress to build railroads when necessary for military purposes. Opinions varied on the question of whether the commerce clause authorized aid to railroads.[206] The law provided that the federal government would enjoy a preference in the use of the lines for the transportation of mail, troops, and munitions, and it would pay no more than "fair and reasonable rates of compensation, not to exceed the amounts paid by private parties." The statute incorporated the Union Pacific Railroad, gave it a right of way through federal territory, and authorized generous land grants as well as financial aid (bonds) to help the railroad build a line extending west from Missouri. The line's western terminus would be met by a railroad heading east from northern California to be built by the Central Pacific, a California corporation. Lawmakers decided against having the federally incorporated Union Pacific build the section extending through California to avoid offending those who doubted the authority of Congress to create a corporation for the purpose of building a railroad within a state.[207] (Many states barred corporations chartered in other jurisdictions from doing business within their borders.) In providing financial aid directly to the railroads the measure was without precedent, though during the 1820s Congress had authorized the purchase of shares of canal-building companies.[208]

One innovation of importance in the long run but little noticed at the time was the formation of the National Academy of Sciences pursuant to a statute of March 3, 1863.[209] This entity was charged with the duty of investigating and reporting on any area of science when asked to do so by a department of the federal government. The Academy grew out of a temporary committee formed by Navy Secretary Gideon Welles for the purpose of providing technical assistance to the navy.[210] The need of a modern government, even one of enumerated powers, for technical competence in a thousand different areas, from the design of bullets to the composition of stamps, justified the introduction of a federal scientific establishment from a constitutional as well as a practical point of view. In time lawmakers and idealists would discover that the guise of inquiry offered an ideal opening for forays into matters beyond the federal sphere.

The chief asset of the federal government in the conduct of the war was the huge population of the North—about 22 million, compared to 9 million in the South. A close second was a vibrant and varied economy, which had already made the United States one of the wealthiest nations on earth.

After the shock of secession produced a panic in New York City, the northern economy drew a deep breath and moved forward, like a great, belching locomotive. The demand for military goods stimulated business in a variety of trades, and the infusion of government cash ushered in good times across the North. The lumber industry of the Great Lakes states exploded; much of the wood ended up in Chicago, which itself swelled mightily during the war. The shoe factories of New England hummed, as did the woolen industry, which could not locate enough workers. Railroads made great profits moving military supplies; eventually they ran short of cars.[211] Iron and coal production jumped and the North built more merchant ships than it had in any previous four-year period. Exports of key agricultural commodities doubled.[212] Wall Street enjoyed a boom in railroad stocks. Contractors who provided the military with supplies became rich overnight—though fraud was so endemic that Congress enacted a law that made them part of the U.S. military establishment so they could be tried by military courts.[213] Whole towns grew up around factories built to supply armaments or equipment to the national government and then disappeared when the war ended.[214] The War Department provided thousands with employment, as the naval yards and arsenals saw their staffs balloon. Industries that produced critical goods saw labor strife as the war progressed and inflation worsened; at one point seamstresses demanded that federal officials impose a minimum wage in their industry or employ them directly and raise their wages. The request was ignored.[215] The U.S. Army broke strikes in war-related industries in New York and Missouri and the federal government operated the Reading Railroad in Pennsylvania after its employees stopped working in a dispute over pay.[216]

Nothing in the North benefited more from the war boom than the bustling entrepot situated on the island of Manhattan. New York City, the nation's largest city since early in the century, received an injection of capital from the war that would place it on a course to threaten London's role as the world's financial capital by 1900. The financial policies of the government, novel and varied as they were, all seemed to have the same incidental effect: pouring more money into the vaults of New York City banks. As soon as the law allowed, the Lincoln administration stored government deposits with private institutions instead of federal subtreasuries. The National Bank Act required "country banks" to maintain reserves equal to at least 15 percent of their total deposits; of this amount, three-fifths could be deposited in one of 17 federally recognized regional banks in major cities. These in turn exercised their right to keep up to half of their own required reserves in New York City banks. When the tax on state bank notes drove them out of circulation in 1865, the number of banks in the national system jumped from 681 to 2,080 in 1877, thereby bringing more money to New York. The war turned trade routes in the Midwest away from the Mississippi River and the South and toward the northeast, funneling the commodities of the nation's breadbasket into east coast ports. The deluge of money helped ensure that capital earned a higher rate of return in New York City than in any other part of the country.[217] Complaints over the financial dominance of the nation's first city—which were heard even before the war—became pervasive.

The booming economy of the North helped provide the federal government with the revenue it needed to fight the war. The War Department exploited the opportunity afforded it, though it took time for the Union war machine to work up a full head of steam. There were not enough rifles to go around, and while the federal government ordered approximately 1.1 million rifles and rifled muskets by July 1862, the guns had to be manufactured before they could be delivered.[218] The situation was rectified over the next 18 months—by 1864 more firearms were being produced than the Union army needed.[219] Modern weapons such as breechloaders were now in the possession of the government, though the War Department remained painfully slow in distributing them until almost the end of the conflict. A vast new bureaucracy was employed to administer the gargantuan tasks of feeding, clothing, sheltering, and arming Union troops. The quartermaster alone employed 7,000 clerks. Overall the federal payroll (not including troops) expanded from 60,000 to just shy of 200,000 by the end of the war, with 136,000 employees in the War Department alone.[220]

The firearms industry was not the only one to feel the benevolent hand of the national government during the war. The railroads and related industries did as well. By 1864 manufacturers were delivering a locomotive a day to the War Department.[221] A January 1862 statute authorized the president to take over the railroads as well their rolling stock, buildings, and equipment. Telegraph lines were also made subject to federal confiscation.[222] The law authorized the president to set railroad rates and provided for the drafting of railroad and telegraph employees into the military if necessary to ensure that the railroads continued to operate smoothly. A commission of railroad representatives and War Department officials met in Washington, DC, in early 1862. It established a system of rates for both passenger and freight traffic. Two cents a mile was paid for the transportation of soldiers. The commission provided benefits to the railroads as well as the Union army; it established connections between lines and made much progress in standardizing gauges.[223] Railroads had to provide rate schedules to the War Department and notify it of any changes.[224] Having obtained reasonable rates, the War Department did not bother taking over the railroads en masse; only a few lines in Pennsylvania and Maryland were turned over to the government (though the Union army took over and operated many railroads in the South).[225] Military Director and Superintendent of the Railroads of the United States Daniel C. McCallum oversaw an establishment that had 25,000 employees by the end of the war. It built railroads of some 650 miles in length. This network was complemented by the U.S. Military Telegraph Bureau, which employed 1,500 operators by 1863.[226]

At the head of the Union organizational effort was Edwin M. Stanton, an intense and able lawyer who succeeded Simon Cameron at the War Department in 1862. Stanton brought intelligence and foresight to the task as well as puritanical zeal. Despite his past as a Buchanan Democrat, Stanton worked closely with radical members of Congress and the Committee on the Conduct of the War, which itself aided the war effort by deploying its subpoena power to investigate matters beyond the reach of War Department.[227] The president took only a modest interest in administrative matters. His mighty contribution to the Union cause arose out of the firmness of his resolve and his ability to manage Congress—much to the chagrin of radicals, who chafed at his unwillingness to embrace their program of vengeance. Lincoln succeeded in steering a middle course between those seeking accommodation and those determined to pound the southern people into dust. In the fall of 1862 the president's leadership qualities were not entirely evident to northern voters. His skills as a military strategist were not universally recognized, either. On the eve of the midterm elections the administration was embarrassed by the failure of McClellan's peninsular campaign. Democrats made much of the federal government's excesses in the area of civil liberties, but the opposition party itself was rent by factions. One favored peace while the other supported the war effort. New York Democrat Horatio Seymour ran for governor on a platform calling for restoration of the Old Union and Constitution. That such a thing was impossible—the South had no interest in reunification—did not prevent him from winning. Democrats also carried New Jersey and Illinois and gained some 25 congressional seats (a majority in Indiana, Ohio, and Pennsylvania). Republicans retained a working majority in the House; they also secured 33 of 52 seats in the Senate.[228] A profoundly negative popular response to the president's September 1862 announcement that slaves in rebel areas would be emancipated allowed Democrats to strengthen their majority in the Indiana legislature. Fearing the majority would imperil the state's war effort, Republicans withdrew in order to deny their opponents the quorum they needed to operate. Republican Governor Oliver Morton refused to call the legislature into session during the next two years; instead, he governed the state as a virtual dictator with the help of loans provided by county governments as well as $250,000 from the War Department.[229]

CONSOLIDATION AND VICTORY

In the spring of 1863, Union troops set out to take Vicksburg, along with Port Hudson, the last remaining Confederate stronghold on the Mississippi River. After moving his men south of the city, landing them on the eastern shore and moving inland, Ulysses S. Grant advanced toward it from the southeast. During May and June a Union siege slowly choked the life out of Vicksburg. With residents reduced to living in caves to avoid Union cannonballs, Grant's men patiently dug the trenches necessary to approach Confederate lines in safety. With its residents starving, the city fell on July 4. A few days later Port Hudson fell, allowing Union shipping to move up and down the Mississippi River at will. The Confederacy had been permanently divided. On July 3, the most critical battle of the war concluded at Gettysburg, Pennsylvania. After Robert E. Lee spent two days attacking Union troops dug in along a small ridge south of the village, he ordered a Confederate division under the command of George Pickett to mount a frontal attack across a wheat field on July 3. The advance across a mile of open terrain was preceded by the loudest artillery barrage of the war—it could be heard in Pittsburgh, on the other side of the state. Pickett's charge resulted in the destruction of half of his division, and the Army of Northern Virginia suffered defeat for the first time. After Union forces narrowly prevented the fall of Chattanooga to Confederate forces, General William Tecumseh Sherman mounted an invasion of Georgia that resulted in the capture of Atlanta and the severing of railroads that provided Lee's troops with grain. After pausing for a time, Sherman and his men marched to Savannah. They left a 60-mile-wide path of destruction in their wake, destroying everything that could sustain or in any way benefit the Confederate army, including farm equipment, railroad tracks, and foundries. Sheep and cattle were slaughtered, and dogs that appeared capable of tracking runway slaves were shot.[230]

The fall of Vicksburg brought Ulysses S. Grant international fame and the command of all Union armies. He joined the Army of the Potomac, which remained under the immediate command of George Gordon Meade, the hero of Gettysburg. In early May 1864, Grant and Meade began a push into Virginia. The men under them repeatedly clashed with the Army of Northern Virginia. Unlike his predecessors, Grant responded to these engagements—which were exceedingly costly—by pushing forward, deeper into Virginia toward the critical railroad junction of Petersburg. The Army of the Potomac sustained 65,000 casualties between May 1 and mid-June 1864, and the loss of the equivalent of an entire army sent the northern public into another bout of despair. Gold rose to unprecedented levels. That Grant had largely replaced his losses, inflicted 35,000 casualties on the rebels, and pushed them back 80 miles was of little consolation to Northerners tired of the war and unable to see a way to victory.[231] Lincoln's reelection prospects seemed poor. Treasury Secretary Salmon P. Chase wanted the nomination of the Republican or Union Party. Radicals in Congress were also less than enthused about the prospect of renominating Lincoln. They convinced themselves that the president was dominated by moderates such as Seward and Thurlow Weed; in fact, it was the other way around.

What really angered radicals was Lincoln's refusal to let Congress impose a harsh form of "reconstruction" on the southern states occupied by Union forces. His preference for letting Southerners organize loyal state governments made them apoplectic. While a radical plan to replace Lincoln as the Republican nominee fizzled before the election year of 1864 opened, Chase continued to plot. Hoping he might yet gain the presidency—an office he had long had his eye on—the Ohioan had Treasury Department employees labor on his behalf. Postmaster General Montgomery Blair wielded the formidable resources of his department in support of the president. Blair also managed to turn the navy yards into "cogs" for the incumbent.[232] When a deluge of endorsements for the president burst forth from northern legislatures, newspapers, and political clubs, the Chase boom went bust. While the nation's leading Republican editors, William Cullen Bryant and Horace Greeley, refused to endorse Lincoln, the president was re-nominated at Baltimore in mid-June 1864 by an entity that now styled itself the National Union Party. The name change stemmed from the hope of gaining the support of "War Democrats"—the wing of the Democratic Party that supported the war. The nomination of Tennessee Senator Andrew Johnson in lieu of the incumbent, Hannibal Hamlin of Maine, also arose from a desire to broaden the ticket's appeal. The platform insisted on unconditional surrender by the South and called for ratification of a constitutional amendment banning slavery throughout the nation.[233] Chase resigned after the convention and returned home to Ohio, where he continued to be a source of difficulty. In a remarkable act of magnanimity, the president nominated his one-time rival to succeed Roger Brooke Taney as chief justice in December 1864.

The fissures that had formed between Lincoln and the radical wing of his party threatened to widen into a chasm when he vetoed the Wade-Davis reconstruction bill in July 1864, in part because it would have banned slavery in the South by statute, something the president believed Congress did not have authority to do. A splinter group nominated John C. Fremont on a platform that held Congress must determine reconstruction policy. It also called for the confiscation of the lands of planters in the South so they could be turned over to former slaves. While Fremont withdrew in September, radicals continued to chafe, and Republicans of every stripe doubted that the president would beat the Democratic nominee, General George McClellan. The markets didn't think much of the president's reelection prospects, either, and the price of gold jumped.[234] Republicans might have taken some consolation in a quiet but noticeable shift that was underway. The electorate had embraced the preservation of the Union and it naturally associated the president with that cause. One observer wrote of his experience traveling on a train in the East. He encountered lifelong Democrats, including men from the Border States, who intended to vote for Lincoln. "They now go for the salvation of the country, which could be secured only by the re-election of Mr. Lincoln."[235] The president maintained the public silence regarding political matters that had been the practice of his predecessors, though he did point out for a Wisconsin judge one likely consequence of a McClellan victory: If the Democrats acted on their promise to disband black regiments, the move would cost the Union army 200,000 men.[236]

Democrats had their own problems. The party convention in Chicago saddled its nominee with a platform that labeled the war a failure and urged the commencement of peace negotiations. In a letter accepting the nomination, McClellan disavowed the plank calling the war a failure.[237] The general's difficulties continued during the fall, in part because his supporters included so many Copperheads who wished to reach an accommodation with an independent Confederacy, such as New York City Congressman Fernando Wood. Democrats repeated old complaints regarding the concentration of public authority. Speaking in Monmouth, Illinois, Clement Vallandigham declared he was "opposed to centralization of power in one government from the Atlantic to the Pacific." He called for the reconstruction of the Union on the basis of state sovereignty.[238] Years of practice had left Americans well-trained in disregarding complaints over the accumulation of power in Washington, and the sympathy of leading Democrats for the notion of an armistice rendered the election of McClellan unpalatable to many. During the late summer and fall of 1864, a steady accumulation of Union victories made Democratic calls for an accommodation look somewhat ridiculous. These included the capture of Fort Morgan in Mobile Bay in August, the fall of Atlanta in early September, and Phillip Sheridan's victory at Fisher's Hill in the Shenandoah Valley a few weeks later. The capture of Mobile Bay was crucial because it closed the last port east of Texas that had been used by blockade runners. Union successes eased frictions among Republicans, and party unity was also strengthened by the resignation in September of Postmaster General Montgomery Blair, a longtime enemy of the radicals.

With a federal establishment four times the size of what it had been when Buchanan left office (not including the army), Republicans had another advantage. Many of the tens of thousands of civil servants in the War and Treasury Departments as well as the Post Office were forced to pay assessments (campaign contributions). In New York City money was openly collected at the customhouse and the post office. The president professed to oppose the practice of extorting money from civil servants but made no discernible effort to stop it. Republican inexperience may have compromised the effort—Edwin Stanton estimated that when they controlled the executive branch during the 1850s, Democrats collected two dollars for every dollar gathered by Republicans.[239] The navy agent in San Francisco admitted that he tried to arrange for the city's navy yard to hire 200 men on the eve of the election. A Democratic editor complained of the futility of a contest against an administration "disbursing millions daily, employing one-third of the active industries of the whole population, and directing the interested energies of a whole army of stipendiaries scattered through every city, town, and village in the land."[240]

Both parties toyed dangerously with the soldier vote. Eighteen states enacted laws allowing soldiers to vote in the field between 1860 and 1864, but complications were many. The soldiers had to be located before they could be provided with ballots, and the War Department ignored requests of New York State officials for information regarding the location of soldiers from the Empire State until the president intervened. Thereafter War Department personnel devoted a great deal of time to ensuring that soldiers could vote in the 1864 election. New York had to amend its constitution and enact a law to ensure that soldiers could vote in the field; Governor Seymour objected on the grounds that fraud would be encouraged. Shortly thereafter military officials discovered Democratic Party operatives were printing and casting soldiers' ballots. When the wrongdoers were tried by military commissions, a New York delegation arrived in Washington to protest that the federal government was usurping the authority of the states. Politicians seeking votes traveled to the front and even visited ships participating in the blockade in violation of regulations that banned campaigning among the troops. When Pennsylvania failed to allow soldiers to vote in 1862, Thaddeus Stevens raised the possibility of enacting a federal law ensuring soldiers could vote in presidential elections.[241]

As the results of the state elections began coming in, it became clear that members of the Union army had no interest in condemning their own work. Pennsylvania went Republican in October; so did Indiana and Ohio. After spending much of the year convinced he would serve only one term, Lincoln now concluded he would win, albeit by only three electoral votes.[242] As Election Day approached, soldiers went home in droves, and the Union lines before Petersburg were seriously depleted for a time.[243] New York soldiers, suspicious of the state's Democratic governor, refused to trust him to count their absentee ballots and returned home.[244]

On the eve of the election, The *New York Times* issued an editorial aimed at the city's well-to-do, many of whom continued to sympathize with the South. It predicted that if McClellan won the election, an armistice would follow, during which the South would obtain needed supplies and foreign support. Thereafter, time and inertia would produce southern independence. The western states would themselves secede and the national government would default on its obligations, including the bonds held by thousands of prosperous New Yorkers.[245] With the telegraph, Americans learned of the verdict quickly. The first report, from Indianapolis, arrived at the War Department at 6:30 in the evening; it showed the president with a lead in the Hoosier state of 1,500 votes.[246] A dispatch from New York indicated Lincoln had carried that state by 10,000 ballots. By midnight it was clear that New England, Ohio, Indiana, Michigan, Wisconsin, and Maryland had voted for the president, thus ensuring his reelection. A late supper of oysters was served at the War Department where the president received telegraph reports; a brass band met Lincoln at the door as he left to return to the executive mansion.[247] News of the endorsement of Illinois for its native son arrived at 1:00 a.m. The overall popular margin was 500,000, with McClellan winning only 12 electoral votes to 212 for the incumbent. The support for Lincoln displayed by members of the Union army was phenomenal; the margin for him among the men in blue was almost five to one among Wisconsin, Maine, Maryland, and Ohio regiments, and more than 10 to one in California and Iowa regiments.[248] Democrats did well among their traditional constituents including immigrants, poor farmers, and the "Butternut" regions of southern Ohio, Indiana, and Illinois. In Massachusetts, Irish Catholic immigrants voted for McClellan at a 9 to 1 ratio. Lincoln in contrast did well among Bay state Congregationalists.[249] New York City went Democratic, and the state almost did as well (Republicans won it by less than a single percentage point).[250] Writing to his diary at his home in Manhattan, Republican lawyer George Templeton Strong reported that "the crisis has been past, and the most momentous popular election ever held since ballots were invented has decided against treason and disunion." He was pleased to report that his "contempt for democracy and extended suffrage is mitigated."[251] Pursuant to a congressional resolution providing that states in rebellion would not be allowed to participate in the presidential election, Vice President Hannibal Hamlin refused to count the electoral votes of Louisiana and Tennessee despite the fact that citizens in those states had erected loyal state governments.[252]

With the election over, all eyes turned again to the constriction of the South. Sherman was midway between Atlanta and the sea, and Grant was slowly choking the life out of Lee's army at Petersburg. During the winter, Union troops cut off the last road reaching the town from the west, and they turned their attention to the single railroad line that still supplied it. With the arrival of March, Lee resolved to make a run for it to join up with Joseph Johnston's forces for an attack on Sherman, who was then making his way through North Carolina. Engagements of March 25 and April 1 saw the Army of Northern Virginia lose almost 5,000 men. Lee attempted to break free one more time. He and his men reached the grounds of Amelia courthouse, 35 miles west of Richmond. After 6,000 Confederates were captured at Sayler's Creek on April 6, Grant and Lee began exchanging notes, but it was not until Confederates found themselves surrounded on April 9 that Lee offered to surrender. The two men met at Appomattox courthouse, where Grant offered to parole Confederates on the condition that they return to their homes and uphold the law. Lee accepted Grant's terms. Arms and artillery were stacked and officers signed statements on behalf of their men promising they would not take up arms against the federal government. Grant issued an order providing for the distribution of 25,000 provisions to his starving countrymen. When news of the surrender arrived in the capital, 800 guns were fired in celebration.

With the war won, the North went on a bender, and stayed on it. The revelry continued during Easter week, but it came to a tragic end when Lincoln was shot in the back of the head by actor John Wilkes Booth on the evening of Good Friday as he watched a play at Ford's Theatre. Abraham Lincoln died the next morning. The assailant and his coconspirators planned to assassinate several members of the administration; other than the president, only Secretary of State William Seward was harmed. He sustained severe injuries but recovered and remained in office until 1869. Louis Wigfall, as dedicated a secessionist as any man, believed Lincoln's assassination to be a disaster for the South.[253] As events would prove, he was right.

While the meaning of the Civil War for American federalism is inextricably tied to the process of reconstruction that followed it, certain truths were evident in 1865. The war had cost 600,000 lives—one of every 50 Americans. In the South, one-fifth of the adult white male population died.[254] The grieving of millions of families, often overlooked by history, would last well into the next century and affect the way many Americans regarded their country, their fellows, and their system of government. Many Southerners never reconciled themselves to Appomattox and viewed their condition as one of subjugation by a foreign power. Some southern towns did not begin celebrating Independence Day again until well into the twentieth century. Many Northerners developed a hatred for all things associated with the rebellion that affected their political views for the rest of their lives. They were determined to exact a price from the men who brought the country so much misery, and if an entire section had to live with the federal government's foot on its neck for years in order to learn the errors of its ways, that was fine with them. The South could—and did—protest what it viewed as violations of the rights of the states, but Northerners scoffed. In their view, they had no reason to fear the concentration of power in a government they dominated.

For a time the war threatened to change the government itself. With a budget of over a billion dollars in 1865 (it had been $63 million in 1860), the federal establishment had grown to proportions that even John C. Calhoun in his darkest moods would not have predicted. At the close of the war, the federal government was the largest employer in the country.[255] Americans labored under the highest tax rates in the world according to one estimate—and they would continue to do so for some time, as the conflict left the nation with a debt of $2.8 billion.[256] Yet the swelling of the federal apparatus abated, so that when the 51st Congress managed to spend a billion dollars between 1889 and 1891, it was a national scandal. The military establishment produced by the war seemed to disappear overnight. The navy had 600 ships in the spring of 1865; by that fall only 115 were in service. The army dropped from nearly a million strong to only 54,000 by the end of 1866.[257]

While the federal establishment lost much of its excess weight in the years after the war, the precedents established during the conflict remained. The Civil War saw the national government make its first foray into financial regulations with its establishment of a network of national banks. State educational institutions received federal funds for the first time and the tax code was deployed to penalize activities viewed unfavorably by Washington. Agriculture won for itself a place at the table with the formation of a department devoted to its interests. These initiatives would serve as important precedents in coming years. Perhaps the most important legacy of the Civil War for the federal system was its revelation of public sentiment—the conviction arrived at by so many in the North that the country was worth preserving. Americans would not countenance the division of their country anymore than the French or the British would have. Woodrow Wilson described this realization and its effects in a 1901 article in the *Atlantic*. As he saw it, the "law of the Constitution reigned until the war came." At that time, "questions were broached to which [the Constitution] gave no answer [and] the ultimate foundation of the structure was laid bare: physical force, sustained by the stern loves and rooted predilections of masses of men, the strong ingrained prejudices which are the fiber of every system of government." The war portended a future in which a confident government would be backed by a force larger than itself. "The sentiment of union and nationality, never before aroused to full consciousness or knowledge of its own thoughts and aspirations, was henceforth a new thing, aggressive and aware of a sort of conquest." The practical consequences of this change were obvious: "A government which had been in its spirit federal became, almost all of a sudden, national in temper and point of view."[258]

Never again would federal officials hesitate to adopt novel policies out of fear that they might trigger nullification or secession. These dangers hovered over the country during the antebellum period. Now federal power might be exercised vigorously without fear of bloodshed or embarrassment. In fact, it already had been—the laws passed by Congress during the conflict "reflected a sea change in constitutional interpretation amounting to no less than wholesale abandonment of states' rights principles that had generally prevailed before the war."[259] Yet, the United States still qualified after the war as what it had always been—a confederated republic. Nor did people stop referring to the United States as a confederation, or as a composite of smaller units. When Secretary of State Hamilton Fish wrote a diplomatic note to his British counterparts in late 1869, he spoke of London's implicit bestowal of belligerent status on the Confederacy (by declaring its neutrality) and the fact that "the United States felt constrained at the time to regard this proclamation as the sign of unfriendliness to *them* [emphasis added], and of friendliness to insurgents."[260] The belief in states' rights survived, even in the North. One historian went so far as to suggest that it took on new strength from the Union war effort, which relied heavily on the state governments and fostered pride in state volunteer units.[261] Nor did the notion of state sovereignty disappear. Illinois revised its state seal in 1867. After some hesitation, the legislature chose to retain the original motto: "State Sovereignty, National Union."

The emancipation of 3.5 million slaves was another consequence of the war—without the trauma of that conflict it is doubtful that ratification of the Thirteenth Amendment could have been secured. Slavery had been abolished in large parts of the South by the Union army well before the end of the conflict. Prodded by Andrew Johnson, all of the slave states abolished it by the time the Thirteenth Amendment was added to the Constitution in December 1865.[262] The liberation of so many human beings would itself bring changes to the federal system. Another consequence of the war that would have great consequences for American federalism was the desolation of the South. Vast stretches of Virginia had been laid waste, as had large areas of Tennessee, northern Mississippi, Louisiana, Georgia, and South Carolina. The central business districts of Columbia and Charleston, South Carolina, were in ruins, as was that of Richmond. During the years after the war, Southerners would abandon their former opposition to federal aid and seek appropriations for the dredging of rivers and harbors as well as land grants for railroads in the hope of reviving commerce in their section. Washington was no longer the enemy, but a benefactor. Federal officials sensed the change in perceptions and exploited it. An often timid government that found its mettle in war began to abandon the reticence that had once been its most notable characteristic.

Chapter 2

THE CONSTITUTION OBSCURED, 1865–1877

RESTORATION

Areas of the South that came under control of the Union army during the war were governed by army officers or military governors appointed by the president. Difficulties arose out of the attempt to establish—or recognize—loyal state governments. The events that resulted in the partition of Virginia gave an early indication of the complexities of this task. In May 1861, delegates of several western counties hostile to secession met at a convention in Wheeling to consider modes of resistance, one of which was the formation of their own state. After the state's voters approved the secession ordinance on May 23, a second convention met at Wheeling. The delegates chose to separate. To comply with the Constitution's ban on carving new states out of old ones without the consent of the latter, they established a loyal government for the entire state so it could consent to separation. The Wheeling convention had no more authority to take this step than Virginia had a right to secede. In May 1862, the new state government—which was composed only of men from the northwestern counties of the state—gave its consent when those same counties proposed to form their own state: West Virginia. When West Virginia applied for statehood, administration officials found themselves divided. Three cabinet members—Gideon Welles, Montgomery Blair, and Attorney General Edmund Bates—thought the Virginia legislature was not competent and lacked authority to consent to the division of the state.[1] Congress followed its own mind when it passed a law in December 1862 providing for the admission of West Virginia to the Union once it amended the state constitution to provide for the gradual emancipation of slaves.[2]

The question of what constituted a competent state government presented itself repeatedly during the war. During 1862 the president appointed military governors for North Carolina, Tennessee, Arkansas, and Louisiana. Although they presided only over the portions of these states under Union control—which sometimes consisted of little more than a handful of counties—they were charged with the task of reestablishing state governments loyal to the Union. While the experiment failed in North Carolina, General Nathaniel Banks arranged for the election of delegates to a state constitutional convention in Louisiana in January 1864. Voters selected members of the legislature, congressmen and senators as well as convention delegates; later that year a congressional delegation traveled to Washington. Delegations from Arkansas and Virginia also sought admission. A former speaker of the House, Banks launched a campaign to convince members of Congress to admit the Louisiana delegation. In early 1865 the president set aside his practice of remaining aloof from legislative matters and gave his skills to the cause. Although they had been on friendly terms throughout the war despite different approaches to emancipation and reconstruction, disagreement over the admission of the Louisiana delegation between President Lincoln and Charles Sumner threatened to boil over that winter. Congress failed to act before the session expired early March in part because Louisiana voters had refused to enfranchise literate blacks. Lincoln expressed surprise and disappointment at the refusal of lawmakers to admit men elected under the auspices of governments he had sponsored.[3]

In a February 1865 speech, Senator Jacob Howard of Michigan explained the thinking of lawmakers responsible for the refusal to admit the Louisiana delegation. He noted that the entity purporting to be the state government had been formed under the auspices of the military and the president. Congress must exercise all the powers of local government within the state until "the federal government has done its duty in the reestablishment of order (and) the revival of loyalty." It could do this only by establishing a provisional government operating under its authority. In doing so Congress would be acting under authority bestowed by the republican government clause as well as its war powers. Howard denied the president alone held power to reconstruct conquered states; Congress must restore civil governments in them as it alone is the "law-giving power of the nation."[4]

Section 5 of Article I provides that "each House (of Congress) shall be the Judge of the Elections, Returns and Qualifications of its own Members." This provision has been interpreted as authorizing each House to deny admission to persons purporting to be the duly-elected representatives or senators of a state. During the war this power was exercised harshly if inconsistently. The 37th Congress (1861–63) included congressmen from districts in Louisiana and Virginia, despite the fact that those states had joined the Confederacy. Louisiana was denied representation in the House during the 38th Congress (1863–65) despite the fact that a large portion of the state was under the control of the Union army and a loyal state government had been established.[5] Andrew Johnson continued to serve in the Senate even after Tennessee seceded. After he was appointed military governor of the state in 1862, Johnson reluctantly arranged for a congressional election in Tennessee at the president's request even though much of the eastern portion of the state remained in Confederate hands. The House of Representatives refused to admit the winner.[6]

Radical Republicans believed that Congress and not the president should control the process of reconstruction; they also insisted that the Constitution's limits on federal authority no longer applied in the South. No radical was as extreme as Thaddeus Stevens, the Pennsylvania ironmonger and congressman who exhibited a moral fervor on matters related to slavery and the South that was reminiscent of John Brown's intensity. He viewed the war as an opportunity to rebuild southern society. Speaking in the House on January 8, 1863, Stevens insisted that Congress could do as it wished in the South. "Whenever a war, which is admitted to be a national war, springs up between nation and nation, ally and ally, confederate and confederate, every obligation which previously existed between them, whether treaty, compact, contract or anything else, is wholly abrogated, and from that moment the belligerents act toward each other, not according to any compacts or treaties, but simply according to the laws of war." With respect to the states in rebellion, the Constitution "has no binding influence, and no application."[7] Congressman George Dunlap of Kentucky was appalled. "Are not," he asked, "those seceded States still members of this Union, and under the laws of this government?" Stevens had no doubt of the answer. "In my opinion they are not."[8] In the future his colleagues would "come to the conclusion that the adoption of the measures I advocated at the outset of the war, the arming of the negroes, the slaves of the rebels, is the only way left on earth in which these rebels can be exterminated. They will find that they must treat those states outside the Union as conquered provinces and settle them with new men, and drive the present rebels as exiles from this country; for I tell you they have the pluck and endurance for which I gave them credit a year and a half ago in a speech which I made, but which was not relished on this side of the House, nor by the people of the free states. They have such determination, energy, and endurance that nothing but actual extermination or exile or starvation will ever induce them to surrender to this Government."[9]

While Massachusetts Senator Charles Sumner and Stevens were fellow travelers in their views of the South, Sumner offered sentiments on the subject of reconstruction in an October 1863 article in the *Atlantic* that were less drastic than those of his colleague. He merely wished to ensure that Congress and not the president oversaw the reestablishment of state governments. The Massachusetts Senator approved of Lincoln's appointment of military governors, yet he insisted that they had no sanction in the Constitution. They did not qualify as military officers "charged with the duty of enforcing martial law." As the southern state governments had ceased to exist, "the way is prepared for the establishment of provisional governments by Congress." In Sumner's view, this route was preferable to military governments established by the president alone, as provisional governments "proceed from the civil rather the military power" and are based upon law. The state governments that formerly prevailed in the South no longer exist and it was incumbent upon Congress to assert its jurisdiction. While their civil societies remained, as organizations having a relation to the Union, the southern states were defunct.[10]

The present question was how, in the absence of loyal governments that could participate in the Union, should "rightful jurisdiction shall be established in the vacated states?" Sumner dismissed the principle upon which the president had acted—that power could be lodged in those citizens who remained loyal—as they were too few in number. He thought Congress should provide for elections under southern state laws existing at the time those states seceded. Congress alone could establish the mechanisms necessary to bring state governments to life, as it is the "natural guardian of people without any immediate government and within the jurisdiction of the Constitution." It derived this power from "the necessity of the case," its war powers, the republican government clause, and the power to admit new states, as the rebel states had ceased to be "de facto" states and were now merely territories.[11] Perhaps the most serious flaw in Sumner's argument was his casual assumption regarding the number of loyal people in the southern states—there was no way for him to know how many were loyal. To assume that they were so few in number as to warrant congressional intervention was a recipe for abuse that could just as easily be turned back on northern states under different circumstances.

Throughout his presidency, Abraham Lincoln displayed an appreciation for the Constitution's limitations on federal authority that infuriated the radical wing of his party. He would not go along with the forcible abolition of slavery outside of the theater of war; nor would he acquiesce in the wholesale confiscation of land in the South. His approach to reconstruction was colored by an awareness that the federal government did not have unfettered discretion to remake the South—at least not if it wished to be thought of as acting within the confines of the Constitution. In his Proclamation of Amnesty and Reconstruction of December 1863, the president took a moderate course. He offered pardons to all persons in the South who swore to protect the Constitution and abide by laws of Congress passed during the rebellion regarding slaves, except senior Confederate civil and military officers as well as those who mistreated prisoners of war. Persons who took the oath would regain all of their former rights except their property right in slaves. When the number of persons in each southern state who took the oath reached 10 percent of the number of persons casting ballots in the 1860 presidential election, said persons could establish a new state government "which shall be republican." Said governments would be recognized "as the true government of the state" and receive the benefit of the republican government clause.[12] Lincoln did not, and could not, promise that the delegations of said states would be admitted to Congress, as the Constitution vests that power in each house alone. Louisiana and Arkansas took the president up on his offer—once 10 percent of the voters had sworn allegiance, they formed provisional governments and sent delegations to Washington where they sought admission to Congress, albeit in vain.

When some in Congress continued to talk of more punitive measures such as the Wade-Davis bill, Senator John Ten Eyck of New Jersey claimed that Lincoln had demonstrated "practical good sense" in offering moderate terms to southerners. As for more radical proposals, he raised the question of authority. "What shall now be done? Shall we reduce these states to territories? Shall we appoint their judges, governors, and other officers? Shall we, in common with insurgents, ignore their status in the Union, and sink the loyal people to a state of pupilage? Would that be constitutional? . . . What right have we to say to Tennessee, to Mississippi or to Texas—the loyal people there—'you no longer constitute a state, but are the people of a territory, your state governments are gone?' " He thought no such right existed. "The functions of state governments may have been suspended, and law and order for a time ignored; still the doctrine of the Constitution is, 'once a state, always a state.' "[13]

Congressman James Ashley of Ohio disagreed. He held that a "state may forfeit its rights as part of the supreme governing power of the Republic. A majority of the electors of any state in this Union may, unquestionably, alter or abolish their written constitution and refuse to establish another in its stead. If they may, as all concede, do this, then the abolition of a state constitution . . . would terminate their right under the [U.S.] Constitution to exercise any part of the governing power of the nation. If a state refuses to maintain a government, then the assumption that 'a state is always a state' is a fallacy as pernicious as it is false." Ashley agreed that the Union had not been dissolved. The ordinances of secession cannot "legally or constitutionally affect the rightful jurisdiction of the national government over the people and territory of such a State." Yet he insisted that those ordinances and acts of rebellion, "sustained by a majority of its citizens, destroys, as a matter of fact, the political organization known and recognized as a state by the national Constitution." Turning to the president's proclamation, Ashley found it objectionable as beyond his rightful authority. "If the old state constitutions and governments of the rebel states are destroyed, then neither the president nor any general under him can, with the military power, establish civilian state governments with such constitutions as they may dictate, without the consent of Congress."[14]

Congressman Henry Winter Davis of Maryland cited *Luther v. Borden* for the proposition that it was the task of Congress alone to ensure that new governments formed in the southern states qualified as adequately republican in nature. Therefore Congress must supervise the establishment of those governments and rule the southern states directly in the interim.[15] J. C. Allen of Kentucky insisted that neither the Lincoln plan nor the Wade-Davis bill had any basis in the Constitution. While southern individuals who participated in the rebellion had forfeited their rights under the Constitution, the southern states had not. These states still had the same constitutions and laws they maintained before the rebellion. The only step that needed to be taken was to replace the current occupants of public offices in the South with persons loyal to the Union.[16]

During the spring and summer of 1864, the Wade-Davis bill moved through Congress. More extreme than Lincoln's Amnesty Proclamation, it provided for the abolition of slavery in the rebel states. It also authorized the appointment of provisional governors by the president with the advice and consent of the Senate. The provisional governors would enroll all white male citizens and U.S. marshals would ask them to take an oath of allegiance to the United States. If half or more swore allegiance—as opposed to 10 percent provided under the president's Amnesty Proclamation—the provisional governor would arrange for the election of delegates to a state constitutional convention. Constitutions drafted by these conventions must include provisions that (1) banned slavery and the payment of Confederate or state debts, (2) proclaimed the state's adherence to federal laws, and (3) declared the state's acceptance of the supremacy of the national government. The bill banned all Confederate Army officers above the rank of colonel as well as senior government officials from voting in elections for delegates to state constitutional conventions.[17] Speaking in support of the bill on June 13, 1864, Charles Sumner explained that the war gave Congress as well as the president dominion over the southern states. While he conceded that conquered regions of the South were under the control of the military, which answered to the president, he insisted that "there is nothing which the president may do as commander-in-chief which Congress may not direct and govern, according to the authoritative words of Chancellor Kent: 'though the Constitution vests the executive power to the president and declares him the commander-in-chief of the army and navy of the United States, these powers must necessarily be subordinate to the legislative power in Congress.' "[18] To some extent Sumner was correct; Congress could regulate the military establishment of the United States. However, the Constitution did not give it—or the president—power to establish terms upon which the rebel states could reestablish themselves within the Union.

The president pocket-vetoed the Wade-Davis bill in July 1864. He issued a proclamation on July 8 explaining his refusal to sign it. Lincoln objected to the measure because he did not want to abolish the civilian governments already in place in Louisiana and Arkansas. Nor did he believe Congress had the power to abolish slavery in the states via statute. The president conceded that the people of the rebel states were free to embrace the plan devised by Congress, and he promised to direct military governors to aid them in that course if they chose it.[19] Senator Ben Wade and Congressman Henry Winter Davis responded with the Wade-Davis Manifesto in the August 5, 1864, issue of the *New York Post*. The two lawmakers complained that the president's veto had frustrated the will of the only entity—Congress—that could reestablish civil governments in the South. They charged that the veto arose out of the president's wish to maintain his own power in states such as Louisiana. It "discards the authority of the Supreme Court" and usurps the power of Congress to "determine what is the established government in a state."[20]

The desire among some Republicans in Congress to take over the process of reconstruction arose in part out of a fear that the admission of southern delegations would restore the Democratic Party to the dominance it had enjoyed between 1828 and 1860. During that time, the party of Jefferson and Jackson controlled both houses of Congress for all but 10 years; it also won six of nine presidential elections. Once they were admitted, southern congressional delegations would form a solid block of Democrats. In combination with their northern brethren, who continued to fare well in the region's cities and in the Ohio Valley, southern Democrats might enable the party to dominate the national political scene once again. Their ability to do so would be enhanced if each black person was counted as whole person in the apportionment of congressional seats instead of as only three-fifths of a person—southern congressional delegations would therefore be increased substantially even if blacks were denied the right to vote.

The fissure between the president and radicals widened in early 1865, with Republican leaders in New England states such as Connecticut moving steadily toward the radical camp and embracing its demand that the southern states be reduced to territorial status.[21] As the war approached its end that spring, the president continued to espouse the cause of moderation. When Secretary of War Edwin Stanton presented a plan subjecting North Carolina and Virginia to military rule, the president ordered him to revise it as Virginia was operating under a civil government.[22] During a celebration in Washington on April 11, the president addressed a boisterous crowd that had gathered on the grounds of the executive mansion. After hailing the victory, Lincoln turned to reconstruction. The president expressed disappointment at the refusal of Congress to admit delegations from Louisiana, Arkansas, and Virginia and thereby recognize the state government that had been established. Lincoln acknowledged the defects of the Louisiana government—it was elected by only 12,000 voters and withheld the vote from blacks. He still favored admission—delay would serve no purpose. "Can Louisiana be brought into proper practical relation with the Union sooner by sustaining, or by discarding her new state government?"[23] On the day of his death, Lincoln was said to have uttered within earshot of Seward his belief that "we cannot undertake to run state governments in all these southern states. Their people must do that—though I reckon some of them at first may do it badly."[24]

The prospects for a seamless transfer to peace changed on the evening of April 14, when a disgruntled southerner discharged a lead ball into the back of the president's head. As life drained from Lincoln's body over the next 10 hours, the chances for peaceful reconciliation dissipated. Andrew Johnson, a states' rights Democrat in past years who had looked up to fellow Tennesseans James Polk and Andrew Jackson, succeeded to the presidency. While his southern colleagues resigned from their positions in the Senate in 1861, Johnson remained—the only senator from a state that seceded to do so. Appointed military governor of Tennessee in the spring of 1862 after Union forces took Nashville, he displayed a willingness to stand up to the slave owners who dominated the western portion of the state. He also proved willing to arrest secessionists and suppress newspapers. Some feared the new president would prove too severe in his dealings with the South. When Ben Wade of Ohio recommended to Johnson that the 12 most prominent Confederates should be tried for treason and hanged, Johnson was said to have asked the Ohio Senator why only 12 men should be sent to the gallows.[25] For a time the new president and the radicals attempted to work together. He allowed the military to go forward with plans to try persons alleged to have been involved in the conspiracy that resulted in Lincoln's death despite the fact that civil courts in Washington, DC, were functioning.[26]

The first signs of rupture appeared on May 29, when the president issued two proclamations that revealed his intentions regarding the South. In the first he set terms for the granting of pardons.[27] In the second proclamation, the president appointed William W. Holden provisional governor of North Carolina. Holden was charged with the task of establishing rules for the election of delegates to a state constitutional convention. Said convention would devise a new state constitution and U.S. military officers were ordered to provide whatever assistance the governor needed. The treasury would appoint collectors and assessors in the state and the postmaster general would reestablish post offices and postal routes. Only persons who took an oath of allegiance and qualified to vote under state laws as they existed before May 20, 1861, could participate in the selection of convention delegates or attend the convention.[28] Shortly thereafter the president issued similar proclamations for other southern states—though not for Virginia, Tennessee, Arkansas, and Louisiana, where civilian governments had been established during the previous administration.

The proclamations stood on dubious constitutional grounds—the president did not have legal authority to force the southern states to adopt new constitutions (nor did Lincoln when he arranged for Louisiana to hold a constitutional convention). As a result, the proclamation served as a dangerous and disastrous precedent. In providing for the holding of constitutional conventions instead of elections to fill state offices, they seemed to indicate Congress could require the abolition of the old state constitutions in the South. Could it also dictate the terms of the new constitutions that would have to be drafted? In providing for the southern states to use their suffrage laws as they existed in 1861, the president—at least in the view of some—established a precedent that authorized the national government to set rules regarding the suffrage in southern states. The charge was inaccurate but it was quickly embraced by radicals, many of whom wanted to force the southern states to enfranchise blacks.

Men such as Charles Sumner had been asking the president to extend the suffrage to blacks since his first days in office, and they seemed to have convinced themselves that they had won the Tennessee Democrat to their cause. Two days after Lincoln's death, Sumner went to the War Department to inquire what arrangements were being made for black suffrage in the South.[29] In the August 1865 *Atlantic*, Edwin Percy Whipple spoke for those who were disappointed that the president had not enfranchised blacks in the southern states. For the claim of a lack of authority, he had no sympathy. "It will not do, at this stage, to say that the Federal government has no right to prescribe the qualifications of voters in the states because, in the case of the whites, it does and must prescribe them; and President Johnson has just the same right to say that negroes shall vote as to say that pardoned rebels shall vote. The right of states to decide on the qualifications of its electors applies only to loyal states; it cannot apply to political communities which have lost by rebellion the federal character of 'states.' " Whipple wanted free blacks enfranchised for several reasons, among them that their presence in the South would bring the region approximately 30 additional representatives in Congress and vastly increase the power of Democrats unless blacks were given some influence over how those seats were filled.[30]

The attitude of persons who held this view stemmed in part from events in the southern states; South Carolina refused to repeal its ordinance of secession and Mississippi refused to repudiate its wartime debts or ratify what became the Thirteenth Amendment. While many of the state conventions were attended by men who had opposed secession, in the Deep South these gatherings included many former Confederates. The president advised the southern states to go beyond the minimum requirements of his proclamations. He knew that each house of Congress alone had the power to admit southern delegations and that Republican majorities would be unwilling to do so if the southern states evinced anything other than moderation and humanity in their attitude toward blacks. Johnson went so far as to tell the provisional governor of Mississippi that the state ought to enfranchise literate blacks. Southern states not only refused to give blacks the vote, they began enacting "black codes" that reduced them to a degraded status. Georgia elected former vice president of the Confederacy Alexander Stephens to the U.S. Senate. The president did not help matters when he allowed southern states to organize militias; he also removed black soldiers from units of the army stationed in the South when southerners complained of their presence.[31]

During the summer ominous noises emanated from radicals and their supporters about the need for Congress to make the final determination as to whether the governments formed in the southern states complied with the republican government clause of the Constitution. In the view of *Harper's Weekly*, the president's proclamations had done no more than to invite persons in each southern state to suggest "what kind of state constitution they wish, leaving Congress to decide whether it is truly republican or not. When Congress approves, then the electors, recognized in the Constitution, become 'the people,' who rightfully exercise all state authority."[32] Most infuriating to *Harper's* were the critics who would have the federal government leave the rebel states to their own devices, thereby defeating the purpose of the war. "Having thus, at the cost of a quarter of a million of lives, an enormous public debt, and a universal derangement of affairs, once more established (its) authority, it is now told that it has no constitutional right to secure it."[33] The *Nation* claimed the guise of legality had already been abandoned; the president should now go all the way. "There is no such officer as a 'provisional governor' known to the Constitution of the United States." Nor was there "any machinery provided by the Constitution for imposing upon States 'that have never been out of the Union' conditions for their re-admission to it." The president was already treating the southern states as mere "conquered territories," so there was no reason for him or Congress to refrain from imposing black suffrage on the South. The "notion that Mr. Johnson cannot interfere with the suffrage in the revolted states is pure doubled-refined fiction."[34] Most Republicans as well as Democrats embraced the president's course. Governor John Andrew of Massachusetts expressed his support for the president's policies and attacked the state suicide theory popular with radicals.[35] Few in the North were ready to impose black suffrage on the South and most Republicans contented themselves with the demand that blacks be accorded economic and legal rights such as the right to enter into contracts and marry.[36]

Even as Democrats and moderate Republicans embraced a middle course, the southern states made their task infinitely harder. Equality before the law had always been a work in progress in the United States, but free men in all parts of the Union had long enjoyed a few basic rights, such as the right to work when and where they chose. In late 1865, the southern states began to deny even that privilege to constrict as much as possible the freedom of movement of emancipated slaves. The legislatures strengthened vagrancy laws to the point of absurdity. An Alabama law provided that servants who proved stubborn or loitered "away their time" were vagrants subject to arrest and fines. Failure to pay would result in their being hired out for up to six months by the justice of the peace; their earnings would go to the county treasury. Persons suspected of vagrancy in Louisiana had to post a bond and promise they would exhibit "good behavior and future industry" or face delivery to the recorder of their parish, who could hire them out for the rest of the year. If that failed, they could be sent to a workhouse or required to labor on public projects, such as roads and levees, for up to six months.[37] A South Carolina law provided for the relatives of blacks who became public charges to pay the cost of maintaining their relation; if necessary all blacks in the immediate area had to contribute.[38] Blacks were also denied the protection of the laws; violence against them was widespread and the perpetrators were rarely prosecuted. The effect of all of this on northerners was searing. As Massachusetts Republican George Hoar later wrote, the strengthened vagrancy laws enacted in the South, "if carried out would have had the effect of reducing the negro once more to a condition of practical slavery. Men were to be sold for the crime of being out of work. Their old masters were to have the preference in the purchase. So the whole Republican Party of the North came to be united in the belief that there could be no security for (blacks) without the ballot."[39]

An article in the *Nation* of November 23, 1865, complained that the president's "excessive tenderness" had roused southerners to "their old audacity." The conventions held in the South to draft new state constitutions failed to protect the rights of blacks; South Carolina newspapers not only opposed schools for blacks but demanded a law barring anyone from educating them. "What Mr. Johnson insists upon is done, and that grudgingly; but he has insisted upon nothing which will prevent the reduction of the blacks to a condition but one degree removed from, and in some respects more marked by physical suffering, than slavery itself, the minute the states are restored to the Union and military force withdrawn." It was now incumbent upon Congress to do its duty or the nation would witness "one of the most tremendous and revolting crimes ever perpetrated by a community laying claims to civilization, and we shall witness the substitution for slavery of a social organization marked by every feature which made slavery politically dangerous."[40]

In a November 1865 letter to the editor of the *Nation*, Maryland Congressman Henry Winter Davis complained that the president's indulgence of southerners had resulted in state governments that scoffed at federal authority, hostility to blacks, and an aristocracy of disloyal whites. Congressional action was necessary, and the republican government clause provided ample authority for it. "Whenever, therefore, the mass of the citizens or any great proportion of them is excluded from political power, yet required to submit to its laws, the government ceases to be republican and Congress cannot recognize it as such." Davis distinguished the case of Connecticut, whose voters had just rejected an amendment extending the suffrage to blacks, on the grounds that there were too few blacks in that state for their disenfranchisement to render the state government anything other than republican in nature.[41] The notion that the republican government clause authorized Congress to impose suffrage requirements on the states was devoid of substance; at the most it obligated the states to maintain functioning legislatures. Between 1790 and 1861 the states had slowly broadened the suffrage to include most white males. During that period no one suggested that the republican government clause authorized Congress to compel the states to accept suffrage requirements it deemed appropriate. As Davis acknowledged, the North itself was not making much progress on black suffrage. In only five northern states in 1867 did blacks enjoy the same voting rights as whites.[42] Between 1865 and 1867 proposals to enfranchise blacks were defeated in Connecticut, Ohio, Minnesota, Wisconsin, and Kansas.[43]

As members of Congress trickled into Washington in advance of the session that would commence in December 1865, both sides realized trouble was imminent. Few expected Congress to sit by quietly while the southern Democrat in the executive mansion allowed his brethren to do everything they could to restore antebellum conditions in the South. Radicals prepared to push for a more assertive congressional role in the southern states, with most citing the republican government clause as authority for the move. At a meeting with Charles Sumner, Gideon Welles was shocked to hear the Massachusetts Senator report that he had scoured everything from the works of Plato to the latest French pamphlets to determine what constituted a republican government.[44]

In his annual message of December 4, 1865, the president reported that conventions had been held in the southern states, "governors elected, legislatures assembled, and Senators and Representatives chosen to the Congress of the United States."[45] (In fact, some southern states were still in the process of reestablishing their state governments.) The 39th Congress convened during the first week of December. Republicans held 136 of 193 seats in the House and 39 of 50 seats in the Senate.[46] Southerners claiming they had been lawfully elected from the states of North Carolina, Tennessee, and Louisiana appeared on the floor of the House of Representatives when the House convened on December 4. The House refused to recognize them as lawfully elected representatives and denied them admission.[47]

From the start, the determination of radicals combined with the ineptitude of the president and the impudence of southern legislatures to push the great mass of Republican lawmakers toward the radical position. In a speech of December 18, 1865, Thaddeus Stevens repeated his claim that the Constitution no longer applied in the South—the states of the region remained outside of the Union and subject to the will of Congress. "Unless the law of nations is a dead letter, the late war between the two acknowledged belligerents severed their original compacts, and broke all the ties that bound them together. The future condition of the conquered power depends on the will of the conqueror. They must come in as new states or remain conquered provinces." If, as some claimed, the southern states never left the Union, Stevens believed the republican government clause applied. It would then be the task of Congress to decide if they had republican governments. In his view the southern states had left the Union, as the Confederate States of America was "an independent belligerent, and was so acknowledged by the United States and by Europe." Stevens insisted that the present governments of the South, sponsored as they were by the U.S. Army, merely obscured the fact that the southern states had been "governed by martial law" since the war. As military rule is "necessarily despotic," it ought to be terminated as soon as possible. "As there are no symptoms that the people of these provinces will be prepared to participate in constitutional government for some years, I know of no arrangement so proper for them as territorial governments." Stevens closed by demanding that the southern states be denied representation in Congress until an amendment was ratified that would "secure perpetual ascendancy to the party of the Union; and so as to render our republican government firm and stable forever." He called for amendments that would change representation from "Federal numbers to actual voters" and reduce the size of the House delegations of states that withheld the vote from blacks.[48]

Congressman James Raymond of New York responded to Stevens three days later. Proprietor of the *New York Times* and a prominent supporter of the president, he denied that the rebel states left the Union—the ordinances of secession never had legal force. Radicals had argued that the southern states could secede even though said acts were illegal, just as a man can commit murder even though it is illegal. Raymond conceded the analogy might be valid if the southern states had repelled northern armies, but as they failed to do so, their actions only "interrupted for a time the practical enforcement and exercise of the jurisdiction of the Constitution." He insisted that the Supreme Court in the *Prize Cases* held only that there were two belligerents; it did not say that the Confederacy was an independent nation. In truth, it was citizens who engaged in rebellion, not states.[49] G. Clay Smith of Kentucky echoed Raymond's claim that people and not states had engaged in the rebellion. He noted that at one point, Confederates had taken control of all of Kentucky except for two cities in the north. Representatives and senators were elected to the Confederate Congress and a rebel state government was formed. Yet Kentucky was never denied representation in the Congress of the United States.[50]

The intricacies of what Lincoln called that "pernicious question"—whether the southern states had seceded—would tax the resources of politicians and historians for years to come, but Raymond and Smith seem to have approached the truth of the matter. Dominant factions took over the machinery of government in the southern states and used them for treasonous purposes, but the southern states did not leave the Union. Of greater importance in early 1866 was another truth: Contrary to the claims of radicals, the president's establishment of certain procedures for reestablishing civil governments did not confirm the federal government's authority to impose any conditions it chose on the South. The Union army could hardly have been expected to turn the South over to anarchy merely because Confederate soldiers laid down their arms.[51] The head of the army—the president—had to invite southerners to reestablish governments and provide some mechanism for them to use in doing so. These actions could hardly serve as precedent for attempts to reform political institutions in the southern states in a way Congress never would have attempted in the North.

The battle intensified when Congress took up a bill to extend the life of the Freedmen's Bureau. Established in March 1865, the Bureau provided provisions, clothing, and fuel for whites as well as former slaves in the South. Bureau commissioners and employees—with the Union army backing them—intervened when necessary to prevent the exploitation of blacks by their former owners. The commissioner of the Bureau was authorized to set aside abandoned lands in the Confederate states for the use of freedmen (up to 40 acres each). They could either rent the land or purchase it.[52] With 850,000 acres of land taken pursuant to the confiscation laws under its control in 1865, the Bureau gave 40 acres—and a mule—to freedmen until President Johnson put a stop to the practice in the summer of 1865. Johnson ordered the Bureau to return all lands to their original owners that had not yet been deeded to former slaves; in doing so he may well have violated both the confiscation laws and the act creating the Freedmen's Bureau. Twenty thousand blacks were evicted from land many thought they owned.[53] Thereafter insult was added to injury, as radicals promised blacks they would receive 40 acres of land only to fail in their efforts to extract the necessary legislation from Congress. Blacks emigrated to army bases in expectation of the bounty only to be disappointed. Some were swindled by whites who sold them croquet sticks for the purpose of marking off 40 acres on the estates of their former masters.[54]

The law giving life to the Freedmen's Bureau constituted an exercise by Congress of its war powers (the Bureau was placed within the War Department).[55] Republican Senator Henry Lane of Indiana objected to it. He was willing to grant the slaves their freedom, afford them legal protections, and grant them the vote if necessary, but he wished "to have no system of guardianship and pupilage and overseership of these negroes."[56] A bill reauthorizing the Freedmen's Bureau moved through Congress with ease in early 1866. The measure went beyond relief in subjecting disputes between blacks and whites to military courts. The president vetoed it. In his veto message, Johnson charged that the bill would "establish military jurisdiction over all parts of the U.S. containing refugees and freedmen." Persons accused of violating the rights of freedmen would be tried by military commissions lacking juries. The president insisted the bill could not be justified as an exercise of the government's war powers as its authority was no longer contested anywhere in the Union. The condition requiring the Bureau's creation—slavery—no longer existed. Never before had the federal government provided housing or the necessities of daily life for citizens. "A system for the support of indigent persons in the United States was never contemplated by the authors of the Constitution." The expense that would be incurred in carrying out the program also rendered it objectionable, as did its provision for the confiscation of land without legal proceedings—a violation of the Fifth Amendment. It would also give the president power to appoint "agents, overseers, or taskmasters . . . in every county and parish throughout the United States containing freedmen and refugees." A chief executive might well use his power over "this numerous class" for "political ends."[57]

An attempt at an override failed by a narrow margin, and Johnson appeared to have won the battle. He proceeded to overplay his hand. When a crowd arrived at the executive mansion to serenade him after the veto, the president announced that he had opposed proslavery leaders such as "the Davises, the Toombs, the Slidells." Now he looked on "as being opposed to the fundamental principles of the Government and as now laboring to destroy them, Thaddeus Stevens, Charles Sumner, and Wendell Phillips."[58] Northerners were infuriated at the comparison. Republicans in Congress began moving toward the radical camp, and by summer the necessary votes were mustered to pass the Freedmen's bill for a second time. When the president vetoed it once more, Congress overrode the veto. The law extended the life of the Bureau to July 1868; it was charged with the duty of helping freedmen and refugees "become self-supporting citizens." Medical stores and supplies of the War Department would be given to persons in need, and lands formerly leased to freedmen in Georgia and South Carolina were to be made available to them for purchase. The law also provided that until civil governments recognized by Congress were reestablished in the southern states, all persons in each of these states would enjoy the right to make and enforce contracts as well as the right to inherit, purchase, hold, and sell real estate. Said persons would have "full and equal benefit of all laws and proceedings regarding personal liberty," including the right to bear arms. The secretary of war would extend military protection to freedmen and military courts were given jurisdiction over all cases regarding their rights, and no variations in punishment would be allowed for persons of color.[59]

The work of the Bureau was of huge importance in the lives of southerners. In its first two years, it distributed 21 million rations, 5.5 million of which went to whites.[60] Congress supplemented the Bureau's work with laws providing for the distribution in the South of supplies, seeds, and excess canned goods accumulated by the War Department.[61] The Freedmen's Bureau invalidated some of the more obnoxious "black codes" such as the harsh vagrancy laws that appeared on the statute books of several southern states in late 1865.[62] The Bureau supported some 3,000 schools (it routed aid provided by charitable groups in the North) and convinced some southern states to revise their legal systems to protect freedmen. It purchased land and sold it to blacks; it also loaned money to them so they could build houses on the tracts they had purchased. On at least one occasion the

Bureau established a minimum wage for freedmen; it also gave them a first lien on crops and impounded harvests to ensure they were paid. To prevent idleness, it also tied blacks to the land by restricting their movements.[63] The agency became less active as time passed. By late 1871 its functions were limited to paying bounties to black soldiers and maintaining a single hospital in Washington, DC.[64] The Bureau confirmed Johnson's dire predictions when its resources were deployed in aid of Republican politicians in the South, but no one could deny that it had saved the lives of thousands of southerners of both colors.

While the Freedmen's Acts constituted extraordinary exercises of federal authority, their novelty was somewhat limited by the fact that they were enacted via the war powers of Congress. Congress could aid those whose means of support had been destroyed by the war, at least temporarily. The acts did not evince a permanent expansion of congressional authority into areas formerly left to the states. The same could not be said of the Civil Rights Act of 1866, which was enacted that spring. No statute enacted thus far in the history of the federal system constituted so profound a usurpation of state authority. To attempt to connect it to one of the enumerated powers was an exercise in futility. Secretary of the Navy Gideon Welles was deeply aggrieved. Writing on the eve of the bill's passage, he complained that it "is consolidation solidified, breaks down all barriers to protect the rights of the states, concentrates power in the General Government, which assumes to itself the enactment of municipal regulations between the states and citizens, and between citizens of the same state. No bill so contradictory and consolidating a character has ever been enacted. The Alien and Sedition Laws were not so objectionable."[65] That federal intervention to protect the rights of freedmen constituted a necessity of the first order was undeniable; that Congress waited until after the law was passed to enshrine the same rights in a constitutional amendment—thereby solving the problem of legality—gave some indication of the chaos and partisan rancor that enveloped the national capital in the spring and summer of 1866.

As devised by Illinois Senator Lyman Trumbull, chairman of the Senate Judiciary Committee, the Civil Rights Act of 1866 provided that all persons born in the United States are citizens—thus reversing, or purporting to reverse, one of the Supreme Court's holdings in *Dred Scott*.[66] All citizens would enjoy the right to make and enforce contracts, sue, testify, inherit property, and purchase and sell land in every state. In his selection of rights, Trumbull seems to have relied at least in part on Justice Bushrod Washington's description in *Corfield v. Coryell* of the rights bestowed on Americans when in states other than their own by the privileges and immunities clause of Article IV, Section 2.[67] All citizens would also receive the full and equal benefit "of all laws and proceedings for the security of person and property, as is enjoyed by white citizens, and shall be subject to like punishment, pains, and penalties." All persons who, under color of law, deprive citizens of the aforementioned rights due to their color or former condition of servitude were guilty of a misdemeanor and subject to imprisonment for up to a year or a fine of $1,000. Federal courts were given exclusive jurisdiction over alleged violations of the act, and persons sued for their actions in carrying out the law were given the right to remove said cases to federal court. This provision was necessitated by the willingness of state courts to try federal officials and soldiers for acts committed while enforcing federal laws. During the Civil War and the years after that conflict, state courts indicted federal troops, officials, and even cabinet officers for acts committed while enforcing federal laws. Congress responded with laws such as the Habeas Corpus Act of 1863 and the Civil Rights Act of 1866 that allowed federal officers and employees to remove cases targeting them to federal court and/or indemnifying them for costs incurred in defending themselves against civil suits.[68]

In a speech of April 4, 1866, Lyman Trumbull claimed that the measure would have no effect at all in most states as they treated their citizens equally in their exercise of rights protected by the act.[69] Senator Garrett Davis of Kentucky denied the right of Congress to make persons citizens—it could only naturalize aliens. Describing the bill as an assertion of jurisdiction by Congress over "civil rights and immunities, and over all the penalties and punishments to which (citizens) may be subjected," he contradicted Trumbull—in most states, North as well as South, there are "discriminations in relation to some of those important concerns against the negro race, made by their constitutions and statutes." Recalling the descriptions of federal authority given by Hamilton in *The Federalist* (#'s 17, 23, and 33), as well as Madison (#39), Davis insisted that the Founders anticipated that laws regulating civil and criminal justice would be left to the states.[70] Few were willing to argue that the law was constitutional. In targeting the black codes that reduced blacks to a position equivalent to slavery, some saw it as enforcing the Thirteenth Amendment. House Republican leader John Bingham believed the bill was beyond the powers of Congress, as did secretary of state William Seward (except the provision making blacks citizens). Seward believed *Dred Scott* was wrong and that blacks already were citizens, though he favored a bill recognizing the fact.[71]

Although it proved to be an exercise in futility, the president vetoed the bill. In his veto message of March 27, 1866, Johnson claimed the attempt to bestow citizenship on all persons born in the United States was either unnecessary or futile (if blacks were not citizens, the bill could not change that fact). Johnson went on to complain that "hitherto every subject embraced in the enumeration of rights contained in this bill has been considered as exclusively belonging to the states." He also objected to the assignment of matters to federal courts over which they had no jurisdiction, and the establishment of a federal police force in the South (commissioners) to enforce the law. As for the claim that the Thirteenth Amendment authorized the measure, Johnson insisted that the amendment was intended only to secure to freedmen the right to enjoy the fruits of their labor.[72] Congress passed the measure over Johnson's veto. Unable to prevent the Civil Rights Act of 1866 from becoming law, Johnson consoled himself by refusing to enforce it.[73]

On April 21, 1866, the president issued a proclamation declaring the rebellion over in all southern states except Texas; a proclamation declaring the same thing of the Lone Star state was issued on August 20 after it established a civilian government.[74] Gideon Welles was pleased. "This closes and disposes of the provisional governors, and the interposition of federal authority in the states which were in rebellion will no longer be necessary."[75] As events would prove, he grossly underestimated the determination of Congress to impose its will on the South. The southern states for their part seemed to be asking for it; at the least they had yet to provide for safety of their populations. A riot in Memphis during May 1866 saw white policemen terrorize blacks. Forty-eight people died before it was over; all but two of the victims were black. More bloodshed followed, this time in New Orleans. Domination of the state government by former Confederates led Provisional Governor James Wells to "reconvene" the constitutional convention of 1864, a move that was no more legal than recalling the Constitutional Convention of 1787 would have been. A state judge issued an order barring Wells from carrying out his plans, but the governor, intent on securing black suffrage, ignored it. When New Orleans Police officers tried to break up the convention on July 30, bloodshed resulted. Thirty-seven persons were killed—34 of them blacks.[76] The melee in New Orleans further antagonized the northern public.

In December, House Republicans began discussing an amendment that would place "beyond the reach of presidential vetoes and shifting political majorities, their understanding of the fruits of the Civil War."[77] They wished to protect the Civil Rights Act against invalidation by the courts, penalize those who supported the Confederacy, prevent the payment of state debts incurred in furtherance of the rebellion, and ensure that southern states allowed blacks to vote. On December 5, 1865, Thaddeus Stevens proposed an amendment to the Constitution: "All national and state laws shall be equally applicable to every citizen, and no discrimination shall be made on account of race and color."[78] The next day John Bingham proposed an amendment authorizing Congress to pass all laws necessary to secure to all persons equal protection of their life, liberty, and property.[79] Over the next several weeks, some 70 proposals to amend the Constitution for that purpose were offered.[80] The Joint Committee on Reconstruction considered a plan that would deny southern states representation until they repealed their black codes and provided civil rights to blacks. Out of its deliberations emerged what became the Fourteenth Amendment. The amendment was embraced by lawmakers out of concern that the Civil Rights Act would be found unconstitutional.[81] Henry Raymond explained his thinking after the amendment was submitted to the states: "I regarded it as very doubtful, to say the least, whether Congress, under the existing Constitution, had any power to enact such a law [the Civil Rights Act of 1866]; and I thought, and still think, that very many members who voted for the bill also doubted the power of Congress to pass it, because they voted for the amendment by which that power was to be conferred."[82] Radicals accepted the measure despite disappointment over its failure to enshrine a constitutional right to vote; moderates accepted it despite misgivings about its broad language because it held out the promise of southern representation in Congress—once the southern states approved it, their delegations would be admitted.[83]

The amendment provided, in part, that all persons born in the United States were citizens and that no state could impair the privileges and immunities of citizens. This provision required that the economic and legal rights that a state afforded to its white citizens, such as the right to hold property, must be extended to its black citizens. The amendment also barred states from depriving persons of life or property without due process of law, i.e., the right to a jury trial, the right to examine evidence, and the right to question hostile witnesses. Nor could they deny persons the equal protection of the laws—they would have to protect blacks as well as whites from violence by punishing wrongdoers and allow blacks access to courts when necessary to protect their rights.[84] As lawmakers could not bring themselves to require the southern states to enfranchise blacks, the amendment penalized states that deprived adult male citizens of the right to vote for any reason other than conviction of a crime or participation in the rebellion by empowering the national government to reduce the number of their representatives in Congress. It also barred all persons from elective federal office who had once served as senior federal officials only to later hold places in the Confederate government. Finally, the amendment barred the southern states from paying their Confederate war debts, abolished the three-fifths rule, and authorized Congress to enact legislation necessary to enforce its terms.

Speaking in the House on May 8, 1866, Thaddeus Stevens conceded that he found the measure in its final form to be inadequate. He would not push his luck, as he knew three-quarters of the northern states would not ratify anything more aggressive (he believed the southern states need not be counted in determining the total number of states needed to ratify it because they were not represented in Congress). Stevens was pleased to report that the amendment still "allows Congress to correct the unjust legislation of the states, so far that the law which operates upon one man shall operate equally upon all. Whatever law punishes a white man for a crime shall punish the black man precisely in the same way and to the same degree. Whatever law protects the white man shall afford equal protection to the black man. Whatever means of redress is afforded to one shall be afforded to all. Whatever law allows the white man to testify in court shall allow the man of color to do the same." Stevens thought that the provision authorizing the reduction of the congressional delegations of states that "exclude any of her adult male citizens from the franchise" was "the most important" portion of the amendment.[85] James Garfield described the amendment as providing "every American citizen, without regard to color, the protecting shield of law." He regretted that it did not require states to enfranchise blacks.[86] Benjamin Boyer, a Pennsylvania Democrat, spoke more truth than he knew when he complained that the first section was "open to ambiguity and admitting of conflicting constructions."[87] In July 1866, the amendment, with its promise of "an equality of civil rights," received the approval of two-thirds of both the House and Senate and was submitted to the states.[88]

In their effort to obtain ratification of the amendment in the northern states, proponents of ratification emphasized section two of the amendment: Ratification would, they promised, reduce southern representation in the House and ensure northern control of the federal government for the foreseeable future. Section 1 entered the headlines when it became tied up with the issue of race. Democrats claimed the vague language of the privileges and immunities clause would be used to bestow suffrage on blacks.[89] In fact, many Republicans expressed disappointment with it precisely because it did not bestow a right to vote—instead they viewed it as providing a constitutional basis for the Civil Rights Act of 1866. The *Chicago Daily Tribune* called the amendment a "re-enactment of the civil rights law" and claimed most northerners found it inadequate due its lack of provision for black suffrage.[90] In Evanston, Illinois, Lyman Trumbull stated that Section 1 "secures civil rights to all citizens of the United States."[91] Emery A. Storrs, a prominent Republican lawyer, explained that the amendment "simply declares the equality of all American citizens before the law; that the black man will be protected in his rights of person and property, as well as the white."[92]

During the fall of 1866, the debate over ratification became immersed in one of the most vicious political campaigns in the nation's history. The president was among the mudslingers. During a meeting at the executive mansion with delegates from the recently held National Union Party convention, Johnson questioned whether the 38th Congress, devoid as it was of southern delegations, had authority to pass any laws at all.[93] Shortly thereafter the president made the fateful decision to give a series of speeches in the northern states. It was the first stump campaign by a sitting president, and it proved to be an unmitigated disaster. The "swing around the circle" had as its ostensible purpose the dedication of a memorial statue of Stephen A. Douglas in Chicago. Traveling by train, Johnson spoke in cities along the route defending his policies. At first he fared well, skillfully explaining his actions and detailing the excesses of Congress. New York City received him enthusiastically. He had the temerity to remind listeners in Ohio that their state had just rejected an amendment that would have extended the suffrage to blacks.[94] In Cleveland hostile crowds succeeded in goading Johnson into an ugly exchange and from that point on his temper regularly led him off track. He spoke of radicals in harsh terms and blamed them for the New Orleans riot. With crowds demanding that Jefferson Davis hang, Johnson hinted that the same punishment ought to be extended to Thaddeus Stevens and Wendell Phillips. By the end of the tour hostile crowds were shouting him down and the president's northern allies such as Henry Raymond abandoned him. James Blaine later wrote that Johnson returned to Washington "personally discredited and politically ruined."[95] Northern Democrats did not take advantage of the schism between Johnson and Republicans in Congress; in state after state in the North, they nominated Copperheads who had called for letting the South go during the war. Radicals played on northern anger at the president and claimed he would use force to obtain the admission of southern delegations to Congress. Wendell Phillips suggested impeaching the president and arranging for a congressional committee to run the government even before the trial concluded.[96]

REVOLUTION

Republicans won overwhelming majorities in both houses of Congress in the 1866 midterm elections; they showed no sign of admitting southern delegations. The capital was filled with talk of returning the South to military rule while new governments acceptable to radicals were devised, despite the fact that the war was now only a memory. When such a measure had been proposed by the Joint Committee on Reconstruction in April, it had been ignored. Eight months later, with the patience of the northern public exhausted, radicals were emboldened. New southern state governments established under congressional supervision could be forced to both enfranchise blacks and ratify the Fourteenth Amendment, which appeared to have stalled with its rejection by Maryland and Delaware.

With radicals dominating each house of Congress, the replacement of civil government in a third of the United States by military rule now awaited. Gideon Welles saw Sumner, Stephens, and other radicals herding lawmakers like so many sheep, and he remarked that it is "pitiable to see how little sense of right, real independence, and what limited comprehension are possessed by our legislators. They are the tame victims and participators of villainous conspirators."[97] Just as the guillotine was about to be dropped on the South's neck, the Supreme Court reminded the country that it possessed a written Constitution and that at one time it had aspired to live under the rule of law. *Ex parte Milligan* arose out of events in Indiana during the last year of the Civil War. Major general Alvin Hovey, commander of the Military District of Indiana, ordered the arrest of Lambdin Milligan and others in October 1864. They were charged with conspiring to release Confederate prisoners of war. After Union soldiers came to his home and took him into custody, Milligan was tried before a military commission at Indianapolis. He was found guilty and sentenced to death by hanging. After the president postponed his execution, Milligan petitioned the U.S. Circuit Court in Indianapolis for a writ of habeas corpus; he claimed the military commission had no jurisdiction over him. When three circuit court judges who heard his request disagreed on the proper response, they certified three questions for appeal to the U.S. Supreme Court: Did the commission have authority to try Milligan? Should a writ of habeas corpus be issued? Should Milligan be released? With Milligan at the steps of the gallows, the high court wrestled with these questions for months until it finally issued its ruling in December 1866.

In his opinion for the majority, Justice David Davis held that Congress had not and could not authorize the establishment of military tribunals for the purpose of trying civilians in areas that were at peace. "This court has judicial knowledge that in Indiana the federal authority was always unopposed, and its courts always open to hear criminal accusations and redress grievances; and no usage of war could sanction a military trial there for any offence whatever of a citizen in civil life, in no way connected with the military service." Noting that "Congress could grant no such power," Davis was pleased to report that it "has never been provoked by the state of the country even to attempt its exercise."[98] Milligan's trial by military commission violated the Constitution because no indictment was obtained from a grand jury and no civil jury heard the case.[99] As for Indiana's close proximity to areas where hostilities had occurred and the possibility that the state might become a theater of war at any moment, Davis stated flatly that "martial law cannot arise from a threatened invasion." It can "never exist where the courts are open, and in the proper and unobstructed exercise of their jurisdiction."[100] Four justices disagreed with the majority on the question of whether Congress could have established military tribunals in the state of Indiana. Their sentiments were encapsulated in a concurring opinion by Chief Justice Chase, who claimed that Indiana was a theater of military operations (Confederate raiders had crossed the Ohio River). Therefore Congress could have, if it wished, established military commissions in the state.[101]

Radicals thought the majority opinion wrong, dangerous, and horribly ill-timed.[102] Republican leaders talked of stripping the Supreme Court of at least a portion of its appellate jurisdiction. The ability of the Freedmen's Bureau to take control of disputes involving freedmen was placed in jeopardy by the decision; even worse, the willingness of Republican lawmakers to follow their leaders and support the abolition of southern state governments was now in doubt. Northern newspapers did not help matters when they interpreted the decision as having mortally wounded the idea of imposing military rule on the South. The *Springfield Daily Republican* of Springfield, Massachusetts, believed that both the majority and the minority of the court agreed on the illegality of military trials of civilians in areas untouched by war where the civil courts were open. With the South at peace, the game appeared to be over: The application of the decision to the southern states must be governed by their condition. "The president has proclaimed them at peace and the civil law in full force." As the civil rights bill "secures the interposition of the United States courts [in aid of] citizens who cannot obtain equal justice in local tribunals, there is not likely to be any very earnest interest for further military rule."[103] Several days later it was apparent that the *Republican*'s editor, Samuel Bowles, had regained his nerve and was ready to embrace extreme measures. In an article entitled "The *Milligan* Case—False Alarms," he consoled readers with the news that Congress could still impose any conditions it pleased before admitting southern delegations.[104]

As the congressional session commenced, the North became increasingly agitated. The president held some responsibility for this; with his removal of numerous Republicans from office he made it clear that the presidency had changed parties as well as occupants with the death of his predecessor. (While Johnson had been nominated on the National Union Party ticket in 1864, his views remained closer to those of Democrats than Republicans.) The South did its part as well—one southern state after another rejected the Fourteenth Amendment as 1866 drew to a close. The increasing likelihood that it would fail unless the southern states could be forced to ratify it pushed lawmakers toward the conviction that military rule was necessary (Thaddeus Stevens' assertion that the amendment could become law with ratification by only three-fourths of the northern states failed to take hold).

The radical fusillade in Congress began before the *Ex parte Milligan* ruling was issued, when Charles Sumner offered resolutions on the floor of the Senate on December 5. One held that "it is the duty of Congress to proceed with the work of reconstruction, and to this end it must assume jurisdiction of the states lately in rebellion . . . and it must recognize only the loyal states or those states having legal and valid 'Legislatures' as entitled to representation in Congress (and) a voice in the adoption of constitutional amendments." Another resolution held that "in determining whether the southern state governments qualify as republican, Congress must follow the definition supplied by the Declaration of Independence, and, in the practical application of this definition, it must, after excluding all disloyal persons, take care that new governments are founded on the two fundamental truths therein contained; first, that all men are equal in rights; and secondly, that all just government stands only on the consent of the governed."[105] Similar rhetoric was heard from other lawmakers, though of course they did not apply such lofty tests to the northern states. As the forces in favor of abolishing the southern state governments picked up momentum, Gideon Welles lamented that Congress was dominated by radicals "who have no more regard for the Constitution than for an old almanac." They seem to believe that "Congress is omnipotent." Radicals proposed to turn upside down a section of the country that was functioning as normally as it had 10 years previously. There was, Welles complained, "nothing to re-construct."[106]

Along with a great many other Americans, Thaddeus Stevens thought otherwise. On January 3, 1867, Stevens proposed a bill providing for military reconstruction that effectively reduced the southern states to territorial status while the army oversaw the formation of new state governments that met the demands of radicals. Speaking in support of the bill, he described *Ex parte Milligan* as even worse than *Dred Scott*. It is "far more dangerous in its operation upon the lives and liberties of the loyal men of this country. That decision has taken away every protection in every one of these rebel states from every loyal man, black or white, who resides there. That decision has unsheathed the dagger of the assassin, and places the knife of the rebel at the throat of every man who dares proclaim himself to be now, or to have been heretofore, a loyal Union man." Such evils would follow because persons accused of assaulting blacks would be tried by civil juries instead of military commissions. In Stevens's view, it was now incumbent upon Congress to act, as the power "to reconstruct the nation, to admit new states, to guarantee republican governments to old states are all legislative acts."

Otherwise, "all our blood and treasure will have been spent in vain." Blacks should be given the vote in the South, as "they form the great mass of the loyal men" in the region. With their aid "loyal governments may be established in most of these states. Without all are sure to be ruled by traitors; and loyal men, black and white, will be oppressed, exiled or murdered." Even worse, every one of the rebel states "is sure to send a solid rebel representative delegation to Congress, and cast a solid rebel electoral vote."[107]

The *Springfield Daily Republican* concluded that reconstruction of the southern state governments was now likely, yet it also held that the argument for its constitutionality—the republican government clause—"amounts to nothing." It noted that the southern states might later reverse the reforms required of them in exchange for admission. Echoing the sentiments of many Republicans, it suggested that perhaps constitutional revisions ought to be embraced instead. "The pending (Fourteenth) amendment embodies some of these, but not all. Equal suffrage is the essential thing."[108] On January 8 the cabinet discussed the question of whether the southern states could be reduced to territorial status; all agreed they could not.[109] No matter. Despite the fact that the southern state governments were now "organized and in full operation," in the words of Gideon Welles, "the lesser lights in Congress are told that they must assist in undoing the work [that] has been well and rightly done by the people interested, and compel the states to go through the process of disorganizing in order to organize."[110]

On the floor of the House, Democrat Lawrence Trimble of Kentucky charged that the military reconstruction bill would "establish in lieu of the governments now in those states, governments to be set up and put in operation by Congress, through the agency of commissioners and military despots with no responsibility to the people, disenfranchising a large portion of the people of that section. The most intelligent and best citizens are to be reduced to serfs. I ask where is the authority, where is the power, under the Constitution of the United States to so treat these same people?" As for claims that the republican government clause authorized the bill, Trimble asked whether it is "republican to deprive these people of the right of suffrage, of any voice in their local affairs?" If enacted, the measure would be a bill of attainder, a violation of due process, and impair the right to a jury trial. It would also violate constitutional provisions for the election of members of Congress and constitute an ex post facto law.[111]

Republican George Julian of Indiana believed the bill did not go far enough, as the southern states had been reduced to territorial status by the war. They "are wholly without any valid civil government, and without any constitutional power to frame such government; and being solely under the jurisdiction of Congress, and having none of the powers and attributes of states, they are necessarily territories of the United States."

They should remain territories so that the "nationalizing" of the region could proceed.[112] Andrew Rogers, Democrat of New Jersey, denied that there was a level of anarchy or lawlessness in the South that would justify military rule. He thought *Milligan*, with its unanimous agreement on the matter of military trials in areas at peace, rendered the bill unconstitutional ("the question involved has been settled").[113]

Frederick Pike, Republican of Maine, suggested that military rule would check the violence that afflicted the region. Three U.S. soldiers had been murdered in October 1865 while guarding cotton in South Carolina. The accused murderers were tried and convicted by a military commission, only to be freed following the issuing of a writ of habeas corpus by a state judge. On returning to their homes in Anderson, South Carolina, they were "received by a general ovation of the people of the place." Pike noted that the Freedmen's Bureau reported numerous murders of blacks in the South. The murderers went free due to the unwillingness of juries to convict them.[114] Congressman William Niblack of Indiana focused on the matter of authority. The president long ago declared the rebellion over and "yet more than a year and a half after volunteer soldiers were mustered out service, because the war had closed, we are met by the declaration in this House that the country is still at war, and that, being thus at war, we are justified in taking military jurisdiction of all the country lately in rebellion, and of suspending the privilege of the writ of habeas corpus throughout its limits."[115]

The military reconstruction bill passed the House on February 20. The *Springfield Daily Republican* held that the measure's violation of the right to trial by jury and its other constitutional defects were matters best left to the courts. As for the necessity of military rule, it conceded that "there are wide differences of opinion." Although it approved the measure, the *Republican* interpreted its passage as meaning—regrettably in its view—that Congress was not going to submit a constitutional amendment to the states that would give blacks the vote.[116] Noting Maryland Senator Reverdy Johnson's claim that only passage of the bill would ensure the admission of southern delegations to Congress, the *Baltimore Sun* insisted that the object of the measure was to keep them out of it and to make sure the South did not vote in the 1868 presidential election. The *Sun* complained that the bill's provision denying the vote to those who participated in the rebellion would disenfranchise a large portion of the white population in the southern states.[117]

The bill that went to the president's desk was a wonder to behold. It began with the assertion that no legal governments existed in the rebel states—a claim that would have come as news to the governments then functioning in the South. It divided the region into five military districts and subjected each of them "to the military authority of the United States."

An officer of the army would preside over each district, and he would have the choice of using either civil or military courts to try persons accused of breaking the law. The people of each southern state were authorized to devise new state constitutions that must be in "conformity with the Constitution of the United States in all respects." Said constitutions were to be drafted by conventions of delegates "elected by the male citizens of said State, twenty one years old and upward, of whatever race" except those disenfranchised for "participation in the rebellion" or "felony at common law." Once a state secured congressional approval of its proposed charter and ratified the Fourteenth Amendment, it would be entitled to representation in Congress. Until the delegations of rebel states were admitted to Congress, "any civil governments which may exist therein shall be deemed provisional only, and in all respects subject to the paramount authority of the United States at any time to abolish, modify, control or supersede same."[118]

The president vetoed the bill. After working on his veto message with Attorney General Henry Stanbery and Jeremiah S. Black (Buchanan's attorney general), Johnson issued it on March 2. The president's objections were familiar: "The military rule which (the bill) establishes is plainly to be used, not for any purpose of order or for the prevention of crimes, but solely as a means of coercing the people into the adoption of principles and measures to which it is known that they are opposed, and upon which they have an undeniable right to exercise their own judgment." Not only did it "palpably conflict with the plainest provisions of the Constitution," the measure flew in the face of a thousand years of experience in the English-speaking world. The commanding military officer in each military district would have absolute power over its inhabitants. "His mere will is to take the place of law." The president noted that the bill gave commanders the choice of holding civil or military trials—or no trials at all. Military officers could make arrests without warrants. Persons in Massachusetts, Pennsylvania, Rhode Island, and New York had resisted federal authority in the past, but the "relations of those states with the federal government were not supposed to be interrupted or changed thereby after the rebellious portions of their populations were defeated and put down." Johnson cited *Ex parte Milligan* for the proposition that martial law can only be imposed in areas where there is an actual state of war: "Peace exists in all the territory to which this bill applies." In addition, the judicial power of the United States can be exercised only by Article III courts. As for claims that the republican government clause authorized the bill, Johnson could have not have been more dismissive. "Can it be pretended that this obligation is not palpably broken if we carry out a measure like this, which wipes away every vestige of republican government in ten states and puts the life, property, liberty, and honor of all the people in each of them under the domination of a single person clothed with unlimited authority?"[119]

The task of squaring the first Reconstruction Act with the Constitution has not become any easier with time. There was something surreal about substituting military rule for 10 republican governments for the purpose of making those governments more republican. Thus the critique of a legal historian: "Not only was it less than obvious what constitutional provisions might support such legislation; on its face the statute seemed a gross breach of Congress's constitutional obligation to guarantee each state a republican form of government, a denial of the constitutional right of representation in Congress, and a perversion of the ratification provisions of Article V. It also raised Article III and jury-trial provision problems already identified in *Ex parte Milligan*."[120] Alas, the time for legal niceties had passed. The *New York Times* conceded the force of the president's message but concluded that his hypocrisy undermined the force of his argument. It explained that the "power exercised by Congress in the premises is identical with the power he exercised on the close of the rebellion. So far as he is concerned, the question at issue relates rather to the agency exercising authority than to the authority itself. And upon this point the people have pronounced a decision from which there is no appeal. They have decided that the final solution of the reconstruction problem belongs to Congress, not to the President; and nothing can be gained by a controversy of which this is the essential part."[121] S. S. Cox, the redoubtable and crafty New York City Democrat (who had formerly represented an Ohio district), provided a balanced assessment of the veto in his autobiography. While he insisted that the South "was subjected to a military despotism, pure and simple," he also held that some conditions on the southern states might be imposed. "Otherwise, a rebellious people might re-establish their former constitutions and laws, and reinstate their disloyal officials."[122] In a March 23 article entitled "Let the Constitution Slide," the *Springfield Daily Republican* again conceded that Congress lacked authority to pass the Reconstruction Act, but it insisted that it would be best if the southern states went along with its terms and bided their time. They should not litigate the measure but instead accept the fact that "Congress is sustained by the states now in possession of the government."[123]

It was inevitable that the southern state governments would seek redress in the federal courts rather than acquiesce in their own destruction. Their efforts were futile. Despite its apparent conflict with *Ex parte Milligan*, the Reconstruction Act was never in any danger from the Supreme Court. Mississippi brought an action seeking an order barring the president from carrying out the terms of the law; the Court held it lacked the power to enjoin the president "in performance of his official duties."[124] When

Georgia sought an injunction barring the secretary of war from carrying out the terms of the law, the high court held that a state lacked standing "to assert merely political interests."[125]

Congress was not willing to leave the Reconstruction Act to the whim of the president. In the Tenure of Office Act of March 2, 1867, it provided that all persons appointed to office with the consent of the Senate would hold office until a successor had been approved by the Senate; cabinet officers would hold their places during the term of the president who appointed them, plus one month. When the Senate was not in session, the president could suspend these officials when evidence indicated they engaged in misconduct or committed a crime; a successor could also be appointed. Once the Senate was back in session, the president had 20 days to present evidence supporting the suspension to the Senate and the suspension remained in effect only if it concurred.[126] The act was designed to keep Johnson from removing Edwin Stanton from the War Department (he was already working with the radicals in secret); it was also intended to keep the president from removing generals who proved too aggressive in enforcing the Reconstruction Act. Congress had debated the question of the removal power at the time it passed the organic act for the State Department (1789). It dispensed with a clause requiring its approval for the removal of senior officeholders, in part because it would weaken the president's ability to control executive branch officers and, in the view of some, infringe on the Article II powers of the presidency.[127] Radical animosity toward Johnson had reached the point that Congress was willing to sacrifice effective management of the executive branch. Some lawmakers objected to the assault; Democrat Andrew Rogers of New Jersey claimed that the bill constituted a diminution of the president's power as commander-in-chief granted by Article II and was therefore unconstitutional.[128]

Johnson weighed in against the bill, albeit in vain. In his veto message, he insisted Congress had usurped the power of the president, in whom the Constitution vested the power to remove senior officials. He cited the above-mentioned 1789 debate in support of this position, the Supreme Court's decision in *Ex parte Hennen*, and congressional debates of the Jacksonian period.[129] Congress passed the measure over Johnson's veto. It also passed another act regarding the executive branch that was equally destructive—the Command of the Army Act (March 2, 1867). The law required the president to issue all military orders through the General of the Army and barred chief executives from removing the occupant of that office. The law also abolished the militias of the states formerly in rebellion.[130] Johnson signed the measure out of fear that the army would be deprived of needed funds (the provision was part of an army appropriation bill).

To ensure that the president did not reduce the Reconstruction Act to a nullity by inaction, the old 39th Congress passed a resolution just before it adjourned providing that the new 40th Congress would meet at noon on March 4. Normally it would not have met until the following December. Within days lawmakers passed the Second Reconstruction Act, which devised the steps Union army officers would follow in arranging for state constitutional conventions in the South. It was passed over the president's veto on March 23.[131] The law provided for commanders of each military district to register as voters in southern states all males over 21 who took an oath affirming they had not been disenfranchised for participating in the rebellion or served in public office before the war and then aided the rebellion; they also had to promise they would support the Constitution and obey the laws of the United States. Once registration had been completed (by September 1, 1867), a plebiscite on the question of whether to hold a state constitutional convention would be held. If a majority supported the idea, an election for delegates would take place. The constitution drafted by each convention would then be submitted to a popular vote; if it won a majority, it would be submitted to Congress for its approval. If approved, "the state shall be declared entitled to representation, and senators and representatives shall be admitted therefrom as therein provided."[132] The process was similar to that which had been used in territories seeking admission to the Union as states.

A majority of the American people proceeded to impose military rule on a minority. In a third of the country, the Constitution had, for all practical purposes, been suspended. The possibilities inherent in a policy of subjecting to military rule states that did not possess governments acceptable to congressional majorities was demonstrated by a proposal of Francis Thomas, a radical Congressman from Maryland. He introduced a resolution providing for the House Judiciary Committee to investigate whether his state had a government adequately republican in form. The state had never seceded. Would New York be next? Ohio? The *Baltimore Sun* believed the episode had more to do with the desire of Maryland radicals to regain control of the state than with any defects in its government.[133] Shortly thereafter, radicals in the state legislature took the hint and started sending memorials to Congress demanding its intervention. The *Sun* was appalled, calling the effort "one of those lamentable exhibitions of frenzied partisanship which would only excite commiseration for the unfortunate men whose desperation is thus evinced, were it not for the fact that in these revolutionary times there is no telling what usurpation might not be attempted." The *Sun* expressed confidence that Congress would not involve itself in Maryland's internal affairs and it insisted that nothing had occurred that warranted federal intervention. It noted that Maryland radicals pushed through a new state constitution during the war, and that the new charter not only withheld the suffrage from blacks but was more restrictive in allotting the vote than its predecessor.[134]

While Maryland avoided the wrath of radicals in Congress, the federal judiciary was not so fortunate. Mississippi editor William McCardle saw fit to criticize Reconstruction; for his trouble he was tried by a military commission. His request for a writ of habeas corpus was denied. McCardle filed an appeal with the Supreme Court pursuant to the Habeas Corpus Act of 1867.[135] The law authorized federal judges to issue writs of habeas corpus when persons were jailed in violation of their rights under the Constitution and provided for appeals in such cases to the Supreme Court. While the justices were considering the matter, Congress passed a law modifying the Habeas Corpus Act of 1867 to strip the high court of appellate jurisdiction over most habeas corpus cases, including McCardle's—Republicans feared the Supreme Court might hold the Reconstruction Acts void.[136] In April 1869 the Supreme Court issued an opinion in which it held it no longer had jurisdiction to hear the case as the Constitution endowed Congress with the power to make exceptions to the Supreme Court's appellate jurisdiction.[137] The decision, which was unanimous, has been heavily criticized for its implication that Congress could reduce the Supreme Court to a nonentity by stripping it of its appellate jurisdiction altogether, but the Constitution's grant of authority could not have been more clear: "In all other Cases before mentioned, the Supreme Court shall have appellate jurisdiction, both as to Law and Fact, with such Exceptions, and under such Regulations as Congress shall make" (Article III, Section 2).

Slowly and fitfully, military reconstruction began during 1867. The state governments then in power came under the supervision of army officials. Voters were registered and convention elections took place. When the president circulated an opinion of the attorney general holding that military officials did not have authority to remove men from state offices in the South, General of the Army U.S. Grant took it upon himself to tell them the circular could be ignored, and he received the support of Secretary of War Edwin Stanton. Generals such as Philip Sheridan continued to remove men from office.[138] Alerted to the conflict over the removal of southern officeholders, Congress enacted the third Reconstruction Act of July 19, 1867. It declared that the intent of the first such act was to pronounce the southern state governments illegal. Said governments continued "subject in all respects to the military commanders of the respective districts." Military commanders could remove any person from any state civil office and appoint replacements.[139] The president vetoed the measure only to have it become law. He objected to its provision for vesting the appointment power in inferior military officers.[140] Secretary of War Stanton helped draft the law;

when the president found out that one of his cabinet members was secretly working with the opposition, he asked Stanton to resign on August 5. When the request was refused, Johnson suspended his Secretary of War, only to have Stanton insist the president lacked authority to impose the suspension.[141]

Meanwhile military reconstruction continued. The generals in command of the military districts of the South usually behaved with prudence. Philip Sheridan removed two state governors and George Meade discharged another, and on occasion military officials transferred civil and criminal cases to military courts. Dan Sickles ordered an end to discrimination in public conveyances in his district (North Carolina and South Carolina). The generals put the machinery for establishing new civil governments in motion: They established new voter lists that included black males and arranged for constitutional conventions to be held in each state. The ban on persons who aided the Confederacy had the effect of disenfranchising many whites.[142] The conventions met during 1867 and early 1868. They devised constitutions that made great improvements over their predecessors, providing for public schools and more fairly apportioning seats in the legislatures. They also bestowed equal political rights to whites and black males, though they did not guarantee integrated schools or ban all forms of private discrimination. The new constitutions were approved in most of the southern states by the spring of 1868. Congress responded by passing two laws admitting the delegations of Arkansas, North Carolina, South Carolina, Florida, Georgia, Alabama, and Louisiana as those states had devised constitutions and governments acceptable to Republican leaders in Washington.[143] Johnson vetoed them only to be overridden.[144] In other states the process slowed due to intransigence; in Virginia the military governor refused to allow the state's proposed Constitution to be submitted to a popular vote. In Mississippi, the state's voters rejected a proposed constitution in 1868.

Radical Republicans succeeded in winning control of the new state governments in the South due to the enfranchisement of blacks and the withholding of the vote from many whites who participated in the rebellion. Southern blacks took to politics with enthusiasm. They enrolled in political organizations such as the Union Leagues and turned out for elections at rates approaching 90 percent. Southern Republicans proved to be a good deal more populist than their northern brethren; the Charleston, South Carolina, Republican Party convention called for equal rights for both races, integrated schools, state care for the aged and poor, debt relief, internal improvements (with contracts parceled out to blacks and whites equally), laws exempting homesteads from debt collectors, and punitive taxation of large estates to promote their sale and widen land ownership.[145]

Once in Republican hands, the new state governments in the South proved humane and forward-looking. They increased funds for schools, hospitals, and asylums. Republican legislatures expanded women's property rights and passed laws banning racial discrimination in public accommodations; they were not enforced. Tax systems were made less burdensome for the poor—property taxes were increased and poll taxes were abolished. Some 6,000 blacks served as state legislators under the radical state governments. They had more difficulty obtaining and holding power at the local level as the daily contact of town and county governments with the citizenry made whites particularly resistant to the idea of turning local offices over to blacks.[146] Blacks also won election to Congress and some, such as Joseph Rainey of South Carolina, won distinction for their oratorical skills. George Hoar later recalled witnessing Rainey best S. S. Cox of New York in a debate on the floor of the House, leaving him "unhorsed and on his back in the arena."[147]

In the fall 1867 elections, blacks provided Republicans with votes in the southern states even as they sustained defeats across the North. It was evident that the Republican surge that began with Johnson's harsh rhetoric in 1866 had reached high tide and was now receding. The losses stemmed largely from the unwillingness of northern voters to support Republicans seeking to modify state suffrage laws to give blacks the vote.[148] Measures that would have enfranchised blacks were rejected in Minnesota, New Jersey, Kansas, and Ohio. Democrats won the Ohio legislature largely because of widespread hostility to a black suffrage amendment that had been defeated overwhelmingly. Ben Wade, among the leading radicals in the Senate, now had no hope of gaining reelection. Democrats also took Pennsylvania and New York. The total vote cast for Democrats in the North exceeded that of Republicans for the first time since before the Civil War (1.62 million to 1.58 million).[149]

Backed by the army, southern Republicans allowed their monopoly on power to corrupt them and the state governments in the South degenerated from a humane advance over their predecessors into a collective disgrace to representative government. In Georgia, Governor Rufus Bullock funded 42 party newspapers with public funds. Enormous amounts of money appropriated for roads simply disappeared. When he began to fear Democrats might win state offices in 1870 and investigate his actions, Bullock used public funds to lobby Congress for a law delaying state elections.[150] Radical legislatures courted business and northern investors aggressively, exempting railroads from taxation, repealing usury laws, and using the power of eminent domain to aid the construction of railroads and factories. In time a close relationship developed between business interests and southern legislatures; many lawmakers served as directors for railroads even as they voted in favor of huge subsidies for them.[151] Corruption and waste on an epic scale followed. The state debt of Louisiana rose from less than $15 million in 1868 to almost $50 million in 1871.[152] The Arkansas state debt increased from $4.8 million in 1868 to $18.7 million in 1871 even as tax rates reached absurd levels. Over $4 million in bonds had been issued to fund the construction of railroads in the state, but corruption and mismanagement limited construction to 93 miles of track by the end of 1871.[153] In 1869 Florida's expenditures for public printing alone was greater than the state government's entire budget in 1860.[154] The huge state debts that resulted would not be paid for decades, and in some cases, the obligations were avoided altogether. Seven southern states repudiated at least part of their debts during the 1870s and 1880s.[155]

While radicals in Congress could take pride in having finally imposed their will on the South, they grew angry with a president whom they suspected of undermining their progress. They were infuriated by reports that Johnson was appointing conservative men to federal offices in the South to weaken the new state governments.[156] They also took offense at the president's attempts to control the activities of military officers who supervised the military districts into which the South had been divided. As early as 1866 there had been talk of impeachment; in the fall of 1867 Radicals finally determined that Johnson should be removed from office. Although somewhat chastened by the results of state elections in the North, radicals moved forward with a project that was generally ignored at the time and universally condemned later. On November 25, the House Judiciary Committee voted 5 to 4 in favor of issuing a report recommending impeachment, citing the president's suspension of Stanton while Congress was in session, thereby violating the Tenure of Office Act. On December 7 the House voted against a motion to adopt the report calling for impeachment, 108–57. The cause seemed to have failed until the president attempted to fire Stanton outright in February 1868.

The House took up impeachment resolutions within two hours of receiving word that the president had again attempted to remove the Secretary of War.[157] On Monday, February 24, it voted to impeach the president, 126–47. The articles of impeachment alleged that the president violated the Tenure of Office Act in (1) issuing an order for the removal of Stanton, (2) failing to comply with the Senate's refusal to concur in Stanton's removal, (3) appointing Lorenzo Thomas to replace him, and (4) attempting to prevent Stanton from holding office. The resolutions also charged the president with attempting to give orders directly to military officers instead of going through the General of the Army (U.S. Grant), as required by the Command of the Army Act.[158] The trial in the Senate began on March 4. The president received invaluable aid from a legal team that easily surpassed the prosecution in experience and skill. Attorney general Henry Stanbery resigned to lead the president's defense, and he was aided by former Supreme Court Justice Benjamin Curtis, William Evarts, Thomas Nelson, and former attorney general Jeremiah Black. Prosecuting attorney Ben Butler confirmed his reputation as a courtroom bully; he berated witnesses and substituted histrionics for argument.[159]

Speaking on behalf of the president, former Supreme Court Justice Benjamin Curtis noted that the Tenure of Office Act provides that cabinet officers remain immune against removal by the executive only during the term of the president who appoints them plus an additional month into the next term. He brushed aside the claim that Johnson was merely serving Lincoln's second term—thereby obligating Johnson to leave Stanton in place for the next president to remove—by suggesting that presidents hold office only conditionally—it passes to another if they die. The law obligated Johnson to leave Stanton in office only until May 15, 1865—one month into his term. As for the question of whether the president violated federal laws, Curtis pointed out that Johnson had ample grounds to believe the Tenure of Office Act was unconstitutional. The former Supreme Court justice suggested that chief executives could violate laws to have them tested in court if they removed duties or powers vested in them by the Constitution.[160] The Tenure of Office Act fell within this category as it impermissibly subtracted from the executive power of the president.[161]

Johnson sought to aid his own cause by nominating John M. Schofield—acceptable to radicals—for secretary of war while the trial was in progress. He also terminated efforts to evict Stanton from the War Department.[162] William Evarts secretly advised Republicans that the president would stop frustrating military reconstruction. The pressure for removal eased with Republican victories in southern state elections and by the time the vote on impeachment was held, bookmakers were predicting acquittal.[163] As the trial drew to a close, radical elements in the North including Union League chapters bubbled over with anger, demanding that Republican senators adhere to what they viewed as the orthodox position of the party. The country remained largely indifferent; it was more interested in the unfolding Erie Railroad War, one of the earliest and most interesting hostile takeovers—or attempted takeovers—in the history of American business. On May 16, the Senate voted on the critical 11th article of impeachment. The decision came down to Senator Joseph Fowler of Tennessee. After the Senator mumbled his response to the query of Chief Justice Chase—some thought he said guilty—Fowler was asked for his answer a second time. He responded, "not guilty."[164] The final tally was 35–19, one vote shy of the two-thirds necessary for removal. The vote on the other articles was now postponed, but for all practical purposes, the trial was over. The effort to remove the president disintegrated. Seven Republican votes against removal made the difference. With the final verdict, Stanton resigned and was replaced by General Schofield.

By the time the impeachment drama concluded, radical governments were in the saddle in most of the southern states. In addition to electing suitably Republican delegations to Congress, they also gave their assent to the long-stalled Fourteenth Amendment. The debate over the amendment in the southern states echoed that which had occurred in the North: Advocates suggested the amendment would provide a constitutional basis for the Civil Rights Act of 1866 while critics claimed it would be used to bestow the vote on blacks.[165] Only the replacement of almost every state government in the South made ratification possible. Congress did what it could to aid the cause; after they rejected the amendment, the state governments of Kentucky, Delaware, and Maryland were subject to congressional investigations, ostensibly because of the excessive influence of former Confederates in those states.[166] Finally, in July 1868, three-quarters of the states approved the amendment and it became a part of the Constitution.

With the 1868 presidential campaign underway, Andrew Johnson issued pardons on July 4—the first day of the Democratic National Convention—restoring rights to all former Confederate officials except persons currently under indictment for treason (Jeff Davis alone was set to be tried on that charge).[167] It was already too late for Johnson to obtain the nomination of his former party as the New York Democracy had not responded to his overtures, and he refused to appease the party by sacking William Seward or Secretary of the Treasury Hugh McCulloch.[168] Other suitors included Chief Justice Chase, who spent the spring writing to editors across the North insisting he had no interest in the Democratic nomination, which was naturally taken as an expression of his interest in the Democratic nomination.[169] Western Democrats favored George Pendleton of Ohio on the strength of his "Ohio idea": paying the interest on bonds in greenbacks instead of gold to lighten the tax burden and stimulate inflation. Eastern mercantile interests were horrified and worked against Pendleton's nomination.

The Democratic convention was called to order at Tammany Hall in New York City on July 4. Persons in attendance included Robert Barnwell Rhett, architect of secession in South Carolina, Nathan Bedford Forrest, tormentor of the Union army—he somehow failed to prevent the massacre of black troops at Fort Pillow—and Wade Hampton, who had served as one of the Army of Northern Virginia's senior cavalry officers. Pendleton led Union general Winfield Scott Hancock and other contenders on the first 15 ballots. When neither Pendleton nor Hancock could obtain the votes of two-thirds of the delegates, the convention settled on former governor of New York Horatio Seymour. As the nominee had come dangerously close to fomenting resistance to the draft while serving as governor of New York, Gideon Welles complained that his fellow Democrats destroyed their chances when they nominated him.[170] The Democratic platform called for the "immediate restoration of all the States to their rights in the Union, under the Constitution, and of civil government to the American people." It complained that the "Radical Party" had "substituted arbitrary seizures and arrests, and military trials and secret star-chamber inquisitions, for the constitutional tribunals" and that it had "disregarded in time of peace the right of the people to be free from searches and seizures."[171]

Republicans nominated U.S. Grant for president that spring; they offered the country a platform that constituted a new low in hypocrisy. While insisting that the "guaranty by Congress of equal suffrage to all loyal men at the South was demanded by every consideration of public safety," it held that the "question of suffrage in all the loyal states properly belongs to the people of those states."[172] The campaign was characterized by virulent racism on the part of Democrats, opportunism on the part of Republicans, and rampant violence in the South. Shortly before the Democratic convention, the party's vice presidential nominee, Frank Blair, issued a letter promising that if his party won the presidency, it would declare the radical governments in the South "null and void" and allow the people of that region to govern themselves.[173] Thereafter he went on a speaking tour, warning of the evils that would result from black enfranchisement in the North. Republicans reminded Americans that their party led the Union to victory. They staged a rally of veterans or "Blue Coats" in Philadelphia on October 2. It took a full day for the assembled veterans to march through the city.[174] Governor Seymour's 1863 address to New York City rioters was liberally quoted, and the presence of former Confederate leaders at the Democratic convention was made known to voters across the North. Republicans also made much of the Democrats' embrace of greenbacks. Conservative and commercial elements embraced the Republican cause to a degree heretofore unseen, providing the party with badly needed funds.[175]

Violence in the South also helped the Republican cause. As everyone in the region seemed to carry a rifle, it was not extraordinary for 300 armed blacks to hike to a political meeting in Camilla, Georgia. A county sheriff met them outside of town and demanded they disarm. When they refused, shooting began and before it was over, eight blacks were killed. The incident was used to remind northerners that southerners could not be trusted to manage their own affairs.[176] Blacks were subjected to intimidation and violence throughout the South. The Ku Klux Klan had been formed in Tennessee in 1866. During the 1868 campaign it assassinated Republican politicians including Arkansas Congressman James M. Hinds and three members of the South Carolina legislature.[177] The military was slow to respond, in part because Johnson had filled the upper ranks with men hostile to reconstruction.

When the October state elections in Indiana and Ohio produced narrow Republican wins, talk among Democrats of replacing Seymour on the ticket was heard; the candidate responded by commencing only the second round of stump speaking by a presidential candidate in American history (Stephen Douglas staged his own tour in 1860). Seymour visited critical states including Pennsylvania, Ohio, Indiana, and Illinois; he denounced Republicans for destroying state bank notes and replacing them with the notes of national banks, which were distributed unevenly across the country. Seymour also pointed out that Republicans had managed to spend $8 billion since 1860. They had placed "a tax-gatherer at every corner and government officials throughout the land."[178] When the presidential election was held in November, Grant won 214 electoral votes to 80 for Seymour. The popular vote margin was 300,000. In the South, six states voted for Grant and two chose Seymour; the others, Virginia, Mississippi, and Texas, were not allowed to participate in the election. (A joint resolution of July 20, 1868, barred states that had not established civil governments recognized by Congress from participating in the presidential election.[179]) The vote was closer than it appeared; a margin of 30,000 in New York and the votes of blacks in the South made the difference (Seymour won a majority of white votes).[180] Grant would have won by a larger margin had blacks in many parts of the South not been prevented from voting.

Realizing how dependent they were on blacks in the South, Republicans moved to amend the Constitution for the purpose of ensuring that blacks would be able to vote throughout the region. In doing so, they acknowledged the ineffectiveness of Section 2 of the Fourteenth Amendment—reducing the congressional delegations of states that prevented blacks from voting was viewed as beset with too many difficulties. They may have been concerned that the broad language of Section 2—it did not refer to race—could be applied to northern states such as Massachusetts that continued to disenfranchise a portion of their male populations via property or literacy tests.[181] Continuing opposition to the enfranchisement of blacks in the North forced Republicans to once again approach the subject indirectly. In 1867–68, Colorado, Connecticut, Kansas, Michigan, Minnesota, Missouri, New York, Wisconsin, and Ohio rejected amendments that would have bestowed suffrage on blacks.[182] What became the Fifteenth Amendment provided that "the right of citizens of the United States to vote shall not be denied or abridged by the United States or by any State on account of race, color, or previous condition of servitude." It authorized Congress to pass legislation necessary to affect this worthy goal. Critics such as Massachusetts Senator Henry Wilson complained that the amendment did not go far enough. Wilson proposed a more far-reaching amendment that would have barred discrimination on the grounds of "race, color, nativity, property, education or creed"—thereby prohibiting the use of property and literacy requirements for voting.[183] Unwilling to embrace universal suffrage for males in their own states, Republicans would have nothing to do with Wilson's draft. The amendment was rushed through Congress in early 1869. Congress helped its prospects with an April 1869 law barring the delegations of Virginia, Mississippi, and Texas until their states ratified the amendment, and the measure was approved by the requisite number of states within a year.[184]

U.S. Grant was sworn in as president on March 4, 1869. He refused to ride in a carriage with Andrew Johnson from the executive mansion to the Capitol.[185] The new president found that he was not the master of Washington any more than his predecessor had been. The Capitol was the center of gravity. Republicans continued to enjoy huge majorities in both houses. In the House of Representatives something of a vacuum developed with the death of Thaddeus Stevens in the summer of 1868. Henry Dawes of Massachusetts exercised the most influence from his post as chairman of the Committee on Appropriations. In the Senate Republicans were led by Zachariah Chandler of Michigan, Roscoe Conking of New York, and Oliver Morton of Indiana. Chandler had used federal patronage to build a dominant political machine in Michigan; he served as the equivalent of the majority whip. The wartime governor of Indiana, Morton was a capable partisan and utterly ruthless in matters regarding the South. Allen Thurman of Ohio and Thomas Bayard of Delaware were among the leading Democrats in the Senate.

In late 1869 Grant signed a bill barring Georgia's delegation from Congress until it ratified the Fifteenth Amendment—in effect rescinding the June 1868 act re-admitting the state. The law also made illegal the barring of legislators from the state capitol on account of their race and provided a method for resolving election disputes in the state. It authorized the governor of Georgia to ask the president to employ the military to enforce the act.[186] Enactment of the measure had been made necessary in the view of Republicans by the state legislature's expulsion of black lawmakers and its admission of former Confederates in violation of the Fourteenth Amendment. In complaining of the law, the *Atlanta Constitution* charged that the "state governments are the mere creatures of Congress and can be overthrown at the will of the dominant party."[187] Brigadier General Alfred Terry, military governor of the district including Georgia, proceeded to replace 24 members of the Georgia legislature with Republicans.

When the Senate took up a bill to extend the life of the Radical government in Georgia by two years, Lyman Trumbull issued a stinging indictment. "The Lecompton swindle was not more iniquitous, when an attempt was made to force it upon the people of Kansas, than would be an act of the Congress which should force the people of Georgia to submit for two years to a government set up by a minority and held against the will of the people."[188] In fact the Georgia bill was worse than Lecompton, as Kansas had not been a state at the time of that episode. The bill failed; another enacted in July provided that Georgia is "entitled to representation in Congress," and the state's delegation was admitted in early 1871.[189]

Virginia, Mississippi, and Texas received similar treatment. After they drafted new constitutions and sent congressional delegations to Washington, new conditions were imposed. A law of January 26, 1870, barred the admission of Virginia's delegation until state officers took an oath promising the state constitution would never be altered to deprive persons of the right to vote. The state was barred from denying citizens the right to hold office on the basis of race; nor could it revoke "school rights and privileges" afforded by the state constitution. Only when the oath was taken would the state's congressional delegation be admitted to Congress and its newly devised civil government be allowed to assume power.[190] Virginia officials bowed to the will of the conqueror, and the state's congressional delegation was admitted later that year.

REDEMPTION

With radical governments in the South growing increasingly corrupt and their ranks marked by internal divisions, the long, bloody process known as "Redemption" began. The whites of each southern state used a combination of political experience, fraud, violence, and sheer numbers to take control of the southern state governments. In states where whites were in the majority, the process moved along quickly; in states with black populations that equaled or surpassed whites, such as Louisiana and South Carolina, only the intimidation of black voters enabled Democrats to regain power. The process often dragged out for several years, as federal officials and military personnel defended blacks and protected the polls with declining effectiveness. The process began with the immersion of the region's former Whigs within the resurgent Democratic Party. The former adherents of Henry Clay and Alexander Stephens took this step with reluctance, but they saw no alternative when the only alternative was the carpetbagger-dominated Republican Party.[191] Democrats proved adept at achieving their ends without giving offense in the North; they devised moderate platforms and entered into coalitions with their opponents.

Tennessee, Virginia, North Carolina, and Georgia were "redeemed"—under the control of Democrats or coalitions—by the end of 1871. In Virginia, a coalition of moderate Democrats and Republicans took over following the end of military rule.[192] Congress contributed to the process of redemption when it passed the Amnesty Act of 1872, thereby relieving almost all of those who participated in the rebellion of the disabilities imposed by the Fourteenth Amendment.[193] That fall Texas Democrats won the state legislative elections. The legislature proceeded to strip the Republican governor of much of his power. Democrats won the legislative elections of 1873 as well, and their gubernatorial candidate prevailed. The incumbent Republican governor responded by convincing the Texas Supreme Court to hold that legislators had been elected illegally and could not hold office.[194] The governor proceeded to barricade himself in the capitol and asked Grant for troops. When the request was denied—twice—he finally gave up his office in January 1874.[195]

Alabama, evenly divided between blacks and whites, was redeemed in 1874. Republicans had covered the state with federal deputy marshals (10 to 25 in each county) as well as agents of the newly formed Justice Department. They made mass arrests under the Enforcement Acts with warrants provided by U.S. commissioners. The tactic prevented whites from suppressing the black vote; it also motivated Democrats to go to the polls. Democrats won the state elections that year in part by pointing to a civil rights bill pending in Congress that would have required the integration of schools in the state.[196] The state would have to wait to get rid of George Spencer, an Iowa native who had won election to the U.S. Senate in 1872 with funds provided by Michigan Senator Zachariah Chandler and the aid of employees in the Mobile and Montgomery internal revenue offices. Spencer provided some 30 members of the legislature with jobs in the federal civil service following his election.[197] Mississippi went over to the Democratic column in 1875 after armed mobs went to the homes of blacks on the night before the state election and warned them not to vote. On taking over the legislature, Democrats impeached the lieutenant governor and secured the governor's resignation by threatening to impeach him. Local black officials were forced to resign at gunpoint.[198]

The process of Redemption in Louisiana was marked by shocking violence, in part because the large numbers of blacks in the state made it difficult for the Democratic Party to regain power by relying on the ballot alone. A "White League" was formed in 1874 for the purpose of intimidating blacks into staying away from the polls. That August, six Republican officials in Red River Parish were murdered. On September 14,

3,500 members of the White League occupied the statehouse after overwhelming forces deployed by the Republican governor. Only federal troops sent by the Grant administration prevented a coup.[199] Irregularities on Election Day in 1874 resulted in two groups claiming to be the duly-elected legislatures of the state. At that point the president sent in federal troops to ensure that the Republicans prevailed, triggering demonstrations over federal intervention at Cooper Union in New York City and Faneuil Hall in Boston.[200]

The Democratic resurgence in the South was aided by the extravagance, waste, and corruption of the Republican-controlled state governments. Democrats organized Taxpayers' conventions to protest excessive spending by legislatures. The tax of $4 for every 100 acres in South Carolina was viewed as excessive at a time when southern farmers had trouble making $300 a year. The cause of retrenchment gained adherents as hard times made it more difficult to earn a living.[201] Almost as soon as they regained control of the legislatures, Democrats moved to limit the political power of blacks, though they did not explicitly disenfranchise them. Poll taxes returned and legislative seats were reapportioned to reduce the number of lawmakers elected from black areas. The Georgia legislature arranged for members of the Atlanta city council to run in citywide elections to keep blacks from winning seats.[202] Democrats also cut expenditures; Florida went so far as to abolish the state's only penitentiary. In many states funds for public education were slashed. To ensure Republicans did not regain power, Democrats perpetrated voting frauds and as they controlled the state governments, prosecutions were not forthcoming. In some states the selection of county officials was taken from voters in each county and given to the state governments to deprive local black majorities of the power to select black officials. Legislatures also reenacted harsh vagrancy laws.[203]

Although violence simmered down after Redemption had been affected, the period between 1866 and 1876 saw blacks slaughtered in droves. By one count, one of every 10 black men who attended one of the state constitutional conventions authorized by the Reconstruction Acts was a victim of violence. Seven were murdered. A Mississippi black man active in the state Republican Party was disemboweled in front of his wife. Armed whites attacked a Eutaw, Alabama, political rally attended by blacks in October 1870; four blacks were killed and 54 suffered injuries. Following the 1872 gubernatorial election, armed blacks held off white attackers for three weeks in Grant Parish, Louisiana. When they retreated to a courthouse, whites forced a black man to torch the roof with kerosene-drenched cotton affixed to a bamboo stick. Blacks exited the building and surrendered, only to be shot. Some 80 blacks died in the worst episode of violence to occur during Reconstruction (the Colfax Massacre).[204] In 1872 a white woman in Alabama was burned alive for the crime of living with a black man.[205] Much of the violence was the work of the Ku Klux Klan, which served as the quasi-military arm of the Democratic Party in the region throughout the period, terrorizing blacks until they learned to stay away from the polls. From 1868 to 1871 the Klan lynched 400 black men in the South.[206] Democratic sheriffs, who were often Klan members themselves, refused to arrest those responsible for bloodshed.

An 1868 report of a committee of the Tennessee legislature explained the power of the Klan in the middle and western counties of the state.

> In these counties a reign of terror exists, which is so absolute in its nature that the best citizens are unable or unwilling to give free expression to their opinions. The terror inspired by the secret organization known as the Ku Klux Klan is so great that the officers of the law are powerless to execute its provisions, to discharge their duties, or to bring the guilty perpetrators of these outrages to the punishment they deserve. Their stealthy movements are generally made under cover of night, and under masks and disguises, which render their identification difficult, if not impossible. To add to the secrecy which envelopes their operations, is the fact that no information of their murderous acts can be obtained without the greatest difficulty and danger, in the localities where they are committed. No one dares to inform upon them, or take any measures to bring them to punishment because no one can tell but that he may be the next victim of their hostility or animosity.[207]

A February 1872 report of a joint committee of Congress revealed the political consequences of this undeclared war on black Americans. In the spring 1868 elections in Orleans Parish, Louisiana, Republicans won 13,973 votes; Klan violence reduced the Republican tally in the parish that fall to just 1178 votes. In St. Landry Parish, registered Republican voters outnumbered Democrats by a margin of 1,071. In the spring of 1868 Republicans carried the parish by 678 votes, yet that fall there was not a single Republican vote cast. Some 200 persons were killed or injured in Louisiana during the weeks prior to the 1868 election. Thirteen blacks were removed from jails and shot, and some 25 corpses were later found in wooded areas of the state.[208] In the end the Klan achieved its purpose; blacks stayed away from polls and Republican state organizations withered as their members suffered threats, injuries, or worse.[209] The inability of the radical state governments in the South to check Klan violence led many in the North to conclude that they were fatally weak and that one way or another, the southern states would return to Democratic control.

Both houses of Congress were held by Republicans until 1875, and Washington did not stand by passively while blacks were hounded into silence and submission. Enacted under the authority of the Fourteenth and Fifteenth Amendments, the Enforcement Act of May 31, 1870, provided that all persons entitled to vote shall be allowed to do so without regard to race or previous condition of servitude. Persons intimidating others to keep them from voting were liable in the amount of $500. Persons acting in disguise to intimidate others, violate the law, or deprive another person of their rights and privileges under the Constitution and laws of the United States were guilty of a felony and subject to imprisonment for up to 10 years. State officers authorized to require persons to perform certain acts before voting (such as proving they were literate) must give all persons an equal opportunity to perform said acts. Federal district courts were given exclusive jurisdiction over violations of the law and the president could deploy the army and navy to enforce it. The law also criminalized fraud in congressional elections. Interference with election officers was made a crime and persons deprived of office due to the exclusion of votes on the basis of race were given the right to file suit in federal court.[210]

In Congress numerous objections to the measure were heard. S. S. Cox deplored the bill's authorization of the use of military force and claimed it was being rushed through to allow the administration to meddle in Virginia state elections. He also objected to the statute's provisions imposing duties on state officers—the Supreme Court had held they cannot be required to enforce federal laws.[211] Congressman Joseph Smith, Democrat of Oregon, believed the measure unconstitutional because it reached private citizens while the Fourteenth and Fifteenth Amendments by their own terms regulated the conduct of state and federal officials. He thought it inappropriate for the federal government to enforce penal laws on a broad scale and objected to the measure's provision for trying alleged violators in federal court. This provision would force defendants to travel hundreds of miles—his state, one of the largest, had only one federal court (in Portland). Smith expected the law to result in the flooding of the states by swarms of federal officials during elections.[212] Eugene Casserly of California saw the measure as an attack on state registration laws. It would require state officials to accept the votes of persons who had not registered if they produced an affidavit, which did not even have to be sworn—failure to do so subjected officials to criminal as well as civil penalties. By requiring officials to comply with state election laws, and providing for the federal courts alone to have jurisdiction over violations, the bill would transfer to federal court all cases involving violations of state election laws. Federal election commissioners and deputies would usurp the role of state officials and seek to "control the elections throughout the Union." Casserly insisted that the law was beyond the authority bestowed on Congress by the Fifteenth Amendment; in his view it prohibited only discriminatory state suffrage laws.[213]

The second Enforcement Act became law on February 28, 1871. Modeled in part on the Naturalization Act of 1870, it provided a mechanism for bringing federal law enforcement officials to any city of 20,000 or more where voter intimidation or fraud in congressional elections was alleged. On the written application of two citizens, federal judges would appoint supervisors to oversee the registration of voters as well as the casting of ballots—they would stand directly behind the ballot boxes if necessary. They were to report any precincts where they were not allowed to watch the casting of ballots. Federal supervisors would "scrutinize, count, and canvass" each ballot in their precinct and forward a set of returns to the chief federal supervisor. These returns would be used in lieu of state returns in the event the two conflicted. U.S. marshals could be deployed to enforce the law. Written ballots were to be used in congressional elections "any law of any state to the contrary notwithstanding."[214] Once again S. S. Cox was among the naysayers. He complained the measure authorized officials to make arrests without warrants or evidence. "It is an unwarranted ex parte use of power, without fairness, and for the worst purposes—the perpetuation of a failing and dishonored party."[215] A law of June 10, 1872, authorized the appointment of election supervisors in rural districts upon the application of voters, but as the measure did not authorize them to arrest violators, it was essentially toothless.[216]

Acting under authority of the 1870 Naturalization Act as well as the second Enforcement Act, federal officials watched the fall 1870 elections in New York City. Tammany Hall–controlled judges were expected to follow their usual custom of naturalizing immigrants by the boatload so they could be voted en masse by Democratic partisans in violation of state election laws. Swarms of federal officials descended on the city and the president saw fit to send two regiments of troops as well as two warships, which were stationed in the waters surrounding Manhattan.[217] Governor John T. Hoffman called the enterprise a "bold attempt on the part of the Federal government to assume absolute control of state and local elections, in order to accomplish partisan ends."[218] As events in New York demonstrated, passage of the Second Enforcement Act had as much to do with Republican frustrations in the North as in the South: only 5 of the 68 cities with populations larger than 20,000 and subject to the law's terms were in the South. Between 1871 and 1894, half of the expenditures for federal election officers were spent in New York State alone.[219]

The Ku Klux Klan Act became law on April 20, 1871. When two or more persons went in disguise on the public highways to obstruct the enforcement of the laws of the United States, intimidate others for the purpose depriving them of the equal protection of the laws, or to prevent persons from voting or advocating the election of others, they were subject to imprisonment.

Military force could be deployed to enforce the law and the president could suspend the writ of habeas corpus when necessary to defeat combinations so powerful they prevent states from affording their citizens the equal protection of the laws.[220] At first Grant resisted attempts to enlist his support for the measure; he went along after Secretary of the Treasury George Boutwell convinced him of its necessity. In a message of March 23, 1871, Grant claimed that the delivery of the mails and the collection of taxes had been threatened.[221] Moderate Republicans continued to resist. Lyman Trumbull declared that he was unwilling to "enter the states for the purpose of punishing individual offences against their authority committed by one citizen against another. We in my judgment have no constitutional authority to do that."[222] Such concerns helped produce the Liberal Republican movement of 1872.[223] The bill was subject to withering criticisms from Democrats, who insisted its provision for the use of the armed forces was unconstitutional. Republican James H. Platt Jr. of Virginia recalled that Democrats supported the practice when it had been utilized to enforce the Fugitive Slave Acts.[224] Ulysses Mercur of Pennsylvania pointed to the conclusions of the Senate Select Committee formed to investigate the Ku Klux Klan: (1) the organization exists, it has a political purpose, and it uses violence against opponents; (2) it protects members against conviction via disguises, secrecy, and perjury on the witness stand as well as in the jury box; and (3) its members number in the hundreds if not thousands. Mercur pointed out that numerous crimes had been committed against blacks in North Carolina, yet no one had been convicted for committing such acts. He believed the measure was authorized by the Fourteenth Amendment: "If a state denies equal protection, the United States government must step in and give that protection which state authorities neglect or refuse to give."[225] Nor was violence limited to blacks; U.S. marshals in the South had been murdered, and some found themselves jailed by state authorities.[226]

Attorney General Amos Akerman began prosecuting Klansmen in North Carolina in the spring of 1871. By December, 49 persons in the state had been convicted of violating the Ku Klux Klan Act.[227] Akerman next turned to South Carolina. Aided by the president's suspension of the writ of habeas corpus in nine counties and the army's detention of scores of persons, the attorney general spent weeks supervising the prosecution of those accused of violating the Ku Klux Klan Act. Juries proved surprisingly willing to convict accused Klansmen. Seven hundred indictments were handed down in Mississippi, though most resulted in suspended sentences. Unfortunately Akerman ran afoul of Secretary of State Hamilton Fish, who complained that he was enforcing the Ku Klux Klan Act too aggressively. He resigned in December 1871 and was succeeded as attorney general by George Henry Williams, who took a more cautious approach. Prosecutions were hampered by a lack of funds. The federal attorney at Jackson, Mississippi, requested additional sums for his office, which was prosecuting some 200 men for violating the Enforcement Acts as well as the Ku Klux Klan Act, only to be denied.[228] During the following year the federal court in Columbia, South Carolina, struggled under an enormous caseload produced by indictments issued pursuant to the Ku Klux Klan Act. With over a thousand indictments yet to be processed, it was warned by the newly established Justice Department that it was spending too much money. Despite a lack of adequate funds and resistance in the South, the Justice Department succeeded in breaking the Klan by 1872, causing violence in the South to drop substantially. The northern public did not rejoice; instead, it viewed the prosecutions and the deployment of the army in South Carolina as confirming its suspicions that the radical Republican governments in the South were fatally weak and destined for failure.[229] In sum, southern violence had forced Republicans in Washington to go to the outer limits of federal authority in response and while congressional majorities proved willing to act, in doing so they eroded their base of support in the North. As events in coming years would demonstrate, federal power had expanded beyond a level the public would accept.

With passage of the Ku Klux Klan Act, the momentum for passing additional laws protecting blacks lapsed. Charles Sumner proposed a civil rights bill in 1871 that would have barred discrimination in public accommodations, trains, schools, and even churches. A weakened bill barring discrimination in public accommodations and trains only—and leaving enforcement to the state courts—passed the Senate in 1872 but died in the House. The Republican governments that remained in the South were under siege, and as the process of Redemption moved forward, one after another disappeared. Republican state officials begged the Grant administration for assistance. The governor of Mississippi asked the attorney general to send troops on the eve of the 1875 state elections; he claimed Republicans could not meet safely. The request was denied and with blacks afraid to leave their homes, Democrats won.[230]

That northerners were losing their taste for reconstruction was demonstrated by the reaction of the *Springfield Daily Republican* to an incident of racial violence in the North. Following the murder of a white family in Henryville, Indiana, three black men were accused of the crime and taken into custody. A mob of approximately 100 whites "masked in the ku-klux manner" broke into the jail, removed the accused, and lynched them.[231] When the *Indianapolis Journal* suggested the possibility of federal prosecutions under the Ku Klux Klan Act, the *Springfield Daily Republican* objected:

> When [members of Congress] placed that act on the statute book, did they contemplate any such use and application of it as is here foreshadowed?

> Did they then understand that they were empowering the president to break into Indiana, or Michigan, or New York, with force and arms; set aside judges and courts; imprison citizens at his discretion and use the great writ to light his cigar while listening to the reports of military jailers? If they did not, we would suggest the obvious prudence of looking over the act, and finding out what its scope really is. Better occasional or even frequent disturbances of the peace than the most profound quiet and good order, if secured by breaking down the organic law and removing the old landmarks of constitutional liberty.[232]

Samuel Bowles, editor of the *Springfield Daily Republican*, was among the leaders of a group known as Liberal Republicans who objected to a second term for Ulysses S. Grant.[233] The alienation of many Republicans from the Grant administration stemmed from allegations of corruption, the bestowing of patronage on the most venal elements of the Republican Party, and the continuing excesses of Reconstruction. Missouri Senator Carl Schurz was the driving force behind the movement. In a September 1871 speech he called for the establishment of a new party built on a platform of civil service reform, lower taxes and tariffs, resumption of specie payments, and the termination of both land grants to railroads and federal supervision in the South.[234] Liberal Republicans favored Lyman Trumbull or Supreme Court Justice David Davis for the party's 1872 presidential nomination. When Liberal Republicans met in May, they made the mistake of compromising on Horace Greeley. The courageous but inconsistent editor of the *New York Tribune* did as much as anyone to aid the antislavery cause during the 1840s and 1850s and his newspaper helped elect Lincoln in 1860. Thereafter Greeley lost his nerve and demanded an end to the war at any cost. A career spent advocating a varied succession of causes including socialism and temperance contributed to the American public's impression of Greeley as a well-meaning but scatterbrained reformer. David Davis accepted the nomination of the National Labor Party even as he continued to serve on the Supreme Court.

Despite widespread disappointment over Greeley's nomination by the Liberal Republicans, Democrats also nominated him when they met at Baltimore in July, albeit with little enthusiasm. His support was strongest among southern whites due to his support for amnesty and an end to Reconstruction—an extraordinary development considering that mere possession of a copy of the *New York Tribune* in the South during the 1850s would have subjected one to a grave risk of incarceration. In his acceptance letter, Greeley declared his opposition to "federal supervision of the internal policy of the several states." Each one "should be left free to enforce the rights and promote the well-being of its inhabitants."[235] The *Atlanta*

Constitution applauded the nomination of the South's old nemesis; it explained that his newspaper, the *New York Tribune*, had "spoken emphatically against any further Ku-Klux or enforcement laws."[236] Thereafter Greeley won the support of a broad spectrum of Americans. Charles Sumner had clashed with the president and lost much of his influence in the Senate; he informed his black supporters in Washington, DC, that he would vote for Greeley. The candidate did himself severe injury during a western speaking tour when he went beyond calls for reconciliation and stated that separation would have been preferable to war.[237] Republicans nominated the president for a second term. The Grant campaign benefited from an array of effective speakers including Oliver Morton, Roscoe Conkling, and John Sherman. Thomas Nast depicted Greeley as a crank in his famous cartoons. The preference of the mercantile interests of the northeast for Republicans was increasingly evident as the party received huge contributions. Narrow Republican victories in Ohio and Pennsylvania promised victory in the presidential contest. It was even worse for Greeley than expected; he won only Georgia, Kentucky, Maryland, Missouri, Tennessee, and Texas (redemption was still a work in progress). In the congressional elections of 1872–73, Republicans won huge majorities in both houses.

Following the election, violence flared up again in the South as the remaining radical governments entered their death throes. Armed whites succeeding in deposing Governor William Pitt Kellogg of Louisiana in September 1874, only to fall back when the administration sent troops to New Orleans at Kellogg's request. When a conservative minority illegally took over the lower house of the legislature in early 1875, federal troops entered the statehouse at the request of Governor Kellogg and expelled enough Democrats to enable radicals to assume control. In no state had governors been viewed as having authority to decide disputes over legislative seats; even Republicans were appalled by Kellogg's actions. The legislature of Ohio joined those of Missouri and Georgia in passing resolutions criticizing the deployment of federal troops in Louisiana.[238] Shortly thereafter, Philip Sheridan worsened the administration's plight with his proposal to try leaders of the white leagues by military commission. Carl Schurz spoke for many when he wondered if such a thing might be tried in the northern states.[239] Sheridan had already strained nerves in the North when he deployed federal troops in downtown Chicago following the great fire of October 1871 without the consent of state officials, as Article IV, Section 4 seemed to require. Illinois Governor John Palmer was so outraged over the president's refusal to order Sheridan to evacuate the troops that he left the Republican Party.[240]

The Louisiana episode further eroded northern support for federal supervision of the affairs in the South. That even Congress was growing tired of the whole business was indicated by its reaction to a proposal of Grant's to intervene in Arkansas. After Democrats took over the state legislature, they adopted a new state constitution. Shortly thereafter, they won the governorship in an election provided for by the new constitution. Incumbent Republican Governor Elisha Baxter and his allies traveled to Washington and sought federal intervention. They claimed that the new state constitution and the recent gubernatorial election held in accordance with its terms were illegal. The provisions of the new charter violating the conditions imposed on the state for readmission of its delegation to Congress lent credence to the charge. In February 1875, Grant asked Congress to authorize him to intervene; he suggested that the new state constitution was null and void and that the governor had been unlawfully deprived of his office.[241] Congress ignored the request.

Fourteen years of Republican hegemony came to an end with the midterm elections of 1874–75. Among the chief causes was the Credit Mobilier scandal, the news of which broke in September 1872. The directors of the Union Pacific Railroad delegated the task of building the eastern section of the line to Credit Mobilier—a company they happened to own—and then vastly overpaid it for the work, thereby greatly enriching themselves. The Union Pacific was reduced to the point of insolvency overnight, leading many to fear it would not be able to pay back the sums loaned to it by the federal government. With a congressional investigation imminent, Credit Mobilier officials distributed stock at reduced prices among a dozen Republican representatives and senators, including James Garfield. Other factors in the loss of the House included impatience with the administration's errors in the South. The repeated deployment of the army, the backing of increasingly corrupt Republican state governments lacking popular support, and congressional investigations of legislative and even municipal elections all presented a novel and unwelcome spectacle to most Americans and one they wished to see terminated. Grant's veto of an "inflation bill" designed to increase the quantity of greenbacks in circulation, a steep and retroactive salary hike for members of Congress, and the economic dislocations that followed the Panic of 1873 also aided the Democratic cause. In the spring of 1874, the Senate passed a civil rights bill that prohibited discrimination in public accommodations and, in the view of some, public schools (a provision required that all persons have equal access to them). The fury of voters in states such as Indiana and Ohio where laws required that the races be educated separately produced additional Republican casualties.[242] When the waves subsided, the party of Jefferson and Jackson had won control of the House of Representatives for the first time since 1856–57. It held 182 of 285 seats. It also won gubernatorial elections in New York and even Massachusetts. The dwindling number of congressional seats held by

Republicans in the South indicated that the party's presence there was now limited to the margins. The party won multiple seats only in Louisiana, Alabama, and South Carolina. It held six Senate seats in South Carolina, Mississippi, and Arkansas—without these it would have lost control of the Senate as well as the House.[243] The lame duck 43rd Congress hurried to fasten a capstone on reconstruction before its term expired in March 1875. The House of Representatives took up the Senate-approved civil rights bill that had cost many members their seats, removed the provision that appeared to ban segregation in the schools, and passed it. The Senate concurred in the changes and shortly thereafter on March 1, the president signed the Civil Rights Act of 1875.[244] The law provided that all persons within the United States shall be entitled "to the full and equal enjoyment" of public accommodations, amusements, and transportation facilities regardless of color. Nor could Americans be barred from jury service on account of their race.[245] Democrats attacked the measure as unconstitutional while Republicans dismissed it as toothless. It was violated with impunity.[246] Two days after the civil rights bill became law, Congress enacted a law giving federal courts exclusive jurisdiction over all cases involving crimes and offenses "cognizable under the laws of the United States."[247]

If it seemed strange that a government that had exhausted public patience in merely trying to check racial violence proposed to go further and protect blacks against discrimination in the marketplace, former attorney general Rockwood Hoar—now in the House of Representatives—provided an explanation. The measure would, he explained, be merely symbolic, at least for a time: "I have no belief that this bill, if enacted into a law, is going to produce any great effect immediately for good or for evil in the states whose representatives most prominently oppose it." Laws, he continued, depend for their enforcement upon juries. Hoar explained that the "value of this act is similar to that of the Declaration of Independence. It will stand as the declaration of the American people that henceforth before the law every citizen of the country is to have equality."[248] In Atlanta, a group of black men attempted to enter pool halls and taverns in an effort to exercise their new rights only to be denied admission. The *Atlanta Constitution* believed the men were "making cases under the civil rights bill"; it was pleased to report that some of the men said to have been involved in the venture not only denied the accusation but condemned the effort.[249]

Senator Thomas F. Bayard of Delaware explored the murky waters of the privileges and immunities clause of the Fourteenth Amendment, the only possible constitutional basis in his view for the Civil Rights Act. "If the government of the United States has the power to enter a state and take control of that vast domain of rights under state regulation which a citizen acquires by virtue of the state laws, which are regulated by the state, which are conferred by the state, which heretofore always in the history of this government have been protected by the state, and the state alone—if the United States can assume guardianship of all those, then the state laws and the state governments are absolutely worse than useless; they are mere laughingstocks existing only at the pleasure of Congress and the executive." Bayard cited the Supreme Court's ruling in the *Slaughterhouse Cases* for the proposition that the Fourteenth Amendment protects only those privileges and immunities bestowed by the Constitution. The states remain free to discriminate in allotting those of their making. As public accommodations were usually established by private citizens, access to them qualified, at most, as a state privilege. Thus the conclusion: The right of a person "to go into an inn or railcar or a theater or concert room, whatever size it may be, belongs to him as a citizen of a state and not as a citizen of the United States."[250] In the Senate Matthew Carpenter of Wisconsin conceded that the Fourteenth Amendment did not authorize the bill as it concerned rights within the domain of the states, but he thought that its requirement for equal access to public accommodations "might be sustained as a regulation of commerce if confined to that commerce over which Congress possesses the power of regulation—commerce with foreign nations, among the several states, or with the Indian tribes." The clause requiring states to allow blacks to sit on juries fared better as it targeted the states and not individuals. Oliver Morton of Indiana thought it was plainly authorized by the equal protection clause of the Fourteenth Amendment: "To give the exclusive right to white men to sit upon juries and to adjudicate upon the rights of colored men is denying to colored men the equal protection of the laws because it is placing the adjudication of their rights exclusively in the hands of another race, filled with a prejudice and passion in many states that would prevent them from doing justice."[251]

The reconstruction amendments and laws played a prominent role in federal litigation during the postwar period. By the time the Supreme Court issued its first major ruling regarding these measures (1873), the personnel of the High Court had changed a great deal since Lincoln's inauguration—only one justice remained who had been appointed by a Democratic president (Nathan Clifford). From 1861 to 1873, Lincoln appointed five justices, Johnson none, and Grant three. On the whole the Supreme Court reflected the nationalizing tone of the Republican Party that was responsible for its personnel. The appointment of two men associated with the Democratic Party did not materially alter the fact. Salmon P. Chase, appointed Chief Justice in late 1864, had been a Democrat for most of his adult life and he continued to flirt with Democrats when afflicted with presidential fever. Yet his decisions only occasionally revealed a fascination with the states' rights doctrine that remained the hallmark of his former party. Justice Stephen Field, appointed in 1863, had also been a Democrat. In time he would display a willingness to invalidate state laws that exceeded that of almost all of his contemporaries on the high court.

While it was tolerant of Congress, the Supreme Court was not subservient. Its decision in *Ex parte Milligan* instilled in radicals a mortal fear that military reconstruction would be held void. Frictions continued thereafter; the justices refused to go on circuit duty in the southern states while they remained under military rule. The refusal of Chief Justice Chase to serve on circuit duty in Virginia made it impossible to try Jeff Davis for treason.[252] To the disappointment of radicals, the Republican-dominated Supreme Court proceeded to void some of the postwar laws designed to protect blacks in several decisions issued between 1873 and 1883. The justices also reduced the scope of the postwar amendments from that which had been contemplated at the time they were added to the Constitution.

In *The Slaughterhouse Cases* (1873), the Court held that the Fourteenth Amendment prohibited the states from infringing only federal privileges and immunities; those bestowed by the states themselves were beyond federal cognizance and thus could be granted or withheld from their citizens for any reason, including race.[253] The litigation arose out of cholera. When 3,000 residents of New Orleans died of the disease during a severe outbreak in 1867, the Louisiana legislature concluded that the discharge of offal by up to a thousand slaughterhouses upstream from the intake valves for the city's water supply was responsible. In March 1869 it passed a law limiting slaughterhouses to an area south of New Orleans and gave a private entity, the Crescent City Livestock Landings and Slaughter Houses Corporation, the exclusive right for 25 years to rent out spaces at the new facility.

New Orleans butchers did not embrace the idea of having to pay rent to an entity handpicked by the state in exchange for doing business. A group of them filed suit. They claimed the law violated the privileges and immunities clause of the Fourteenth Amendment and the matter reached the Supreme Court. Justice Samuel Miller, a former physician who knew well the need for public health measures, wrote the decision. In his opinion for a 5–4 majority of the Court, Justice Miller held the law did not violate the Fourteenth Amendment. He asserted that no one disputed the right of a legislature to determine the appropriate location for potentially injurious activities, such as the burial of the dead, the storage of gunpowder, or the slaughtering of animals. Such matters were left to the states and appropriate for their regulation on the "principle that every person ought to use his property (so) as not to injure his neighbors."[254] As for the Fourteenth Amendment, Miller noted that it provided that all persons born within the United States and subject to its jurisdiction are citizens of the United States and citizens of the state wherein they reside.[255] It thus established two levels of citizenship—state and federal. The privileges and immunities clause of the Fourteenth Amendment protected Americans in their capacity as citizens of the nation from state violations—the states could not violate rights bestowed by the U.S. Constitution.[256]

For the idea that the Fourteenth Amendment authorized the national government to prevent state governments from discriminating in their allotment of rights devised by them among their own citizens, Miller had no sympathy. Was it, he asked, "the purpose of the Fourteenth Amendment, by the simple declaration that no state should make or enforce any law which shall abridge the privileges and immunities of citizens of the United States, to transfer the security and protection of all the civil rights which we have mentioned, from the states to the federal government?"[257] Miller thought not. To answer the question in the affirmative would invite Congress to legislate to protect said rights, "whenever in its discretion any of them are supposed to be abridged by state legislation." It would also "constitute this court a perpetual censor upon all legislation of the states, on the civil rights of their own citizens, with authority to nullify such as it did not approve as consistent with those rights, as they existed at the time of the adoption of the amendment."[258]

What rights did Miller believe constitute the privileges and immunities enjoyed by citizens as bestowed by the national government via the Fourteenth Amendment, and therefore protected against the states? Citing *Crandall v. Nevada*, he held they included the right to pursue claims against the national government, seek federal employment, access to seaports and federal offices, use of the navigable waters of the United States, and the right to seek the "care and protection of the federal government" while on the high seas or in areas of federal jurisdiction.[259] Justice Field dissented. He thought the privileges and immunities clause of the Fourteenth Amendment required states to hand out state-based privileges without discriminating. What Article IV, Section 2 "did for the protection of the citizens of one state against hostile and discriminating legislation of other states, the Fourteenth amendment does for the protection of every citizen of the United States against hostile and discriminatory legislation against him (by his own state) in favor of others, whether they reside in the same or different states."[260] Field's argument appears stronger than Miller's as discriminatory state laws that targeted a portion of a state's citizenry had more to do with the enactment of the Fourteenth Amendment than the rights listed by Miller in the majority opinion, i.e., access to the navigable waters of the United States.

In sum, the Fourteenth Amendment as originally understood was intended to require the states to hand out privileges and immunities in a fair manner without discriminating.[261] The contrary view made the struggle over ratification rather pointless and, at some level, absurd. As Justice Field noted, if the clause had been intended to prohibit the impairment of only privileges and immunities enjoyed by Americans in their capacity as citizens of the nation, such as the right to reach seaports, the Fourteenth Amendment was a "vain and idle enactment, which accomplished nothing, and most unnecessarily excited Congress and the people on its passage."[262] The opinion received little attention in the press, perhaps because it appeared to do no more than confirm the common belief that states possessed authority to regulate businesses within their borders.[263]

Three years after reading the privileges and immunities clause of the Fourteenth Amendment out of the Constitution, the Supreme Court narrowed the scope of the First Enforcement Act in *U.S. v. Reese*.[264] State election inspectors were indicted for violating Sections 3 and 4 of the act in a Kentucky municipal election—they refused to accept a ballot cast by William Garner, a black man, because he failed to produce proof that he had paid a tax. In holding Sections 3 and 4 of the act unconstitutional, Chief Justice Morrison R. Waite (he succeeded Salmon Chase in 1874) explained that the law appeared to penalize inspectors when they rejected votes for any reason, when the Fifteenth Amendment barred discrimination only on account of race.[265] (Section 3 imposed penalties on election officials who wrongfully prevented someone from casting a ballot when they had the right to do so; Section 4 penalized citizens who prevented others from casting a ballot.) The decision was widely supported due to growing distaste for Reconstruction and the belief, common even in the North, that Congress had gone beyond the Constitution in imposing its will on the South.[266]

Also in 1876, the Supreme Court voided the indictments of over a hundred men involved in the Colfax Massacre in Louisiana as failing to properly allege criminal activity prohibited by federal law—they did not state that the accused were acting under state authority (they were not); nor did they disclose what constitutional rights had been violated. In his opinion for the majority, Chief Justice Waite held that the equal protection clause and the First Enforcement Act targeted only state action.[267] In 1883 the Court held void Section 2 of the Ku Klux Klan Act of April 20, 1871.[268] Several men were indicted under the act for removing four blacks from the custody of law enforcement officials and assaulting them, thereby denying them the equal protection of the laws. Justice William Woods claimed that the Fourteenth Amendment concerned only state action, while Section 2 of the above-mentioned act went further and imposed penalties on private individuals who conspired to deny others the equal protection of the laws. It was therefore without any basis in the Amendment and thus unconstitutional.[269] If states denied blacks equal protection of the laws by failing to prosecute those who committed crimes against them, how else could Congress remediate the situation other than providing for the prosecution of the perpetrators in federal court? Prosecution of individuals would have been consistent with the purpose of equal protection clause. As one historian wrote, "a strong argument can be made, on the basis of the origins of the equal protection clause, that private lynching was among the evils that Congress was meant to have power to forbid."[270] That same year the Supreme Court held void Sections 1 and 2 of the Civil Rights Act of 1875 in the Civil Rights Cases.[271] In his opinion for the Court, Justice Joseph Bradley explained that nothing in the Fourteenth Amendment authorized Congress to ban discrimination in public accommodations, conveyances or places of public amusement as these facilities are private institutions. "Until some state law has been passed, or some state action through its officers or agents has been taken, adverse to the rights of citizens sought to be protected by the Fourteenth Amendment, no legislation of the U.S. under said Amendment, nor any proceeding under such legislation, can be called into activity; for the prohibitions of the Amendment are against state laws and acts done under state authority."[272] Bradley went on to state that the Court was not addressing the question of whether Congress could bar discrimination in public conveyances moving between states under its commerce clause powers.[273] Justice John M. Harlan dissented; he claimed that as "railroads, inns, and places of public amusement are agents or instrumentalities of the state," discrimination by them violates the equal protection clause Fourteenth Amendment.[274] Nor did he accept that claim that Congress must wait until a state violated the amendment before enacting legislation designed to protect rights bestowed by it.[275] Harlan's claim that railroads, inns, and places of public amusement qualify as agents of the states was not credible, though it was true that railroads and inns had a common law duty to serve the public. The *Atlanta Constitution* was delighted with what it called a "righteous and welcome decision." It claimed that Georgians were united in the belief that the "social equality contemplated by this infamous and malignant bill could never, and should never be put into practice." The *Constitution* noted that during the eight years since passage of the Civil Rights Act, blacks had entered white theaters in Atlanta on only two occasions, and that no one in the state of Georgia had ever been convicted of violating the law.[276]

Another provision of the Civil Rights Act of 1875 survived judicial scrutiny—the provision barring discrimination in jury selection was upheld in *Strauder v. West Virginia*, when the Supreme Court invalidated a state law limiting jury duty to whites as a violation of the equal protection clause.[277] In *Ex parte Siebold*, the high court held the remaining sections of the Enforcement Acts of May 31, 1870, and February 28, 1871, constitutional. It refused to invalidate the conviction of five Maryland election judges for preventing federal election inspectors from supervising the polls. The high court turned aside claims that the laws under which the men were indicted impermissibly imposed duties on state officials. Justice Bradley explained that Congress can enforce state laws and punish state officers for violating those laws "when, in the performance of their official functions, state officers are called upon to fulfill duties which they owe to the U.S. as well as the state," especially when, as in the case of elections for the House of Representatives, "Congress has plenary and paramount jurisdiction over the whole subject." Bradley also noted that with the Enforcement Acts, Congress had in effect adopted the laws of the state; it "simply demands their fulfillment."[278]

The country's acquiescence in the Supreme Court's narrow reading of the Reconstruction amendments and statutes stemmed from the fact that it had long since lost interest in the whole enterprise. The rampant corruption that characterized the radical state governments and the numerous episodes of military intervention by the Grant administration led the North to long for the day when it could forget the entire experiment. As the *Springfield Daily Republican* stated in December 1874, there "is a growing recognition in all quarters here of the truth that manipulation of the southern states from Washington has been a failure. Perhaps it would have been, even it had not been so grossly abused; but the abuses have insured its failure, and insured, also, the disgust of the North, and the certainty that, either by this administration or the next, the opposite policy will be tried." Thus the conclusion: "uncertain and risky as it may be, both the states and the people of the South must be left to work out their own peace and salvation."[279]

This sense of popular disillusion gave Democrats hope as the presidential campaign of 1876 began. So did revelations regarding "whiskey rings" in several Midwestern cities including St. Louis, Milwaukee, and Chicago. Internal revenue service employees accepted bribes from distillers in exchange for helping them avoid millions of dollars in taxes, usually by making false measurements of whiskey or distributing more tax stamps than the distillers had purchased. Such practices had been occurring since the Civil War but a higher degree of organization was brought to the enterprise during the Grant administration. In 1874 Treasury Secretary Benjamin Bristow began an investigation of the activities of revenue officials in St. Louis and indictments were eventually filed against 47 distillers, 60 rectifiers, 10 wholesalers, and 86 internal revenue agents. There were 230 indictments in all.[280] The trail led to Grant's personal secretary, General Orville Babcock, who tried to avoid justice by demanding a military trial, apparently in the belief that his army colleagues would impose a light sentence. To the amazement of the country, the president granted the request; even worse, he arranged for an officer who was a friend of Babcock to oversee the investigation. Federal attorneys in St. Louis refused to turn evidence over to military officials, greatly infuriating the president. Grant responded by having the Attorney General issue an order barring the Justice Department from using the testimony of persons involved in conspiracies who had agreed to testify in exchange for a reduced sentence. As much of the evidence in the whiskey ring investigations was obtained in this manner, the order severely undermined prosecutions of the perpetrators.[281]

Grant's unwillingness to fire men who had been implicated in wrongdoing until they were practically in handcuffs worsened the North's contempt for him, and by the last year of his second term, he was despised by citizens of every section. Democrats chose Governor of New York Samuel J. Tilden, famous for his exposure of the Tweed Ring in New York City. Thomas A. Hendricks, governor of Indiana, received the vice presidential nomination. Mindful of northern concern that a Democratic president would not be adequately vigilant in protecting the rights of blacks, Tilden issued a letter in October in which he promised to enforce the Fourteenth Amendment.[282]

James G. Blaine enjoyed frontrunner status in the contest for the Republican presidential nomination for much of the last two years of the Grant administration. Speaker of the House until Republicans lost their majority in the 1874 midterm elections, the change in control was particularly unfortunate for Blaine as it enabled his opponents to investigate his somewhat questionable dealings with railroads. With reports of his leaning on the lines for compensation hanging over his head, Blaine led his competitors on the early ballots when the Republican convention met at Cincinnati in June, but he was eventually surpassed by Ohio Governor Rutherford B. Hayes, whose reputation for probity was exactly what the party needed.

Hayes studied law under Joseph Story and later defended persons accused of being runaway slaves in Cincinnati. During the Civil War, he served with the 23rd Ohio volunteers and was wounded four times. As governor of Ohio in the years after the conflict, Hayes helped establish the Ohio State University and secure the state's ratification of the Fifteenth Amendment. He subsequently returned to the practice of law. With their fortunes suffering in 1875, Republicans convinced Hayes to run in the gubernatorial election of that year; his narrow victory made him an instant frontrunner for the Republican nomination in 1876. The party of Lincoln gave its candidate a platform that spoke to resolved issues—it claimed the United States was a "nation, not a league"—and others that were unresolved: "The permanent pacification of the southern section of the Union and the complete protection of all its citizens in the free enjoyment of all their rights, are duties to which the Republican Party is sacredly pledged."[283]

As the fall campaign unfolded, Republicans did not emphasize the need to protect blacks. Instead, the austere and abstemious Hayes issued a letter promising civil service reform and self-government in the South. He also announced that he would limit himself to a single term. The Republican press made much of Hayes's reputation for honesty—much to the irritation of the incumbent. The party's best speakers, such as Oliver Morton, James Blaine, and Roscoe Conkling, campaigned for Hayes; Michigan Senator Zachariah Chandler ensured that Republicans emphasized civil service reform even as he extracted contributions from federal employees. Civil servants in Washington, DC, had to pay 2 percent of their salaries to Republican Party officials collecting money for the campaign.[284] In the South federal employees worked on behalf of the Republican cause. James Tyner of Indiana was made postmaster general so he could distribute post office largesse in his home state.[285] Robert Ingersoll was among the most effective Republican speakers; at Cooper Union he issued a warning to New Yorkers: "Recollect that the men who starved our soldiers and shot them down are all for Tilden and Hendricks. All the hands dipped in Union blood were in the Democratic Party."[286] William Wheeler, the Republican vice presidential nominee, claimed that southerners regarded the Civil War amendments as the French regarded the German annexation of Alsace-Lorraine—an object attained by military force that would someday be reversed. Administration officials leaked information from Tilden's tax records to reveal his large income (he was a successful attorney) in the hope of eliciting envy among voters.[287]

A severe economic downturn was in progress at the time of the election. Some believed hard times and falling prices might be eased by increasing the amount of greenbacks in circulation. Eastern mercantile and creditor interests opposed the idea; they insisted the country must return to the gold standard as soon as possible, and the Resumption Act of 1875 promised to achieve that end by 1879. As hard times lingered, the Greenback Party formed; it sought to postpone resumption and circulate more greenbacks, thereby reversing, or so it was hoped, the decline in prices then in progress. Greenbacks nominated Peter Cooper, a New York philanthropist, for president. While Cooper had no chance of winning, Republicans lived in mortal fear of the possibility that the new party would win enough votes to cost them one of the critical states in the Midwest. Fortunately for Republicans, Tilden was no more sympathetic to diluting the currency than they were—though they still accused him of being a closet inflationist.[288]

It remained to be seen if the Greenbacks would gather enough votes from northern farmers who normally voted Republican to give Democrats the presidency.

Southern farmers were another matter. In the fall of 1876, the Republican domain in the South had been reduced to South Carolina, Louisiana, and Florida. Fewer than 5,000 federal troops remained in the region. In mid-October Grant declared South Carolina to be in a state of insurrection and sent additional troops to the state. He cited the proliferation of "rifle clubs" as well as the Governor's request.[289] Whites were unbowed; they refused to disband their rifle companies despite being ordered to do so. By Election Day blacks in the state had been thoroughly intimidated—many if not most stayed home rather than risk their lives despite a last minute show of force at the polling places by federal troops.[290]

New York as well as South Carolina was the scene of an enlarged federal presence on Election Day. Hordes of federal election inspectors descended on the Empire State. Under the provisions of the Second Enforcement Act, federal officials could appoint supervisors for every poll in any urban congressional district if two or more voters in that district claimed electoral frauds were about to be perpetrated. U.S. marshals and assistant marshals could also be deployed. As New York City now saw massive frauds perpetrated by Tammany Hall and other Democratic organizations at every election, the Grant administration flooded the city with federal personnel to ensure that Democrats did not vote ineligible persons en masse. It spent $300,000 for 2,300 deputy marshals and over 100 supervisors. John Davenport, the chief supervisor of federal elections in the city, went so far as to take out ads in newspapers warning the populace that jail awaited persons who tried to vote illegally.[291]

When the results of the October state elections in the Midwest became known, Republicans winced. While they won Ohio by some 6,600 votes, they lost Indiana by 5,000 ballots despite flooding the state with cash. Victory in New York and at least two southern states was now an absolute necessity. At first glance it appeared they had come up short. By midnight on Election Day, November 7, it was apparent that Tilden had won New York, New Jersey, Indiana, and Connecticut as well as most of the South, thereby obtaining a narrow majority in the electoral college.[292] His majority of the popular vote approached 250,000. On the morning after the election, Benjamin Hayes believed he had lost. Dan Sickles realized that Republicans still had a card to play. The New York lawyer was among the most notorious and fabulous characters to appear on the American political stage during the nineteenth century. A Tammany Hall Democratic congressman before the war, Sickles had once been a close ally of James

Buchanan; in 1859 he gained notoriety for shooting his wife's lover and successfully employing the novel defense of temporary insanity. That he was able hit his target despite his condition said much for his marksmanship, or at least his imagination. As a major general in the Union army, Sickles almost lost the Civil War single-handedly when he had troops under his command take an exposed forward position at Gettysburg in violation of orders given to him by General Meade. He barely avoided being court-martialed. Ulysses Grant barred him from field duty for the remainder of the war, but Sickles managed to obtain appointment as a commander of a military district in the South during Reconstruction. Following a stint as minister to Spain, he returning to New York City and dabbled in Republican politics.

As he examined the incomplete returns, it dawned on Sickles that Republicans could still win the election even without New York and Indiana if they carried South Carolina, Florida, Louisiana, and Oregon. All of these states were close and as yet unresolved. Sickles took it upon himself to telegraph the Republican-controlled election boards in each of these states with his conclusions, and the insights of the New Yorker were not lost on the recipients of his message. Tilden appeared to have a small lead in South Carolina until the state election board discarded the votes of two counties on the grounds of voter intimidation, thus giving the state to Hayes. In Florida, the state canvassing board also threw out enough votes to wipe out a small lead for Tilden. In Louisiana Tilden held what appeared to be an insurmountable majority of 6,300 votes. After the head of the state election board—who also happened to be surveyor of the port of New Orleans—found his inquiries with Democrats regarding a bribe had been ignored, he threw the state to the Republicans by tossing out the votes of two entire parishes and discarding votes in 22 others (15,000 in all). Complicating matters was the Republican elector in Oregon who forgot to resign from his postmastership before the election—federal employees were prohibited by law from serving as electors. If his vote was barred and Hayes won the other disputed states, two candidates would both earn 184 votes in the electoral college and the election would be decided by the Democratic-controlled House of Representatives.

On December 6, the electors of each state met and cast their votes. In the state capitals of Oregon, Louisiana, Florida, and South Carolina competing slates of electors voted for the candidate they claimed had won; state governors or other officials certified one of the two slates and forwarded the certificates to Congress.[293] (In Oregon the state constitution designated the secretary of state as the official who would certify the results.) Attention now focused on Washington. Article II, Section 1 of the Constitution provides that the "President of the Senate shall, in the presence of the

Senate and House of Representatives, open all the Certificates, and the Votes shall then be counted." Normally the vice president serves in that role, but Henry Wilson died in 1875. Succeeding to the position was the president pro tempore of the Senate, Thomas White Ferry, Republican of Michigan. All of America wondered what Ferry would do. What could he do? Did have any discretion in deciding which slate of electors to count?

Republicans worked themselves into fits over the possibility that Ferry, a first-term senator with no legal experience, would be talked into doing something rash by Senate Democrats. What they feared most was that Ferry, or, more likely, the House and Senate, would decide to investigate the returns of one or more states. The tarnished battle cry of states' rights was now deployed by members of the party of Lincoln—Congress had no right to look into the integrity of the process by which states certified their electors. Democrats in contrast embraced a view of the powers of Congress that seemed exceedingly and uncharacteristically generous—it could investigate the process by which states appointed their electors. They had precedent on their side—four years earlier, Congress had investigated the returns of Louisiana. At a joint meeting of the House and Senate Judiciary Committees, lawmakers agreed to draft a bill providing for the dispute over electoral votes to be submitted to a commission consisting of five senators, five representatives, and five Supreme Court justices. Its rulings would prevail unless rejected by both Houses of Congress. Republicans opposed the idea at first, fearing it would result in the election of Tilden. The ambivalence of party leaders toward Hayes, the conviction of James G. Blaine that his ambitions might best be served by a Republican loss, and the indifference of the president combined to cause Republicans to accept the measure. Following a debate in which lawmakers discussed the question of whether Congress had authority to investigate the returns of the states, the bill became law on January 29, 1877.[294]

The Electoral Commission included two justices viewed as Republicans (Samuel Miller and William Strong) and two viewed as Democrats (Nathan Clifford and Stephen Field) as well as five senators (three of whom were Republicans) and five representatives (three of whom were Democrats). Pursuant to the law's provisions, the four appointed justices would pick the fifth themselves, and speculation focused on Justice David Davis of Illinois. With each party holding seven seats on the Commission, Davis might well have decided the issue in favor of Tilden but Illinois Democrats nominated him for the U.S. Senate. Davis resigned from the high court after he was elected to the Senate on January 25. Instead of Davis, Justice Joseph P. Bradley was the fifth Supreme Court justice appointed to the commission. Nominated for a seat on the high court by Grant in 1870, Bradley was a loyal Republican as well as an experienced attorney. The counting of electoral votes by the president pro tempore of the Senate now proceeded; when objections to the vote of a state were made the matter was referred to the Electoral Commission. The votes of four states ended up in the hands of the commission: South Carolina, Florida, Louisiana, and Oregon. The 15 men upon whom the election would turn had their first meeting in the chambers of the Supreme Court on February 2. The outcome of the dispute became apparent when the Commission decided against investigating the returns. Instead it limited itself only to questions of law regarding the certificates that had been turned over to it by Ferry.

It was at this point that the concern over states' rights became a matter of consequence. Republicans may have been hypocritical in defending the prerogatives of the states when they claimed that neither Congress nor entities created by it had authority to investigate the returns, i.e., whether votes had been wrongfully discarded or suppressed, but they were, alas, correct. As Justice Bradley pointed out, the Constitution gave each House power over returns in the election of its members in explicit words, but it gave them no such power regarding presidential elections.[295] (Section 5 of Article I provided that each "House shall be the Judge of the Elections, Returns and Qualifications of its own Members.") Republicans were not entirely consistent in their sudden embrace of a strict construction of the powers of Congress granted by the Constitution; the Electoral Commission itself had no basis in the powers listed in Article I and it imposed non-judicial duties on members of the Supreme Court.

When Democrats offered to present evidence of irregularities in Florida and Louisiana, the commission refused to hear it.[296] The *Atlanta Constitution* was incredulous: "We cannot see how the Commission can ascertain 'which is the true and lawful electoral vote' of a state, if it does not go behind the returns."[297] The Commission proceeded to vote on each state separately, and the Republican slate in each of the four states prevailed 8–7. Bradley voted with Republicans lawmakers and two other justices (Samuel Miller and William Strong). The Senate agreed with the Commission's verdict on Florida but the Democratic House rejected it on February 12. Under the provisions of the law, the Commission's rulings prevailed unless rejected by both houses. Being the judicious lawyer that he was, Samuel Tilden read the writing on the wall and began packing for a trip to Europe.[298] The Senate affirmed and the House rejected the Commission's verdicts in favor of Republican electors in Louisiana on February 16 and Oregon on the 23rd. The Senate's acceptance of all three Republican electors from Oregon turned on the right of the two remaining electors to name a third after the one who happened to be a postmaster resigned, and the secretary of state's certification that these men were the duly-named electors of the state. Members of the Democratic-controlled House realized they had a losing hand, as Ferry would likely count the votes in accordance with the recommendations of the Commission. With talk of a filibuster in the air, a bargain was reached. It provided for the following: withdrawal of federal troops from the South, termination of Washington's support for Republican state governments in South Carolina and Louisiana, the appointment of a southerner as postmaster general, Republican support for internal improvement appropriations benefiting the South including funds for levees along the Mississippi River, and (some claimed) federal land grants for the Texas and Pacific Railroad. In exchange, southern Democrats would accept the rulings of the electoral commission and acquiesce in the election of a Republican speaker.[299] The withdrawal of the army was the key element, though at the beginning of 1877 there were only 4,300 troops in the South (a handful of soldiers remained in the region in coming years). It was not until the early morning of March 2 (4:00 a.m.) that a joint session of Congress finally declared Hayes the victor.

The excesses of Radical Reconstruction might well have been avoided if the national government had barred Confederates from participation in public life as the price of their treason, enacted an amendment explicitly bestowing the suffrage on blacks throughout the country, and used arms to preserve that right. Unwilling to take these steps, the North settled for the destruction of state governments, poorly drafted and ineffective amendments, and usurpations of state authority that were both futile and disastrous. The first experiment in federal omnipotence had failed miserably; the consequences of that failure would last for over a century.

Chapter 3

FEDERALISM IN THE GILDED AGE, 1877–1901

PECUNIARY ISSUES

During the last quarter of the nineteenth century, the federal government involved itself in matters not included among its enumerated powers, including education, agriculture, and labor. An intricate web of financial relationships between the American people and their national government grew steadily, as federal policies in a variety of areas affected the daily lives of citizens. The distinguishing characteristic of the period was the primacy of pecuniary issues. Politicians convinced voters that their material well-being depended on the maintenance of federal policies, thereby gaining influence over, if not control of, the votes of millions. The Jeffersonian image of a rural electorate immune to monetary considerations, allowing only the best interests of the nation to guide its votes, receded further into the background. The growth of the power of the national government over the lives of citizens was not driven by strictly cynical political motives; Republicans saw federal action as necessary to promote national development. Democrats also embraced federal initiatives that would have been unheard of in the 1850s. The machinations of politicians did not accelerate the process of centralization nearly as much as industrialization and the growth of trade. As more Americans went to work in factories, the number of voters who saw their livelihoods as dependent on tariffs for protection from cheap foreign labor went up accordingly. Americans found their fortunes increasingly subject to the vagaries of the marketplace, and in turn, a government whose powers, few as they were, included the authority to regulate interstate and foreign commerce and the right to tax imported goods.

As centralization progressed, the presidency declined in importance and power moved to Congress and in turn to committees. Congress suffered from a decline in standards and competence. Antebellum debates that equaled in skill those seen in Parliament gave way to indifference, cigars, and newspapers. Legislation was devised by committees meeting in private and then passed along party lines with little examination. Gilded Age lawmakers were not nearly as corrupt as history has portrayed them, but accepting stock from and even lobbying on behalf of businesses with an interest in legislation was routine in the national and state capitals—though such actions were hardly advertised and often hidden.

The period between 1877 and 1901 has been characterized as a Republican-dominated era, but the party of Lincoln found itself on the defensive in the closing decades of the nineteenth century. It gave the period its defining policies and then spent years defending them against growing opposition. In four of five presidential elections from 1876 to 1892, Democrats won a majority of popular votes; during the same period they usually enjoyed majorities in the House of Representatives. Only twice between 1874 and 1896 did the same party control Congress and the presidency. The period was also characterized by sectional conflict that worsened as the century progressed—the South and West complained bitterly over what they saw as political domination and economic exploitation by the Northeast. Political activity grew increasingly ruthless. As Democrats used intimidation and control over election machinery to root out the last vestiges of black Republican strength in the South, Republicans acted to stem the revival of the Democratic Party in the North. Democrats often matched Republican vote totals in states such as Rhode Island and Connecticut but gerrymandering prevented them from enjoying the fruits of their labor. In 1880 Republicans won 1.8 million votes in northern congressional elections resulting in the election of 90 representatives, while Democrats won 1.6 million votes in the North but elected only 20 representatives.[1]

The parties remained evenly matched even as their bases evolved. The South became more Democratic as the century progressed until Populism cut into the party's support in the region during the 1890s. In the northern cities, Democrats lost the stranglehold they enjoyed before the Civil War, and immigrant Catholics, perhaps the strongest bulwark of the party during the 1850s and 1860s, did not always give it their complete support. Republicans enjoyed support in cities such as Philadelphia, Cleveland, Cincinnati, and Chicago, though New York City invariably provided Democrats with a dozen or more congressmen every two years. In the

North Democrats benefited from high levels of support among the urban poor, farmers hostile to increased public expenditures and taxes, and those who were not enthused over the metamorphosis the national government appeared to have undergone during the 1860s. Republicans on the other hand did well with more prosperous voters in the North as well as those who saw high tariffs as necessary to the development of the nation's industries or the preservation of their jobs.[2] The Republican Party's association with the Union cause in the Civil War—each of its presidential nominees from 1868 until the end of the century was a veteran—gave it an advantage that took decades to dissipate. Many farmers who had been lifelong Democrats until the late 1850s continued to support Republicans after the war. They would prove to be an unstable constituency.

Enormous federal expenditures during the Civil War helped trigger a boom in the North that lasted into the early 1870s. High commodity prices followed, only to tumble with the end of the Franco-Prussian War in 1871. Enormous fires at Chicago and Boston in 1871 and 1872 inflicted additional strain on the economy, as did the outbreak of an equine virus that killed thousands of horses. To some degree the economy had been straining under a fierce headwind since the war—the steady reduction of the money supply through the withdrawal of greenbacks resulted in higher interest rates. After the crash of the Vienna Stock Exchange, European investors began dumping their American railroad stocks, and talk of a bust was heard on Wall Street. When New York bankers refused to bail out Jay Cooke and Company in September 1873 (it had been unable to sell bonds of the Northern Pacific Railroad), the investment firm closed its doors. Announcement of the news on the floor of the New York Stock Exchange triggered a panic and trading was suspended on Saturday, September 20. The exchange remained closed for 10 days. A run on the city's banks followed. New York City banks saw their reserves fall from $50 million to $17 million. Seeking to provide reassurance to the country, the president traveled to Manhattan where he took up residence at the Fifth Avenue Hotel. Along with Treasury Secretary William Richardson, he listened as local bankers and merchants begged him to deposit $40 million in greenbacks in the city's banks. Claiming a lack of authority, the president refused to comply. Instead the Treasury Department redeemed government bonds, thereby providing the market with a needed infusion of cash.[3] Several national banks in New York City saw their reserve requirements drop below the minimum required by law as depositors made steep withdrawals. As the shock spread through the financial system, banks throughout the country suspended payments (withdrawals), depriving businesses of capital and causing some to miss their payrolls. The crisis eased by the end of the year but not before a wave of business failures had commenced.

The Panic of 1873 led to a depression that lasted for seven years. While the gross national product increased in every year but one during the decade, the spike in unemployment warrants use of the term *depression* to describe the period. It saw prices drop sharply and resulted in thousands of workers traveling the country in search of jobs and sustenance. By 1875, 500,000 Americans were unemployed (the number would reach a million), half of the nation's railroads had failed, and two-thirds of the iron mills were idle.[4] In New York City a quarter of the workforce was without employment in 1874. In the Midwest strikes broke out among railroad workers and labor violence in the anthracite coal region of eastern Pennsylvania resulted in the hanging of 20 miners. Leaders of the nascent labor movement demanded public works that would provide jobs to the unemployed. Authorities in New York City became nervous over boisterous labor meetings, and a "work or bread" rally at Tompkins Square in early 1874 was broken up by the police.[5]

The federal government remained passive in the face of these dislocations until it was called on to act when striking railroad workers proposed to shut down the nation's railroads. The lines had engaged in withering competition with each other during the years following the Civil War. The price to ship 100 pounds of farm products between Chicago and New York dropped from 50 cents to 18.[6] Many lines found they could not cope and went bankrupt. Having slashed rates, railroads sought to cut wages in 1877 to remain afloat, even as they allowed more men to stay on the payrolls than they could use. Railroad employees, having already sustained multiple wage cuts, were not inclined to accept another and strikes commenced. When strikers shut down the Baltimore & Ohio in West Virginia July 1877, the state found itself unable to restore train service as it had, like many other states, reduced its militia to nearly nothing to save money. A survey of February 1878 revealed that many states had all but disbanded their militias: Maine counted only 883 men, Florida had 60, Oregon had 49, and Indiana had only three—all officers.[7]

West Virginia Governor Henry Matthews had all of four companies at his disposal, two of which were said to be in sympathy with the strikers. With no other options available, Matthews asked the president to send federal troops.[8] The president sent 300 marines despite the fact that they had not been paid for several weeks—he was engaged in a standoff with the Democratic-controlled House over the latter's insistence on attaching to an army appropriation bill a measure barring marshals from using federal troops to enforce federal law. The marines found West Virginia at peace when they arrived. In Maryland members of the inadequately trained state militia shot and killed nine striking railroad workers, thus incurring the wrath of mobs that seemed to be ruling over large parts of the state.

Following the shootings, members of the militia—many of whom had barely reached their 20s—hid in private homes and changed into civilian clothes to avoid death at the hands of vengeful strikers. At the request of Maryland's governor, the president authorized officials at Fort McHenry to deploy troops if necessary but peace arrived before U.S. soldiers had to intervene. Pennsylvania also suffered violence. Mobs in and around Pittsburgh destroyed 2,000 train cars belonging to the Pennsylvania Railroad.[9] The state proved incapable of restoring order; like Maryland and West Virginia, it had to request federal assistance. Trains did not begin moving until the end of July, and even then they had to be covered with troops.

At points further west, July was marked by shocking violence as strikers forcibly prevented the railroads from operating. Wary of tangling with the national government, strikers allowed locomotives hauling the mail to proceed. The tactic proved futile when the federal judiciary embraced a novel legal tactic that would prove in time to be among the most notable exercises of federal power between 1860 and 1930. Numerous railroads were in the temporary custody of federal receivers while their owners went through bankruptcy proceedings. Judge Thomas Drummond of the U.S. District Court in Chicago ordered receivers having custody of the property of bankrupt railroads to operate the lines despite the strike. He issued an injunction directing U.S. marshals to inform mobs that obstructing trains constituted contempt of court—an extraordinary novelty in that contempt orders were normally directed at parties to suits or persons named in court orders.[10] When unruly crowds ignored the injunction, Judge Drummond requested the aid of federal troops, and the president complied. Hayes thought so highly of Drummond's injunction that he recommended the tactic to federal judges around the country.[11]

On July 26, a battle at 16th Street in Chicago between U.S. troops and the state militia on one side and striking railroad workers on the other resulted in 10 deaths. By August 3, the application of force and the use of replacement workers or "scabs" broke the railroad strikes. The wage cuts that caused them remained in place. More than 100 persons died in the violence. The well-to-do were appalled. With memories of the Draft Riots and the French Commune still fresh—workers in Paris had taken over the city briefly following their country's defeat in the Franco-Prussian War—they feared that the future would bring class war. Some called for enlarging the army.[12] The states increased spending for their militias and the War Department built formidable armories in the larger cities. (The mercantile classes of some cities built armories at their own expense.) U.S. Grant noted the irony of using federal troops in the North—many of the same politicians who bitterly criticized military rule in the South were enthusiastic about the use of the army to stem labor violence in their own states.[13] When the cabinet debated whether to allow federal troops to be deployed in states not yet declared by their governors to be incapacitated by domestic violence (as the Constitution seemed to require), Secretary of State William Evarts observed that the "Ten Commandments would not have been made if they were not to be broken."[14] On the whole the president took a moderate approach. Only small numbers of U.S. troops were deployed and they tended to remain in the background while state militias brought the strikers to heel.[15] Hayes did not grant all requests for federal troops and he proved an exacting lawyer when he haggled with governors over the statutory and constitutional prerequisites for federal assistance—outbreaks of lawlessness were not enough to warrant intervention in his view. Still, he may have granted more requests than the facts warranted.[16]

For most of 1877, the attention of the new president was focused on the South. His attitude was illustrated by a conversation he had with R. A. Alston of Georgia, who was seeking appointment as a U.S. marshal. After Alston assured Hayes that he would obey the Constitution, the president explained that what he really wanted to know was whether Alston would enforce the Thirteenth, Fourteenth, and Fifteenth Amendments. The Georgian gave a contradictory answer, although he didn't seem to realize it. "I might as well be frank with you Mr. President; we southern people have accepted those amendments as absolutely as the people of the North, but the negro must always occupy the position in society to which his brain and his muscle entitle him, and no amount of legislation can change it." Hayes found the answer acceptable; he did not protest when Alston added that "the people of the South never intended to be governed by negroes."[17] In April 1877 the president withdrew troops from South Carolina and Louisiana, causing the besieged carpetbag/Republican state governments to collapse, thereby allowing Democrats to take over both states (they claimed to have won state elections the previous fall). In exchange, Governor Wade Hampton of South Carolina promised to respect the constitutional rights of blacks; Louisiana citizens made the same vow. Both promises went unfulfilled.[18] The abandonment of Louisiana so infuriated Republicans that the president lost the support of much of his party and never regained it.

The president was undeterred. Eager to promote national reconciliation, he appointed Democrats to federal offices in the South. In September 1877 Hayes toured Virginia, Tennessee, Alabama, and Georgia and was well-received.[19] Despite the warm reception, the president knew a struggle was coming; he had called a special session of Congress for the following month to extract an appropriation for the army. The previous Congress had been unable to provide one, as the Democratic-controlled House insisted on adding a clause that would bar use of the army to enforce federal laws. The president and the Senate refused to acquiesce and the session expired in March 1877 without an appropriation for the army. In the new 45th Congress, Democrats once again controlled the House while Republicans maintained a narrow majority in the Senate. The battle lasted through the first half of 1878. Hayes allowed the Posse Comitatus Act to become law; it banned the use of the army "for the purpose of executing the laws" or as a posse comitatus except when specifically authorized by Congress or the Constitution.[20] The determination of southerners to ensure the excesses of Reconstruction were not repeated served as the driving force behind the law; the frustration of westerners with the often arbitrary response of army personnel to violence on the Plains also contributed to its passage.

A War Department order of October 1878 revealed just how large a loophole existed in the Posse Comitatus Act. It listed some of the laws that authorized the use of the army to enforce the laws. They included the Ku Klux Klan Act and statutes applicable to crimes committed in the Indian territories, extradition measures, and even quarantine laws.[21] When violence in the Arizona territory exceeded the capacity of local law enforcement officials in the spring of 1882, President Arthur asked Congress to amend the Posse Comitatus Act, as he believed it barred him from responding. The Senate Judiciary Committee did not agree. Speaking on behalf of the Committee, Senator George F. Edmunds explained that it found several laws that seemed applicable, including Section 5286 of the Revised Statutes, which banned persons in the United States from organizing military expeditions into foreign countries (the violence had spilled into Mexico). He also cited Section 5298, which authorized the president to deploy the army whenever the law could not be enforced via normal judicial processes.[22] That there were numerous statutes that authorized use of the army to enforce the laws was also illustrated by the fact that it was deployed in response to domestic disturbances on approximately 125 occasions between 1877 and 1945. In 1899 U.S. soldiers deployed in response to labor strife at Coeur d'Alene, Idaho, arrested and detained over a thousand members of a coal miners' union, some for more than four months.[23]

While the First Enforcement Act provided authority for using the Army to defend blacks attempting to exercise their political rights, the will no longer existed. In the fall of 1878, Democrats in the South forcibly prevented blacks from voting. Federal marshals arrested persons alleged to have intimidated blacks, but juries proved unwilling to convict those charged.[24] The intimidation of black voters in the South helped Democrats win majorities in both houses in Congress—something the party had not achieved since 1856–57. Seeking to weaken the federal law enforcement apparatus, the Democratic-controlled House once again refused to appropriate money for the army during the winter of 1878–79. Hayes responded by calling the new 46th Congress into session in March 1879. A bill that passed in late April included a rider banning federal marshals from preventing violence during congressional elections. Hayes vetoed the measure on April 29. He rejected similar bills on May 12 and May 29. Democrats responded by placing appropriations for judicial expenses (including payment of marshals, their deputies, and supervisors of elections) in a separate judiciary bill, thus allowing them to appropriate money for the army. The judiciary bill limited the use of armed force in elections; it was vetoed by the president on June 23. As Democratic lawmakers sensed the futility of attempting to impose their will on the president, the House tried one last time to gain a victory. It passed a bill providing money for marshals alone that included the same rider limiting the use of force, only to see it vetoed on June 30.[25] Marshals and deputy marshals thereafter went unpaid.

As Hayes noted in his diary, "the object of this struggle is the removal of national authority in any efficient form from the polls, even at national elections. State authority, with force at its back, both military and civil, is to be permitted to remain but all national authority, whether military or civil, is denied."[26] There was no question of constitutionality in the view of Hayes; Congress is expressly authorized to regulate House elections.[27] As the struggle progressed, the president gained the upper hand, at least in the eyes of the public.[28] A final clash occurred in June 1880, when Congress passed a law depriving deputy marshals of the power to make arrests outside of their own precincts and stripping them of legal protection for acts performed in the course of executing the laws. Hayes vetoed the bill on June 15, 1880.[29] Federal election officials continued to appear in cities and towns of 20,000 or more at the time of congressional elections until a Democratic Congress and president ended the practice in 1894.[30] By the end of the century, southerners had almost completely eradicated the black vote in congressional as well as state elections, thereby giving Democrats in the House at least two dozen seats that should have gone to Republicans. Thus, the denial of suffrage to blacks was no mere state issue.

Rutherford Hayes had declared he would serve only one term; the jockeying for succession began before his presidency was a year old. Roscoe Conkling, John Logan of Illinois, and Donald Cameron of Pennsylvania led a movement favoring a third term for U.S. Grant. James Blaine sought the nomination, as did Treasury Secretary John Sherman. Despite an aggressive deployment of treasury offices—he fired several employees after learning they supported Grant—Sherman fared poorly when Republicans met in Chicago.[31] He could not obtain the support of the more than one hundred delegates whom he controlled thanks to treasury offices. Blaine may have had the most support of any candidate going into the convention, but his forces could not overcome those supporting Grant. The delegates turned to a compromise candidate, Congressman James Garfield of Ohio.

Before the Civil War, Garfield studied law and then enjoyed a brief career as a preacher. He served with the Army of the Cumberland and won distinction for his service at Chickamauga, after which he was made a major general. Elected to Congress in 1862, Garfield served on the Electoral Commission in 1876. He enjoyed a reputation for honesty though he was also alleged to be something of a trimmer.[32] New York Republican Thomas Platt suggested that Garfield lacked "moral courage," though he conceded that the Ohioan was "perhaps the ablest parliamentarian in Congress" as well as a "born orator" who could "sway the multitude as no other man of his day could."[33] The Democrats had the good sense to nominate another Union general, Winfield Scott Hancock. At Gettysburg, Hancock ordered the construction of the convex defensive line from Cemetery Ridge to Little Round Top that proved impregnable. His nomination was well-received, though the selection of William English for vice president raised eyebrows. The Indiana lawyer was best known for his authorship of the infamous English bill of 1858, which offered Kansans a gargantuan land grant if they would accept statehood under the proslavery Lecompton constitution. (The offer was declined.) Republicans nominated the deposed collector of the port of New York, Chester A. Arthur, for vice president. Arthur had been sacked by Hayes after he failed to implement reforms at the New York Customhouse, which in addition to being the single largest patronage plum in the country, was beset by gross inefficiencies. While his firing made him something of a martyr in the eyes of the Stalwart wing of the Republican Party, Arthur was more than a machine politician. He served as legal counsel for a slave in famous *Lemmon* case that saw the New York Court of Appeals reject the notion that the privileges and immunities clause of Article IV, Section 2 endowed slaveowners with a right of transit—they did not have a right to bring their slaves with them as they traveled through northern states.[34] The nomination of Arthur was a sop to the Stalwarts who had favored Grant, but Garfield was more than happy to allow his running mate to manage the campaign. Arthur proceeded to impose assessments on all federal employees—including judges—to raise money.[35]

Aware that Republicans could no longer contest any of the southern states, Garfield focused his energies on the North. During August he traveled through Ohio, Pennsylvania, and New York, speaking to large and enthusiastic crowds. Garfield took a hard line with the South; like many Republicans he was intensely frustrated with southern attempts to weaken the federal law enforcement apparatus established during Reconstruction.

He had been among those who had once been ready to abandon sectional confrontation. Now Garfield and his party took it up again with fervor.[36] The Republican platform revealed this anger with its frank declaration that the "Solid South" must be "divided by the peaceful agencies of the ballot."[37] Republican speakers warned that U.S. bonds would lose value if Hancock won.[38] They also suggested that the abolition of protection would result in the loss of jobs.[39] Democrats appeared to be caught unprepared.

The *Nation* found the whole scene a bit much; it claimed the country was not interested in the campaign or the tariff question and that even the players were only going through the motions. "There is no real interest among the managers on either side in any question of the day, and their debates in the campaign are like the battles of the Italian condottieri, which were fought under contract, and sometimes lasted a whole day without injury to life or limb. When they rush furiously at each other about the 'Solid South,' and the tariff, and State rights, it is in order to entertain and move the spectators and earn their pay, and not by any means to give vent to passions or convictions of their own. They are about as well prepared to fight on one subject as another. If the orator thinks the audience would like him to groan over the fate of the poor negro hiding in the swamp, he is ready for that question; but if the audience shows signs of doubting whether the negro is in the swamp, the orator is ready to groan over the threatened extinction of American industry (via the removal of tariffs); and he can groan as deeply over the one as the other."[40]

If the country was indifferent, Republican incumbents were not. They had held the reins of power in the executive branch for 20 years and profited immensely as the federal establishment ballooned. They were not ready to give up their offices. Writing in the *Nation*, Republican National Committee member John M. Forbes warned that if Democrats regained power, it would take three presidential terms to remove them, as they would have the 138 electoral votes of the "Solid South," 80,000 officeholders and the use of "any needful parts of the salaries (of federal employees), say, in the whole, $24 million per year."[41] The Republicans themselves were proving hard to dislodge. Enormous pressure was brought to bear on civil servants for contributions; in Pennsylvania federal officeholders received a second and then a third notice demanding assistance. One circular warned that "at the close of the campaign we shall place a list of those who have not paid in the hands of the department you are in."[42] Following Republican losses in the October state elections, an additional assessment of 1 percent was imposed. The contributions were considerably higher among officeholders in the customhouses of the North and especially in Maine "where there was a general belief that tenure was dependent upon payment."[43]

Republicans were most concerned about Indiana. Much of the funds spent in that state were provided by postal contractors who had sent fraudulent petitions to Congress to obtain an increase in the number of mail routes in the West (the Star Route frauds).[44] Ill-gotten gains formed only a part of the pile of cash or "soap" that was used to buy votes in the Hoosier state. Financier Jay Gould was said to have provided much of it at the request of Garfield himself.[45] In November Republicans won Indiana by 7,000 votes, probably through mass bribery.[46] Garfield won a clear majority in the Electoral College (214–155) but his popular vote majority was only 9,500 votes out of 4.9 million cast. Many Democrats suspected that the election had been stolen. Republicans regained control of the House but the Senate was deadlocked. Every southern state voted Democratic.

James Garfield was shot in a Washington, DC, train station on July 2, 1881, and died after two months of inept medical treatment. Before the shooting, the president found himself almost completely consumed by the task of bestowing federal offices in a manner that would please congressional leaders and mollify his own supporters. The wing of the Republican Party that had supported Grant for president in 1880—the Stalwarts—was generally annoyed with Garfield's appointments. James Blaine was appointed secretary of state over Levi Morton, the favorite of Stalwart leader Senator Roscoe Conkling. Far more damaging was the president's replacement of Collector of the Port of New York Edwin Merritt with William Robertson. Conkling, who considered himself head of the Republican Party in New York, believed he had received assurances from Garfield that incumbent officeholders in the state would be left in place. Following the inauguration, Garfield succumbed to pressure brought on him by Blaine—Conkling's archenemy—and sacked Merritt. Conkling and New York's junior senator, Tom Platt, resigned from the Senate to express their displeasure. They did so expecting to be returned to their posts by the New York legislature. The administration aided opposing candidates with federal patronage and as the battle promised to drag out over the summer, Platt withdrew. He was followed a short time later by Conkling.[47] The episode has been cast as a chapter in the history of the spoils system; it also demonstrated that federal offices were plentiful enough to enable presidents to overawe legislatures.

In the South, Garfield discarded Hayes's practice of appointing Democrats as a goodwill gesture. Instead both he and Arthur gave patronage to Republicans and independents.[48] They devoted enormous resources to winning the support of Virginia Senator William Mahone, an independent, who held the balance of power in the Senate. Mahone's plunder included 200 treasury jobs, 1,700 places in the post office, the Norfolk

Naval Yard, and 70 positions in the state's federal courts.[49] In other southern states Arthur provided Populists with jobs in an attempt to undermine the Democrats.[50] Arthur also distributed places with an eye on the 1882–83 congressional elections. The administration estimated that Republicans would need to win approximately 20 House seats in the South to hold their narrow majority. Despite a generous deployment of patronage, the party was routed and Democrats took back the House in the 48th Congress, with a majority of 70. Arthur's luck in the North wasn't much better. He allowed most of the cabinet to resign following Garfield's death and his appointments satisfied neither Blaine's followers nor those of Conkling.

The problem of federal patronage had only worsened since the Covode Committee report of 1860 demonstrated how the Buchanan administration used federal offices and contracts to buy support for its proslavery policies from editors, delegates, and elected officials.[51] Lincoln was harassed at all hours by men demanding employment. He found to his chagrin that he was spending much of his time trying to fill offices in a manner acceptable to lawmakers and other politicians. The sharp expansion of the federal bureaucracy provided vast resources for Republican Party bosses. Between 1861 and 1871 new entities such as the Department of Agriculture, the Bureau of Education, the Bureau of Statistics, and the Internal Revenue Service were added to the federal establishment. By 1877 the navy yards and arsenals employed 15,000. In the west there were 90 regional land offices, and 135 customhouses employed tens of thousands. In 1877, 38,000 postmasters held office, and that number did not include the contractors who worked for the Post Office—15,000 by one estimate. Overall, 64,000 Americans derived support from the Post Office.[52] The coasts were watched by 950 lighthouse keepers, and 130 inspectors examined steamboats. Large mints operated in several cities.[53] An 1888 report of a Senate committee led by Senator Francis Cockrell of Missouri counted 171,746 employees, over half of whom worked for the Post Office.[54] A supplement to the same report issued a year later documented gross inefficiencies in many departments and the employment of more persons than necessary; despite the arrival of copying machines and carbons, executive departments continued to employ clerks for the purpose of copying documents by hand.[55]

The chief plumb was in the North—the New York City Customhouse. As of 1888, it employed 1,585 persons.[56] The resources of that institution were deployed ruthlessly though not always with effect. An 1872 congressional investigation revealed that Collector Thomas Murphy had offered federal offices to local politicians including one William Atkinson in the hope of getting a slate of his choosing sent to the state Republican convention of 1870. Atkinson, who was the leader of the Republican organization in his district, refused the offer. The vote at the local caucus was 234 for the winning slate and only 34 for the "customhouse ticket." In a last-ditch effort to get customhouse delegates admitted, the local federal pension agent, William H. Lawrence, appeared at the Republican state convention in Saratoga with a document that he said proved the customhouse ticket had won the caucus vote. When Atkinson objected, he was fired from his own position as captain of the watch of the New York City post office.[57]

With the presidency in eclipse following the Civil War, Congress inserted itself into the process of appointments and removals. The incursion began with the National Bank Act of 1863, which provided that the president could remove the comptroller of the currency only with Senate consent.[58] The Tenure of Office Act made Senate consent a prerequisite to the removal of any official whose appointment required Senate approval. Andrew Johnson responded by suspending officials when the Senate was not in session (as the law allowed), and then sending it nominations of new appointees and explanations for the suspensions on its return. With the exception of the dispute over Stanton's removal, the Senate generally approved the nominations, thus acquiescing in the removals. In April 1869, with Johnson back in Tennessee, Congress enacted a law modifying the Tenure of Office Act so the president no longer had to submit reports to the Senate explaining his removal of underlings. The Tenure of Office Act was finally repealed on March 3, 1887.[59]

Congressional dictation in the matter of offices was largely an informal affair. Lawmakers who were members of the same party as the president notified him of persons in their districts or states that deserved appointment and their requests were usually granted. George Hoar recalled that each senator and representative "was followed like a highland Chieftain 'with his tail on' by a band of retainers devoted to his political fortunes, dependent upon him for their own, but supported at the public charge."[60] State political machines placed a high value on Senate seats due to the control each senator enjoyed over federal patronage in his home state. Thus one historian's description of the Senate as a "federation of state bosses."[61] By 1880, senators controlled all federal patronage in their states if they were members of the same party as the president, with the exception of postmasterships, which were left to the dictation of congressmen. If the state had two senators of the same party, they split the available patronage between them.[62] Roscoe Conkling dominated the Republican Party of New York for a decade due to his control over almost all of the 7,000 federal offices in the state.[63] In their appointments, Grant and Arthur did little more than carry out the personnel decisions of lawmakers. The rapaciousness of members of Congress resulted in almost the entirety of the federal establishment serving as a prize to be won or lost at elections. Oliver Morton resented the epithets hurled at Republicans during the 1872 campaign; when the party gathering scheduled to take place in Philadelphia was labeled an "office-holders convention," he predicted that there would be more "office-seekers" at the Liberal Republican convention in Cincinnati.[64] One contemporary dismissed the 1876 contest as a battle "between 80,000 officeholders and 500,000 office seekers."[65]

The federal spoils system gave executive branch officials enormous influence over state nominating conventions, newspapers, and members of Congress. It did far more than Congress or the Supreme Court to concentrate power in the hands of the national government. Many viewed a professional civil service, insulated from political pressure, as the appropriate remedy. Exams had first been used on a limited basis in 1853. The Joint Select Committee on Retrenchment proposed a comprehensive system of exams and terms of service for federal employees in 1867. Four years later Congress authorized the president to establish a commission for the purpose of devising hiring rules.[66] The Civil Service Commission was formed shortly thereafter; it submitted draft rules to the president in December 1871. Competitive exams began the following spring under boards of examiners established in each department. When Congress refused to put civil service rules into the form of statutes and set aside money for the effort, Grant disbanded the boards in 1875.[67] During the Hayes administration, the New York Customhouse began using exams, the scores upon which served as a basis for hiring. Upper level vacancies were filled only by persons already employed in the Customhouse. The practice was later adopted by other customhouses across the country, as well as the post offices. The Interior Department also implemented exams and promotions based on competence.

On June 22, 1877, Rutherford Hayes issued an executive order prohibiting assessments and barring civil servants from participating in the "management of political caucuses, conventions or election campaigns."[68] *Harper's Weekly* approved, explaining that "almost any leadership is better than that of an official class of the selfishly interested." Some complained that it was "monstrous" for the president to bar men from participating in the political process, but *Harper's* did not agree. "Do these opponents think it any less monstrous that officeholders should go to conventions and into committees armed with rewards and punishments to carry their objects, which those who are not officeholders cannot have, and which the officeholders have only because they hold places under the government?" *Harper's* explained that 1,300 places at their disposal enabled New York Customhouse officials to control the city's Republican

Central Committee (92 of its 158 members were civil servants), which itself ran the state party. An entity that "Republican voters must support or give victory to the Democrats," is a "closed corporation, the seat of which is the Customhouse and other national offices in New York." The situation was much the same in Massachusetts and other states: "The organization is maintained by the federal patronage and it is virtually invincible."[69] In his autobiography written in the early 1880s, *Twenty Years in Congress*, James Blaine took issue with the idea that the federal government controlled an inordinate amount of patronage. In the cities, where the customhouses wield "vast influence," the federal payroll was far smaller than that of the municipal governments. He conceded that in most congressional districts there was "scarcely any patronage known except that of the postmasters."[70]

In the spring of 1878, Hayes modified his order regarding the political activities of federal employees so they could make political contributions. It is doubtful the employees sought the right to part with a portion of their meager salaries. Politicians, on the other hand, had been bending the president's ear for months over the troubles his order had brought upon them. State bosses in particular lamented the reduced utility of local federal offices.[71] The collector of customs in Chicago complained of the absence of federal employees at the Illinois state Republican Convention of June 1878: "Heretofore such gatherings have had a good many agents of the executive, whereas this (one) was without them and being deprived of them, the platform is without the customary personal laudation of the president."[72]

In his last annual message, Hayes acknowledged that the problem of federal patronage was becoming more severe with the growth of the civil list.[73] He was undoubtedly a friend of civil service reform, though his reputation suffered when it was revealed that members of the Louisiana returning board that wrongfully awarded him the state's electoral vote in 1876 had received federal places for themselves and members of their families.[74] Hayes's peers in the Republican Party were much less sympathetic to the idea of removing the civil service from the hands of politicians, even when the spoils system and its discouraging effect on voters imperiled their own fortunes. When the fall 1880 state elections in Maine went against Republicans, the *Nation* expressed hope that Republican senators would see the folly of machine politics and embrace the cause of reform. "The rule of Mr. Conkling in New York, of General Logan in Illinois, and of Mr. Blaine in Maine is, as has often been remarked, a copy, and a poor one, of the device by which Tweed mastered the ignorant of New York City. If it could succeed in the larger field of state and federal politics we might well despair of the government. The extent to which it has already miscarried seems to show that we are near the end of it, and if this be true the failure in Maine may be fairly set down as, in more senses than one, a blessing in disguise."[75]

That many still did not see the light was demonstrated by a letter to the editor of *The Nation* of December 1880. The author attacked proposals to allow civil servants to remain in place as long as they exhibited "good behavior" on the grounds that such a policy would result in an "aristocracy of office-holders." Permitting the "same set of men" to continue in office indefinitely would create "in the mind of the officeholder the idea that he owns the office, and, instead of being a public servant, he becomes a master, haughty towards those whom he ought to serve."[76] The warning would prove to be something of a prophecy; still, the present situation was corrupting elections and impairing the efficiency of the executive branch. James Blaine was among the unconverted—he opposed the order barring officeholders from participating in conventions. When the national government follows the federal civil servant home "to tell him whether in hours which are his own he shall devote his time to the efforts of inventive genius, or whether he shall attend religious or spiritual meetings or political meetings, or shall do anything else, the government, in my opinion, is a tyrant." The *New York Times* disagreed. It approved the president's order barring civil servants from caucuses and conventions "because it is perfectly proper for him to protect the great body of his fellow citizens from any interference with their equality of political rights, based on and made possible by the conditions of public employment." It held out the possibility that the order might be rescinded if civil service reform was put into effect.[77]

In 1880 civil service reformers supported Garfield; they were disappointed over his failure to endorse the cause in his inauguration speech.[78] The assassination of the president by a disgruntled office seeker gave momentum to the cause of reform, as did the difficulty of filling a burgeoning civil list through personal contacts—it was now approaching 150,000 positions. In January 1882 the *Springfield Daily Republican* expressed relief that two civil service reform measures were under consideration. It predicted that a merit system would enable one western congressmen who had obtained "places since December for twenty men, three women and one boy" to give "some portion of his time to the legislation of the country."[79] The final impetus arrived with the 1882 midterm elections, which gave the House back to the Democrats. A lame-duck Republican Congress, eager to protect Republican officeholders against what it expected would be a Democratic president following the 1884 presidential election, took the bit in its teeth.[80] Democrat George Pendleton sponsored the bill that became law. During the congressional debate that preceded its passage, he claimed that the civil service had degenerated into a "great political machine," the exertions of which "at least twice within a very short period in the history of our country have robbed the people of the fair results of presidential elections."[81] The Pendleton Act became law on January 16, 1883. It established a Civil Service Commission that would set rules for hiring and promotion and devise exams to be taken by applicants. Hiring would be based on exam scores. The law provided that civil servants were under no obligation to make political contributions but it did not ban them.[82] Arthur issued an order implementing the law on May 7, 1883; among other things it barred persons in the civil service from compelling underlings to perform political work or contribute to political funds.[83] The law applied to only 11 percent of federal employees following its enactment but the president was authorized to increase the portion of federal employees subject to its provisions. At first it covered only the largest facilities, including 11 customhouses and 23 post offices.[84] It did not apply to collectors, marshals, and district attorneys and other senior officials as presidents were viewed as needing the power to fire senior-level personnel if they were to control their administrations. Persons receiving appointments in the classified civil service continued to be members of the same party as the president; the only difference was they also scored well on exams.[85]

The law improved the civil service in the decades after its enactment. Although the Pendleton Act itself did not impede the president's authority to remove lower level employees, its provision for hiring based on exams reduced the motive to empty offices—those within the U.S. Civil Service could no longer be filled with party hacks regardless of their qualifications. The question of whether Congress could enact laws limiting the president's removal power was addressed by the Supreme Court in 1886. In *U.S. v. Perkins*, the justices held that a law barring the president from removing naval officers except on the approval of a naval board was constitutional. In his opinion for the Court, Justice Stanley Matthews pointed to Section 2 of Article II, which authorized Congress to vest the president with the power to appoint inferior officers: "The constitutional authority in Congress to thus vest the appointment implies authority to limit, restrict and regulate the removal by such laws as Congress may enact in relation to the officers so appointed."[86] Forty years later the Supreme Court held void an 1876 law requiring Senate consent for the removal of first-, second-, and third-class postmasters; Chief Justice William Howard Taft explained that presidents must be able to fire their subordinates if they were to have any hope of controlling them.[87] Why this logic applied to senior officials who were often little more than figureheads but not to the lower level civil servants who implemented the policies of the national government, Taft failed to explain.

What civil service reform did not do was remove executive branch employees from the political process. Almost all federal employees could still be fired at will and the use of exams did not prevent presidents from selecting competent men and women from their own party instead of the opposition. Nor did it prevent the use of federal offices to control party nominations. As Chester Arthur angled for the 1884 Republican nomination, he had Secretary of the Navy William Chandler use federal offices to gain the support of southerners.[88] The Louisiana delegation at the 1884 Republican national convention included a surveyor, deputy surveyor, naval officer, customhouse clerk, sub-treasurer, district attorney, two revenue collectors, and a deputy collector along with a member of Congress and a state senator. Only one delegate was not on a public payroll.[89] In time southern delegations at Republican conventions—packed with federal officeholders—would enable the executive branch to wield enormous influence at these affairs.[90] In 1898, the *New York Times* observed that "for many years the Federal [civil] service in the South, when the Republicans were in power, has been run, not for the public benefit, not even to influence elections, but . . . to manufacture delegations to national conventions."[91] Southern Republicans proved willing instruments of the political managers of several presidents because (1) federal offices were their only sustenance—they no longer had access to state offices, and (2) they owed their positions to the chief executive and not Republican members of Congress (there were none from the South).

Grover Cleveland issued an order early in his administration barring federal officeholders from using "their official positions in attempts to control political movements in their localities." He explained that "the influence of federal office holders should not be felt in the manipulation of political primary meetings and nominating conventions."[92] A message of the president to the superintendent of the Mint advising against the participation of employees in political conventions was ignored.[93] Despite his support for reform, Cleveland permitted mass removals of Republican officeholders. First assistant postmaster Adlai Stevenson won popularity with party members in all parts of the country with his removal of thousands of Republican postmasters even before their terms under the Tenure of Office Act expired.[94] His work would eventually bring Stevenson the vice presidency and his family political prominence for a century. Cleveland proved flexible enough to allow a party that had been out of power for 24 years to enjoy the fruits of its labors. By one estimate, 40,000 out of 52,600 fourth-class postmasters were dispatched during his first term, along with 100 of 111 collectors, 64 of 70 marshals and 22 of 30 territorial judges.[95]

Like Jackson, Polk, Pierce, and Buchanan, Cleveland was not above using federal offices to stamp out dissent in the Democratic Party; he deployed them for the purpose of undermining Populists and other splinter groups.[96] Prior to the 1893 Nebraska State Democratic convention, applicants for postmasterships were informed that voting for pro-silver nominees would place their appointments in grave jeopardy.[97] Despite the demands of his party, Cleveland made some contributions to the cause of reform; he enlarged the Civil Service from about 14,000 to 27,000 places.[98] He also wrestled the Senate into submission over the Tenure of Office Act. In compliance with the terms of the law, the president suspended officials he wished to replace and submitted nominations for their successors to the Senate. When the Senate asked for papers detailing the reasons he wished to replace the U.S. attorney for southern Alabama, the president refused, insisting it had no right to papers reflecting executive deliberations. The term of the U.S. attorney expired during the interim; the Senate relented and confirmed his successor.[99] Abuses continued under Cleveland's successors, even as the U.S. Civil Service was expanded to include a larger portion of the federal payroll. Within 18 months of Benjamin Harrison's inauguration in March 1889, his administration removed 32,000 of 55,000 fourth-class postmasters.[100]

The survival of the spoils system made the addition of new federal activities problematic. Speaking on the floor of the House in May 1892 regarding a bill to provide rural free delivery of mail, Congressman Benjamin Enloe reported hearing of odd stories regarding the turnout at a recent Republican state convention in his home state of Tennessee. When it assembled, "the post offices were deserted all over the state by the postmasters and the offices were left in charge of the assistants." The postmasters were in Nashville, along with the district attorneys and the internal revenue collectors. Even the "U.S. marshals rallied their forces there." Enloe complained that many of the proposals for new federal activities, such as establishing rural free delivery, agricultural warehouses, and public ownership of railroads and telegraphs, would, if enacted, greatly worsen the problem of federal patronage. He saw a pattern that involved making as many Americans as possible dependents of the national government so they could be manipulated. Federal operation of the railroads would ensure "that every railroad employee in the U.S. would be a 'striker' for the administration."[101]

At the turn of the century progress in protecting federal employees from political pressure continued, albeit in fits and starts. A little less than half of all federal employees were included in the U.S. Civil Service in 1897.[102] William McKinley became president that year; he dared to remove some offices from it.[103] McKinley issued an executive order in July 1897 barring the removal of persons in the Civil Service from their offices except for just cause. The reasons had to be stated in writing. The order did not apply to senior officials whose appointments required Senate consent or U.S. attorneys.[104] Theodore Roosevelt served on the U.S. Civil Service Commission. His investigation of activities at the Baltimore post office led him to call for the removal of 25 employees for acts committed in the 1891 municipal election, but no action was taken.[105] As president he fired Republican boss Lincoln Avery after Avery collected assessments from employees at a Michigan customhouse.[106]

If the ability of collectors and postmasters to dominate local nominating conventions through their ability to flood them with federal employees formed the most pernicious aspect of the spoils system, the propensity of federal officials to use jobs and contracts to influence the press was a close second. The practice reached the height of its effectiveness during the antebellum period, when presidents from Jackson to Buchanan bestowed postmasterships and other jobs on newspaper editors and then expected them to provide favorable coverage of their administrations. The dependence of most newspapers on government largesse resulted in the control of a sizeable portion of the nation's media by public officials and politicians. The rise of large, independent newspapers during the 1840s and 1850s eased the problem, but all too often smaller newspapers remained dependent on state or federal patronage for survival.

On taking office in 1861, Secretary of State Seward removed State Department printing contracts from Democratic editors and gave them to Republicans.[107] Lincoln appointed almost 50 editors to office—nearly matching the record of Andrew Jackson, who was justly castigated for introducing the practice on a wide scale.[108] Early in his administration, Lincoln arranged for James Buchanan's former editor, John W. Forney, to establish the *Daily Morning Chronicle* in Washington. (Forney had defected from Democratic ranks over slavery issues.) The newspaper was expected to counter the influence among federal troops of critical editors such as James Gordon Bennett of the *New York Herald* and Horace Greeley of the *New York Tribune*. The *Chronicle* was distributed widely among Union soldiers, creating sizeable profits for Forney. Government printing contracts also helped. If the *Chronicle* was not quite an administration organ, it was close.[109] As with the spoils system, some of the most egregious abuses were perpetrated in the South during Reconstruction. Ten Republican newspapers in South Carolina had so few subscribers in 1873 that they were almost completely dependent on federal printing contracts for income.[110] Federal money did not satiate the state's Republican printers; the state government had a printing bill that year larger than those of Iowa, Massachusetts, Pennsylvania, and Ohio combined.[111] The end of Reconstruction deprived the region's Republican newspapers of their places at the public trough and they quickly failed.[112]

In 1867, 54 newspapers held contracts with the State Department for printing the laws of the United States. Others printed revenue stamps used by the Department of the Treasury. Andrew Johnson distributed contracts and postmasterships with the expectation of obedience one would expect from an old Jacksonian Democrat, but editors in the North who received federal largesse were not shy about criticizing the president. Grant gave postmasterships to editors in Elmira, Syracuse, Saratoga, and Niagara Falls, New York. Printers in Canton and Troy, New York, were made collectors. Grant tried to make the editor of the *National Republican* a police commissioner in Washington; the effort failed when Congress abolished the police board to prevent the appointment of the editor, who happened to be under indictment at the time.[113] The practice of issuing State Department printing contracts to newspapers was terminated by an act of May 8, 1872, effective in 1875.[114] Hundreds of editors in each state continued to serve as postmasters. If the party press was dying, the presidents of the time did not seem to know it. Rutherford Hayes was pleased to recall his administration did not maintain its own newspaper (most of its predecessors had), but he freely gave offices to editors such as William Henry Smith, whom he saw fit to serve as the collector in Chicago.[115] Benjamin Harrison gave places to several editors including Charles E. Fitch of the *Rochester Democrat and Chronicle*—he was appointed collector at Buffalo in February 1890. The *Springfield Daily Republican* assured its readers that the president "now has the Republican press of the Empire State from the Harlem River to the falls of Niagara well in hand."[116]

Despite its awareness of the corrupting influence of federal largesse on civil servants and newspaper editors, Gilded Age America accepted appeals to the pecuniary interests of voters as a matter of course. Voters were told repeatedly that the maintenance of a particular federal policy would either secure their fortunes or ruin them. The most common source for predictions of doomsday or the Promised Land was the tariff. The Civil War saw tariffs reach unprecedented levels, which the country accepted on the assurance they would be temporary. By the time the last hike went through in June of 1864, the average rate had reached 47 percent.[117] Following the conflict, farmers demanded reductions but their pleas were in vain. Writing in January 1867, correspondent Georges Clemenceau charged that "protectionism is rampant in this country. When an industry is interrupted for a couple of weeks, importation of foreign goods is given as a reason, and men set to work on framing a new tariff. Owing to this custom, the people have been made to pay ridiculous prices for items of primary necessity, the treasury has been defrauded of the customs duties, which are no longer collected when they become exorbitant, and a few big men in the east have grown exceedingly rich."[118] In 1874, the *San Francisco Bulletin* complained of high rates on eastern goods, but it did not demand their abolition. Instead it favored protection for California's products. "If we are compelled to buy Pennsylvania coal and iron at advanced rates, Pennsylvania should be forced to drink our wines and brandies."[119] The United States would have benefited from a moderate policy of protection at least during the early phase of industrialization; the development of its iron and woolen industries had been hurt in the decades before the Civil War by the free-trade policies of the national government embodied in the Walker Tariff of 1846 and thc Tariff of 1857. During thc Civil War, ratcs moved beyond what beyond would have been appropriate and they remained at absurd levels for almost the entirety of the next 70 years. Congress extended protection even to raw materials, thereby raising costs for manufacturers.[120]

In early 1867 revenue commissioner David Wells devised a bill to lower rates. Congress went in the opposite direction despite the fact that the government was running a surplus. In the House of Representatives, Michael Kerr of Indiana sounded a theme that would be heard for the rest of the century when he charged that manufacturers "had applied, and not in vain, to government to compel people to trade with them and to pay them twice or thrice as much for their merchandise as it was intrinsically worth." Amounts paid for goods beyond their cost "without the duty is so much paid as a bounty or gratuity for the temporary advantage of the home producer or manufacturer of such articles." He pointed to a report that showed Americans labored under a higher per capita level of taxation ($11.46) than Britain ($10.92) or France ($7.97).[121] One estimate held that between state property taxes, which fell hard on farmers, and tariffs, which depended heavily on taxation of "necessaries" such as coffee, sugar, and salt, the poor paid somewhere between 70 and 90 percent of their "average annual savings" in taxes.[122]

The Tariff Act of March 2, 1867, was a product of many forces, chief of which was the woolen industry, which expanded sharply during the Civil War to meet an increased demand produced by the shortage of cotton. A December 1865 convention of woolen manufactures and wool farmers met in Syracuse, New York. It drafted the woolen schedule that was included in the act. The schedule's distinguishing feature was a steep increase in rates over levies that had already risen dramatically during the war. Rates on the most popular grade of woolens increased to almost 50 percent. Woolen cloth, dress goods, and carpeting now came with a total tax of 60 to 70 percent, while blankets and flannels carried a total rate of 80 to 100 percent. Proponents justified high rates as compensation for the high duties on wool imports. Wool farmers did not obtain any visible benefit from the tax on the raw material, as the price of raw wool continued to decline.[123]

With the annual surplus closing in on $100 million in 1870, the need to cut taxes was obvious. Congress abolished most of the remaining wartime internal taxes via a law of July 14, 1870, and the income tax was phased out as well. Falling prices deprived farmers of income, and they resented the levies imposed on "necessaries." The rates on these items were lowered. The tariff on imported steel—used in rails—was raised to $28 a ton, which was more than the cost of a ton of steel in Britain. The capacity of even small industries to exploit protection was demonstrated by the high rates on fine marble that enabled quarry owners to raise their prices 80 to 150 percent—all to benefit a tiny area of Vermont where the mineral was extracted.[124] That even the mercantile Northeast had something less than complete affection for protection was evident from the resolutions passed at a Worcester, Massachusetts, Republican convention in October 1871. They demonstrated that maritime New England, where support for high tariffs had always been lukewarm, had changed course. The resolutions condemned a navigation law that made it illegal to buy foreign ships and the "high tariff taxes on materials" that made it "impossible to build them." The *Springfield Daily Republican* suggested that the Worcester resolutions indicate "the strong desire of Boston to regain her ocean traffic, and the fact that she has found the navigation law and the tariff law obstacles in her way." After noting that the portion of foreign commerce moving on American ships had dropped from two-thirds in 1860 to less than a third, the *Daily Republican* complained of the coal duty that impeded the importing of cheap coal from Nova Scotia. The duty of $1.25 per ton "almost doubles what would be the price of the Pictou (Canadian) coal." It noted that the shoe and boot industry, the second largest employer in the United States after agriculture and especially prominent in New England, suffered from the steep protection imposed on raw materials such as rubber and leather.[125]

In 1872, with a presidential election on the way, Congress sought to head off complaints over the tariff by cutting rates an average of 10 percent.[126] Three years later on March 3, 1875, Congress was able to rescind the cuts without complaint due to a loss of revenue produced by the depression that followed the Panic of 1873.[127] After remaining dormant for a time, the issue of tariffs flared up again in the early 1880s. Ten years of declining prices for agricultural commodities eroded the willingness of farmers to pay high prices for manufactured products. Republicans were quick to refine their arguments; mindful of the labor vote, they insisted that protection enabled manufacturers to pay higher wages. Democrats such as Abram Hewitt agreed that some protection was necessary if factory hands were to continue to receive higher pay their equals in Europe (their pay was 50% higher than that of their counterparts in Britain).[128]

A surplus of $125 million made revision necessary. In early 1882 Congress established a Tariff Commission to postpone serious discussion of rate cuts. To the surprise of nearly everyone the Commission proposed a 20 percent reduction in rates despite the fact that it was staffed by manufacturing executives including the secretary of the Wool Manufacturers' Association.[129]

After Republicans lost control of the House in the 1882 midterm elections, the lame duck session of the 47th Congress enacted what became known as the "Mongrel Tariff" of March 3, 1883. Rates were cut by, on average, 1.5 percent.[130] Before the law went through, Mississippi Senator Lucius Q. C. Lamar issued a stinging indictment of protection. He wondered how a country so sensitive to the corrupting influence of public employment could embrace a policy that made every voter's livelihood subject to the impulses of congressional majorities:

> Sir, we have had a great deal to say of late about the corruptions growing out of the vast patronage of the government. The source of this evil was held by both Mr. Calhoun and Mr. Webster to be in the dependence of sixty thousand people, who held employment under the government, upon those in power for their sustenance. They believed that a power so unlimited and despotic over this numerous and powerful corps of officeholders would corrupt and debase those who composed it into the supple and willing instruments of power, and at the same time work a fearful change in the character of the government itself. Now this protective system produces precisely the same result that Mr. Webster and Mr. Calhoun saw in the workings of official patronage. It has obtained control of the capital and labor of industry, and bound it, through its interest, to the support of the party in power.

Lamar recalled that "according to the declarations of the advocates of high duties, the laborers in these manufactures built up by protection depend for their bread upon the rate of taxes levied in this bill. If what they say is true, all this vast amount of capital and the operatives, amounting according to their representations to over a million persons, are hanging in suspense for their food and clothing and shelter and supplies for their wives and children, as well as employment at all, upon a vote of ayes and noes."[131]

If protective tariffs purchased hundreds of thousands of votes, river and harbor appropriations won tens of thousands. Before the Civil War they peaked under the Fillmore administration. They were justified variously under the commerce clause, the territories clause, and the war powers. To the great irritation of Whigs, Republicans, and Great Lakes Democrats, the Pierce and Buchanan administrations rejected many of these appropriations as unconstitutional and federal funding barely extended beyond navigational aids during the late 1850s. While these expenditures all but disappeared during the war, they multiplied rapidly following Appomattox. Reconstruction saved Republicans from the unhappy task of arguing constitutional law with their southern counterparts, who had in the years before the war easily demonstrated that none of the enumerated powers had been added to the Constitution so that Congress could provide money for dredging the nation's waterways. With the southern impediment removed, river-and-harbor appropriations flowed easily through Washington during Reconstruction; most of these appropriations went for projects in the northern states. In fiscal year 1870 the South received just over 5 percent of the funds expended.[132] A statute of July 11, 1870, provided money for 28 different projects in Minnesota and Wisconsin; Maine also did well. Only a handful of places in the South received aid.[133] The degradation of antebellum improvements along southern waterways during the war led southerners to discard their constitutional scruples and join the "great barbecue" at Washington. If pork was to be distributed, it would be distributed universally. The Mississippi River was the leading candidate for aid in southern minds and properly so. Northerners did not have to be told how critical the waterway was to the commerce of the Midwest as well as the South; they had fought a war to retain access to the mouth of it. Yet northerners did not realize following the war how complete the destruction was—the loss of levees along the river had resulted in the inundation of whole counties. By 1858 there were already a thousand miles of levees along the river, though sandbars at its mouth remained a problem—one ship had to wait 83 days to enter it from the Gulf in 1859. During the war numerous levees were destroyed. When U.S. Grant cut levees during the siege of Vicksburg, thousands of acres were flooded.[134]

With navigation on the nation's central waterway hampered by snags, hidden shallows, and shifting sands, talk was heard in Congress of establishing a commission that would focus solely on improvements along the Mississippi. Two groups pushed for its establishment; while both wanted to see the creation of a stable and safe shipping channel, one wanted resources devoted to flood control as well.[135] After much bickering, Congress established the Mississippi River Commission on June 28, 1879. The act's preface indicated what clauses of Article I, Section 8 were thought to authorize the endeavor: "It shall be the duty of said commission to take into consideration and mature such plan or plans and estimates as will correct, permanently locate, and deepen the channel and protect the banks of the Mississippi River; improve and give safety and ease the navigation thereof; prevent destructive floods; promote and facilitate commerce, trade and the postal service."[136] The Commission was given the duty of investigating various methods proposed for flood control but constitutional concerns led lawmakers to bar the commission from spending money to protect property or reclaim flooded lands. Instead it was to focus on creating a stable shipping channel. It could build levees, but only when necessary to protect navigation and commerce on the river itself.

Commenting on an 1882 discussion of a bill appropriating funds for the Commission, the *Nation* was pleased to report that the "most noteworthy thing in the debate thus far is the general abandonment by the Democrats of their old sensitiveness about states' rights." Of the need for federal funds, thc *Nation* had no doubt. "The states . . . cannot meet the difficulty . . . the general government alone has the legal power and the money to do all that needs to be done. . . . [I]t is hardly possible that the constitutional duty of keeping rivers navigable, derived from the power to regulate interstate commerce, does not include the duty of keeping the waters of a great river within its banks, so that it shall not overflow vast tracts of country, and besides destroying enormous amounts of property, making its channel unapproachable for hundreds of miles by any species of vehicle." Noting recent floods—600,000 acres of farmland were under water—the *Nation* complained that "the Mississippi, in the condition in which it has been for the last two or three months, does not serve the purposes of interstate commerce. On the contrary, it cuts off the inhabitants of three or four States from the use of it for commercial purposes altogether, besides producing, in one of the richest agricultural regions in the Union, the effects of the ravages of an invading army."[137] A proposal to appropriate funds for the reclamation of land flooded by the Mississippi received a more negative reception. The *New York Times* labeled as "ridiculous" the claim that flood control was beyond the capacity of the states. Federal aid should be limited to improving navigation on the river.[138] An act of August 2, 1882, provided $4.9 million for improvements on the Mississippi; it stipulated that levees were to be built with federal money only when necessary to aid navigation.[139] During the coming years advocates of federal funds for flood prevention would offer a variety of arguments, the most ingenious of which may have been the claim that federal government bore an obligation to see that its property—the river itself—did not damage that of others. During the early twentieth century, the Mississippi River Commission began spending funds on flood control despite a lack of statutory authority.[140] It was not until 1917 that Congress authorized the use of federal funds for flood control.[141]

Although flooding would remain a problem, federal improvements on the river restored it to use in short order. By the early 1880s, navigation was so easy that traveling on it bored at least one contemporary. Mark Twain complained that the "national government has turned the Mississippi into a sort of two thousand mile torchlight procession." Improvements had "knocked the romance out of piloting." With these "abundant beacons and the banishment of snags, plenty of daylight in a box and ready to be turned on whenever needed, and a chart compass to fight the fog with, piloting, at a good stage of water, is now nearly as safe and simple as driving stage, and is hardly more than three times as romantic."[142] The improvements stimulated commerce and helped raise a devastated portion of the South from the desolation that enveloped it in the years after the war. The annual tonnage of goods passing through New Orleans went from 6,857 in 1875 to 453,681 in 1880.[143] The city jumped from 11th to 2nd among American ports in the quantity of goods handled. The achievement was especially notable in light of the fact that the extension of the eastern trunk lines to the Mississippi, in combination with the war, resulted in Midwestern farmers shipping their crops to east coast ports by rail—they did not return to their prewar practice of transporting the harvest to New Orleans by water. During the late nineteenth century, federal appropriations made possible critical improvements throughout the country, from the harbors of the east coast and shipping channels on the Great Lakes to the Missouri River and the waterways of the Northwest.

Not all river-and-harbor appropriations of the Gilded Age were useful. Their lack of utility to any end other than enhancing the ability of lawmakers to provide employment for voters was indicated by the fact that the names of the bodies being improved were not exactly familiar. The *New York Times* commented on this development in August 1879: "The curious student in geography will find in the river and harbor appropriation bills of the last five or six Congresses repeated biennial mention of rivers and harbors which are never heard of anywhere else." Perhaps the "maps of the schools" should "be amended and expanded by following the topography of the river and harbor appropriation bills." The editorial lamented that "no matter what else may fail, or what important public measure may be killed for want of time, the river and harbor appropriation bill always goes through without debate, under a suspension of the rules, if necessary, but it goes through because every member sees in it a chance to distribute the public money among his constituents."[144]

The political utility of these appropriations was demonstrated by the accomplishments of Miles Ross, Representative of New Jersey. He secured appropriations for the improvement of the Shrewsbury River following his election to Congress in 1878. Much of the money ended up in his pockets as well as those of other members of the local ring; Ross used part of his share to purchase his re-nomination from delegates at his district's Democratic convention. Enticements were necessary in part because Ross had promised to serve only one term, but he was still in office at when his practices were detailed in a *New York Times* article of July 1882. Survey work on the river provided employment for the sons of local politicians as well as others whose assistance was needed during political campaigns. The enterprise might have received more approval had it improved navigation on the Shrewsbury; in fact, it may have worsened it. Mud dredged from the river was taken upstream a quarter mile and dumped—it then moved downstream with the current. In Keyport Harbor, dredged soil from the front of a dike was placed in the back of it, causing the dike to collapse and filling in the hole from which mud had been removed.[145]

Ross was not alone in his avarice. A Minnesota Congressman was found to have secured appropriations for the improvement of waterways he used to float logs from the northern woods to his mills.[146] William Hepburn of Iowa complained of lawmakers obtaining appropriations benefiting their own homesteads. One colleague secured money to improve his own "harbor" despite the fact that it was "but the merest and most meager landing-place in which a steamboat could tie up to a stubbing post occasionally if there was a passenger to be landed, or if it happened there was a hogshead of tobacco to take on."[147] In his two-volume survey of the American political system, *The American Commonwealth*, Lord Bryce observed that the purpose of these appropriations, although "nominally in aid of navigation," was to "turn a stream of public money into the state or states where each improvement is executed." Bryce viewed the surplus as among the chief sources of the problem. America, he wrote, "is the only country in the world whose difficulty has mostly been not to raise money but to spend it."[148] The greed of members of Congress proved too much for Chester A. Arthur, who issued a widely applauded veto of an $18 million river-and-harbor bill on August 1, 1882. The president insisted that numerous projects for which the bill provided money were not conducive to the common defense or the general welfare; nor did they promote commerce among the states.[149]

Congress overrode the veto the day after it was issued.[150] The country sided with the president. A *New York Times* editorial of August 2 complained that it had been "many years" since "purely local jobs began to creep into this annual measure providing nominally for improvements upon rivers and harbors for the benefit of national commerce." As for the source of the problem, the *Times* pointed to logrolling. "Each member who asked more for his district was constrained to allow more for other districts, and thus we see the dimensions of the river and harbor appropriation advancing with steady but increasing strides from less than $4 million in 1870 to nearly $20 million this year."[151] As occurred with the tariff, parts of the country that were not favored by these appropriations did not call for their abolition; instead they wanted their share of the favors.

The *San Francisco Bulletin* lamented the neglect of the Sacramento River and the Joaquin River, both of which "needed dredging badly." They had "just as valid claims" as the Mississippi and the Missouri.[152] The *Nation* observed that the affinity for pork barrel spending seemed to be a bipartisan disease. "Democrats and Republicans will lustily abuse one another when the question is which party shall have the offices. They fight one another tooth and nail on the stump and at the polls. But when it comes to draining the treasury, a large majority of the chosen men of one party will harmoniously cooperate with a majority of the other like a band of brothers. They fight for the first seats at the table and embrace in the gutter."[153] The insistence of the House on overriding Arthur's veto proved costly. In November 1882 Republicans lost their majority in the midterm elections in large part due the drubbing they took in the press over their addiction to pork barrel spending.

While river-and-harbor appropriations provided jobs and tariffs promised higher wages and profits, those programs lacked the elegant simplicity of veterans' pensions, which placed federal revenue directly in the pocket of the voter—thus the appeal of military pensions after the Civil War. With the South lost to the opposition, generous pensions for Union Army veterans helped the Republican Party remain competitive in critical Midwestern states, where control of the presidency and Congress was often decided. Born of good intentions and necessity alike, the program degenerated into the most politicized and decrepit federal endeavor of the nineteenth century. Congress established the first pension for disabled veterans in 1790. The first service pension—benefits for the able-bodied as well as the injured—was introduced for Revolutionary War veterans in 1818. As of 1861, some 10,709 veterans were collecting a monthly check from the federal government.[154] During the Civil War, 2.2 million men served in the Union army; 364,000 were killed, leaving almost two million veterans who could look forward to receiving a monthly check from the government if they lived long enough.[155] The first pension act for Civil War veterans was enacted on July 14, 1862. It provided pensions of $8 and $30 a month, respectively, for privates or officers who suffered a disabling wound in the war; family members could succeed to the pension on the veteran's death if he died of a wound suffered in the war.[156]

By June 1872, the pension rolls included 95,405 disabled veterans as well as 113,518 widows and orphans, and 176,000 claims were being adjudicated.[157] Fraud quickly became a problem. The Secretary of the Interior claimed that one in four claims proved to be fraudulent on investigation and an estimate of 1873 held that $100,000 would have paid all the legitimate claims that year, but the actual appropriation was four times that amount as men collected pensions who had no disability.[158] The enterprising pension agents who had plagued Washington since the 1850s exacerbated the problem. They convinced lawmakers to push through private acts designating individuals for pensions at a monthly rate determined by Congress. Private acts were rarely preceded by investigations of any kind and the applicants for these measures—many of whom had already been turned down by the Pension Bureau—did little to substantiate their claims. Lawmakers approved the private bills of their colleagues to ensure that their own passed. As Benjamin Enloe of Tennessee explained in 1890, "if a government army mule were to come here and get his name on this calendar on Friday and some member were to propose a pension for that mule . . . there would not be a word of objection from any member here, because the objecting member would know that if he objected to the mule's bill the member presenting it would object to his."[159] The excesses of the pension agents responsible for these measures won them praise instead of contempt; after an Iowa pension attorney was convicted of defrauding the bureau of pensions, he was elected mayor of his hometown.[160]

In March 1875, Ulysses Grant found it necessary to veto the equalization of bounties bill. On the pretense that veterans who enlisted early in the war for three years had been underpaid—they received only $100 bounties while men who signed up later received larger amounts—the bill provided for gargantuan payments to three-year men, the cost of which was variously estimated between $60 and $100 million. Presidential secretary Orville Babcock, a Union army veteran himself, mishandled the veto message in the hope of preventing its publication.[161] Thereafter pension applications declined until 1879. The drop stemmed in part from the Consolidation Act of March 3, 1873, which allowed disabled veterans to apply for benefits that had already accumulated but only if they did so within five years of the date of their discharge. If they failed to file before the expiration date passed, they could still receive a pension, but not the accrued benefits running back to the war.[162]

Pension agents, tired of scouring the country for new cases, began to press for a new arrears act that would remove the five-year limitation. Their labors were rewarded with the Arrears of Pensions Act of January 25, 1879.[163] Pensions issued for injuries sustained during the war now commenced from the date of discharge or death and not the date of application, resulting in a vastly larger lump sum payment, even for those already on the pension lists. The widow of a soldier killed at Bull Run was now eligible for a lump sum payment of $1,728. If her late husband had been an officer she would have been eligible for $7,000.[164] This was a staggering sum at a time when the average American did not earn $500 a year. Some lawmakers realized Congress was opening Pandora's Box.

On January 16, 1879, Justin Morrill of Vermont warned the Senate that "nearly all the pensions that have been granted are to be reopened and a new account taken by the Commissioner of Pensions."[165] The *Nation* labeled the Arrears Act a "piece of demagogy of which a great many members of Congress saw the mischief," and claimed lawmakers passed it hoping the president would veto it. It reported that the Treasury Department was already contemplating a new bond issue to pay for the measure and predicted even that would only encourage more profligacy. "It is to be feared that the necessity of meeting the deficit may again open the floodgates of financial folly."[166] One Union army veteran wrote to the *Nation* of his disgust with the whole business. He complained that it is the "bummers, deadbeats, drunkards, shirks, cowards and bounty jumpers of our late war who are now the greatest part of the honored pensioners of our demagogue-depleted treasury." The veteran blamed the problem on "members of Congress with political aspirations" who feel they must look after "the soldier vote."[167] As applications poured in and the treasury emptied, Congress amended the Arrears Act to limit arrears to those who applied for pensions before June 1, 1880; pensions granted on applications filed after that date would commence only with the date of application.[168] Republicans called for repealing this limitation in their 1884 platform.[169] The Arrears Act proved more costly than even its critics had expected. The number of applications exploded and the cost of pensions went from $27 million in 1878 to $65 million in 1885.[170] Other than interest on the national debt, the expense of paying 325,000 pensioners—most of whom were voters—was the largest item in the budget.[171]

During the 1880s, the Grand Army of the Republic (the "G. A. R.") made its name as the first lobbying organization in American history that succeeded in extracting vast sums from Congress to enrich an element of the population at the rest of the country's expense. Formed in 1866, the organization remained quiescent until its leaders realized that northern lawmakers and Republicans in particular were mortally afraid of it. The G. A. R. received aid from the *National Tribune*, a Washington, DC, newspaper founded by claims agent George Lemon. The *Tribune* bullied lawmakers into loosening the federal purse strings for the benefit of veterans. During the Garfield and Arthur administrations, the G. A. R. worked with Commissioner of Pensions W. W. Dudley to develop lists of persons in each state who might be eligible for benefits but who had not yet applied.[172] Persons nominated for pension commissioner were confirmed by the Senate only after a withering confirmation process in which the senators satisfied themselves that the nominee would not be too rigid in evaluating applications. By the late 1880s, the commissioner tended to be not only a veteran but also one who had been disabled by wartime injuries. Dudley lost a leg at

Gettysburg. Benjamin Harrison's pension commissioner, James Tanner, lost both legs at Second Bull Run.

The use of tariffs and pensions to buy votes in the north was largely a Republican phenomenon; proposals to dilute the currency for the purpose of increasing prices were usually though not always the province of Democrats and various third parties. During the Civil War prices rose about 75 percent and wages rose about 50 percent. The "wage price squeeze" inflicted widespread hardship, though it was eased by a wartime boom that produced thousands of new jobs.[173] Inflation was produced in part by the issuance of greenbacks that were not backed in gold. With the end of the conflict, financial interests seeking to check the rise in prices sought the resumption of specie payments and the withdrawal of all greenbacks at the earliest possible date. They also wanted to ensure that the federal government paid its wartime debt in gold and not greenbacks. The support of industry for the withdrawal of greenbacks was far from unanimous; Pennsylvania coal and iron interests saw the benefits of inflation, and so did debt-ridden railroads. Labor and rural elements, which had embraced hard money during the antebellum period, now began to support greenbacks and inflationary monetary policies.[174]

The Johnson administration reduced the paper in circulation from $737 million to just under $600 million. When a financial panic in London of May 1866 spread to America and property values dropped, farmers blamed the upheaval on the contraction of the money supply.[175] Andrew Johnson allowed his conservative Secretary of the Treasury Hugh McCulloch to continue withdrawing greenbacks from circulation even as he himself embraced George Pendleton's Ohio idea.[176] The Ohio Democrat called for paying off the five-twenty bonds in greenbacks, thereby saving the government money—greenbacks were cheaper than gold—and enabling it to cut the burdensome wartime taxes that remained. Such a policy would also inject paper currency back into circulation, expand the money supply, and produce, or so it was thought, inflation and higher commodity prices sought by farmers.[177]

In 1869 Congress moved in the opposite direction. It enacted a law promising to pay most government debts in gold.[178] During his first term, Grant allowed the Treasury Department to redeem some bonds with greenbacks to aid western Republicans who were receiving a tongue lashing from farmers, many of whom were struggling with mortgages and falling commodity prices.[179] The Panic of 1873 led many business leaders, especially in the iron industry, to discover the virtues of inflation and they called on the administration to issue more greenbacks. In early 1874 Congress drafted a bill increasing the quantity of national bank notes and greenbacks in circulation (by a maximum of $64 million), but after a fierce campaign against the "inflation bill" led by Protestant ministers and liberal reformers, the president vetoed it. The nation was shocked and Republican politicians were appalled, as they feared the president had given Democrats an issue that would enable them to win the midterm elections.[180] Their fears were confirmed when the Democrats won a majority in the House of Representatives for the first time in 18 years. Following the election, the lame duck Republican Congress devised a measure designed to unite the wings of the party—it had been badly split between hard money elements and inflationists angry over the veto of the inflation bill. The bill eased the requirements for entities wishing to join the national bank system; it also promised to secure the resumption of specie payments, with an effective date of January 1, 1879. While most at the time regarded the promise as a hollow one—the Treasury did not have enough gold to redeem all of the greenbacks in circulation—the bill was passed by both houses of Congress.[181]

The president signed the Resumption Act of January 14, 1875. Greenbacks would be reduced to $300 million by January 1, 1879, and were expected to disappear completely after that date as a one dollar note could be exchanged for one dollar in gold.[182] To the surprise of nearly everyone, the deadline was met. Greenbacks did not disappear. In the midterm elections of 1875, state elections largely turned on the prospect of resumption. In Ohio and Pennsylvania it was the votes of the cities hostile to greenbacks and inflation that enabled Republicans to win narrow victories, while Democrats improved over their past performances in the coal and iron regions of both states. Ironmongers now embraced resumption and hard money. While some commercial elements had clamored for increasing the quantity of greenbacks in circulation during the years immediately after the Civil War, the business world became virtually unanimous in its opposition to the idea after passage of the Resumption Act, and remained so for the rest of the century.[183] Still, as late as 1884, the Republican campaign textbook described the party as the "Father, Friend and Guardian of the Republican greenback"; it also blamed Democrats for the contraction of the money supply.[184]

During the 1850s and 1860s, silver coins were rarely used and few were minted. As they were worth more than their face value, they tended to disappear from circulation. With European nations moving toward a gold standard, there seemed to be no reason for the United States to continue to use silver. In February 1873, Congress omitted silver coins for use in the domestic trade when it listed the types of coins to be issued by the Mint.[185] Production of silver increased after 1873 and its price dropped. Mining interests sought the coinage of silver in the belief that increased demand would boost prices. In part due to their longtime hostility to paper money, inflation-seeking farmers—many of whom had always been lukewarm in their support of greenbacks—embraced silver. Numerous Republicans in the Midwest also embraced the coinage of silver during the late 1870s, including James Garfield.[186] With the forces of inflation growing in strength and Democrats in control of the House, a bill providing for the coinage of silver passed the House in early 1878. The Senate revised the measure so it only required the treasury to buy $2 million to $4 million in silver in each month. The Bland-Allison Act became law on February 28, 1878.[187] The administration responded by purchasing the minimum amount of silver required by the law. The price of silver continued to drop as the western mines turned out more of it and by 1886 the silver in a dollar coin was worth only 78 cents, causing people to redeem silver dollars in gold, leaving the federal government to bear the loss.[188] The Bland-Allison Act did not produce inflation. Even as silver began to replace greenbacks as the favored tool of inflationists, the Greenback Party appeared to be on the verge of establishing itself as a viable third party during the late 1870s. In 1878 Greenback candidates polled over a million votes and elected 15 members to the House of Representatives, though many of the candidates were longtime Democrats.[189] The potency of currency manipulation as a political tool would continue to grow in coming years, as depressed commodity prices would weigh on farmers for the rest of the century.

FEDERAL NOVELTIES

The federal spoils system, protective tariffs, river-and-harbor appropriations, and the conversion of the currency question into a political dispute all contributed to the expansion of the pecuniary relationship between the American people and their national government. If Alexander Hamilton's claim that a power over a man's support brought with it a power over his will did not apply on every occasion, American political development during the Gilded Age attested to its fundamental validity. Civil servants sought to ensure the reelection of those to whom they owed their places, and voters supported those who promised to enhance their material well-being with tariffs, public works jobs, pensions, or inflation produced by a debased currency. All of these measures were long familiar to Americans, and few critics still bothered to claim that protection and river-and-harbor appropriations were beyond the authority of the federal government. There were other more novel federal initiatives during the Civil War and the period following it, some of which did go beyond the powers listed in the Constitution.

On May 15, 1862, Congress established a Department of Agriculture.[190] A search of Article I for the power that authorized such a department would have been a futile exercise. Nevertheless, its activities multiplied during the next 40 years. An 1877 law appropriated $18,000 for the hiring of entomologists; they were to report on Rocky Mountain locusts "and the best practical means of preventing their reoccurrence."[191] After the boll weevil spread east across the South from Mexico—it often cut cotton harvests in half—appropriations were for made in the hope of controlling the infestation.[192] A weather bureau, established in 1870, was transferred to the Department of Agriculture in 1890. By that time the Department oversaw 2,400 employees; about half of its budget went for research. On the eve of World War I, the Department of Agriculture was among the world's leading research institutions—it investigated everything from diseases of crops and animals to the physiology of insects and hybrid seeds.[193] Its supporters viewed the Department of Agriculture as a great success. Grover Cleveland's second secretary of agriculture was not a fan. Despite being an agriculturalist himself, Julius S. Morton viewed the Department as a bloated source of patronage and obtained authority to cut hundreds of jobs.[194]

Agriculture Department employees began examining infected cattle in 1877. A Veterinary Bureau was established in the Department in 1883 and in 1884 a bureau of animal husbandry followed. It was "to prevent the exportation of diseased cattle, and to provide means for the suppression and extirpation of pleuropneumonia and other contagious diseases among domestic animals."[195] The secretary of the treasury was authorized to establish rules regarding the transportation of livestock. In 1887 Congress enacted a law authorizing the Department of Agriculture to establish quarantine stations, carry out inspections, and if necessary destroy infected cattle.[196] While the bill being debated, Congressman Adoniram Warner of Ohio expressed his objections: "That there is any authority under our Constitution to go into the states, enter upon farms and go into stockyards and seize cattle and slaughter them under any pretense or for any great purpose, would not have been claimed or thought of twenty years ago." He conceded that Congress could regulate the movement of cattle among the states (presumably because at that point they qualified as interstate commerce), "but that is the exercise of a very different power from that proposed in this bill, which sends the agents of this government into the states and supplants the local authorities and takes supreme control of matters which I believe the people can much better, and certainly much more economically, manage themselves."[197] Benton McMillin of Tennessee objected because the bill would authorize Department of Agriculture officials to enter dwellings without probable cause—thereby violating the Fourth Amendment. "These agents of the Agriculture Department, above all law, above the Constitution, if they desire to do so, in violation of all rights of citizens, in every homestead in the state, are permitted to range at will." They will appear "armed with that Department's autocratic proclamation of war of extermination against his stock; and if you resist them you are dragged to federal court, and may be fined $500 and imprisoned one hundred days." McMillin insisted that the federal government could not touch cattle until they were moved out of state.[198] While lawmakers could question the constitutional basis for the program, they could not dispute its results—pleuropneumonia was wiped out by 1892.[199]

Congress also saw fit to involve itself in education despite the fact that Article I did not mention that subject either. The Morrill College Land Grant Act became law on July 2, 1862. It provided land in the West to each state (30,000 acres for each representative and senator), with proceeds from the sales of said lands to be used for the establishment and operation of agricultural colleges.[200] The use of land sale revenue stemmed from the belief that it was not subject to the limitations on congressional authority that applied to general revenues, which could be spent only on subjects related to one or more of the enumerated powers. The land grant colleges introduced a more scientific approach to farming, yet in time farmers began to feel the program benefited students more than them. Some states went so far as to abolish their land grant colleges. Seeking to demonstrate that its generosity could benefit farmers as well as students, Congress passed the Hatch Act in 1887, which established state-operated agricultural experimental stations.[201] The law provided for these entities to operate in association with the agriculture colleges for the purpose of researching plants, animals, diseases, and the "comparative advantage of rotative crop growing." The commissioner of agriculture obtained reports from the stations regarding their experiments and distributed them at no charge. Forty-three stations were in existence by the end of 1888.[202] The stations were also funded out of land sale revenues. A law of August 8, 1894, required the states to provide the Department of Agriculture with information regarding the stations so it could determine if the revenues turned over to them had been spent in accordance with the requirements of the 1887 law.[203]

A second Land Grant College Act enacted in 1890 increased the amount of land sale revenue provided to land grant colleges. It provided that states could not discriminate against blacks in admitting persons to colleges funded with land grant revenue, though they were given the option to establish separate schools for blacks, and several southern states did so.[204] The increased donations made possible by the law motivated the states to begin spending more of their own money. The number of land grant colleges grew from 36 in 1890 to 65 in 1900, and the number of students attending these schools grew during the same period from 6,147 to 39,505.[205] Whatever doubts members of Congress had over its power of appropriation at the time of the Morrill Act, they dissipated by the turn of century. In May 1900 Congress enacted a law providing for grants of general revenue to the states for the support of agricultural colleges whenever land sale revenues proved inadequate.[206]

While Civil War era lawmakers embraced the notion of turning land sale revenues over to the states for educational purposes, they found the idea of establishing a department of education more difficult to accept. When a bill for that purpose was proposed in early 1867, Senator Daniel S. Norton of Minnesota warned that a department of education would assume "control of the school systems of the various states." Garrett Davis of Kentucky did not believe Congress had the competence to "take under its care and management the subject of education." The bill struck him as "more of a device to create offices and patronage and to make drafts on the Treasury than anything else." He believed there were too many bureaus and he was willing to get rid of a half dozen of them: "This thing of Congress drawing into the vortex of the power of the national government so many subjects and interests that, according to my judgment, belong peculiarly to the states, and were intended to be left exclusively to state management, and that can be so much more wisely and successfully and beneficially managed by the states than by Congress, is a very mistaken policy."[207]

On March 2, 1867, the bill to establish a department of education became law. It authorized the new Department to collect and diffuse statistics regarding the "progress of education in the several States and Territories."[208] The commissioner was given the duty of reporting on the states' use of land sale revenues in operating land grant colleges. The Department of Education's life was a short one; it was renamed the Office of Education and transferred to the Department of the Interior via a law of July 20, 1868.[209] George Hoar recalled that when he arrived in the House of Representatives in 1869, the Office of Education "was exceedingly unpopular, not only with old strict constructionists, who insisted on leaving such things to the states, but with a large class of Republicans."[210] Hoar embraced a federal role in education. The Massachusetts congressman proposed a bill distributing land sale revenues for the benefit of common (primary) schools. Senator Justin Morrill blocked consideration of the measure, as he wanted land sale revenues reserved for the land grant colleges devised under the act that bore his name.[211]

While the claim that the territories clause gave the federal government authority to spend land sale revenues for purposes beyond the enumerated powers had been hotly disputed from the time it first appeared during the 1820s until the Civil War, no one denied the existence of a general legislative power in the western territories. Congress could ban items or conduct in the West that it could not have prohibited in the states. A law of 1862 criminalized polygamy, but enforcement proved difficult as the occurrence of a "polygamous ceremony" was hard to prove.[212] The Edmunds Acts of 1882 and 1887 strengthened the prohibition; in an effort to remove all traces of what was regarded as a scourge, they also made cohabitation, adultery, and fornication crimes and disincorporated the Mormon Church. Polygamists were stripped of the right to vote and sit on juries.[213] In practice Congress delegated at least a portion of its authority to the territorial legislatures, though as the struggle over polygamy indicated, it was not shy about enacting laws covering every aspect of life when the assemblies in the territories failed to act. Nor was it reluctant to invalidate territorial laws it deemed injurious.

Perhaps the most significant exercise of the authority of Congress in the West occurred under its war and postal powers—the funding and construction of railroads. The Pacific Railroad Act of July 1, 1862, provided for the construction of a transcontinental railroad.[214] The law proved inadequate: Its terms were too harsh and investors stayed away from the project. A second Pacific Railway Act became law in 1864; it doubled the land grant and provided mineral rights.[215] The Union Pacific, which proceeded west from Missouri, and the Central Pacific, which moved east from California, were each granted large swaths of land along the line as well as financial aid. Pursuant to the terms of the Pacific Railway Acts, federal officials served on the board of directors of the Union Pacific until the line finished paying back its federal loans (bonds) in 1897.[216] Congress also incorporated and provided land—but not money—to entities hoping to build three other transcontinental lines; only one was completed (the Northern Pacific). Numerous other lines also obtained land grants in the West—future profits from the sale of the real estate aided the sale of the bonds, the proceeds from which funded construction. Fraud was rampant among the western land grant railroads; the lines cost three times what they should have due to the greed of promoters and the lack of federal oversight. Railroads ended up owning vast swaths of the West when states as well as the federal government proved too exuberant in their willingness to give away land. The lines received one-fourth of Minnesota and Washington, as well as one-fifth of Wisconsin, Iowa, Kansas, North Dakota, and Montana.[217]

Railroads were not alone in benefiting from federal largesse. At least 15 million acres passed from the Interior Department into private hands each year from 1873 to 1887.[218] The independence of the western pioneer has been made the stuff of legend and lore, but the settlers of the trans-Mississippi region were not shy about demanding federal assistance. Their primary demand was for water and if Congress could not enact a law making it rain, it could aid the cause of irrigation. The Desert Land Act of March 3, 1877, was designed to encourage Americans to purchase and irrigate large farms in the West.[219] It provided for the sale of up to 640 acres at 25 cents an acre to anyone who filed a declaration indicating "he intends to reclaim a tract of land, not exceeding one section, by conducting water upon the same, within the period of three years thereafter." Irrigated lands totaled 3.6 million acres by 1890.[220] During the drought of the late 1880s, Congress authorized surveys for irrigation in the Plains states. The Carey Act of 1894 provided a land grant of up to a million acres to states in the West that agreed to irrigate it and sell it to farmers.[221] The measure enriched companies that built irrigation channels and triggered a land boom, but its inadequacies led to demands that the federal government fund irrigation directly. Both parties endorsed the idea during the presidential campaign of 1900.[222] California lawyer George Maxwell led a powerful irrigation lobby—the Irrigation Congress—that received ample funds from the western railroads.

In 1901 Senator Francis Newlands of Nevada proposed a bill authorizing the federal government to build irrigation canals in the West. Representative Roswell Flower of New York wondered whether Congress ought to irrigate land when farmers were struggling under the burden of an agricultural surplus. He thought the program would be too expensive and believed irrigation was best left to the states.[223] Such wisdom was of another time and when Theodore Roosevelt embraced the bill, it moved through Congress with relative ease. The Newlands Act became law on July 17, 1902.[224] It provided for the use of land sale revenues to fund irrigation projects in semiarid states in the West, with general revenues to be used if the former proved inadequate. By the fall of 1906, 23 major projects were underway and $40 million had been spent. Eight hundred miles of canals had been dug.[225] The Reclamation Service built dams on some rivers and sold the electricity. The irrigation program received widespread approval despite the expense involved, in part because commercial interests operated under the impression that it would enable farmers to cultivate the entirety of the West, "from the Mississippi to the Pacific."[226] Advocates sold irrigation projects as the equivalent of rivers-and-harbors projects in the East—a comparison that would prove all too accurate in coming years, as their locations were often determined by political considerations instead of merit. In time westerners would discover that their rivers did not hold limitless amounts of water. Federal reclamation projects were also hobbled by numerous mistakes: Soil was irrigated that was far too acidic to be farmed and officials vastly underestimated the amount of water necessary to cultivate semiarid lands. Those enticed to work the reclaimed land often gave up after a few years due to the harsh conditions and rigorous loan terms.[227] An attempt to irrigate a large area of western Nevada by diverting water from the Truckee and Carson Rivers failed due to a lack of water, but not before Reclamation Service officials tried to take over Lake Tahoe—one of the most scenic bodies of water on the continent—to divert its waters to the failing project. After securing control of a small dam on the lake, the Bureau threatened to flood the lands of locals if they did not sell their lots. Thereafter officials altered the lake level, causing floods and subjecting the federal government to lawsuits.[228] The episode constituted an early example of the havoc that federal agencies could inflict far from Washington when they received inadequate supervision. Still the reclamation program proved critical to the settlement of wide areas in the West. The Roosevelt Dam on the Salt River in Arizona made the settlement and growth of Phoenix possible, and dams in Idaho and Colorado made farmland out of what had been desolate and barren country.

The mountain states owed their early development to mining, though the profits tended to move out of state and their populations remained small for decades after the available minerals had been extracted. The industry received invaluable aid from the reports of the U.S. Geological Survey. Established in 1879, it classified the public lands and identified mineral deposits.[229] Gold and silver brought people to Nevada and Colorado, while copper was the attraction in Arizona and Montana. In the Pacific Northwest, the lumber industry prospered exploiting lands that had been sold indiscriminately by the federal government. In the western Plains cattle was the first enterprise—aided in great part by the willingness of cattlemen to fatten their animals on public land without paying for the privilege and the willingness of the federal government to let them. This oversight was forgivable; allowing them to do the same on Indian lands was not. When the cattle kings started stringing barbed wire across thousands of acres they had not bothered to purchase, Grover Cleveland forced them to change their ways. The cattle barons controlled the Wyoming Territory for a time, just as the Southern Pacific dominated California and the copper kings ruled Montana. Flaws and all, the western territories formed and matured, adding a new section with new interests to the nation. Six states in the West obtained admission in 1889–90; Utah in 1896—after it agreed to ban polygamy—Oklahoma in 1907, New Mexico and Arizona in 1912. A Union of equals had grown from 13 to 48 states. "The greatest experiment in colonial policy and administration of modern times had been brought to a conclusion successful beyond the wildest dreams of those who inaugurated it."[230]

Farming on the Great Plains was made possible by the confinement of Indians to reservations, railroads, barbed wire, and special growing methods that accounted for the shortage of water. The federal government sent in the army to route the Indians, gave financial assistance to railroads, and funded irrigation projects. What it did not do was provide adequate law enforcement personnel. The western territories did not have enough courts and judges as Congress proved unwilling to spend adequately on a subject for which there was no immediate political benefit. Turnover among underpaid judges, U.S. attorneys, and marshals was rampant. Courts often lacked the money needed to operate. Federal judges in the West had to ride circuit like the lawyers who appeared before them. "Courts on wheels" were seen as late as 1903 (with marshals often serving as judges) and in Alaska judicial proceedings took place on boats during the summer months.[231] Where the law was absent, vigilantism appeared.

The relationship between the history of American Indians and the development of the federal system is a complicated one. Broadly speaking, the federal government bestowed rights on Native Americans in exchange for the right to push them farther West and then allowed states as well as corporations and private citizens to violate those rights. In no area of American life except race relations was a vigorous exercise of federal power needed more, and in no other area was federal authority so hotly opposed and so utterly anemic. Generals who earned their places in history smashing the armies of the Confederacy to pieces found themselves outwitted, outgunned, and outlasted by prospectors, cattle barons, and land-hungry farmers in the West. Philip Sheridan might have been able to cleanse the Shenandoah Valley of rebels, but he could not keep prospectors from flooding the Sioux reservation in the Black Hills when gold was discovered there in 1875.[232] The May 1868 Treaty of Fort Laramie gave the Black Hills to the Sioux but the treaty was violated within a year by crews of the Northern Pacific Railroad.[233] Such failures stemmed largely from the fact that the million-man Union army of the Civil War had disappeared. In 1868 a regular army of only 26,000 troops occupied perhaps 100 posts throughout the west.[234] The Indian Bureau was hampered by patronage and the insistence of many of its employees on defrauding the population they were expected to serve. Management of Indian relations was so haphazard that federal officials often entered into treaties with Indian tribes and then failed to inform Army officers in the West of these agreements. Peaceful tribes were herded onto reservations where they were often left to starve, while violent Indians were rewarded with food in an attempt to appease them.[235] Army officers failed to prevent white attacks on Indians or Indian attacks on whites, and all too often they responded with more force than was necessary.

The Grant administration pursued a "peace policy" under which it encouraged Indians to become self-supporting even as it demanded that the last few nomadic tribes in the West remove themselves to reservations or face the U.S. military. Native Americans received industrial and agricultural training in schools funded by Congress and supervised by a newly established commission that was itself dominated by prominent ministers and leaders of various Protestant denominations. These men had been lobbying federal officials for years to let them take the lead in Indian policy in the belief that they could succeed where Washington had failed and turn Indians into self-sustaining, law-abiding Americans. The Grant administration and Congress were only too happy to comply. Their enthusiasm stemmed in part from the relentless lobbying campaign of the leading Protestant denominations; it may also have arisen out of the frustration of lawmakers with the need to appropriate money to meet every conceivable expense of those living on reservations, from the pay of blacksmiths and carpenters to the cost of maintaining tools. The effort enjoyed only mixed success. During the 1870s, Texans became infuriated with the Grant administration's peace policy and its reversal of an earlier decision to remove all Indians from their state. They also took offense at the army's restraint—it repeatedly defeated Indian war parties in battle and then failed to apprehend their members. Raids across the Red River into the state from the Indian Territory (present-day Oklahoma) as well as incursions from New Mexico further strained the patience of Texans. Finally, the Texas Rangers—state law enforcement officers—took it upon themselves to bar Indians from entering the state.[236]

An act of March 3, 1871, provided that in the future no Indian tribe within the United States would be recognized as an independent nation with whom the federal government could enter into treaties.[237] The act was consistent with earlier Supreme Court decisions holding the tribes did not constitute independent nations or sovereign entities, as well as the language of the commerce clause, which provided for the regulation of commercial activity with Native American tribes and foreign nations separately.[238] Complicating matters was the legal status of the individual Native American. In *Elk v. Wilkins* (1884), the Supreme Court ruled that Indians were not citizens, and this ruling remained in effect until citizenship was bestowed by federal statute in 1924.[239] An 1885 law subjected all persons on Indian reservations to trial in federal court for serious crimes such as murder. The Supreme Court upheld the law, explaining that Native Americans remained under the "political control" of the federal government and the states.[240] The 1887 Dawes Act divided some but not all tribal lands among their members.[241] The law proved highly beneficial to whites, as about two-thirds of Indian lands were transferred to them during the next 50 years.[242] It did not achieve its intended purpose of assimilating Indians into American society; among other problems, the law provided for the distribution of land in the Great Plains that was not suitable for farming, at least not in small lots. During World War I the

Interior Department began giving land patents to those Native Americans who were deemed worthy by "competency commissions." It had to terminate the practice when it was found that the patents were being sold almost as soon as they were issued. The cause of assimilation led to absurd attempts to stamp out the remnants of Indian culture; at the end of the century the Commissioner of Indian Affairs barred Native Americans of both sexes who lived on reservations from wearing their hair long.[243] The sufferings of Native Americans at the hands of Indian Bureau officials gave an early demonstration of the perils faced by any group unfortunate enough to become dependent on the federal government.

Federal power grew in myriad ways during the period after the Civil War. Advances were made in Congress through broad constructions of the powers of the national government listed in Article I, Section 8. Advocates of states' rights and a strict construction of these powers often perceived major departures in even modest legislation, but they often failed to convince the country to refrain from novelty, experiment, and consolidation. Four episodes—the debate over appropriations for the Centennial Exhibition, the expansion of postal functions, federal intervention in public health regulation, and the use of the tax code to penalize an unpopular industry—give some idea of the steady if chaotic expansion of federal authority during the Gilded Age.

In early 1876 Congress took up a bill to appropriate $1.5 million for the Centennial Exhibition in Philadelphia scheduled for that summer. Some lawmakers doubted the authority of Congress to devote money to a subject that did not appear related to any of the enumerated powers. Precedent helped the cause of the bill; in 1861 $2,000 was devoted to an American exhibit at an industrial exhibition in London; five years later funds were set aside for a similar event in Paris.[244] Proponents of the bill's legality embraced a broad spending power. Their ranks included Democratic Congressman Thomas L. Jones. In his view, the powers of the states could not be maintained with the aggressiveness of past years: "Why, sir, how is it that Congress appropriates money to build great hospitals for the sick and wounded and aged soldiers and sailors of the Union? There is no definite power in the Constitution to build a hospital. How is it that Congress grants pensions and appropriates millions every year to pay for them? The specific power is not in the Constitution; the word pension cannot be found in the instrument. How was it that even yesterday this House passed bill giving a salary for life to a feeble and paralyzed judge, retiring him before the limitation in time fixed by law?" In his view, these appropriations derived authority from the general welfare clause—"one of the enumerated powers of the Constitution." It bestowed ample authority for Congress to spend money in aid of the exhibition at Philadelphia.[245]

Charles Joyce, a Vermont Republican, disagreed: "I emphatically deny the doctrine that the Constitution either in letter or spirit authorizes Congress to make a gift or to loan money to any individual or corporation for any purpose whatsoever." Some claimed Congress could appropriate money for any project that would promote commerce. Joyce warned that if this was so, "Congress may charter fairs and agricultural shows in every county in the Union." After complaining that the people of Vermont were already "groaning under a load of taxes [imposed by] state, town and village, which is grinding them down to the very earth," Joyce charged that that the Democratic majority had backed down on its promise to "squander no more of the national treasure, and cut down the extravagant expenditures of the government."[246]

Veterans' hospitals and pensions as well as the debt produced by the war had all occurred in the exercise of the war powers of Congress—they did not need to be justified via a broad spending power. Nathaniel P. Banks of Massachusetts—a former Republican speaker of the House who had defected to the Democrats—dismissed the idea that the general welfare clause bestowed authority for the bill; instead he believed the United States could enter into compacts with other nations, and that an invitation to participate in an exhibition constituted such a compact.[247] Lucius Q. C. Lamar of Mississippi insisted that the general welfare clause "contains no substantive or affirmative grant of power to Congress." It is only "a restriction upon the powers which are grouped around it, and it means that Congress shall have power to lay and collect taxes and duties only for the objects therein prescribed—the common defense and general welfare." He thought the commerce clause authorized the appropriation—if Congress could spend money to explore the Arctic Ocean in the hope of stimulating commerce, it could spend money to "bring the commerce of the world to our own shores."[248] Congress passed the bill and it became law on February 16, 1876.[249]

The spending power question would continue to be debated in the coming years, with varying degrees of enthusiasm and sincerity. Many Republicans and a few Democrats acted under the impression that it had been resolved and that the old Madisonian view—that the general welfare clause did not provide a broad spending power and Congress could appropriate money only for subjects listed in Article I, Section 8 of the Constitution—had long since been discredited.[250] If anything, the contrary was the truth. During ratification, proponents of the Constitution did not inform the states that the general welfare clause bestowed a broad spending power. In the Federalist #41, James Madison suggested that it bestowed no powers of any kind. Consequently, Democrats had little difficulty demonstrating that a broad spending power via the general welfare clause was a figment of Alexander Hamilton's vivid imagination. Leaders of the opposition parties, including Henry Clay and William Seward, also dismissed the notion of a broad spending power.[251] When pushing federal expenditures for projects such as river-and-harbor projects, lawmakers cited the commerce power as authority for these measures. By 1861, the view that Congress enjoyed a broad power of appropriation had been all but abandoned.[252]

No one disputed the power of the national government over the mails. Article I, Section 8 authorized Congress to establish "post offices and post roads." By the middle of the nineteenth century, the inefficiencies of the post office were already legend; during the 1840s it was almost abolished due to excessive charges and the lower rates of private carriers.[253] Most federal employees toiled in the Post Office, even though free delivery did not arrive until 1863, and then only in the cities. The campaign to extend free delivery to rural areas began in 1879 with Illinois editor John M. Stahl. Progress was slow but steady. Towns of 20,000 or more were included in the system in 1887.[254] The idea of delivering mail at no charge even in the countryside encountered a surprising amount of resistance in a nation that was still largely rural. In 1892 its chief promoter in Congress, Tom Watson of Georgia, assured critics that it would both increase federal revenues and extend "the blessings of culture, refinement and education" to the "remotest confines of the republic."[255] Benjamin Enloe of Tennessee objected to the idea of adding to the "66,384 postmasters we already have." Such persons would, if hired, "become active agents for the administration in power, as our postmasters generally are."[256] An experimental program was begun in 1896 over the objections of many, including President Cleveland. By 1905 over 32,000 rural routes were in operation serving over 12 million persons despite the resistance of postmasters. They wanted to continue a system that forced people to come to their post offices, which were often located in general stores they owned.[257]

A more controversial proposal occurred in response to Western Union's control of most of the country's telegraph lines. In December 1869, Representative C. C. Washburn of Wisconsin called for the federal government to either buy the lines of Western Union or set up its own and charge low prices for the use of them, with the post office operating the network. He estimated the cost of building a government network to be $10 million—less than the amount "that was so cheerfully voted away to pay for Alaska [1867]." Washburn's ire seems to have originated in the cost of sending a 10-word telegraph message from the national capital to Lacrosse, Wisconsin—three dollars.[258] The federal government owned the first telegraph line in the country and operated it for a time, but sold it in 1847.[259] Congress funded the construction of a transcontinental telegraph line in 1860.[260] When the idea of having the post offices operate telegraphs surfaced in 1872, James Garfield, normally a friend of federal authority, was appalled. "I greatly dread," he wrote, "the postal telegraph scheme and its effects on the government in the direction of centralizing its power."[261] Two years later Garfield listened as New York lawyer Grosvenor Lowrey told a congressional committee there were constitutional difficulties in the proposal. As Garfield recalled, Lowrey "advanced the idea that the original purpose of the post office, as provided for in the Constitution, was to send parcels and packages and not to send intelligence and [he] asserted that the telegraph was not an incident to the power of establishing post offices and post roads."[262] As the *Springfield Daily Republican* described it, some of the opposition seems to have stemmed from the "serious danger" that would arise out of "creating 20,000 new offices to be put under partisan control."[263] Edward Rosewater, editor of the *Omaha Bee* and a former telegraph operator for Western Union, argued in favor of the proposal. As government employees cannot strike, publicly operated telegraph lines would, he explained, eliminate the possibility of labor discord in a business that was critical to the national economy.[264] The nation's telegraph system remained in private hands.

In 1873 President Grant endorsed the idea of "postal savings depositories."[265] The appeal of postal savings banks stemmed from the fact that private banks often failed (many went under during the depression of the 1870s), thereby rendering their notes worthless and depriving depositors of their savings. The successful implementation of the idea in Great Britain revealed that it could work, and demand for such a program rose even as state banks made a comeback after the Civil War—there were 4,405 by 1900—perhaps because most remained small and unsteady. (National banks, barred by law from expanding across state lines, numbered 3,731 in 1900.)[266] *Harper's Weekly* endorsed the idea of postal savings banks in 1886. It suggested that depositors could be paid 1 or 2 percent interest—no more lest Americans be discouraged from investing in more profitable ventures—out of funds to be raised by investing the deposits in U.S. bonds.[267] The *Springfield Daily Republican* took a different view. While conceding that "thrift is a virtue so necessary to contented citizenship that government is bound to encourage it by the foundation of institutions for promoting savings," it opposed postal savings banks. The states should authorize the establishment of savings banks, as Massachusetts had. "In a federal republic like our own, and under our Constitution as it exists, the social concerns are mostly left to the care of the states, and to the states properly belong the nurture and regulation of savings banks." The savings of people should remain in their states and finance local improvements and not go to Washington to be used for the purchase of bonds. The

Springfield Daily Republican noted that Massachusetts had 165 banks serving 738,000 depositors, almost all of which survived the depression of the 1870s without having to suspend payments.[268] Postal savings banks remained a prominent issue; the Populists embraced them during the 1890s and in 1908 the Republicans endorsed the idea in their platform of that year. Democrats did as well, on the condition that the deposits of said banks would not be funneled into Wall Street.[269] A Postal Savings Bank Act became law on June 25, 1910; the institutions thereby established never posed a serious threat to savings banks.[270]

The most novel exercise of the postal power during the Gilded Age may have been its use to suppress obscene materials. Obscenity had long been banned by the states; Congress entered the field in 1842 when it banned the importing of obscene prints.[271] In an effort to protect members of the Union army, in 1865 Congress banned obscene as well as "vulgar and indecent" materials from the mails.[272] The prohibition was strengthened by an 1872 statute.[273] An act of 1873 known as the Comstock law expanded this prohibition to include equipment or drugs used to induce abortions or prevent conception and all persons were barred from importing these items. Mere possession of them was banned in Washington, DC, and the territories.[274] While these laws constituted an extraordinary use of the power to establish post offices and roads, they were not subject to criticism in Congress due to the realization that only the national government could exercise a "police power" over the mails. If the national government did not have to transfer explosives or poisons, presumably it did not have to transfer items whose destructive qualities were of a more abstract nature. It was perhaps inevitable that a power to interdict obscene materials would be abused. The chief perpetrator was one Anthony Comstock, a New York City dry goods clerk who seems to have been equally troubled by depictions of the human form and the frailties of human nature. Comstock first gained fame when he secured the prosecution of suffragist Victoria Woodhull for violating state obscenity laws. She had dared to write a newspaper article disclosing details of the extramarital affair of Henry Ward Beecher and Elizabeth Tilton. Comstock used his connections with the bankers influential with the Grant administration and the scandal-induced weakness of Republicans in Washington to push through the above-mentioned 1873 law that bore his name. His willingness to mail tawdry postcards to lawmakers also helped. Thereafter Congress created a new office—special postal agent—and Comstock was appointed to the position. He spent the next 40 years entering homes and businesses in New York City without a warrant and arresting those who possessed obscene materials. Comstock incarcerated Frank Leslie until the editor agreed to refrain from printing advertisements for books he found objectionable.[275] When he obtained the conviction of "marriage reform" advocate Ezra Hervey Heywood for mailing obscene materials and the defendant was sentenced to two years at hard labor, Bostonians rallied in protest at Faneuil Hall and the president pardoned Heywood.[276] By the late 1880s Comstock was reduced to harassing New York City art dealers over items such as a Rodin statue.[277] Congress continued its efforts even after Comstock destroyed his credibility; in 1897 it banned the transportation of obscene materials across state lines via common carriers or express companies.[278] As late as the 1920s, postal and customs inspectors were destroying copies of James Joyce's *Ulysses* and other books they viewed as obscene.

If obscenity could be barred from the mails, why not other corrupting materials? In a message of July 29, 1890, Benjamin Harrison urged Congress to deploy the postal power against lottery tickets. He explained that the "use of the mails is quite as essential to the (lottery) companies as the state license. It would be practically impossible for these companies to exist if the public mails were effectively closed against their advertisements and remittances. The use of the mails by these companies is a prostitution of an agency only intended to serve the purposes of a legitimate trade and a decent social intercourse."[279] Congress complied with his request and enacted a law of September 19, 1890, barring the use of the mail to distribute information regarding lotteries. Even newspapers advertising lotteries were barred from the mails.[280] Two years later the Supreme Court upheld the law. In his opinion for the high court, Chief Justice Melvin Fuller explained that prior to ratification, the states could use their police powers to prevent the use of the mails for pernicious ends. With the adoption of the Constitution, a power over the mails as complete as that formerly possessed by the states passed to Congress. Nor did the ban on newspapers advertising lotteries impair the freedom of the press. "The circulation of newspapers is not prohibited, but the government declines itself to become an agent in the circulation of printed matter which it regards as injurious to the people."[281]

As Congress deployed the postal power to protect citizens from vice, it utilized the commerce power to protect them from disease. Prior to the Civil War it had required customs officials to comply with state quarantine laws. In May 1866 lawmakers contemplated enlisting the federal government in the effort to limit the spread of a cholera epidemic. Republicans differed even among themselves over the question of whether that task should be left to the states. An 1870 yellow fever epidemic in the South led Congress to consider passing a quarantine law; southern Democrats resisted due to constitutional concerns. The tide began to turn after yellow fever outbreaks in 1873 and 1876. On April 29, 1878, the National Quarantine Act became law. It authorized the Marine Hospital Service to work with state authorities in imposing quarantines and required U.S. diplomatic personnel in foreign cities to provide information regarding outbreaks of disease in those cities.[282] Yet another yellow fever outbreak hit the southern states during 1878. The outbreak cost 15,000 lives. An 1879 Senate Report held that Congress lacked authority to interfere with quarantine regulations of the states, yet it also insisted that Congress could "regulate commerce as to prevent the importation of contagious or infectious diseases from foreign countries and from one state to another."[283]

In December 1878 President Hayes called for the establishment of a national sanitary administration that would "not only control quarantine, but have the same sanitary supervision of internal commerce in time of epidemics, and hold an advisory relation to the state and municipal health authorities, with power to deal with whatever endangers the public health, and which the municipal and state authorities are unable to regulate."[284] Not everyone saw the need for national intervention. When Congress took up a bill to establish a national health board with quarantine powers, Congressman William Fleming of Georgia wondered if the national government could assume jurisdiction over everything that killed large numbers of people. "If yellow fever has slain its thousands, quackery has slain its tens of thousands. If we have the power to enact quarantine laws to prevent yellow fever, then we have the power to put down quackery by prescribing the qualifications of every practitioner of medicine in the Union. There is no difference in the cases. In each case the object is to protect the health and lives of our people. But who believes that we have the power to regulate the practice of medicine in the states? And yet we have the power to do it if we have the power to enact quarantine laws."[285]

The *New York Times* claimed that the outbreak of 1878 along the lower Mississippi cost $100 million in losses. Yet the "authorities of New Orleans and Memphis have, with amazing supineness, neglected to do anything to prevent a repetition of the terrible experience." It "behooves the national authority to make rigid regulations for internal as well as external quarantine. Its powers in that regard depend upon its right to regulate commerce, which is as complete in respect to communication between states as to that with foreign countries." The *Times* called for the quarantine of districts where the epidemic exists "by the interruption of all interstate communication with them."[286] On March 3, 1879, Congress established the National Board of Health.[287] It was assigned the task of obtaining "all information on all matters affecting the public health." The board would report to the next Congress regarding a plan for a national public health organization, with special attention being given to the subject of quarantine and "the possibility of a national quarantine system." When southerners continued to insist that Congress did not have authority to impose quarantines even as they demanded that the federal government eradicate pleuropneumonia among cattle, the *Chicago Daily Tribune* suggested that they seemed to be favoring aid for "sick cows" over aid for "sick men." In the view of the *Tribune*, "if the Government cannot interfere to prevent yellow fever, it has no right to eradicate pleuropneumonia."[288] A law of June 2, 1879, authorized the Board of Health to cooperate with the states to prevent the introduction of contagious diseases into the United States or from one state into another. It empowered the president to impose quarantines through the Board of Health even when states would not.[289] A Senate report of 1882 credited the Board with limiting the damage wrought by an 1879 outbreak of yellow fever. It noted that money appropriated for the new agency was often turned over to local officials who used it to construct quarantine facilities and fund the enforcement of their own measures. The report claimed that appropriations for lighthouses, the Lifesaving Service, and steamboat inspections, as well as laws barring explosives from steamboats, confirmed the legality of measures designed to protect the health of those engaged in interstate commerce.[290]

Unfortunately the Board of Health ran afoul of vested interests. Louisiana officials took offense when it attempted to oversee the wholly lackadaisical efforts of that state to prevent its ports from serving as conduits for disease. Officials at the Marine Hospital Service resented having the power to oversee quarantines taken from them. The law authorizing the Board to oversee quarantine-related issues was not reauthorized in 1883, and its duties returned by default to the Marine Hospital Service, to which they had been assigned in 1878.[291] The development of the Marine Hospital Service itself constituted an extraordinary chapter in the history of American federalism. Originally established in 1798 to serve members of the merchant marine on the east coast, it was funded by a tax on the wages of seamen until 1884, when a tonnage tax was imposed. During the early nineteenth century marine hospitals were established at inland points inland such as Louisville, Kentucky, to serve those who worked aboard steamboats. Although the Civil War resulted in the destruction or abandonment of many hospitals, the service survived and was reorganized in 1871.

In 1888 Congress appropriated $100,000 to eradicate yellow fever.[292] An 1890 law authorized the secretary of the treasury to issue regulations and appoint inspectors to effect said regulations when cholera, yellow fever, or smallpox exists in one state or territory and threatened to spread to another.[293] During the following year, the Marine Hospital Service began examining immigrants arriving in New York City to ensure they did not suffer from infectious diseases. The office of the Superintendent of Immigration oversaw the treatment of immigrants following its establishment in 1891.[294] In 1909, 8,649 immigrants were treated at a marine hospital established on

Ellis Island, New York. Overall, more than 50,000 persons, most of whom were sailors, received treatment at marine hospitals that year. The division of domestic quarantine, established under the Quarantine Act of 1893, investigated typhoid fever in Chicago and Omaha, yellow fever in New Orleans and Laredo, and bubonic plague in California.[295] The law also abolished the moribund National Board of Health and authorized the Marine Health Service to enforce quarantine regulations. In 1901 labs devoted to the investigation of communicable and infectious diseases were established. During the following year, federal entities performing work related to the public health were consolidated within the new Public Health and Marine Hospital Service, which replaced the Marine Hospital Service in 1902.[296] This entity was renamed the Public Health Service by a 1912 law that authorized it to investigate "diseases of man" and "conditions influencing the propagation and spread thereof" including "sanitation, sewage and the pollution of navigable streams and lakes."[297]

The need for federal regulation of other activities previously left to the states was less apparent. The dairy industry, long limited by the difficulty of preserving its products, came into its own during the 1880s, only to suffer what it considered illegitimate competition from manufacturers of oleomargarine, a cheap substitute for butter. Made from animal fats or vegetable oils, lawmakers and lobbyists sensitive to dairy interests insisted it was a health threat. In fact it was not—while oleomargarine was adulterated on occasion, so was butter and virtually every other food product. Still, seven states banned it.[298] In 1886 Congress considered a bill to impose punitive taxes on oleomargarine. The use of the tax power to punish and deter activity otherwise beyond the reach of the federal government had some precedent; state bank notes had been effectively banned via prohibitory taxes. Senator Wilkinson Call of Florida explained that the Constitution does not require that taxes fall equally on all industries; nor does it require that federal taxes be consistent with the "law or the policy of the states."[299] Congressman William Oates of Alabama derided the oleomargarine bill as "full of hypocrisy and false pretence." It purported "to be a bill to raise revenue, when in fact its purpose is not to raise revenue but to break down and destroy one branch of industry to foster and build up another." What right, he asked, "has Congress to prohibit the raising of sorghum or the making of glucose, beet, and maple sugar?" None that he could see. "Discriminations by Congress (in) favor of the industries of our own people against foreign competitors are familiar to every reader of our statutes, but discrimination as between rival industries of our own people is a new and vicious departure."[300] The *Chicago Daily Tribune* scoffed—oleomargarine was unfit for human consumption. In its view, "the constitutional argument against the bill is a makeshift resorted to in default of other means to kill it by delaying action."[301] The bill passed and became law on August 2, 1886. It imposed steep license taxes on manufacturers, wholesalers, and retailers of oleomargarine as well as a five cent tax on each pound manufactured and a two cent a pound tax at the point of sale.[302]

With the door ajar, other interests rushed forward to tax their competitors or foes out of existence. Farmers had long blamed futures exchanges for low crop prices. During the early 1890s Congress considered bills imposing punitive license taxes on dealers of futures and options. An 1890 bill offered by Senator John J. Ingalls of Kansas—who was under fire from Populist farmers angry over crop prices—would have imposed a $1,000 license tax on futures and options dealers and required them to post a bond of $50,000 with collectors.[303] When a similar bill was proposed in 1892, Congress Amos Cummings of New York objected. He pointed out that the exchanges where these dealers worked were incorporated and regulated by the states. The measure was little more than a "low attempt to circumvent the Constitution. It wipes out not only state boundaries, but it interferes with the private rights of citizens. If you can regulate the making of private contracts in the states, what can you not do?" He conceded that Congress licenses liquor dealers and taxes commodities such as whiskey and tobacco, but insisted that "it neither taxes nor interferes with bargains (in those industries) nor tries in any way to regulate the manner of dealing. It makes a distinction between wholesale and retail dealers, but never interferes with the terms of sale." Cummings noted that the report of the Agricultural Committee endorsing the bill labeled it a revenue measure, yet the bill described its object as relieving "the producer of the destructive competition to which he is now subjected by the offering, upon the exchanges, of illimitable quantities of fiat or fictitious products by those who do not own and have not acquired the right to the future possession of the articles which they pretend to offer and sell."[304] The bill failed. So did a proposal to impose steep taxes on compound lard—composed of lard and cottonseed oil. The measure required those who sold compound lard to pay a steep tax and to label it. Congressman Thomas Stockdale of Mississippi believed Congress was once again contemplating using the tax power to drive out of existence what it could not ban directly. Advocates of the measure "use the Constitution as a pretense; that is, you use the article of the Constitution authorizing Congress to raise revenue, not for the purpose of revenue, but to get at another object, which is to burden one industry that another may flourish; to drive one class out to give [a] place to another more favored class, which is, I say, using the Constitution in the letter to violate it in spirit."[305]

In time these concerns would be rendered moot by the use of the commerce power to regulate the sale and manufacture of foodstuffs and other agricultural products. Before that occurred, the question of whether

Congress could use its tax power to favor certain domestic producers over others reached the Supreme Court in 1904. In *McCray v. U.S.*, the Supreme Court held that Congress could burden goods with prohibitory taxes.[306] In an opinion written by Justice Edward Douglass White, the high court upheld the 1886 oleomargarine tax and another one imposed in 1902. White insisted it was not the Court's place to speculate regarding the motives of Congress that led it to enact legislation.[307] He conceded that the tax served to repress or discourage the manufacture of oleomargarine by making it more expensive. As the manufacture of oleomargarine was not a fundamental right, Congress was within its powers in imposing a punitive tax on it.[308]

With centralization surging forward during the 1870s and 1880s and politicians of both parties lending their support to experimentation in Washington, some suggested that questions of federal authority no longer dominated national politics. In June 1879 the *Nation* insisted Republicans and Democrats did not differ at all on questions of federal power: "the art of suddenly forgetting all the principles one has propounded when they are going to operate to the disadvantage of one's party or section, is now cultivated by politicians of all classes." It lamented the perception advanced by newspapers and politicians that Republicans cared not a whit for the prerogatives of the states and believed they exist "only by the sufferance of the Union." The *Nation* also dismissed as false the belief that Democrats "are endeavoring to throw off all the authority of the general government by a certain old and pernicious heresy known as 'states' rights.'" It cited the 1876 election dispute, when Republicans insisted Congress did not have the power to investigate the actions of state officials and Democrats held that it did, as evidence for the proposition that "there is not the slightest foundation for the view that one party is especially in favor of and the other opposed to states' rights."[309]

A February 1880 article in the *Atlantic* suggested that the parties still differed on matters of federalism, though both had accommodated themselves to the concentration of authority in Washington. The Civil War had the effect of "immensely strengthening the recognized powers of the national government, and giving it a hold on the hearts of the people it never had before." States' rights survives "but only as a sentiment associated with the beaten rebellion." Among southerners "the younger generation does not understand it, or care for it. The intelligent whites have made use of it to some extent under the cry of 'home rule,' to release themselves from the consequences of negro suffrage; but it is not the living force in the convictions of great masses of people which it used to be. In its place there has come what the Democrats call 'opposition to the centralizing tendencies of the Republican Party.' This opposition is scarcely formulated, however, into a political creed, and no Democrat ventures to give it the old discredited name of state sovereignty. The existence and strength of the tendency towards nationalism are clearly shown by its avowal by one political party, and by the hesitancy of the other to antagonize it with the counterpoise of states' rights."[310]

As evidence of the "centralizing movement" in progress, the *Atlantic* cited the "multitude of projects of legislation brought forward every winter at Washington, the assertion by the Republican Party of the duty of the government to protect the citizen in his right of suffrage, and the impossibility of conducting state canvasses on state issues."[311] It predicted this trend would continue as citizens would demand stronger federal election laws—the New York voter would not acquiesce in the "suppression of the vote of his party in a dozen parishes on the Red River" because the congressman elected would help establish policies "antagonistic to his views."[312] The *Atlantic* predicted that in the future, centralization would produce novelties including legislation protecting railroad investors and passengers, as well as national marriage and divorce laws due to the problems created by conflicting state laws on the subject. The national government was also likely to aid the construction of roads and canals and establish a postal telegraph system. The federal courts would probably be strengthened "to enable them to protect the rights of citizenship." Authority for all of this would be found in the Constitution as the "instrument admits of very expansive interpretations."[313] The *Atlantic* insisted centralization would not threaten individual rights. Nor would it enable the wealthy to dominate the country, as "the great majority of the voting population will always be composed of men of small means or no means, and the national government will be their servant, and not the tool of great capitalists and corporations."[314]

David Dudley Field, counsel for L. P. Milligan in *Ex parte Milligan* and one of the nation's leading lawyers (as well as the brother of Supreme Court Justice Stephen Field), took a more critical view of the trend toward centralization in a May 1881 article in the *North American Review*. He began with the tariff: "There is not a city in any of the states, there is not a village along the rivers, and scarce a hamlet among the hills, that does not look to Congress more than to its own legislature to determine the occupations of its people. Mills all over the land are built or left to decay, furnaces are lighted or extinguished, as parties or factions, or the shifting influences of private interests, swing to and fro at Washington." Field listed what he saw as congressional excesses: the use of the postal power by Congress to enable telegraph companies to run lines across states against their will, the appointment of federal officers (15,000 in 1876) to oversee state elections, and the federal prosecution of state officials for violating state election laws. "Worst of all, in flagrant defiance of the Constitution," in 1867 the southern states were placed "under military rule, reducing them to the condition of subject provinces, opening the way to misgovernment by aliens and thieves beyond the dreams of Roman proconsuls." He derided the use of the term "police power" to describe the authority remaining with the states "as if these great commonwealths which, according to the theory, divide the attributes of sovereignty with the United States, and which make most of the rules of property and of conduct under which we live, had been reduced to the condition of a body of police officers!"[315]

Field also disparaged the Legal Tender Acts and the abuse of tariffs. "Congress has an undoubted right to collect duties on imports, but it has no right to foster one branch of industry at the expense of another; and when it uses its lawful power to accomplish indirectly what it cannot do directly, it violates the Constitution."[316] He blamed the situation on members of Congress, who were held accountable only to voters in their districts—thus measures designed to secure their reelection such as the Arrears of Pensions Act and river-and-harbor bills that enriched the constituents of lawmakers at the expense of the rest of the country. In describing the latter, Field charged that "a member from a district whose people want employment, and a plentiful disbursement of public money, expects to win popularity and votes by giving them the opportunity. These constituents of his contribute little money to the treasury, but get much out of it."[317]

Speaking at the University of Michigan in June 1887, Supreme Court Justice Samuel F. Miller expressed his appreciation for the federal system. Contrary to the assertions of some, the Civil War amendments had not substantially altered it. "With the exception of the special provisions in them for the protection of the personal rights of the citizens and the people of the United States and the necessary restrictions upon the powers of the states for this purpose, with the additions to the powers of the general government to enforce those provisions, no substantial change has been made. The necessity of the great powers conceded by the Constitution originally to the federal government, and the equal necessity of the autonomy of the states and their power to regulate their domestic affairs, remain as the great features of our complex form of government."[318] The *Springfield Daily Republican* thought the speech significant in light of the "popular idea, at least within the Republican Party . . . that the war affected through these amendments and in general great changes in the relations of the states and the general government, that it 'settled the states' rights issue.'" It acknowledged Republican fears that the appointment of Democrats to the Supreme Court "may unsettle the issue." The article concluded that while it was fortunate that the "southern view" of states' rights, including the right of secession, had been "put down" by the Civil War, "the states were the original sovereignties. They yielded certain powers to a central government for the common good; all other powers they reserved to themselves."[319]

Democratic politicians continued to adhere to a more restrained conception of federal power than Republicans—certainly they wished to leave that impression. Writing in 1886, New York City Congressman S. S. Cox claimed that the issue of federal power remained the fault line of American politics. "Whatever their names, there will ever be two schools of political philosophy, and two parties in this country accepting their doctrines; one with Federal tendencies for a strong centralized government, distrustful of the people, and the other seeking local governments and strictly defining the sphere of national powers to national necessities."[320] In its 1888 platform, the Democratic Party announced that "chief among its principles" was the "maintenance of an indissoluble Union of free and indestructible states" and "devotion to a plan of government regulated by a written Constitution, strictly specifying every granted power and expressly reserving to the States or people the entire ungranted residue of power."[321] Even more than political parties, the sections remained divided in their attitudes toward federal authority. Writing in 1904, George Hoar recalled that during his 35 years in Congress, southerners "opposed the construction of the Constitution which has prevailed in New England and throughout the North" and to which he himself was devoted.[322] Late-nineteenth-century constitutional law textbooks produced by northern scholars such as Thomas Cooley emphasized the limits on state power imposed by the Fourteenth Amendment and other provisions of the state and federal constitutions, while those of southerners such as John Randolph Tucker embraced state sovereignty.[323]

While Gilded Age Americans saw themselves as divided in their attitudes toward federal authority as their forebears had been, Lord Bryce observed a fairly stable federal system that was evolving with the country. He thought the "states' rights spirit has declined" in part because the "material interests of every part of the country are bound up with those of every other."[324] Bryce recalled that in the months and years following Appomattox, many in Europe thought the states might be reduced to non-entities—the "federal system was virtually at an end." As events proved, "none of these apprehended results followed. The authority of the central government presently sank back within its former limits." At present, states' rights "are in question only so far as certain economic benefits might be obtained by a further extension of federal authority; nor has either party an interest in advocating the supersession of state action in any department of government."[325] Bryce noted "the growing strength of centripetal and unifying forces," including finance, trade, and communications. He also perceived a trend among champions of the dispossessed and impoverished farmers—they increasingly promised federal action because they saw the federal government as the only entity "strong enough and wide-reaching enough to give effect to their proposals." The future, he believed, would see a continuation of centralization at the expense of states' rights.[326]

Bryce did not believe that novel interpretations of the Constitution would be resorted to in order to enhance federal power because the "interpreting authority" was "composed of lawyers imbued with professional habits."[327] Yet he went on to concede that since the Civil War, "the broad construction view of the Constitution (has) practically prevailed."[328] He cited as examples the legalization of paper money and the Interstate Commerce Commission. The trend toward centralization dated from before the Civil War and it had only been slowed by Nullification and similar incidents. The national government's ability to "stimulate and depress commerce" via its power over the currency, finance, tariffs, and transportation had caused Americans, particularly those employed in manufacturing, to look to it and not to the states. The country would acquiesce in the further concentration of power in Washington due to a heightened sense of patriotism, the respect in the North for the government that saved the Union—and southern awe of it for the same reason—as well as "the great army of federal office-holders who look to Washington as the center of their hopes and fears."[329]

THE INDUSTRIAL ABYSS AND THE SOUTHERN REVIVAL

Between 1870 and 1900, the population of the United States doubled from 38 to 76 million people, in part due to the arrival of 11 million immigrants. The percentage of Americans living in cities rose from 27 to 40 percent. Population growth and urbanization went hand in hand with and contributed to the advance of manufacturing. The American Industrial Revolution hit its stride after the Civil War, producing fantastic amounts of wealth, generating improvements in the quality of life that benefited all and stimulating the growth of cities that contained some of the worst slums on the face of the earth. By the end of the century America had the world's highest per capita income. The earliest beneficiary of the Industrial Revolution was the farmer. The arrival of harrows, reapers, and threshers reduced the amount of time necessary to produce a bushel of wheat from three hours in 1830 to less than 10 minutes in 1900.[330] The number of farms tripled between 1860 and 1910, when there were six million. Railroads now reached into or at least approached every county to remove the farmer's bounty—35,000 miles of tracks in 1865 grew to almost 200,000 in 1900. As corporate America matured, the middle class expanded greatly during the period—the ranks of managers went from 750,000 to two million in 1910 and 4.4 million in 1920.[331] Consumer goods and conveniences flooded the marketplace and changed the way people lived—by the mid 1890s, New York City had

12 telephone exchanges, each handling 150,000 calls a day.[332] At the turn of the century women comprised a fifth of the workforce.

Among the consequences of industrialization for the federal system was the fact that it created a population that was, if more prosperous most of time, also more susceptible to economic downturns. Laborers improved their lot during the second half of the nineteenth century—annual industrial wages increased by 70 percent to $573.[333] At the same time many persons earned so little that they barely survived. Following an 1883 investigation, Illinois officials concluded that a quarter of the laborers in the state did not make enough to avoid want. Conditions in the South—where laborers earned only 70 percent of the incomes of their counterparts in the North—were even worse. Laborers everywhere toiled for 10 or 12 hours a day. They looked to the legislatures for assistance. During the years after the Civil War, seven states passed laws limiting the workday to eight hours; they did not devote much energy to enforcing them and the statutes themselves were riddled with exceptions.[334] Democrats were more sympathetic to labor than Republicans though the leadership of the party had close ties to railroads and other corporate interests. Tammany Hall remained at the head of the Democratic Party in New York City and it obtained laws improving working conditions for streetcar workers and establishing arbitration for some labor disputes between 1887 and 1893.[335] In neighboring New Jersey, Democrats devised a system of arbitration for labor disputes only to see it gutted when Republicans took over the state government.[336]

Congress did not concern itself with the grievances of laborers due to a lack of jurisdiction, though lawmakers assured that protective tariffs would raise wages. In 1868 Congress passed an eight-hour law for the benefit of mechanics and laborers working for or on behalf of the federal government.[337] Letter carriers were given an eight hour day in 1888.[338] An eight-hour day law applicable to all federal employees was passed in 1892.[339] In December 1871 Congressman George Hoar proposed a bill appointing a commission to investigate wages and hours, as well as "the social, educational and sanitary condition of the laboring classes of the United States, and to show how the same are affected by existing laws regulating commerce, finance and currency."[340] Over a decade passed until Congress established the Bureau of Labor in 1884 to collect the information sought by Mr. Hoar.[341]

Labor's chief goal was increased pay. At least a thousand work stoppages occurred in every year but one from 1886 until the end of the century, and most stemmed from disagreements over compensation.[342] Union membership peaked in 1886 at a third of the workforce.[343] When strikes occurred, employers often responded by bringing in immigrants or blacks as replacement workers. Railroad strikes in 1886 brought train traffic to a halt in large parts of the West. Cities were denied shipments of food for a time.[344] Strikers resisted violently when the governors of Texas, Missouri, Arkansas, and Kansas ordered railroad managers to send trains on their way. The episode led some to call on Congress to pass legislation providing for the voluntary arbitration of labor disputes on the interstate railroads. Lawmakers acquiesced in 1888.[345]

The contrast between the modest pay of the new laboring classes and the vast fortunes being accumulated by a relative few produced congressional speeches that sounded as if they had been written by French or German radicals. On March 31, 1886, Democratic Congressman Andrew Jackson Caldwell of Tennessee spoke in apocalyptic terms. "We are," he announced, "on the threshold of the last great conflict for the disenthrallment of men." For what benefit, he asked, "are the victories of the ages if at last man by the power of money may be forced to work like a slave all his days and still go naked and hungry?" What benefit is liberty, he asked, "if under its glittering wheels the multitude writhes in the abject slavery of starvation, ignorance, and vice? Are the many ever to be in some form the slaves of the few? The very triumph of our republicanism, our prosperity under free government, has developed a new enemy to the rights of the many. The aggregation of capital in corporate bodies and the accumulation of money in private hands is unprecedented in the history of the world, and menaces the perpetuity of our institutions." Caldwell noted that " 'prophets of ill omen' had predicted that as our population became dense, the area of public lands filled up, the struggle of life more intense, the conflict, so called, between labor and capital would, with universal suffrage, render property insecure, revolutionize society, and overthrow our democracy. If our institutions cannot stand this final test they are a failure." What was the solution? Strengthening labor unions. "The victory of the medieval burghers and craftsmen of England will be repeated in the triumph of our trade-unions and cooperative-associations over monopolists, money-kings, and bosses."[346]

Extremes of poverty and wealth were consequences of the Industrial Revolution. Another consequence was the expansion of the activities of the state governments. Industrialization and urbanization first took hold in the North, and the state and local governments responded by expanding their activities in the areas of law enforcement, education, public works, utilities, and public health. As a result the state tax burden exploded—it tripled in five northern states during the 1860s. During the term of Governor Reuben Fenton (1865–67), New York established eight teacher colleges as well as boards of charities and health. It also devised housing standards for New York City.[347] During the 1870s the number of public high schools in the United States grew from 200 to 800.[348] Massachusetts provided new services to its farmers, including the suppression of livestock diseases, bounties to agricultural societies, a board of agriculture, and a dairy bureau.[349] The expansion of government functions enlarged state bureaucracies, thereby providing new opportunities for patronage and strengthening political machines.[350] As the duties imposed on them increased, the state governments were often rendered ineffectual by powerful interests that succeeded in corrupting them. The fantastic quantities of wealth produced by industry, mining, and trade gave men the capacity to buy state legislators by the dozen while the increasing materialism of the period and a decline in ethics made public officials more susceptible to bribery. The pressure imposed on state legislatures by corporate interests was severe. The Southern Pacific dominated California, silver ruled Nevada, and lumber wielded great influence in Michigan. The Anaconda Copper Company ruled Montana while cattlemen imposed their will in Wyoming. Land speculators held dominion over the New Mexico territorial legislature.[351] Larger states such as Ohio and New York were usually spared domination by a single interest due to the presence of multiple industries within their borders.[352] If interests seeking favorable treatment did not offer bribes, lawmakers learned to demand them. In some states such as New York, they introduced "strike bills" designed to hurt the interests of powerful corporations—once paid, legislators would cease efforts to pass the offending law.

Railroads dominated many states. Three lines—the Rock Island, the Santa Fe, and the Missouri Pacific—oversaw Kansas politics.[353] William Allen White described the situation that existed in Kansas and other states during the 1880s: "A state boss collected money from the railroads, the packing houses, the insurance companies, and the banks in his state. This money he sent to his henchmen in the counties, who distributed the largesse to their followers, who controlled the county conventions. The object and aim of all county conventions was to control the nomination of those Republicans who would run for the legislature and the state senate. When they were elected, as all good Republicans were, they would follow the boss. On most matters they were free; but where legislation touched the banks, the railroads, the insurance companies, or the packing houses, they were bound in honor to vote with the boss, and for his candidate for U.S. Senate. So over the United States, our senators went to Washington obligated to the large corporate interests of their states."[354]

While Republican machines in the northern and western states depended on contributions from businesses as well as state and federal employees, Democratic machines in the cities relied more heavily on the patronage provided by municipal offices. Their almost complete control of abject populations enabled urban bosses to dispense with any pretense of honesty or efficiency, and the problem grew worse as the century neared its end. In 1890 a former president of Cornell University described American city governments as the "worst in Christendom: the most expensive, the most inefficient and the most corrupt."[355] The high point in municipal corruption was already 20 years past. Democrat William Tweed dominated New York City in the late 1860s and early 1870s. He and his cohorts at Tammany Hall determined that all bills submitted to the city must be inflated by at least half. Before its members were indicted, the Tweed ring stole at least $30 million from the city. A courthouse designed to cost $250,000 was not finished until $13 million had been spent.[356] Tweed maintained power by providing jobs, sustenance, and medical care to the city's poor. They returned the favor by providing him with votes and ignoring his misdeeds. While Tweed died in jail in 1878, Tammany Hall survived and prospered, in no small part because of the patronage it was able to dole out in the form of 12,000 municipal jobs available during the 1880s.[357] A *Harper's Weekly* article of October 24, 1891, calculated that Tammany had four times as many places to offer as local federal establishments provided Republicans. Through its alliance with liquor interests and its management of "the immense venal vote of the city" Tammany controlled the state Democratic organization. This in turn enabled it to cast the vote of the largest state in the Union at Democratic national conventions. Thus, "although only a local organization, it is by far the greatest power in the national Democratic Party."[358]

City governments across the country began exhibiting familiar traits: levying high taxes and refusing to control expenditures. This development stemmed in part from the fact that most urban voters were too poor to pay taxes. By one estimate, only 17 percent of Bostonians paid property taxes at the turn of the century. These voters were indifferent to the growing tax burden. To them the city governments were a source of sustenance; that the more prosperous complained of their taxes was of no consequence. Spending on relief exploded in the cities during the second half of the nineteenth century. The rise in expenditures to maintain those without other means of support stemmed in part from the rank poverty of the cities; it also arose out of the desire of urban politicians to purchase votes. In time states were forced to intervene as the explosion in municipal spending after the Civil War combined with the depression of the 1870s to bring many cities to the verge of bankruptcy. By the end of the century, over 40 of the 68 largest cities in the North operated under charters that fixed their maximum tax rates.[359] Several states amended their constitutions to limit the borrowing power of municipal governments.[360]

Electoral corruption grew to epidemic proportions in cities and rural areas alike. The going rate in upstate New York State in 1880 varied between $10 and $27, depending on the town.[361] In New York City a surplus of impoverished men lowered the rate to $2 a voter. By one estimate, 20 percent of the votes in New York City were for sale during the late nineteenth century, if one combines an estimate of those bribed and those placed on party or public payrolls at the time of elections. "Vote buying shops" appeared in the cities throughout the North: runners would escort persons voting illegally to the polls, ensure they voted properly, and then give them slips that could be redeemed for cash. One estimate held that a tenth of the electors of New Hampshire were ready to sell their votes to the highest bidder in 1876. Voters were manipulated and intimidated as well as bribed; planters voted sharecroppers and farmers dictated the votes of farmhands.[362]

While the adoption of the secret ballot was the most common remedy for electoral corruption, New York conservatives took a more direct approach following the Tweed Ring scandal—disenfranchisement of the poor, at least with respect to the municipal offices whose occupants handled city revenue. The New York legislature passed a resolution amending the state constitution for that purpose in 1877 but the approval of successive legislatures was needed to pass amendments and Republicans lost control of the statehouse to Tammany-led forces before the next session.[363] Conservatives had little success in keeping municipal governments in the largest cities out of the hands of vote-buying political machines for the rest of the century and these organizations saw their influence reach new heights when cities such as New York were flooded with a new wave of impoverished immigrants during the 1880s and 1890s.

The consequences of training citizens to expect to be paid for their votes was not lost on all Americans. In an 1890 speech, former federal judge and Union army general Walter Gresham charged that "those who spend money in corrupting voters and bribing officers are more dangerous enemies to the republic than were the men who engaged in the unsuccessful rebellion against it."[364] At the turn of the century, George Hoar repeated a sentiment common before the Civil War when he warned that corruption forms "the most formidable peril to any government and, if it be not encountered and overcome, fatal to a republic."[365] Republicans such as Hoar seemed to miss the irony of denouncing electoral corruption even as they promised voters policies designed to enrich them. What was the difference between promising tariff protection for woolens to the voters of Massachusetts—many of whom worked in textile factories—and simply bribing the residents of lower Manhattan?

As it was associated with dependence and electoral corruption, public relief for the unemployed remained inadequate. State governments had yet to involve themselves in this endeavor—the maintenance of poorhouses and other forms of aid were left to county and city governments. On at least one occasion talk of a federal role was heard. In December 1874, with the economy in the midst of a severe downturn, the Grant administration's organ, the *National Republican*, floated the idea of increasing funding for federal public works to provide jobs for the unemployed. The reaction of the press was universally negative. *Harper's Weekly* called the plan

> a suggestion for jobbery and corruption on the largest scale, and for an enormous extension of the patronage, that is, the power of bribery. It is, moreover, a confusion and forgetfulness of the proper function of government. To develop the paternal element is to weaken the robust self-dependence which is the palladium of the American system. There may be great public services which the government may wisely undertake, as it carries the mails, and supports schools, light-houses, and quarantine. But each of these is to be considered upon its merits and the fair probabilities of each case, and they are very different from a system of colossal public works and enterprises—canals, roads, telegraphs, expresses—which leads straight to a concentration of almost resistless force in the hands of the government, fosters vast corruption and directly threatens public liberty.

Nor was that all. "It is a proposal to retain power by the old Roman imperial method, from which Napoleon borrowed his scheme, of feeding and amusing people at the public cost."[366] *Harper's* need not have worried; nothing was heard from the Grant administration on the subject.

While the North moved forward despite great dislocations among its populace, the South struggled to rebuild. The devastation was widespread. Almost half the region's farm machinery had been destroyed during the Civil War. As late as 1879, the business district of Charleston, South Carolina still had not been rebuilt.[367] Southerners turned to the federal government for the same type of aid it had parceled out so generously in the North and West. Southern congressional delegations, though overwhelmingly Democratic, sought money for levees, harbor improvements, and railroads—precisely the sort of projects they had once denounced as unconstitutional. In an extraordinary bit of timing, northern lawmakers discovered the value of economy in early 1877, just as Democrats were completing their takeover of southern congressional delegations. When lawmakers in the House led by Indiana Democrat William Holman pushed through a resolution against additional subsidies for private corporations, it appeared for a time that the "great barbecue" was over.[368]

Southern Democrats held to their demands. They focused on money for levees along the Mississippi River as well as subsidies and land for the Texas & Pacific Railroad, which wanted to build a southern route to California. Although the line was eventually connected to the Southern Pacific, thereby providing a southern route to the west coast, this was achieved by railroad promoters and not Congress.[369] The problems of the region went deeper than transportation. Thomas Jefferson's vision of a nation of freeholders tilling modest farms was far from a reality in the postwar South. Instead of property owners, the region's farmers had become sharecroppers, renting small lots and mortgaging their crops in advance. One-third of the farmers in the cotton belt were sharecroppers in 1880; two-thirds in 1920.[370] In the case of blacks, the problem stemmed in part from the unwillingness of whites to sell them land. From the planter's viewpoint, the sharecropper system was in some ways superior to slavery. Men contracted with planters to farm a portion of their land; in exchange they received one-half of the harvested cotton crop, or one-third if the planter provided fertilizer and implements. The system freed planters from the need to supervise those tilling their lands and transferred risk to their tenants, many of whom were former slaves.[371]

The southern economy began to move forward during the 1880s and 1890s. The loosening of the federal spigot helped. Congress appropriated $8 million for improvements on the Mississippi River between 1891 and 1906. It spent $7.5 million to improve the harbor at Galveston. Railroad construction boomed and exports from the South almost doubled between 1880 and 1901. The number of cotton mills in the region more than doubled during the last two decades of the century.[372] By 1910, the quantity of coarse cotton yarns produced in southern mills exceeded that of New England.[373] The South had advantages that beckoned northern industry including proximity to raw materials, a mild climate, water power, and lower wages—40 percent lower than wages in New England by one estimate. A lack of labor laws and unions also helped. The workday in the factories of North Carolina was said to be 24 percent longer than in those of Massachusetts.[374]

Living conditions for blacks remained poor. Many left the region for places such as Kansas. In time northern mercantile interests frowned on the exodus, believing it would reduce the supply of cheap labor in the region and reduce the value of their own investments. Steamboat lines responded by lifting rates beyond what most blacks could afford.[375] Black political participation slowly disappeared, though the House of Representatives included a black congressman from North Carolina as late as 1901 (George H. White).[376] The most severe blow came with the adoption by many states of the "Mississippi Plan." In 1890 Mississippi adopted a new state constitution. It limited the suffrage as well as jury duty to males over 21 who could pay a poll tax and read a section of the state constitution or explain it to the satisfaction of election officials. John Coit Spooner of Wisconsin commented on this hopelessly subjective test on the floor of the Senate in December 1890: "There are many of us on this side who, according to the Senators on the other side, do not understand the Constitution. No man ought to be given the power to decide as a test of anyone's right to vote whether he understands the Constitution or not, certainly unless it is first made dead certain that he understands it himself. What utter folly! We have great courts to construe the Constitution. Every day in the history of every state, questions arise as to what the instrument means, and grave lawyers, trained in the law, accurate and acute, spend hours and sometimes weeks, in arguing one way and another way, as to what a provision in the Constitution means."[377]

The Supreme Court held that nothing in the Mississippi constitution violated the Fourteenth Amendment in *Williams v. Mississippi* (1898).[378] The case grew out of the indictment of a black man by an all-white grand jury. He claimed the state constitution's limitation of the suffrage and jury duty to certain persons violated the Fourteenth Amendment. The Supreme Court did not agree. In his opinion for court, Justice Joseph McKenna held that the provision fell within the power of the Mississippi legislature because it was not limited to one race. Its terms were not themselves discriminatory.[379] Other southern states followed Mississippi's lead and imposed literacy and property requirements for voting.[380] Property tests for the suffrage had a long history in America, but it was apparent that the goal of the latest version of these laws was to disenfranchise blacks. Yet many poor whites also lost the right to vote. The suffrage requirements in the Louisiana constitution of 1898 resulted in the disenfranchisement of almost a quarter of the state's white voters.[381] As a result of these changes, the electorates of several southern states remained smaller in 1930 than they had been in 1880. Some of the pressure came from Populist farmers who had grown tired of combating planters who "voted" their black tenants by the dozen. In an attempt to preserve the vote for poor whites, South Carolina exempted from property and literacy requirements all those whose had held the franchise before the Civil War, as well as their male descendants. The measure was modeled on a Massachusetts law designed to allow poor native-born residents to vote while depriving immigrants of the right to vote.[382] Other southern states followed South Carolina's example. The tactic proved successful in preserving the suffrage for illiterate and impoverished whites while keeping blacks disenfranchised until the Oklahoma constitution's grandfather clause was held void by the Supreme Court in 1915.[383] As whites consolidated their control of the southern state governments, a more virulent strain of racism began to prey on southern society. During the late nineteenth century, southern legislatures began requiring the separation of the races in public areas and on trains and steamboats. Nine states adopted laws providing for the separation of the races in public areas by 1907.[384] Ten cities in the South passed or expanded the scope of laws segregating public accommodations between 1900 and 1911. The scourge of racial lynching multiplied near the end of the century, with an average of 187 a year in the 1890s and 92 a year during the following decade.[385]

If the South appeared unique in its problems of race, the farmers of that section suffered along with those of the rest of the nation from low prices for agricultural commodities. The cost of a pound of cotton dropped from

83 cents in 1865 to 11 cents in 1880 and 10 cents in 1890.[386] The price obtained for a bushel of corn at the Chicago Board of Trade fell from 75 cents in 1869 to 38 cents a decade later and only 28 cents in 1899.[387] Hardships in rural America were exacerbated by a national financial system that made money scarce in the South and West—few persons in these areas had the resources necessary to buy the bonds that were a prerequisite to joining the national banking system and issuing bank notes.[388]

Agitation among farmers peaked in the Plains states. Induced by federal homestead laws and preemption acts, settlers poured into western Kansas, Nebraska, and Colorado during the years following the Civil War. Many bought their land with mortgages or borrowed against their property to expand their acreage. A real estate boom ensued as the region received unusually large amounts of rainfall in the early and mid-1880s. The bubble burst in 1887. In the months before the crash, towns in western Kansas saw real estate change hands on an almost weekly basis. That summer rainfall in the region dropped, returning to normal levels. Multiple crop failures followed, and half the residents of western Kansas returned east between 1888 and 1892. As the farms of the Plains states were heavily mortgaged, defaults exploded. As much as 90 percent of the farmland in some Kansas counties passed into the hands of loan companies.[389] The farmers of the Plains states began to look to the political system for relief.

Southern cotton farmers also became restless. C. W. Macune converted the Texas Alliance from a social organization into one dedicated to improving the profits of cotton farmers.[390] Chapters in other states were formed and in time these merged with the Texas Alliance to form the Farmers' Alliance. Its members held a meeting in 1889 in St. Louis; it called for the expanded use of greenbacks, the free and unlimited coinage of silver, a ban on futures speculation and government ownership of railroads, and abolition of the national bank system. The national banks earned the wrath of farmers in part due to their refusal to accept land as collateral for loans—they were barred from doing so by federal law. By 1890 the Farmers' Alliance had a million members. It sought solutions to the crop lien system and its members talked of cooperatives. Working with Democratic Party organizations in the South, the Farmers' Alliance won control of eight southern legislatures in 1890. Eighty-four candidates endorsed by the Alliance (many of whom were longtime Democrats) won election to Congress.[391] In some southern states Democrats co-opted the Alliance by adopting its agenda, much as Jacksonian Democrats had once co-opted the agenda of the Workingmen's Party.

Democratic leaders, both in the South and at the national level, were far more conservative than supporters of the Alliance would have preferred. The 1892 Democratic nomination of Grover Cleveland, who was fiercely anti-silver, spurred farmers to form a new party, the Populists. Its presidential candidate, James Weaver, received over a million popular votes and the electoral votes of Kansas, Colorado, Idaho, and Nevada. Following Cleveland's victory, Populists formed their own parties in the South, taking on the Democratic organizations that had dominated southern states since the end of Reconstruction. In 1894 North Carolina Populists won both houses of the state legislature and elected three congressmen who served alongside three Democrats, two Republicans, and one independent.[392] Overall, nine Populists were elected to Congress in 1894.[393]

More important than their candidates were their proposals to save farmers from the vagaries of the market. In mining the federal quarry, Populists hoped to extract what farmers no longer had access to in the marketplace, and what many believed was their right: more credit. Southern Populist leader Dr. Charles Macune proposed what became known as the sub-treasury plan at the St. Louis meeting of the Farmers' Alliance in December 1889. It provided for the federal government to issue certificates to farmers at the time they deposited their crops in warehouses to be built at government expense. The certificates would be worth up to 80 percent of the deposited crops and could be used as collateral for loans. Warehouses would be located in each county producing an annual crop worth $500,000 or more. They could charge farmers up to 1 percent interest and the certificates had to be redeemed within a year or the crops would be sold at auction. It was thought that the one year period would give farmers enough time to find an adequate price for their crops. A bill establishing a sub-treasury system was proposed in Congress. The plan did not have any real hope of success, but some lawmakers spoke highly of it. Their arguments for the constitutionality of the measure relied heavily on precedent. In a speech of August 1892, Populist Congressman John Davis of Kansas recalled that national banks deposit bonds in the treasury and receive 1 percent notes "on twenty years' time, renewable when due if the bankers desire it." This, he announced, "is the bankers' sub-treasury plan." Nor were the national banks the only recipients of federal largesse. Owners of gold and silver could store these metals in government vaults, where they were guaranteed against loss. Merchants stored imported goods in government warehouses at no charge and did not pay the tariff until the goods were sold. The system constituted a "sub-treasury plan for the benefit of importers." Distillers did not pay the 90 cent a gallon tax on whiskey until it was sold—before that time they were allowed to store it in a government warehouses for a small fee. If the whiskey was sold abroad, no tax was paid. "This is the distiller's sub treasury plan." Why, Davis asked, may farmers and planters not "ask the general government to furnish warehouses and elevators in which to store a portion of the grain and cotton crops, in order to hold them from the markets until needed for consumption?"[394]

Davis assured that the sub-treasury would remain in operation only until the money supply expanded and farmers could find other sources of credit. As for the question of authority, he returned to past practice. "A Constitution which permits sub-treasury plans, with loans and gifts of money to bankers, bullionists, whiskey men and others, surely will not object to similar plans for the benefit of the common people." Davis may have spoken more truth than he knew when he asserted that "what the people of this country urgently need and earnestly demand will usually be found constitutional."[395] It was a far cry from allowing businesses to store items in government warehouses for the convenience of the Treasury Department to building warehouses that were of no use to the federal government and then loaning money to those who used them. As for the notes issued by the federal government to national banks, they were secured by bonds deposited with the treasury. The practice did not, admittedly, have a valid basis in either the coinage or the commerce power, at least as those powers were originally understood.

The sub-treasury plan was subjected to derision in the press. The *Springfield Daily Republican* complained that the recent growth in government functions had produced a belief that the "government can do anything, that an act of Congress can cure all evils, that the state must be the great burden-bearer." Thus, members of the "Farmers' Alliance rush to Washington asking Congress to issue greenbacks, coin silver and loan them money on land or crops, and so cure the depression from which all the agriculture of the world is suffering." The sub-treasury plan constituted "reliance on government to do that which no government on earth has power to do—that is, repeal the universal law of supply and demand." As long as "the food products of the world are more than the world needs, the farmer will suffer from low prices."[396]

Democrat Benjamin Enloe of Tennessee spoke in opposition to the sub-treasury bill on May 28, 1892. The measure was a form of "class legislation, at war with the fundamental principles of the government, as laid down by Thomas Jefferson and promulgated by the farmers in their resolutions at St. Louis and Ocala, in which they declare that they favor 'equal rights to all and special privileges to none.'" The sub-treasury system could be made consistent with that doctrine only by authorizing "any owner of any species of property, which would furnish equally good security for a debt, to turn it over to the government and make the government take proper care of it for one year, or a shorter period, and loan him eighty percent of its value." There is, he continued, "not a word or line in the Constitution which authorizes the government to loan money to the people, and there is nothing in it from which such power can be implied. We are told that it has loaned money, and that Congress may do anything under the 'general welfare' clause which the majority may think would promote 'the general welfare.' If that be true, then the other provisions of the Constitution are meaningless and useless."[397] Why not, he continued, arrange for the federal government to simply hand out money instead of taking the trouble to loan it? "If this language of the Constitution can be stretched to authorize the loan of money to the people it can be stretched to authorize the gift of it. I think precedents may be found for giving away the public money, but I suppose it will hardly be argued that we ought to follow such precedents and give the public money to individuals or classes."[398]

Enloe suggested that if sub-treasury proponent Tom Watson of Georgia "follows out his own argument to its legitimate conclusion . . . he will soon find himself not merely in the Republican camp, but he will find that he has charged right through the Republican line, and is leading it in the work of centralizing the government. I admit, however, that the gentleman is perfectly consistent in all this, if he wants a strong centralized government controlled by the office holding and tax eating classes instead of a republic controlled by the uncorrupted and patriotic suffrages of the majority of the people."[399] In the end the sub-treasury scheme died a quiet death, though not before the Committee on Ways and Means issued a report dismissing the proposal as a wasteful, centralizing piece of class legislation that would increase speculation in farm commodities, destabilize the currency, and provide another means for politicians to buy votes. "How far it would be wielded to control his (the citizen's) action in elections would depend upon the integrity or unscrupulousness of those officers who depend upon the administration for their official existence or the size of their salaries." The report also condemned the measure as violating the Constitution—none of the enumerated powers authorized the loaning of money by the federal government to private businesses.[400]

FEDERALISM, REGULATION, AND THE GILDED AGE SUPREME COURT

Farmers were more interested in laws controlling railroad rates than the sub-treasury plan. Beginning in the late 1860s, they demanded that the legislatures regulate the charges of railroads and grain warehouses. Between 1869 and 1874, Illinois, Iowa, Wisconsin, and Minnesota passed laws establishing railroad commissions that imposed rates on railroads.[401] Whether the Supreme Court would allow these commissions to regulate rates on interstate lines remained a question. At the time of Salmon Chase's appointment as Chief Justice (1864), the Supreme Court appeared to have determined that the states could regulate interstate commerce when their statutes did not conflict with federal law or touch subjects that were appropriate for national regulation. This somewhat vague standard had been devised in *Cooley v. Board of Wardens* (1851).[402] Some questioned the conversion of an enumerated power into a ban on state legislation; if Congress alone could regulate interstate commerce, why did the Constitution not vest exclusive power over that subject in Congress, as it had with regard to the capital? Article I, Section 10 barred the states from enacting several types of laws; it said nothing regarding commerce. In *Steamship Co. v. Portwardens*, the Supreme Court held void a tax imposed by Louisiana on ships entering the port of New Orleans (1867).[403] The law was held unconstitutional in imposing a duty on tonnage, something that the Constitution expressly prohibited. The Court also held the measure invalid as a regulation of interstate commerce. In his opinion for the majority, Chief Justice Chase took the position that the states could not move beyond health laws and police regulations in regulating interstate commerce within their borders.[404] The test devised in *Cooley* appeared to be abandoned; it did not matter if the subject was appropriate for state regulation—except for the subjects noted above, the states could not regulate interstate commerce.[405]

In *The Daniel Ball* (1871), the Supreme Court expanded the scope of the commerce power to entities that operated entirely within a single state.[406] The Grand River runs west from the central portion of lower Michigan until it empties into Lake Michigan. Steamboats including the *Daniel Ball* worked the river between Grand Rapids and Grand Haven. Federal statutes of 1838 and 1852 imposed safety requirements on steamboats using the navigable waters of the United States. These vessels had to be inspected and obtain federal licenses. In the spring of 1868, the U.S. attorney in Michigan filed a libel of accusation against the steamer *Daniel Ball* for operating without a federal license. The owners claimed that as the vessel was limited to waters within the state of Michigan that were not navigable waters of the United States, it was beyond the scope of the commerce power and federal regulations of steamboats. They pointed out that the vessel did not so much as enter Lake Michigan to turn around, as it drew only two feet of water. Therefore they did not need to obtain a license for the *Daniel Ball*. The owners conceded that the vessel transported Michigan goods destined for points outside of the state as well as goods from other states between points within Michigan.[407]

In his opinion for the Court, Justice Stephen Field held that rivers are navigable in law if they are navigable in fact, and that such waters qualify as the "navigable waters of the U.S. when they form in their ordinary condition by themselves, or by uniting with other waters, a continued highway over which commerce is or may be carried on with other states or foreign countries in the customary modes in which such commerce is conducted by water." As the Grand River forms, via its connection to Lake Michigan "a continued highway for commerce, both with other states and with foreign countries," it is "brought under the direct control of Congress in the exercise of its commercial power." The *Daniel Ball* also engaged in interstate commerce because it carried goods that originated in or were destined for other states. Field explained that the Court was "unable to draw any clear and distinct line between the authority of Congress to regulate an agency employed in commerce between the states, when that agency extends through two or more states, and when it is confined in its action entirely within the limits of a single state. If its authority does not extend to an agency in such commerce, when that agency is confined within the limits of a state, its entire authority over interstate commerce may be defeated."[408] The decision foreshadowed a line of cases in which the high court held that Congress could regulate entities operating wholly within a single state when doing so was necessary to the effective regulation of interstate commerce.

Morrison R. Waite was appointed Chief Justice in early 1874 after Grant bungled the nominations of other candidates. A respected lawyer, Waite served at the Geneva Arbitration of 1871–72. During his tenure as Chief Justice, the Court took a modest approach, leaving state legislation in place when it could and refusing to read prohibitions into the Constitution that did not exist. The first major commerce clause decision of the high court during Waite's tenure was issued in 1877. In the *Granger Cases*, the Supreme Court took up the question of whether the states could regulate the charges of grain warehouses and railroads. In his opinion for the majority in the lead case, *Munn v. Illinois*, Chief Justice Waite held that an Illinois law setting maximum charges for grain elevators and warehouses did not violate the Constitution.[409] Nor did the railroads commission laws and rates at issue in the companion cases.[410] Waite turned aside the suggestion that the Illinois law constituted an impermissible regulation of interstate commerce. He pointed out that the 14 warehouses owned by the plaintiffs were all located in Illinois: "Incidentally they may be connected with interstate commerce, but not necessarily so. Their regulation is a thing of domestic concern, and, certainly, until Congress acts in reference to their interstate relations, the state may exercise all the powers of government over them, even though in so doing it may indirectly operate upon commerce outside its immediate jurisdiction."[411] Attorneys for the warehouses also claimed the law violated the Fourteenth Amendment's due process clause. In response, Waite pointed out that in Great Britain, where statutes protecting due process rights had been on the books for centuries, Parliament had long regulated the prices of common carriers and warehouses. Congress, which had always operated under the constraints of the due process clause of the Fifth Amendment, authorized Washington, DC, officials to regulate rates at private wharves in 1820 and the rates of hackney carriages in 1848. "From this it is apparent that, down to the time of the adoption of the Fourteenth Amendment, it was not supposed that statutes regulating the use, or even the price of the use, of private property necessarily deprived an owner of his property without due process of law."[412] The rates of grain elevators and warehouses could be regulated as well as they were affected with a public interest—farmers in several states depended on them. Nor would the Court take upon itself the review of the rates set—legislatures were free to perform that function without supervision. "For protection against abuses by legislatures the people must resort to polls, not to the courts."[413] Justice Field dissented. He insisted the law violated the due process clause of the Fourteenth Amendment without offering anything to substantiate this claim, perhaps because due process clauses had not been used previously to invalidate laws regulating rates. Instead he insisted that only when some privilege had been bestowed by public authority had the right to control prices followed. As for usury laws—apparent evidence of the right of legislatures to regulate the charges of strictly private entities—Field insisted that the motivation for such measures "had long ceased to exist."[414] The companion cases revolved around the same issues. In *Peik v. Chicago & Northwestern*, the Supreme Court held that a Wisconsin law regulating railroad rates did not violate the Constitution.[415] Chief Justice Waite explained that as railroads also constituted property affected with a public interest, their rates could be fixed by legislatures. If the rate "had been improperly fixed, the legislature, not the courts, must be appealed to for change."[416]

The *Springfield Daily Republican* applauded the *Munn* ruling, though it expressed surprise that the appellants did not cite the *Dartmouth College* doctrine and claim the law impaired the value of their corporate charters—a favorite tactic during the antebellum period. As for the claim that the law constituted a regulation of interstate commerce, the *Daily Republican* pointed out that the "states retain their internal powers, in the absence of any exercise of the federal jurisdiction."[417] The real defect in the ruling was not immediately apparent. In describing the Illinois grain elevators as a virtual monopoly and claiming they were affected with a public interest, Chief Justice Waite seemed to be implying that the rates and prices charged by other types of businesses could not be regulated.[418] The public interest dichotomy had no basis in American history or case law—all types of businesses were subject to having their rates or prices set by governmental entities—yet it would survive to create havoc.[419]

In *Wabash, St. Louis & Pacific Railway v. Illinois* (1886), the Supreme Court held the states can ban rate discrimination only on railroad routes wholly within their borders. The alternative would result in "embarrassments upon interstate transportation." The commerce clause had been adopted to prevent such abuses.[420] Historians have suggested the *Wabash* case, by driving states from the field, stimulated the movement for federal regulation of the rates of interstate railroads.[421] Eight years earlier in 1878, the high court barred the regulation of interstate commerce by the states even for so noble a purpose as securing racial equality when it held void a Louisiana law barring racial discrimination on steamboats.[422] The Chief Justice explained that chaos would follow if each state could regulate common carriers on the Mississippi River, as it goes through or touches so many states. As for the lack of a conflicting federal law, Waite asserted that federal inactivity constituted a declaration that the area shall remain free of regulation of any kind.[423] Silence may have implied consent in the rest of the world, but not in Washington.

As the Supreme Court proceeded to apply its rather arbitrary doctrines to an ever-growing maze of state commercial regulations, the personnel of the Court began to change. Southerners were once again being appointed. John Marshall Harlan of Kentucky was elevated to the Supreme Court in 1877 after swinging the Kentucky delegation to Hayes at the 1876 Republican national convention in Cincinnati. Harlan had served in the Union army and was a typically nationalistic Republican in his views. Lucius Q. C. Lamar was of another stripe. After drafting Mississippi's ordinance of secession, he served in the Confederate army and reached the rank of colonel before illness forced him to resign. Jeff Davis appointed him minister to Russia but Lamar never reached St. Petersburg. Following the conflict, Lamar taught law at the University of Mississippi. He was elected to the House in 1872 and the Senate in 1877. Lamar's eloquent eulogy of Charles Sumner in April 1874 made him a national figure. The Mississippi lawyer brought to Washington a deep well of knowledge of the Constitution and its original understanding at a time when such acumen was badly needed, as many Republicans appeared ready to read the document—or at least Article I, Section 8's enumeration of the powers of Congress—into oblivion. Would the Republican majority in the Senate acquiesce in the appointment of their nemesis to the Supreme Court? It did not appear likely when Grover Cleveland sent Lamar's nomination to the Senate in late 1887. Some lawmakers such as John Sherman believed Lamar—then serving as secretary of the interior—held too narrow a view of national power.[424]

If confirmed, Lamar would be the first person nominated by a Democratic president to take a seat on the high court since 1858. Many Republicans in Congress and in the North did not want the nomination to be approved, primarily because of the nominee's service in the Confederate army. Lamar's prospects were aided by the realization that whether it was him or someone else, the place would likely go to a southerner, as the vacant seat was assigned to the fifth circuit in the southeast and each seat was traditionally given to a person residing within its circuit. (The justices were still doubling as appellate and district court judges.) Lamar's conservative outlook on economic questions may have helped his cause; he had been one of the few southern lawmakers to resist the expanded use of greenbacks and the reintroduction of silver. Some perceived him as more nationalistic in outlook than other southerners.[425] Republicans had a narrow majority in the Senate, and for a time approval of the nomination seemed in doubt. Northern senators received letters from Union army veterans who opposed the nomination. Some complained that there were too many former Confederates holding high positions in the federal government. Republicans were said to fear Lamar would shortly be elevated to chief justice, as the retirement of Morrison Waite was said to be imminent.[426] As the final verdict drew closer amid wild charges of "Calhounism," some claimed Lamar was anti-labor. On January 10, the Senate Judiciary Committee issued a majority report opposing confirmation.[427] The former senator prevailed in the end; his nomination was narrowly approved 32–28 on January 16.[428]

Later in 1888, the president nominated Melvin Fuller to replace Chief Justice Morrison R. Waite. A 55-year-old Chicago lawyer long active in the Illinois Democratic Party but without judicial experience, Fuller encountered no difficulty in obtaining the approval of the Senate and the press applauded his appointment. In 1889, Benjamin Harrison appointed David Brewer of Kansas to the high court. Despite hailing from Kansas, the epicenter of Populism, Brewer would take the lead in attacking railroad rate regulation. With its new personnel, the Supreme Court invalidated state laws more frequently, either as violations of due process or as impermissible regulations of interstate commerce. Just before Fuller's appointment, the Court had held that states cannot ban the importation of liquor by wholesalers.[429] The Court continued along this line in *Leisy v. Hardin*, when it severely limited the right of the states to ban the sale of liquor (1890).[430] The case arose out of events in Keokuk, Iowa. The city marshal confiscated 300 barrels of beer pursuant to the state prohibition law. Leisy & Company, the Illinois liquor dealer that shipped the beer to Iowa, brought suit against the marshal seeking to recover the confiscated property. After a trial court ruled against it and the Supreme Court of Iowa refused to reverse the ruling, Leisy filed a writ of error with the Supreme Court seeking to have the Iowa law held void. In his opinion for the Supreme Court, Chief Justice Fuller suggested that the failure of Congress to either enact its own regulations of liquor sales or authorize the states to address the subject constituted evidence of an intention that it should remain free of all regulation.[431] Henceforth, only after liquor imported into a state has been removed from its original package could state prohibition laws act on it.[432] The law constituted an impermissible regulation of interstate commerce and was therefore void.[433]

In a dissent joined by John M. Harlan and David Brewer, Justice Horace Gray complained that the Court had long recognized the right of states to prohibit the sale of liquor.[434] The Court's willingness to interpret the silence of Congress as evidence of its intention to bar the states from acting did not pass muster, either. The commerce power was only paramount and not exclusive; therefore, the states need not leave the field of interstate liquor sales until Congress has entered it.[435] Commenting on the *Cooley* standard for state regulations of commerce—that they could not touch subjects appropriate for national regulation—Gray pointed out that even the legislatures found it difficult to apply one rule on the subject of liquor over an area as large as a state—thus the popularity of local option laws: "It is manifest that the regulation of the sale, as of the manufacturer of such liquors manufactured in one state to be sold in another, is a subject which, far from requiring, hardly admits of a uniform system or plan throughout the United States."[436]

Leisy elicited an exceedingly negative response from the public. In Kansas—a dry state—officials continued to arrest "original package" liquor dealers even as a local federal judge released them following habeas corpus proceedings. The judge finally issued an injunction restraining state officers from making further arrests. The governor responded by urging "resistance." He ordered the state attorney general to fight "until all means of lawful redress are exhausted."[437] The *North American Review* endorsed a bill moving through Congress that would authorize the states to regulate the sale of liquor within their borders. It believed that Congress should not exercise its power over that business, as "no law having uniform application throughout the country would be either acceptable or equitable, considering the diversity of public sentiment in the several states on this subject."[438] The Wilson Act of August 8, 1890, provided that intoxicating liquors transported into a state were subject to the laws of that state even if transported in the original package.[439] The Webb-Kenyon Act of March 1, 1913, went further and banned the importation of liquor into dry states.[440]

Congress had no interest in using its commerce powers to regulate spirits; it had a great deal of interest in using its commerce power to encourage development, if one judged from the statute books. Among the most common types of federal public laws to be enacted during the decades after the Civil War were measures authorizing the construction of a bridge across a river. These laws set minimum height requirements and declared the bridges to be lawful structures to prevent lawsuits alleging they constituted impediments to navigation.[441] As Congress provided legal protections for bridges, it also regulated what passed beneath them. It had imposed safety requirements on steamboats since 1819, and an 1871 law listed materials to be used in the construction of the floating palaces. The act required the installation of fire hoses before vessels could receive a customs license. Materials such as nitroglycerine were not to be transported on passenger boats. Watchmen were to be employed for the purpose of warning passengers and crew of fires and other hazards.[442]

It was that which passed on many of the bridges—railroads—that would, by the end of the century, demand the most attention from Congress. During the Civil War the federal government asserted its authority over the lines, though it took over only a handful near the capital and in the South. While the war powers were adequate to that purpose, a dispute over a railroad in New Jersey led Congress to act under its commerce powers in 1866. The Camden & Amboy Railroad enjoyed an effective monopoly over land-based transportation between Philadelphia and New York City—the nation's two largest cities—pursuant to a charter provided to it by the state of New Jersey. The charter barred the state government from authorizing the establishment of another line through the state between New York City and Philadelphia or allowing another railroad to compete with the Camden & Amboy.[443] The Camden & Amboy protested bitterly when the War Department began arranging for the delivery of troops and supplies to Washington, DC, from the northeast through New Jersey via a cumbersome route involving steamships, the Camden & Atlantic and the Raritan & Delaware Bay railroad lines. The Camden & Amboy obtained an injunction from a state court barring the Camden & Atlantic from transporting passengers and freight between New York and Philadelphia unless it turned over to the Camden & Amboy all money it received for providing said service.[444] The order constricted the transportation of men, equipment, and foodstuffs to the capital for the duration of the war.

Frustration in Washington over the city's inadequate railroad connections with the Northeast grew steadily. The problem became acute when waterborne transportation came to a halt—in 1862 Confederates blockaded the Potomac River; in 1864 it froze. The quantity of wheat and hay arriving in the capital dropped below the minimum levels necessary to sustain the Army of the Potomac and the need for action to assure that railroads could operate unimpeded by state charters became painfully obvious.[445] In early 1865, a bill was proposed to authorize railroads to serve the government and the public and receive compensation for their services without being encumbered by the demands of other roads under the color of state charters. In defending the bill, Senator James Nye of Nevada complained that "Washington may be invaded and destroyed, but not a citizen or soldier can cross New Jersey to the relief of the capital, unless he consents to come in the way and at the time dictated by the Camden & Amboy Railroad."[446] Solomon Foot of Vermont summarized the constitutional issues raised by the bill. Could a state grant exclusive privileges to common carriers that restrict interstate commerce in the absence of a conflicting federal law? Can Congress regulate common carriers under its commerce clause powers for the purpose of eradicating these restrictions? Foot answered the latter question in the affirmative: "Congress may set aside any such special and exclusive legislation when it at all restricts, impedes or impairs the facilities of travel and trade and commerce between or among the states." It was free to set railroads "upon the same footing" in carrying passengers and freight regardless of "any inhibition which have been imposed by local state enactment." Foot cited *Gibbons v. Ogden* in support of the proposition that states may not grant monopolistic privileges that impair interstate commerce.[447]

James Garfield charged that "New Jersey has said there shall be no commerce between Washington and New York beyond what one road is able and willing to carry. Who will deny that this is, pro tanto, an interdiction of commerce—a decision that all the surplus business over and above what the Camden & Amboy road can do, shall not be done at all?"[448] On March 31, 1866, Garfield charged that rates for travel within New Jersey were artificially low because the Camden & Amboy was charging high rates for persons passing from New York City to Philadelphia. Non-residents subsidized the train travel of citizens of New Jersey. Garfield acknowledged that thus far Congress had acted under its war and postal powers with respect to railroads, "but there is another power which should not be overlooked. I mean the power to regulate commerce between the states."[449] When some in Congress talked of authorizing construction of an "air line" railroad from the northeast to Washington, Camden & Amboy's general counsel, Joseph T. Bradley—a future Supreme Court justice—objected. He insisted that the commerce power did not authorize Congress to enter the states for the purpose of building railroads or authorizing others to build them. Within the states the federal commerce power was, in his view, limited to navigation.[450]

A law of June 15, 1866, designed to "facilitate commercial, postal, and military communication among the several states" authorized every railroad in the United States to carry "all passengers, troops, government supplies, mails, freight and property on their way from any state to another state, and to receive compensation therefor, and to connect with roads of other states so as to form continuous lines for the transportation of the same at the place of destination."[451] The law did not translate immediately into improved connections between New York City and Washington; nor did the expiration of the charter of the Camden & Amboy in 1869. The problem was not resolved until additional lines built by private interests began operating during the 1870s.

Authorizing railroads to operate free of encumbrances imposed by the states was one tool available to Congress in responding to abusive practices such as those of the Camden & Amboy. If the commerce clause empowered Congress to prevent the states from discriminating against railroads, did it also authorize Congress to ban the lines themselves from discriminating against their customers? Could Congress regulate the rates charged, at least on interstate lines? Attorney General Henry Stanbery thought not. In an opinion of December 30, 1867, he took up the question of whether Congress could fix tariff rates charged by domestic telegraph companies, as it had for interoceanic ones. He answered it in the negative, leaving Congress in the position of being able to fix telegraph rates outside of the United States but not within it. "Certainly the telegraph is not so clearly a vehicle of commerce as the railroad, and if, as I suppose, Congress has not the power to regulate the charges upon a railroad, it cannot have a like power over telegraph communication."[452]

Six months later, in June 1868, the House Committee on Roads and Canals took the opposite view when it issued a report endorsing federal regulation of railroads. In its view, the commerce power might be exercised over railroads as fully as it had been exercised over steamboats. It warned that leaving the matter to the states would make the lines susceptible to attempts to steer traffic to politically connected railroads. The hardships inflicted on New York City by Cornelius Vanderbilt in response to difficulties between his lines and the New York Central revealed the chaos that was inevitable if the matter was left to the caprices of railroads and the state politicians on their payrolls.[453] (In early 1867, Vanderbilt refused to allow New York Central freight to complete its journey into Manhattan along his lines, the Harlem and Hudson River Railroads, imperiling the city's economy for a time.) The Committee noted that the board of directors of one of the railroads involved in the New York dispute had taken refuge in a vessel off of Manhattan to avoid the jurisdiction of New York State courts. It had no doubt of the right of Congress to regulate the lines to "secure the safety of passengers and such regularity and system in the running arrangements and connections as to secure the most prompt transportation of passengers and freight."[454]

While the *Dartmouth College* ruling and the line of cases that followed it hampered the ability of legislatures to regulate railroads (the contract clause was thought to bar the states from enacting laws impairing the rights bestowed by the lines' corporate charters), the Committee noted that the clause did not apply to Congress—it was free to enact regulations that modified or impaired the value of the charters. The Committee explained the failure of Congress to regulate fares on steamboats—some saw this as evidence that the commerce clause did not bestow authority to regulate the rates of common carriers—by pointing out that competition limited the fares charged by the steamers. There was no danger of monopolies assuming control of waterborne transportation; many railroads on the other hand went through areas where there was not another line for hundreds of miles.[455] The minority of the Committee issued a report embracing a narrow view of the power of Congress over railroads; it noted that Congress had never regulated the "manner and terms upon which the agents of commerce shall cooperate."[456] The *New York Times* reacted favorably to the majority report; it suggested that the "notoriously unsatisfactory management" of transportation between New York and Washington led the Committee on Roads and Canals to take up the subject. The *Times* favored federal regulation of the lines, as it would reduce costs and improve service. It would also put an end to the "ability of a wealthy corporation, with the help of a corrupt state legislature, to impose unjust charges and to inflict continual annoyances."[457]

While the Committee on Roads and Canals did not propose legislation in its report, bills to establish a commission authorized to regulate railroad rates were proposed in the House during the 1870s. In March 1874 William Arthur of Kentucky expressed his belief that Congress did not have the power to regulate rates. Permissible regulations of commerce included only those that concern "safety, equality, and freedom of commerce, imperiled and fettered under the Articles of Confederation." Arthur thought it significant that federal steamboat laws "leave the carriers free to fix their own, price, fare, and freight." He pointed out that Alexander Hamilton, John Marshall, and Joseph Story gave the commerce clause broad interpretations, yet even they had never suggested it included a power to set rates for transportation. If Congress fixed railroad rates, how long would it be before it fixed the "merchantable price or equivalent for the goods, wares, and merchandise carried, which are equally the instruments and subjects of the commerce designated, equally subject to the exercise of the power, and even in a greater degree, and in more respects, the objects of high prices, excessive exactions, and vexatious monopoly?" Arthur cited several Supreme Court decisions holding that the commerce power was not exclusive but was held by Congress concurrently with the states and insisted that the states could enforce the common law duty of railroads to charge reasonable rates.[458]

Arthur was correct in suggesting that the commerce clause had not been viewed as authorizing the regulation of rates. The clause had been added to the Constitution to deprive states of the power to impose tariffs on each other's goods.[459] Its drafters saw the clause as authorizing Congress to regulate the waterborne transportation of goods with measures such as navigation laws that favored American shipping for the purpose of compelling other nations to trade with the United States on equitable terms.[460] The commerce power was rarely used for that purpose in the nation's early years. Beginning in the 1820s, Congress acted on the view that the clause bestowed a creative as well as a regulatory power when it funded the construction of turnpikes and canals and began making river-and-harbor appropriations. Its regulatory enactments under the commerce clause continued to be limited to water-based trade.

Congressman John Reagan, Democrat of Texas, served as the driving force behind the movement for a rate bill during the 10-plus years it took to overcome the resistance of the railroads. The former postmaster general of the Confederacy served in the House between 1857 and 1861; on his return to the floor of that chamber in December 1875 he was greeted with catcalls and worse by his northern counterparts. An orthodox Jeffersonian Democrat, Reagan attacked what he saw as excessive fees paid to railroads in exchange for carrying the mails as well as protective tariffs.[461] He was an unlikely sponsor for the role of chief advocate of one of the most significant expansions—or exercises—of federal power to occur during the nineteenth century. Reagan won over some critics with his vote in favor of an electoral commission during the crisis of 1876–77; thereafter he was appointed chairman of the House Committee on Commerce. James Hopkins of Pennsylvania proposed a railroad rate bill in early 1876 that barred rebates and discrimination. Reagan proposed a similar measure in early 1878. He described the bill as designed to "prevent a discrimination in charges for freight by railroad companies against shippers; that is, that no higher rates shall be charged to one shipper than to another." It would also ban the practice of charging more for shorter hauls as well as pooling (the sharing of profits by railroads).[462]

Speaking on May 11, 1878, Representative Edward Bragg of Wisconsin turned to original intent. He did not believe the framers "ever intended that Congress should make laws regulating the rates that a wagon might charge for transportation if it happened to pass over a state line." He believed the bill was being pushed by Pennsylvania iron and steel interests who resented paying high charges to railroads carrying their products. Bragg cited the *Federalist* for the proposition that the commerce power has been granted to Congress only to bring an end to state-based tariffs. He then turned and conceded Congress had authority to enact the measure, but he insisted that it would stifle competition among railroads.[463] Clarkson Potter of New York spoke of the significance of such a measure being pushed by Democrats, thus far the party of strict construction and states' rights: "It shows how things are changing politically as well as otherwise."[464]

The *Nation* labeled the "Reagan anti-discrimination bill" one of the "most momentous steps ever contemplated by the national government." If Congress "has the power to legislate on the subject of transportation at all, it may in the future interfere to a much greater degree than is now proposed." It supported the measure as a solution to both railroad rate wars and the problem of monopoly.[465] In some parts of the country there was nary a sign of monopoly. The main lines had been undercutting each other for years. Rate wars preceded and led directly to the Railroad Strike of 1877. Industry leaders repeatedly organized pools to establish rates and limit competition, only to have one or more lines break the agreement and return everyone to a condition of relentless price-cutting. Large shippers exacted discounts from the railroads, leading the lines to impose higher rates on their other customers to make up for the loss. While the utility of federal regulation eventually dawned on railroad executives, for years they did their best to frustrate the cause, failing to appear before congressional committees when called to testify and claiming a lack of knowledge regarding matters with which their positions made them familiar. At one point John Reagan concluded that the transcripts from congressional hearings had been stolen. Railroad interests funded the candidacies of men running against lawmakers who favored rate regulation. They succeeded in defeating several of them, including Congressman James Hopkins, who lost his seat in 1876.[466]

The cause of rate regulation suffered when Republicans won the House in 1880. When Democrats took the House back in 1882, John Reagan regained his position as chairman of the Committee on Commerce and introduced another railroad bill in December 1883. Progress was slow due to divisions in the House over the question of whether the law should be enforced by courts or a commission. Reagan favored the former; his opponents insisted that method would succumb to excessive litigation costs. The House passed the railroad bill in January 1885 but the Senate refused to act on it, preferring a bill proposed by Shelby Cullom of Illinois. It provided for a commission and lacked a long and short haul clause prohibiting higher charges for shorter trips. The two houses stood deadlocked when the session expired in March.[467]

During the summer and fall petitions demanding passage of a rate bill poured into Washington, and Republicans as well as Democrats realized action was necessary. The frenzy was somewhat surprising in light of the fact that railroad rates dropped by a fifth between 1882 and 1886. As it became more likely a bill of some kind would pass, many railroads began to embrace federal rate regulation as experience taught them that voluntary efforts to coordinate rates, such as pooling, did not work.[468] Some saw federal regulation as a way of ensuring that the national government would take action to keep labor strife from interrupting railroad service.[469]

In early 1887, John Reagan prepared for additional hearings to build support for his bill even though it had already passed the House. When the Senate passed the Cullom bill, a stand-off appeared likely until Reagan accepted a commission. Cullom went along with a long-and-short-haul clause as well as an anti-pooling clause. The measure became law on February 4, 1887: "All charges made for any service rendered to or to be rendered in the transportation of passengers or property as aforesaid, or in connection therewith, or for the receiving, delivering, storage, or handling of such property, shall be reasonable and just."[470] Railroads had to post rate schedules and adhere to their published rates. Offenders were liable for damages plus attorney's fees, and persons suffering harm retained the choice of filing a complaint with the Commission or bringing suit. The guilty would pay up to $5,000 for each offense. The Interstate Commerce Commission (ICC) devised under Section 11 received authority to investigate the management of all common carriers subject to the act (those operating interstate lines). The president would appoint five commissioners with the advise and consent of the Senate; the commissioners were subject to removal only in cases of "inefficiency, neglect of duty (or) malfeasance in office."[471] The law also barred interstate railroads from giving "any undue or unreasonable preference" to passengers. Some saw this provision as a barring racial discrimination. Their illusions were quickly dispelled when the ICC ruled in April 1887 that the railroads could limit blacks to colored cars so long as they were equal in quality to those provided to whites. It explained that "public sentiment, wherever the colored population is large, requires separation of the races."[472] Railroads continued to segregate passengers; they did not provide blacks with facilities equal in quality to those assigned to whites.[473]

The country reacted to the law with guarded approval; many cities and towns feared they would be penalized by the long-and-short-haul clause. Some but not all pools disappeared and accounting practices improved. Secret deals multiplied after 1890. The Commission's glacial pace in handling complaints impeded the law's effectiveness; between 1887 and 1900 cases remained before the ICC for an average of four years.[474] The commission took a hit in 1897 when the Supreme Court ruled that the law did not authorize it to set rates.[475] In his opinion for the Court, Justice Brewer claimed that the power to prescribe rates is not a judicial or an administrative function; the language of the law did not reveal the existence of any such power and none would be inferred.[476] The commission could bar rate increases it found unreasonable, but it could not impose its own.[477] In his autobiography, Shelby Cullom complained that the courts had gutted the law—they "robbed it by judicial construction of much of its intended force." He thought Congress intended that the Commission should have the power to set rates after due investigation following a complaint and a hearing.[478]

Confusion over the scope of the commerce power marked the decade-long debate over the railroad rate bill; it also haunted discussion of a measure to establish a board that would arbitrate labor disputes involving railroads engaged in interstate commerce. Senator John Randolph Tucker of Virginia objected to the bill on the grounds that the labor relations of the lines were not within the jurisdiction of Congress. "Because the Baltimore & Ohio Railroad carries flour and passengers from Maryland to Missouri, which is interstate commerce, it does not follow that the contract of employment in Baltimore between the company and its ticket agent there is subject to regulation by Congress, or to the jurisdiction of the federal courts." Whether a labor contract is valid, "what it means, whether the wages are fair, or the hours of labor are just, or the company or its officers are harsh, cruel, or unjust, or discharge an employee against right—there are questions collateral to commerce and transportation, and which cannot under the power to regulate commerce be controlled by Congress or be adjudicated by federal courts."[479] Despite Tucker's objections, the measure establishing a board of arbitration became law on October 1, 1888.[480]

If Congress could prevent railroads from using their control over transportation in large areas of the country to gouge farmers and other customers, could it regulate other industries that suffered from the problem of monopoly? With protective tariffs removing foreign competitors from the marketplace in many fields, all that stood between industry giants and complete domination was the stifling of domestic competition. As early as 1879, Standard Oil, an Ohio corporation, obtained control of 90 percent of the domestic supply of refined oil. It exploited its position to extract concessions from railroads and customers—though it also consistently lowered its prices throughout the last two decades of the century. Standard evaded an Ohio law barring it from operating outside of the state by placing foreign companies it controlled in the hands of a trustee. In 1892 the Ohio Supreme Court ordered the trust dissolved; Standard responded by moving to New Jersey, which permitted corporations formed therein to do business in other states. Even more significantly, New Jersey allowed holding companies. While the increased use of holding companies led to the demise of trusts as a popular form of corporate organization, these monster entities remained known as trusts.

Trusts were formed in at least 10 processing industries in addition to oil, such as sugar refining. Action at the national level seemed problematic to some. As George Hoar put it, "many of the evils caused by trusts, or apprehended from them, can only be cured by the action of the states, but cannot be restrained by Congress, which can deal only with international or interstate commerce."[481] Restraints of trade and monopoly had been condemned by the law for centuries. By the summer of 1890, 27 states and territories had enacted statutes barring or restraining monopolistic conduct.[482] These proved ineffective in part because monopolies extended across state lines.

States had little motive to investigate trusts based in their cities as they drew wealth from other parts of the country; they also had trouble mustering the political will to investigate entities that exercised enormous influence over legislatures.

In January 1888, Representative Richard Guenther of Wisconsin called for federal action against trusts that manipulated the price of articles in interstate commerce. The *Springfield Daily Republican* could not see it. "This would seem to be straining the commerce clause of the Constitution quite beyond the range of reason or vision."[483] In late 1889 Ohio Senator John Sherman proposed a bill banning restraints of trade. The Senate Judiciary Committee reported negatively on the bill; two of its members thought it unconstitutional.[484] Sherman defended the bill on the floor of the Senate, describing it as a "remedial statute to enforce by civil process in the courts of the United States the common law against monopolies." If Congress can regulate commerce, surely it can protect it and if necessary "nullify contracts that restrain commerce, turn it from its natural courses, increase the prices of articles, and therefore diminish the amount of commerce."[485] He described the bill as designed to prevent persons from combining to prevent competition.[486] John Tyler Morgan of Alabama surprised the Senate with his support for the bill. He claimed to be one of the "states' rights school of politicians" who "stand here for the purpose of trying to protect the states of this Union against encroachment on the part of the federal government." Yet he conceded that in "this matter concerning trust and combinations and conspiracies, I must say I think the states are utterly derelict." He blamed the failure of states to act on "lethargy" inspired by "a too confident reliance upon the powers of Congress to remedy public evils."[487]

Was state indolence now the standard by which the constitutionality of federal acts was to be judged? Senator Richard Coke of Texas did not think so. He thought the bill went beyond the scope of the commerce clause in targeting manufacturers. Interstate commerce "commences only when the product gets into the hands of the common carrier for transportation to another state and ends as soon as it reaches its destination."[488] James George of Mississippi was a member of the Judiciary Committee; he also thought the bill had no warrant in the Constitution. The mere entry of manufactured goods into interstate and foreign commerce did not, in his view, give Congress authority to regulate manufacturers. Otherwise, Congress could also regulate the pursuits of the "planter, the grazier, the manufacturer, the mechanic, the immense operations of the colerics, and miners and furnaces of the country; for there is not one of these vocations the results of which may not become the subject of interstate commerce." George believed the bill regulated the disposition of goods before and after but not during the time they were subjects of interstate commerce (in transport).[489] The Mississippi senator later changed course and endorsed the bill after Sherman amended it so that it was limited to interstate combinations in restraint of trade.[490]

The bill passed both Houses of Congress and became law on July 2, 1890.[491] "Every contract, combination in the form of trust or otherwise, or conspiracy, in restraint of trade or commerce among the several states, or with foreign nations, is hereby declared to be illegal." Violation of the law constituted a misdemeanor, subjecting guilty parties to fines of up to $5,000 and a year in prison. U.S. attorneys could also bring actions in equity in federal court to prevent and restrain violations of the law. Aggrieved parties could file suit and seek treble damages. The law proved defective in several ways; it appeared to go beyond the common law's prohibition of unreasonable restraints of trade to include any restraint. As George Hoar pointed out, many actions taken in the course of commercial activity constitute a restraint of trade; even the establishment of a partnership restrains the partners.[492] The Justice Department did not jump at the opportunity presented to it. The law had been on the books for a year before Attorney General William Miller asked U.S. district attorneys to determine if there were any violations in progress in their states. The limited resources of the Department of Justice hampered enforcement of the law. The Department employed only 18 lawyers in Washington, DC; they occupied the upper quarters of a bank building where the government rented space. Seven cases were initiated during the administration of Benjamin Harrison; the first victory occurred in a suit against a coal mine operators in Tennessee. Justice Department lawyers considered filing suits against the bobbin, drug, and oleomargarine trusts but no action was taken. Grover Cleveland's attorney general, Richard Olney, did not embrace the Sherman Antitrust Act as he saw it as poorly drafted and likely to be ineffective.[493]

Corporations also evaded the Sherman Act by forming holding companies or merging—thereby removing the necessity for a contract or agreement among independent entities. When E. C. Knight Company contracted to purchase sugar refineries in Philadelphia, the country faced the prospect of having a single entity control 98 percent of the sugar refining industry. The U.S. attorney for the eastern District of Pennsylvania filed suit. The bill sought an order enjoining the merger on the grounds that it would enable Knight to obtain control of the price of sugar, and that the contract for the purchase of the refineries therefore constituted a restraint of trade. The Circuit Court held the evidence did not show a restraint of trade, and its ruling was upheld by the Circuit Court of Appeals. The Supreme Court agreed and held that the Sherman Antitrust Act did not apply to manufacturing.[494] In his opinion for the Court, Chief Justice Melvin Fuller explained that "commerce succeeds to manufacture, and is not a part of it." Nor does the fact that an article is manufactured with the intent to export it to another state "make it an article of interstate commerce, and the intent of the manufacturer does not determine the time when the article or product passes from the control of the state or belongs to commerce."[495] As for the argument that the Defendant intended to gain control of sugar manufacturing to determine its price in the national marketplace, Fuller refused to consider the possibility. "It does not follow that an attempt to monopolize, or the actual monopoly of, the manufacturer was an attempt . . . to monopolize commerce, even though, in order to dispose of the product, the instrumentality of commerce was necessarily invoked."[496] In fact it did follow—why would the Defendant seek a monopoly over manufactured sugar, if it did not seek to control the price of it? With his insistence that no evidence indicated there was an attempt to monopolize commerce, Fuller seemed to conceded that if a manufacturer did attempt to restrain interstate trade, it actions would come within the scope of the commerce clause and the Sherman Act. In his dissent, Justice John Harlan conceded that the scope of the commerce clause did not extend to manufacturing, yet he also insisted Congress could remove impediments to interstate commerce, whatever the source.[497] In his view the majority opinion held that while states cannot impede interstate commerce, entities of their creation—corporations—could.[498] The effect of the decision was somewhat dampened four years later when the high court held that an agreement among a group of manufacturers to sell a product at or above a price agreed on by all violated the Sherman Act.[499] While the *Knight* decision was viewed as retrograde and unduly restrictive almost from the time it was issued, it did have the rare quality of clarity—manufacturing was beyond the scope of the commerce clause. The principle would remain in force for decades.

In *Swift v. U.S.* (1905), Justice Oliver Wendell Holmes provided rhetoric if not a formal method of analysis that would eventually aid the Supreme Court in bringing most economic activity, including manufacturing, within the scope of the commerce clause. In his opinion for the high court, he held that a conspiracy among purchasers of livestock to avoid bidding against each other came within the scope of the Sherman Act and the commerce clause as the movement of cattle from the range to the consumer constituted "a current of commerce among the states."[500] The beef trust—so called despite the fact that it controlled only 60 percent of the market—was thereby dissolved. In the past, only the passage of goods or services across state lines endowed Congress with authority over them under the commerce clause—a state's border served as a sort of trip wire for federal jurisdiction. If interstate commerce constituted a body of water instead—a current—that extended from the source of the product to the home of every American, it was easy to see how judges would use that analogy to extend the authority of Congress to economic activity that took place solely within a single state.

Despite the fact that the commerce clause powers of Congress as originally understood did not encompass the production of goods or agriculture, its extension to those subjects was inevitable and probably necessary, as large corporations and trusts eluded the authority of the states to such an extent that they operated in a market that was practically devoid of any public authority capable of checking their excesses.

The need for federal regulation of monopolies in the American marketplace became more evident at the turn of the century, as the number of industrial trusts multiplied by a factor of nine between 1898 and 1901 to 185.[501] The vagueness of the Sherman Antitrust Act made the law difficult to administer and the problem only worsened with the passage of time. In *U.S. v. Trans-Missouri Freight Association*, the Supreme Court read the statute literally—it barred all restraints of trade and not just unreasonable ones, despite the railroads' argument that this interpretation conflicted with the intent of Congress.[502] It therefore held illegal a contract among 18 railroads setting rate charges. In dissent Justice White noted that not all contracts restraining trade were viewed as violations of the common law and pointed out that the Supreme Court had previously disregarded the literal language of statutes to avoid giving them an unreasonable meaning.[503] The Supreme Court reversed course in Standard Oil of *New Jersey v. U.S.* (1911), holding that the Sherman Act barred only unreasonable restraints of trade.[504]

THE NATIONAL PORK BARREL

From 1860 to 1880, the Republicans won six consecutive presidential elections. As the 1884 contest approached, most observers realized the party was likely approaching the end of its winning streak. Senator John Sherman sought the Republican nomination; his cause was hurt by the fact that his wife was a Roman Catholic.[505] President Arthur damaged his own slim prospects when he fired the collector at Boston and replaced him with a candidate viewed as a partisan hack, thereby alienating the influential Massachusetts delegation.[506] James Blaine had been the leader of the Republican Party for over a decade. Believing he could not carry New York, the former secretary of state did not seek the nomination.[507] Rank-and-file Republicans would not have it, though, and they chose him over Sherman and Vermont Senator George F. Edmunds, a skilled lawyer and enemy of the spoils system.

Democrats chose New York Governor Grover Cleveland over Senator Thomas Bayard of Delaware, whose prospects were crippled by his defense of secession as a young lawyer. Cleveland enjoyed a reputation as a reformer; Tammany Hall bitterly opposed his nomination. In the general election Democrats claimed their opponents had been corrupted by too many years in power. They produced a map showing federal lands that had been granted to railroads during the past 20 years (139.4 million acres).[508] The seedy relationship between Republicans and railroads was embodied in Blaine himself, and Democrats were quick to make much of allegations that had been hovering over him for a decade. He likely received compensation from railroads in exchange for pushing legislation favorable to them through Congress. Republicans warned that Democrats would remove protective tariffs despite the fact that Cleveland had done nothing to warrant such a charge. The issue divided Democrats, with easterners embracing protection and farmers demanding an end to it. The party straddled the issue in its platform—it dropped its traditional demand for a revenue-only tariff.[509] Republicans also claimed that Democrats would abolish military pensions, imperil the rights of blacks, abolish the Fourteenth and Fifteenth Amendments, and weaken the Supreme Court.[510]

Blaine's relationship with railroads led several of the leading newspapers and periodicals in the northeast that usually supported Republicans to embrace Cleveland. These included the *New York Times*, *New York Herald*, *New York Evening Post*, and *Harper's Weekly*.[511] Reform Republicans—known as "Mugwumps"—also supported the New York governor. When Republicans pointed out that Cleveland's record of public service was not long, Carl Schurz observed that there were friends of Blaine who must "wish that his had been a little shorter."[512] The Republican candidate struggled under numerous handicaps, one of which was the hostility of the president—the Postmaster General would not allow party officials collecting assessments into post offices.[513] Blaine's disadvantages were mitigated by the support he received from Irish Catholics. Blaine's mother was Roman Catholic and the candidate himself had demonstrated a willingness to speak of Great Britain in disparaging terms—always a good strategy for those seeking the Irish vote. As the election would turn on New York, which now teemed with hundreds of thousands of Irish Catholics, the support of this group—which had voted Democratic since the party's birth—might well decide the contest. Blaine may have been on his way to a narrow victory until a one of a group of Protestant clergymen meeting with the candidate assured him that they would not join the growing number of Republicans who were supporting Cleveland. He and his cohorts did not "propose to leave our party and identify ourselves with the party whose antecedents have been rum, Romanism and rebellion." While it was not clear Blaine heard the remark, a supporter of Cleveland did. It was relayed to the country along with Blaine's failure to distance himself from it. His support among Irish Catholics dropped through the floor.

As a chapter in American political history, the campaign was notable both for its revelation of rampant anti-Catholic feeling and the introduction at the national level of abject pandering to ethnic groups whose priorities seemed to have little connection with the best interests of the United States. As a chapter in the development of American federalism, the significance of the election of 1884 arose out of the machinations of Pension Bureau employees. Perhaps not until the middle of the following century were the electoral consequences of placing as many Americans as possible on the federal payroll demonstrated so clearly. The pension list expanded sharply following the Arrears Act of 1879— it included 325,000 persons by 1885.[514] The distribution of pensioners in the northern states could not have served Republicans better if they had told veterans where to live—in the early 1880s 40 percent of the persons on the pension rolls lived in the critical states of New York, Pennsylvania, Ohio, Indiana, and Illinois—along with over half of those with applications pending.[515] A sizeable portion of the northern electorate took notice when Republicans told them in the fall of 1884 that military pensions would not survive a Cleveland administration.[516] The head of the Pension Bureau, W. W. Dudley, resigned from office in September, but the resignation was not effective until November 10. He went to Ohio and Indiana to campaign for Blaine while continuing to receive his salary. The *Nation* complained that while in the Midwest, Dudley used the Pension Bureau "as a bribe for votes." It was "openly announced that pensioners who voted for Blaine would be given precedence in having their claims heard at Washington, and with this announcement there was spread the naturally following intimation that a pensioner who voted against the Republican candidate would have to wait a long time for a hearing on his claim."[517] As voters still used colored ballots provided by the parties, it was easy for observers to see how citizens voted. Hordes of special pension agents from the Pension Bureau arrived in Ohio and aided Dudley in his work.[518] They promised that pensions would be "promptly adjusted" for veterans who voted Republican.[519]

Between Union army veterans concerned about their pensions and northern workers fearful of losing protective tariffs, the Republican Party wielded a pecuniary influence over the northern electorate that dwarfed the bribery of immigrants that was now a regular Democratic tactic in the section's cities. As everyone expected, the election turned on New York. Grover Cleveland won the state by 1149 votes. Blaine's late loss of support among the state's Irish Catholics may have made the difference; support given by many New York Republicans to the Prohibition Party may also have cost him the state. The defection of so many reform-minded Republicans to Cleveland and widespread unemployment aided the Democratic cause, as did the repression of the black vote in the South. Five southern states with black majorities voted for Cleveland.[520]

The first session of the 49th Congress convened in December 1885. Republicans held the Senate. They gained 20 seats in the House in the

1884 elections but they were still in the minority. The party now held only eight congressional seats in the South.[521] Writing just after the election, S. S. Cox confidently reported that the "pendulum is again swinging toward decentralization."[522] He could not have been pleased when the Cleveland administration found itself fighting efforts to further expand the pecuniary relationship between the national government and the American people. The first battle revolved around an attempt to push yet another gargantuan pension bill through Congress. The president's lack of enthusiasm for packing the pension list was revealed in a veto message of May 8, 1886, when he decried the congressional habit of approving claims that had already been denied by the Pension Bureau.[523] Illinois Senator John Logan served as Blaine's running mate in 1884; he did as much as anyone to promote a sense of entitlement among Union army veterans. Logan reacted to what he saw as the president's hostility to veterans by demanding a pension for every man who served the Union cause during the war. Congress refused to take the hint. It continued to send the president hundreds of special pension bills approving the applications of Union army veterans that had been denied by the Pension Bureau or increasing pensions already granted. By the end of the century these acts were so numerous that two volumes had to be issued listing the laws enacted by each Congress; one contained public laws while the other listed private acts, almost all of which were laws granting pensions to individual veterans or their widows, or increasing the size of the monthly payments. By mid-August 1886, Cleveland had vetoed more than 100 of these measures. Most of the meritorious claims had long since been granted during the two decades that had elapsed since Appomattox. Applicants now included a man who fell from his horse and injured his ankle while on his way to enlist and another who was injured by a cannon on the Fourth of July while home on leave.[524]

During the second half of 1886, the Grand Army of the Republic put its shoulder to the wheel. With its membership now at 269,000 (it would reach 427,000 by 1890), it was the most powerful lobbying organization in the country. Claiming it had discovered thousands of veterans residing in poorhouses, the GAR pushed for enactment of a law providing monthly checks to all disabled veterans, regardless of the source of the disability—it need not have been suffered in the war.[525] The desire of Republicans and assorted Democrats to reduce the surplus and ease the pressure to cut tariffs helped produce the required votes and a dependent pension bill passed in early 1887. It provided a monthly payment of $12 to any Union army veteran who had served three months, received an honorable discharge, and suffered from a disability that left him unable to support himself via physical labor. The arguments offered in favor of the measure revealed a political culture that been severely warped by the growing contrast between wealth and poverty. In the view of Charles H. Grosvenor, Republican of Ohio, "it was the men who carried the musket at $16 a month and slept in the swamps of the South; in the open air; and filled their system with the seeds of disease, from which they never recovered, that saved the credit of this nation and made the men of New York the millionaires that they are; that enable them to grasp the industries of this country by the throat; to build up monopolies that are today the monuments of their grasping tendencies, and yet they turn about and through their organs denounce the efforts of the friends of the soldiers to save these men from the poor-house."[526]

The president was unable to see the debt. He vetoed the dependent pension bill on February 11, 1887. In his view the measure amounted to a service pension bill that would result in payments to all veterans. Cleveland pointed out that service pensions had been provided to veterans of the Revolution and the War of 1812 long after those conflicts were over and when the recipients were in their dotage (1818 in the case of the Revolutionary War and 1871 in the case of the War of 1812). "So far as it relates to the soldiers of the late Civil War, the bounty it affords them is given thirteen years earlier than it has been furnished the soldiers of any other war; and before a large majority of its beneficiaries have advanced in age beyond the strength and vigor of the prime of life." Veterans already received preferential treatment in public employment and those who had become destitute had access to soldiers' homes operated by the War Department. In light of past frauds, Cleveland was confident that the measure would, if passed, "put a further premium on dishonesty and mendacity." Worst of all, it would increase the burden on taxpayers. Many cities and towns still had not paid off the debts they incurred to pay bounties to soldiers during the war. The nation had been toiling under the weight of wartime taxes for over 20 years, and demand for their abolition was growing.[527]

Despite the efforts of the Grand Army of the Republic, Congress failed to override the veto. Many Americans were relieved. The *Nation* blamed the bill on the widespread belief among members of Congress that "the ex-soldiers of the Union army are open to bribery, and that their votes may be captured by special appropriations for them as a class from the public treasury." The veterans were viewed as "so mercenary in their character that they would support any public man who voted them money, and oppose any public man who voted against any such grant." The *Nation* was pleased to report that such beliefs were not confirmed by the facts. Lawmakers who settled on the idea of sponsoring huge pension bills as a means of political survival often met with defeat.[528] *Harper's Weekly* blamed the pension problem on the surplus. "The advocates of every extraordinary scheme hope to snatch a part of the surplus, and those whose views of public policy require the maintenance of a large surplus (advocates of high tariffs) naturally teach the desirability, not of limiting taxation to the needs of the government, and of restraining the public expenditure, but of spending profusely for every purpose to which any semblance of public concern can be given." The spending scheme that took precedent over all of the others was the "movement for further pensions." Pension agents were primarily responsible for it; their long-term goal was "to place upon the list of public support every person who served for any time in the army or navy, and with them a certain range of their relations."[529]

The second battle over the pecuniary relationship between the national government and the American people that occurred in 1887 revolved around the desire of lawmakers to aid victims of drought in the Southwest. Thirty thousand persons were left destitute by a severe shortage of rainfall that affected western Texas in 1887. Lawmakers took up a bill to provide farmers in the stricken region with seeds. There was some precedent for the idea even if it lacked any basis in the Constitution. Members of Congress had been sending seeds to their constituents since the 1850s. In 1867 Congress authorized the purchase of $50,000 worth of seeds for distribution in the South by the Freedmen's Bureau; in 1875 it appropriated $180,000 for the distribution of seeds in areas of the Plains states affected by a grasshopper plague.[530] Advocates of a bill appropriating $10,000 for the distribution of seeds in drought-stricken Texas were confident it would become law. Senator Richard Coke of Texas normally opposed novel exercises of federal authority. When he announced to the Senate that he supported the bill, George Hoar asked him to cite constitutional authority for the appropriation. Caught short-handed, Coke responded, "not at this time." Laughter echoed through the chamber. After an awkward exchange revealed the Texas legislature was then in session and considering modes of relief, Coke noted that Congress spent money every year distributing seeds. Therefore "it is but right that it should make a special application of some of the seeds thus purchased in a district . . . so needful of them as the one in Texas." Hoar, amused that he had demonstrated the inconsistency of one of the Senate's leading strict constructionists, expressed his hope that "if the Senate voted to furnish seed to Texas, Texas would furnish constitutional law to the Senate." He was willing to be generous in the interim, though, and announced that he would vote for the bill "with great pleasure."[531]

Lawmakers expecting the president to sign the bill received an unpleasant surprise. In a veto message of February 16, 1887, Cleveland announced that he could "find no warrant for such an appropriation in the Constitution." He did not believe "that the power and duty of the general government ought to be extended to the relief of individual suffering which is no manner properly related to the public service or benefit."

Federal aid in cases such as the Texas drought would only encourage "the expectation of paternal care on the part of the government and weaken the sturdiness of our national character." Cleveland closed by noting that the Commissioner of Agriculture already received a large annual appropriation for the distribution of seeds—two-thirds of which went to members of Congress so they could forward them to their constituents. If they wished, lawmakers could ask the Commissioner to send their allotments to Texas.[532] Members of Congress did not appreciate the suggestion. The Agricultural Commissioner asked them to donate their seed allotments—some 1.22 million packages had been given to them—but over the next two days lawmakers waived their right to only 13,000 packages.[533] The *Nation* applauded the veto; in its view the seed bill was born of "the same principle as that of the pension bill, that the government ought to come to the help of anybody who is in distress." In its view relief ought to come from private parties or the Texas legislature.[534]

The fortunes of 30,000 Americans were involved in the seed bill; several hundred thousand veterans had an interest in pension legislation. These were nothing in comparison to tariffs, on which the livelihoods of millions of Americans turned—or at least that is what politicians claimed. After years of simmering beneath the surface, the issue of protection boiled over in 1887. That year the federal government had receipts of $336 million, about two-thirds of which were derived from tariffs, and expenses of $242 million. Surpluses were nothing new, but with the excess approaching $100 million it was evident the time for action had arrived.[535] Democrats as well as Republicans had stood in the way of a downward revision of rates even though cuts had been regarded as inevitable since the 1882 Tariff Commission suggested them. In 1884, Illinois Democrat William Morrison, chairman of the Committee on Ways and Means, called for passage of a bill imposing 20 percent reductions across the board; the measure failed when Samuel J. Randall of Pennsylvania and 40 pro-tariff Democrats objected. When Republicans used the issue of protection successfully in the 1886 midterm elections—they gained a dozen seats in the House, including Morrison's—some Democrats began to regard the issue as toxic.[536] Still the surplus continued to grow—it was expected to reach $140 million by the end of 1888. The federal government had already increased its purchase of bonds and some thought it should redeem the greenbacks remaining in circulation. Others favored reducing internal taxes on whiskey and tobacco. When it became evident that the alternatives were unworkable or inadequate, talk turned again to tariff cuts. In the fall of 1887 strange rumors began to circulate that Cleveland was going to devote the entirety of his annual message to a plea for lower rates—it had been the practice of chief executives to use their annual messages to report on the activities of each department.

The move was viewed a risky, but with the exception of a handful of pro-tariff lawmakers led by Samuel J. Randall of Pennsylvania, Democrats began to warm to the idea, in part because they believed the president had not provided effective leadership in legislative matters thus far.[537]

The message began with what had been a common assumption: "The theory of our institutions guarantees to every citizen the full enjoyment of all the fruits of his industry and enterprise, with only such deduction as may be his share toward the careful and economical maintenance of the government which protects him." Taking more than this from the citizen "is indefensible extortion and a culpable betrayal of American fairness and justice." After noting that the federal government expected to report a surplus of $113 million for the current fiscal year, Cleveland turned to the source of the problem—high tariffs. Not only had they caused the government to take in more than it needed, they forced people to pay more for domestic as well as foreign goods, as manufacturers increased prices on protected products to reflect the lack of competition. Prices were even higher in those industries that were dominated by a single company or group of companies. The president dismissed the endless debate over the comparative virtues of free trade and protection, saying that "it is a condition which confronts us, not a theory." He closed by telling Congress that a duty was owed to the American people to reduce taxation "to the necessary expenses of an economical operation of the government and to restore to the business of the country the money which we hold in the Treasury through the perversion of governmental powers."[538]

As the message was read by the clerk in the House of Representatives, lawmakers gradually stopped talking among themselves and went dead quiet as they realized the president had devoted the entirety of his message to a single subject.[539] The *Nation* applauded the president's courage. Republican charges that Democrats had avoided taking a position on the issue were no longer valid. "The gun has been fired and will be heard in every corner of the country."[540] It was said that the president's message made the tariff issue more of a party question than it had been at any time since the period before the Civil War, with Democrats committed to free trade and Republicans to protection.[541] Still the fissures that existed in both parties remained just as evident in 1888 as they had been in 1887. Republican-leaning farmers despised tariffs that did not profit them at all but increased the prices they paid for consumer goods and farm equipment (though sheep owners prized the tariff on wool). The merchants of New York and Boston saw little advantage in a policy that reduced foreign trade. Those who worked in northern factories and mines may not have shared the outlook of their employers, but the two groups were equally susceptible to the argument that reduced tariffs would bring a flood of foreign goods produced by cheap labor. The arrival of manufacturing in the Democratic South increased support for protection in the region that had long been the most hostile to it. In an effort to slow a movement that was obviously building steam, James Blaine revived an idea Henry Clay used in an attempt to preserve high tariffs rates—distribution. He suggested that Congress use the proceeds of the tax on whiskey to provide the states with grants, which they could use to reduce real estate taxes. The *Nation* was appalled; it thought such an expenditure fell outside the scope of even the general welfare clause. If Congress could distribute money to ease the tax burden, perhaps it should raise revenue "to make good the losses of sheep owners from dogs, or to help lower the railroad fares of the suburban population, or to supplement wages in the coal districts, or to provide everybody whose earnings are below $600 a year with a winter overcoat." The possibilities were endless. "There is no end to the folly or extravagance to which this theory of surpluses might lead."[542]

What became known as the great tariff debate of 1888 took place in the House of Representatives that spring. It revolved around the Mills bill, which the Committee on Ways and Means reported favorably on in March. It lowered rates an average of 7 percent. The bill cut tariffs on necessaries and imposed specific rates (per yard or per pound) in an effort to reduce fraud. The free list was expanded. It was a moderate start to be sure but Democrats hoped it would be followed by further reductions.[543] A key constituency was alienated from the beginning—wool had been included on the free list, thereby making "every farmer who owned sheep a protectionist."[544] Manufactured products lost protection, as did woolen goods. High rates for sugar and cotton textiles remained. Consequently, support for the bill divided along sectional lines, with southerners embracing it and northerners opposing it.

The debate began when Roger Mills of Texas arose from his seat at 1:00 p.m. on the afternoon of April 17 and addressed the House.[545] The chairman of the Committee on Ways and Means began by noting that tariffs currently averaged 47 percent—compared to 19 percent in 1861. Mills recalled Justin Morrill's assurances during the Civil War regarding a steep tariff hike: "this is intended as a war measure, a temporary measure." Yet, Mills continued, 20 years later, "instead of the rate of taxation being reduced to meet the wants of an efficient administration of government in time of peace, it continues to grow and fill the coffers of the government with money not required for public purposes, and which rightfully should remain in the pockets of the people." He complained that most of the wartime internal taxes had been repealed, while tariffs, which fell heavily on the poor, remained. "Was the tax of three percent on women's and children's clothing paid by the manufacturer more oppressive than the tax of 82% on both foreign and domestic goods of the same kind paid by the consumer?"

He thought the United States could produce nine-tenths of the manufactured goods consumed by Americans more cheaply than Great Britain—manufacturing jobs would survive lower tariff rates. The Texas congressman denied that enhanced profits made possible to industry by protection were passed on to laborers in the form of higher pay. Mills cited the Commissioner of Labor's annual report for the proposition that wage costs of American manufacturers were modest. While it cost $2.51 to produce a pair of five-pound blankets, the portion of that cost arising out of labor was only 70 cents. The tariff on that same pair of blankets was $1.90.[546]

Benton McMillin of Tennessee claimed that protection had destroyed the American merchant marine and the carrying trade. These industries prospered before the Civil War; following Appomattox they suffered due to a decline in international trade and an increase in the cost of protected raw materials needed for the construction of ships, such as iron, copper, and steel. Turning to the widespread belief that certain industries depended on the tariff for survival, McMillin complained that "we are striving to teach our people concerning tariffs and almost everything else that they cannot prosper in their business pursuits (unless) they are fortified by United States statutes; we are trying to inculcate in them the belief that upon Congress depends the amount of their wages, the number of hours which they shall labor and their prosperity or adversity in their industrial pursuits."[547] On April 24, Julius Burrows of Michigan assailed the Mills bill as a "deformity" that had been "nursed by the harlot of free trade." He warned that it would subject "the great wool growing interest of the country . . . to a ruinous foreign competition which will surely prove its ultimate destruction." He blamed the 1883 reduction of the wool tariff for the decline in the number of sheep in the United States. Burrows denied that tariffs were paid by consumers in the form of increased prices—on the contrary, they produced lower prices. Prices had been dropping for years—he thought protection itself was responsible for this trend. Burrows suggested—as Henry Clay had 60 years previously—that in stimulating industry and creating manufacturing jobs, protection increased the size of the domestic market for agricultural commodities. He did not believe that other nations were likely to buy large quantities of American crops.[548]

On April 25, Democrat William Bynum of Indiana conceded that wages had increased since protective tariffs had been instituted during the war, but so had wages in Britain, which had much lower tariffs. Protectionism ruled in France and Germany, yet those countries had lower wages than either Britain or America. American manufacturers did not benefit from protection to the extent claimed; high rates on copper forced them to pay more for that critical resource than their European competitors despite the fact that the country had the world's most ample supplies of copper. Overall the United States produced more manufacturing goods and agricultural commodities than it could consume—therefore it would benefit from lower tariffs and more international trade.[549] Thomas M. Browne, an Indiana Republican, cited articles in the *Glasgow Herald* and the *London Ironmonger* that treated the president's message as an endorsement of free trade. He charged that Democrats planned on reducing protective tariffs to the absolute minimum necessary to maintain an adequate revenue. Browne warned that internal taxes and the sugar tariff could pay for all but $30 million of the previous year's expenditures. He conceded that tariffs had increased the cost of some goods but he insisted that the cost of many items had fallen, including plate glass, iron, woolens, and cotton goods.[550]

At the end of April, with the newspapers publishing speeches from the great tariff debate in Washington and editors proclaiming it a landmark in American oratory, the *Springfield Daily Republican* ran out of patience. Instead of packed galleries and awestruck reporters witnessing the greatest forensic battle since the Webster-Hayne debate, a largely empty chamber endured a series of flat monologues. "The honorable members are not addressing themselves to the business at hand, but in the main are reading long manuscripts to empty seats in order to waste time and figure in the record. There is the biggest display of 'buncombe' now on exhibition that the national capital and the American people have ever seen." During the previous week, Congressman Nathan Goff of West Virginia addressed six of his fellow Republicans while nine Democrats were occupied on the other side of the chamber. What was so important as to cause scores of representatives to be absent during the debates? Horse races.[551]

Nelson Dingley, Republican of Maine, addressed the less-than-capacity crowd on May 3. He insisted that tariffs actually decreased prices by enabling manufactures to establish themselves and reach an advanced state of efficiency—thus saving Americans the cost of importing items such as steel from foreign countries. Dingley claimed that wages in Massachusetts were 77 percent higher than in Britain because of protective tariffs—they stimulated manufacturing and "diversified employments." He denied that tariffs impaired the ability of foreigners to purchase American products (by reducing their profits on the sale of their own goods), as they, like everyone else, always sought the lowest price. Protection assisted foreign trade because it enriched Americans and enabled them to buy more goods.[552] The tariff debate of 1888 was built on syllogisms, but Dingley's argument may have constituted a high point in the accumulation of specious arguments. If protection did not enable manufacturers to raise prices, why did its proponents assure that it limited the effects of cheap foreign labor? If protection reduced the income of foreign countries by reducing their sales in America, then it followed that they could not buy as many American products. Wages in the United States were higher than in Britain, but was this because of tariffs or other factors? Two truths were plain: manufacturers wanted high tariffs so they could raise prices, and on the enactment of high tariffs, they did.

On May 3, William H. Martin of Texas claimed there "are few articles of necessary consumption" that the people of his district had to buy that were not subject to protective tariffs, including farm equipment. Tariffs made up $16.45 of the $35 price of a stove; $12 of the $27 price of two carpets; and $4.20 of the $12 cost of sewing equipment (thread, needles, thimbles, and a scissors).[553] On May 17, Clifton Breckinridge of Arkansas pointed out that in the cotton textile industry, wages made up only 21 percent of the cost of the product, but tariff rates for textiles started at 35 percent and went up—the industry's claim that present tariff levels were necessary to cover the cost of labor was without validity.[554] On May 17, S. S. Cox deflated the windy syllogisms that were blowing through the House by offering a few of his own. "Ireland has no snakes. Ireland has low wages. Snakes make wages high." The United States, he continued, "is infested with tramps. The U.S. has high wages. Therefore tramps make wages high." As for the fear of foreign competition that ran through the arguments of his opponents, Cox found it hard to believe that "a country that that obtains 250,000 patents a year had anything to fear from foreign competition."[555]

On May 17, Speaker of the House John G. Carlisle of Kentucky concluded the debate with a searing indictment: "There is not a monarchical government in the world, however absolute its form or however arbitrary its power, that would dare to extort such a tribute from its subjects in excess of the proper requirements of the public service; and the question which Congress is now compelled to determine is whether such a policy can be longer continued here in this country, where the people are supposed to govern in their own right and in their own interest." Carlisle insisted that improvements in productivity had produced a worldwide decline in prices—tariffs had nothing to do with it. Nor did he accept the claim that protection had reduced the cost of steel rails, as their price had fallen in parts of the world that lacked protection, such as Britain. As for talk of establishing a home market for farmers, Carlisle pointed out that the United States simply did not have the population to buy all of the crops grown each year. "What the American farmer most needs is a home market in which he can purchase supplies as cheaply as his competitors purchase theirs'." With the House full for once, the Speaker closed: "Let us diminish the cost of production in our agricultural and manufacturing industries, not by diminishing the wages of labor, but by reducing taxation upon the necessaries of life and upon the materials which constitute the basis of our finished products, and by removing, as far as we can, the restrictions which embarrass our people in their efforts to exchange the fruits of their own toil which they do not need for the commodities of other countries which they do need." The House erupted in applause.[556] The Mills bill passed the House on July 21, 162–149; three Republicans joined the Democratic majority in sending the measure to the Senate.[557] There it died a quiet death, and the country prepared to hear the same arguments all over again, as a presidential election was already in full swing.

Annoyed by the Mills bill, manufacturers and many of their employees were less than sympathetic to the president. Cleveland also had much to fear from the "soldier vote." With Union army veterans comprising over 10 percent of the northern electorate, it was apparent that the president had a serious political problem on his hands.[558] In addition to the veto of the dependent pension bill, veterans were annoyed over his rejection of measures passed by Congress approving the applications of individuals seeking pensions. The president vetoed 228 private bills; 175 of them concerned injuries sustained outside of the military.[559] On the other hand, he signed 1,453 private bills, more than any of his predecessors. Egged on by the Republican Party and the GAR, veterans, or at least those who claimed to speak for them, denounced the president. They also took offense at the return of Confederate battle flags captured by Union forces to the southern states and the appointment of Lucius Q. C. Lamar to the Interior Department and later the Supreme Court.[560] Even a law increasing pensions for Mexican War veterans caused offense, as some of the recipients served in the Confederate army. With so long a bill of indictment, the increase in annual pension expenditures from $56 million to $80 million received little notice.

Benjamin Harrison, a former Indiana senator and onetime brigadier general in the Union army, received the Republican nomination largely due to the importance of the Hoosier state to Republican prospects. The party dropped the equivocal language of its 1884 tariff plank and issued one endorsing "the American system of protection." It also demanded the payment of "just pensions."[561] The candidate made it clear that if he was elected, veterans would once again be given the keys to the treasury: "it is no time now to use an apothecary's scale to weigh the rewards of the men who saved the country."[562] As the campaign unfolded, the tariff was the main issue. Speaking to delegations that visited him at his home in the first "front porch" campaign, Harrison insisted that a protective tariff was needed to protect American workers from cheap European labor. He cast the Mills bill as the first step toward a revenue-only tariff.[563] Harrison spoke to 110 delegations that visited his home in Indianapolis between July and November. He explained his refusal to commence a speaking tour by saying that he had "great risk of meeting a fool at home, but the candidate who travels cannot escape him."[564] In light of a September poll showing Cleveland ahead in Indiana, Harrison may have been wise to remain in the Hoosier state. The Republican National Committee responded by flooding Indiana with campaign literature and speakers.[565] Republican politicians visited workplaces such as the shipyards of Maine, explaining the advantages of protective tariffs. Contributions from manufacturers enabled Republicans to flood the North with thousands of speakers and pamphlets, most of which concerned the tariff. In return Republican politicians dared to promise upward revisions of the tariff. Manufacturers held rallies against the Mills bill and free trade, with the understanding that employees would be wise to attend. In time it became unclear whether the Republican Party was the tail or the dog. Trade organizations such as the American Iron and Steel Association not only contributed to the campaign but also won control of delegations and local nominating conventions.[566]

As the Empire State now decided presidential elections, the prospect of frauds in Democratic-controlled New York City deprived Republicans of a great deal of sleep. In an effort to combat it, the Republican National Committee invested $100,000 in its own census of the city's population. It offered to pay up to $2,000 to those who provided evidence resulting in the conviction of persons engaging in illegal registration or voting. Republican Party headquarters in Manhattan accumulated piles of paper containing the names and addresses of registered voters that reached halfway to the ceiling. The irony of all of this was not lost on the *New York Times*, which thought the anti-corruption posture was an odd one for a party that "for years bribed voters with the proceeds of tariff bills made in their interest and as they demanded."[567] Matt Quay, Republican senator of Pennsylvania and manager of Harrison's campaign, oversaw the anti-fraud effort. He convinced New York City police officers to provide him with certified copies of returns from the precincts before they were delivered to city hall, as Democrats had previously doctored returns to the extent necessary to produce victory. While Republicans were carrying out a task that should have been performed by state officials, their work helped produce a relatively honest election.[568]

The contest may have turned on the Irish Catholic population of New York, which saw the president in a new light after a British diplomat made the error of stating in a letter to an American that he believed Cleveland's reelection would best serve the interests of Great Britain. The letter was promptly turned over to the newspapers and the president sustained a blow to his reelection chances, as Irish Catholics were loathe to do anything they were told would please Great Britain.[569] Harrison won New York by 13,000 votes and Indiana by 2,348 votes, thereby obtaining a small majority in the electoral college. Cleveland won the popular vote by 96,000. The ballots of veterans proved decisive in several states.[570] How many votes Republicans lost to voter suppression in the South is unknown; the lure of tariffs almost enabled them to carry Virginia and West Virginia. Democrats claimed wrongdoing cost them New York, in part because their gubernatorial candidate won 13,000 more votes in New York City than the president.[571] Tammany Hall's failure to support Cleveland may have been a more critical factor. In Indiana the victory was said to have cost Republicans at least $60,000. The treasurer of the Harrison campaign, former pension commissioner W. W. Dudley, provided directions to the state's Republicans as to how the money should be spent. "Divide the voters into blocks of five and put a trusted man with the necessary funds in charge of these five and make him responsible that none get away and that all vote our ticket."[572] Bloomington, Indiana, Republicans deployed floaters (citizens of other states). They also approached the polls on Election Day with two or three blacks in tow, placed ballots in their hands, and waited while they voted. Compensation followed confirmation of service.[573] Allegations of electoral fraud led state officials to commence proceedings against W. W. Dudley. The local U.S. attorney managed to bring the prosecution to a halt after a summons had been issued.[574] In 1889 the Attorney General of the United States lobbied against a Senate resolution providing for an investigation of frauds in the state; he went so far as to advise a Republican Senator as to how the effort might be derailed.[575]

Republicans won control of both houses of Congress and the presidency for the first time since 1872. They used their majorities to take up novel legislation concerning education and voting rights. In one of the greatest miscalculations in American political history, Republican leaders also pushed through an upward revision of the tariff. A generous pension bill also became law. The new tariff was prepared by Ohio Congressman William McKinley, chairman of the House Committee on Ways and Means, and Senator Nelson W. Aldrich of Rhode Island. Trade organizations such as the National Association of Wool Manufactures devised the critical schedules.[576] With the exception of iron and steel-manufacturing areas in Pennsylvania, Ohio, and Illinois that were its main beneficiary, the McKinley tariff bill nauseated much of the country, including many Republicans. While the matter was under discussion in Congress, George Fithian of Illinois pointed out that tariffs were now so high that American manufacturers charged more for a great variety of products at home than abroad despite the cost of transporting them overseas. An American-made steel spade cost $9.20 in the United States and $7.86 in Europe. He thought the variation stemmed from the fact that imported spades were subject to a 45 percent tariff.[577]

Vermont Senator Justin Morrill complained bitterly of critics who dared to quote his Civil War–era assurances that protective tariffs were temporary measures necessary to fund the war effort. He explained that he did not realize the full cost of the war at the time he insisted those tariffs would be temporary. In his view, protection would be necessary so long as the national debt remained and there were still Union army veterans on the planet.[578] Senator John H. Mitchell of Oregon suggested that Americans had little to gain from competing on the open market with the laborers of Europe. In Britain annual wages among employees in the cotton textile industry were barely half of what their American counterparts made ($180 v. $330).[579] The McKinley Tariff Act of October 1, 1890, pushed rates up to an average of 49.5 percent. Cotton clothing now came with a 50 percent ad valorem tax. The duty on barley increased from 10 to 30 cents to protect farmers in the North against their Canadian competitors.[580] The act also imposed a steep duty on opium designed to discourage its use. In perhaps its most novel feature, the act provided for a bounty—a cash payment—of two cents a pound to planters for growing sugar.[581] This provision was designed to compensate them for the repeal of tariffs on imported raw sugar. William Holman of Indiana was appalled: "Here we have a new departure, one thoroughly un-American, sugar on the free list and the whole people taxed to pay the wealthy planter of Louisiana two cents on every pound of sugar he produces." He expected the program would cost $8 million a year.[582] While the Tariff of 1894 abolished the bounty, the legality of the program as well as that of an 1895 appropriation carrying out its terms (for payments to those who complied with the program while it remained in force) came before the Supreme Court during its 1895–96 term. *Harper's Weekly* expressed hope that the law would be held void. Noting that the payments had been branded an exercise of a broad spending power, it warned that "if this contention is sustained by the courts, the limitations of the Constitution are swept away, and by merely appropriating money to carry them out, Congress may exercise all the powers that the states were supposed to have reserved to themselves." *Harper's* feared the "vast extent of socialistic legislation" that might follow and suggested that only the federal system had thus far prevented the adoption of socialist programs in the United States similar to those in Europe. It charged that lawmakers had already proposed bills giving money to states and cities for purposes as varied as public works programs designed to employ the jobless and the irrigation of farmland.[583] The case before the Supreme Court arose out of the refusal of a disbursing officer of the treasury to issue payments to sugar planters on the grounds that the 1890 law was unconstitutional. A planter obtained a writ of mandamus requiring the official to make the payments, and the matter was appealed. The Supreme Court affirmed the Circuit Court's order granting the writ. In doing so it held the 1895 appropriation to be within the equity powers of Congress. In his opinion for the Court, Justice Rufus Peckham explained that sugar planters had made investments in the belief that the bounty would remain in place for 15 years. As for the question of whether Congress could appropriate money for any purpose conducive to the general welfare, Peckham explained that it need not be answered immediately. "A decision on that question may be postponed until it arises."[584] The federal government had long exercised equity powers to compensate those who sustained damages due the conduct of its agents and employees; during the 1850s, a Court of Claims was established to adjudicate such matters. Equity did not require compensating the sugar planter who filed suit as he did not claim he had grown sugar, or even additional sugar, because of the bounty held out before him. It would not be the last time that the high court would bend over backwards to avoid ruling on the spending power question. For most of the country, it was the McKinley Tariff's high rates and not the bounty that gave cause for offense. Americans were flabbergasted at the effrontery of Republicans. Journalist George William Curtis remarked that "even Henry Clay would have blushed."[585] Many Americans blamed the law for a steep rise in prices that began even before it was passed. The rates were so steep they depressed imports and reduced federal revenues. Combined with economic dislocations, they wiped out the surplus.[586]

With Republicans in control of both the legislative and executive branches, the more idealistic members of the party pushed two bills that had been stalled for years. The first concerned aid for primary schools. The idea was born in the years after the Civil War, when the widespread desolation and poverty that gripped the South left many children unable to obtain an education. Public schools had just begun to appear in the region before the war. Following Appomattox, radical state governments in the South appropriated more money for schools even as they turned them, along with everything else under their control, into sources of patronage and plunder. Thousands of children across the South remained without access to adequate schools. It was with them in mind that George Hoar proposed a bill in 1870 providing federal funds to the states for education. Lawmakers could be forgiven it they thought it significant that the subject was not found among the enumerated powers. Hoar handled the question of authority by shrouding it in a fog of generalities. In matters unrelated to commerce and "confessedly of domestic regulation and concern" the test of constitutionality of a particular exercise of federal power depended on the answer to the following question: Is the exercise of it "essential and indispensable to the maintenance of republican government?" Whatever is necessary "to enable the persons entitled to share in the government, to exercise the duty and right devolved upon them by the Constitution, is within the power of Congress to secure by law, if it is not otherwise accomplished." If the republican government clause could be used to decapitate the state governments, apparently it could be used to compensate those that were unwilling to adequately fund their own schools. Hoar cited Bureau of Education statistics indicating 1.3 million Americans over the age of 20 were illiterate in 1860. He believed Congress had long used its power under the general welfare clause to aid agriculture and manufactures—the Department of Agriculture would spend $175,000 in the current fiscal year. Education was "not only essential to agricultural and manufacturing supremacy" but also "equally essential to strength in war." Hoar claimed that under his bill the federal government would provide aid only when the states failed to act.[587]

An education bill that turned land sale proceeds over to the states for the funding of primary schools passed the House in February 1872; it did not receive serious consideration in the Senate. Before it passed, Congressman Mark Dunnell of Minnesota cited the practice of making land grants to new states for schools as a precedent for the bill. (In addition to putting aside land for schools, a college, and a capital, laws admitting states to the Union often reserved to them 5% of the proceeds of land sales within their borders, with the proviso that said funds were to be used for roads and canals or schools.) John T. Harris of Virginia suggested the measure was another step in the process of centralization, and one that would "force upon the country mixed schools."[588] Over the next two decades, Republicans did a great deal of talking on the subject of education and very little acting. Ulysses S. Grant suggested an amendment requiring the states to establish and maintain free public schools in his seventh annual message of 1875.[589] Rutherford Hayes was presumptuous enough to suggest in his first annual message that the wisdom of federal aid to schools "is no longer a question."[590] The 1880 Republican platform addressed the question of legality with the requisite ambiguity: "the work of popular education is one left to the care of the several states, but it is the duty of the national government to aid that work to the extent of its constitutional power."[591] During the 1880 presidential campaign President Hayes called for federal education subsidies. In an August 11 speech at Columbus, Ohio, he suggested that the western and southern states were too impoverished to educate the entirety of their youth. Ignorant voters, he warned, were "powder and ball for the demagogues."[592] During a stop in Canton, Ohio, the following month, Hayes cited the territories clause as authority for turning land sale revenues over to the states for education. He claimed that out of a school-age population of five million, only 2.7 million southern youths were enrolled in schools. The *Nation* was less certain of the constitutionality of aid, even for the benefit of blacks: "The moral obligation to do something in the premises may be derived from the fact that the negroes have been given the suffrage, but the legal power cannot be got in this way."[593] Northern Republicans were not alone in seeking aid for education; of 60 petitions sent to Washington during 1877–79 that endorsed the idea, 56 came from the South. Numerous organizations in the region lobbied for aid, including the Peabody Fund.[594] Much of the work was performed by Peabody's agent, J. L. M. Curry, who had been an orthodox states' rights Alabama congressman during the 1850s.

In 1880, former slave states spent a total of 12 million dollars for education, but two-thirds of that amount was appropriated by just two states—Missouri and Maryland. The northern states spent six times the South's total.[595] In December 1880, the Senate passed an education bill 41–6 (there were 20 abstentions). Devised by one-time Union army general and Rhode Island Senator Ambrose Burnside, it provided the states with grants for primary schools.[596] Henry Teller of Colorado pointed out that illiteracy rates in the North and South were 7 percent and 45 percent, respectively.[597] George Vest of Missouri objected to Section 9 of the bill, which required the states to report to the Bureau of Education regarding the number of schools, teachers, and students within their borders. "I should like to ask the friends of the measure why it is that the national government, through its commissioner of education, is to inquire into the appropriations made by the legislature of a sovereign state? What has the general government to do with the acts of the legislatures of the respective states in regard to appropriations for a system of education?"[598] The measure died in the Democratic-controlled House.

Two months later, in February 1881, Albion Tourgee, a North Carolina lawyer and author of northern antecedents, took up the cause in an article in the *North American Review*. Citing the threat of ignorant voters—by his estimate 24 percent of whites and 90 percent of blacks in the South were illiterate—he called for federal education subsidies. As for the issue of legality, Tourgee claimed that numerous exercises of federal authority in the past, including the Department of Agriculture, the coastal survey, scientific expeditions, the signal service, and military academies, were "beyond the purview of a written Constitution." Resorting to the Hamiltonian doctrine that the national government possessed certain inherent powers common to all nations, Tourgee insisted that the power "to provide for the education of the people, to secure the intelligence of its electors and thereby prevent its own disintegration and destruction, is one of these incidents of national existence." The war powers could also be deployed for the purpose, as the nation's "right to self-defense, the implied power to maintain itself, was not exhausted by the struggle to put down rebellion. It equally exists as to any impending evil." Tourgee called for the distribution of federal funds to states on the basis of illiteracy rates, with the money to go directly to teachers under a "thorough system of inspection and supervision of the schools thus assisted." Congress should retain authority to ensure that state-approved textbooks did not glorify the rebellion or defend secession. Federal aid would produce more intelligent voting, assist laborers in their efforts to protect themselves from fraud, and stimulate the growth of both manufacturing and the Republican Party in the South. Federal generosity would also erode the "states' rights dogma" as it would present the federal government "in an entirely beneficent light."[599]

While the country was not quite ready for a national government that sponsored propaganda celebrating its virtues, several school measures were talked of in Washington in early 1882. John Logan sponsored a bill that would have devoted all revenue from taxes on distilled spirits to an education fund from which money would be distributed to the states according to population, thus diverting more money to the North than one based on illiteracy rates. Senator Zebulon Vance of North Carolina sponsored a measure that would have abolished liquor taxes and allowed the states to increase their taxes on alcohol so they could devote more money to their schools. Senator Henry Blair of New Hampshire, chairman of the Committee on Education and Labor, proposed a bill that would devote $15 million from general revenues to the states—including those in the North—according to illiteracy rates, with the funds to be spent on primary schools. The program would cease after 10 years.[600] The *Springfield Daily Republican* approved of the Blair bill; it thought any law enacted on the subject should require the states to make similar appropriations themselves as a condition for obtaining federal funds—the southern states needed to be taught "the value of self-taxation as an investment."[601]

It was Blair's bill that would capture the imagination of Republicans during the 1880s. More than once it won the approval of the Senate only to die in the Democratic House. The version presented in December 1883 provided for the use of up to one-tenth of the funds for the training of teachers. It listed the subjects that could be taught using said funds. It also required that each state accepting federal grants spend an amount on its common schools equal to at least one-third of its federal allotment. Instruction would be free to all children "without distinction of race, color, nativity or condition in life." Another clause assured that the states could provide each race with separate schools. State governors were to submit reports describing the disbursement of grant money. States with illiteracy rates under 5 percent could spend money on industrial schools as well as common schools.[602] The 1884 Republican campaign textbook devoted an entire chapter to Democratic attempts to obstruct passage of the Blair bill.[603]

Southerners were conflicted over federal education subsidies. Many objected to the Blair bill; they believed it would, like Henry Clay's distribution schemes, sop up revenue and make it easier for Congress to maintain protective tariffs. Others rationalized support for the bill on the grounds that it would be unfair for the South alone to bear the burden of educating blacks.[604] Approximately half the region's senators voted for the measure when it came up for votes in 1884, 1886, and 1888.[605] The Blair bill tended to receive the support of old line Bourbon Democrats from the Deep South while earning the opposition of border state and populist Democrats. In the House, Democrat John G. Carlisle of Kentucky served as speaker from 1883 until 1891; he blocked consideration of the Blair bill repeatedly. He went so far as to pack the Committee on Education with members known to oppose it. Texans opposed the Blair bill in part because proceeds from their state's huge endowment of public lands were viewed as more than adequate to fund its common schools.[606] Lucius Q. C. Lamar, senator from Mississippi, endorsed the Blair bill in March 1884. He explained that the South was rebuilding at a slow pace. Lamar insisted that the southern states could be trusted to use the money to benefit the races equally.[607]

Such assurances were not enough for Shelby Cullom of Illinois, who announced he would vote against the bill unless it was amended to ensure fair treatment of blacks.[608] James George of Mississippi explored the question of authority. He conceded that Madison had been right in the debate over the meaning of the general welfare clause but he insisted "that construction was no longer possible." Congress had always operated under the view that it possessed a broad spending power. In support of this assertion, George cited appropriations for the military academies, the Centennial Exhibition, and relief of persons hit by crop failures. George was careful to insist that because education was one of the "reserved rights of each state," the power of Congress over the subject ended with appropriations.[609] Joseph Hawley of Connecticut pointed out that the federal government could condition grants in ways that eroded state control over schools. The Blair bill would tempt states to acquiesce in changes or face the loss of substantial amounts of money. Hawley objected to the provisions for federal supervision—even the textbooks would have to be submitted to the secretary of the interior. He dismissed the idea that state consent made legal what would otherwise be illegal: "To impose upon a state these regulations or virtual commands, it is virtually admitted, would be unconstitutional; but the consent of the state having been obtained, it is alleged to be constitutional. That consent only changes it from rape to prostitution. I hold that a state has no power to give the national government an extension of its control over that state's affairs. A single state cannot surrender any fraction of its powers." The alternative view would allow Congress to bring any subject under its purview by a "judicious distribution of money."[610]

Benjamin Harrison endorsed the Blair bill during the 1888 campaign, and its time seemed to have arrived when Republicans won majorities of both houses of Congress as well as the presidency that fall. In his first annual message of December 1889, the new president endorsed federal subsidies for primary education in the South. As for the legal difficulties, Harrison conceded that federal aid to the states for primary education thus far had taken the form of land grants: "In that form the constitutional power of Congress to promote the education of the people is not seriously questioned. I do not think it can be successfully questioned when the form is changed to that of a direct grant of money from the public Treasury."[611] The state of public education remained poor in the South at the time of Harrison's inauguration. A Virginia woman wrote to the editor of the *Springfield Daily Republican* claiming the teachers of her state had to wear rubber shoes and waterproof jackets due to rain penetrating the dilapidated log cabins that were all the schools boards would provide.[612]

With victory in sight, proponents of the Blair bill were appalled to find that the North seemed to be turning against the idea. One critic claimed that the South was now wealthy enough to fund its own schools. He lamented "the disposition to fall back upon the general government for everything" and claimed it was "the most alarming tendency in [the] American character at the present time."[613] Despite Senator Blair's request, the New Hampshire legislature refused to endorse his bill.[614] John Coit Spooner of Wisconsin was precisely the sort of broad-minded northern Republican who could be expected to approve the measure and he had in the past. Now with the bill's prospects better than they had been in years, the senator turned on it. It would, he charged, give money to northern states that did not need it and provide a disproportionate amount of money to white schools in the South at the expense of black ones even though illiteracy rates were higher in black areas. It would also cause southerners to expect the federal government to fund their schools.[615] Albion Tourgee opposed the measure as having inadequate safeguards to prevent southern legislatures from giving white schools an inordinate share of the funds.[616]

Southerners were also split. Senator Richard Coke of Texas made easy work of the notion that an appropriation subject to conditions would be less intrusive than a federal law that directly regulated common schools. "So far as the consent of the states accepting this bill can convey, the power and jurisdiction of Congress over their common schools will be perfect and complete. Jurisdiction, in its most general sense, is defined to be the 'power to make, declare, or apply the law.' In every section of this bill Congress makes law for the government and administration of common schools of the states, and the bill erects a tribunal to declare and apply that law, thus furnishing every element that enters into the definition of federal jurisdiction."[617] John W. Daniel of Virginia embraced the Blair bill; he thought it a constitutional exercise of a broad spending power. He conceded that his conclusion might have differed "if we were debating this subject in 1790 rather than in 1890" but he thought the numerous acts of Congress that struck him as based on a broad spending power changed the case. Daniel believed he could no more insist that Congress adhere to its original limitations than he could insist that a steamboat captain follow the Mississippi River's old route across dry land. He proceeded to describe a long list of statutes providing relief to citizens in distress that he believed proved the existence of a broad spending power. He welcomed federal aid as prosperity in the South was limited to areas near rail lines. States need not accept the money; the federal government would not supervise education in the states; the law did not require the races to be educated together; only non-sectarian schools would receive aid and the measure deferred to local authorities in the subjects to be taught. Daniel noted that the provision requiring the states to submit their textbooks to the Department of the Interior had been dropped.[618] Senator John Taylor Morgan of Alabama objected to the bill because it would require southern states to raise taxes to provide the money necessary to match federal grants. His own state would have to increase expenditures for education from $527,319 to $1.6 million by the seventh year of the program. The law would also drain the federal treasury and require additional taxes. Morgan thought it odd that so many senators complained of the plight of farmers and then proposed programs that would result in higher taxes being imposed on them.[619]

The Blair bill failed of passage for the final time on March 20, 1890, when it was defeated in the Senate, 37–31. Henry Watterson of the *Louisville Journal-Courier* was ecstatic: "the bait is refused, the snare has been laid in vain."[620] Having discarded its earlier support for the measure, the *Springfield Daily Republican* applauded the vote. It announced that "a halt was called today in the Senate to the program of extravagance and interference with local rights, which has prevailed during the present session of Congress."[621] The significance of the bill's defeat while the government was in the hands of the party of Lincoln was not lost on the paper's editors. After a decade of campaigning on promises to educate southern blacks, Republicans would have to drop the idea, as their credibility on the matter had been destroyed. "As a bit of buncombe, it had quite a run."[622] After the turn of the century the southern states finally committed themselves to public education, and their spending on it tripled during the period between 1900 and 1913.[623]

The second novel measure pushed by Republicans in 1890 also concerned the South. Republicans watched with dismay as southern whites drove blacks out of the political process during the 1870s and 1880s. As a result the number of Republican congressmen from southern states dropped to a handful. Many Republicans believed they had been repeatedly denied majorities in the House of Representatives by the intimidation and disenfranchisement of blacks in the southern states. Not only were Republicans losing up to 24 seats in House elections, they were also deprived of as many as 38 votes in the electoral college—a huge number in the razor-thin presidential elections of the era.[624] The abolition of the three-fifths clause contributed to this development by increasing the size of southern delegations. With blacks harassed into staying away from the polls even in areas where they enjoyed majorities, what should have been Republican districts returned Democratic congressmen elected by small numbers of whites. The seventh district in South Carolina routinely sent Democratic representatives to the House despite having 33,000 black voters and only 7,700 white voters.[625]

In his first annual message of December 3, 1889, Benjamin Harrison urged Congress to enact laws that "will secure to all our people a free exercise of the right of suffrage and every other civil right under the Constitution and laws of the United States." He had no doubt that the federal government possessed "the power to take the whole direction and control of the election of members of the House of Representatives." The black man "should be protected in all of his relations to the Federal Government, whether as litigant, juror, or witness in our courts, as an elector for member of Congress, or as a peaceful traveler upon our interstate railways."[626] The question of authority appeared to be an easy one. Article I, Section 4 of the Constitution empowered the states to determine the "Times, Places and Manner" of elections for representatives and senators but it also provided that Congress "may at any time by Law make or alter such Regulations, except as to the Places of Choosing Senators." In a March 1889 *Harvard Law Review* article, E. Irvin Smith acknowledged that in the *Federalist* #59, Alexander Hamilton assured that House elections would be left to the states under all but extraordinary circumstances. Smith noted that an 1842 law apportioning House seats that required all representatives to be elected from districts was regarded as unconstitutional.[627] It was not enforced until after it was reenacted in 1862.[628] What was involved in the phrase "time, place and manner?" Smith thought it authorized Congress to enact laws that would contribute to the "accuracy and fairness of the result." Moreover, the reconstruction amendments provided broad authority for the federal government to interfere when the franchise was denied on racial grounds. As for the use of literacy tests, Smith acknowledged that northern as well as southern states continued to use them: Massachusetts thereby reduces its voting population "one-sixteenth."[629]

In December 1889, Henry Cabot Lodge, a Massachusetts congressman in his second term, proposed a bill expanding federal oversight of congressional elections. In a speech of June 26, 1890, he described the measure. Modeled on the Naturalization Act of 1870 and the second Enforcement Act, it provided for federal courts to appoint a chief election supervisor on the petition of citizens. The supervisor and other federal employees under his command would watch registration and voting. Federal boards of canvassers would canvass the voting and send returns to federal courts that would certify them and forward the results to the clerk of the House of Representatives. In the event the results certified by state and federal authorities conflicted, the person certified as the victor by the latter would be deemed to have won the election. Lodge cited the steep drop in the overall vote in southern states during recent years as evidence of vote suppression.[630]

The prospects of the Lodge bill improved during the spring of 1890 as the House investigated multiple cases of electoral fraud and bribery in southern congressional districts.[631] Southern congressmen were apoplectic over the prospect of the Lodge bill's passage; observers feared violence would break out on the House floor.[632] Congressman Thomas R. Stockdale of Mississippi saw the bill as the means by which the Northeast hoped to protect the tariffs she used to extract money from the South. "It is not negro domination but New England and negro domination mixed we fear—a domination of avarice using the colored men as tools to force the South to pay tribute to New England and the North, and that, too, by creating enmity between the races that did not exist before." He warned the federal government would fill the South with partisan election officials who would manipulate black voters to secure congressional seats for Republicans. The bill would also place an irresistible temptation before judges. Stockdale complained that a majority of white Americans were Democrats, and that Republicans held power only because they were supported by almost all blacks.[633]

Congressman John Hemphill of South Carolina denied that Congress had the power to regulate state elections in the manner provided by the Lodge bill. He quoted resolutions passed by the Ohio legislature after Congress required district elections in 1842: Congress "has no right . . . to prescribe the manner, time, or place of holding elections for its members, except in case where the legislatures of the states shall refuse or fail to make provision for the same." Federal election supervisors who engaged in fraud would remain above the law, as the states cannot prosecute federal officials for acts committed in the performance of their jobs. Hemphill complained that the bill provided for a federal official in each judicial district who would have the power to appoint as many subordinates as he pleases "who shall attend the polls at a compensation of five dollars a day to carry out the instructions of their political boss." He charged that northeastern Republicans were trying to eliminate electoral corruption in other parts of the country even as they used fraud to carry elections in states such as Connecticut.[634]

On July 2, 1890, the bill passed the House, 155–149.[635] Even as the Republican-controlled Senate prepared to take up the measure, delegates at the 1890 Mississippi state constitutional convention debated the best means to eliminate the last vestiges of black political participation in the state. Nine different provisions designed to indirectly deprive blacks of the vote were under consideration, including gerrymandered districts, literacy tests, poll taxes, and property requirements for the suffrage. (Indirect means were sought to avoid running afoul of the Fifteenth Amendment.) As most of these devices were still used in the North as well as the South, convention delegates expected they would survive a challenge in court. The availability of such measures demonstrated that laws designed to eliminate voter intimidation could do nothing for those denied the franchise. Thus the warning of the *Springfield Daily Republican*: as long as the states retained the power determine the eligibility of voters, the whites of the South would find ways to keep blacks from voting regardless of the presence of federal agents at the polls.[636] Southerners were unwilling to take any chances; they began to call for a regional boycott of northern products if the Lodge bill passed, thereby scaring the daylights out of the North's commercial interests, who had already been ambivalent about the bill.[637] Almost overnight, support for the measure disintegrated. *Harper's Weekly* concluded that prudence was the better part of valor. While insisting that legal authority for the bill is "indisputable," it concluded that the "redress provided by the election bill is so subversive of cherished traditions and convictions, and so certain to exasperate instead of remedying the evil, it is so plainly a resort to unusual legislation solely for a supposed party advantage, so evident of a straining of the spirit of the Constitution, however conformable to the letter—that it is in the highest sense unwise and inexpedient." *Harper's* cited a black North Carolina preacher's assertion that the bill would hurt blacks 364 days of the year in order to help them on the 365th. Most important of all, the bill would not achieve its stated purpose.[638] The *Springfield Daily Republican* cited the testimony of federal election commissioners who claimed the measure could be enforced only if federal troops were stationed "at every precinct on election day." It also wondered about the bill's potential as a source patronage and mischief—even in Springfield, Massachusetts, federal officeholders would be present at every poll. It concluded that the states were already improving their election procedures by adopting measures such as the Australian ballot. As the bill would only worsen sectionalism, election procedures were best left to the states.[639] For the first time since the 1850s, the South appeared to be getting the better of its perennial nemesis. As support for the bill evaporated, the *Atlanta Constitution* credited the boycott. "There is a North of politics, and a North of business and progress. The latter—the real North—grasped the situation at once, and its sober second thought is beginning to find expression."[640]

In the Senate the Lodge bill sustained a blow when consideration of it was postponed so the McKinley tariff bill could be considered. Randall Lee Gibson of Louisiana offered a withering indictment when it finally came up for consideration in December 1890. He called the bill "a partisan measure intended to create a huge machine to control the elections of the people in the interest of the Republican Party." Gibson asked what the reaction would be if "every judge and every supervisor in the country was a Democrat" armed with authority to appoint "supervisors, assistant supervisors, deputy marshals, and returning boards." Could it not "be said truthfully that they would constitute a Democratic machine to control elections on behalf of the Democratic Party? Every Republican in the country would denounces it as un-American, unconstitutional, and a perversion of the functions of government."[641] John Coit Spooner of Wisconsin defended the bill the next day (December 20). He pointed out that federal supervisors had watched elections in New York City almost continuously since the early 1870s and that on occasion they had appeared in Chicago, Cincinnati, and St. Louis.[642] Spooner denied that the bill provided for judges to exercise non-judicial powers—courts routinely used writs of certiorari to review the actions of assessors and county boards to determine if they acted beyond the scope of their statutory authority. He pointed out that winning candidates in northern congressional districts often won 30,000 votes. Of the 45 districts whose congressmen won with fewer than 15,000 votes, all but five were in the South. After attacking the suffrage provisions in the state constitution then being prepared in Mississippi, Spooner conceded that blacks could be denied the right to vote "by a law or a rule which applies equally, such as an honest educational test, to black and white alike."[643] In January 1891, attempts to arrange a vote on the Lodge bill failed, in part due to a filibuster. Democratic senators left the Senate to deprive it of a quorum.[644] Efforts to pass the Lodge bill ceased. Four years later, Democrats exploited their control over both branches of Congress and the White House to abolish the federal apparatus set up during Reconstruction to supervise elections in cities with populations of 20,000 or more.[645] The next effort to restore voting rights to southern blacks would not occur for decades, when persons born in 1890 were in their dotage. Southern states proceeded to adopt their own versions of the "Mississippi Plan" and imposed burdensome literacy requirements for voting, thereby removing the suffrage from most blacks and a large portion of whites as well.

While Republicans allowed a chance to restore black voting rights to slip through their fingers, they were not as cavalier in the matter of pensions.

Congress now operated under the burden of a staggering number of private pension bills—1,388 either providing pensions or increasing benefits were passed by the 51st Congress.[646] With Republicans again controlling the executive branch, advocates of pensions sought to exploit their opportunity. Harrison's first commissioner of pensions, James Tanner, announced that he favored pensions for all needy veterans and that he believed those already given were too small—each one would be reviewed with an eye on increasing it. Tanner proceeded to increase pensions across the board in violation of an order from the secretary of the interior. A senator who had not applied for it received a check in the amount of $4,300 in arrears. Amid growing criticism in Congress and the press, Tanner resigned in September 1889.[647]

Three months later in his first annual message, Benjamin Harrison called on lawmakers to enact pension legislation; he claimed that veterans across the country were "dependent upon public aid." Harrison though it inconsistent "with the national honor" to allow them to "subsist upon the local relief given indiscriminately to paupers instead of upon the special and generous provision of the nation that they served so gallantly and unselfishly."[648] Republican congressional leaders wanted to provide every Union army veteran with a pension. Their generosity may have stemmed from the stance of the Grand Army of the Republic; in 1888 the 22nd encampment of the GAR in Columbus, Ohio, passed a resolution demanding service pensions.[649]

Republican leaders in Congress realized that the country was not ready to place every Union Army veteran on the federal payroll; instead they took up a dependent pension bill of the type vetoed by Cleveland. The *Springfield Daily Republican* thought even that was going too far; it warned lawmakers were flirting with disaster. If the bill passed, "a vastly greater number of undeserving cases will thereby gain access to the public bounty, to the further upsetting of healthy habits of industry and saving among the people, and the heightening of that discontent among the laboring taxpayers which is now manifesting itself in threatening proportion."[650] Congressman Edward Lane of Illinois objected to placing wealthy veterans on the pension rolls and thereby collecting money from impoverished taxpayers who were far less affluent.[651] Joseph Washington of Tennessee was not enthused about the bill; he cited the claims of its proponents that it would double the number of pensioners from 500,000 to a million by the end of 1892. He thought the bill would, despite its apparent limitations, provide a pension to any veteran who wanted one. He complained that the poor of the country had already paid over a billion dollars in taxes to fund pensions for former federal employees (almost all of whom were veterans).[652] Protests were in vain. The Dependent Pension Act of June 27, 1890, provided a monthly stipend to all persons who served 90 days or more and suffered from a permanent mental or physical disability that prevented them from engaging in manual labor. The disability need not arise out of a wound suffered in the war.[653]

The Grand Army of the Republic was pleased with its victory; its Pension Committee called the law "the most liberal pension measure ever passed by any legislative body in the world" and claimed it would place every Union army veteran on the roles whose health was not "practically perfect."[654] The amount spent on pensions annually went from $89 million in 1889 to $157 million in 1893.[655] Two of every five dollars spent by the federal government was going to veterans by the mid-1890s.[656] The *New York Tribune* estimated that some 750,000 persons would obtain pensions. It predicted that "a voting population of twelve million will not long consent to pay more than half the entire revenues to a twentieth of their number."[657] In fact the pension rolls had 966,000 names by 1893.[658] In the critical Midwest, the number of pensioners grew from less than 200,000 in 1889 to over 300,000 in 1892.[659] The large increase stemmed from several factors, including the willingness of some to discover, as one historian of the period wrote, "ailments which would have passed unnoticed but for the pension laws." Thus his conclusion that the law stimulated "dishonesty and dependence and failed to discriminate between the deserving and undeserving."[660]

The political potential of a pension system that placed one of every 12 voters on the federal payroll was revealed in the comments of Charles H. Grosvenor of Ohio in the House of Representatives on December 14, 1894. He claimed that on the eve of the 1892 presidential election, the deputy commissioner of pensions appeared in congressional districts where the candidates were running evenly, and explained "the principles of the administration of the Pension Bureau" to the voters. The tactic nearly won a district for Republicans that normally returned a majority of 4,500 for Democrats. Nor was it unusual; Grosvenor claimed Pension Bureau employees appeared regularly at county seats on Election Day. He wanted to remove the pension system—and the Pension Bureau—from the nation's political life. Otherwise politicians would continue to manipulate veterans at every election. "One million voters in the country is a very large number, even in a country that votes twelve million people, distributed as the soldiers of this country are. They are a formidable element in our politics; and to place that great number of men in a condition or position where they fall under obligation to one political party or another, to place them in a position where they feel that they are in danger by any action of either party, is a system of coercion, and of bribery, so to speak, necessarily incident to such a condition, that is a disgrace upon the whole country." He thought the solution was to simply give every veteran of the Union army a pension, apparently oblivious to the possibility that lawmakers would simply move on to the next means of bribery—an increase in benefits.[661]

The Dependent Pension bill became law four months before the election of 1890, the McKinley Tariff only four weeks before it. In July a former governor of Kansas assured Republicans that if they would cut tariff rates, there wouldn't be enough Democrats in his state "to conduct an election."[662] Alas, his colleagues in Washington did not listen. The McKinley Tariff pushed rates to almost 50 percent and the country was in an ugly mood. Prices were going up; store clerks and drummers were said to be explaining to farmers' wives that everything cost more because of the McKinley Tariff. The recipients of this information naturally shared it with their husbands, thus turning the midterm election, at least according to one observer.[663] The prospect of an increase in the tariff on tin-plate led to increased purchases of it and in turn higher prices. Chicago meatpackers passed the cost on to the public when they increased the price of canned meats in November 1890.[664]

The result was one of the worst slaughters in American political history. The number of Republican congressmen dropped from 166 to 88. Democrats won 235 seats in the House. Republicans expanded their majority in the Senate only because of the admission of six states in the West (North Dakota, South Dakota, Montana, Wyoming, Idaho, and Washington). Democrats won a majority of congressional seats in the North for the first time since 1856–57 (113–83). Even in New England they gained 10 seats. The slaughter stemmed from many factors, including Republican support of prohibition forces in the Midwest. The casualties included Joe Cannon of Illinois and William McKinley, whose defeat may have stemmed from the gerrymandering of his Ohio district. The Populist-controlled Farmers' Alliance fared well, winning (in combination with Democrats) control of eight southern legislatures.[665] Several Populists were elected to Congress. In explaining the results, the *Springfield Daily Republican* pointed squarely at the McKinley Tariff: "the people are opposed to this new doctrine of protection—the commercial isolation of this among all other nations. They are decidedly against the employment of the taxing power of the government to build up the fortunes of the trusts and the favored few at the expense of the many."[666]

A national convention of Populists (the "People's Party") met at Omaha in 1892, making the presidential contest of that year a three-party contest. The Populist convention included more than angry farmers seeking to dilute the currency; also present were labor advocates. Ignatius Donnelly, a one-time Minnesota congressman who had embraced every political fad since the Civil War, spoke to the delegates of a litany of national sins. These included electoral intimidation and corruption, purchased newspaper editors, labor's failure to obtain the right to organize, the use of immigrant labor to keep wages low, and a "hireling standing army" that broke up strikes.[667]

The convention nominated James Weaver for president. A former Union army general and Iowa congressman, Weaver had been a member of the Greenback Party in the 1870s and 1880s. Republicans talked of nominating James Blaine or William McKinley; the incumbent president did not want to run again. Harrison had resisted the demands of party bosses for consideration in the distribution of jobs, and the resulting acrimony sapped his enthusiasm. Indignation finally moved Harrison to seek another term. He relied heavily on southern delegations—loaded down with federal employees—in his successful attempt to claim the Republican nomination at Minneapolis in early June. *Harper's Weekly* complained that 130 federal officeholders served as delegates at the Republican national convention and charged that "under our spoils system, such votes are virtually bribed."[668] William Pitt Kellogg's claim that the North favored Blaine and that Harrison won only because of the support of Republican officeholders in the South may have been an exaggeration—in truth, the North was divided—but the episode did not motivate a party that had already soured on the incumbent.[669] The platform reeked of defiance; it asserted that the "prosperous condition of our country is largely due to the wise revenue legislation of Congress." On all products made in America, there should be a tariff "equal to the difference on wages abroad and at home."[670]

The Democratic nomination fell to Grover Cleveland, who set in motion an extraordinary series of events with his 1887 tariff message. The 1888 debate over protection unmasked the system as an elaborate fraud; the 1888 election revealed that it was nonetheless a politically compelling one; the 1890 tariff and the midterm election demonstrated that it was in fact possible to exhaust the patience and credulity of the American people. Cleveland was heartened by the results of the midterm contests even as the rise of the Populists alarmed him and other conservative Democrats. His only rival for the nomination was David Hill, his successor as governor of New York. Hill's chances took a hit when his allies at Tammany Hall scheduled the state Democratic convention for early 1892 so that heavy snow would keep farmers from attending and allow Tammany to control the selection of delegates for the national convention. The move was viewed as underhanded and hurt Hill.[671] Democrats met at Chicago in late June and nominated Cleveland. They avoided the issue of silver—many wanted it coined again in the hope it would produce inflation—and focused on the tariff. The platform denounced protection "as a robbery of the great majority of the American people for the benefit of the few." It claimed that tariff levies higher than necessary for the actual revenue needs of the government were unconstitutional and promised "that the collection of such taxes shall be limited to the necessities of the government when honestly and economically administered." The platform also called for legislation "by Congress and state legislatures" improving safety practices among the railroads. The ambiguity regarding what level of government should act was not an accident; along with everyone else, Democrats were increasingly uncertain as to the extent to which Congress could regulate railroads under its commerce powers. The platform also called for the enactment of state laws barring sweatshops, contract convict labor, and the employment of children under 15 in factories. Seeking the support of farmers tired of the deflationary policies of the national government, Democrats also called for the repeal of the 10 percent tax on state banks notes—a move that would have allowed state banks to once again flood the nation with their own currency.[672]

Republicans were hampered by a variety of problems. With the exception of agricultural commodities, prices had increased since the enactment of the McKinley Tariff and Americans remained annoyed with the party that appeared to be responsible for this development. Harrison alienated labor when he sent federal troops to restore order at the Coeur d'Alene silver mines in Idaho in July. He also sent troops to Buffalo, New York, when a strike by railroad switchmen led to violence beyond the capacity of the state militia. The Republican cause was also hurt when a strike at the Carnegie Steel Works outside of Pittsburgh disintegrated into violent clashes that saw 10 slain and 60 wounded (no federal troops were involved). The strike began in the summer and extended into the fall, competing with the presidential campaign for headlines in the newspapers. More damaging than the strike itself were the wage cuts imposed on Carnegie employees during a period of prosperity—perhaps protection did not mean higher wages for industrial workers after all.[673] Republicans were also divided by intra-party frictions over Harrison's appointments. Maine Republican Congressman Thomas Brackett Reed claimed that he had only two political enemies in his home state and that the president released one from the penitentiary and appointed the other collector at Portland.[674] Cleveland won the election; he carried the South and northern swing states including New Jersey, Illinois, and Indiana, and even more safely Republican states such as Connecticut, Wisconsin, and California. James Weaver won a million popular votes and 22 electoral votes in the normally Republican West. Democrats won both houses of Congress for only the second time since James Buchanan was president.

LABOR AND MONEY

By the time Grover Cleveland took office for a second time, the agricultural depression that fueled the growth of Populism had been in progress for five years. Reduced demand for American grain abroad worsened the problem, and the impaired purchasing power of the American consumer—many of whom were farmers—caused the economy to sputter and then stop altogether. A panic began with the recall of gold by European banks, many of whom had been leery of the American market ever since the Sherman Silver Purchase Act of 1890—Would the United States turn its back on the world and go it alone with a bimetal money system? Prices dropped through the floor and companies wilted overnight. The National Cordage Company—the "twine trust"—went under in the spring of 1893; so did the Philadelphia and Reading Railroad. Other major lines followed, including the Erie, the Northern Pacific, the Union Pacific, and the Santa Fe Railroad (they declared bankruptcy). Within two years a quarter of all railroads had gone into receivership. Six hundred banks failed during the summer of 1893.

As the economy went over the edge, the federal government faced its own financial crisis. In 1890, a Republican Congress and president embraced the methods of their foes and agreed to debase the currency to ensure passage of the McKinley Tariff and secure the loyalty of the new silver-mining states in the West. The Sherman Silver Purchase Act obligated the government to buy 4.5 million ounces of silver each month with treasury notes—about twice as much as it has been required to buy under the Bland-Allison Act of 1878. John Sherman justified his support for the measure on the grounds that it weakened demand for the free coinage of silver.[675] The law authorized the redemption of treasury notes in either gold or silver.[676] People naturally chose the former as it was more valuable. Government vaults emptied and for a time the law threatened to drive gold out of circulation. Many feared that silver would replace gold as the nation's currency—a serious problem in light of the fact that foreign debts could not be paid in silver.[677] The problem reached a crisis level during the summer of 1893, as banks, depleted of their gold reserves, began to fail. The president called Congress into special session in August for the purpose of repealing the Sherman Silver Purchase Act. The goal was achieved later that fall, but it did nothing to stop the drain of gold from the treasury, as the economic downturn was causing individuals and banks to hoard the metal. Two bond issues produced inadequate revenues and a default was avoided only through a deal that saw the government purchase three and a half million ounces of gold from a consortium led by J. P. Morgan. The exchange stopped the flow of gold to Europe. Morgan's involvement seemed to confirm the suspicions of western and southern Democrats that the conservative wing of the party was allied with Wall Street and Republicans in a conspiracy to contract the money supply and reduce them to destitution.

The economy continued its nosedive in early 1894 and by that summer, four million jobless Americans were roaming the country looking for work. The unemployment rate among manufacturing workers exceeded 15 percent and may have reached 20 percent. Wages dropped through the floor and wheat prices fell to 50 cents a bushel. Cotton sold for only six cents a pound. Strikes were common and usually futile. The burden of relief fell, as it always had, on cities and counties. New York City increased its appropriation for public improvements to a million dollars. Thirty-four towns in Massachusetts funded public works projects for the purpose of aiding the unemployed between 1893 and 1896.[678] Several cities turned land over to the poor so they could grow their own food.[679]

Some thought that Washington should act—if Congress could spend a billion dollars on a steel navy and military pensions, surely it could spend something on the indigent laborers of the country. The prospects for increased federal spending on public works as a way to provide jobs were not good, even if some prominent politicians such as Roger Mills of Texas endorsed the idea.[680] Observers did not expect Cleveland to cooperate; he had warned of the dangers of "paternalism" in his inaugural address—people should not expect to be supported in any form by the national government.[681] As the depression worsened, some Americans refused to take no for an answer. Bypassing the state capitals, they looked to Washington to do something for the unemployed. Among those making demands was one Jacob Coxey. An Ohio merchant, he was appalled by the condition of the roads in the Midwest. He took up the cause of improving them to aid commerce. In the early 1890s he established the Good Roads Association and called on Congress to spend $500 million improving roads. When that idea failed to take hold, Coxey devised a program under which towns would deposit bonds with the Treasury Department in exchange for money that could be used to fund improvements including schools and libraries as well as roads, with the bonds to be paid off within 25 years. Advocates promised that the infusion of cash would also produce inflation. Alas, the "good roads bill" went nowhere in Congress. Coxey organized a march on Washington by the downtrodden; 17 different groups set out for the capital. Large groups of unemployed men in the West commandeered trains in the hope of reaching the capital; federal judges responded with injunctions ordering them to cease-and-desist. Most of them never crossed the Mississippi. When Coxey and his men reached Washington—there were no more 100 persons in total—they were treated to a vicious assault at the hands of the municipal police as their leader tried to address them from the steps of the Capitol. *Harper's Weekly* was appalled by the entire episode; in defending the injunctions issued by federal judges, it complained that a stern response by the federal government was required because the nation's governors had failed to carry out their duty to repress violence. Their passivity had resulted in "bodies of vagabonds and tramps formed for the purpose of marching on Washington, with the avowed intention of breaking the law and intimidating Congress."[682]

Federal injunctions were deployed against striking railroad employees as well as the unemployed, despite a lack of clear jurisdiction. At the time of the railroad strikes of 1877, the federal courts had been able to act aggressively as many of the railroads were bankrupt and in the legal custody of court-appointed receivers—those who damaged railroads were destroying property that was, at least for the moment, in the possession of the U.S. government. During the 1880s, federal judges began injunctions targeting persons interfering with railroads even when the affected lines were not bankrupt.[683] These injunctions usually targeted interference with the mail, which was transported by trains. There had been calls to use the Sherman Antitrust Act against labor as early as the summer of 1890, when a newspaper correspondent recommended its use against New York Central Railroad employees who had gone on strike. The *Springfield Daily Republican* was appalled. "It would be a very singular comment indeed if this law, which was professedly aimed at combinations of capital, should be first invoked against organized labor." The law had been on the books for two months "and meantime all sorts of trusts and syndicates and pools and capitalistic cabals have been operating and have been organized to operate on the people, and not a word has been said about applying the law in these cases."[684] The law was first used in response to a strike by Attorney General William Miller. In 1892 he instructed the U.S. attorney in Louisiana to seek an injunction pursuant to the Antitrust Act targeting strikers in New Orleans on the theory that they were impeding interstate commerce. The judge conceded that the law as drafted targeted corporate abuses, but he insisted that its language was broad enough to encompass combinations of labor that served to restrain trade. Richard Olney, who would succeed Miller as attorney general, criticized the tactic. He would later use it with fervor.[685]

The year 1894 saw over half a million Americans go on strike; many of the work stoppages involved the railroads. A work stoppage on the Great Northern Railroad led Judge James Jenkins of the U.S. Circuit Court for the Eastern District of Wisconsin to issue a rather extraordinary injunction in April 1894—it barred the line's employees from going on strike on the theory that doing so constituted interference with interstate commerce and a violation of the Sherman Act. To quit working for the railroad would place one in contempt of court. A House subcommittee issued a report finding that the order constituted a gross abuse of power and lacked any basis in the law; it conceded that Jenkins's conduct did not warrant impeachment as there was no evidence of "corrupt intent."[686] The House Judiciary Committee endorsed the report. It recommended a bill barring federal judges from requiring specific performance in disputes over labor contracts or otherwise forcing persons to work (the measure did not become law).[687]

While Jenkins had overreached, the fact remained that striking employees often refused to limit themselves to work stoppages. Some forcibly prevented replacement workers from crossing picket lines—they wished to ensure that their employers ceased functioning until they were provided with wages they deemed acceptable. Others tried to prevent their employers from doing business with companies whose employees were on strike, despite the fact that secondary boycotts were illegal. The widespread use of these tactics inevitably affected interstate commerce. The Pullman Company, located just south of Chicago, manufactured passenger cars that were used by most of the railroads. In dire financial straits, the lines reduced their orders, and Pullman found itself starved of customers. It cut pay repeatedly, reducing its employees to a threadbare existence. It still had to slash the payroll, and even then it operated at a loss.[688] In May 1894 Pullman employees went on strike and forcibly prevented their employer from operating with new hires. The American Railway Union, representing 150,000 railway employees, met in Chicago that spring and voted to stage a secondary boycott—its members would stop handling trains with Pullman passenger cars, effective June 26. When those participating in the boycott were fired—railroad managers did not think highly of employees selecting cars they would handle—the boycott evolved into a general strike among railroad workers. Within three weeks, 20,000 were on strike in Chicago and another 40,000 were on strike at points further west. On June 29, strikers stopped a train at Hammond, Indiana, and forcibly detached two Pullman cars. The next day crowds in Chicago—which included large mobs of unemployed persons as well as strikers—began stopping trains. The nation's transportation system broke down and deliveries of livestock and grain came to a halt. Factories stopped operating due to a lack of coal and hospitals ran out of ice.[689]

Attorney General Richard Olney proceeded to lay into the strikers like a Kansas cyclone hitting a wheat field. After the Postmaster General complained that strikers were blocking the movement of train cars containing mail, Olney instructed the district attorney in Chicago to apply for an injunction ordering the strikers to allow mail trains to move unmolested. The railroads had been at least partially responsible for the problem; they had attached Pullman cars to virtually every passenger train carrying mail in the hope that by impairing the activities of the Post Office as well as their own, the strikers would incur the wrath of the national government. The unions responded by allowing Pullman cars to move when they were attached to trains that also contained mail cars.[690]

Olney had expressed doubt on the question of whether the Sherman Antitrust Act could be applied to labor organizations. When the district attorney in Chicago obtained an injunction ordering the strikers to cease and desist interfering with the mails and the transportation of freight across state lines in part by pointing to the law, Olney change course and recommended this approach to other district attorneys around the country, albeit with some reluctance.[691] U.S. marshal J. W. Arnold proceeded to Blue Island, Illinois on July 2, where strikers occupied a large railroad yard. He read the injunction to them, only to be ignored. Instead they went to work blocking the tracks. The next day Arnold reported that that mail trains were unable to move and that strikers had disobeyed the injunction. By July 6 mobs had taken control of the stockyards as well as tracks belonging to the Rock Island Railroad. Nearly 1,000 railroad cars had been destroyed.[692] The failure of the mobs to comply with the injunction led Olney to take more drastic steps. After securing a statement from the U.S. marshal and a federal judge asserting that federal troops would be needed to enforce the court order and get mail moving, he took it to the president and asked him to send the army to Chicago.

Cleveland granted Olney's request. He ordered federal troops to aid marshals seeking to ensure the railroads in Illinois could operate. The order cited the inability to move of trains containing mail and the need to enforce federal law; it did not mention the Sherman Act. Fourteen thousand soldiers arrived in Blue Island, the Chicago stockyards, and at Grand Crossing on July 5. Despite the fact that the state militia was not deployed in its entirety in Chicago until July 6, Governor John P. Altgeld was furious over the president's decision to send federal troops. Along with Chicago Mayor John Hopkins, Altgeld provided critical aid in helping Cleveland carry Illinois in 1892. The two men believed federal intervention to be unnecessary and illegal; both suffered severe political damage due to Cleveland's decision to send troops. Four Democratic governors sent the president a telegram calling his actions a betrayal of the Democratic Party's traditional opposition to centralization.[693] Those governors who were facing violence on their own railroads feared—or at least professed to fear—federal intervention in their own states. Governor James Hogg of Texas sent Cleveland a telegram insisting that his state "is able to control the situation and enforce the law and protect rights guaranteed by the state and federal constitutions and she will do so. You are notified that you may not feel called upon by the plea of any alarmist to use United States troops here unless requested by state authority."[694]

On July 5, Governor Altgeld sent the president a telegram demanding the withdrawal of federal troops from Chicago and claiming their presence was not authorized by federal law or the Constitution. He denied that the chaos had moved beyond the ability of state officials to control it and noted that three regiments of the state militia had been stationed in the city. Altgeld concluded with the absurd claim that trains were not running because the railroads could not find anyone to operate them. The president responded with his own telegram. Cleveland insisted that he had acted in accordance with federal law and the Constitution "upon the demand of the Post Office Department that obstructions of the mail should be removed, and upon the representations of the judicial officers of the United States that process of the federal courts could not be executed through the ordinary means, and upon abundant proof that conspiracies existed against commerce between the states."[695] Altgeld responded the next day with yet another telegram; he claimed the president had assumed unilateral power to decide when a disturbance warranting federal intervention exists. The governor asserted that statutes authorizing the use of federal troops predicated their deployment on the failure of state militias to quell violence.[696]

While Governor Altgeld and President Cleveland debated the law, matters continued to disintegrate in Chicago and across the nation. Trains as far away as the west coast and the Mexican border were stopped by strikers.[697] Crowds in Chicago were now ransacking and destroying property unrelated to the railroads, including buildings used the prior year for the Columbian Exposition. On July 8, the president issued a message justifying his decision to send troops to Chicago: the mail was obstructed, it had been impossible to enforce the laws through normal judicial processes, and federal property was in peril. Cleveland admonished all persons in Illinois destroying property to return to their homes before noon on July 9.[698] The message seems to have been issued in a belated attempt to comply with the terms of the Militia Act of 1807, which required the issuing of a proclamation ordering insurgents to disburse prior to deployment of the army.[699] It was not until mid-July that trains operating under military guard were able to move in and out of Chicago. The strike sputtered to an end but not before Eugene Debs, head of the American Railway Union, was arrested along with three others for contempt of court (violating the injunction) and conspiracy. Debs was found guilty and served six months in jail. Twelve persons died in the Chicago rioting; over 500 were arrested.[700]

In the weeks after the incident, recriminations were many. While labor saw the president as having betrayed it, the press endorsed his conduct and criticized Altgeld. *Harper's Weekly* accused the governor of criticizing the president while failing to do his own job. It claimed the entire incident need not have occurred if he and other governors had fulfilled their responsibility to maintain order.[701] In December 1894, the U.S. Strike Commission—formed by Congress following the events in Chicago—issued its report. It recommended the formation of a permanent strike commission with powers over railway labor disputes similar to those the Interstate Commerce Commission had over rates.[702] It suggested giving federal courts authority to compel the railroads to accept the decisions of the commission; unions should be required to expel members who engage in violence; union members ought to be exempt from liability for judgments against unions. The Commission called on the states to adopt arbitration systems, prohibit yellow dog contracts (under which employees promised to refrain from joining unions), and advised railroads to recognize unions.[703]

The Supreme Court had the last word on the use of injunctions to curtail labor violence when it reviewed Eugene Debs's appeal of the denial of his request for a writ of habeas corpus.[704] In its ruling of May 1895, the Court upheld the order denying the writ. The bill of complaint alleged that four defendants, all officers of the American Railway Union, organized a boycott of Pullman and sought to bring it into effect by conspiring to prevent 22 railroads from engaging in interstate commerce.[705] In his opinion for a unanimous court, Justice David Brewer held that federal courts had jurisdiction over the strike via the federal commerce and postal powers, the right of courts to use their powers in equity to remedy nuisances that cannot be immediately abated in other ways, the right of the United States to invoke legal and equitable remedies in the protection of its property, and the sovereign right of a government to protect the public welfare.[706] Brewer closed by stating that the high court would offer no opinion on the question of whether the Sherman Antitrust Act provided a basis for injunctions targeting those who interfered with railroads even though it had been the basis for the lower court's decision.[707] The decision has been derided for its assumption of "an implied power that would have made Hamilton and Marshall gasp."[708] Perhaps critics protested too much. The violence against railroads had brought interstate commerce in large parts of the country to a halt and it threatened to throw thousands out of work while factories awaited deliveries of coal. It constituted the greatest emergency the nation had faced in 20 years.

In the July 1895 *Atlantic*, Henry Fletcher asserted that the federal government should establish a department of transportation and "take cognizance of the relations of the transportation companies" with their employees, stockholders, and customers. He noted that railroads as well as laborers were suffering in the current climate of unrestrained competition—156 were in receivership as of June 1894. More effective regulation of rates was needed, as much to protect the lines and their investors from rate wars as to protect shippers. In Fletcher's view, it was the labor problems facing railroads that were in the most immediate need of attention. In taking up this issue, the federal government would have to determine whether violent strikes that impeded rail traffic constituted criminal conspiracies. Could it fix wages as well as rates in light of the fact that railroads are affected with a public interest? Should federal judges continue to try strikers who violate their injunctions without the benefit of juries?[709]

The federal government's reaction to the Pullman strike combined with repeal of the Sherman Silver Purchase Act to alienate the president from large sections of his own party. Labor never forgave Cleveland for what it saw as the unwarranted and illegal use of federal troops to break a strike. It was also offended by the fact that Eugene Debs had been tried for contempt without benefit of a jury. Some mistakenly viewed this as a violation of his right to a jury trial despite the fact that the Circuit Court was exercising its equity jurisdiction, an area of the law in which juries had never been used. Western and southern Democrats took offense at the repeal of the Sherman Silver Purchase Act. The hostility of many Democratic constituencies to the president was not eased by Cleveland's failure to exploit the party's control of Congress to obtain a substantial reduction in tariff rates. The problem stemmed from divisions within the party and not a failure of leadership on the president's part. As editor Josephus Daniels recalled, there were "scores of Democrats who espoused (a) 'tariff for revenue only with incidental protection,' meaning they wanted some gravy for manufacturers or others in their district."[710] Due in large part to the influence of protectionist Democratic Senator Arthur P. Gorman of Maryland, Congress produced a tariff that reduced the McKinley Tariff's rates only slightly. The Wilson Tariff of 1894 resurrected the income tax in the hope of moving more of the tax burden to the upper end of the income scale (2% on incomes above $4,000).[711] The president was appalled by the failure of the Democratic Congress to demonstrate more courage. He allowed the bill to become law without his signature, realizing as he did that Congress was not likely to produce anything better if forced to make another attempt. The Supreme Court modified the Wilson Tariff shortly thereafter in *Pollock v. Farmers' Loan and Trust Company* (1895) when it held the income tax void due to the failure of Congress to apportion it among the states.[712] In the view of the high court, since real estate taxes had to be apportioned (as they were direct taxes), so did income from real estate.[713]

In the 1894 midterm elections, Republicans took back the House. Following the election, the matter of the currency rose to the fore once again after the federal government had to sell bonds at what were viewed as exorbitant rates in order to replenish its gold supplies. With the Democrats in disarray and the economy in a state of collapse, the discontent that had been building in the South and West for years erupted. Farmers demanded a return to silver and they refused to take no for an answer. Vital to their demands were the myths built up in support of them. Populists devised an elaborate account of a conspiracy believed to have lasted decades to explain what was only an accident of history. Prices declined during the last 30 years of the century due to improvements in productivity, a relatively small increase in the amount of gold mined each year, and the adoption of the gold standard in Europe and South America.[714] Some claimed deflation arose out of the 1873 decision of Congress to stop coining silver.[715] As William F. Parrett of Indiana explained in the House in 1890, the demonetization of silver in 1873, "perhaps the greatest financial calamity that ever has ever befallen mankind," occurred because of the influence of bondholders who wanted to redeem in gold what they had paid for with paper. "An opportunity was presented for converting their bonds and other accumulations into a form representing over twofold the actual amount of property and labor which, under an honest system of financiering, they had represented or could ever represent; and this opportunity was seized with the avidity of a hungry beast of prey." The result was a severe retraction of the money supply and deflation. "Where it before took one horse to pay a debt it now took two." (In fact the money supply grew, but at a modest rate.[716]) The solution was obvious, at least to Parrett. "I hold that the free coinage of our present silver dollar would not be a fraud upon any class of our people, but an act of simple, unmixed justice to all; and that instead of over-flooding us with domestic money it would simply supply the volume of currency so earnestly demanded and so much needed by the people to infuse life, energy and activity into the waning and drooping business of the whole country."[717]

It seemed plausible enough, at least until the Sherman Silver Purchase Act caused gold to disappear and the government came within a fortnight of defaulting on its debts. Still the nation's farmers pressed their cause as the depression of the 1890s spread misery across the country. Bimetallism affected Republicans almost as much as Democrats, in part due to their need for the support of western states, where it was thought that inclusion of silver in the currency would stop the long decline in its price and give the mining industry a more substantial return on its investment. If enough silver had been coined, it might have produced inflation, though driving gold out of circulation and scaring away European capital would have invited disaster. The introduction of new supplies of gold to the market finally produced a hike in prices starting in 1897. After declining a little more than 1 percent a year from 1879 to 1897, prices rose about 2 percent a year from 1897 to 1914.[718]

The country did not know it was near the end of the deflationary tunnel in the mid-1890s and so the demand for silver rose to a deafening roar. Disappointed over their performance in the 1894 elections, Populists focused on silver and dropped their other priorities. They spent much of 1895 and 1896 telling impoverished farmers that their inability get higher prices for their wheat, corn, or cotton stemmed from the inadequate growth of the money supply—a condition that could be reversed by the coinage of silver. Silver forces began to take over Democratic machinery in state after state despite the president's use of federal offices to slow their progress.[719] Postmaster General William L. Wilson complained that to reason with those favoring the coinage of silver "is as impossible as to talk down an angry cyclone." Silver advocates turned away from those whom they had long followed, "and rally behind the loudest and emptiest demagogues who can rail at 'Goldbugs,' denounce Wall Street, and shout free silver."[720] By the end of June 1896, silver forces had won control of 18 of 23 state Democratic conventions held to select delegates to the party's National Convention in Chicago.[721]

Although no one suspected it at the time, the main beneficiary of the revolution within state Democratic organizations would be William Jennings Bryan, a 36-year-old Nebraska newspaper editor. Elected to Congress from Nebraska in 1890, Bryan was only the second Democrat sent to the House by that state. On arriving in Washington, he called for strengthening the Interstate Commerce Commission and basing rates on the actual value of the railroads and not their capitalization, as the latter was often inflated and used to justify higher charges. Bryan demanded the revival of the income tax as well as appropriations for irrigation projects. The Nebraska congressman was among the earliest to suggest that the federal government insure bank deposits. He supported Cleveland in 1892 but soon thereafter departed from party orthodoxy when he decided to make a name for himself on the silver issue. Bryan's comments on the subject were typically demagogic. He believed the act of 1873 demonetizing silver was the product of an international conspiracy that had bribed lawmakers into taking that momentous step to keep gold expensive, thereby causing a depression and enabling it to buy failing businesses.[722] After a hopeless attempt to win election to the U.S. Senate in 1894, Bryan spent the next year and a half working with pro-silver Democrats throughout the country, helping them win control of their state conventions.

By June 1896, Bryan was angling for the Democratic presidential nomination, though he was considered a dark horse at best. Party leaders in Washington, DC, were aware of his oratorical skills but the rest of the country remained ignorant of his gifts. The early front-runner was Richard P. Bland, a former Democratic congressman from Missouri. Bland was the head of the pro-silver wing of the party, author of the Bland-Allison Act of 1878, and the odds-on favorite for the nomination as late as the Fourth of July.[723] The convention met at the Chicago Coliseum on July 7. When it approved the majority report of the Committee on Credentials seating the pro-silver Michigan delegation (and expelling a slate devoted to the gold standard), silverites obtained a two-thirds majority and control over the nomination.[724]

Senator Ben Tillman of South Carolina addressed the convention on July 8. He claimed that the people of the South and West had been impoverished by the national financial system and could not buy goods from the factories of the North, leaving their workers idle.[725] Shortly thereafter, Bryan spoke. He began with conciliation when he moved to table resolutions condemning the Cleveland administration. Defying the Supreme Court, he insisted the income tax was constitutional. Bryan complained that the country had waited 20 years for an international agreement on bimetallism; he charged that those who counseled patience did not want an agreement. It was time to act, as the deflation wrought by gold had inflicted far more harm than even tariffs: if "protection has slain its thousands, the gold standard has slain its tens of the thousands." In his view, the movement in the Democratic Party toward silver stemmed from a determination that the American people and not foreign powers should decide the nature of money in the United States. He believed Democrats would win the upcoming election as Republicans had made it clear they would not go along with bimetallism unless England and other nations agreed to it. "We will restore bimetallism and let England adopt it because the United States has led the way. We shall answer their demand for the gold standard by saying to them: 'you shall not press down upon the brow of labor this crown of thorns. You shall not crucify mankind upon a cross of gold.' "[726]

North Carolina editor Josephus Daniels recalled that silver delegates were enthralled, "standing (and) shouting as if lifted out of themselves." Gold Democrats, on the other hand, "sat like stone men, seeming to look upon the frenzied throngs as if the shouters were beside themselves. They couldn't understand it. To them free silver was heresy, and they thought there was nothing but free silver in Bryan's speech."[727] Daniels explained that there was more to the frenzy than money or inflation: "The truth is, free silver was the expression of the hope for legislation of a people who had been through the panic and hard times and were seeking to strike at government by privilege. There were thousands who did not know anything about free silver and did not care anything about it who were enthusiastic for Bryan."[728] As Bryan finished, he was placed on the shoulders of two of the more burly delegates and paraded through the hall. Several hundred delegates worked themselves into a frenzy over the prospect of inflation and, at some abstract level, vengeance.[729]

The next day balloting for a nominee began. Richard Bland took the early lead, but Bryan gained with every ballot and finally won the vote of two-thirds of the delegates and the nomination on the fifth.[730] Gold Democrats walked out of the convention rather than acquiesce in the selection of the "Boy Orator of the Platte." The platform proclaimed the right of the United States to determine for itself what should qualify as money. It noted that the first Congress coined silver dollars and demanded "the free and unlimited coinage of both silver and gold at the present legal ratio of 16 to 1 without waiting for the aid or consent of any other nation. We demand that the standard silver shall be a full legal tender, equally with gold, for all debts, public and private." The platform went on to express the party's opposition to the issuing of bonds in time of peace, as well as the use of injunctions by federal judges in labor disputes as "arbitrary interferences by federal authorities in local affairs." The platform called for approval of a bill pending in Congress that would provide jury trials in federal contempt cases arising out of strikes. In an indication of the practical effect of civil service laws, it also condemned "lifetime tenure" for executive branch employees.[731] Later that summer, Populists held their own nominating convention and nominated Bryan. Gold or "National Democrats" nominated former Illinois Governor John M. Palmer in September. Their platform dismissed the one issued by regular Democrats in July as a "reckless attempt to increase the price of silver by legislation to the debasement of our money standard." The demand for a law depriving courts of the right to issue injunctions was dismissed as an attack on the independence of the judiciary.[732]

The fight for the Republican nomination was considerably less dramatic. Ohio Governor William McKinley's stock went up as the economy worsened—many believed that more protection, such as that embodied in the 1890 tariff that bore his name, would bring an end to the depression. House Speaker Thomas Brackett Reed sought the nomination, but he was hobbled by a lack of enthusiasm for his candidacy among Republican congressmen, many of whom chafed at his domineering ways and his lack of generosity in the matter of pork barrel appropriations.[733] Benjamin Harrison also made a half-hearted attempt to gain the nomination, but his hopes were dashed when Mark Hanna, McKinley's campaign manager, secured control of the southern delegations.[734] Lacking federal offices with which he might have matched Hanna's resources, Harrison had no hope of regaining the support of delegates of southern states who had proven so critical to his successful effort in 1892. Perhaps the most serious trouble for McKinley came from eastern bosses led by Matt Quay. They tried to stop him by fielding favorite son candidates when he refused to promise them federal offices for distribution among their supporters (Quay himself wanted to be appointed secretary of the treasury).[735] McKinley was duly nominated, causing Silver Republicans to walk out in protest. They did not stage their own convention. At McKinley's behest the platform included a clause offering a slim ray of hope to pro-silver voters; it called for an international agreement on the coinage of silver. With one eye on veterans, Republicans denounced the Pension Bureau for striking names from the pension rolls.[736]

New York boss Thomas Platt dismissed McKinley as "simply a clever gentleman, much too amiable and much too impressionable to be safely entrusted with a great executive office."[737] Of more concern to easterners was McKinley's history of flirtation with silver; he had made troubling comments on the subject as recently as 1894 and he voted for the Silver Purchase Act of 1890. Still the Republicans presented an attractive candidate to the country. A 52-year-old lawyer, McKinley had served with the 23rd Ohio Regiment during the Civil War and saw action at Antietam. He was an avowed protectionist. As a youth McKinley watched his father's iron business suffer along with others in Niles, Ohio, during the 1850s and he blamed their difficulties on the hostility to protection of Democratic congressional majorities in Washington. Elected to Congress in 1876, McKinley retained his distaste for free trade. After he lost his House seat in 1890 he went home and served two terms as governor. In that position McKinley signed laws providing protection to railroad and streetcar workers; he also went along with a measure imposing fines on employers who prevented workers from joining unions. His sympathy for labor did not prevent McKinley from deploying the state militia to keep railroads running after coalminers attempted to prevent West Virginia coal from entering the state.[738]

Republican leaders were dismissive and contemptuous of Bryan. John Hay called him a "half-baked glib little briefless jack-leg lawyer . . . grasping with anxiety at that $50,000 salary, promising the millennium to everybody with a hole in his pants and destruction to everybody with a clean shirt."[739] The hostility of Republican Party leaders to Bryan was driven by fear—of what exactly, beyond an expanded currency, it was hard to say. Looking back in 1900, on the eve of another Bryan candidacy, the *Atlantic* suggested that the real danger stemmed from the "state of mind" evident in the 1896 Democratic platform. It displayed "a perilous belief held by hundreds of thousands of voters, that the owners of wealth in this country are oppressing, through the law, those who have no wealth, and especially those who till the earth and who labor with their hands." The article conceded that it is "unhappily, true that wealth and prosperity, created and fostered by law, are doing nothing to dissipate this belief; on the contrary, they are doing everything in their power to confirm it." In the view of the *Atlantic*, "the first and the most important cleavage between voters separates those who believe in the use of the taxing power to promote commerce (tariffs), and to increase the gains that come from commerce, from those who are at war with special privileges that are already conferred by law or that are threatened, and whose enmity against what they call the money power will inevitably gain force so long as the accomplishment of their immediate object (a reduction in rates) is postponed."[740]

The McKinley campaign did nothing to indicate its candidate would close the fissure that had formed over 30 years; on the contrary it called for more protection. Given a choice between Republicans—who insisted that foreign trade would be sacrificed by free silver even as they proposed to burden it with tariffs—and Bryan, conservative Democrats chose the former. Rumors abounded of federal officeholders who had been removed from office for aiding the Bryan campaign.[741] Democratic newspapers in the Northeast, Midwest, and even the South came out against Bryan.[742] The great commoner's support among the giant dailies of Gotham was limited to William Randolph Hearst's *New York Morning Journal*—even Joseph Pulitzer's staunchly Democratic *New York World* condemned the silver plank. Hearst provided the Bryan campaign badly needed assistance. He had the *Journal*'s press turn out thousands of pages of campaign literature for the Democratic nominee.[743]

During late August Bryan toured upstate New York where he drew huge crowds. One day saw him speak to 10,000 in the afternoon and 13,000 in the evening. The crowds were "unquestionably enthusiastic." Republicans were advised to take notice.[744] The audiences in the West and South were even larger: 50,000 at Columbus and 30,000 at Toledo. Twenty thousand men on horseback honored Bryan when he visited Lexington, Kentucky, and his reception in North Carolina was said to have surpassed one given Henry Clay. Burning tar barrels marked his route from Asheville to Raleigh.[745] The candidate would travel over 18,000 miles before the campaign was over, making up to 30 speeches a day. Estimates put the number of persons who heard him speak at figures as high as five million.[746] Despite the enthusiasm, most observers did not give Bryan much of a chance in the eastern states, for the simple reason that labor failed to see how it would benefit from inflation—on the contrary, Republicans had some success in arguing that inflation would hurt wage earners.[747]

Bryan assured workingmen that inflation would stimulate the economy and called for federal arbitration of labor disputes. He pointed out that McKinley had embraced silver while in Congress between 1876 and 1890.[748] Speaking at Madison Square Garden in September, Bryan quoted Republican John Sherman's 1869 assertion that contraction of the currency would result in hardship for all but the "capitalist out of debt, or a salaried officer, or a annuitant." He also quoted 1876 remarks from James Blaine: the establishment of a single gold standard "would produce widespread disaster" and have "a ruinous effect on all forms of property except those investments which yield a fixed rate of return." In Minneapolis later that fall,

Bryan cited John Sherman's 1890 assertion that the currency needed to expand by at least $50 million every year.[749] Visiting West Virginia in late September, Bryan told the residents of Martinsburg that banks should not have the power to issue money; he pointed out that Jefferson had called "banks of issue" more dangerous than a standing army. Bryan assured listeners at Harper's Ferry that in seeking the coinage of silver, he merely wished to restore the financial system that had been in place until 1873.[750] Americans remained skeptical of plan that would impair foreign trade if the United States alone embraced the coinage of silver. The *Atlanta Constitution* acknowledged this fear when it claimed to have located a British financial expert who assured that if America embraced silver, the rest of the world would follow.[751]

McKinley refused to take to the road; he was forthright enough to admit he could never match Bryan's energy. He had already conducted his own tour in 1894 when he traveled widely speaking on behalf of Republican candidates; in the process he earned a reputation as an effective speaker and advocate of Republican policies. Now the country came to him. Fifty thousand heard the candidate speak from his front porch at his home in Canton, Ohio, on the day word of his nomination arrived.[752] The work Mark Hanna performed may have been the most novel aspect of the campaign. The Cleveland ironmonger raised $3.5 million from corporations by scaring the daylights out of them with tales of free trade and inflation. He used the money to fund two campaign headquarters, one in New York City and one in Chicago. One hundred workers toiled in the mail room of the Chicago office; they distributed 200 million documents during the campaign.[753] Hanna dispatched trainloads of voters to McKinley's home in Canton to hear the candidate. The delegations found themselves treated to liquor or non-alcoholic drinks, depending on whether their home state was wet or dry.[754] Shelby Cullom thought 50,000 to 75,000 persons gathered outside McKinley's home on the day he visited Canton that fall.[755] McKinley had been suspect on the money question in the eyes of some Republicans; yet he held fast and ignored Hanna's pleas to endorse the gold standard, preferring to focus on the tariff. Other Republican speakers stressed the consequences of the rampant inflation that would be produced by the coinage of silver; it would diminish the value of savings and pensions.[756] Thomas Brackett Reed claimed the gold standard had been in place since 1531. He warned that there was too much silver to coin it at a 16:1 ratio to gold. If Bryan had his way, gold would be driven out of circulation.[757]

Harper's Weekly complained of the "promise held out to debtors that free coinage will enable them to get rid of their debts by paying them in debased currency."[758] Republicans suggested that with their hostility to railroads and banks, Bryan and his followers posed a threat to property. In pushing this line they received invaluable aid from William Allen White, the 28-year Kansan who edited the *Emporia Gazette*. After he published several articles disparaging Populists as extremists, the young upstart found himself rolling in the dirt one night, courtesy of a motley gang of elderly farmers.[759] White had been walking home from the post office when he was accosted; now he went to his office and penned the article that would become famous: "What's the Matter with Kansas?" Dripping with sarcasm, it professed to encourage Kansans to use the legislature to ease their plight and alter the laws of supply and demand. "We have a shabby, wild-eyed, rattle-brained fanatic who has said openly in a dozen speeches that 'the rights of the (railroad) user are paramount to the rights of the owner;' we are running him for Chief Justice, so that capital will come tumbling over itself to get into the state." The law might also be used to wipe out debt. "Legislate the thriftless man into ease, whack the stuffing out of the creditors and tell the debtors who borrowed the money five years ago when money 'per capita' was greater than it is now, that the contraction of currency gives him a right to repudiate."[760] The McKinley campaign thought the editorial perfectly captured the disdain the country ought to feel for Bryan and his ilk. It distributed over a million copies of the editorial.[761]

Some observers thought Bryan would have won if the election had been held in the weeks after his nomination. The fall campaign gave eastern manufacturers time to explain to their employees why they had nothing to gain from inflation. Some relied on fear. Josephus Daniels recalled a sign he saw outside of a Connecticut establishment during a campaign swing with Bryan: "This factory will be closed on the morning after the November election if Bryan is elected. If McKinley is elected, employment will go on as usual."[762] Overall the tales of intimidation of employees seem to have been exaggerated. The middle class of the North and East did not need to be threatened; it accepted the notion that the depression would worsen with the adoption of bimetallism. Polls of employees of Midwest manufacturers such as the John Deere Company revealed strong majorities for McKinley.[763] As the election approached, McKinley was said to be a 3:1 favorite, though fears lingered among conservatives of both parties over the possibility that labor would be seduced by the Great Commoner.[764]

Bryan won much of the South and West but lost the northern and central states, including Illinois (where he was born), North Dakota, Minnesota, Iowa, and Wisconsin. He also managed to lose traditionally Democratic states including Delaware, Maryland, West Virginia, and Kentucky. McKinley won most of the large cities of the North; Bryan was the first Democratic candidate to lose New York City and Brooklyn since 1848.[765] While McKinley's popular vote margin was modest (51 to 47%) his large majority in the Electoral College gave the illusion of a great victory. Republicans won majorities in both the Senate and the House; 40 seats in the latter were held by Populists or Silver Democrats. Democrats charged that Republicans spent thousands of dollars bringing men into large cities where they voted for McKinley. They also complained of widespread intimidation of employees. Perhaps the most important factor was the rise in farm prices—wheat reached a three-year high in December—as it lessened the appetite of farmers for radical measures.[766] The return of German Americans to the Republican Party after an exodus of several years caused by Republican flirtation with the prohibition movement also proved critical.[767] *Harper's Weekly* rejoiced in what it called "the defeat of socialism." The nation had, it explained, been spared the sight of publicly operated railroads, telegraph, and telephone companies.[768]

For over 30 years, politicians of all stripes had tampered or proposed to tamper with the currency. As the October 1896 *Atlantic* pointed out regarding fiat money, "by far the larger portion of our public men—the very men who are now doing excellent service against the absurdity—have at one time or another dallied with it."[769] In that sense the divisions of 1896 were somewhat contrived. Where the election of 1896 differed from its predecessors was in the exploitation of the precarious economic condition of Americans. As the *Atlantic* put it, "this campaign has taken a more dangerous form than any preceding one, because so direct and so essentially dishonest an appeal has been made to the envy of the mass of men, and a candidate for the presidency has himself appealed directly to the class feeling of the discontented."[770]

Yet Bryan had been correct in the central insight of his campaign—the inadequate growth of the money supply had inflicted tremendous hardship. While his prescription would have been economically destructive in risking a flight of gold and in the harm it would have inflicted on creditors and consumers, as an exercise of federal authority the coinage of silver would not even have risen to the level of novelty—the national government was after all charged with the duty of regulating the coinage and Congress had proved more than willing to exercise that power in the past. Still the *Atlantic* was correct in perceiving something new in a presidential candidate's appeal to the "class feeling of the discontented." In time other candidates for national office would embrace this approach; the connection between their chosen remedies and the enumerated powers would prove more far elusive than anything seen in 1896.

Shortly after taking office, continuing revenue problems led McKinley to call a special session of Congress for the purpose of increasing tariff rates. The Republican Congress enacted the steepest tariff in the country's history, with rates reaching an average of 52 percent. The Dingley Tariff of July 24, 1897, removed wool from the free list in a bid for the western votes that had been lost to silver in 1896.[771] Woolen manufacturers received ad valorem rates of 55 percent to compensate them for the duty on the wool.[772] Twenty-one goods carried duties of greater than 125 percent including dress goods, blankets, worsted woolens, and flannels.[773] With the economy improving, the increase in tariff rates did not elicit widespread protests. Nor did the country mind the administration's lackadaisical enforcement of the Sherman Antitrust Act despite the appearance of trusts in numerous industries. The Erdman Act of June 1, 1898, constituted the sole exercise of federal power over the economy possessed of any novelty to be implemented during the McKinley administration.[774] The act strengthened the mechanism established 10 years earlier for the voluntary arbitration of labor disputes involving common carriers engaged in interstate commerce. Of more significance was the law's provision barring common carriers from making membership in company-sponsored unions a condition of employment (some railroads established company unions as a way of undermining the power of independent unions). Nor could railroads discriminate against employees who were members of unions. The connection between labor contracts and interstate commerce was less than clear; in 1908 the Supreme Court announced it did not see one and held the law void.[775]

Prosperity returned as the century approached its end; the Alaska gold strike produced higher prices, easing the plight of farmers and enhancing the president's prospects for reelection. It also increased the price of silver and decreased the price of gold, enabling Congress to enact a law of March 14, 1900, making the return to the gold standard official. It was received with little protest. The law also allowed each national bank to issue more notes as currency; the end result was an increase in the amount of national bank notes in circulation from $223 million in 1898 to $433 million in 1904.[776] Republicans thus embraced expansion of the money supply by government fiat after gaining power by attacking the idea. The increase in the money supply aided the economy; so did an increase in spending necessitated by the Spanish-American War. Nominated again in 1900, William Jennings Bryan continued to demand the coinage of silver but with the return of prosperity the cause no longer registered with the public. In search of a new issue with which he might drum up indignation, Bryan focused on imperialism and trusts. Like many Americans he had been uneasy over military intervention in Cuba and the Philippines and he opposed the idea of making them colonies of the United States. The issue of trusts held more promise. With the *Knight* decision's assertion that Congress could not reach manufacturers still fresh in the public mind, Bryan asserted that those entities operated in a twilight area that existed between the jurisdiction of the federal government and that of the states. Democrats may have hurt themselves when they added a silver plank to their platform, as the party's conservative wing responded by announcing its refusal to support Bryan.[777]

Republicans ignored the silver issue and emphasized Bryan's hypocrisy in charging imperialism—he did valuable work in getting the Treaty of Paris ratified—and reminded Americans that the economy had shown marked improvement. "Four more years of the Full Dinner Pail" served as the slogan for the president's reelection campaign; it also confirmed that Republicans were aware of the need to emphasize the economic well-being of voters. McKinley appeared to be moving serenely toward victory until a strike among Pennsylvania coalminers involving 134,000 men threatened trouble in late September. Bryan pointed to the mere 90 cents a day the miners received as evidence of the failure of protection to aid labor.[778] Sensing trouble, Mark Hanna pressured the mine owners to cut a deal. They did so at the end of October, giving their employees a 10 percent hike in pay. McKinley won a more definitive victory than he had in 1896, with a popular majority of 900,000 (though he still obtained only 52% of the popular vote). Bryan won the South again but his take in the West was limited to four silver states. The Republicans retained control of both houses of Congress. Ten months later, in September 1901, an anarchist, one Leon Czolgosz, shot the president in the stomach at Buffalo, New York. Like Garfield, McKinley was a victim of the healing arts of his time—when Thomas Edison offered the president's physicians an X-ray machine in the hope it might show the bullet's location, they refused.[779] After lingering for eight days, the president died, leaving his office to 42-year-old Theodore Roosevelt, the former governor of New York who had been placed on the ticket in 1900 at the behest of state boss Tom Platt, who was desperate to get his young charge out of the state.

Chapter 4

THE PROGRESSIVE ERA AND AMERICAN FEDERALISM, 1901–1921

THE EROSION OF STATE AUTHORITY

When the Supreme Court upheld an Illinois law establishing rates to be charged by grain warehouses in *Munn v. Illinois* (1877), it turned aside two arguments offered by the warehouses: (1) the measure constituted an impermissible regulation of interstate commerce and (2) it violated the due process clause of the Fourteenth Amendment.[1] The first, considered earlier in this work, held some validity as the warehouses stored grain delivered to Chicago from several states. The second was completely devoid of merit. The phrase *due process* had been borrowed from Great Britain, where it required officials of the crown to comply with certain procedural safeguards when subjecting persons to criminal sanction or taking their property. It did not apply to Parliament. Most of the states included due process clauses when they drafted constitutions during the 1770s and 1780s; there is no evidence they viewed them at that time as limiting the power of legislatures. When state courts began holding void laws viewed as impairing property rights, they claimed the statutes violated "natural law" or other abstract political doctrines. The democratic trends of the early nineteenth century made this approach untenable, and state judges began claiming that state laws viewed as overly burdensome regulations of property conflicted with one more provisions of the state or federal constitutions, such as the contract clause. It was not until the 1850s that they began applying the due process clauses of the state constitutions to state laws with anything approaching regularity. When they did so, their decisions were harshly criticized by other state court judges.[2]

In its original sense, the due process clause of the Fifth Amendment merely barred the federal government from depriving persons or groups of procedural protections enjoyed by other citizens when subjecting them to trial.[3] The Supreme Court applied the due process clause of the Fifth Amendment to an act of Congress for the first time in 1856; the law remained in place.[4] One year later in *Dred Scott*, it held the Missouri Compromise's ban on slavery void on the grounds that it violated the property rights of slaveholders that were protected by the due process clause of the Fifth Amendment.[5] The high court erred badly in using the clause to invalidate a statute that excluded slavery from most of the territories, as legislative bodies had long banned items deemed injurious, such as explosives. The Fourteenth Amendment's due process clause extended the assurance of procedural protections to the states, but it did not widen its scope.

The warehouses in *Munn* claimed the due process clause of the Fourteenth Amendment barred the establishment of rates without a hearing. In an opinion written by Chief Justice Morrison R. Waite, the majority held that because they were affected with a public interest, the rates of the warehouses were subject to regulation of their rates despite the lack of a hearing.[6] In dissent, Justice Stephen Field argued that a power to set the rate of return that might be obtained on a particular form of property would render hollow the bar against the taking of property without due process of law.[7] Field had a point; the ability of legislatures to reduce the value of property of all kinds via burdensome regulations has only become more apparent since the *Munn* decision. Yet the ability of legislatures to adversely affect the value of property by regulation did not bring such cases within the scope of the due process clause.

The refusal of the Supreme Court to widen the scope of the due process clause of the Fourteenth Amendment to limit the regulatory power of the states did not stop lawyers from citing it. They seemed to have viewed it as appropriate conclusion for any appeal filed over state economic regulations. This tactic earned a rebuke from Justice Samuel F. Miller in *Davidson v. New Orleans* (1878): "It would seem, from the character of many of the cases before us, and the arguments made in them, that the clause under consideration (the due process clause) is looked upon as a means of bringing to the test of the decision of this court the abstract opinions of every unsuccessful litigant in state court of the justice of the decision against him, and of the merits of the legislation on which such a decision may be founded."[8] This penchant for labeling any regulation that seemed to burden property a violation of due process received encouragement from state courts, which began holding numerous state economic regulations void as conflicting with due process clauses in state constitutions. The New York Court of Appeals held void on these grounds a statute prohibiting cigar manufacturing in tenements in 1885.[9] In 1895, the Illinois Supreme Court invalidated a law limiting the work day of women to eight hours as a violation of the due process of the state constitution.[10] As Roscoe Pound noted in a 1909 article, usury laws had long limited the amount of interest lenders could charge, and no one suggested they violated due process.[11] The U.S. Supreme Court took the bait in 1890 in *Chicago, Milwaukee & St. Paul Railway v. Minnesota*.[12] In 1887 the state of Minnesota established a railroad commission whose decisions regarding rates were not subject to judicial review. Shortly thereafter farmers filed a complaint with the commission alleging that the Chicago, Milwaukee & St. Paul charged 2.5 cents a gallon to transfer milk from Northfield to St. Paul and three cents a gallon for the same trip from Owatonna even though the two towns were equidistant from St. Paul. The commission ordered the railroad to charge 2.5 cents a gallon for both routes without holding a hearing and the railroad refused, causing the commission to seek a writ from the Minnesota Supreme Court requiring the railroad to comply with the order. The railroad claimed that the state legislature could not delegate its rate-making power to a commission and that the rate imposed by the commission constituted a taking of property without due process of law. The Minnesota Supreme Court ruled for the commission, and the railroad brought a writ of error in the U.S. Supreme Court.[13]

The Supreme Court ruled in favor of the railroad. In his opinion for the majority, Justice Samuel Blatchford explained that the law establishing the Minnesota Railroad and Warehouse Commission did not provide the railroad an opportunity to contest its findings.[14] If, he explained, a company is "deprived of the power of charging reasonable rates for the use of its property, and such deprivation takes place in the absence of an investigation by judicial machinery, it is deprived of the lawful use of its property, and thus, in substance and effect, of the property itself, without due process of law."[15] Justice Joseph Bradley wrote a dissent that was joined by Justices Lucius Q. C. Lamar and Horace Gray. He complained that the decision "practically overrules *Munn*," which stood for the principle that the setting of rates for railroads and other public accommodations qualified as a "legislative prerogative and not a judicial one." So was the question of what qualified as a reasonable rate. Prior cases established that legislatures can set rates and they can delegate that power if they wish. In Bradley's view there was "no deprivation of property" but instead "merely a regulation as to the enjoyment of property, made by a strictly competent authority, in a matter entirely within its jurisdiction."[16] The decision and others that followed it enabled railroads to use litigation to delay and often defeat attempts to impose rates on them. Farmers' Alliance organizations were infuriated with the decision; Populist leader Ignatius Donnelly compared it to *Dred Scott*.[17] What became known as the "Milk Rate Case" may well constitute one of the most important turning points in American legal history, as it inaugurated the era of judicial supervision of the decisions of administrative agencies and a long period in which this power was abused, usually for the benefit of railroads.

In 1893, the legislature of Nebraska enacted a law imposing maximum railroad rates. After failing to obtain relief before the state railroad commission and the Nebraska Supreme Court, Union Pacific and other railroads sought relief in U.S. Circuit Court; they claimed the law's tariff schedule would, if implemented, deprive them of the ability to earn a reasonable return. The Circuit Court agreed and issued an injunction barring the state from enforcing the law, and its ruling was upheld by the Supreme Court in *Smyth v. Ames* (1898).[18] In his opinion for the high court, Justice Harlan explained that even when rates are imposed by legislatures themselves, they are subject to judicial review to ensure that the railroads received a reasonable rate of return.[19] Calculations regarding a reasonable rate must be based on the "fair value of the property," which was to be arrived at by considering, among other things, the public's right to reasonable rates and "the probable earning capacity of the property under particular rates prescribed by the statute."[20] As the Nebraska law would have deprived the railroads of a reasonable return, the Circuit Court was correct in issuing the injunction.[21] Whether legislatures, commissions, or anyone could forecast what railroads would earn in the future was open to question; courts hardly seemed qualified to perform that task. Farmers were often unreasonable in demanding lower rates for transportation in areas that did not provide enough traffic to support reductions, but the newfound ability of railroads to use the courts to defeat the public's right to control rates constituted a strange legacy for an amendment designed to protect former slaves.

In *Allgeyer v. Louisiana*, the Supreme Court again held a law void in part on due process grounds; it was also offended by what appeared to be an attempt by a legislature to reach parties outside of the state.[22] The statute barred persons within the state of Louisiana from obtaining marine insurance from companies that failed to comply with the state's insurance regulations. Speaking for the Court, Justice Rufus Peckham pointed to the term "liberty" as used in the due process clause of the Fourteenth Amendment. He claimed it included the "right of the citizen to be free in the enjoyment of all his faculties; to be free to use them in all lawful ways; to live and work where he will; to earn his livelihood by any lawful calling; to pursue any livelihood or avocation, and for that purpose to enter into all contracts which may be proper, necessary and essential to his carrying out to a successful conclusion the purposes above mentioned."[23] Peckham held that the purchase of insurance from an out-of-state company was "a proper act, one which the defendants were at liberty to perform and which the state legislature had no right to prevent, at least with reference to the federal Constitution. To deprive the citizen of such a right as herein described without due process of law is illegal." The doctrine of liberty of contract was born. Although rooted in nothing more than the minds of imaginative lawyers, it would eventually grow to monumental proportions and threaten to strip the states of the ability to regulate all types of economic activity.

The Supreme Court held void a state labor law on due process grounds alone for the first time in *Lochner v. New York* (1905).[24] The Defendant baker was convicted by the state of New York of violating an 1895 law barring employees of bakeries from working more than 60 hours a week or 10 hours a day; after his conviction was upheld by the New York Court of Appeals, he filed a writ of error in the U.S. Supreme Court. Justice Peckham held for the majority that the law "interferes with the right of contract between the employer and employees" that arises out of the due process clause of the Fourteenth Amendment.[25] He distinguished the matter before the Court from a recent case in which it upheld a Utah law limiting miners to an eight-hour day on the grounds that mining was more dangerous than working in a bakery. Peckham conceded that each state possessed police powers under which it can legislate to protect the health, safety, and morals of its citizens; however, if such a law regulates contracts of labor between employers and employees, it must qualify as "a fair, reasonable and appropriate exercise of the police power of the state" or it would be held void as unreasonably and arbitrarily interfering with liberty of contract.[26] Peckham found the law to be unreasonable as bakers were as capable of determining their own hours as persons in other trades, and there was no evidence that the work of a baker was particularly hazardous—therefore the law did not qualify as a reasonable health or safety measure designed to protect persons in that occupation.[27]

Justice Harlan filed a dissent that was joined by Justices Edward White and William Day. As he conceded state laws regulating hours of employees could be held void if they were unreasonable, Harlan acquiesced in an approach that made the Supreme Court the arbiter of maximum hour laws. All that was left for him to do was to insist that the New York law was reasonable, thereby making the dispute between the justices appear suspiciously close to a substantive argument over the law's merits, such as would occur between legislators debating a bill. Harlan quoted a professor for the proposition that the work of bakers "is among the hardest and most laborious imaginable."[28] Justice Oliver Wendell Holmes issued a dissent that made it clear the Court was exercising a veto power over state legislation it disliked, rather than applying the law. "It is settled by various decisions of this Court that state constitutions and state laws may regulate life in many ways which we as legislators might think as injudicious or if you like as tyrannical as this, and which equally with this interfere with the liberty to contract. Sunday laws and usury laws are ancient examples. A more modern one is the prohibition of lotteries. The liberty of the citizen to do as he likes so long as he does not interfere with the liberty of others to do so the same, which has been a shibboleth for some well-known writers, is interfered with by school laws, by the post office, by every state or municipal institution which takes his money for purposes thought desirable, whether he likes it or not."[29] The Supreme Court had upheld laws impairing economic freedom on numerous occasions. "Some of these laws embody convictions or prejudices which judges are likely to share. Some may not. But a constitution is not intended to embody a particular economic theory, whether of paternalism and the organic relation of the citizen to the state or of laissez faire. It is made for people of fundamentally differing views and the accident of our finding certain opinions natural and familiar or novel and even shocking ought not to conclude our judgment upon the question whether statutes embodying them conflict with the Constitution of the United States."[30]

The *New York Times* applauded the ruling; it was pleased to report that the "tendency of state legislatures, under the pressure of labor leaders and professional agitators, to enact laws which interfere with 'the ordinary trades and occupations of the people' is sharply checked by this decision." It agreed that there was no reasonable basis for a legislature to conclude that the hours of bakers ought to be limited. "There are a thousand occupations to which the argument that the workman must be saved from the consequences of his own inclinations would apply with equal or greater force."[31] Some saw the law as yet another example of what would later be called "rent seeking"—the use of public authority by interest groups to obtain a competitive advantage.[32] The law had been pushed by the New York Bakers' Union, the members of which already worked fewer than 10 hours a day. They resented the competition of unorganized immigrants who toiled for long hours in the small bakeries of New York City.[33] Still, the origins of the law had no bearing on its constitutionality. Not only did the ruling deny the people of New York the benefit of a law they had the right to enact, it applied a test the continuing use of which would subject all state economic regulations to invalidation if they appeared unreasonable to the members of the Supreme Court. An article in the *Yale Law Journal* expressed fear that the period in which courts deferred to legislatures and presumed laws were valid until the contrary was demonstrated had come to an end. With the *Lochner* ruling, the high court appeared to have approached "a little nearer the legislative border line that it has hitherto. The old writers on the Constitution dreaded such an approach, and the (Constitutional) Convention, though of course with no thought of the Fourteenth Amendment and its accompanying police power, rather heartily rejected the proposal to vest in the judiciary a qualified negative on all legislation."[34]

The high court did not apply the doctrine of liberty of contract with vigor in the years following *Lochner*. In 1908, the Supreme Court upheld an Oregon law setting a maximum of 10 hours a day for women working in laundries and factories.[35] The case was notable for the brief filed by Louis Brandeis, attorney for the state of Oregon. It cited studies and investigations of bureaus of statistics, commissioners of hygiene, and factory inspectors revealing the deleterious effects of long hours on the health and well-being of women.[36] It was a document that would have been more appropriately considered at a hearing of a legislative committee investigating the subject of women and labor, as it addressed the merits of Oregon law (whether there was a need to limit the hours worked by women). Given the Court's test for determining the constitutionality of state economic legislation, i.e., its reasonableness, Brandeis had no choice. Justice Brewer accepted the invitation offered by Brandeis; he concluded that a woman's "physical structure and a proper discharge of her maternal functions—having in view not merely her own health, but the well-being of the race—justify legislation to protect her from the greed as well as the passion of man."[37]

Although there was a great gnashing of teeth over the Supreme Court's use of the doctrine of freedom of contract for the purpose of invalidating state regulations, this weapon was rarely used before 1920. In 1913 Charles Warren counted a grand total of three cases in which state laws concerning "social justice" had been held void as violations of the Fourteenth Amendment between 1887 and 1911: *Allgeyer v. Louisiana*, *Lochner v. New York*, and *Connolly v. Union Sewer Pipe Co.* (1902). On the other hand, Warren acknowledged that the high court held 34 state laws regulating the charges of railroads and other businesses void as "confiscatory" and violations of the due process clause during the same period.[38] That there was still a negative reaction to these decisions stemmed in part from the fact that the invalidation of a single law discouraged the enactment of similar measures by other states. It also arose out of the fact that the hopelessly subjective legal doctrines used in cases such as *Lochner* promised a future pregnant with judicial mischief. As George Alger wrote in the March 1913 *Atlantic*, "no other country in the world permits its courts to test to approve or condemn legislation by the application of any vague concept such as 'natural and inherent principles of justice', or by the interpretation of phrases incapable of approximately exact meaning which lawmakers can know in advance.

In theory at least, the continuance of a constitutional system for governing ninety millions of people on such a basis involves peril, if not disaster."[39]

The ability of railroads and other entities to contest the legality of state laws in federal court was limited, at least in theory, by the Eleventh Amendment. At the time of ratification, the Constitution included disputes between states and citizens of other states among the types of actions that could be brought in federal court. Some advocates of ratification dared to assure such suits would never be brought; when they were, Congress and the states enacted the Eleventh Amendment specifically barring them. In *Osborn v. Bank of the United States* (1824), Chief Justice Marshall evaded this bar when he ruled that citizens of other states could accomplish the same end by simply naming state officials and not states as defendants.[40] Litigants followed the path Marshall suggested. Suits by citizens against their own states—far more critical to the enforcement of civil rights legislation—remained beyond the jurisdiction of the federal judiciary as they did not appear among the types of suits federal judges were authorized to hear by Article III, Section 2. The Supreme Court reaffirmed the lack of jurisdiction of federal courts over suits against states by their own citizens in *Hans v. Louisiana* (1890), though it erred in citing the Eleventh Amendment as authority for this prohibition instead of simply pointing out that Article III did not include these actions in its list of suits involving states that might be brought in federal court.[41] In his opinion for the high court, Justice Bradley quoted assurances made by Federalists during ratification to the effect that states would not be dragged by citizens into court—whether their own or of other states—against their will.[42]

When a deluge of state rate laws enacted just after the turn of the century threatened their profits, the railroads sought to undermine what remained of the doctrine of state immunity. Two of the most remarkable clashes between federal and state authority since the Civil War resulted. When railroads obtained a federal injunction barring North Carolina from enforcing a 1907 law lowering rates, the governor announced that the order violated the Eleventh Amendment and that it would be ignored. State officials jailed railroad employees when they attempted to impose rates on the public higher than the rates established by state law—much to the embarrassment of the Justice Department and the administration of Theodore Roosevelt. When the Minnesota legislature enacted a law imposing rates on the railroads in 1907, the legislature purposely avoided assigning the task of enforcing the rates to a state official, thus depriving the lines of the ability to name that official as a defendant—as was necessary under *Osborn* to bring a suit in federal court contesting the legality of the rate law. The lines responded by devising a stockholder suit in equity against their own corporate officers. The prayer for relief requested that the U.S. Circuit Court in Minnesota bar corporate officers from complying with the law; it also asked the Court to issue an injunction barring the state Attorney General, Edward T. Young, from enforcing it. The suit was plainly an evasion of the Eleventh Amendment, but Circuit Court Judge William Lochren issued the injunction.[43] Young defied the order when he filed suit in state court seeking to have the rate ruling enforced; he was held in contempt of court by Judge Lochren. When Young appealed to the U.S. Supreme Court for a writ of habeas corpus on the grounds that the Circuit Court did not have authority to issue the injunction, it ruled against him. In his opinion for the majority, Justice Peckham held that the Circuit Court could hear the case, as it involved federal questions (alleged Fourteenth Amendment violations).[44] As for the claim that the Eleventh Amendment barred the suit, Peckham explained that officials engaging in unconstitutional acts were not acting under the authority of the state, and that "the state has no power to impart to (Young) immunity from responsibility to the supreme authority of the United States."[45]

In a blistering dissent, Justice Harlan pointed out that the purpose of the suit was to "tie the hands of the state."[46] The machinations of the railroads were also unnecessary—they could have contested the constitutionality of the rate law in state court and, in the event rulings adverse to them were issued, they could have appealed them to the U.S. Supreme Court.[47] Nor did he believe that the Fourteenth Amendment modified "in the slightest degree" the Eleventh Amendment.[48] In his view, the Circuit Court had no authority to prohibit the Minnesota attorney general from seeking an order in state court enforcing the rate law.[49] In a companion case, the majority affirmed a Circuit Court's order granting a writ of habeas corpus for a railroad employee who had been jailed by North Carolina officials for attempting to collect rates that exceeded those set by the state's rate law.[50] By World War I, the states routinely found themselves subjected to suits brought in federal court by their own citizens as well as those of other states when federal questions were involved (state officials were named as defendants). While this development constituted a usurpation of state authority, it was likely appropriate in the long run as the supremacy of the federal system depended on the ability of persons to quickly and efficiently vindicate their constitutional rights that had been infringed by states. To require them to litigate their claims in state court first would have left their rights subject to the caprices of state court systems that had never been known for their efficiency of fairness. State judges could deprive litigants of the right to seek relief in federal court by refusing to issue orders that could be appealed. Nor could the Justice Department serve as an effective substitute for private parties, as it lacked the resources necessary to litigate every state violation of rights bestowed by the Constitution.

Facilitating federal lawsuits against states in cases of constitutional violations qualified as an appropriate step; in theory no group should have benefited more from this development than blacks. The Fourteenth Amendment had been enacted for their benefit, but the members of the Supreme Court proved increasingly resistant to the idea of applying it in a manner consistent with that purpose. By the 1880s, the privileges and immunities clause had been whittled to almost nothing. In *Yick v. Wo* (1886), the Supreme Court revealed a latent streak of vigilance when it held void a San Francisco ordinance barring the operation of laundries in wooden buildings unless one obtained permission from the city.[51] In an era of disastrous urban fires, the measure seemed to constitute a reasonable fire regulation, but the Supreme Court (Stanley Matthews) held that the law, while neutral on its face, had been applied in a discriminatory manner against Chinese immigrants, thus violating the equal protection clause. Some 200 Chinese had been denied permission to operate wooden laundries, while 80 or so whites had been allowed to do so.[52] The Court also cited the power enjoyed by the San Francisco Board of Supervisors with respect to wooden laundries: It need not investigate said laundries or explain its rulings.[53] In truth, the law, even with its discriminatory application, did not violate the equal protection clause, at least in its original sense—the clause had been adopted to compel the states to protect blacks from violence and ensure that they could vindicate their rights in court. The privileges and immunities clause would have been a better fit for the right to operate a laundry than the equal protection clause, or at least it would have been if the Chinese immigrants had been citizens.

Ten years after *Yick Wo*, the Supreme Court issued one of its most famous nineteenth-century decision affecting matters of race: *Plessy v. Ferguson*.[54] An 1890 Louisiana law required railroads to carry black and white passengers in separate train cars. Homer Plessy was ejected from a train car designated for whites. Louisiana officials arrested him for violating the state's Separate Train Car Act; trial and conviction followed. Plessy appealed to the U.S. Supreme Court, claiming the Louisiana law violated the Thirteenth Amendment and the due process, equal protection, and privileges and immunities clauses of the Fourteenth Amendment. He did not base his claim on the fact that the cars designated for blacks were of an inferior quality to those occupied by whites.[55] Louisiana attorney general Milton Cunningham argued that the law was consistent with the privileges and immunities clause because "it does create any inequality between the citizen of the State and the citizen of the United States or between citizens of differing race and color. By its terms it provides equal privileges to all on all the railroads engaged in intra-state transit." If the right to travel in train cars containing both races constituted a privilege at all, it was not, in

Cunningham's view, among those national privileges protected by the Fourteenth Amendment.[56] The Supreme Court upheld the law. Writing for the majority, Justice Henry Brown conceded that the Fourteenth Amendment was intended to enforce "absolute equality" before the law among the races. Reality itself prohibited the country from complying with this requirement in its most literal sense; nor was it reasonable to assume that the framers of the Fourteenth Amendment sought to eradicate all racial distinctions. "It could not have been intended to abolish distinctions based upon color, or to enforce social, as distinguished from political equality, or a commingling of the two races upon terms unsatisfactory to either." Brown insisted that laws requiring separate facilities "do not necessarily imply the inferiority of either race to the other." He pointed out that separate schools had been provided to each race without protest "even by courts of states where the political rights of the colored race have been longest and most earnestly enforced."[57]

Brown distinguished the Louisiana law from the one held void in *Yick Wo* on the grounds that it was, in light of the "established usages, customs and tradition of the people," a reasonable regulation. "We cannot say that a law which requires the separation of the two races in public conveyances is unreasonable, or more obnoxious to the Fourteenth Amendment than the acts of Congress requiring separate schools for colored children in the District of Columbia, the constitutionality of which does not seem to have been questioned, or the corresponding acts of state legislatures."[58] As for the claim that the law constituted a stamp of inferiority on blacks, Brown offered a rather inane response—if such a thing happened it would be because "the colored race chose to put that construction upon it."[59] The truth was that persons of every race were likely to put that construction on it. John Harlan dissented. He thought the law conflicted with the Fourteenth Amendment without stating what provision of it had been violated.[60] Harlan suggested that the measure impaired the freedom of blacks and whites to travel together.[61] While many believed whites to be the superior race, "in view of the Constitution, in the eyes of the law, there is in this country no superior, dominant, ruling class of citizens. There is no caste here." Harlan predicted that the ruling would prove to be as "pernicious" as *Dred Scott*.[62]

Blacks were furious. When a Boston chapter of the National Colored League convened at the African Methodist Episcopalian church on Charles Street, a minister declared that he would arrange for his sons to learn Spanish so they could emigrate to Latin America. Another speaker noted that a majority of the justices were Republicans. He complained that the party of Lincoln had done nothing even as lynching grew into a plague during the past five years. Another warned that the South was once again "getting the upper hand in this country." Repeal of the Fourteenth and Fifteenth

Amendments would be next, he predicted.[63] The *Atlanta Constitution* was delighted with the ruling. It insisted that separate accommodations for the races would work no hardship for blacks; they were necessary as there were "many negroes who challenge the respect of the white people of the South." Northerners who criticized laws such as the one upheld by the high court were, it charged, simply ignorant of actual conditions in the southern states.[64]

Although *Plessy v. Ferguson* has been treated as an equal protection case, that proposition was a difficult one as the clause's original object had been to obligate states to protect blacks from violence and give them access to courts. A more likely candidate would be the privileges and immunities clause, at least in its original, pre-*Slaughterhouse* meaning. In 1823, Justice Bushrod Washington suggested that the original privileges and immunities clause in Section 2 of Article IV included a right to "pass through other states."[65] In *Crandall v. Nevada* (1868), a case decided by the Supreme Court on the eve of the ratification of the Fourteenth Amendment, Justice Nathan Clifford held that the citizen has a right to come to the seat of government and a right to "free access to its seaports" and its offices.[66] It was no great leap to suggest that the privileges and immunities clause of the Fourteenth Amendment barred states from enacting laws that burdened the ability of its citizens to travel by condemning them to inferior accommodations aboard common carriers. A right of access tantamount to a license or privilege also arose out of the common law duty of common carriers to serve the public. Under the Louisiana law, blacks enjoyed a right to travel that was inferior to that possessed by whites due to both the inferior quality of the accommodations afforded them and their separation from the rest of the citizenry. While the measure on its face did not discriminate so much as separate, in the context of American society, where the white race had labored for three centuries to impose a badge of inferiority on the black race, the justices would have been within their rights to consider the law's likely result and to hold it void as a violation of the privileges and immunities clause of the Fourteenth Amendment.

The difficulties in the case were all the more pronounced because the Fourteenth Amendment did not explicitly prohibit all discriminatory laws. At the time the amendment was drafted, Congress had considered and then dispensed with language that would have explicitly barred the states from varying in their treatment of their citizens according to their color.[67] Instead it sought only to ensure that blacks received the protection of the law, access to courts, economic and legal rights (via the privileges and immunities clause), and the full panoply of safeguards afforded those faced with the loss of liberty or property, such as jury trials. The Supreme Court weakened even these modest provisions when it (1) held that the equal protection clause did not authorize Congress to sanction private citizens for violence against blacks unless they acted under state authority and (2) held that only a handful of rights incidental to national citizenship were protected by the privileges and immunities clause. In light of the abject failure of the Supreme Court to apply the Fourteenth Amendment effectively for the protection of blacks, the question arises as to whether the amendment proved completely pointless. In 1935 Andrew McLaughlin went so far as to write that "one is tempted to say that, for the main purposes in the minds of its originators, the amendment has been a complete failure."[68] In truth it was worse than that. When the Supreme Court's use of the due process clause for the purpose of invalidating state economic and social legislation is considered, the conclusion that the amendment had proved thus far to be a disaster for American federalism—and the American people—seems hard to deny.

While the Fourteenth Amendment served as source of a veto power over state economic legislation, judicial interpretations of the commerce clause also centralized public authority at the national level. The high court used it to limit the ability of states to tax and regulate the railroads, even in the absence of federal legislation. Yet the justices also embraced what some viewed as a restrictive view of the powers of Congress under the commerce clause. Between the Supreme Court's vigilance in preventing the states from regulating interstate commercial activity and its unwillingness to allow Congress to reach all economic activity that affected interstate commerce, some perceived a "no man's land" between the two jurisdictions in which businesses were free to abuse the public.[69] This view became pervasive after the Supreme Court held that the commerce clause did not extend to manufacturing in *U.S. v. Knight* (1895).[70] At the same time the high court upheld morals legislation enacted under the commerce clause powers of Congress, leaving federal lawmakers in the odd position of being able to legislate on matters of morality but unable to enact laws viewed as more directly related to commercial activity.

In the *Lottery Case* of 1903, the Supreme Court upheld by a 5–4 vote an 1895 federal law banning the interstate transportation of lottery tickets.[71] In his opinion for the majority, Justice Harlan held that lottery tickets qualified as articles of commerce because of their economic value, at least before the drawing.[72] If states could ban lotteries within their own borders, "why may not Congress, invested with the power to regulate commerce among the several states, provide that such commerce shall not be polluted by the carrying of lottery tickets from one state to another?" In doing so, Congress was not usurping the power of the states but rather ensuring that their laws were effective.[73] As for the idea that the power to regulate did not include a power to prohibit, Harlan pointed to a May 29, 1884, law banning the transportation of diseased cattle across state lines.[74] In the view of the majority, the commerce power "is complete in itself" and subject to no limits other than those in the Constitution.[75]

Chief Justice Melvin Fuller wrote a dissent that was joined by three other justices. He believed that Congress could bar lottery tickets from the mails but denied it could criminalize the transportation of them across state lines. In his view, lottery tickets resembled policies of insurance in that they created a contractual relationship. Fuller cited *Paul v. Virginia*, in which the Supreme Court held that the creation of insurance contracts did not constitute interstate commerce, for the proposition that the mere transfer of a contract across state lines did not bring it within reach of the federal commerce power.[76] He complained that "an invitation to dine, or to take a drive, or a note of introduction, all become articles of commerce under the ruling in this case, by being deposited with an express company for transportation."[77] Fuller insisted that the transportation of lottery tickets differed from moving diseased animals across state lines because the latter are "in themselves injurious to the transaction of interstate commerce."[78] An article in the *Harvard Law Review* noted one ramification of Congress joining the states in enacting "police" legislation that was startling. If the commerce power could be used to ban lotteries, it could also be used to establish them, thereby preempting or invalidating state laws prohibiting them.[79] As originally understood, the power of Congress over interstate commerce authorized it to prohibit only those items that directly imperiled the transportation of goods, e.g., laws banning explosives from ships. There is no evidence that the Founders viewed the clause as bestowing a general police power over all goods and services transported or purchased across state lines.[80]

In 1908, the Supreme Court invalidated part of the Erdman Act of 1898.[81] That law barred interstate carriers from discharging an employee for being a member of a union. In his opinion for the Court, Justice Harlan held that there is "no such connection between interstate commerce and membership in a labor organization as to authorize Congress to make it a crime against the United States for an agent of interstate carrier to discharge an employee because of such membership on his part."[82] Justice Joseph McKenna dissented. He cited a Senate committee's finding that the establishment of a labor commission in Britain and the strengthening of labor in that country had helped to prevent strikes: "Where the (labor) associations are strong enough to command the respect of their employers, the relations between employer and employee seem most amicable."[83]

The assertion was, to say the least, debatable. More importantly, labor relations had always been within the province of the states. To the extent that unions gained legal protections during the nineteenth century, they were indebted to state legislatures and courts. On the other hand, if the national economy did not depend on peaceful labor relations in key industries, such as railroads and coal mines, it required that those industries continue to function at all times. The national and state governments had two choices before them in preventing interruptions in these industries: facilitating agreements between employers and employees or using force to ensure that those industries could function when employees staged strikes and used violence in an attempt to prevent the use of replacements. The unwillingness of the country to continue embracing the second alternative would eventually result in it accepting the first, almost unconsciously.

THE DISCOVERY OF NATIONAL AUTHORITY

Theodore Roosevelt ascended to the presidency at an auspicious time. An accomplished historian and reformer, the 42-year-old New Yorker had served on the U.S. Civil Service Commission under Harrison and Cleveland and was assistant secretary of the navy at the time the Spanish-American War began. While occupying that office Roosevelt confided in William Allen White regarding his disgust with the "plutocracy" that Mark Hanna was establishing in the country via an alliance of government and business.[84] With the arrival of war, Roosevelt resigned from office, organized a volunteer cavalry regiment, and saw combat in Cuba. In the fall of 1898 he was elected governor of New York. During his two-year term Roosevelt helped secure reenactment of a repealed civil service law, as well as an increase in the number of factory inspectors. He also signed legislation regulating sweatshops, strengthening the state railroad commission, establishing a tenement housing commission, and requiring the use of air brakes on rail cars.

Roosevelt's progressive nature was tested within months of his elevation to the presidency when 50,000 anthracite coal miners went on strike in eastern Pennsylvania seeking a pay hike of 10 to 20 percent. Eighteen thousand bituminous coal miners staged a sympathy strike a short time later. United Mine Workers President John Mitchell suggested arbitration but the mine owners, led by George Baer of the Philadelphia and Reading Railroad, would not go along. They held firm even when Mitchell offered to waive the miners' demand for union recognition if the owners would raise wages and reduce the workday from 10 to eight hours. Having succumbed to a wage hike at the behest of Mark Hanna during the presidential campaign of 1900, the mine owners were determined to persevere. As the coal mine industry was barely profitable, they feared that the pay hike demanded by the miners would mean ruin.[85]

With fall and cool weather approaching and fuel supplies across the country running low, Americans took notice of the drama unfolding in

Pennsylvania. Fears worsened as it became clear that no resolution to the impasse was apparent. The Pennsylvania militia prevented labor violence from shutting the Homestead Works in 1892, but, intimidated by the coal miners, it stood by impassively when violence erupted at the mines. Lawyers and politicians competed with each other in devising ways for the state or federal government to restore the production of coal. An Illinois judge suggested that the Pennsylvania legislature enact a law setting wages or condemn the mines and operate them itself.[86] While addressing the New York state Democratic convention, former governor David Hill suggested the federal government take possession of the mines via eminent domain; despite great effort he failed to demonstrate any relationship between such an endeavor and any of the enumerated powers of Congress. The convention endorsed the idea. *Harper's Weekly* was appalled. "Mr. Hill . . . has caused the Democratic Party of the great state of New York to commit itself officially to such an extension of the Federal government's right of eminent domain as no Federalist, Whig, or Republican has ever dared to claim for it." If such a program was enacted, the same treatment might await any industry that angered the public. "A case no less strong, or a stronger case, for the interposition of the federal government can be made for bituminous than for anthracite coal; for the use of electricity considered as a generator of power or light; for iron-mines; for salt-mines; for the applications of steam to land and water communications; for building materials, and for all articles of food."[87]

The general counsel for the Delaware, Lackawanna and Western Railway—one of the owners of the mines—wanted Attorney General Philander Knox to obtain an injunction under the Sherman Antitrust Act against the United Mine Workers. Others suggested that the coal strike, being a restraint of production and not trade, remained beyond the scope of the law.[88] The railroads who owned the mines did not appreciate the distinction; they lobbied Attorney General Philander C. Knox to seek an injunction, as Richard Olney had eight years earlier at the time of the Pullman Strike. George Baer made the same request of the president.[89] Once the injunction was violated, the mine owners hoped the president would send in troops to enable them to operate with replacement workers. Roosevelt ignored the request.

As the strike lingered, miscreants dynamited bridges and destroyed train cars. Violence in the coal region of eastern Pennsylvania resulted in the deaths of 21 persons and provided ample motivation for those contemplating work at the mines to refrain from doing so.[90] In early October, the prospect of a coal shortage led a New York City utility raised its rates 15 percent.[91] The hike was rather modest in light of the fact that the price of coal had gone from $5 to $20 a ton.[92] With the country on the cusp of cold weather, the president called representatives of each side to the house on Jackson Place in Washington where he was staying while the White House was under repair. After confessing his lack of authority to impose a solution on them, Roosevelt insisted there were three parties to the dispute: the owners, the miners, and the public. John Mitchell repeated his readiness to accept arbitration while George Baer claimed 15,000 to 20,000 miners were ready to provide the coal the country needed if they received the protection of federal troops. As William A. Stone, governor of Pennsylvania, claimed the state militia could handle the strikers (as yet it had not), the president ignored the suggestion. The conference failed to resolve the impasse.[93]

The Pennsylvania National Guard—about 10,000 men—was finally deployed in its entirety in early October.[94] The mines remained closed, much to the chagrin of *Harper's Weekly*, which blamed the governor of Pennsylvania for failing to deploy the forces necessary to allow miners who were willing to work to do so.[95] Desperate to avoid the widespread suffering that would arrive with cold weather, the president let it be known that he might arrange for the governor to ask him for assistance; at that point he would send in the army. While Roosevelt later claimed he would have arranged for soldiers to operate the mines and sell coal at the "regular price," it was not clear at the time whether he intended to pursue this course or simply use troops to enable mineworkers willing to work to do so.[96] Restoring peace to enable commerce to continue had some precedent; a search for a statute or provision of the Constitution that authorized the operation of industrial facilities by federal troops in peacetime would have been futile.

It has been said that the mine owners were chastened when they were told of the president's plan to have the army operate the mines, but it is not clear that they knew of it. Secretary of War Elihu Root met with J. P. Morgan in an effort to convince the financier to bring the mine owners to the table; he did not mention the president's threat to use the army. Morgan acquiesced and shortly thereafter the owners accepted the appointment of a commission that would consider the miners' grievances. The miners agreed to allow the commission to investigate the matter and went back to work at the end of October. Five months later the commission gave them a pay hike averaging 10 percent, cut workday hours to nine, barred discrimination against miners belonging to the UMW, denied the demand for union recognition, and recommended a 10 percent increase in the price of coal. The commission rejected the idea of compulsory arbitration as beyond the authority of the national government.[97]

The strike was viewed as a victory for unions and it was said to have aided the growth of the labor movement. It saw the federal government move from its former insistence that critical industries be allowed to function regardless of labor discord to the role of a mediator that sympathized with labor.[98] Many in the union movement did not view the strike and its resolution as a victory despite the fact that the United Mine Workers had won their second pay hike in three years, this time by enlisting the national government in its effort to coerce the mine owners. It was not long before the president clashed with public employee unions. As early as 1896, Postmaster General William L. Wilson complained that the three unions representing postal employees had "learned their strength." He predicted that thereafter, post office employees would not "tolerate any discipline that interferes with their comfort, or omit any occasion to secure the increase of salary or privileges."[99] Roosevelt antagonized civil servants when he reinstated an employee of the Government Printing Office who had been dismissed over his failure to join the Central Labor Union. Viewing the order as effectively requiring that the Printing Office remain an open shop—men and women need not join a union to work there—other employees were furious; some talked of going on strike.[100] Despite the president's efforts, the Government Printing Office as well as the navy yards remained de facto closed shops.[101] Roosevelt also issued an order providing that while employees of the Government Printing Office could join unions, the rules of these organizations cannot "be permitted to override the laws of the U.S."[102] Labor organizations were most annoyed by the "gag rule" of January 31, 1902. It barred executive branch employees from lobbying members of Congress for pay raises or the passage of legislation favorable to them.[103] As if the relationship between the president and labor was not already soured, Roosevelt deployed federal troops in the Arizona territory in 1903 in response to violence during a miners' strike; he also sent them to Nevada when labor violence led the governor to ask for them.[104]

Three months after McKinley's death, the 57th Congress met for its first session. Republicans enjoyed comfortable margins in each house, though the Democratic presence in northern cities was growing. Chicago elected three Democrats, the New York City area 13, and even Boston sent a Democrat to Congress. Ohio and Pennsylvania were overwhelmingly Republican, as was upstate New York, New England, Minnesota, Iowa, Kansas, and the west coast. The southern sections of Indiana and Illinois remained Democratic, as did the South. As it would for the next decade, the party of Lincoln governed by retreating; it enacted just enough constructive legislation to appease the forces of progress. The demand for a more aggressive regulation of business, and especially trusts and railroads, forced Republicans to wield federal power more aggressively than they would have liked. It soon become obvious that the most significant impediment to reform legislation was not Bourbon Democrats from the South but instead a faction of highly talented and highly disputatious Republican lawyer-legislators in the Senate. Men such as John Coit Spooner of Wisconsin and Joseph Foraker of Ohio seemed to operate under the impression that the federal government could not so much as glance at the railroads or any other business until a hearing before a federal judge had been held, and the lesser lights of the chamber were usually incapable of refuting their elaborate, if often specious, arguments. Spooner had served as counsel for the Chicago, Minneapolis & Omaha and had made a fortune defending railroads from what he regarded as the depredations of legislatures. Foraker embodied the somewhat disjointed nature of the Republican party—a fierce defender of the rights of blacks, the former governor of Ohio and Union army veteran saw nothing wrong in accepting money from large corporations while using his position in the Senate to defeat legislation designed to bring them to heel.

The matter of trusts was now the primary issue before the country, mainly because they had exploded in number, from 20 in 1898 to 185 in 1901.[105] The first steps taken by the Roosevelt administration were modest. A Department of Commerce and Labor was established via an act of February 14, 1903; it housed a Bureau of Corporations armed with the power to subpoena corporate records.[106] The Bureau was sold as an entity that would aid the Justice Department's antitrust investigations; in that regard it proved to be something of a disappointment. When the federal district attorney in Chicago asked for assistance in an investigation of meatpackers including Armour & Company, the Commissioner of Corporations did nothing more than provide a list of persons who might have information. On being asked for additional help, the Bureau tried to take back what it had already given by warning Justice Department attorneys that the information it provided was confidential. When indictments were obtained, the Bureau issued a report exonerating the meatpackers. A trial commenced in 1906; the defendants sought an acquittal on the grounds that they had complied with the Bureau of Corporation's investigation.[107] Federal Circuit Court Judge J. Otis Humphrey proceeded with the trial in equity but held that the packers were entitled to immunity against criminal prosecution on the grounds that the evidence against them had been obtained by the Bureau of Corporations.[108]

In his first annual message, the president called for more effective regulation of trusts; he also suggested that perhaps the solution was to leave them in place.[109] This approach would have constituted a step backward to the period before the Sherman Act. The Expedition Act of 1903 aided the Justice Department's antitrust prosecutions by giving them first priority on the dockets of federal courts. The effort was still hobbled by a lack of resources; thus far fewer than a dozen attorneys were devoted to the effort by the national government. They had to go up against entities that could deploy small armies of lawyers. Proceedings against the Northern Securities Company, which owned the two dominant railroads in the Northwest, began in early 1902. After a trial court ordered the dissolution of the company, the ruling was appealed to the U.S. Supreme Court, which affirmed the order in March 1904. The merger of the Great Northern and Northern Pacific railroads into a single holding company qualified as a restraint of trade and the merger would have to be reversed.[110] Justice Edward Douglass White dissented (along with Chief Justice Fuller, Rufus Peckham and Oliver Wendell Holmes); he denied that the commerce power included the right to regulate the ownership of stock in a state corporation.[111] Justice Holmes interpreted the majority opinion as subjecting any entrepreneur who dared to initiate a new industry to prosecution for violating the Sherman Act, as the entrepreneur would necessarily enjoy a monopoly in the new field, at least for a time. He claimed that under the ruling, the existence of a railroad in an isolated area constituted a restraint of trade because it discouraged others from building lines in the vicinity.[112] Holmes pointed out that the Sherman Act said nothing regarding competition, and suggested that under the logic of the opinion of the majority, even partnerships were illegal.[113]

Some in Congress talked of requiring trusts or corporations that engaged in interstate commerce to obtain a federal license before doing so, while others went further and advocated a federal incorporation law. Between 1900 and 1914, lawmakers proposed 67 bills providing for federal licensing or incorporation.[114] Confusion over the extent of federal authority haunted the effort. In May 1900, the House Judiciary Committee endorsed an amendment to the Constitution that would have authorized Congress to incorporate and dissolve entities seeking to engage in interstate commerce.[115] In 1902, the U.S. Industrial Commission issued a report that called for requiring all corporations engaged in interstate commerce to register with a bureau to be established in the Treasury Department and provide it with information that would be used to levy a franchise tax on their earnings. The bureau would have authority to review the financial records of corporations and share the information contained therein with the public. If these measures proved inadequate, federal incorporation of the "great corporations and combinations" should be considered, along with hiking the franchise tax on state corporations to the point that these entities would be compelled to reorganize under federal law. It would then be possible "to apply to corporations any degree of publicity or restriction that might be authorized." In the interim, states should enact laws barring restraints in production, over-capitalization and price discrimination.[116]

Bills proposed by Congressman Charles Littlefield in 1901 and 1903 would have required corporations to file information including their capitalization and bylaws with the Treasury Department. Lawmakers criticized the 1903 bill—a watered-down version of its predecessor—as it did not apply to corporations already in existence and removed the criminal sanctions established by the Sherman Act.[117] It passed the House easily (99 members did not vote) perhaps because the members knew full well it would die in the Senate.[118] In late 1904, Commissioner of Corporations James R. Garfield issued a report proposing federal incorporation of trusts and federal licensing of other corporations that did business across state lines. Disclosure of financial information such as the amount of outstanding stock would also be required. Garfield cited "piratical" state incorporation laws that encouraged evils such as watered stock and suggested that federal intervention would protect the public against fraud. In his view, the desire to attract business led states to enact inadequate corporation laws. Garfield conceded that whether Congress could authorize a corporation to do business in a state against its will remained a question.[119] The *Wall Street Journal* claimed that corporations supported the idea as they preferred to be regulated by a single entity instead of 45. It cited the example of insurance companies, which have, "by bitter experience, come round to this view and are now working for federal control."[120] The inability of federal prosecutors to use evidence obtained by the Bureau of Corporations at the 1906 antitrust trial of Chicago meatpackers increased calls for federal licensing of trusts—they could be broken up before being allowed to participate in interstate commerce—as the threat of criminal sanctions seemed ineffective.[121] By 1908, even financiers such as Henry Clews embraced the idea of placing corporations under the exclusive supervision of the federal government.[122]

As 1904 opened, Republicans were uncertain about the president—should he be nominated for a full term? Annoyed by the Northern Securities prosecution ever since its announcement rattled Wall Street in 1902, many in the party would have preferred Mark Hanna, who had obtained election to the U.S. Senate. The president won applause for his handling of the coal strike; Americans also appreciated his success in obtaining the right to dig a canal through the newly formed nation of Panama. Still, Hanna's death in February 1904 may have prevented an unpleasant fight, though the president had already done much to undermine Hanna's prospects when he replaced two-thirds of federal officeholders in the South, thereby securing the loyalty of the southern delegations at the Republican national convention. Hosting Booker T. Washington at the White House was more than mere show—the country's leading black public figure advised the president regarding appropriate candidates for federal offices in the southern states. The president was thereby able to undermine Mark Hanna's support among black Republicans in the South.[123]

To maintain the support of Republican senators annoyed with the prosecution of trusts, the president ceded control over federal patronage to them. They used it to enhance the power of their own political machines and thwart the cause of reform. This state of affairs did not stop Roosevelt from denouncing machine politics.[124] In a January 1906 article in *North American Review*, Wayne MacVeagh charged that the "national government has drifted into a condition of practical alliance with these 'bosses' because they have had practical control of almost all of the nominations for Congress." Almost every person in Pennsylvania who received a federal appointment "was the avowed persistent and reckless opponent of that decency and honesty in politics for which President Roosevelt has courageously battled all his life." The same thing was occurring in other states.[125] On the eve of the 1904 campaign, the White House let it be known that George B. Cortelyou, chairman of the Republican Party, would be nominated for postmaster general after the election, thus ensuring that Republican Party workers would obey Cortelyou—at least if they wanted a job when the campaign ended.[126]

With Hanna's death, the president appeared to be on his way to another term before the campaign even started. Unwilling to let events take their natural course, the administration engineered a pension giveaway designed to secure the veterans' vote. Congress had toyed with the idea of finally enacting a service pension that would have given a monthly stipend to all men who served in the Union army. When the end of the session arrived in March 1904 and lawmakers failed to pass a service pension bill, the Commissioner of Pensions issued an order interpreting the Dependent Pension Act of 1890 and its provisions regarding disabilities. A person's age would now constitute evidence of disability—any veteran 62 years of age or older now qualified for disability benefits of at least six dollars a month. The order was a departure from the text of the statute though only an extension of prior practice; previously veterans had to reach 65.5 years before citing their age alone as evidence of disability.[127]

The Nation was appalled. In its view the failure of the service pension bill indicated that "both Congress and the country [have] shown plainly enough that they did not care to have further pension laws placed upon the statute-books, [yet] the same end has been attained by an unexampled perversion of the existing pension rules." It charged that the "shocking feature of the new rule is the way the executive has thereby usurped the functions of Congress." In its view, the president gave the 1890 Pension Act "a construction which Congress never intended to allow." The willingness of the president to go beyond even his party's leadership in Congress in the business of buying votes was equally surprising. *The Nation* did not expect that "Mr. Roosevelt would uphold the hands of the pension grabbers, or that he would do so by reading into laws passed years ago the present intentions of his party leaders in their anxiety for votes." The president's "willingness to abuse his undoubted right to interpret the statutes of Congress is another sign of what has been termed his 'lawlessness' of mind." *The Nation* predicted that the measure would fail to satiate the appetite of the GAR and that veterans would demand pension increases in the near future. "Why stop now? Have not the veterans the right to feel that they own the government and can bend it to their will?"[128]

Republicans assembled at the Chicago Coliseum in late June and nominated Roosevelt for a full term. They completed their work under the gaze of Mark Hanna, or at least a huge portrait of the late senator that had been affixed to the rafters. Democrats selected a conservative for the first time in 12 years—Judge Alton B. Parker of the New York Court of Appeals. Parker had been among the few New York Democrats who had supported William Jennings Bryan in the contests of 1896 and 1900, thus the acquiescence of the Great Commoner in his nomination.[129] The campaign proceeded in something of a stupor; with the economy faring well and agricultural prices increasing, the country was content. More than a few former Bryan supporters favored the president while conservatives troubled by Roosevelt's propensity for castigating wealth and his alleged "lawlessness" supported Parker. *The Nation* summed up the attitude of this latter group when it complained that Roosevelt had "flung himself upon the raw passions of the country, instead of appealing to its reasoned convictions." He has "created a sort of Tory Democracy, fed on promises of a social heaven on earth." It concluded that he had "proved recreant to his antecedents and training, and has so made himself the protagonist of all who are for hazardous experiment, lawless method, swollen outlay, and a dulled sense of honor in public affairs." His defeat would, it concluded, "be good for the country."[130] What had provided cause for annoyance? In addition to the antitrust prosecutions, there was the matter of Panama. After Columbia failed to ratify a treaty granting the United States the right to dig a canal with the requisite speed, Roosevelt encouraged Panamanians to rebel against Bogota and sent the U.S. Navy to prevent Columbian troops from putting down the revolt. There was also Roosevelt's speech regarding the "criminal rich" offered in Spokane, Washington, in 1902. Many regarded it as a dangerous, ill-advised attempt to placate radicals.

After presiding over a languid campaign, Judge Parker shocked the country on the eve of the election when he charged that Republican Party chairman George Cortelyou was extorting huge contributions from the trusts. Bribed or beaten, they contributed so steep tariffs would continue: "undue protection so that riches may be unfairly acquired; contribution of riches so acquired that undue protection may be continued and extended."[131] The president angrily denied the charge of blackmail and demanded that Parker provide evidence to support his charge. According to one account, the candidate obtained the information from Cleveland's secretary of war Daniel Lamont. When Parker asked Lamont to substantiate the charge, Lamont refused, sinking whatever dim hopes the Democratic nominee had for victory.[132] A New York state investigation later confirmed that insurance companies had made ample contributions to the Republican National Committee and that an aide of Cortelyou approached Standard Oil executives seeking money—with the assurance that the president's attitude on antitrust matters had evolved.[133] Roosevelt coasted to victory, winning 56 percent of the popular vote and the electoral vote of every state outside of the South and border areas. Republicans won almost two-thirds of the seats in each house of Congress.

As members of the 59th Congress arrived in Washington in December 1905, the president called for laws strengthening the administration's ability to investigate corporations engaged in interstate commerce without saying why such legislation was necessary or how current statutes were deficient. He thought the Interstate Commerce Commission ought to be empowered to issue rates following investigation of those proposed by railroads, though he was quick to add that judicial review of ICC rulings should be preserved. Railroads should be required to install signals at all street crossings. Mindful of the fact that no one seemed quite sure of the outer limits of national jurisdiction anymore, the president called for an employers' liability act "applicable to all industries within the scope of the federal power." Roosevelt saw no difficulty in asking Congress to address the excessive hours of railroad employees, but he conceded that that the national government has "as a rule, but little occasion to deal with the formidable group of problems connected more or less directly with what is known as the labor question, for in the great majority of cases these problems must be dealt with by the state and municipal authorities, and not by the national government." Congress did have plenary authority over the District of Columbia, and Roosevelt thought it "should see to it that the City of Washington is made a model city in all respects, both as regards parks, public playgrounds and proper housing regulation." Roosevelt called for the Department of Commerce to investigate child labor conditions, though again he conceded "that these problems can be actually met in most cases only by the states themselves."

On the matter of insurance—many wanted it subjected to federal regulation—the president confessed his uncertainty on the question of authority. He suggested that Congress "consider whether the federal government has any power or owes any duty with respect to domestic transactions in insurance of an interstate character. That state supervision has proved inadequate is generally conceded." Roosevelt also called on Congress to pass a law barring corporations from making political contributions and requiring the publication of the names of persons making contributions as well as the amounts given. The president applauded the Newlands Reclamation Act; he claimed it had created "communities of freeholders." In fact it had created a small population of struggling farmers dependent on the continuing generosity of Washington. Roosevelt complained of a problem in the federal bureaucracy that would eventually become legend—the vaunted civil service rules were making the termination of incompetents all but impossible. The requirement that a hearing be held before civil servants could be dismissed often prevented their termination "because of the reluctance of heads of departments and bureau chiefs to go through the required procedure." The president also called for federal regulation of food safety.[134]

Roosevelt's agenda was an ambitious one, but at no point during his administration was he the master of Congress. The president proposed and the Senate disposed. In this regard he was the inferior of his predecessor, though McKinley had no interest in pushing Congress in a progressive direction. Thus the lament of the *Nation*: "One [can] only think of McKinley's unfailing skill in that regard! He had an instinctive feeling for the congressional way of looking at all questions, and seldom failed to adjust himself to it with the nicest tact. Whenever he stroked Congress, the resulting purr was audible; but Mr. Roosevelt seems usually to elicit such angry spittings and clawing as we now see."[135] The president's propensity for outbursts resulted in his being ignored by the Senate bulls and House Speaker Joe Cannon, who was old enough to have witnessed the Lincoln-Douglas debates the year Roosevelt was born.

Many lawmakers believed more stringent railroad regulations were necessary. During Roosevelt's first term, they enjoyed only limited success. The Safety Appliance Act of 1903 strengthened an 1893 statute's provisions requiring the use of air brakes on railroad cars.[136] The Elkins Act of 1903 outlawed the giving or accepting of rebates in freight transportation and subjected rail lines to sanctions if they did not adhere to publish rates.[137] The law owed its passage at least in part to the desire of the railroads themselves to abolish rebates. It was thought that the measure would put an end to discrimination in favor of large shippers, though it remained to be seen why those who shipped more should not pay lower rates. In late 1905 Congress took up a railroad rate bill strengthening the Elkins Act's prohibition of rebates. It also would have limited court review of ICC rulings to procedural issues and barred courts from suspending ICC orders during the review process. Conservatives opposed depriving the courts of the power to review all aspects of ICC rulings, especially those concerning rates. Many progressives found the bill inadequate as they wanted the ICC authorized to issue rates without waiting for a complaint to be filed. In an opinion prepared at the request of Stephen Elkins, chairman of the House

Committee on Commerce, Attorney General William H. Moody concluded that a law depriving the courts of the power to review rate rulings would violate the due process clause of the Fifth Amendment. He held that a law authorizing the Interstate Commerce Commission to establish rates in advance would not violate the Constitution so long as Congress provided it with a standard to be used in fixing rates.[138] Ohio Senator Joseph Foraker disagreed: "Congress has no power to delegate to a commission, except in an administrative way, authority to make rates, because that is a delegation of a legislative power pure and simple, and you cannot find a rule in any of the books or in any of the decisions that will uphold it."[139] Former attorney general Philander C. Knox, now a Pennsylvania senator, sided with Moody: "Is it not the true rule that while you cannot delegate the entire legislative power, Congress may prescribe a rule and leave the application of the rule in specific cases to an administrative body, so if the act of Congress provided that rates should be fair and just and reasonably remunerative, or used any other definition that it might see fit to impose, it could delegate to the Commission the power to apply that rule to specific cases as they arise?"[140] Foraker insisted that charging a commission with a duty to devise something so vague as a "reasonable" rate would leave it with "a discretion that is legislative in its character."[141]

John Coit Spooner suggested that the clause limiting the scope of court review of ICC orders constituted a diminution of the judicial power, something Congress could not do. He pointed out that Article III extended the judicial power to all cases in law and equity arising under the Constitution or federal laws; therefore Congress could not strip the federal courts of any of the tools of equity jurisdiction.[142] Spooner conceded that Congress could withdraw jurisdiction from the federal courts over the entire class of cases arising out of ICC orders, but it could not subdivide that jurisdiction between federal courts and commissions.[143]

Conservatives including Spooner held out for an amendment explicitly preserving judicial review of ICC orders and, after delaying for a time, the president went along. The Hepburn Act of June 29, 1906, authorized the ICC to impose rates when it held hearings on complaints brought before it—the Commission was no longer limited to merely barring the lines from imposing proposed rate increases. It still had to wait for a complaint to be filed by private parties—it could not revise rates on its own initiative. The law also barred the issuing of free tickets to persons other than railroad employees. Free annual passes given to members of legislatures and other government officials were enormously valuable—and enormously corrupting—as railroads constituted the only form of long-distance transportation available in many areas. The law tightened the ban on the use of rebates, thereby earning the support of railroads seeking to eliminate the last vestiges of competition. It also extended the ICC's jurisdiction to rates charged by ferries, bridges, terminals, and express companies.[144] The Hepburn Act barred railroads from carrying their own products, thus forcing them out of businesses such as mining. A provision of the statute known as the Carmack Amendment provided that when goods were damaged while being transported by multiple carriers, the first carrier would be liable to the owner of the goods.[145] This provision was upheld by the Supreme Court in 1911.[146] Justice Horace Lurton explained that in protecting the shipper, the law facilitated commerce.[147]

With its provision authorizing the ICC to impose rates, the Hepburn Act converted federal control of railroad rates from theory into fact. The country's first experiment in price controls would bear fruit in unexpected ways in the years after the law's enactment. Investors began to avoid railroad stocks as the ability of the lines to raise rates was effectively checked, and the decline in their market value impaired the ability of the lines to obtain loans. In time this would have a devastating effect, as railroads required huge amounts of money to properly maintain equipment and rolling stock. The ICC turned down requests for rate increases or allowed only token hikes in 1913, 1914, and 1915. A deluge of state regulations of railroads enacted during those years—many by Democrats who had not controlled legislatures in several northern states for decades—further burdened the lines.[148] In 1913, Congress established parcel post—depriving the railroads of their own express business which had been hugely profitable—while forcing the lines to carry the same packages as part of the U.S. Mail, the rates for which were set by Congress. The move constituted a subsidy for department stores in the view of one critic, as they were the major beneficiaries of artificially low rates for the transportation of parcels.[149]

Also in 1906 Congress abolished the common law fellow servant rule. Instead, the railroads themselves would be liable for all damages resulting when their employees suffered injuries or death due to the negligence of their coworkers. Contributory negligence would no longer serve as bar to recovery though damages could still be reduced to account for it.[150] The Supreme Court held the law void in 1908.[151] In his opinion for the Court, Justice Edward White dismissed the idea that "one who engages in interstate commerce thereby submits all his business concerns to the regulating power of Congress."[152] Thus the defect of the Employers' Liability Act: It addressed all the activities of carriers engaged in interstate commerce "and is not confined solely to regulating the interstate commerce business" in which these entities engaged. It therefore "includes subjects wholly outside of the power of Congress to regulate commerce."[153] A second Employers' Liability Act became law in 1908; it applied solely to railroad employees working on interstate lines.[154] It was upheld in 1912.[155] In his opinion for the Court, Justice

Willis Devanter explained that the law would "impel the carriers to avoid or prevent the negligent acts and omissions which are made the bases of the rights of recovery which the statute creates and defines; and, as whatever makes for that end tends to promote the safety of the employees and to advance the commerce in which they are engaged, we entertain no doubt that in making those changes Congress acted within the limits of the discretion confided to it by the Constitution."[156] A similar exercise of the commerce power occurred with a 1907 law limiting the hours of railroad employees: no more than 16 consecutive hours on duty; when the maximum is worked, it must be followed by 10 hours off-duty.[157] In 1911, the Supreme Court held that the law fell within the powers of Congress; Justice Charles Evans Hughes explained that the hours worked by railroad employees have "a direct relationship to the efficiency of the human agencies upon which protection to life and property necessarily depends."[158]

The year 1906 also saw Congress also enact laws requiring the inspection of meat products and drugs that were transferred across state lines. A law of 1891 provided for the inspection of pork and beef destined for export after several European countries banned American pork products as unsafe.[159] Thereafter inspectors examined cattle and swine but problems remained. The embalmed meat scandal that occurred during the Spanish-American War made it clear that task of improving sanitary conditions in the meatpacking industry had not been completed. Investigations early in the century revealed that the remains of diseased cattle and even rats had been added to canned meat products. When a bill providing for the inspection of meatpacking plants received consideration in the House in the spring of 1906, Edgar Crumpacker of Indiana cited what he viewed as the original understanding of the commerce clause in arguing against the constitutionality of the measure. The commerce power was granted to Congress only "for the purpose of guaranteeing the absolute freedom of traffic among the people of all the states. It was feared at the time of the adoption of the Constitution that the states, prompted by selfishness, might establish barriers against the commerce of other states and enact such hostile regulations as would separate them into as many independent commercial provinces as there were states in the Union." In Crumpacker's view, "police laws and regulations were reserved to the states and the people, and by police laws and regulations I mean laws for the protection of the public health, the public morals, and the public peace." Turning to food products, Crumpacker conceded that while Congress possessed no express authority to provide for their inspection, "it does have the incidental power to protect interstate and foreign commerce against abuse by those who would impose upon the public in the sale and transportation of impure and unwholesome foods and other things that are universally regarded as immoral or unfit for commerce."[160]

In his view, "commodities must enter the channels of commerce before the federal government has any authority over them."[161] Crumpacker pointed out that for several years 180 federal inspectors had been inspecting the Chicago meatpacking houses, yet the horrors described in Upton Sinclair's *The Jungle* had occurred anyway. He thought the federal government could do no more than bar the entrance of impure meats into interstate commerce and provide for a system of inspections when the meat is tendered for transportation, though he conceded such a system would likely be impractical.[162]

Crumpacker's colleagues did not embrace his narrow view of the commerce clause. In funding inspections of meatpacking plants, they received ample motivation from Upton Sinclair's graphic depiction of the lack of regard for the public displayed by the Chicago packing houses. *The Jungle* was said to have caused Senator Nelson Aldrich of Rhode Island to drop his opposition to the measure.[163] An appropriation of June 30, 1906, provided for federal inspection of all animals before they entered slaughterhouses or meatpacking plants as well as the destruction of animals found to be diseased. It required that the meat of slaughtered animals be inspected and tagged or marked with words indicating that it had passed inspection. Interstate common carriers were barred from carrying meat products that had not been inspected and marked. Inspectors were to have access to slaughterhouses at any time to ensure they complied with sanitary requirements to be established by the secretary of agriculture.[164]

Along with deficient meat products, the country was also plagued by mislabeled food and drugs. By 1890, 25 states had enacted pure food laws. Unfortunately these statutes failed to establish effective mechanisms for their enforcement. In 1899 the National Pure Food Congress recommended uniform legislation to the states for enactment; a year later it endorsed a bill proposed by Representative Marriott Brosius of Pennsylvania that would provide for federal regulation of food products entering interstate commerce.[165] The food and drug industries relented in the face of universal support for the measure; they also hoped to see more exacting state laws preempted and believed the measure would enhance sales by reassuring the public regarding the safety of their products.[166] The Pure Food and Drug Act of June 30, 1906, prohibited the introduction into any state or territory from any other state or territory misbranded or adulterated articles of food or drugs. Regulations were to be issued for the inspection of food and drugs transferred across state lines.[167] The law was upheld by the Supreme Court in 1911. Justice Joseph McKenna explained that articles qualifying as "enemies of commerce" may be seized wherever they are found.[168]

The deluge of federal laws regulating economic activity led to litigation over alleged conflicts between these measures and state regulations. Several state laws regulating railroads were held void on the grounds they conflicted with the Hepburn Act. One invalidated law required railroads to provide cars to shippers within 72 hours of receiving a request for them—the Supreme Court viewed it as going beyond the Hepburn Act's provision that cars be provided in a "reasonable time"[169] Until the 1930s, the Supreme Court took the attitude that the entry of Congress into a particular field of commercial regulation barred the states from entering it, even when state laws on the subject did not directly conflict with federal statutes.[170] Later in the twentieth century, when federal power was advancing on so many fronts, the federal judiciary would display uncharacteristic modesty and begin to inquire in its interpretation of federal laws as to whether Congress intended to bar state laws on the same subject when it enacted regulations of particular areas of the nation's economic life.[171]

The second session of the 51st Congress saw Congress contemplate its most remarkable incursion yet into the realm of labor relations. Child labor plagued all parts of the country, especially the South. Three of 10 workers in southern textiles mills in 1900 were under 16. For a time Alabama was the only state in the region with a law limiting the practice; it repealed it in 1895 at the insistence of a Massachusetts textile firm that was building a factory in the state. By 1912, every southern state had passed laws limiting child labor, but these still allowed children over 12 to labor up to 16 hours a day.[172] Indiana Senator Albert Beveridge was one of the new breed of progressive Republicans who followed the president and not the party's more conservative elders in Congress. At the short congressional session of 1906–7, he proposed to amend a bill barring child labor in the capital with a provision that would have barred interstate carriers from transporting across state lines items produced by child labor. The Indianapolis lawyer pointed out that almost two million children under the age of 16 worked during 1900.[173] He conceded that some states had taken steps to limit the evil. Still Beveridge insisted federal action was necessary. He pointed to what would later be called the "race to the bottom": states competing to maintain the most lax regulatory environment in the hope of attracting businesses and employers. "If one state passes good laws and enforces them and another state does not, then the businessmen in the former state are at a business disadvantage with the business men in the latter state." He assured that his bill would not bar cotton from interstate commerce merely because it was harvested by children.[174]

Senator Isidore Rayner of Maryland asked if Congress possessed authority to bar goods from interstate commerce that were not made by members of labor unions. Beveridge answered in the affirmative—it could bar anything from interstate commerce.[175] When the Indiana senator pointed out that Congress had already banned items such as lottery tickets from interstate commerce, Charles Fulton of Oregon responded that the articles banned would have had a deleterious effect on persons who might otherwise have purchased them. "Is there not a vast distinction between that and simply refusing to allow to be transported in interstate commerce an article, against which no charge of that character can be made, merely because some particular character of labor has been employed in making it?"[176] Beveridge responded that lottery tickets were not intrinsically harmful.[177] Augustus Bacon of Georgia asked whether Beveridge agreed that obscene material qualified as harmless because there is nothing destructive in the paper upon which it is printed. Beveridge answered in the negative.[178] John Coit Spooner distinguished lottery tickets from the products of child labor by insisting that the former produced an evil at the location to which they are sent or delivered, while the latter involved an evil at the factory where the items produced by child labor were made.[179] Congressman Herbert Parsons of New York sided with Beveridge. He pointed to a recent court decision—*Swift v. U.S.*—and claimed that for the purposes of federal jurisdiction, it was enough for an article to enter the "current of commerce" that extended from the manufacturer to the home of the consumer.[180] No child labor legislation was forthcoming in the 51st Congress. Pressure would build in coming years, in no small part because of the determination of northern lawmakers to prevent what they considered unfair competition from southern states with lax labor standards.

There were other activities thus far regulated by states that some saw as candidates for federal regulation during the Roosevelt presidency. Some thought Congress should regulate the insurance industry. An 1869 Supreme Court ruling, *Paul v. Virginia*, had long been viewed as standing for the principle that the creation and sale of insurance policies did not qualify as interstate commerce.[181] Former assistant attorney general James Beck called for federal regulation of life insurance in 1905. He complained of the "capricious and arbitrary" terms imposed on insurance companies by the states in exchange for the right to do business within their borders. Once admitted, their right to do business "exists only by sufferance, and is liable to immediate destruction by the mere whim of a state official."[182] In his 1906 annual message, Theodore Roosevelt called for ratification of an amendment authorizing Congress to regulate marriage and divorce.[183] In a 1906 article in the *North American Review*, Wilbur Larremore explained that the states were increasing the grounds upon which divorces could be obtained. Yet some refused to recognize divorces in other states when the grounds cited were not recognized by their own laws, resulting in endless complications for the people involved. Even worse, "the conflict of laws entails varying personal status and legitimacy of children on different sides of domestic geographical lines."[184] Larremore thought the conflict warranted either a constitutional amendment authorizing Congress to preempt these laws and regulate the subject itself or the drafting of uniform laws that could be recommended to each state. He noted that a movement supporting uniform state laws in certain areas had already made progress—29 states had adopted a uniform negotiable instrument law. Larremore preferred a constitutional amendment, though he acknowledged that even abiding by the forms of the Constitution would offend "states' rights purists" who regarded marriage as a state matter.[185]

With the pace of centralization picking up speed, the *Sewanee Review* examined the process in 1908. In describing what he called the "New Federalism," author P. Orman Ray wrote of a "spontaneous, almost instinctive, looking to the federal government as the only source whence might come a panacea for the various maladies affecting the body politic."[186] The rise of the West contributed to this development; the western states seemed to view the federal government as their benefactor in part because unlike the states on the eastern seaboard, they had been created by it. A new sectionalism born of the perceived dominance of the South and West by eastern industries and banks led those sections to seek measures that would limit the dominance of the East, such as postal savings banks.[187] The embrace of federal authority had manifested itself in all sorts of novelties, including quarantines, efforts to control the boll weevil, the Interstate Commerce Commission, distribution of Weather Bureau reports, proposals to establish merchant marine subsidies, congressional appropriations to improve inland waterways and the Reclamation Service's efforts to irrigate dry lands—the "most stupendous paternalistic undertaking of modern times."[188] The increased prominence of labor in national politics had also produced innovations at the federal level, such as the law limiting the hours of railroad employees.[189]

Secretary of State Elihu Root discussed the process of centralization in a December 12, 1906, speech before the Pennsylvania Society of the City of New York. "It is plainly to be seen that the people of the country are coming to the conclusion that in certain important respects the local laws of the separate states . . . are inadequate for the due and just control of the business and activities which extend throughout all the states, and that (the) power of regulation and control is gradually passing into the hands of the national government."[190] Nor was the process of centralization complete. "We are urging forward in a development of business social life which tends more and more to the obliteration of state lines and the decrease of state power as compared with national power; the relations of the business over which the federal government is assuming control, of interstate commerce with state commerce, are so intimate, and the separation of the two is so impracticable that the tendency is plainly toward the practical control of the national government over both."[191] If the states wished to preserve their roles, there must be "an awakening on the part of the states to a realization of their own duties to the country at large."[192] If they persisted in keeping laws on their books that enabled monopolies or permit child labor, or allow their marriage laws to conflict sharply with those of other states, they would be "promoting the tendency of the people of the country to seek relief through the national government and to press forward the movement for national control and extinction of local control."[193] Root closed by warning the states that if they failed to provide legislation necessary to meet new conditions, "constructions of the Constitution will be found to vest the power where it will be exercised—in the national government."[194]

The *North American Review*, although not traditionally hostile to federal authority, was less than impressed. It dismissed the idea that the "gradual passing of control in the hands of the national government meets with the approval of the sober sense of the people" as "purely assumptive." It is "also 'useless' according to the Secretary of State, to inveigh 'against the extension of national authority in the fields of necessary control.' Against constitutional extension of such authority? No. To that there is no objection. It is the admittedly unconstitutional extension that makes for apprehension; that is, admittedly, unconstitutional until 'constructions' shall be found. When, if ever, that sinister prophecy shall have come to pass, there will be no occasion to stand steadfastly for or inveigh against a Constitution that will have become as dead as the laws of Medes and Persians."[195]

Two episodes that occurred during the second Roosevelt administration revealed that the federal government was not yet omnipotent. The first saw a municipal government defy the president for a time; the second witnessed a vital sector of the economy bring itself and the nation to the brink of disaster while federal officials stood by and watched. Labor interests in California had long been hostile to emigrants from the Orient, whom they suspected of depressing wages. At their behest, Congress imposed a moratorium on "Chinese laborers" in 1882.[196] While immigration from China slowed, the number of Japanese persons arriving on the west coast increased sharply during the closing years of the century. In October 1906, the City of San Francisco condemned the children of Japanese immigrants to separate schools, similar to those already established for students of Chinese descent. Japan was irate over the move; her relations with the United States had already been strained by the president's role in ending the Russo-Japanese War. Roosevelt was infuriated by the actions of officials of the San Francisco school board, but as occurred with the coal strike, the federal apparatus included no tools with which he might have imposed his will. Some thought a U.S.-Japanese treaty of 1894 requiring the United States to provide aliens of Japan with all the privileges it afforded its own citizens rendered the separate schools illegal; they suggested that Japanese residents of San Francisco seek an injunction barring the city from establishing separate schools for their children. In truth the privileges contemplated by the treaty did not include the right to attend the same schools as whites. The president was reduced to lobbying the San Francisco School Board to modify a policy that promised to humiliate a rising power and threaten U.S. interests in the Pacific. His pleading was in vain for a time. Amid complaints of some that California was engaging in "nullification," San Francisco officials agreed to refrain from establishing separate schools for the children of Japanese aliens. Japan promised to stop issuing passports to citizens wishing to emigrate to the continental United States.

In the fall of 1907, shares on the New York Stock Exchange took a hit when an attempted takeover of the United Copper Company failed and two brokerage houses went under along with a bank. As trust companies and banks tottered on the edge, the annual shortage of currency that struck New York banks every fall when money flowed west to pay for the purchase of the harvest nearly proved disastrous. When the Knickerbocker Trust Company failed, frightened depositors began withdrawing money from the city's other financial institutions, many of whom were unable to meet the sudden demand for cash and had to suspend withdrawals—they had used deposits to purchase securities. J. P. Morgan met with leading bankers in the library of his Manhattan home; he succeeded in getting them to contribute funds for the purpose of propping up failing institutions and thereby prevented a national calamity. The New York Stock Exchange itself had been on the verge of closing when Morgan lent it $25 million. An infusion of European gold brought on by declining prices for securities and the availability of clearing house certificates helped shorten the period of suspension that followed the crisis.[197] Some blamed President Roosevelt for the entire episode; the markets began sputtering after a federal judge imposed a $29 million fine on Standard Oil for antitrust violations in August. After he was alerted to the crisis, the president allowed the Treasury Department to increase its deposits of customs revenue in New York City banks but the infusion of $25 million was far from adequate.[198] In time the Panic eased but some banks did not resume specie payments until the end of the year. The crisis produced a widespread conviction that federal officials would have to take a more active role in regulating the money supply and limiting the effects of panics than waiting by the telephone to see what prescriptions were devised by Manhattan bankers and their cohorts in Europe.

Democrats gained 28 House seats in the 1906 midterm elections. Yet Roosevelt remained popular and with the economy surging forward despite Wall Street's hiccup, most observers expected Republicans to prevail in 1908. Roosevelt had decided against running again. Although Senator Joseph

Foraker, Governor Charles Evans Hughes of New York, and even Joe Cannon had been spoken of as successors to the president, the nomination fell to Secretary of War William Howard Taft. The president was said to fear that the nomination of one of the party's "reactionaries," such as Foraker or Cannon, would cost it the election. A successful Ohio attorney who later served as solicitor general and as a federal judge, Taft presided as governor-general in the Philippines during the early years of the century. During his stint in the Far East he turned down a Supreme Court nomination.

The Democratic nominee in 1908 was William Jennings Bryan. Since 1896, the country had moved steadily toward his positions. During the same period Bryan weakened his personal authority by devoting his time to the editorship of a radical agrarian screed, *The Commoner*. He also undermined his position as a leader of his party by picking unnecessary fights and taking positions that would have been extreme for any politician—such as his advocacy of public ownership of railroads—much less a contender for the presidency. He seemed to have believed that all persons associated with corporations should be ostracized. John D. Rockefeller's donation of money to the University of Nebraska won his hearty opposition.[199]

Flaws and all, many Democrats suspected that Bryan's chances were fairly good in 1908—certainly better than they had been in 1896 or 1900. The country was moving toward the Democratic Party in outlook (or at least that of its progressive wing), and the Republican nominee was far less attractive than his two predecessors had been. Bryan aided his cause by dropping his demand for public ownership of the railroads. When Democrats met in Denver in July, the Nebraska editor easily won the nomination. The convention devised a platform that indicated the party of Jefferson and Jackson was beginning to embrace national authority. It called for the organization of a national health bureau with "power over sanitary conditions connected with factories, mines, tenements, child labor and other such subjects as are properly within the jurisdiction of the federal government and do not interfere with the power of the states." The platform also endorsed federal regulation of telephone and telegraph companies (including their rates) and the establishment of a Department of Labor. It also recommended arming the ICC with the power to initiate changes in railroad rates. Another plank endorsed jury trials in contempt of court cases arising out of strikes. Democrats favored laws barring corporate campaign contributions and limiting individual contributions. Another plank embraced federal insurance of bank deposits—a sensitive issue at a time when at least 100 banks failed every year (it proposed to require national banks to pay into a guarantee fund). Democrats paid homage to states' rights, claiming they were "opposed to centralization, implied in the suggestion, now frequently made, that the powers of the general government should be extended by judicial construction." The platform insisted "there is no twilight zone between nation and state in which exploiting interests can take refuge from both" and it endorsed "federal remedies for the regulation of interstate commerce and for the prevention of private monopoly." A plank complained of an increase in the size federal bureaucracy—100,000 jobs had been added in the previous six years, compared to only 10,000 during the McKinley and Cleveland administrations.[200]

Republicans found their own reasons to complain of the federal civil service—many believed the president used it to sew up the nomination for his chosen successor, much the way Andrew Jackson had 72 years earlier.[201] In truth the president allowed Taft's campaign manager to do the needlework; places in the Post Office served as threading. First assistant postmaster general Frank Hitchcock resigned to manage the Taft campaign. Although he did not rely as heavily on patronage-dependent southern delegations as Republican kingmakers had in the past, newspapers charged the president was allowing the Taft campaign to buy delegates with Post Office largesse. Roosevelt angrily denied the charge, but as late as May the Republican senators of New Jersey—both of whom had refused to succumb to pressure to endorse Taft—found that nominations of their favorites for places in the Post Office had been delayed.[202] At the Republican convention in Chicago, 125 delegates were federal officeholders—about one-tenth of the total.[203] In a bid to head off the threat posed by Democratic advocacy of federal deposit insurance, the Republican platform endorsed postal savings banks. It also acknowledged the need for tariff revision, a reduction in the hours worked by railroad employees, and called for an investigation of the working conditions of children and women. Vague language enabled the party to avoid stating how far it was prepared to go in extending national authority: labor laws would be "pursued in every legitimate direction within federal authority to lighten the burdens and increase the opportunity for happiness and advancement of all who toil."[204] The Platform Committee rejected a plank that would have endorsed the curtailing of labor injunctions despite the fact that it was supported by Roosevelt and Taft; it also rejected one that explicitly embraced a lower tariff.[205]

The campaign failed to catch the nation's attention during its early weeks, as Americans were more concerned with baseball's pennant races. The battles between the Chicago Cubs and the New York Giants in the National League and the Detroit Tigers and the Cleveland Naps for the American League title transfixed the country during September and early October. Bryan assured the nation he was the candidate to continue the reforms begun by Roosevelt. Following the Republican convention, Taft resigned from the War Department and commenced a two-month vacation. By the end of summer Bryan appeared to be winning—some polls found him leading in New York, which remained all-important.[206] With a confident Bryan making scores of speeches throughout the nation, Taft relented and took to the road himself. When leading Democrats began to suspect their candidate might win, they tried to convince business leaders that Bryan would refrain from placing irresponsible men upon the Supreme Court. Party leaders asked Bryan if he could provide the necessary assurances only to have him refuse.[207] Bryan's suggestion that no business should be allowed to control more than 50 percent of any particular market did not win him friends on Wall Street, either. A more popular suggestion was his call for removing tariff protection from items produced by trusts. Bryan also wished to require corporations to obtain a federal license if they controlled one-quarter or more of the market, which he saw as preferable to the Republican plan for the centralized regulation of corporations from Washington.[208]

Labor organizations supported Bryan. He returned the favor by calling for the exemption of unions from antitrust laws. Taft, he charged, was the "father of government by injunction."[209] In response, Taft insisted that during his stint as a federal judge (1892–1900), he had only issued injunctions against secondary boycotts and attempts to harm the property of employers.[210] Bryan also called for a law requiring the national banks to establish a guarantee fund to pay depositors in the event one of them failed; any bank in the country should be allowed to join the plan if it chose. The fund would be derived from a tax on participating banks. Republicans feared the measure enough to devote 10 pages in their 1908 campaign textbook to explanations offered by various figures as to why the plan was a bad idea. Their arguments were atrocious. One critic insisted that deposits were merely investments and appropriately subject to risk like any other. It was also said that depositors did not need insurance as they could select the bank where they placed their savings. Why, one critic asked, should one type of creditor have the credit he or she extended be insured? Should conservative rural banks be required to insure speculative city banks?[211]

Taft sought to blunt the appeal of deposit insurance by embracing a proposal to allow post offices to enter the banking business—a step that arguably constituted a more revolutionary exercise of federal power than merely forcing banks to pay into a guaranty fund.[212] While he refused to promise reductions in tariff rates, the Republican nominee assured advocates of cuts that they would be "given a hearing" and that revisions of some kind would be embraced, with reductions on at least some items.[213] Taft embraced federal incorporation of large businesses—something that would have vastly expanded federal regulation of the nation's economic life, as it would have enabled Washington to supervise everything from stock issues to corporate finance.[214] He also accepted the need to base railroad rates on the value of each line's physical assets instead of its capitalization. While speaking in Kansas, Taft credited the tariff for the rise in the price of wheat from 49 cents to 92 cents a bushel since 1896.[215] The Republican candidate received aid from Post Office, Interior, and Treasury employees who went on unpaid leave to campaign for him.[216] On Election Day Bryan exceeded Alton Parker's take in 1904, but he still won only 43 percent of the vote. He carried the South, Kansas, Nebraska, Colorado, and Nevada. The rest of the states went to Taft. Republicans won a healthy majority of House seats, and their position in the Senate remained dominant. The issue of bank deposit insurance disappeared beneath the waves. It would not reappear for a quarter of a century, after many boats had sunk.

The presidency of Theodore Roosevelt came to an end four months later in March 1909. It was obvious that something important had happened over the previous seven and a half years, but no one was certain of what exactly had occurred. Congress had used its commerce power in new and different ways to regulate railroads, food products, and drugs, and the Justice Department began the work of making the Sherman Antitrust Act a reality. Under the authority of an 1891 law, the president classified some 150 million acres of federal lands as national forests.[217] One novelty ignored at the time that would have important benefits later was the establishment of the National Bureau of Standards (it was actually established six months before Roosevelt became president). The Bureau investigated a bewildering variety of subjects and helped set standards that aided a numerous industries, including the construction trades.[218] The consequences of a lack of national standards were revealed in a 1904 conflagration that destroyed much of Baltimore's central business district. Fire departments in nearby states sent equipment but much of it proved useless due to the fact that their hoses did not fit the city's hydrants. Perhaps the most significant change was in the president's rhetoric; Roosevelt had said things never uttered previously by an occupant of the White House. At the dedication of a House of Representatives office building in April 1906 he spoke of the need for a federal income tax and inheritance taxes. These were not needed to raise revenue, but to reduce the share of national wealth in the possession of those at the top of the income scale. "I feel that we should ultimately have to consider the adoption of some such scheme as that of a progressive tax on all fortunes, beyond a certain amount, either given in life or devised or bequeathed upon the death of the individual—a tax so framed as to put it out of the power of the owner of one of these enormous fortunes to hand on more than a certain amount to any one individual."[219] The movement to limit the incomes of Americans stemmed from a desire the check the accumulation of power in the hands of a few, but the inevitable consequence of diverting billions of dollars from private citizens to Washington would be to greatly expand the power of the national government. There was more than a little irony in the president decrying the accumulation of wealth at the upper end of the income scale, as he scrupulously avoided doing anything about the one federal policy that had the effect of transferring hundreds of millions of dollars each year from American consumers to manufacturers—the protective tariff. Whether he had any real interest in revision is doubtful; in 1906 he won support for the Hepburn rate bill by promising to leave rates alone.[220] Roosevelt later claimed that "the only people who wanted me to take up the tariff were the people who ardently desired to divert attention from the what I was doing about the trusts, for instance, or who wished to block all the progressive movements which I had inaugurated."[221] It is doubtful that the millions of consumers who paid artificially high prices for goods fell into this class.

William Howard Taft deferred to Republican leaders in Congress from the beginning. His fondness for playing golf regularly in Beverly, Massachusetts, where he rented a house, contributed to the transfer of power back to the Capitol. Speaker Joe Cannon was at the height of his power in the House while the Senate was dominated by Finance Committee Chairman Nelson Aldrich and his allies. These men were determined that the special session called for March 1909 to revise tariff rates would not result in reduced levies. The House passed a bill that lowered some rates but increased others, largely due to the insistence of the Speaker. Foodstuffs including sugar carried higher rates when the bill reached the Senate. Nelson Aldrich proceeded to increase rates on a variety of items, and when a group of young progressive-minded Republicans including Wisconsin Senator Robert M. LaFollette rebelled, they were "read out" of the party by their elders. LaFollette appealed to the president, who promised to demand reductions once the measure went to a House-Senate conference committee. After the committee made some token cuts to accommodate Taft, he went along with the bill.[222] The average rate dropped slightly, but rates on some 600 items increased.[223]

The Payne-Aldrich Tariff of August 5, 1909, had been produced by manufacturing lobbyists and looked it. Advocates of high rates justified them as necessary to compensate manufacturers for the difference between the domestic and foreign cost of production, as well as the need to ensure that they received a "reasonable" profit. The chemical industry, withering under the heat of German competition, obtained higher duties on chemicals and dyes. A lone manufacturer of pliers in New York State obtained higher rates to discourage the purchase of pliers from its foreign competitors. A New England Senator secured a doubling of the duty on gloves.[224] Progressive Republicans from the Midwest claimed party leaders had backed down on a promise made during the 1908 campaign to lower rates. The president inflicted needless injury on himself when he defended the Payne-Aldrich Tariff as "the best tariff bill the Republican Party has ever passed."[225]

He repeated the error during a Lincoln Day speech in February 1910 when he insisted the law was in no way related to the increase in prices that was inflicting a hardship on many Americans. The president forever linked himself with the rent-seeking element of his party when he vetoed a bill reducing wool duties from 44 to 29 percent on August 17, 1910; he later vetoed several other bills reducing tariffs on certain items because they had not been recommended by the newly formed tariff board.

The president took a more enlightened approach to antitrust questions, albeit one that evinced an indulgent view of federal authority. In a December 16, 1908, speech Taft called for a law that would go beyond the Sherman Act's vague definition of the conduct it outlawed ("restraints of trade") and list prohibited acts. In early 1910 he called for incorporating trusts under federal law and limiting the ability of states to regulate them. As for doubts over the power of Congress to incorporate corporations for the purpose of engaging in interstate or foreign commerce, the president pointed out that it had already been exercised in the case of national banks, railroads, and companies that constructed bridges over waterways separating states.[226] Some claimed Taft exhibited a more tolerant attitude toward trusts than his predecessor, perhaps because in one of its first acts, the administration authorized the New Haven Railroad to take control of the major lines in New England.[227] Yet the Taft administration initiated about 70 antitrust suits, compared to 40 under Roosevelt.[228] The Mann-Elkins Act law of June 18, 1910, established a Commerce Court endowed with jurisdiction over all cases arising out of ICC orders. Many thought it a weak creature that would be controlled by the railroads. The law authorized the ICC to investigate and act on its own complaints as well as those of shippers—thus giving it the power to initiate rate changes and granting progressives the victory they had been denied in 1906. Telephone and telegraph rates were added to the ICC's jurisdiction.[229] The measure only became law over the opposition of Progressive Republicans when Democratic votes were obtained in exchange for statehood for Arizona and New Mexico.[230] Progressives thought the measure did not go far enough—they wanted the ICC authorized to supervise the issuance of railroad stock and calculate rates based on the value of the assets of the railroads and not their capitalization. Congress passed a bill abolishing the Commerce Court in August 1912; it was vetoed by President Taft.[231]

The Taft administration and congressional Republicans pushed outward the lines of federal jurisdiction in an effort to keep abreast of the progressive wave. Congress established a postal savings bank system on June 25, 1910.[232] The political ramifications of having a publicly operated bank were revealed when progressives sought to outbid the administration by authorizing the bank to pay up to 2.5 percent interest—they had to settle for 2 percent. They tried and failed to add an amendment requiring post offices to invest deposits locally.[233] The question of what relation accepting deposits had to delivering the mail received only perfunctory examination. Work begun during the administration of Theodore Roosevelt to prevent corporate America from corrupting the political process continued. A 1907 law barred corporations organized under federal law as well as national banks from contributing money "in connection with any election to any political office." All corporations were barred from making contributions in elections for federal offices.[234] The Corrupt Practices Act of June 25, 1910, imposed organizational and financial disclosure requirements on "political committees"—groups that included the national committees of parties, congressional campaign committees, and all entities "which shall in two or more states influence the result or attempt to influence the result of an election in which representatives in Congress are to be elected."[235] A measure of August 19, 1911, limited candidates in House elections to maximum expenditures of $5,000 and those in U.S. Senate elections to a maximum expenditure of $10,000.[236] In *Newberry v. U.S.* (1921), the Supreme Court held void the provision of the law limiting expenditures in primary campaigns.[237] In his opinion for a 5–4 majority of the Court, Justice James McReynolds explained that while Section 3 of Article IV bestowed a power over congressional elections on the federal government, said power did not extend to primaries.[238]

The introduction of primaries undermined the century-old practice of federal officeholders descending en masse on local nominating conventions to work the will of the president. James Buchanan tried to drive Free Soil Democrats in the North out of office by using postal and customhouse workers to deny them re-nomination; Cleveland enlisted federal workers in a futile attempt to root out pro-silver Democrats. As recently as 1904, Roosevelt used federal offices in the South to turn what had been Hanna delegations into a huge block of delegates loyal to the president. In 1910 the administration deployed federal offices for the purpose of depriving Progressive Republicans of re-nomination. Its task was complicated by the fact that primaries had replaced nominating conventions in several states, and even the largest post office or customhouse could do little to defeat the popular will when it was expressed at the ballot box. In those states that continued to allow party conventions to select nominees, progressives were often able to match the resources of federal machines with state patronage. As a result Taft's effort failed miserably. Party divisions combined with the Payne-Aldrich Tariff to produce Democratic victories in many states that had not elected a Democrat in generations. The year 1910 saw Maine send its first Democratic senator to Washington since 1852.[239] Democrats won the House for the first time since 1892 (with 225 seats to 165 held by

Republicans) and took over several northern state governments, including those of Massachusetts and Connecticut. Forty incumbent Republicans in the House lost reelection bids. The main cause seems to have been the Payne-Aldrich Tariff; many associated it with a steep rise in prices. A Democratic editor thought his party more unified than it had been since the 1830s—it was no longer haunted by sectional issues or "economic fallacies."[240] When the 62nd Congress went to work in late 1911, its priorities revealed that progressive forces were taking control of both parties.

The law establishing a Children's Bureau qualified as the most notable innovation. The notion of a federal entity devoted to children was said to have originated with Lillian Wald and Florence Kelley, two New York City social workers, who came up with the idea after reading a newspaper article about federal appropriations aimed at eliminating diseases among farm animals. Progressive Republican William E. Borah of Idaho proposed a bill for that purpose in December 1911. The Bureau would collect information regarding "all matters pertaining to the welfare of children and child life among all classes of our people, and shall especially investigate the questions of infant mortality, the birth rate, orphanage, juvenile courts, desertion, dangerous occupations, accidents and diseases of children, employment [and] legislation affecting children in the several states and territories." Senator Joseph Bailey of Texas was appalled: "We have for a hundred years or more left these matters concerning children to the proper authorities, which are the mothers, fathers, and guardians, and in that hundred years we have reared such children as the Senator from Idaho; and a system which has produced him does not need much apology or much amendment." Of the suggestion that the Bureau would merely collect information, he knew better. "Men who are familiar with the course of legislation understand perfectly that these matters come first in the shape of requests for statistics, and they are invariably followed then by legislation."[241] Senator Borah defended his bill on January 8, saying that he only wished to see the national government collect and distribute information to the states.[242] He did not envision Congress enacting laws on the subject of children. Borah insisted that the youth of the country are an appropriate subject of national interest. "Under present economic conditions there are thousands and thousands of children who will never be capacitated or fit for the discharge of the duties of citizenship unless they receive some aid, some comfort, some support, or some direction from someone. Who is more interested in this than the national government, which must, in time, if they live, depend upon them for support and for protection?" Noting that the federal government already collected information regarding hogs, he insisted that the "Constitution was not made for hogs alone, but also for men."[243]

On January 24, 1912, Senator Bailey charged that it was a "novel and . . . a dangerous doctrine that the federal government has the power . . . to obtain information which will enable the state governments to execute their functions." Besides, he continued, each state had a right to know "only just as much, about [its] own people and their conditions as it chooses to know." Bailey denied that the people of Texas had the right to "force upon the people of Idaho an unwelcome knowledge of their condition." Ignorance, it seemed, was bliss. Montana Republican Joseph Dixon hinted at the driving force behind the bill. After conceding that only the states could bar child labor, he insisted that "the thing that will do more than anything else to bring a stop to it is to turn on full publicity, to let in light on the conditions that we know go on every day in all of the great industrial centers of this country."[244]

The children's bureau bill passed the Senate on January 31. In the House, Congressman James Cox of Ohio insisted that as the Census Bureau already collected information beyond "the mere enumeration of inhabitants," there can be no "constitutional objection to our creating another bureau to carry on the same character of work." If no authority existed for the children's bureau, Congress ought to discontinue appropriations for the following bureaus at once as their relationship to the enumerated powers was also doubtful: Education, Mines, Animal Industry, Soils, Labor, Entomology, Biological Survey, Fisheries, and Ethnology. Cox noted that the Bureau of Labor had discovered children working nightshifts from 6:45 p.m. to 6 a.m. and manufacturers who kept their youthful employees awake by spraying them with water.[245] The bill passed the House later that day and was signed by the president. The law provided that officials collecting information could not enter homes unless they obtained consent.[246] During its early years, the Bureau tried to convince the states to register every live birth and to make efforts to reduce infant mortality. It also lobbied states to form their own children's bureaus.[247]

With progressives holding the balance of power in both houses of Congress, legislation enacted under the commerce power touched a bewildering variety of subjects. The Mann Act of June 25, 1910, imposed criminal sanctions on persons who transferred women across state lines for immoral purposes including prostitution and debauchery.[248] Although an exercise of the commerce power, the law was enacted in part to comply with the Convention for the Suppression of White Slave Traffic, a treaty ratified by the Senate in 1905. It also arose out of widespread and greatly exaggerated fears over the extent of prostitution, forced and otherwise, in the nation's cities. Officials contributed to the hysteria with irresponsible comments regarding the extent of the problem; the U.S. attorney in Chicago claimed a single syndicate scoured the American countryside and the nations of Europe looking for innocent victims.[249] The law was considered a revolutionary departure at the time, but the Immigration Act of 1875's ban on importing women for prostitution and an 1860 statute that barred the seduction of female passengers aboard steamboats arguably provided solid precedents for the measure.[250]

While the bill was still before Congress, Charles Bartlett of Georgia objected to it as unconstitutional. It would sanction those who merely purchased train tickets for women so that they might cross state lines. "The delivering of a ticket to a person in the state of New York or giving a passenger a ticket by which he can board in the state of New York a train or a vessel and go to some other state is not interstate commerce." Bartlett distinguished statutes barring lottery tickets and diseased cattle from interstate commerce on the grounds that those items are inherently destructive. A person traveling for the purpose of committing a crime on the other hand does not qualify as inherently noxious; it is only what that person does after reaching their destination that causes harm.[251] On the whole the bill received little resistance in Congress, perhaps because southern lawmakers, who would have been most likely to oppose a measure that might provide precedent for a child labor bill, did not wish to appear to be standing in the way of efforts to limit prostitution.[252] In *Hoke v. U.S.*, the Supreme Court upheld the Mann Act.[253] In his opinion for the Court, Justice James McKenna suggested that persons as well as things can serve as articles of commerce. He justified the intrusion of Congress into an area formerly left to the states—the repression of prostitution—by claiming that the states can only control the problem within their own borders. The act was in his view similar to the Pure Food and Drug Act in barring nefarious activities from interstate commerce. That the measure concerned morals and not commerce was no defect, as the commerce power is "complete in itself."[254]

That the law was constitutional did not make it wise. In targeting the transportation of women for immoral purposes as well prostitution, it authorized U.S. attorneys to prosecute men who merely traveled across state lines in the company of women with whom they had a romantic attachment or with whom they hoped to establish one. The Justice Department considered limiting prosecutions to only cases involving prostitution. Under pressure from religious leaders, it continued to try both men and women who made the mistake of crossing state lines in the company of members of the opposite sex and who either offered or accepted gifts, meals, or free travel from their companions. Some women reacted by avoiding interstate travel with their suitors; others exploited the law and helped produce a small industry devoted to blackmail. Men and women accused of violating the measure resorted to marriage to avoid conviction as married persons could not be compelled to testify against their spouses.[255]

Authorities also used the Mann Act to target persons who flouted social norms. Black boxer Jack Johnson served time in prison for violating the law after traveling across state lines with a woman who was not his wife and who had worked as a prostitute in the past. The woman happened to be white, as were many of the boxers defeated by Johnson, thus earning him the hatred of a broad spectrum of Americans. The newly formed Bureau of Investigation in the Justice Department tapped into this hostility when it devoted an inordinate portion of its resources to enforcing the Mann Act—and pursuing Johnson—while neglecting more obvious duties such as the protection of blacks against lynching.[256] The Bureau expanded sharply in size to aid prosecutions of the law and its agents worked closely with state enforcement officials for the first time.[257] In warping the priorities of law enforcement officials and involving the federal government in matters neither it nor any public entity should have bothered with, the Mann Act provided a grim preview of the waste and abuse associated with Prohibition.

Jack Johnson was also at the center of another novel exercise of the commerce power. Animosity toward the nation's most famous boxer led Congress to enact a law of July 1912 that banned the interstate transportation of films or photos of prize fights (the Sims Act). They were also barred from the mails.[258] The law stemmed in part from a desire to prevent entrepreneurs from showing a film that depicted the July 4, 1910, victory of Johnson over Jim Jefferies, who was white.[259] When blacks attempted to celebrate the victory that night, they were met by mobs of angry whites and riots ensued in cities and towns across the country. The violence enabled lawmakers to convince themselves that in pushing through the Sims Act, they were acting to preserve order and not merely to gratify the racial vanity of whites. The law was violated routinely during the 1920s, when white boxers again dominated the sport. It was repealed in 1940.

Among the novel exercises of federal power that occurred during the Taft administration was a law of May 13, 1910, that established a Bureau of Mines and gave it the task of conducting investigations for the purpose of improving mine safety. The measure did not establish safety requirements for mines.[260] In April 1912 Congress imposed a tax on phosphorus matches (two cents per 100 matches) designed to drive them out of existence.[261] The Department of Commerce and Labor was divided into two new departments, evincing the government's sympathy to a constituency growing in importance. The Labor Department was to "foster, promote, and develop the welfare of the wage earners of the United States . . . improve their working conditions, and . . . advance their opportunities for profitable employment."[262]

On taking over the House in late 1911, Democrats took steps to demonstrate they were not hostile to the nation's veterans. Four years earlier

Congress had given statutory authority to the 1904 order of the Commissioner of Pensions designed to place every Union army veteran on the federal payroll.[263] Persons who served 90 days or more during the Civil War and had reached the age of 62 were eligible for a pension of $12 to $20 a month. As the pension rolls still contained the names of almost a million persons, the political utility of the law was obvious. By 1915, 93 percent of Union Army veterans still on the planet were receiving benefits.[264] With pensions now available to all men who served in the army during 1861–65, lawmakers realized that the only remaining means to derive any political benefit from pensions was to increase them. The Democratic House took up that Herculean task in early 1912. Several measures received consideration, including the Sherwood pension bill that would have increased the minimum monthly payment by two-thirds—from $12 to $20. Courtney Hamlin of Missouri was proud to say that after years of Republican exploitation of the issue, "the most liberal, equitable, and just bill ever introduced in Congress for the old soldiers is taken up as the first bill of general legislation by a Democratic House."[265] When some objected to the expense involved, Democrat James Post of Ohio suggested that the estimated cost of $75 million could be recouped through retrenchment. The War and Navy Departments in particular seemed ripe for slicing. "We can build fewer dreadnoughts to deteriorate to worthlessness in less than a decade. The great army and navy appropriations, approximating $300 million annually, can easily be curtailed without impairment to the national defense."[266] That the United States might need its warships in the coming years seemed a remote possibility. The act that emerged from Congress in May 1912 provided for relatively modest increases in pensions payments.[267] An interesting postscript to the conversion of veterans' benefits into a political football during the period between 1870 and 1912 occurred with the demand of federal civil servants for pensions. The cry was first heard in the 1880s; a Senate committee report of 1888 cast aside the idea, observing that as persons outside of the government were not placed on "retired lists," there was no reason those in the public service should be.[268] When talk of pensions for civil servants was again heard in 1912, Representative Dan Stephens of Nebraska recoiled at a future in which executive branch employees, after doing the political bidding of their benefactors for 100 years, began to wield their power on behalf of themselves. "There are hundreds of thousands of government employees scattered throughout the United States. When these folks with a vote demand of Congress favorable legislation along the line of pensions for public servants, just what will happen to the principal idea that our government is for, of, and by the people? It will cease to be so, and will be a government of, for, and by the pensioners. If Congress refused an increase in pensions they would defeat [its members] for re-election, and elect instead a Congress that would grant it. We now pay a tremendous total of about $200,000,000 a year for war pensions, and the Philippine war veterans are not yet on the rolls to any extent. Add to these war pensioners the civil pensioners, and the end can easily be seen. This government, strong as it is, cannot resist a stranglehold like that. I feel that all of the people owe the war pensioners all they get, for all of the people were back of the war, but this public-service pension is another matter, and will naturally follow a life tenure of office for government employees."[269] Pensions for federal employees in the Civil Service arrived eight years later in 1920—annual payments of up to 60 percent of their salary was provided to those who had reached the age of 70 and toiled within the Civil Service for 15 years of more.[270]

The possibility of executive branch employees using their political power for their own ends increased with passage of the Lloyd-LaFollette Act of August 24, 1912.[271] The law barred the removal of persons in the civil service "except for such cause as will promote the efficiency" of the service and gave them the opportunity to contest the removal. It also bestowed the right to organize or join unions on postal workers by barring the termination of them for said membership, though this protection did not apply when they joined unions that obligated them to go on strike. The law also reversed Roosevelt's executive order barring federal employees from lobbying. Following its enactment executive branch workers joined unions affiliated with the American Federation of Labor, which encouraged their consolidation within a single entity, the National Federation of Federal Employees. The incidence of union membership among federal employees remained low—less than 20 percent. For a time the belief that sovereign governments, whether state or federal, could not renounce or relinquish their own powers via labor contracts checked the power of public employee unions.[272] In time that safeguard began to erode as well.

In the eyes of the public, neither the accomodation of labor interests nor the progressive legislation enacted under the commerce clause redeemed the conservative Republicans who dominated both the Senate and the executive branch. The continued gouging of consumers through absurdly protectionist tariffs caused fatal offense to many. While federal power had expanded dramatically in recent years and been deployed in ways pleasing to progressives, the fact remained that its most consequential exercise remained the massive transfer of wealth made possible by high tariff rates. None of this might have mattered if unity within the Grand Old Party could be maintained, but growing tensions between party elders and progressives posed a grave risk of rupture.

DEMOCRATS AND NATIONAL AUTHORITY

By late 1911, it was apparent that the president's prospects for reelection were not great. Pained by rising prices, the country looked with displeasure on his embrace of the Payne-Aldrich Tariff. Progressive Republicans were alienated by Taft's decision to side with conservatives in the intra-party battle that was growing more bitter by the month. By the summer of 1912, the likely outcome of the presidential election was known to everyone. Still it was the most critical and dramatic year in American history since 1865. It saw a former president try to position himself as a radical critic of his handpicked successor and the sitting chief executive wield patronage to secure his re-nomination in what constituted a last hurrah for the old federal spoils system. The year 1912 also witnessed a future president gain his party's nomination through a defect in the nascent primary system that enabled a political boss to override the verdict of the people of his own state. Through it all ran a debate over the appropriate role of the federal government in American life that saw the Democratic Party turn away from its century-old fixation with states' rights.

The driving force in 1912 was the Progressive movement. Its roots went back to the Granger laws of the 1870s and the civil service reforms of the 1880s. After the turn of the century the movement took on a new momentum and became a powerful influence, if not a dominant one, in both parties. Its priorities included the improvement of tenements and measures designed to enhance public health.[273] Progressives also sought minimum wage laws for women and children, the first of which was enacted by Massachusetts in 1912.[274] States enacted laws limiting working hours despite *Lochner*. As many workplaces had become spectacularly dangerous—U.S. Steel's South Works in Chicago saw 46 employees killed and 368 permanently disabled in 1906—progressives also sought workmen's compensation acts and laws regulating workplace safety.[275] Some legislatures limited the use of labor injunctions. Twenty states provided monthly payments to single women with dependent children by 1913.[276] One aspect of the Progressive movement later abandoned was its determination to limit government waste. In 1884, New York State barred cities and counties from incurring debt greater than 10 percent of the assessed value of the property contained within their borders.[277] The example was followed in other states around the country. Some states imposed income taxes as they were less regressive than property taxes. The first decade of the twentieth century saw increased funding for education, especially in the South.

Progressives also focused on reforming the political process in the hope of driving corruption out of government. They viewed the Australian or secret ballot, civil service laws, direct primaries, the initiative, referendum, and recall as devices through which the influence of bosses and lobbyists might be overcome. A series of newspaper and magazine articles of 1905 and 1906 that revealed the extent to which commercial interests had corrupted legislatures and municipal governments gave new momentum to the drive for political reform. Aided by the public's negative reaction to these revelations, reformers succeeded in loosening the grip of corporations over state legislatures; perhaps the most famous revolt took place in California, where the Southern Pacific's stranglehold over the state government came to an end. The Progressive movement enjoyed more successes in some states than others; in those states that had not suffered a plague of public corruption, it contributed little. Massachusetts maintained its long tradition of responsive government throughout the late nineteenth century despite urbanization and the rise of powerful industrial concerns; consequently it did not require or witness an upheaval of the type that occurred in so many other states.[278]

The most important progressive reform for the federal system was the Seventeenth Amendment's transfer of the power to elect U.S. senators from legislatures to the electorates of each state (though 29 states had already provided for a popular vote in the election of U.S. senators by 1909).[279] The Seventeenth Amendment arose out of the corruption of state legislatures by corporate interests who were thought to exercise too much influence in the election of senators. It also stemmed from the growing problem of the two houses of legislatures being deadlocked over the election of U.S. senators and depriving their states of representation in the U.S. Senate for weeks, months, and even years. By one count, there were over 70 such deadlocks between 1870 and 1913.[280] Even friends of federal authority such as George Hoar decried the popular election of senators as undermining their role as the guardians of the rights of the states.[281] In truth there is little evidence that this change made any difference—senators had not been more vigilant in their defense of the prerogatives of the states than their colleagues in the House. The popular election of senators did make them more fearful of voters. While their energies had once been devoted to providing patronage for state legislators and aiding corporate interests, senators now sought to please electorates, often through the embrace of initiatives such as aid for farmers that bore no connection to any of the powers listed in Article I. The replacement of state nominating conventions by primaries as a means for parties to select their nominees was the second most critical progressive-inspired reform for American federalism as it eroded the ability of federal employees to use their numbers to control party nominations. The trend began in South Carolina in 1896.[282]

Among the intellectual leaders of the Progressive movement was Herbert Croly. His work, *The Promise of American Life* (1909), had a profound effect on Theodore Roosevelt. Croly argued that the cause of reform must include an effort to ensure that prosperity reached all Americans. He seemed to believe that the widespread existence of poverty stemmed not from dislocations produced by the new industrial order but from a failure of some kind on the part of American government. "Our democratic institutions became in a sense the guarantee that prosperity would continue to be abundant and accessible. In case the majority of good Americans were not prosperous, there would be grave reasons for suspecting that our institutions were not doing their duty."[283] If, he explained, "the American people are not getting a 'Square Deal,' it must mean that they are having the cards stacked against them, and in that case the questions of paramount importance are: who are stacking the cards? And how can they be punished?"[284] With the important exceptions of protection and trusts, no one was "stacking the cards." Croly did not see the abolition of protection as the answer to the problem he perceived; instead he suggested that the national government must expand its policy of discrimination beyond the tariff—"a plain case of preferential class legislation"—to include "the average man."[285]

To discriminate effectively, the federal government would have to assume a degree of power it had not heretofore enjoyed. "Under existing conditions and simply as a matter of expediency, the national advance of American democracy does demand an increasing amount of centralized action and responsibility." The states, he explained, were not competent "to deal effectively in the national interest and spirit with the grave problems created by the aggrandizement of corporation and individual wealth and the increasing classification of the American people." Americans would have to discard their "tendency to oppose each proposal to increase the powers of the federal government 'as an unqualified evil.'"[286] In Croly's view, the "distinction between domestic (intrastate) and interstate commerce makes the carrying out of an efficient national industrial policy almost impossible."[287] It therefore had to be abolished and power over all commerce vested exclusively in the national government. The ICC must be empowered to order changes in services provided by all corporations and the prices charged by them.[288] He noted that while corporations once preferred state regulation as they could dominate the legislatures, they increasingly desired federal control.[289] The federal government should take possession of railroads and industries that had degraded into monopolies and the tax power ought to be used to deprive corporations of excessive profits. A graduated inheritance tax of up to 20 percent ought to be imposed to mitigate "existing inequalities." Labor unions should receive recognition and nonunion labor should be banned.[290]

Theodore Roosevelt had been speaking of the prescriptions of Croly for years, and he embraced them with a new relish in 1910. Already disenchanted with his successor, he sought to place himself at the head of a movement that regarded the president as a hopeless reactionary. Speaking at Osawatomie, Kansas, on August 31, 1910, Roosevelt announced that he stood for the "Square Deal." This meant more than "fair play under the present rules of the game." It also required that "those rules (should be) changed so as to work for a more substantial equality of opportunity and of reward for equally good service." His remedies included "workmen's compensation laws and both state and national laws to regulate child labor and work for women." Roosevelt insisted that the gap he perceived between the jurisdiction of the states and the national government must be eradicated. "There must be no neutral ground to serve as a refuge for lawbreakers, and especially for the lawbreakers of great wealth, who can hire the vulpine legal cunning which will teach them how to avoid both jurisdictions. It is a misfortune when the national legislature fails to do its duty in providing a national remedy, so that the only national activity is the purely negative activity of the judiciary in forbidding the states to exercise power in the premises."[291] Two weeks later in Syracuse, Roosevelt cited *Lochner* as a case in which the Supreme Court had constricted the right of the states to regulate labor conditions and the *Knight* case as one in which it had pushed back the boundaries of federal authority. To those who claimed he was mounting a dangerous attack on the federal judiciary, he cited Lincoln's disavowal of *Dred Scott*.[292]

In a February 21, 1912, speech at the Ohio Constitutional Convention at Columbus, Roosevelt embraced the recall of judicial decisions at the state level.[293] Left unclear was whether he was willing to apply this remedy to the federal judiciary. In a letter to Secretary of War Henry Stimson, Roosevelt conceded that there had never been a corrupt Supreme Court justice, but he insisted that a chief justice such as Taney "is a far worse influence to the country than a President like Pierce or Buchanan, and there should be some possibility of removing him." Roosevelt complained that he had seen "well-meaning judges, such as Peckham, Fuller and Brewer, whose presence on the Supreme Court was a menace to the welfare of the nation, who ought not to have been left there a day." As for the solution to the problem, the ex-president admitted that he was "not prepared to say what, if anything, should be done as regards the federal judiciary." In a March 1912 speech in which he complained of "judicial nullification," Roosevelt suggested that his own state of New York ought to amend its state constitution to provide for the reversal of decisions by the state Court of Appeals (the highest court in the state) when it invalidated state laws on due process grounds.[294] Roosevelt conceded that most of the legislation favored by progressives would have to be achieved at the state level. In a February 1911 essay, "Nationalism and Progress," he called on the legislatures to abolish sweatshops, require that every worker had at least one day of rest each week, provide for safety inspections of "factory, workshop, mine and home," and ensure that children had access to adequate playgrounds and were spared from the need to labor. The states should also "supervise the conditions of tenement-housing and limit the hours worked by women."[295]

Roosevelt might have been content to continue advocating progressive measures in his capacity as a private citizen if Wisconsin Senator Robert M. LaFollette, the progressive candidate for the Republican nomination, had not collapsed while giving a speech in early February 1912. Roosevelt declared his own candidacy later that month. LaFollette refused to abandon the race, and so the Republicans found themselves split into three camps at the start of what was expected to be a difficult year. Roosevelt eventually gained the upper hand as the leader of the progressive wing of the party, but the stern advocate of centralization ran straight into the brick wall of machine politics and federal patronage. Many states still had not adopted primaries, thereby leaving control of the delegate selection process in the hands of bosses and their cohorts in Washington. Several states that had established primaries continued to leave the selection of delegates to national conventions to state caucuses or conventions—the results of the primaries in these states were therefore meaningless. In the South the party faithful had access to federal offices alone, making them easy prey for the president's lieutenants. The sparse public establishments of many western states made them susceptible to the machinations of federal officeholders as well. The Republican bosses of the northeast also continued to rely heavily on federal offices as Democratic machines increasingly controlled municipal and even state governments. Unwilling to risk their sole remaining source of patronage, they packed state nominating conventions with Taft men.[296]

Roosevelt complained of the manipulation of federal employees in a note to Henry Kohlsaat, to which he attached a letter sent to Oklahoma postmaster Newton Figley by officials in Washington. It illustrated how federal offices were used to control political activity at the state level. "The commission of N. S. Figley, postmaster at Hastings, Oklahoma, will expire on February 28, 1912. When last inspected this office did not appear in a satisfactory condition, and unless the postmaster can be relied upon to raise the service to a higher standard of efficiency, it is believed that he should not be re-appointed." The author went on to ease any concerns Figley might have by describing the steps he could take to ensure he retained his position. "I hope that you have your office in first-class condition, and will continue to have it so. If you will bring a delegation to the state and district conventions instructed for Taft and Harris, I will see that you are reappointed."[297] Despite the claims of Roosevelt partisans, the president did not rely on machine-controlled nominating conventions alone in meeting the challenge of his predecessor. Taft won the New York and Indiana primaries by decisive margins. By the end of March he had secured the support of 265 delegates to 27 for his predecessor.[298] When Roosevelt won primaries in Pennsylvania, Illinois, and Nebraska, the president went on the attack in an April 25 speech in Boston, calling the recall of judicial decisions a threat to judicial independence that would expose "to the chance of one popular vote questions of the continuance of our constitutional guarantees of life, liberty and property and the pursuit of happiness."[299] Despite Roosevelt's rally, the president held a narrow plurality of delegates by early summer.[300] One the eve of the Republican Convention in Chicago in June 1912, the party's National Committee met to adjudicate disputes over the delegations of several states. Roosevelt received only 19 of the seats in dispute instead of the 100 or so he thought he deserved. The incumbent president was re-nominated easily, though many delegates sat on their hands rather than vote.[301] Robert M. LaFollette was hardly an objective observer, but he was right in claiming that Roosevelt "never had anything like a majority of the honestly-elected delegates to the convention."[302] That did not stop the former president from setting up his own third-party campaign in the hope that he might yet return to the White House. Following Taft's nomination, Roosevelt's supporters resolved to meet again in Chicago that August. They did so as the Progressive Party.

Indiana Senator Albert Beveridge gave the critical speech of the Progressive convention. He implied that it was incumbent on the national and state governments to see that no child went hungry and no laborer remained jobless. "We have more than enough to support every human being beneath the flag. There ought not to be in this Republic a single day of bad business, a single unemployed workingman, a single unfed child." In addition to eradicating the business cycle, Beveridge proposed to ensure that more of the nation's earnings reach those at the bottom of the scale. "We mean not only to make prosperity steady, but to give to the many who earn it a just share of that prosperity instead of helping the few who do not earn it to take an unjust share. The Progressive motto is, 'Pass Prosperity around.'"

Nor would the caring hands of government be withdrawn when men and women reached the end of their working lives. "What is to become of the family and of the laboring man whose strength has been sapped by excessive toil and who has been thrown upon the industrial scrap heap?" Beveridge did not say what level of government he believed ought to aid the elderly. Instead he announced that the Progressive Party had made a remarkable observation. It believes "that the Constitution is a living thing, growing with the people's growth, strengthening with the people's strength, aiding the people in their struggles for life, liberty and the pursuit of happiness, permitting the people to meet all their needs as conditions change."[303] Implicit in the assertion of growth was the notion that amendments giving new powers to the national government would not be necessary—new constructions of the Constitution would serve the same purpose and enable federal officials to meet the challenges that faced the country.

On the speech's conclusion, the convention broke into sustained applause. Progressives gave Roosevelt a platform that was less utopian than the rhetoric offered by Beveridge, but one that was still beyond anything yet offered by a major party in the United States. It complained that states competed against each other to pass the most lax regulations in an effort to lure industry and advocated the assertion of federal authority over those problems "which have expanded beyond the reach of individual states." It belittled the "extreme insistence" on states' rights by Democrats in their platform and claimed it "demonstrates anew" the inability of that party "to understand the world into which it has survived or to administer the affairs of a union of states which have in all essential respects become one people."[304]

Prescriptions included minimum health and safety standards for the workplace as well as the "exercise of public authority of state and nation, including the federal control over interstate commerce and the taxing power, to maintain such standards." Even Progressives, it seemed, could not bring themselves to assign proposed endeavors to the various levels of American government. The platform also endorsed bans on child labor, a minimum wage for women, "one day's rest in seven for all wage workers," and the "protection of home life against the hazards of sickness, irregular employment and old age through the adoption of a system of social insurance adapted to American use." Once again, it failed to state what level of government ought to perform these tasks. The platform also embraced unions and referendums on laws invalidated by state courts for the purpose of reversing said rulings. The country also needed a graduated income tax as well as one on estates. Owing to the frustration of many Progressives over the machinations of the White House in the primary campaign, the platform endorsed legislation "forbidding federal appointees from holding office in state or national political organizations, or taking part as officers or delegates in political conventions for the nomination of elective state or national officials."[305]

The Socialist Party, by now approaching the height of its influence, could hardly outbid the Progressives, but it made an honest effort. Nominating Eugene V. Debs for president, it called for public ownership of the railroads, telegraph, and telephone companies and the "immediate government relief of the unemployed by the extension of all useful public works," with persons employed therein working an eight-hour day at "prevailing union wages." Employment bureaus, loans to the states for public works, and a graduated income tax were also embraced. Socialists recommended a "non-contributory system of old age pensions, a general system of insurance by the state of all its members against unemployment and invalidism and a system of compulsory insurance by employers of their workers, without cost to the latter, against industrial diseases, accidents and death."[306] With some 450 members of the party holding public office in 1911, including 56 mayors and a congressman, Socialists instilled a deep fear in the other parties of what might be done if the sense of deprivation thought to lay deep in the hearts of the poor was properly exploited.

The Democratic Party was in some ways the most archaic of the four entities competing in 1912, despite the fact that it had the longest history of advancing—or at least professing to advance—the agenda of middle America. In a year that would award the party that offered the most viable solutions to the problems of the twentieth century, the party of Jefferson and Jackson appeared at times reluctant to move beyond the pieties of the nineteenth. Throughout much of 1911, the favorite for the Democratic nomination was Woodrow Wilson. He embodied the party's conflicted outlook. Born in Virginia and raised in Georgia and the Carolinas, Wilson made his way to the northeast where he became a professor at Princeton in 1890. After a brief term as school president, he was elected governor of New Jersey in 1910. The state's bosses saw in the thin-lipped academic a figurehead who would both win the trust of voters and allow them to continue their nefarious activities. For their trouble they received a primary law that undermined their ability to dictate party nominations, a corrupt practices act that made it more difficult to squeeze money from corporations, and a public utilities act that made it harder for gas and electric companies to gouge the public. The governor had his hand in all of it, and the New Jersey bosses were more than willing to support his presidential candidacy—anything to get him out of the state.

Wilson demonstrated a capacity for appeasing dueling constituencies that would be a hallmark of successful Democratic politicians during the twentieth century. Following the 1904 election he opined that the Bryan wing of the party should be "utterly and once for all thrust out of Democratic councils."[307] Wilson counted himself a progressive and his work in New Jersey confirmed the fact; yet he also embraced a restrained approach to federal authority. In his 1906 treatise, *Constitutional Government in the United States*, Wilson warned that a federal child labor law would establish such a broad precedent that it would effectively remove all limits on federal authority with respect to "every particular of industrial organization and action." The only "limitations Congress would observe (after passing a federal child labor law), should the Supreme Court assent to such absurd extravagancies of interpretation, would be the limitations of opinion and circumstance."[308]

Wilson conceded state regulation of business had been inadequate but he insisted that the answer was more effective state laws and possibly reorganization of the state governments. He expressed hope that Americans would reform and invigorate the state governments instead of allowing them to atrophy, just as the states themselves had abandoned their attempts to micromanage their cities.[309] The party's conservatives—those who had supported Cleveland both before and throughout the latter's second term—saw Wilson as one of their own, though their enthusiasm cooled as the primaries began. Southern Democrats appreciated the New Jersey governor's lineage; his campaign was managed by a group of young southerners who had moved to northeastern cities to pursue careers in the law or the newspaper business, including Walter Hines Page, William McCombs, and William G. McAdoo.[310]

In the early months of 1912, it appeared that Wilson had peaked too early. With Roosevelt's entry into the race, the main rationale for the governor's candidacy—that he was the one Democrat moderate enough to win the support of Republicans—vanished.[311] As the Wilson tide ebbed, the Champ Clark tide rose. As Speaker of the House, the Missouri Congressman was the nation's highest-ranking Democratic public official. He had played a critical role in stripping the previous House speaker, Joe Cannon, of his dictatorial powers several months before the Republican electoral debacle of 1910. Clark's prospects improved steadily in early 1912 even as he refused to campaign—Wilson, on the other hand, made hundreds of speeches as he traveled across the country. Clark enjoyed two huge advantages that Wilson could not match: the support of William Jennings Bryan, still the most influential Democratic politician in the country, and the aid of William Randolph Hearst, the nation's dominant newspaper magnate.[312] Clark won primary after primary during the spring of 1912, rolling up a total margin over Wilson of more than 300,000 votes.[313]

Democrats met at the Fifth Regiment Armory in Baltimore in late June 1912. Southern delegations supported Congressman Oscar Underwood of Alabama, chairman of the Committee on Ways and Means. Tammany Hall boss Charles Murphy supported Judson Harmon, governor of Ohio. On the first ballot, Clark won 440 votes, Wilson 324, Harmon 148, and Underwood 117. Thereafter Clark obtained additional support and won majorities on ballot after ballot, but he could not reach the required two-thirds. On the 10th ballot, Charles Murphy switched New York's vote from Harmon to Clark, but the move backfired as it offended Bryan, who loathed machine politicians.[314] Bryan responded by transferring his support from Clark to Wilson on the 13th ballot. The hypocrisy evident in this move was not lost on Clark, who recalled that Bryan sought the support of Murphy and Illinois boss Roger Sullivan in 1908 despite having devoted years to a futile attempt to have Sullivan removed from the Democratic National Committee.[315] Bryan's move appeared pointless for a time as his supporters remained with Clark and the Missourian continued to win majorities on ballot after ballot. Wilson's friends began to urge the governor to withdraw. Wilson called North Carolina editor Josephus Daniels to ask if he should release his delegates. Daniels told Wilson he was sure to be nominated, as Sullivan would soon swing Illinois to Wilson and bring Tom Taggart and Indiana with him.[316]

The suspense extended outside the convention. The country followed the balloting with a degree of enthusiasm normally reserved for prize fights and baseball games, with men "standing around the billboards of newspapers in great crowds, watching the Baltimore struggle."[317] The break finally came on the 43rd ballot when Roger Sullivan cast the 58 votes of Illinois for Wilson, triggering a great roar through the hall—the delegates knew the issue had been decided.[318] The Clark forces were furious, as their candidate had won the Illinois primary with more than 70 percent of the vote (218,483 to 75,527).[319] The ability of Sullivan to overrule the voters of his state stemmed from the fact that delegates were not obligated by law or party rules to cast their ballots in accordance with the results of the primary vote. The move may have stemmed from the support of Wilson forces for Sullivan's delegation in a fight over which of two groups should be admitted from Illinois (the other delegation, the one that was barred, may well have had the stronger claim).

The switch gave Wilson a majority of the delegates. It was not over yet; Sullivan let it be known he would go back to Clark on the 46th or 47th ballot if Wilson did not win the nomination before that time. Southerners who had supported Underwood now fell in line behind Wilson; so did northern delegations.[320] The New Jersey governor finally gained the required two-thirds vote on the 46th ballot.[321] The vice presidential nomination went to Thomas Marshall, governor of Indiana, possibly as the price paid for the support of Indiana boss Tom Taggart.[322] Wilson knew well the origin of his victory and said as much when he confided to Sullivan that he could "never forget Illinois."[323] While numerous historians have credited Bryan for Wilson's nomination, in fact it was the northern bosses who played the decisive role.[324] Clark was bitter and he had reason to be. The Missourian had won majorities on eight ballots, and he was the first Democrat to be denied his party's nomination after receiving a majority of the votes at a presidential nominating convention since Martin Van Buren had fallen short in 1844.[325]

The Democratic Party had turned a corner, but it allowed the Nebraska populist who helped keep it in the wilderness for 16 years to write its platform—the fifth time he had done so.[326] Bryan began with a call for tariff reform; he repeated the old canard dating to Calhoun's time, that the federal government had no power to collect duties for any purpose other than revenue. He proposed a complete ban on corporate campaign contributions and limits on individual contributions. The possibility of rural credits (loans to farmers) should be investigated, along with a measure authorizing national banks to issue mortgages on farm property. Bryan also endorsed federal aid to state and local governments for the construction of postal roads and the extension of rural free delivery.[327]

The Democratic candidate accepted his party's nomination in a speech at Sea Girt, New Jersey, on August 7, 1912. Wilson began by suggesting that tariffs should only be as high as necessary to obtain the revenue necessary to meet expenditures. After denouncing present antitrust laws as "ineffectual," he suggested that action on the "labor question" was necessary but refused to offer any specifics. The governor had work to do on this front; in 1909 he had the temerity to suggest that labor unions impeded improvements in productivity.[328] Wilson thought more money should be spent on developing the nation's waterways. He also called for the national government to promote agricultural and vocational education "in every way possible within its constitutional powers."[329]

The preeminent issue of the campaign was the tariff, perhaps because the cost of living had gone up 20 percent between 1901 and 1910 while wages remained static for most of the period.[330] The Republican debacle of 1910 owed much to inflation, which many blamed on the tariff even though it may have arisen out of an increase in the production of gold.[331] Republicans felt compelled to include a plank in their platform insisting that there was no relationship between the high cost of living and protection.[332] In September, the Democratic National Committee set up an exhibit at 29 Union Square in New York City entitled the "Tariff Chamber of Horrors." The centerpiece was a mock home with furniture that included placards indicating the tariff on each item, e.g., 85 percent for dining room chairs. A card next to an American-made typewriter featured its domestic price ($90) and its foreign price ($55). A dress from a mill owned by a senator (Henry Lippitt of Rhode Island) carried a card indicating that the duty on its cloth ranged from 35 percent to 51 percent. It carried a price of $2.75 in the United States and $1.87 in Britain. Political cartoons, statistics, and quotes rounded out the exhibit.[333] The candidate held up an American-made sewing machine that sold for less abroad ($18) than at home ($30) and began to speak. "You will observe that there are exhibited in this room articles which are sold very much cheaper in other countries—articles of American manufacture—than they are sold in this country, which shows that America is already able to compete in foreign markets, that America has already adjusted her methods of manufacture, her skill, her resources, her brains to the markets of the world, and that at the same time American industry is taxing itself upon practically everything that it uses so heavily as to be at an unnatural advantage in the markets of the world." After leaving the tariff exhibit and moving on to Union Square, Wilson pointed out that workers in the mills of Lawrence, Massachusetts, received an average wage of $8 per week, "and those starvation wages from the point of view of the American cost of living were paid in one of the most protected industries in America." In perhaps his most perceptive remark, Wilson insisted that "to free the government we have to get it disentangled from the interests who profit by the tariff, because the chief trouble with the tariff is not that it has been protective, for it has been much more than protective. It has been one of the most colossal systems of deliberate patronage that has ever been conceived." Wilson promised that he would he call a special session of Congress following his inauguration to revise the tariff.[334]

Wilson turned to the labor question on October 4 in a speech at the Peru, Indiana, railroad station. Denying Republican claims that tariffs had increased wages, he insisted that unions had produced that result—despite the fact that, as he put it, "the organization of labor is not yet legal in the U.S. Anything else can organize. Capital can organize and be sustained by the courts, because sustained by the law. But the organization of labor is not recognized by the law. The courts of this country have held that employers can dismiss their employees for the single reason that they belong to a labor union."[335] Wilson offered no labor program of his own. Like Roosevelt, he had a faculty for describing problems facing the nation while refusing to state what could or should be done to address them at the federal level.

With the Republican vote split, a Democratic victory was inevitable and everyone knew it. Theodore Roosevelt did his best to reach the bantam fighter who seemed to be dancing circles around the Grand Old Party and the Progressives. In a speech at the San Francisco Coliseum on September 14, he belittled Wilson's assertion that the "story of liberty is a history of the limitation of governmental power" as a bit of outworn Jeffersonian dogma. "To apply it now in the United States at the beginning of the twentieth century, with its highly organized industries, with its railways, telegraphs and telephones, means literally and absolutely to refuse to make a single effort to better any one of our social or industrial conditions." Noting Wilson's promise to use the tax power only to obtain revenue, Roosevelt claimed his opponent "is against its use to put of existence the poisonous match industry; he is against its use for the purpose of preventing opium coming into the country; he is against its use for preventing wildcat banking [state bank notes]—in short, he is against its use in every case we now use it to tax out of existence dangers and abuses."[336]

While speaking in Arizona, the former president promised he would call a special session to deal with social welfare issues. Roosevelt conceded that several elements of the Progressive platform, including a minimum wage for women, a ban on child labor, and an eight-hour day law, could be implemented only at the state level. He insisted that Congress ought to act where it could, though even here was noticeably vague. "In the first place, the government itself should be made a model employer; we should have a workmen's compensation act, an act providing for the minimum wage, in short all those things applied to the government service, in the Navy Department, at Panama, everywhere. In the next place, so far as we have power over interstate commerce, the laws should be applied there, too, that is, to the workmen engaged in interstate commerce. In the third place, the City of Washington should be made an example city." Congress ought to turn its attention to "taking care of those people in Washington . . . by enacting into law for the District of Columbia every proposition that the Progressive platform holds, as regards social and industrial justice, so that instead of going as we do now to Germany or Denmark as examples of the successful working of these measures, we shall be able to turn to the federal District of Columbia and shall treat that as an experimental laboratory in social and industrial science, through which we intend to better build up this nation as a whole."[337] The Taft campaign was almost passive in comparison; it relied on time-proven tactics such as campaign posters claiming the last Democratic president (Cleveland) removed 40,000 persons from the pension rolls and cut the pensions of "tens of thousands" of veterans.

Wilson managed to obtain a huge majority in the Electoral College despite winning only 42 percent of the popular vote. He received 100,000 fewer votes than Bryan had in 1908. Democrats won control of both houses of Congress; the Senate fell to them for the first time since 1892. Their presence in northern cities continued to grow with the burgeoning populations therein; Chicago gave the party six congressional seats and Boston five.[338] In a March 1913 article in the *Atlantic*, Francis Leupp wondered if the Republican Party would ever be able to accommodate itself to the goal of "industrial justice" sought by Progressives. He noted that many saw the Constitution itself as impediment, and suggested that in light of charter's expansion by construction over the past 40 years for Republican ends, there was no reason it could not be stretched a bit further for Progressive ends. "If we are able to maintain a federal quarantine in spite of local political boundaries; if the freedom of interstate commerce can be used to nullify the police powers of a state respecting the liquor traffic, or to split aggregations of private capital into fragments with an antitrust statute; if any product of human labor, from a box of phosphorus matches to a state bank note, can be taxed out of existence at the option of Congress, why must we assume that 'constructive statesmanship' may not yet evolve, and judicial 'interpretations' ratify, a mode of readjusting some of the relations of employer and employed in our industries generally?"[339]

On taking office, the president called a special session of Congress for the purpose of revising the tariff. Prospects for substantial revisions were good not only because Democrats controlled both houses but also due to the ratification of the Sixteenth Amendment, which authorized federal income taxes—lost tariff revenue could be replaced with the proceeds of a tax on incomes. (In truth the imposition of income taxes preceded ratification of the Sixteenth Amendment; a 1909 law imposed an income tax on corporations.[340]) The cause was also aided by a large class of freshmen in the House willing to be led and by the fact that southern Democrats hostile to protection chaired most of the key committees. The president gave momentum to the cause when he broke a century of tradition and read his tariff message before a joint session of Congress on April 8, 1913. Lamenting the establishment of an "exclusive market" for the benefit of manufacturers, Wilson called on lawmakers to "abolish everything that bears even the semblance of privilege or any kind of artificial advantage, and put our business men and producers under the stimulation of a constant necessity to be efficient, economical and enterprising, masters of competitive supremacy, better workers and merchants than any in the world."[341] Congress itself proved to be less than the picture of efficiency, as it required six months to hammer out a bill. Democrats divided among themselves over tariffs on wool and sugar; under prodding from the White House they agreed to allow wool duty-free and to reduce the levy on sugar to one cent a pound. Agricultural machinery, clothing, and shoes were placed on the free list. Products made by trusts including steel also came in duty-free. Duties on cotton textiles remained prohibitive due to the influence of southerners.[342] The House passed the measure on May 8 along party lines, 281–139. To everyone's surprise the Senate dropped rates further to an average of about 25 percent.[343] To compensate for the lost revenue, an income tax of 1 to 6 percent was imposed on incomes of more than $4,000.[344] The law allowed deductions for business expenses, interest paid on debts, state taxes, and losses incurred in trade. Interest paid on state and federal bonds was excluded from taxation as income.[345] Prices dropped following the law's enactment. Of more significance in the long run was the gradual replacement of the tariff by the income taxes—paid largely by the wealthy—as the major source of federal revenue. The Revenue Act of 1916 resulted in persons with incomes over $20,000 paying over 95 percent of federal income taxes.[346] Even after high tariffs returned during the 1920s, income taxes provided over two-thirds of federal revenues.[347] With most voters no longer feeling the pinch, their insistence on economy in federal expenditures would dissipate, as the taxes necessary to pay for them fell only on the backs of the wealthy. The experience of the cities would be repeated at the national level: with income taxes paid by only a minority of citizens, the electorate began to look upon the national government as a generous benefactor instead of a ruthless tax collector.

The extension of federal power over the nation's banking system with passage of the National Bank Acts of 1863 and 1864 did not alleviate periodic shortages of credit. In 1906 a commission formed by the American Bankers' Association reported that the present system "does not expand with the need for currency in the crop-moving period, causing stringency, nor contract when the uses for currency are less extensive, causing redundancy."[348] The Panic of 1907 gave further impetus to the cause of reform, as it demonstrated that New York banks were dangerously susceptible during the fall when money was transferred to the West to pay for crops. The Aldrich-Vreeland Act of May 30, 1908, increased the money supply by allowing national banks to issue circulating notes based on municipal bonds as well as commercial paper.[349] The act also established a National Monetary Commission, which proposed a national reserve system in January 1912.

Congressional Democrats began fashioning their own plan for a reserve system shortly after the 1912 election. Led by Carter Glass of Virginia, chairman of the House Banking and Currency Committee, they had no interest in setting up a great central bank that would be controlled by private interests; instead they proposed a decentralized system of reserve banks, each of which would operate independently. Wilson agreed to endorse the measure. On June 23 he asked Congress to enact the a bill that would establish a publicly supervised and decentralized reserve system that would maintain an elastic currency and ensure all parts of the country had adequate credit resources. Bankers objected, preferring the Aldrich Plan's provision for a private central bank and 15 branches controlled by member banks. Southern and western lawmakers wanted to provide for short-term agricultural credits.[350]

Speaking in support of the bill on September 10, 1913, Carter Glass recalled that five times in the last 30 years, "financial catastrophe has overtaken the country." All too often, credit had not been available when it was needed. "The lack of cooperation and coordination among the more than 7300 national banks produces a curtailment of facilities at all periods of exceptional demand for credit." Of the federal reserve board, Glass assured that "no capital stock is provided; no semblance of acquisitiveness prompts its operations; no banking incentive is behind it, and no financial interest can pervert or control [its actions]. It is an altruistic institution, a part of the government itself, representing the American people, with powers such as no man would misuse." He claimed that most of the powers conferred on the board had long been exercised by the secretary of the treasury or the comptroller of the currency. The federal reserve board itself would not perform banking functions. The system would provide credit resources for farmers and it would reduce interest rates in the South and West, where they often reached 12 or even 15 percent, compared to only 3 percent in New York.[351]

Elihu Root was serving his sole term in the Senate. Secretary of war under McKinley and Roosevelt and secretary of state during the latter's second term, Root had also practiced corporate law in New York City, where he became well-acquainted with the attitudes and mindset of the city's bankers. Root spoke in opposition to the federal reserve bill on December 13. He pointed out that nations had been prone to issuing excessive quantities of currency in order to appease those caught up in speculative manias. In his view those who supervised the federal reserve would face enormous pressure to inject too much money into the system, especially during bull markets. The framework of the system would facilitate the issuing of excess currency. He also objected to the federal reserve system as an ill-advised delegation of the power of Congress over the currency and as pledging the credit of the United States to every national bank. It would also encourage speculation by bankers.[352]

A combination of Republicans and conservative Democrats in the Senate reduced the power of the federal reserve board over member banks. It lost the power to set discount rates and instead could only veto changes member banks proposed to make.[353] In the House-Senate conference committee that worked out a final measure to be passed by both chambers, a provision that would have required deposit insurance was stricken at the behest of House Democrats who viewed it as inadequate.[354] The Federal Reserve Act of December 23, 1913, set up a reserve system of 12 districts, each with a federal reserve bank located in a major city within it. National banks were obligated to join; state banks were not. The federal reserve banks would accept deposits from member banks; they could also discount notes and sell bills of exchange as well as government bonds. In addition to being obligated to keep half their reserves in district reserve banks, member banks had to deposit bonds with them in exchange for federal reserve notes. A Federal Reserve Board of seven members appointed by the president had the right to examine the books of member banks. It possessed authority to issue notes redeemable in gold at the Department of the Treasury or in gold or other lawful money at any federal reserve bank. The secretary of the treasury could deposit federal funds in reserve banks but was not obligated to do so. Federal reserve notes replaced the notes of national banks as the primary currency; they were backed by commercial but not agricultural paper. The law dispensed with the National Bank Act's bar against issuing mortgages secured by farm land, though the terms for loans remained formidable—the loans had to be repaid in five years and could not exceed half of the land's value. Most important of all, the federal reserve banks would loan money to member banks during credit shortages.[355] The reserve districts proved to be poorly drawn; as some were in areas devoted to a single crop, member banks within them all demanded money at the same time each year. It was said the cities selected as locations for the reserve banks had been picked because a banker anywhere in the country could reach at least one of them via an overnight night train trip.[356] With passage of the law, the federal government had become the bank of last resort and the backstop in the event of future panics.

With little direct connection to the Treasury Department, the Federal Reserve Board joined the Interstate Commerce Commission as one of only two relatively autonomous federal agencies.[357] The reserve system achieved its goal of providing greater elasticity in credit and promoting the spread of banks to more areas of the country. National banks in the South and West could now borrow money from the federal reserve banks at cheaper rates than they formerly obtained from the banks of Manhattan. The system transferred control over the monetary system from New York to Washington and the 12 regional federal reserve banks. It also signaled the arrival of a period when officials would engage in more direct and energetic manipulation of the nation's money supply, thus adding another element to the ever-growing pecuniary relationship between individual Americans and their national government. Federal reserve notes were not backed 100 percent in gold (instead there was only a 40% reserve requirement). During the coming years, officials reduced the loan reserve requirements of member banks, enabling them to make more loans, and thereby inflating the money supply. Between 1914 and 1920, inflation skyrocketed as national banks greatly expanded their lending. The Federal Reserve banks contributed to the problem by keeping interest rates at artificially low levels, in part due to the need to encourage the sale of bonds during World War I. When they raised rates in 1919 and 1920 to tame runaway inflation, farmers protested and politicians howled. In one sense the reserve system did not go far enough; by allowing state banks to remain outside of the system, it preserved a situation in which the savings of millions of Americans were dependent on the uneven and haphazard regulations of the states.[358]

Some viewed the federal reserve system as a Populist measure designed to provide more credit in rural areas. New York bankers certainly viewed themselves as unfairly targeted. Yet the national government had been subsidizing the great banks of Manhattan for decades—albeit out of necessity—by selling them bonds and depositing money in them. It also assisted if not directly subsidized the great trusts by imposing tariffs that made it expensive if not impossible for Americans to purchase goods from their foreign competitors. The new administration now sought to add its own contribution to the campaign to limit unfair trade practices and check the monopolistic behavior of the trusts. The Federal Trade Commission Act of September 26, 1914, established a Trade Commission that replaced the Bureau of Corporations.[359] It possessed authority to investigate corporations and issue cease-and-desist orders. The law sought to eliminate unfair methods of competition such as mislabeling and conspiracies to maintain prices as well as boycotts. The Commission proved ineffective for several years, in part because of the people placed on it. The Clayton Antitrust Act of October 15, 1914, barred practices that "substantially lessened competition," as well as price discrimination and tying agreements.[360] Many of the acts it prohibited had already been held restraints of trade under the Sherman Act; to some extent the 1914 law simply codified rulings of the federal courts.[361] Factors that led to the law included a desire to advise businesses in advance of illegal practices, the goal of avoiding protracted litigation, and the problem of trusts setting the terms of their own dissolution and thereby ignoring the interests of consumers. The measure as finally enacted appeared to have had its teeth removed and was largely ineffective; instead of an outright ban on price discrimination it merely barred discrimination with intent to "substantially lessen" competition or promote monopoly. In accepting a weak antitrust bill, the president was said to have embraced the approach of Roosevelt over his own—monopolistic practices would be targeted by a commission while trusts and other combinations would not be subject to a new and vigorous antitrust effort. In time the vagueness of the Clayton Act proved that it was a potent law if a poorly drafted one. It made it possible for courts to punish virtually any act designed to give the perpetrator a larger share of the market. The law asked the courts to distinguish between competitive and non-competitive acts, and they were not endowed with the expertise necessary to perform that task.[362]

A meaningless clause of the Clayton Act stemmed from a 1908 Supreme Court decision. In the *Danbury Hatters' Case*, the high court held that the Sherman Act's bar of restraints of trade applied to labor unions. (The United Hatters of North America and the American Federation of Labor staged a boycott of a hat manufacturer.)[363] Section 6 of the Clayton Antitrust Act provided that "the labor of a human being is not a commodity or article of commerce" and that the antitrust laws were not to be construed as barring labor unions from "lawfully carrying out the legitimate objects thereof." It proved to be of little benefit because no court had ever held labor constituted an article of commerce. Section 20 barred the issuing of injunctions by federal judges in labor disputes "unless necessary to prevent irreparable injury to property, or to a property right, of the party making the application." In response, employers pointed to lost profits as the property right that was at risk for irreparable injury.[364] Section 22 required jury trials in contempt of court cases arising out of strikes.

The Democratic Congress also turned its attention to the railroads; the discussion that took place revealed that some viewed corporate securities and even stock exchanges as within the scope of the commerce power. Railroad capitalization had long complicated the task of devising appropriate rates; the lines wished to have rates based on their bloated valuations in order to enable them to charge higher rates, while reformers such as Robert M. LaFollette sought to have valuation based on physical assets alone.[365] Section 16 of the Mann-Elkins Act of 1910 authorized the establishment of a commission to investigate railroad securities.[366] In its report of November 1911, the Railroad Securities Commission called on Congress to enact laws requiring full disclosure of all relevant financial information by the lines before they floated new stock or bond issues. If such measures proved inadequate, federal incorporation of all railroads ought to be considered.[367]

Some wished to go beyond railroads and regulate stock issues of all corporations. During Taft's presidency, the states began enacting blue sky laws designed to prevent fraud; they required the disclosure of information to the public by those offering securities. In 1914, Oklahoma Democratic Senator Robert L. Owen proposed a bill directed at the stock exchanges. Inspired by the Cujo Committee report, the measure barred the use of the mail, telephone, or telegraph to relay information regarding stocks traded on exchanges that did not meet certain conditions. These included disclosure of information regarding corporations and stock issues; the exchanges would also be required to incorporate. Even newspapers containing stock quotes from exchanges that did not comply with the law would be barred from the mails. One lawyer told the *Wall Street Journal* the measure was an attempt to use the postal power to do indirectly what Congress lacked authority to do directly—regulate the exchanges.[368] Members of the Cincinnati Stock Exchange sent a telegram to Ohio Senator Theodore Burton in which they claimed the bill would destroy the securities market.[369] Exchange leaders in New York were also appalled; they claimed the measure would impair their ability to discipline members and called on Washington to regulate the issuance of fraudulent securities by going after corporations directly instead of focusing on them.[370] Thus their preference for an alternate measure proposed by Congressman Sam Rayburn of Texas that required the railroads to submit financial information to the ICC and obtain its approval before they issued new stock or bonds or bought other lines. Rayburn defended his bill on the floor of the House in June 1914. While he denied that its purpose was to protect owners of railroad stocks (an end viewed by many as beyond the commerce power), the Texas congressman pointed out that the lines routinely took on too much debt "to the great detriment of the small stockholder." Rayburn claimed his measure was designed to aid the ICC in formulating rates. The actual worth of railroads—their capitalization—served as a constant source of debate and discussion at ICC hearings, and he believed that "the government has the right to say whether this evidence shall be fictitious."[371] Charles L. Bartlett of Georgia noted that the removal of authority to regulate railroad acquisitions from the states could result in the merger of Kentucky's two main lines, despite a state law that prohibited them from combining.[372] While neither bill passed, witnesses testifying before Congress seemed to realize what was at stake—as the *New York Times* put it, even the Rayburn bill was viewed as the "entering wedge to policies which many thoughtful people believe must sooner or later extend to all companies issuing securities."[373]

The Democratic Party in 1913 continued to derive most of its support from farmers. The agrarian sensibilities of its members ruled its thinking until well into the twentieth century. The view of government held by farmers had changed with the passage of time—from an aversion to public expenditures of all kinds it evolved into an appreciation of (1) the value of roads, railroads, and dredged rivers in getting their products to market; (2) tariff protection to prop up crop prices, though they rarely had any effect; and (3) centralized control of credit and currency to prevent deflation and ensure that farmers had access to the credit they were certain they deserved. Unwilling to wait and see if increased credit resources would be available under the Federal Reserve System, farmers demanded rural credits—federally subsidized loans. In a letter read to House members by one of his aides, the president insisted that the government "should not itself be drawn into legislation for credits based on farm mortgages," as it was "unwise and unjustifiable to extend the credit of the government to a single class of the community."[374] The administration remained adamantly opposed even as a Rural Credits Commission was formed in 1913 and bills were proposed in 1914. As late as 1915 the president objected to what he regarded as "class legislation" designed to favor one group at the expense of others. Farmers became more determined to secure their own bank system. The damage inflicted on the cotton market by World War I caused southern farmers to embrace the idea of federal assistance.[375]

The farm lobby and the lawmakers who spoke for it did their best to present a rural credits bill as a measure that would simply let farmers help themselves. Speaking in the House on February 17, 1914, Georgia Democrat William S. Howard described a system of agricultural banks that would be owned, operated, and managed by farmers: "Under this bill a small number of farmers in a given section can organize a local rural bank with a small capital, whose operations are confined to a small district." A farm-land board would adopt rules and regulations governing the operation of farm land banks. A national farm land bank would "act as a clearing house and reserve agent for all the state and local farm land banks and . . . issue and sell collateral trust bonds or national land bank bonds." Said bonds would be secured by mortgages and deeds of trust on farmland.[376] With an election looming, Wilson dropped his former opposition and went along with the Federal Farm Loan Act of July 17, 1916.[377] When lawmakers initially proposed to buy $250,000 worth of bonds from each bank, Wilson insisted that the amount be increased to $500,000.[378] Congress ended up providing $750,000 to each land loan bank. Persons seeking loans had to organize farm loan associations that would borrow funds on the security of farm land. The associations were liable for mortgages issued to shareholders. Each land bank was authorized to make loans to farmers at below market rates (up to a maximum of 6%). The *Atlanta Constitution* promised that the measure would "benefit ten people where the Federal Reserve Act benefited one."[379]

The federal government had entered into the business of making loans to members of critical electoral groups.[380] This innovation, as much as the use of grants and direct aid later in the century, involved the national government deeply in the affairs of citizens, drained the treasury and, most important of all, warped the marketplace—subsidized activities grew more expensive, thus stimulating the need for more loans. In the case of farmers, it inaugurated a period in which government-backed loans helped maintain an artificially high farm population, worsened the glut of agricultural products, depressed their prices and in turn farm income—exactly the opposite of the goal of these programs. In a February 1917 article in the *Atlantic*, Myron T. Herrick charged that the Farm Loan Act's "intent to subsidize rather than finance agriculture is quite evident." The system "is designed to draw funds from the U.S. Treasury and to issue bonds backed by the government for granting loans to its beneficiaries at low interest rates."[381] Nor did he see any connection between the Constitution and the federal farm loan program—the banks were designated as government depositories and as financial agents of the treasury solely for the purpose of evading legal objections. Herrick charged that the measure delegated to a bureaucracy the right to pledge the government's credit in indefinite amounts.[382] In a 1921 case, the Supreme Court held that the bonds issued under authority of the Farm Loan Act were legal.[383] Justice William R. Day explained that the power of Congress to establish banks when necessary to the exercise of its enumerated powers was well-established. It could also determine the duties and purposes of said banks. Day noted that a provision of the law required the land banks to invest 5 percent of their capital in U.S. bonds. He also offered the rather implausible suggestion that the land banks enhanced the government's ability to raise money.[384] Charles Evans Hughes, then in private practice, prepared an argument claiming that the general welfare clause provided ample authority for the program, but as the issue did not come up in the case, he never submitted the brief.[385] The Farm Loan Act proved a success, at least for those farmers who could meet its somewhat stringent requirements for loans, and it did not drain the treasury. Over a billion dollars in loans were issued by 1925 and the bonds sold by the farm boards became a popular investment—due in part to their tax-exempt status and the steep tax rates imposed on other sources of income during World War I.[386] Further assistance was provided to farmers via the Warehouse Act of August 11, 1916, under which designated warehouses could issue receipts to farmers in an amount equal to up to 80 percent of the value of the crops deposited therein; the receipts could be used as collateral for loans.[387] That an idea vilified when it was known as the sub-treasury scheme in the 1890s could become law with little protest 20 years later indicated how far the country had moved.

Congress had long distributed land sale revenue to the states for agricultural colleges. In 1900 it enacted a law providing for more homestead grants; to replace the lost land sale revenue that formerly went to land grant colleges, it provided that any shortfalls would be met by payments out of the treasury.[388] Thus, the fiction that land sale revenues were exempt from the Constitution was discarded, and a subject beyond the enumerated powers was funded with general revenues. The door to the federal treasury remained only slightly ajar thereafter until 1911 when Congress enacted the first grant-in-aid statute. It provided grants to the states for the maintenance of forests near the headwaters of navigable streams.[389] The Smith-Lever Act of 1914 appropriated $480,000 for instruction in agriculture and home economics; states had to appropriate an amount equal to or greater than the federal grant they received. Each state seeking a share of the funds was required to submit its plans for teaching the above-mentioned subjects to the secretary of agriculture.[390] The chief bulwark of American federalism—the limitation of federal activity to the powers listed in Article I—had been breached. Lawmakers rushed through the gap, though they continued to cite one or more of the enumerated powers as authority for novel appropriations when possible. Such was the case with the revival of a federal presence in road construction.

The nation's roads had long been a disgrace. At the turn of the century, there were only 200 miles of paved roads outside of the cities.[391] The arrival of the automobile stirred in the public a new demand for improved roadways, as it did little good to have the latest Packard when it was difficult to drive across three counties without getting stuck. After South Carolina lawyer James Byrnes won election to Congress in 1910, he drove from his home state to the national capital; it took him a whole day to cross Virginia.

In bad weather, he spent four days getting from Aiken, South Carolina, to Washington, DC.[392] The revival of federal involvement in road construction began with an 1893 law that appropriated $10,000 "to enable the secretary of agriculture to make inquiries in regard to a system of road management throughout the U.S."[393] The office of road inquiry was formed shortly thereafter; it later became the Bureau of Public Roads. The Bureau provided technical advice regarding road construction to state officials. Its employees spent much of their time lobbying Congress to establish a national highway program.

At the turn of the century the "Good Roads Movement" called on state governments to supervise and fund the construction of roads and impose new taxes for the maintenance of them. It asked Congress to assist in the endeavor. Several states in the Northeast and Midwest took over the task of road-building from counties, and funding for roads increased by a factor of 10 between 1902 and 1915.[394] Constitutional concerns delayed federal action until a March 1, 1912, appropriation provided money for the improvement of rural roads over which mail was or might be delivered, despite arguments that the matter ought to be left to the states.[395] In 1914 the Lincoln Highway Association enlisted the aid of auto manufacturers, road construction companies, and the public in a scheme to obtain federal funds for the building of a national highway to be named for the 16th president.[396] Other entities that lobbied the national government to fund road construction included the National Grange, the Country Life movement, and farmers annoyed at having proposed rural delivery routes rejected by the Post Office due to the poor condition of the designated roads.[397] By 1916, Americans owned at least 4.8 million cars.[398] They too saw the wisdom of a measure that promised to reduce flat tires and breakdowns.

Following Wilson's election, Congress took up a grant-in-aid bill in designed to promote road construction. James Byrnes spoke in favor of the measure in February 1914. While he believed that "it is the duty of a state to build and maintain its roads," he held that "if the federal government is to use the roads of the states in discharging its governmental functions of carrying and delivering the mails, it should aid and cooperate with the states in the construction and maintenance of the roads." He acknowledged that "in the South there were many who regarded it as paternalism and as an encroachment upon the powers of the states, while in other sections, as well as in the South, it was argued that constitutionally the government could not aid in the construction of highways. A still larger body of men contended that if the government ever embarked upon such an undertaking it would go into bankruptcy." More recently, "these constitutional objections have disappeared. It is conceded that the government has the power to construct and maintain post roads, military roads, and roads used for interstate commerce, and if it has the power to construct them it has the power to aid the state in constructing such roads. The pork-barrel fears have also been so greatly allayed that today the sentiment in favor of federal aid is as universal as the enthusiasm for good roads."[399] Byrnes later cited the wear that was imposed on the sand and clay roads of South Carolina by trucks from out of state in support of federal funds for the construction and maintenance of public highways.[400] The notion that Congress had authority to fund road construction had been embraced in Washington for a brief period during the early nineteenth century, when lawmakers provided funds for turnpikes including the Cumberland Road. Federal aid for roads disappeared by the late 1840s, as Democratic majorities in Congress refused to buy into the fiction that the commerce clause bestowed authority to carve up the country with roads and canals. Doubts over the commerce clause as a source of authority for appropriations of money for roads may explain why the Good Roads Act of July 11, 1916, by its own terms constituted an exercise of the postal power—though the idea that a power to establish post offices constituted authority for road-building had also long been doubted. The law appropriated $75 million over five years to aid states in the construction of "rural postal roads."[401] Urban areas were excluded and the states had to agree to maintain the roads. Any rural route "over which the U.S. mails now are or may hereafter be transported" was eligible for funds. States grasped at the offer; some removed clauses that barred deficit spending from their constitutions so they could make the appropriations that were a condition for obtaining federal funds.[402]

The Smith-Hughes Act of February 23, 1917, provided matching grants for vocational education.[403] To obtain funds, states had to establish or designate boards that would work with the newly formed federal Board for Vocational Education. These boards had to submit to federal officials detailed plans describing the facilities where the instruction would take place and explaining how instructors would be educated in their areas of expertise. Minimum standards for teacher qualifications would be devised by the federal Board. Within 15 years over a million students were attending schools that received federal funds. Half studied trade and industry, a quarter studied agriculture, and the remainder devoted themselves to home economics.[404] In 1916 Congress appropriated money for the promotion of sanitation and health in rural areas.[405] By 1930 demonstration projects had taken place in 204 counties in 24 states.[406] The legality of the grant-in-aid appropriations passed during the second decade of the century received precious little discussion in Congress. When the matter was raised, proponents pointed to the laws turning land sale revenue over to the states that dated from the Civil War, i.e., the Morrill College Land Grant Act of

1862, despite the fact that the new grant programs involved general revenues and not land sale receipts.[407]

Democrats proved less willing to wield federal power aggressively in other areas. The number of lynchings that occurred each year had dropped from its turn-of-the-century peak but remained high and prosecutions were rare. Some talked of a federal anti-lynching law, and federal action seemed both necessary and appropriate—it was for such problems that the equal protection clause had been designed. No legislation was forthcoming; while Democrats had evolved in their attitudes toward federal authority in other areas, they continued to oppose efforts to assert national power for the benefit of blacks. During the 1912 campaign Woodrow Wilson assured Oswald Villard, editor of the *Nation*, that blacks would receive appointments and promised to speak out against lynching but he insisted that the problem was beyond the purview of the federal government.[408] Despite the fears of some, blacks in the federal civil service were not turned out en masse by the Wilson administration. Those who remained in the employ of the national government were treated to the spectacle of segregated government offices, beginning with the Bureau of the Census, the Post Office, and the Bureau of Printing and Engraving. Some officials assigned black workers to separate offices prior to 1913; the Wilson administration departed from previous practice in making it official policy.[409] Applicants for federal places were required to submit photos so that their race would be known.[410] Going to such lengths to gratify the prejudices of civil servants and cabinet officers constituted a waste of tax dollars as well as a viciously immoral practice, but the policy was put into effect with nary a protest from the press. Even more appalling were the excuses; officials cited the need to protect blacks from discrimination. The president was said to believe that black men and white women must be separated. Wilson's thinking was revealed by his response when Villard asked him to appoint a national commission on race. Wilson refused; he believed such a move would alienate southern senators.[411]

Somewhat more surprising was the president's acquiescence in the use of federal offices by local political machines in their attempts to fight the cause of reform. Wilson had long professed to oppose "boss politics.[412] In the South the president had received critical support from reform elements. They sought the administration's assistance in the form of federal jobs, but received only crumbs. Instead "courthouse cliques" or other groups linked to railroads or liquor interests received federal patronage, strengthening them immeasurably.[413] Perhaps because of its fear of the opposition, the administration allied with the strongest faction of the party in each state, which tended to be the local Democratic machine.[414] Such was its concern that the administration refused to add more jobs to the U.S. Civil Service.

The 1914 midterm elections were the first held following enactment of the Seventeenth Amendment, which provided for the popular election of senators. The Democratic majority in the Senate grew but the party lost 60 seats in the House. Republicans did well throughout the North despite the continuing presence of Progressive candidates on the ballot. A sense of unease regarding the president's reelection extended into 1916, and these fears were in part responsible for the attempt to gratify the farm lobby with the Federal Farm Loan Act. The party's other key constituency, labor, awaited its turn. The president had been sympathetic to the extent that the federal system allowed it. He sent troops to intervene in a Colorado mine strike in 1914 at the request of the governor but the soldiers disarmed private guards employed by the Colorado Fuel and Iron Company as well as strikers. The Department of Justice refused to prosecute contempt cases against unions that initiated strikes. It also turned down requests to have federal marshals protect private property at risk during work stoppages, even after federal judges issued injunctions barring the destruction of said property. The Justice Department took the position that unless the property was in the custody of the federal government, it did not have authority to deploy marshals for the protection of said property even when ordered by courts to do so.[415] Legislative action aiding labor included the Clayton Act's limitation of the use of injunctions and its provision for jury trials in contempt cases, an eight-hour day law for employees of federal contractors, and the Seaman's Act of March 4, 1915.[416] Congress began regulating the treatment of seamen in 1790 when it enacted a law requiring written contracts stating the duration of voyages and establishing minimum provisions for each sailor.[417] Laws regulating the relations of sailors with their employers have been described as exercises of the admiralty jurisdiction of Congress despite the fact that the only reference to admiralty in the Constitution is in Article III, which describes the structure and jurisdiction of the federal judiciary.[418] Others viewed laws regulating the wages and working conditions of seamen as exercises of the commerce power; if this description was accurate, they constituted a precedent for labor legislation of extraordinary potential.[419] The 1915 Seaman's Act established maximum hours and the minimum provisions that must be provided to each seaman; it also mandated safety measures such as lifeboats and reduced the severity of punishments to which sailors were subjected for desertion and disobedience.[420]

In 1914, lawmakers also took up a bill banning items produced by child labor from interstate commerce. Wilson withheld his support because he regarded it as beyond the authority of Congress. In a note to aide Joseph Tumulty, the president agreed to see a group of prominent lawyers who supported the bill; he confessed that he expected their efforts to secure his support for the cause would be in vain, as "no child labor law yet proposed has seemed to me to be constitutional."[421] Southerners opposed the bill while northerners embraced it, in part because the use of child labor in the South exacerbated the sharp wage gap between the two sections that was causing manufacturers to move to southern states where labor costs were lower. Congressional hearings saw representatives of textile manufacturers in the South warn that passage of the measure would deprive poor families of income and reduce many of them to destitution. *U.S. v. Knight* was cited for the proposition that manufacturing remained beyond the scope of federal authority.[422] Manufacturers opposed the bill in part because they realized if Congress could ban items from interstate commerce because they were produced by children, it might assume the right to ban items because they were produced by persons laboring more than eight hours a day or receiving less pay than Congress thought adequate.[423] A child labor bill passed the House in February 1916 but appeared doomed to failure in the Senate until Progressives let it be known to one of the president's aides that their support for Democrats in the upcoming election depended on passage of the bill. Wilson pleaded with Senate Democratic leaders to allow the chamber to vote on it. With less than complete enthusiasm they granted his wish. The Senate passed the measure and the president signed the Child Labor Act of 1916 on September 1. It barred the shipping or delivering for shipment in interstate or foreign commerce any article produced at an establishment that employed children of 14 years of age or younger or children between 14 and 16 who worked more than eight hours a day. The Labor Department was authorized to inspect any facility producing goods for interstate commerce to determine if the act was being violated.[424]

As the events surrounding its passage demonstrated, the Child Labor Act had more to do with the importance of Progressives to the Democratic coalition than labor, though the removal of children from the workforce was prized by unions as relieving downward pressure on wages. Labor would receive its own gift from Democrats in 1916, but the gratuity was not one that had been sought. Rather it constituted an ad hoc response to a crisis, and a somewhat unseemly bid for votes on the eve of an election many expected the president to lose. In the summer of 1916 four railroad unions agreed to stage a strike commencing on Labor Day after the railroads refused to agree to a new contract cutting the standard workday from 10 hours to eight with no cut in pay and time-and-a-half for overtime (150% of the normal hourly wage for each hour worked overtime).[425] Believing that an export boom gave them the upper hand, the unions refused to have the dispute mediated by the newly formed Board of Mediation and Conciliation that had been established for the purpose of resolving railroad labor disputes despite the fact that it had already established a good track record.[426] Anticipating a strike, the railroads asked the president to provide deputy marshals to help them protect their property but he refused. On August 18 railroad officials met with the president. When they asked to have the matter submitted to mediation, the president compared them to a former student of his who claimed that Wilson's refusal to give him a passing grade would result in the death of his invalid mother. The strike was the fault of the railroads in the president's view, just as the failing grade was the fault of the student.[427] The next day, Wilson issued a public statement calling on the railroads to grant the unions' demand for an eight-hour day immediately; he suggested the matter of overtime pay ought to be referred to a commission.[428]

As Labor Day approached with no solution imminent, Wilson was reported to be seeking higher freight rates for the railroads in the hope it would convince the lines to accept an eight-hour day. There was talk of adding additional commissioners to the ICC to ensure it approved an application for a rate increase. The *Nation* recalled that no politician at the national level had ever lost an election due to the hostility of a labor union and called on the president to stand up to the railroad brotherhoods.[429] As the major lines prepared reorganization plans that would enable them to continue operating with only a fifth of their normal workforce, the president addressed a joint session of Congress. He asked lawmakers to enact a law making the eight-hour day "the legal basis alike for work and wages" among those operating trains engaged in interstate commerce; he also requested legislation explicitly authorizing the ICC to increase rates to help the lines meet the increased costs that would come with a wage hike.[430] Congressman William C. Adamson proposed a measure designed to meet the president's request. New York Republican William S. Bennet warned of the precedent the bill would set: "Today you are trying to fix the pay of 400,000 men employed in one industry, to give them an increase of twenty-five percent. If you fix the pay of those 400,000 men today, you must fix the pay tomorrow of the remainder of the 2,000,000 in that industry. If you fix the pay of the 2,000,000 men tomorrow, within a short time you will have to fix the pay of every employee of every factory in the U.S. that manufactures goods to go into interstate commerce."[431] Congressman James Heflin of Alabama defended the president—Wilson was only trying to prevent a strike before it occurred while his predecessors waited to act until work stoppages began.[432] In the Senate Porter McCumber of North Dakota wondered, "if every employee of a railway company [is] engaged in interstate commerce? Is the man who drives the president of the railway to his office engaged in interstate commerce? Where is your dividing line? For instance, we will say that the people who operate the trains are certainly engaged in interstate commerce; but is the switchman, the telegrapher, are the coal handlers, engaged in interstate commerce?"[433]

The bill became law on September 3. It provided that effective January 1, 1917, eight hours "shall be deemed a day's work and the measure or standard of a day's work for the purpose of reckoning the compensation for services of all employees of common carriers via railroad."[434] Additional work would require compensation at 150 percent of the normal hourly rate. After signing the measure, the president traveled to Hodgenville, Kentucky, to accept on the nation's behalf a cabin designed to replicate Abraham Lincoln's birthplace. He was greeted along the route by delegations of trainmen expressing their gratitude for the law.[435] The *New York Times*, which normally supported the administration, was less enthused. It charged that the "blackmailing of the whole nation under the threat of a strike, the extortion from the nation's legislature of a special act granting the demands of the brotherhoods without time to inquire into its justice or practicability, puts upon the country an intolerable humiliation. It reduces 100,000,000 people to a condition of vassalage no longer permitted to make laws that freely express their will, but held up, as the highwayman's victim is held up, and forced to instant compliance with the terms imposed upon them by the leaders of organizations comprising only 400,000 of their number."[436]

The *Washington Post* regretted the circumstances that produced the measure but complemented Wilson for resolving the standoff, as a bad law can be modified or repealed, but a nationwide railroad strike "once in effect, could not be called off before it had worked immense loss and hardship. It is the old alternative of clinging to a theory or facing and mastering a condition."[437] The *Chicago Daily News* did not agree. It warned that "a peace so purchased, a peace of this contemptible quality, must necessarily be temporary, fear ridden (and) futile."[438] In an editorial that October endorsing Wilson's opponent, the *North American Review* noted an overlooked effect of the Adamson Act—it would likely result in higher railroad fares and rates for the president's own supporters. "It was he, the President of the United States, who deliberately proposed the mulcting of the great body of his constituency, the millions of low-paid workingmen, farmers, professional men, teachers, clerks, saleswomen and toilers in sweat shops no less than the well-to-do, in the interest, not even of a class, but of a class within a class, comprising four hundred thousand voters, without cost to the companies or to the shippers, who were to comprise the other parties to the conspiracy."[439] The question of what causes prices to rise or fall is a complicated one, but it may presumed that the railroads did not propose to absorb themselves the full cost of the pay hikes that resulted from the law. As Republicans found when they imposed steep tariffs, putting money into the pockets of certain voters inevitably required taking it out of the pockets of others.

The railroads tested the law in court; a federal judge held it unconstitutional on November 22. After the matter reached the Supreme Court, the justices did not issue a ruling immediately. With railroad unions threatening yet another strike, they relented in March 1917. A five-man majority found the law constitutional.[440] In his opinion for the Court, Chief Justice Edward White explained that "if acts which, if done, would interrupt, if not destroy, interstate commerce may be by anticipation legislatively prevented . . . the power to regulate [commerce] may be exercised to guard against the cessation of interstate commerce threatened by a failure of employers and employees to agree as to the standard of wages, such standard being an essential prerequisite to the uninterrupted flow of interstate commerce."[441] He noted that the commerce power had already been used to regulate the relationship between railroads and their employees via the Hours of Service Act, the Safety Appliance Act, and the Employers' Liability Act.[442]

Justice Mahlon Pitney authored a withering dissent that was joined by Justice Willis Van Devanter. In his view the law conflicted with the due process clause of the Fifth Amendment, which, like the Fourteenth Amendment, protected freedom of contract.[443] A more substantial objection stemmed from the law's lack of a relationship with the commerce clause powers of Congress. As Pitney noted, the law "removes no impediment or obstruction from the way of traffic or intercourse, prescribes no service to the public, lays down no rule respecting the mode in which service is to be performed, or the safeguards to be placed about it, or the qualifications or conduct of those who are to perform it. In short, it has no substantial relation to or connection with commerce, no closer relation than has the price which the carrier pays for its engines and cars or for the coal used in propelling them." The measure was instead a regulation of the "internal affairs of common carriers, precisely as if an act were to provide that the rate of interest payable to the stockholders [should be] decreased." Pitney suggested that the Hours of Service Act of 1907 derived its constitutional basis from the fact that there is a direct relationship between hours worked by railroad employees and the safe operation of railroads. The same was true of the Employers' Liability Act of 1908, which was upheld on the theory that it would cause employers to avoid negligent conduct, thereby producing increased safety for the traveling public as well as employees. The notion that there was a relationship between increased pay of railroad employees and safety was "fanciful." It was no more reasonable than the assumption that forcing the railroads to pay 25 percent more for locomotives would promote safety. Nor did the setting of railroad rates by public authorities provide a precedent for the law. "Every member of the public is entitled to be served, and rates are established by public authority in order to protect the public against oppression and discrimination. But there is no common right on the part of the trainmen to demand employment from the carriers, nor any right on the part of the carriers to compel the trainmen to serve them."[444]

The opinion was greeted with relief by many Americans. Some—including railroad officials—dared to predict that the survival of the Adamson Act ensured that the country would never again have to endure a railroad strike.[445] Writing in the *Cornell Law Review*, Charles Burdick suggested that the path now seemed open for Congress to regulate wages in any industry when labor strife threatened to interrupt interstate commerce.[446] If the Adamson Act seemed an unprecedented exercise of the commerce power, it also constituted yet another expansion of the ever-growing pecuniary relationship between Congress and the American people. Railroad employees were added to civil servants and pensioners as persons whose fortunes depended on the generosity of Congress. The nation's manufacturing workers had also been in this position as well for the last half century, or at least they were told as much by advocates of protection. The political consequences of this state of affairs were demonstrated in a prescient article in the *Atlantic* of February 1915, when author Samuel O. Dunn attacked the increasingly popular idea of having the national government take over critical industries including railroads, coal mines, telegraphs, and telephones. Such a momentous step would, he warned, make the wages paid in those industries a political issue—as it must be with four million persons added to the federal payroll.[447] Persons working in those critical industries, as well as their family members and friends, would favor or oppose lawmakers merely because they supported, or failed to support, their demand for wage hikes. "To inject the wages and conditions of employment of from two to four million voters into politics would be to inject a most corrupting and demoralizing influence. Elections and legislation should turn on questions affecting the welfare of the entire public, never on issues affecting the selfish interests of but a part of it."[448] That workers in publicly owned industries would vote for whomever promised them higher wages and disregard other issues seemed a harsh charge, but 50 years of tariff politics demonstrated that Americans were more than willing to let their fortunes determine their votes. The Adamson Act revealed that Congress did not have to take over an industry to exercise political influence over its employees; it could simply enact laws regulating wages within it.

During early 1916, with the child labor bill still in doubt and the idea of a federal law imposing higher wages on the railroads still unimagined, the upcoming presidential election promised to turn on events overseas. The European powers commenced a war in August of 1914; within a year it settled down into a stalemate that saw both sides suffer a million casualties or more each year. German U-boats began sinking passenger vessels in the Atlantic, and the president had to threaten war before the Imperial Navy suspended the practice. Americans of Irish and German origin as well as many others—most of the country west of the Appalachians, in fact—believed the British were trying to manipulate the United States into going to war and opposed participation in the conflict. Progressives saw the war as threatening their agenda. Other Americans recalled that German troops rounded up and shot civilians in Belgium—a country they had invaded merely because it provided a suitable route into northern France—and the Imperial Navy's sinking of passenger ships and insisted that the French and British should be supported in their effort to defeat Germany.

The president knew that war would be politically disastrous. Progressives would likely decide the election. They had not returned to the Republican Party, but they had not joined the Democrats either. The cessation of U-boat attacks on American ships enabled the president to walk back from the brink of war with Germany; still he had taken steps to put the country on a war footing, thereby alienating many Progressives. Most offensive to the peace camp was the president's January 1916 tour of the country urging "preparedness" and the expansion of the army pursuant to the National Defense Act of 1916.

The first of several moves by the president in 1916 that helped secure his relationship with Progressives was his nomination of Louis Brandeis for the Supreme Court in January. The move elicited a grotesque overreaction from conservative lawyers such as former president Taft and Elihu Root.[449] Brandeis had made the mistake of habitually placing his formidable legal talents on the side opposite railroads and other powerful institutions; for his trouble he was treated as a radical. He had also served as an advisor to Wilson during the 1912 campaign and was a prominent opponent of trusts. Six former presidents of the American Bar Association wrote letters to the Senate claiming Brandeis was unfit for the high court. It was true that the Kentucky-born lawyer played a role in converting federal courtrooms into legislative chambers with the famous "Brandeis brief" he filed in the *Muller* case. Yet, if the reliance on social science data as a guide to interpreting the Constitution seemed odd, the fact was that Brandeis had been forced into that position by the Court's holding in *Lochner* and other cases that the constitutionality of economic regulations depended on their reasonableness. Perhaps the only legitimate grounds for criticism was the role Brandeis played in denying the railroads badly needed rate increases. When ICC hearings were held at the customhouse in New York City in 1910, the "people's lawyer" used a combination of demagoguery and junk science to convince the commissioners that the financial problems of the lines could be solved through more efficient management—the railroads should not be granted the rate hikes they sought. Brandeis treated the hearings as a trial and railroad executives as defendants. He brought in manufacturing executives to testify regarding the efficiencies that might be obtained by using assembly-line techniques despite the fact that they had no relevance whatsoever to the operation of railroads.[450]

The Senate Judiciary Committee approved the nomination on a party line vote, 10–8. It appeared for a time that the Kentucky-born lawyer would join that group of men who had elicited the disapproval rather than the approbation of the Senate. The fact that the nominee was Jewish did not help matters. Senator Lee Overman of North Carolina, temporary chairman of the Judiciary Committee, was said to be inclined to vote against Brandeis. Time worked in favor of the nominee. His opponents could come with nothing more than a preference for representing unions rather than corporations, and the nomination went through, 47–20.[451] The support of Progressives for the president was also strengthened by the successful nomination of U.S. District Judge John H. Clarke of Ohio for another vacancy on the Supreme Court. They were also appreciative of the fact that Wilson brought the 10-year struggle over a child labor bill to a successful conclusion. With farmers grateful for the Farm Loan Act and railroad workers satiated by the Adamson Act, the bases seemed to have been covered.

Republicans remained in disarray in large part because the Progressive party refused to disappear. Theodore Roosevelt tried in secret to obtain the nomination of both parties. When the Progressives alone nominated him, he refused to accept the honor and the new party lost what little cohesiveness it possessed. Republicans settled on Charles Evans Hughes, who had been appointed to the Supreme Court in 1910 by Taft following a successful stint as governor of New York. While on the high court Hughes exhibited an appropriately deferential outlook toward legislative bodies, both state and national, and Republicans could claim with some justice that he represented the forward-thinking wing of the party, or at least what was left of it. The party aided their candidate with a platform that embraced all the latest innovations in federal power, including vocational education and the child labor bill.[452]

The Republican cause was hurt by divisions within the party over how far the country should go in preparing for hostilities that might never occur. Northeastern Republicans wanted to move forward with an expansion of the armed forces, while Midwest Republicans opposed the idea. The greatest impediment to the Republican campaign was Hughes himself, or rather his refusal to enlighten the country as to what his policies might be. Whether this stemmed from the reticence of a former judge (Hughes resigned from the Supreme Court to run) or merely the conviction that he did not need to risk his election with specifics remains unknown. Instead the candidate satisfied himself with denunciations of the president's policies, and structured them in such a way as to reveal almost nothing about what he thought should be done.[453] Editor William Allen White later recalled taking a walk with Hughes in Estes Park, Colorado, in the spring of 1916. The former justice asked White how he should express his "sympathy with the Progressive movement." White rattled off a list of measures Hughes could endorse, including old age pensions, a maximum hours law for women, a minimum wage law, and the child labor bill. Hughes proceeded to discuss these items in detail but he refused to say what he thought of them. Nor did he mention them afterwards. "The pressure from the right was with him, always, in his campaign, and he had not time nor strength to beat it down."[454]

When Democrats held their national convention in St. Louis in mid-June, the delegates commended the president for maintaining the peace. The platform announced the party's support for the child labor bill (it had not yet been approved by Congress), a federal bureau of safety in the Department of Labor, suffrage for women, money for road construction, an expanded role for the national government in assisting persons seeking employment, and a law prohibiting the shipment of prison-made goods across state lines.[455] The revolutionary legislation enacted during July and August enabled Democrats to claim they had enacted every major plank of the 1912 Progressive platform. Former members of that fading party announced their support for Wilson.[456] For a time it appeared it would not be enough. As the fall campaign began Hughes was expected to win by most people, including the bookies. The Republican victory in the September state election in Maine cemented this conviction. While unwilling to divulge his own plans, Hughes castigated the president in harsh terms. He dismissed the Adamson Act as a "force bill" and claimed that "the demand by the administration for such legislation as the price of peace was a humiliating spectacle. It was not only a serious misuse of official power but a deplorable abdication of moral authority." The administration did not even investigate the matter as it promised, but instead sat on its hands until the eve of the strike and then demanded that Congress give the railroad unions all they wanted. Hughes thought the matter should have been submitted to mediation. He dismissed the child labor law as ineffective and suggested the issue was one for the states.[457] In a September 30 speech, the president claimed credit for keeping the United States out of the war and his support rose immediately. Democrats nationwide embraced the phrase "he kept us out of war." William Jennings Bryan managed to serve as both Secretary of State and as head of the peace faction until he resigned in anger over what he saw as the president's aggressive conduct toward Germany. Nevertheless he campaigned enthusiastically, secure in the belief that Wilson was more likely to avoid war than Hughes. Democrats also profited from Theodore Roosevelt's pronouncements regarding the need to aggressively defend the country's neutral rights. Wartime prosperity and shortages in Europe further aided the president's cause—farmers profited immensely from the high prices they obtained for their crops (Russian exports of grain had been curtailed). The endorsements of farm organizations helped the president as well.[458] Wilson won the election, with 9.1 million votes to 8.5 million for Hughes. The Electoral College margin was razor-thin and the contest was the first decided by California. It appeared that Democrats had succeeded in building the South-West coalition they had tried and failed to construct in 1896.[459] William Allen White claimed the lack of appreciation for Progressive issues displayed by Hughes proved fatal in the Plains and the Midwest.[460] The Democratic majority in the House dropped to six, but the party retained a healthy majority in the Senate.

The attitude of Progressives toward federal power was revealed in an article published in the *Sewanee Review* on the eve of the election. Author Wilmer T. Stone contrasted the American system, which he saw as ridden by greed, public corruption, and labor strife, with those of the great nations of Europe. Germany provided a striking contrast as its "claim to greatness lies principally in its ideal of economic justice between the various classes of her population; in the disinterested reverence of and service to the state on the part of all."[461] He claimed the support of the laboring classes in Germany for the war effort arose out of the fact "that the government has been an instrument for the furtherance of their economic welfare."[462] France possessed a government that derived popular support from the ample infrastructure it provided, including roads, canals, state forests, rural credit institutions, public utilities, abattoirs, and a national school system.[463]

Stone turned to the United States and offered a view of the future that revealed how far Progressives had strayed, or proposed to stray, from the American political tradition and in particular its federal system. He predicted that the national government would eventually condemn and buy the nation's mineral sources, as well as oil, gas, and water power sites. This would be followed by the gradual disappearance of state lines "and a gradual transference of all economic control, by constitutional amendment if necessary, to the central government." Stone also expected to see federal regulation of labor conditions, including minimum wage and maximum hour laws, public employment bureaus, and federal insurance covering death, disability and unemployment, as well as a national system of roads and federal supervision of education.[464] He acknowledged that an expanded central government controlled by the type of politicians who plagued the country at present would be a disaster. "With the horrible examples of pension abuses, the pork barrel, the army and navy wastes, municipal grafts and franchise stealing, one can imagine what would happen if our present type of politicians got their fingers in national insurance, railroad management, and coal and iron production. However, there is a new type of public man—statesman rather than politician—coming into power, and a great awakening in public interest in civil affairs has already brought some minor changes in political organization, especially in city government."[465] Alas, Stone did not see fit to identify any of these "statesmen." He acknowledged that constitutional changes might be necessary for the national government to take up the duties he proposed to assign to it; perhaps "a great national disaster" might result in the calling of a constitutional convention for the purpose of enhancing federal authority. In the alternative, "piecemeal changes may so break the spell of tradition, that a Congress of the new progressive type of statesmen may voluntarily take such a step."[466]

FEDERALISM AND THE WEIGHT OF WAR

World War I was not the "great national disaster" Stone contemplated, but it accelerated the process of centralization. Once it became clear in late July 1914 that efforts to preserve the peace would fail, Treasury Secretary William G. McAdoo convinced the New York Stock Exchange to suspend trading to prevent Europeans from liquidating their American assets and draining the nation's gold reserves. It remained closed for four months, though limited informal trading continued and large amounts of gold were transferred overseas.[467] More serious dislocations arose out of a severe reduction in trade with continental Europe. The national government attempted to instill confidence by entering the insurance business; on September 2, 1914, Congress established the Bureau of War Risk Insurance in the Treasury Department. It was authorized to insure American ships and cargo against the risk of war whenever private parties could not obtain it in the private marketplace on "reasonable terms."[468] The availability of insurance could not alter the fact of a blockade imposed on Germany by the Royal Navy. As President Wilson had declared America neutral, the country possessed the legal right to continue trading with Germany so long as the goods involved could not be devoted to the war effort. Britain professed to comply with the 1909 Declaration of London and its protections for neutral shipping, but it expanded the list of contraband items subject to seizure beyond the categories contemplated by that agreement. The Royal Navy detained ships heading for neutral ports on the theory that goods contained therein would ultimately reach Germany. All trade between America and Germany, even indirect trade, was brought to a halt. In sum the British violated—obliterated—the neutral rights of the United States. Some called on the president to suspend sales of munitions to Great Britain. He chose not to do so; thereafter the United States supplied the

British and French with enormous quantities of arms. In 1915 the State Department dropped its opposition to loans to belligerents, and American banks began making huge loans to Britain and France. Two billion dollars would be loaned to them by the spring of 1917. Much of the funds came back to the United States as payment for war supplies, and the economy received a boost from the explosion in trade with the Allies.

In early 1915, Great Britain added foodstuffs to the list of items it refused to allow neutrals to ship to Germany; in response the Germans imposed a submarine or "U-boat" blockade of the British Isles. The German navy commenced attacking and sinking passenger ships. On May 1 the Germans warned the United States that Americans should not travel on ships of belligerents. Six days later on May 7, a U-boat sank the British steamer *Lusitania* off the coast of Ireland, and 1,198 passengers died, including 124 Americans. Before the war was over, 209 Americans would lose their lives to U-boat attacks. Wilson responded to the sinking of the *Lusitania* by sending the Germans a note insisting they abandon unrestricted submarine warfare and pay reparations for the lost lives. The Germans claimed the ship was carrying contraband and insisted that circumstances justified surprise U-boat attacks on all shipping. In response Wilson issued a second note demanding that the Germans promise to refrain from such acts in the future and denying circumstances existed that warranted the sinking of passenger ships. The note was phrased too aggressively for Secretary of State William Jennings Bryan, who thought Germany had a right to prevent contraband from reaching Britain and France. Bryan resigned; Wilson and new Secretary of State Robert Lansing sent the Germans two additional ultimatums that all but threatened war. Following the sinking of the British liner *Arabic* in August 1915, the German ambassador promised that ocean liners would only be sunk once noncombatants had been removed to safety. Thereafter the U-boats concentrated on freight traffic for the balance of 1915. In March 1916, an unarmed passenger ship with Americans aboard was torpedoed in the English Channel; with the United States threatening to cut off diplomatic relations, the Germans again renounced surprise submarine attacks on the condition that the United States force the Allies to respect international law. Wilson refused to accept the condition, but U-boat attacks ceased.

During the spring and summer of 1915, Republican leaders including Henry Cabot Lodge and Theodore Roosevelt arrived at the conclusion that American involvement in the war was inevitable in light of the U-boat warfare being waged by the German navy. They called for increased military spending to strengthen the army, which had been underfunded for years. Bitter splits broke out within both parties over the question of preparedness. In the fall of 1915, the administration recommended the establishment of a large reserve army (the "continental army") under the supervision of the War Department in part to avoid the problems that occurred during the Civil War when reliance on state-based volunteer units hampered the war effort. Some wished to establish a national army and require universal military service in part because they believed it would help immigrants acclimate themselves to the United States.

There were also questions regarding the role of the state militias—now known as the National Guard. During the past 30 years, the National Guard had evolved into a powerful interest group, and it succeeded in extracting ever larger sums from Congress. At the time of the Spanish-American War, Army officials discovered that members of the National Guard had been given wholly inadequate training despite generous federal aid to the states. The Guard blocked an effort by Secretary of War Elihu Root to establish a federal reserve force at the time of passage of the Militia Act of 1903. With the onset of hostilities in Europe, the perceived ineptitude of the National Guard and the widespread view that it could not be deployed outside of the United States led some lawmakers to turn again to the idea of a federal reserve force.[469] Southern Democrats opposed the idea. Many were old enough to recall Reconstruction, and they had no desire to establish a large national army that could be deployed by a different president in their section. Democrats on the House Armed Forces Committee proposed to simply have the War Department give vast quantities of equipment to the National Guard. The two sides found themselves at a standstill until Democratic Congressman James Hay of Virginia devised a compromise plan. It provided for the expansion of state National Guard units that would receive equipment and training from the federal government; in exchange, they would submit to oversight by the War Department.[470] In essence, the plan constituted an enormous grant-in-aid program designed to avoid constitutional difficulties: in accepting federal aid, the National Guard in each state freely subjected itself to federal standards for training, equipment, and organization. The National Defense Act of June 3, 1916, also increased the size of the regular Army. It provided that the Army of the United States consisted of the regular Army as well as a new Volunteer Army and the National Guard. It authorized the president to draft members of the National Guard whenever Congress authorizes the use of the land forces of the United States.[471] The law's lack of a provision for a reserve or "continental" army was regarded as a victory for anti-preparedness Democrats.[472]

The navy was also increased in size. A bill providing for the construction of dreadnoughts passed after the Battle of Jutland revealed the utility of these large warships. Congress also provided subsidies for the merchant marine. Before the Civil War, mail packet steamer companies had received generous payments in exchange for promising to allow the government to convert their ships for the use of the navy in time of war. No subsidies were forthcoming in the years after Appomattox, and the U.S. merchant marine declined steadily over the next half-century despite numerous proposals to have Congress provide subsidies to encourage shipbuilding. In his second annual message Wilson endorsed the idea; he cited aid for railroads as precedent.[473] Thc idea was now popular in the South as well as in New England (which had been pushing it for years) as the southern states depended heavily on foreign consumers of cotton. Fear that war would find the United States without adequate tonnage led Congress to pass the Shipping Act of September 7, 1916. It established a U.S. Shipping Board that would build, purchase, or lease vessels through the Emergency Fleet Corporation.[474] The Shipping Board was also authorized to regulate the rates of water-based common carriers (rates had jumped during the war). The act gave the Shipping Board authority to purchase ships for only five years; at that time its powers would become regulatory only. The vessels built by the Board were to be suitable, "as far as the commercial requirements of the marine trade of the U.S. may permit, for use as naval auxiliaries or Army transports." The board was barred from taking an ownership interest in ships already engaged in foreign or domestic commerce unless they were about to be removed from service. Subsequent legislation gave the Board authority to take vessels from their owners, and in October 1917 it commandeered all ships over 2,500 tons. The Shipping Act did not do much to stimulate American shipbuilding; by 1926, the percentage of goods sent abroad that traveled in American ships remained less than 25 percent.[475]

The inability of Germany to grow enough grain, or obtain it from eastern Europe, made the entry of the United States into World War I inevitable. The Germans realized they were racing against the clock even as they halted U-boat attacks in the spring of 1916. Their only hope was to cut off shipping to Great Britain so a shortage of food would force it to seek an armistice before continuation of the war by Germany became impossible. In late 1916, Germany's military leaders decided to resume unrestricted submarine warfare if peace efforts failed. Thereafter the German ambassador in Washington made inquiries with Wilson regarding his willingness to mediate. The president tried to bring the parties to the table, but to no avail. The die was cast when the German ambassador informed Secretary of State Lansing that unrestricted submarine warfare would resume on February 1, 1917. Shortly thereafter Wilson disclosed the contents of the Zimmerman telegram. Sent by the German foreign office to the German ambassador to Mexico, it directed him to inquire regarding an alliance in the event that America entered the war. The return of the southwest United States to Mexico was to be dangled before Mexican officials. The American people reacted with anger as well as disbelief and the episode gave additional momentum to the president's campaign for preparedness. When three American merchant vessels were sunk by German U-boats in March 1917, Theodore Roosevelt called for war, and Americans resigned themselves to the necessity of intervention. Reports of the weakening of the Allies may have pushed the president toward the conclusion that intervention was necessary. A special session of Congress was called for April and the National Guard was called into service. The president addressed a joint session of Congress on April 2; he asked for a declaration of war. Congress complied on April 6. It came not a moment too soon for Britain; the U-boat campaign against shipping in the Atlantic had been so effective that in early April it had only three weeks worth of grain left in reserve.[476]

The task of financing the war effort had begun the previous year. In September 1916 Congress doubled the income tax from 1 to 2 percent and the surtax on incomes over $20,000 was increased to 13 percent. A new tax on the "capital, surplus and undivided profits" of corporations was also imposed along with an increase in the estate tax to 10 percent.[477] Income tax rates for the wealthy were increased repeatedly during the war and by early 1919, the maximum rate for individuals reached 78 percent.[478] Government bonds were sold at only 3.5 percent interest—below the rate people received on their savings accounts—necessitating, or so it was thought, a propaganda drive aimed at getting people to buy bonds. In the end not enough revenue was raised, so that the federal deficit was growing by almost a billion dollars a month by 1918. The war accelerated the replacement of tariffs as the main source of federal revenue by income, profit and estate taxes, which provided 75 percent of all federal revenues when the war ended—a reverse of the situation before the war.[479]

To ensure industries producing items necessary to the war effort had adequate capital, Congress established the War Finance Corporation (WFC) via a law of April 5, 1918.[480] The WFC extended credit to banks that had provided loans to businesses engaged in operations contributing to the war effort. Before the conflict ended it extended $306 million in loans. It also involved itself in the promotion of American exports by providing financial assistance to exporters.[481] The Federal Reserve took steps to make it easier for banks to issue loans, such as lowering their reserve requirements. The money supply increased by 75 percent from 1916 to 1920 and the consumer price index almost doubled.[482] A Capital Issues Committee operating under auspices of the Federal Reserve Board (and later the War Finance Corporation) curtailed access to credit for entities not producing goods related to the war.[483] It was endowed with de facto authority over proposed stock and bond issues—the stock market avoided issues that had not received the Committee's approval. It also supervised the loan applications of businesses and municipalities.[484] Before the war ended, the Capital Issues Committee estimated that American investors spent some $500 million a year on fraudulent stock issues.[485] Just before its authority lapsed, Committee Chairman Charles S. Hamlin called on Congress to enact laws protecting investors against "worthless or doubtful securities."[486] In early 1919 the House took up a bill requiring the disclosure of certain information in each prospectus and advertisement for the sale of securities; it did not become law.[487]

In 1917, the U.S. Army ranked 17th in the world in size (107,641).[488] The first step taken to correct this situation following America's entry into the war was a draft via the Select Service System Act of May 1917.[489] Under the prodding of the law, three-quarters of the men inducted into the armed forces joined the new volunteer army.[490] The decision of War Department officials to rely on a new national army instead of the National Guard stemmed from legal difficulties as well as organizational problems. The Constitution provided that the militias could be called by Congress "to execute the Laws of the Union, suppress Insurrections, and repel Invasions" (Article I, Section 8, paragraph 15). This provision led some to the conclusion that the Constitution did not authorize Congress to send the National Guard overseas—its members would have to be inducted into the Army first.[491] The First Infantry Division reached France in June 1917. During the coming months, a succession of troopships brought American doughboys to French ports. While the American and British navies were able to sharply reduce the amount of tonnage lost to U-boat attacks by the end of 1917, the situation facing the Allies in the field deteriorated. The Russians had abandoned the war that fall and the signing of the Treaty of Brest-Litovsk enabled the Germans to send 50 divisions to the western front. By the spring of 1918, they were able to deploy 192 divisions against 178 Allied divisions, though they were of inferior quality due to manpower and equipment shortages.[492]

While the Civil War saw the federal government take over railroads in theaters of war and break up strikes on a handful of occasions to ensure that factories producing war materiel continued to function, to a large extent the northern economy was allowed to function free of federal interference. The federal government borrowed and spent enormous quantities of money in the North and compelled its young men to serve in the army but manufacturers remained free to produce what they wished. World War I saw the federal government compel industries to produce ammunition and equipment for the army and restricted their use of vital resources for goods not essential to the war effort. This unprecedented exercise of national authority stemmed from the fact that the material needs of the army, navy, and the country's allies vastly exceeded those of the war department during the Civil War. Washington not only asserted jurisdiction over the railroads but exercised it and when necessary it set prices for agricultural commodities and other goods to ensure that they would be produced in necessary quantities. In sum, while the federal government contented itself with being the largest consumer of northern industrial goods during the Civil War, it insisted on serving as floor manager of that great factory known as American industry during World War I.

While American troops made their way across the sea, Congress enacted laws authorizing the national government to supervise large portions of the economy to ensure that it produced adequate supplies for both America and its allies. In July 1917 it established the War Industries Board, in part to counter the suspicion that committees of industrial leaders formed under government auspices were engaging in industry-wide collusion to elevate and maintain higher consumer prices. The Board was not given the power to fix prices; it proved ineffective for a time. After Bernard Baruch took over the War Industries Board in early 1918, it was reorganized. Thereafter it pressured and cajoled various industries to set prices at levels it deemed acceptable and directed the conversion of manufacturing facilities so they could produce goods needed for the war effort.[493] It also restricted the use of critical materials in consumer goods; the amount of steel used in corsets was reduced and toy manufacturers were barred from using tin. In January 1918, the Fuel Administrator ordered factories producing goods not essential to the war effort to close on Mondays for nine weeks.[494] Products were also standardized to reduce waste; the number of plow sizes was reduced from 376 to 76.[495] When necessary, the War Industries Board enlisted other departments in its attempt to regulate prices, such as the Railroad Administration (offenders were barred from shipping their goods via rail) or the Fuel Administration, which could deny coal to those who earned the enmity of the WIB. The imposition of industry-wide prices via agreements brokered by the Board favored large manufacturers and added to growing suspicions that widespread violations of the antitrust laws were occurring under the guise of war.[496] The prices set were high, thus providing large profits for industry. On the other hand, U.S. Steel and the leading automakers backed off of price hikes when Baruch threatened to take over their factories.[497]

The railroads had proven unequal to the task of meeting the relatively modest needs of the military during the Spanish American War—boxcars clogged tracks throughout the southeast—and mobilization in 1917 quickly overwhelmed the lines. Railroad managers blamed the situation on years of inadequate investment in maintenance due to the reduced profits inflicted by rate regulation. The failure to invest in rolling stock and new equipment had disastrous consequences in the fall of 1917.[498] The railroads broke down under the strain of war, depriving critical war-related industries of coal and steel. Making matters worse, the unions took offense when the ICC denied a request for a rate hike in December 1917, as they expected to share in the windfall. They threatened to go on strike—apparently the Adamson Act would not ensure peaceful relations between railroads and their workers.[499] The president finally threw in the towel at the end of December, when he issued an order taking over the railroads pursuant to the authority provided by a 1916 statute empowering him to take over any system of transportation in time of war.[500] Some complained over the president's actions—the 1916 statute had been enacted in response to a war scare that followed raids into the United States by Mexican general Pancho Villa (he and his men killed 18 Americans during an attack on Columbus, New Mexico). The railroads feared the government would retain control of the lines after the war and possibly even take over ownership of them. The severe financial problems of the major lines complicated their mobilization for the war effort. Congress intervened in early 1918, when it passed a law authorizing federal loans to the railroads; federal officials were empowered to impose rates on the lines without holding hearings.[501] The law was explicitly made an exercise of the war powers and included an expiration date of 21 months after ratification of the treaty of peace, in part to lessen fears that the federal government would retain control of the lines after the war. A director general of the railroads took over the day-to-day management of the lines, raising both rates and wages. With the administration's encouragement, union membership in the railroad industry grew exponentially during the war.

The war altered the market for agricultural commodities. When the price of cotton dropped from 11 to 4 cents a pound in 1914, the administration agreed to a plan under which farmers received government loans equal to up to 75 percent of the current cotton price upon depositing cotton at licensed warehouses. Farmers found the plan inadequate. In March 1915 the British government added cotton to the list of goods it barred from German ports, though it promised to either allow all cotton purchased by German buyers before March 2 to reach the continent or to purchase the cotton itself. This assurance did not allay American concerns. The Wilson administration feared that southerners would join other elements in Congress in demanding that an arms embargo be imposed on Great Britain. The president registered his objections with British officials and shortly thereafter they entered into a secret agreement to buy enough cotton to assure that its price reached at least 10 cents a pound.[502] Northern farmers enjoyed a bonanza once Turkey cut off Russian grain exports that formerly went through the Black Sea. With the automobile steadily replacing the horse, feed crops were no longer needed and millions of acres were converted to wheat and corn by farmers hoping to take advantage of sky-rocketing prices.

The Lever Act of August 10, 1917, authorized the federal government to fix the price of wheat and coal.[503] Northern farmers were infuriated that the law set prices for their own staple crop but not for cotton—an indication of the influence of southerners in Congress and in the White House. The law set the price of wheat for the 1918 crop at two dollars a bushel. It also required a license of all persons or entities that either grew, processed, or sold food items and provided for its revocation when the law was violated. Section 15 barred the use of food, feeds, or fruits in the production of distilled spirits, which were made subject to confiscation. The law stemmed in part from the fact that farmers were holding grain—often at warehouses built for them by the national government—to see how high prices would go. The American people, exasperated with high food prices, demanded that something be done.[504] The Lever Act also arose out of the belief that the prices of agricultural commodities would have to be subjected to controls if foodstuffs were to be apportioned among the American people, the Allies, and troops in the field. As Henry Cabot Lodge explained, "we must have one agent to buy for the powers allied with us against Germany." He cited the fact that the Allies went into the Chicago Board of Trade the previous year and bid wheat up to a "perfectly abnormal price."[505]

Senator Frank Kellogg, a Minnesota Republican, thought the measure was within the powers of Congress, as he could see "no difference between the power to conscript property to equip and feed an army and the power to encourage production, to regulate prices, and to protect the people, in order that their power may be greater in time of war—in other words, whenever it is necessary to preserve the national life—Congress may do it."[506] The Food Administration purchased foodstuffs for the army as well as America's allies. It enjoyed an effective power to fix the prices of many goods simply because it was the largest purchaser in the marketplace. The Food Administration was able to avoid rationing; instead it convinced the public to voluntarily reduce its consumption of beef and wheat products. On occasion it issued orders curtailing the consumption of food products, such as hens—killing them was barred in February 1918. The order remained in effect for four months.[507] Distributors operated under rules that kept them from gouging the public while assuring them of reasonable profits. The system worked well at first; it enabled the United States to triple its exports of bread, meat, and sugar. In time it degraded into something of a boondoggle, as high prices for agricultural products were maintained by administrative fiat and loans were provided to the Allies ($10 billion in total), enabling them to buy American foodstuffs at inflated prices.[508] The Food Administration relied on volunteers to enforce regulations such as a ban on consuming meats on Mondays. The end of the line was reached in 1919 after peace had returned and the Agriculture Advisory Board—always sensitive to the needs of farmers—sought a 20 percent hike in the government-set price of wheat. The president refused.[509]

Similar problems beset the coal industry. The Lever Act authorized the president to set coal prices and the wages of miners. The Fuel Administration investigated the industry, but in the end the price of coal was not fixed—desired levels were obtained via suasion. Electricity was conserved through the closing of plants not critical to the war effort and limitations imposed on the use of electricity for advertisements and signs. Still there were coal shortages by 1918. Officials broke a strike among coal-miners with an injunction issued pursuant to the Lever Act.[510] No one contemplated taking over the telephone and telegraph industries until a strike made action imperative. A Joint resolution of July 16, 1918, provided the necessary authority, and the president issued an order bringing these two industries under the control of the postmaster general.[511] Telephone and telegraph rates remained subject to federal control until 1919. The federal government made its first foray into housing when it established the U.S. Housing Corporation to build homes for workers in critical war-related industries. It built 6,000 dwellings under authority provided by a law of July 8, 1918.[512] The return of peace did not see Washington leave the field; the Housing Corporation was still in existence in 1930.

With the arrival of the war came strikes—4,450 in 1917 alone. Many occurred in the lumber industry where men were seeking an eight-hour day. Discontent worsened as prices skyrocketed and laborers found it difficult to keep pace. When strikes occurred in the munitions industry—which was growing fat on war profits—the public was outraged. After Smith & Wesson employees went on strike in the summer of 1918, the national government took over the company's Massachusetts factory. A strike by machinists in violation of an agreement brokered by the Labor Board led the president to inform the strikers they would be barred from working in any war-related industries for a year and their draft deferments would be revoked. The administration aided workers when it could, using its power over contracts for military supplies and construction to cajole employers into providing a "living wage," an eight-hour day, and equal pay for women when they did the same work as men. It also aided the cause of unionization by pressuring employers to recognize unions and negotiate with them. The administration refused to grant the demand of unions building military camps for "closed shops" barring nonunion laborers but it allowed the use of cost plus contracts to compensate construction companies for the higher wage costs that followed when they recognized unions.[513] The War

Department had barred the use of cost plus contracts during the Civil War precisely because of the expense that would have been incurred. Allowing these contracts—which all but invited contractors to slow their work and inflate their costs—testified to the growing power of contractors and labor; their eventual use by government at every level in the United States would result in the gouging of generations of taxpayers.

In an attempt to reduce labor strife and ensure that critical industries had enough employees, Congress established the National War Labor Board in early 1918; it oversaw a staggering array of bureaus including the Women in Industry Service, the Bureau of Industrial Housing, and the Working Conditions Service. The U.S. Employment Service had its roots in a 1907 law that gave the Bureau of Immigration and Naturalization authority to establish an information division for the purpose of promoting a "beneficial distribution of aliens" among the states.[514] The Bureau had employment offices in 93 cities by the time the United States entered World War I. These were considered inadequate by some and during Wilson's first term there was talk of establishing an agency devoted solely to the end of helping the unemployed find jobs.[515] During the war the U.S. Employment Service was established; by October 1918 it had opened 832 local offices for the purpose of finding places for workers.[516] New York City alone had 29. The Employment Service did not limit itself to finding places for applicants in war-related industries.[517]

The work-or-fight order of May 1918 endowed War Department officials with the power to determine which industries and occupations qualified as necessary to the war effort. Bartenders, waiters, hotel clerks, and doormen found they had to seek employment in industries more directly related to the war or enlist. Their jobs were often taken over by women. Officials inexplicably decided that movie actors toiled in an industry critical to the war effort while professional baseball players did not. As a result, the 1918 baseball season was cut short and the World Series had to be played during the first week of September. Provost marshal Enoch Crowder complained of "slacker marriages"' entered into by some to take advantage of the exemption for married men and War Department officials talked of investigating marriages entered into after the selective service law took effect. Registrants accused of not having useful employment or of being idlers had to appear before draft boards and provide an adequate explanation or face induction into the army. The Employment Service used the work-or-fight order as a "weapon" to move men from less critical industries to those where manpower shortages were creating serious problems—rifle and ammunition plants suffered from a deficit of workers, as did the coal mines.[518]

In December 1917, the president established the Committee on Public Information. It paid artists, writers, actors, and professors for their assistance in convincing the public of the necessity of pounding Imperial Germany into dust. Seventy-five thousand orators—the "four minute men"—gave speeches celebrating the war effort and 100 million documents were distributed with the same end in mind.[519] The Committee engaged in various activities designed to enlighten Americans as to the work being performed on their behalf. It prepared articles for newspapers and published the Official Bulletin, which described the daily activities of federal agencies. The Committee established a Division of Work with Foreign-Born, which itself sponsored Loyalty Leagues in the ethnic neighborhoods of the northern cities. It also surveyed foreign language newspapers for evidence of disloyalty. Perhaps the most questionable of all the propaganda activities of the federal government was the effort to alter the curriculums of public schools to ensure they instilled support for the war. The federal Bureau of Education worked with the Committee on Public Information and the ominously-named Board for Historical Service to distribute materials drafted by college professors to be used in high schools. These pamphlets celebrated what their authors saw as the ideals of the United States and its allies and attacked those they associated with Germany. At one point a proposed syllabus was rejected because it failed to defend the British colonial system with enough vigor—an odd twist for a country that owed its existence to the refusal of its founding generation to be ruled by London.[520] The effectiveness of the program was undermined by the limited resources of the Bureau of Education; as late as the fall of 1918, it was still compiling a list of the nation's schools.[521] The war powers of Congress have been aptly described as exceedingly broad; it may take for military purposes any and all national resources. It was hard to see how even this definition encompassed the preparation of course materials for public schools with the goal of manipulating students.

More serious problems arose out of the Espionage Act of 1917 and the Sedition Act of 1918. The first, enacted on June 15, 1917, imposed jail for up to 20 years on those aiding the enemy, obstructing recruiting, or inciting others to refuse military service, whether via the spoken word or in writing.[522] The Espionage Act also barred materials violating its provisions from the mails. The Senate debated the espionage bill in 1917. When Progressives doubtful of the legality of the measure proposed to read the First Amendment literally, Republican LeBaron Colt of Rhode Island refused to go along. "Is not the liberty of the press subject to limitation? Is there any right enumerated in the first ten amendments of the Constitution that is not subject to the limitation of the police power for the protection of society?" Henry Cabot Lodge sided with Colt; William E. Borah of Idaho did not. "It is not within the power of Congress to limit the right of the freedom of the press. If the fathers intended anything, beyond question it was to prevent Congress from passing any law, because that is the language—it shall pass no law—limiting the freedom of the press. Will anybody deny that this is the law after it is passed, and will anybody deny that it limits the freedom of the press? If so it is in the very teeth of the language of the Constitution. Does (the bill) not clearly provide in advance of publication that unless the censor—to wit, the president—consents, either directly or through his regulations, that upon certain subjects publication shall not be had? Now, you may, if Congress has any jurisdiction at all, punish for results of publication, but you cannot set up as censors."[523]

Senator Lee Overman of North Carolina asked Borah whether Congress could punish those who "publish news about the movements of the army, news about where a submarine base is located, news calculated to injure the United States, to give information to the enemy, and to injure the United States in the conduct of the war?" Borah thought not—"the Constitution makes no exception."[524] The Senate refused to follow Borah over the edge; just as Congress could make laws regarding speech by, for example, establishing a code of military conduct to maintain order in the army, it could make laws barring persons from disclosing information regarding the army's location or inciting soldiers to leave the service. When the appeal of a man convicted of violating the Sedition Act came before it—he distributed leaflets objecting to recruiting—the Supreme Court refused to hold the law void and affirmed the conviction.[525] Justice Holmes conceded that the First Amendment may well have been designed to merely bar prior restraints of the press; he insisted that there were many types of speech that remained beyond its scope, such as words designed to cause a panic.[526]

If the absolutist position was impractical, the events of the next two years led many to wonder if the Espionage Act had been drafted with enough care. U.S. attorneys prosecuted persons who criticized the war on the theory that their criticisms were intended to impair recruiting.[527] Part of the problem stemmed from the excessive discretion vested in federal district attorneys; they received almost no instructions from the Justice Department regarding acts that violated the law, so that actions permissible in one jurisdiction were not in another.[528] Looming over these prosecutions was a sea change in the way the nation viewed the war, or at least the way it was viewed by those who saw themselves as responsible for public opinion. Questions regarding American involvement, once so pervasive, were now viewed as vaguely treasonous. In a December 1917 article in the *Atlantic*, author James Harvey Robinson complained that the term "disloyalty" was being applied "with the utmost abandon." He was appalled at the attacks on those who dared to express regret that America had entered the war. The application of the word "treason" to those who merely lamented the country's involvement in the conflict "is to use that expression in just the sense it was designed to preclude—namely, constructive treason."[529]

The Sedition Act of May 16, 1918, expanded the types of comments that would subject one to prosecution.[530] For the duration of the war, the law imposed criminal penalties on all persons who "shall willfully utter, print, write or publish any disloyal, profane, scurrilous, or abusive language about the form of government of the United States, or the Constitution of the United States, or the military or naval forces of the United States, or the flag of the United States, or the uniform of the Army or Navy of the United States." It also imposed criminal penalties on persons making false statements regarding the success of the armed forces, or comments designed to obstruct the sale of government bonds. If such a law had been on the books in the 1780s, its prohibition of criticism of the nation's form of government might have prevented the Constitution from coming into existence. The administration went along with the Sedition Act in part to head off attempts to enact a court martial bill that would have subjected at least some persons accused of disloyalty to military trial. The court-martial bill was itself the work of Oregon Democratic Senator George Chamberlain. In support of the constitutionality of the measure, Chamberlain cited past acts of Congress authorizing the use of court-martials for civilians who violated the laws of war by engaging in espionage or acting as saboteurs. Its opponents attacked the measure as violating the Sixth Amendment right to trial by jury; the president charged that it would "put us upon the level of the very people we are fighting and affecting to despise."[531]

The actions that won Americans the attention of federal district attorneys during the next two years gave sedition laws a bad name. One book was banned even as the Committee on Public Information used it for propaganda purposes; a Vermont minister received a 15-year sentence for suggesting Christ had been a pacifist; the son of the Chief Justice of New Hampshire was jailed for writing a letter in which he endorsed the German explanation for U-boat warfare.[532] Charges were brought under the Espionage Act over a movie that depicted atrocities committed by British soldiers during the Revolutionary War.[533] Postmaster General Albert S. Burleson barred the *Nation* from the mails in September 1918; he was quickly reversed by the president. Pursuant to authority bestowed by the Espionage and Sedition laws as well as an 1879 statute classifying the mails, he also revoked the second class mailing privileges of 22 Socialist newspapers—a move that effectively banned them, as it was too expensive to circulate issues via first class mail.[534]

Speech was not the only area in which the national government overreached. A Commission on Training Camp Activities was formed for the purpose of ensuring that army inductees were not lost to venereal disease. When it was determined that the problem stemmed in part from civilians near army bases, the Commission turned to educating these persons regarding "social hygiene." When that did not work, the Commission established "moral zones" around military bases and expelled prostitutes from them. In some places officials resorted to incarcerating prostitutes residing in cities and towns that hosted military bases under the authority of state "social hygiene" laws; women of suspect morals in these areas were also incarcerated. Forty-three detention houses built with federal aid housed some 15,520 women against their will between 1918 and 1920.[535]

The surveillance network that came into existence may have constituted the most pernicious and regrettable federal enterprise during the war. Much of the work was performed by federal agencies including the Justice Department's Bureau of Investigation, the Post Office, Customs, Internal Revenue, the Secret Service, the Bureau of Immigration and Naturalization as well as the Office of Naval Intelligence and the Military Intelligence Division of the Army. Phones were tapped without warrants (the practice dated from the administration of Theodore Roosevelt).[536] Perhaps even more ominous was the formation of amateur, self-appointed law enforcement organizations that involved thousands of Americans in watching their fellow citizens and reporting what they viewed as disloyal activity to the federal government. These entities included the Liberty League, the Home Defense League, the National Security League, and the American Protective League (APL). The last was the most powerful; the Bureau of Investigation acquiesced in its formation by a Chicago advertising executive because it viewed itself as short of funds.[537] The APL had branches in 600 cities by June 1917. Its members went so far as to wear badges to give the false impression they were law enforcement personnel.[538] Members of these organizations obtained evidence illegally that was subsequently allowed as evidence at trial—it would not have been had it been secured by marshals or other employees of the Justice Department. Woodrow Wilson informed Attorney General Thomas W. Gregory of his objections to organizations such as the American Protective League; he also spoke to Postmaster General Burleson of his misgivings over the latter's practice of barring certain newspapers from the mails. The president's complaints were ignored.[539]

At the close of hostilities in November 1918, the Justice Department ordered an immediate end to spying by private surveillance organizations; some ignored the directive.[540] A series of bombings that terrified the country during the first half of 1919 led to their revival. A bomb arrived at the home of the mayor of Seattle in April 1919; thereafter mail inspectors found 34 bombs. One was addressed to the Postmaster General and another to the Attorney General.[541] On June 2, 1919, bombs exploded in eight American cities; the front of the house of Attorney General A. Mitchell Palmer was caved in by one and another detonated at the home of the mayor of Cleveland. Investigators found a gun at the scene of the Palmer bombing that belonged to an Italian-born anarchist. Palmer had thus far been something of a moderate since his appointment as attorney general in March 1919, urging U.S. attorneys to drop some espionage cases and ordering the release of defendants. He refused to reestablish the civilian surveillance organizations. All that now changed. A peacetime security apparatus now came into being. It targeted immigrant radicals and anarchists. A Radical Division was set up in the Justice Department; it was soon renamed the General Intelligence Division and it proceeded to collect information regarding American citizens and aliens. Its establishment inaugurated a shift in the control of the domestic surveillance capabilities of the national government from military authorities to the Justice Department. The American Protective League came back to life, albeit of its own volition. J. Edgar Hoover, head of the Bureau of Investigation, finally choked the life out of the APL in 1924 when he issued an order barring civilians from performing domestic surveillance work on behalf of the Justice Department.[542]

Justice and Labor Department personnel conducted enormous raids of Communist Party meetings. While the citizens found in those gatherings could not be prosecuted for wishing to acquaint themselves with the doctrines of Karl Marx, the aliens who attended could be deported. Under the Alien Act of 1918 federal officials did not have to go to court to remove aliens from the country if they belonged to an organization that advocated the violent overthrow of the government. Even before the law's enactment, the national government barred un-naturalized German immigrants from approaching military installations, factories, docks, or other facilities deemed critical to nation's infrastructure. They were also barred from owning firearms.[543] When members of the Union of Russian Workers met in various cities on November 7, 1919, federal and state officials conducted raids, netting several hundred aliens, and 249 were deported and sent to Russia on a single boat on December 21, 1919.[544] Five thousand persons were taken into custody during 1919 and many of the aliens among them were turned over to the Bureau of Immigration and Naturalization so they could be deported.[545] The momentum behind the raids lessened when prominent Republican lawyers such as Charles Evans Hughes began to offer their services to aliens slated for deportation—rather than fight, the Department of Labor cancelled most of the deportation orders. The failure of radical violence to materialize on May 1, 1920, after it had been predicted by the attorney general also helped deflate the red scare.[546]

Americans believed much of what they were told about the presence of Communists in part because labor strife, itself allegedly linked to radicals, reached new proportions following the end of the war. Four million workers participated in 3,000 strikes during 1919, as prices continued to rise faster than wages.[547] Thirty-five thousand shipyard workers went on strike in

Seattle on January 21 and a general strike in the city commenced on February 6. A strike in the steel industry over 12-hour days was broken with the use of strikebreakers. Before it ended, federal officials tried to intimidate U.S. Steel by warning that the strikers might be allowed to bring a complaint before the War Labor Board.[548] Federal troops appeared in Gary, Indiana, and Justice Department agents infiltrated the steelworkers' union.[549] That summer a strike among railroad workers made it almost impossible to reach California by land. In New York City, strikes brought the streetcars to a halt, paralyzed the garment trade, and shipping suffered as harbor workers went on strike. A strike in the coal mines in November 1919 threatened the nation's fuel supply; it included 394,000 coalminers. Attorney General A. Mitchell Palmer broke the strike with an injunction issued pursuant to the Lever Act, though the war had been over for a year. At one point Palmer feared the law would expire before the strike had been broken; he asked Congress to extend it.[550]

In the spring of 1918, the German army prepared for what its commanders knew would be the final year of the war—either it would take Paris and force the Allies to seek an armistice, or the lack of adequate supplies of food would bring the German war machine to a grinding halt. The Germans launched an offensive in late March, hoping to break through between the British and French armies and take Amiens. The offensive stalled at the end of April, but not before Allied lines had been pushed back 30 miles. The advance was renewed at the end of May, only to be checked. U.S. Marines stopped the Germans at Belleau Wood on June 4, denying them access to the road to Rheims. Had they reached it, the Germans would have doubled their railroad capacity. The final German offensive began on July 15. At first it appeared it would not be stopped, but the French and Americans threw a fatal counterpunch, made heavier by the weight of five fully armed, fully manned American divisions. The German army now began the slow process of retreat, harassed by tanks, Spanish influenza, and the gnawing suspicion that defeat was inevitable with 250,000 Americans arriving in France each month. By the end of August the allies had reached the Hindenburg line. Shortly thereafter the German army was pushed back into its own territory, where it promptly disintegrated. An armistice was signed on November 11.[551]

Victory came not a moment too soon—a pandemic in 1918 crippled the American military establishment as the war drew to a close. The same Spanish influenza that decimated the German Army first struck America in the spring; a second outbreak in the fall decimated army camps and forced officials to suspend inductions—a draft scheduled for September had to be cancelled. Troopships heading to Europe had to hold burials at sea to dispose of the remains of the scores of men killed by the disease. The outbreak revealed that the federal public health apparatus remained inadequate. At the time the war began, the Public Health Service operated quarantine facilities, a hygienic laboratory (which itself produced vaccines), and the Marine Hospital Service. The duties of the Public Health Service expanded rapidly after the United States entered the conflict, and the agency itself was made a part of the army. Its ability to respond to the influenza outbreak was constrained by the deployment of thousands of doctors and nurses overseas, the lack of effective vaccines, and the short-sightedness of Surgeon General Rupert Blue. Even after being warned of what was coming, he failed to quickly devote funds to researching vaccines. The New England states had demonstrated that the effects of outbreaks could be limited by the rapid deployment of medical personnel, but their example was not repeated at the national level. Instead the Public Health Service limited itself to the deployment of available physicians (about a thousand) and arranging for the publication of innocuous warnings and statements in the newspapers. It did not impose quarantines even after San Francisco officials demonstrated their effectiveness. At least 675,000 Americans died in the pandemic. Twelve years later after another influenza outbreak demonstrated that more resources need to be devoted to public health measures, Congress renamed the Hygienic Lab the National Institute of Health and inaugurated a more aggressive phase in its efforts to protect the public.[552]

Americans were thrilled over the victory of their men-in-arms; they were also deeply frustrated with the war's excesses at home. Inflation, strikes, and dislocations produced by the wartime economy and the disillusionment of Progressives led to Republicans taking both houses of Congress in the 1918 midterm elections. In December 1918 the president left for France to devise a peace treaty with his reputation already tarnished. Once in Paris, the president proved no match for his French and British counterparts, who used the Treaty of Versailles to impose savage and punitive terms on the German people, including a $5 billion indemnity as well as reparations. Wilson prevented the French from annexing the Saar region of southern Germany, and David Lloyd George's attempt to saddle his former enemies with the full cost of the war was thwarted. In addition to reparations, the Treaty of Versailles also provided for a Permanent Court of International Justice at The Hague and a League of Nations.

Members of the Senate objected to the Treaty in large part because it seemed to obligate the United States to defend the borders of every country on the face of the earth. More than a few Americans detected the ceding by the United States of a portion of its sovereignty.[553] Senators of both parties wished to amend the treaty to disavow the obligation to defend other country's borders, but the president would accept no amendments. The approval of the two-thirds of the Senate was unavailing despite a speaking tour mounted by Wilson that resulted only in his being incapacitated by a stroke. Without a treaty, Congress had to enact a joint resolution in March 1921 terminating the war with Germany. It provided that any federal law set to terminate with the end of the war should be interpreted as if the war came to an end on the day the resolution went into effect (March 3, 1921), with the sole exception being the Food Control Act of October 22, 1919.[554] A separate peace treaty between Germany and the United States was agreed to by both sides in 1921.[555]

As occurred after the Civil War, the process of climbing back down from the perch of its war powers proved an enormously difficult task for Congress. By the time the conflict was over the railroads were in desperate financial straits. Treasury Secretary William G. McAdoo served as Director General of Railroads following their takeover by the federal government. He ordered multiple wage increases beginning in April 1918; to pay for the hikes, freight and passenger rates were increased as well. McAdoo forced the railroads to employ more persons than they needed. By the time the war was over the railroad industry was heavily unionized, subject to cumbersome and inefficient work rules, and burdened with too many workers.[556] In the days and months following the armistice, many embraced a proposal to have the federal government take ownership of the railroads and operate them itself (the "Plumb plan").[557] The railroad unions favored the plan (it was drafted by their general counsel), as did many farmers, albeit for contrary reasons—the former saw it as ensuring high wages and favorable work rules, thus increasing costs, while the latter saw it as ensuring lower rates.

While Congress was not prepared to go that far, the Esch-Cummins Transportation Act of February 28, 1920, embodied the belief that what the railroads needed was more oversight.[558] The law returned the railroads to their owners. It also gave the ICC authority to ban railroad lines from abandoning unprofitable routes despite the fact that the country had had built too many lines during the last third of the nineteenth century. The Esch-Cummins Act authorized the ICC to supervise the offering of new securities by railroads as well as their finances. The ICC once again obtained authority to set rates in advance without waiting for a complaint to be filed by private parties, though it was expected to ensure a fair return for railroad stockholders as well as fair rates for shippers. The law also appropriated $300 million for loans to the railroads and extended the jurisdiction of the ICC to railroads operating within a single state. A Railroad Labor Board came into being; the unions were required to give it an opportunity to resolve disputes before they initiated strikes. Congress contemplated but ultimately discarded an amendment to the act that would have prohibited railroad strikes and made decisions of the Labor Board binding on both the lines and the unions. Struggling to maintain pace with runaway inflation, railroad workers staged wildcat strikes unauthorized by their own unions in the spring of 1920. Deprived of materials, factories curtailed operations and food shortages loomed until the Wilson administration leaned on the newly staffed Labor Board to resolve the impasse.[559] At the end of July, it granted wage increases of 20 to 27 percent in an episode all too reminiscent of the events of 1916 that led to the Adamson Act—and authorities were not sure even that would be enough to bring men back to work. Industry observers predicted an enormous hike in rates would be needed to pay for the increase in labor costs.[560]

The Esch-Cummins Act also required the railroads to pay a tax of 50 percent on all earnings in excess of 6 percent, with the proceeds to be used as a revolving fund for the benefit of less-lucrative lines. The Supreme Court upheld the recapture provision on the grounds that as Congress had authority to limit railroad rates, it could confiscate profits that exceeded what it considered to be a reasonable rate of return.[561] The decision was the last in a series of commerce clause cases involving railroads that saw the high court acknowledge that the regulatory powers of Congress had limits and at the same time accept legislation that seemed to obliterate them.[562] Deprived of a large portion of their profits by the recapture clause and squeezed between farmers seeking low rates and unions demanding high wages, the railroads took Congress up on its offer of financing and asked the ICC for a loan of $625 million in May 1920.[563]

While railroads eventually recovered and did well during the 1920s, the Esch-Cummins Act had negative economic consequences, one of which was the inability of railroads to terminate routes. They were also subject to constant pressure to lower rates. Two Republican presidents lobbied the railroads to lower rates during the 1920s, and one was willing to allow the lines to offer reduced rates to farmers alone. Farm groups went so far as to seek repeal of provisions of the Esch-Cummins Act requiring the ICC to consider railroad finances in setting rates—that the lines would go bankrupt in the event of such a modification was of little consequence.[564] A Republican Congress and president enacted the Railway Labor Act of 1926, which has been called "the first federal law to guarantee the right of workers to organize without interference."[565] The law established procedures for railroad employees to decide whether to join unions. It also made yellow dog contracts, under which employees promised to join company unions or refrain from joining unions of their choosing, unenforceable in federal court. It also barred the railroads from interfering in the election of union representatives and provided elaborate mechanisms for resolving disputes over pay. The law abolished the Labor Board, leaving the lines and the unions to work out their differences without federal officials looking over their shoulders. Business interests as well as farmers viewed the move as a step backward, as they feared that the large eastern lines would acquiesce in wage increases and respond with rate hikes, as under the recapture clause they had to cede profits in excess of 6 percent to the ICC anyway.[566] The Supreme Court upheld the law against legal challenge in 1930. In his opinion for a unanimous court, Chief Justice Charles Evans Hughes explained that in protecting interstate commerce, Congress could "facilitate the amicable settlement of disputes which threaten the service of the necessary agencies of interstate transportation."[567] The consequences of the law for labor relations and the federal government were obvious, at least to one observer: "The power to regulate commerce may now, without violence to precedent, be extended to include labor relations in other industries."[568]

The federal tide remained high in other areas as well after the war. The Employment Service survived the arrival of peace and the Women in Industry Service became the Women's Bureau. A joint resolution of January 4, 1921, resuscitated the War Finance Corporation so it could assist "in the financing of the exportation of agriculture and other products to foreign markets."[569] Under the authority of the National Defense Act of 1916, the national government constructed a dam at Muscle Shoals on the Tennessee River to provide power to plants that manufactured nitrates for explosives. Federal officials tried to sell the plant to private interests for a time during the 1920s. When they failed to find a buyer, they took it off the market. At one point Congress passed a bill providing for the federal government to operate the plant but it was vetoed. In an effort to encourage the construction and operation of power-generating dams by private interests, Congress established a federal Power Commission in 1920. It was authorized to license persons and corporations to construct and operate dams, reservoirs, transmission lines, and other installations "for the development, transmission and utilization of power across, along from or in any of the navigable waters of the United States, or on U.S. public lands."[570]

In 1922, representatives of seven western states entered into the Colorado River Compact providing for distribution of waters to be diverted from the Colorado River. Arizona refused to ratify the compact as it was unsatisfied with the share apportioned to it and the other states in the Lower Division (California and Nevada). Congress approved the agreement. Six years later, it authorized the secretary of the interior to construct and operate a dam on the Colorado River for the purpose of controlling floods, improving navigation, storing and delivering water for the reclamation of public lands, and for the generation of electricity "as a means of making the project herein authorized a self-supporting and financially solvent undertaking."[571] Arizona brought suit in the Supreme Court contesting the constitutionality of the 1928 act. In his opinion for the Court, Justice Brandeis held that the law fell within the commerce power of Congress, as studies indicated the dam would improve navigation on the river both above and below the dam.[572] While that prediction proved wildly inaccurate, the Hoover Dam was completed in 1936. The largest public works project in American history and the crowning achievement of federal reclamation efforts, the dam greatly accelerated the development of California. Water diverted by the Hoover Dam and the electricity it generated made the explosive growth of the Los Angeles area possible. It provided the power needed to operate California's aircraft plants during and after World War II.[573] Additional dams and reclamation projects led to the cultivation of the central California valleys that would eventually produce a large portion of the nation's vegetables.

With the war's end, Washington made a perfunctory attempt to extract itself from the merchant marine business. A law of June 5, 1920, required the U.S. Shipping Board to sell the huge fleet of merchant steamers built or purchased for the federal government's use during the war.[574] The fire sale reached a peak in 1926, when 348 ships were sold. The federal government continued to operate passenger as well as cargo ships during the 1920s even as it sold off its stock. A barge line on the Mississippi River remained a federal operation as no one wanted to buy the vessels. During the 1920s the Shipping Board loaned money to private citizens or entities for the construction of ships.[575] Congress subsidized fledgling airlines by giving them generous payments for transporting the mail. It also provided funds for the construction of airports. A national network of emergency landing strips was in place by 1925. The Air Commerce Act of 1926 required airlines to obtain a federal license before sending their planes across state lines.[576]

During the period between 1910 and 1922, the Supreme Court embraced a tolerant approach to state and federal legislation, up to a point. It did not follow through on the threat implicit in *Lochner*—that state laws regulating hours and working conditions in all but the most dangerous occupations were unconstitutional impairments of liberty of contract. On the contrary, it upheld virtually all of the state laws regulating labor relations the constitutionality of which was at issue in cases brought before it during this period.[577] Among the few exceptions to this trend was the ruling in *Coppage v. Kansas* (1915), when the Supreme Court held void as impairing liberty of contract a Kansas law barring the use of yellow dog contracts, under which laborers agreed to refrain from joining unions.[578] Justice Pitney explained that there was no connection between the measure and any permissible field of state legislation, such as safety, morals, or health—therefore the freedom of laborers to decide whether to join unions could not be violated.[579]

The barrage of legislation enacted by Congress during the Taft and Wilson Administrations under the guise of the commerce clause largely escaped the censure of the high court, though there were exceptions. In 1916 Congress tested the court's patience with two pieces of landmark legislation purporting to regulate interstate commerce; one, the Adamson Act requiring overtime pay for railroad employees, survived judicial review.[580] The other, the Child Labor Act of 1917, did not. In *Hammer v. Dagenhart*, the Supreme Court held the law void.[581] In his opinion for the majority, Justice William Day claimed that in the past, laws barring persons or things from interstate commerce targeted activities that had destructive effects after they crossed state lines, such as lottery tickets, impure food, and adulterated drugs.[582] The evil of child labor occurred before the goods produced entered interstate commerce. No harm was inflicted on people in other states: "The goods shipped are of themselves harmless."[583] Nor could Congress use the threat of denying their businesses access to interstate commerce to compel the states to pass regulations it deemed necessary. The commerce clause was not adopted to give Congress authority to eliminate conditions or laws that gave businesses in some states a competitive advantage over businesses in other states.[584] Justice Holmes wrote a dissent that was joined by three other justices. He insisted that "it does not matter whether the supposed evil precedes or follows the transportation. It is enough that in the opinion of Congress the transportation encourages the evil."[585] The ruling bitterly disappointed many—it had been thought that the Court might finally move beyond the reactionary posture that had characterized its decisions during the early years of the century. Many anticipated a reversal of the opinion, just as occurred with the Legal Tender Cases.[586]

Congress refused to leave the field. In February 1919 it enacted a law imposing a 10 percent excise tax on the net profits of businesses that used child labor.[587] The Supreme Court refused to indulge Congress in this subterfuge and it held the law void in *Bailey v. Drexel Furniture* (1922).[588] William Howard Taft, who had been appointed chief justice in 1921, wrote the majority opinion (there was one dissent). He insisted that Congress could not use the tax power as a pretext to regulate subjects beyond its sphere. If such a thing were allowed, all Congress would have to do, "in seeking to take over to its control any one of the great number of subjects of public interest, jurisdiction of which the states have never parted with, and which are reserved to them by the Tenth Amendment, would be to enact a detailed measure of complete regulation of the subject and enforce it by a so-called tax upon departures from it. To give such magic to the word 'tax' would be to break down all constitutional limitations of the powers of Congress and completely wipe out the sovereignty of the states."[589] During oral argument, Justice McReynolds asked Solicitor General James Beck if Congress could impose burdensome taxes on wheat to discourage production of that crop; Beck answered in the affirmative.[590] The ruling produced the most severe anti-court reaction in years. Senator Robert M. LaFollette proposed an amendment authorizing Congress to reverse Supreme Court decisions holding federal laws void, and the question of whether to provide a formal method for checking the justices served as a leading issue in the presidential election of 1924.

Also in 1922 the Supreme Court held void a law imposing punitive taxes on grain futures trades that were not executed in accordance with the statute's provisions.[591] In his opinion for the high court, Chief Justice Taft explained that like the excise tax invalidated in *Bailey v. Drexel Furniture*, the futures tax constituted an attempt to use the tax code to reach subjects reserved to the states. Nor could it be upheld as an exercise of the commerce power, as it was not limited to interstate sales of grain for future delivery.[592] Lawmakers responded with such a law, which the Supreme Court upheld in 1923.[593] Chief Justice Taft explained that as speculation in grain had adversely affected interstate commerce, interstate sales of it were properly subject to federal regulation.[594] Perhaps the most notorious chapter in the 60-year effort to use the tax power to evade the limits on federal authority occurred with the enactment of a tax on cocaine and opium in 1914. The Harrison Narcotic Act imposed draconian criminal penalties on anyone who did not purchase these drugs with a prescription issued in the course of legitimate medical practice, complete the appropriate paperwork and pay the tax.[595] Congress enacted the measure to comply with the terms of the Hague Convention of 1912. The Supreme Court upheld the law.[596] In his opinion for the Court, Justice William Day claimed that the penal nature of the act was a mere incident to the end of raising revenue despite the fact that the tax was only a dollar a year.[597] Chief Justice White wrote a dissent joined by three other justices in which he endorsed the decision of the Court of Appeals, which held the measure beyond the powers of Congress.[598]

It has been said that the Progressive movement, although checked by courts and other conservative forces within the country, expired largely due to the stresses of war.[599] It may have been a victim of its success. Herbert Croly's belief that federal intervention was required to see that the riches of American industrialism were distributed more equitably was embraced in Washington; the result was an unseemly battle of powerful interest groups determined to use the federal apparatus to acquire for themselves a privileged position at the expense of the rest of American society. Farmers obtained loans at cheaper rates than other Americans paid and sought laws setting food prices at levels that would enable them to gouge consumers. Railroad unions sought drastic increases in wages even if they required imposing higher train rates on the public and manufacturers used the opportunity provided by the suspension in enforcement of the Sherman Act to establish cartels and engage in price fixing. The pork barrel, tariff, and pension politics of the late nineteenth century had simply been expanded to include more groups. The result was vastly increased federal spending, higher taxes, destructive regulations, and severe inflation. All was not lost for progressives, though; the template for federal control of the economy that had been developed during the war might have been removed from public view by the mid-1920s, but it was not discarded. It would remain available for the next "emergency" that justified its use.[600]

Chapter 5

PLACES AT THE TROUGH, 1921–1933

MUTUAL EXPLOITATION: THE INTEREST GROUPS

The great upheaval in the federal system that occurred between 1910 and 1920 was not reversed during the following decade. The pace of centralization slowed during the 1920s, but federal involvement in agriculture, labor relations, and education continued to expand. Grant-in-aid programs flourished. Federal law enforcement capacities expanded and became more intrusive while the Supreme Court used its amorphous doctrines to invalidate a wide variety of state laws.

These changes occurred under the watchful eye of an electorate that underwent the most dramatic expansion in American history. In August 1920, the Nineteenth Amendment became law: "the right of citizens of the United States to vote shall not be denied or abridged by the United States or any State on account of sex." As with the popular election of senators, the states embraced this reform before it was enshrined in the Constitution. The western states were the first to give women the vote. In the east, the hostility of various groups including immigrant males slowed its progress. Referendums proposing to give women the vote were firmly rejected in Pennsylvania, New Jersey, New York, and Massachusetts during 1915—in the Bay State, only 35 percent of voters voted in favor of extending the suffrage. Southerners opposed the idea, largely because they feared that it would increase agitation among blacks for the vote. One senator explained that while southern men were more than willing to use violence to keep enfranchised black males from the polls, they would be unable to bring themselves to strike black women. A suffrage amendment failed in the

House in 1915; 171 of the 204 majority votes rejecting it were cast by Democrats.[1] Unwilling to offend southerners, the president avoided the issue. Both party platforms endorsed state legislation granting the vote to women in 1916.[2] What became the Nineteenth Amendment remained stalled until the spring of 1919 when the Senate and House each approved it. With the South an almost solid block in opposition, ratification by the states remained in doubt until Tennessee went along in August 1920.[3]

George Madden Martin wrote two articles for the *Atlantic* during the mid-1920s that suggested the enfranchisement of women would accelerate the process of centralization. In a June 1924 article, she pointed to the work of the Women's Joint Congressional Committee: It helped make the Women's Bureau permanent, aided passage of both the Sheppard-Towner Law (federal grants for maternal care) and the Voight Act barring the shipment of filled milk in interstate commerce.[4] The Committee fought in vain for a child labor amendment and sought a uniform divorce law. It also advocated the distribution of $85 million among the states for educational purposes. Martin thought women tended to look to the federal government for needed reforms because they regarded the states as dominated by political machines. The words "states' rights" are "interwoven in the minds of the great proportion of American women with things sinister and ominous and fraught with menace." The author blamed this in part on association of the term with the Civil War as well as on the unwillingness of women to exercise the patience necessary to achieving reforms on a state-by-state basis. Martin claimed the American woman "thinks of Uncle Sam's money" as inexhaustible and that people received something for nothing when it is obtained from the federal government—without acknowledging that, as the previous 60 years illustrated, the same could be said of men.[5] Martin took a harsher line the following year, when she complained that women have "overlooked the purpose and proper limits of government." They had secured measures that are "alarmingly increasing the official class, and unduly and unwisely burdening the taxpayer." She suggested that women's organizations were being manipulated by groups including social workers, which convinced them to lobby for larger expenditures for social programs.[6]

The connection between the enfranchisement of women and the growth of social programs was embodied in Julia Lathrop, chief of the Children's Bureau. After the Bureau issued a report in 1916 revealing high mortality rates among infants as well as women at childbirth, she campaigned for federal grants to the states for maternal and infant medical care. In 1918, Congresswoman Jeanette Rankin proposed a bill for that purpose. With the support of the Harding administration and lawmakers cognizant of the newly obtained electoral power of women, advocates pushed the measure through both houses of Congress and the Sheppard Towner Act became law in November 1921.[7] Support for the bill by a wide variety of women's organizations proved critical in its passage. So did the widespread belief that action designed to maintain the health of the nation's youth was necessary if the national capacity for self-defense was to be maintained. The law required states seeking federal grants to set up agencies to oversee the program and provide appropriations at least equal in size to federal matching funds. Under the act, 2,978 prenatal care centers were established. The program was overseen by a federal Board of Maternity and Infant Hygiene in the Children's Bureau. The Board investigated subjects relating to children and published information and bulletins. The law lapsed in 1929, in part due to the hostility of the American Medical Association, which believed that the nurses and social workers carrying out the act were taking business away from physicians.[8] The enfranchisement of women helped produce larger appropriations for social welfare programs at the state level even in the South, where public establishments had historically been smaller. Southern states provided generous subsidies for maternal education, in part to qualify for federal grants under the Sheppard-Towner Act.[9]

Women helped elect a Republican to the White House in the 1920 presidential election, though the winning candidate did not call for the establishment of new social programs. The contest instead revolved around the League of Nations, and it turned largely on the disillusion of the American people over events of recent years, including the dislocations of the war, the red scare, and strikes. Democrats met in San Francisco in June. Two of the president's lieutenants, Robert G. McAdoo and A. Mitchell Palmer, sought the party's nomination, but with Wilson delegates split between the two men, the convention chose the candidate favored by the bosses, James M. Cox, governor of Ohio. The platform endorsed the League of Nations while acknowledging the possibility of limiting the responsibilities of the United States within it. That much had changed during the past 30 years was demonstrated by the fact that the party that had once opposed the Blair bill now included a plank in its platform demanding federal funds for schools. "Cooperative federal assistance to the states is immediately required for the removal of illiteracy, for the increase of teachers' salaries and instruction in citizenship for both native and foreign-born." The platform also called for increased federal spending on vocational training and the U.S. Employment Service.[10] It claimed the railroads had operated more efficiently under government management during the war: "economies enabled operation without the rate raises that private control would have found necessary, and labor was treated with an exact justice that secured the enthusiastic cooperation that victory demanded."[11] The platform would have included the promise of a large bonus to veterans of the just-concluded war had the effort not been checked by Carter Glass.[12]

Republicans met in Chicago in June. When none of the leading candidates for the nomination managed to obtain a majority of the delegates, party bosses turned to Ohio Senator Warren G. Harding. They tried to foist Wisconsin Senator Irving Lenroot on the delegates as the vice presidential nominee, but a rebellion on the floor resulted in the nomination of Massachusetts Governor Calvin Coolidge. In its platform the party spoke to concerns over centralization while at the same time vowing to continue all of the latest innovations. It promised that the Federal Farm Loan Act would remain and called for the voluntary arbitration of labor disputes by an "impartial tribunal" as well as a law barring the products of convict labor from interstate commerce. A federal anti-lynching law was endorsed as was federal aid to the states for "vocational and agricultural training." The platform also embraced the federal child labor law then on the books, though it conceded other means of addressing the evil might be needed if the law was held unconstitutional (it was).[13]

During the summer and fall, 600,000 Americans traveled to the Marion, Ohio, home of Warren Harding to hear him speak from his front porch. The tactic was designed to cause people to associate Harding with another Ohioan, William McKinley, and the relative serenity of turn-of-the-century America. Harding went so far as to have McKinley's flagpole installed in his front garden. Many educated Americans viewed Harding as hopelessly out of his depth. H. L. Mencken claimed that the Ohio senator wrote "the worst English that I have ever encountered." It reminded him "of stale bean soup, of college yells, of dogs barking idiotically through endless nights."[14] A listless campaign saw both candidates take equivocal stands on the League of Nations. The great middle of the country—or at least the northern middle—embraced the decency and conservatism of the onetime newspaper editor at the head of the Republican ticket and he won a huge majority in the popular vote: 16 million to 9 million for Governor Cox. Harding even managed to win New York City. With the Progressive Party largely in abeyance, Republicans won large majorities in both houses of Congress.

Americans would eventually learn that the new president was surrounded by what one critic called "a set of third rate, small-town grafters."[15] The administration of Warren Harding would be remembered for corruption, but during his short term the president pursued a policy of retrenchment that served the wishes of the country. The federal workforce was cut and expenditures were reduced by a third.[16] The Revenue Act of 1921 abolished the excess profits tax and cut the maximum surtax on incomes to 50 percent. It also increased the corporate tax rate from 10 to 12.5 percent. The transfer of the tax burden to the wealthy was not reversed; the estate tax remained and it was increased to a maximum of 40 percent in June 1924.[17]

Cities and counties had long provided relief to the indigent, and they increased their budgets for public works projects to alleviate unemployment during the Wilson years. During the winter of 1914–15, 91 cities provided work for the jobless. In early 1915, Theodore Roosevelt called on Congress to employ Americans on river-and-harbor and reclamation projects and to establish a federal clearinghouse for state unemployment bureaus.[18] When a short-lived but severe depression struck in 1921 (unemployment reached 11.9%), many thought it was time for the federal government to involve itself in the matter. The president held a conference on unemployment at the White House. While it described joblessness as "primarily a community problem" to be handled by municipal governments, the conference called for coordination among employment agencies. States should expedite construction projects, and Congress should pass a road construction bill under consideration. The conference also endorsed a proposed federal bond issue, with the proceeds to be loaned to cities for the construction of public works.[19] While the proposal was ignored, the U.S. Employment Service aided the jobless through offices located throughout the country (269 in July 1920), as well as through the subsidies it provided for similar entities established by the state governments.[20] In 1923, over 2.8 million persons applied for jobs through the U.S. Employment Service.[21] While appropriations for it dwindled, the Employment Service still had offices in 11 states in 1928.[22] The administration took steps to "manage" the economy, among the most notable of which was Secretary of Commerce Herbert Hoover's attempt to replace competition with coordination in leading industries. He encouraged the establishment of industrial and trade organizations that sought to eliminate waste and labor strife. These were modeled on similar entities established during the war under the auspices of the War Industries Board. In some cases, the Federal Trade Commission endorsed codes devised by these groups that may have violated antitrust laws. Hoover saw himself as something of a national salesman and sought ways to promote U.S. sales abroad such as providing credit for exports.[23]

Some elements of American society fared poorly during the 1920s. Labor took a step backwards, as union membership declined and employers fought to reestablish the open-shop.[24] Public employee unions suffered badly in the wake of the Boston police strike of 1919. Attempts were made to repeal the Lloyd-LaFollette Act, which bestowed the right to join a union on federal employees. The general strike of 1926 in Great Britain saw members of government trades unions refuse to work, leading politicians of both parties in the United States, including Franklin D. Roosevelt, to declare that public employees should not be allowed to assume the right to strike.[25] While American businesses once opposed federal regulation of labor issues, they now saw in the new federal agencies formed during and after the war an ally in their battle to check the power of unions. In June 1922, the Railway Labor Board recommended a cut in wages. 400,000 railroad workers responded by going on strike. In addition to objecting to the wage cuts, the workers also wanted to base promotions on seniority—thereby depriving the railroads of the ability to award their best employees and shape their workforces. President Harding lobbied the railroads to strike a deal; when that failed he asked the banks upon which the lines depended for financing to pressure their clients. The lines refused to budge, in part because they were unwilling to cede control over promotions. As the strike continued, strikers tarred-and-feathered replacement workers and sabotaged tracks, causing trains to derail. With the delivery of coal and food hampered, the president allowed Attorney General Harry Daugherty to obtain a sweeping injunction from U.S. District Court Judge James Wilkerson in Chicago based on the Sherman Antitrust Act and the national government's postal powers.[26] It barred interference with the operation of the railroads and prohibited the encouragement of persons "to abandon the employment" of the lines via telephone, letter, word of mouth, or through "interviews to be published in newspapers."[27] The injunction may well have constituted a violation of the First Amendment; its broad terms appalled observers across the country. The injunction contributed mightily to the disintegration of the strike.[28]

With the national government in control of anti-labor forces, union leaders sought relief at the state level. Unions had made a practice of exhorting the public to avoid businesses whose employees had gone on strike. Arizona enacted a law that prohibited judges from targeting this practice with injunctions. The Supreme Court held it void in 1921.[29] In his opinion for the majority, Chief Justice Taft explained that "a law which operates to make lawful such wrong as is described by plaintiffs' complaint deprives the owner of the business and the premises of his property without due process, and cannot be held valid under the Fourteenth Amendment."[30] The law did not make wrongful acts lawful. It merely limited the remedies employers could avail themselves of—they could still sue strikers for damages arising out of the loss of business. Taft also took the view that the law violated the equal protection clause.[31] In dissent Justice Mahlon Pitney insisted that states could enact statutes providing equitable remedies, refrain from doing so, or enact said laws and then withdraw them without violating the Constitution.[32] The *Nation* did not think highly of the Court's decision. "In the present case the people of a sovereign state undertook to say that, in practical effect, certain tactics were to be considered legal—or at least that they were not to be enjoined. This the Supreme Court has now held they cannot do and hereafter no state legislature, nor indeed Congress, can prescribe rules of conduct in this field of human relationships without the chance of an irreversible veto from the Supreme Court."[33]

Federal judges continued to target strikes. Between 1918 and 1928, they issued 389 injunctions in cases involving labor disputes, almost all of them at the request of employers.[34] The use of the labor injunction remained a prominent political issue. In 1930, federal judge John J. Parker saw his Supreme Court nomination go down in flames over his alleged penchant for issuing injunctions in response to strikes. In 1932 Congress passed a law providing that injunctions could be deployed against strikers by federal courts only when "unlawful acts were threatened and will be committed" or when law enforcement officials were unable to protect the complainant's property. It listed a variety of activities against which the use of injunctions was specifically barred. The Norris-LaGuardia Act also expanded the right to a jury trial in contempt cases and made unenforceable yellow dog contracts in which employees promised to join a company union or refrain from joining one of their own choosing. The law exempted union officers from liability for the acts of union members.[35]

If some federal officials were not willing to let the states regulate labor disputes as they saw fit, others—members of Congress—were willing to throw money at them. The first grant in aid law of 1911 had been enacted for the benefit of forests along navigable streams. It was followed by similar matching programs benefiting agricultural science, home economics, vocational education, and road-building. A law of March 28, 1918, provided the U.S. Public Health Service with money to be used to limit the spread of venereal disease near military bases.[36] A Social Hygiene Board was established via a law of July 8, 1918.[37] It was assigned the task of protecting the armed forces against venereal diseases and a million dollars was appropriated for grants to states for the purpose of limiting their spread. An act of July 11, 1919, provided funds for veterans to undergo vocational rehabilitation.[38] In June 1920, Congress made all persons injured in industrial accidents eligible for vocational rehabilitation at state-operated institutions funded with the assistance of the federal government.[39] States had to provide their own appropriations equal to or larger than the federal grant to qualify for federal funds. Proposed courses had to be submitted to a federal Board of Vocational Rehabilitation for approval. When a bill to renew the program came before Congress in 1924, lawmakers revealed varied attitudes toward it. John Marshall Robsion, a Kentucky Republican, defended the measure; he pointed out that 225,000 persons were disabled each year by industrial accidents. He noted that it cost $200 to $300 a year to maintain dependents in public institutions—why not rehabilitate them so they can become employable and thus an asset to the nation instead of a liability? He was pleased to report that the number of states funding rehabilitation programs had grown from six to 36 since the program was initiated. The government was spending millions each year to save crops from the ravages of the boll weevil and the tobacco worm. Why not do as much for humans? In Robsion's view, the problem of injured workers constituted a national problem as it involved the "efficiency of our citizenship." He insisted the positive results of the program for the man who benefited from it would be "reflected in his attitude toward government and his attitude toward his fellow man. An independent, self-supporting citizen in a satisfactory wage-earning employment is much less inclined towards radicalism and much less likely to be influenced by the agitator."[40] Henry St. George Tucker of Virginia was less enthused. "Why should the two governments (state and federal) do the same thing at the same time, when only one can legally do it, and when the cost of having two overhead charges, with all that means in rents, employments, medicines and so forth, must be greatly increased?" Tucker complained that he repeatedly found the same agency in both Richmond and Washington: both had an agricultural extension division, agricultural experiment stations, a commission or bureau of fisheries, a board of health, a highway commission (a bureau of public roads in Washington), and a board or bureau of education.[41] Tucker's protests were in vain—a law reauthorizing the vocational rehabilitation program was enacted in June 1924.[42]

In 1921, Congress renewed the highway funding program begun in 1916. The importance of these appropriations was demonstrated during the war when the poor condition of the nation's roads slowed the movement of military supplies and troops. Under the 1921 act, the United States could pay no more than 50 percent of the cost of building either intercounty or interstate highways.[43] By the end of 1921, half of all road projects in progress were receiving federal money; 250,000 persons were employed in road construction.[44] The program increased state spending so much that by 1930 more than half of the total debt of the states stemmed from highway spending.[45] Federal grants for highway construction to Arkansas, Kansas, and Maine were suspended to force these states to replace patronage ridden bureaucracies with civil service systems.[46] The federal government spent $100 million a year on roads between 1918 and 1930.[47] In 1924, Congress provided grants to the states for the purpose of establishing programs designed to limit the spread of forest fires.[48] Federal grants also aided the states in their attempts to control a variety of agricultural pests. While the utility of these measures was generally beyond dispute; it was not clear the same could be said of a 1931 appropriation designed to encourage the destruction of coyotes and wolves.[49] By 1932, annual federal grants totaled $232 million.[50]

As with earlier grant-in-aid statutes, little discussion of the question of authority took place in Congress during the 1920s before it enacted laws providing the states with money. Proponents of the Sheppard-Towner Act cited appropriations to limit the spread of animal and crop diseases and asked, as lawmakers had at the time Congress considered establishing a Board of Health, if the government was to provide aid for sick animals but not sick people? Opponents focused on substantive rather than legal objections; in their view the measure would create an army of bureaucrats that would intrude in American homes and take business away from the nation's physicians.[51] Horace Towner, Republican Congressman of Iowa, was one of the sponsors of the Sheppard-Towner Act. In a June 1922 speech, Towner insisted that a broad spending power had been embraced from the beginning. In support of this claim, he cited the arguments of Alexander Hamilton and Joseph Story as well as the 1793 appropriation to aid residents of Santo Domingo following a hurricane. Towner also pointed to the Farm Loan Board, the Children's Bureau, the Public Health Service, reclamation projects, the Department of Agriculture, and the Smithsonian Institution as evidence of a broad spending power.[52]

Three states refused to accept funds made available to them for maternal care pursuant to the Sheppard-Towner Act. One of them, Massachusetts, filed suit in the Supreme Court seeking to enjoin federal officials from carrying out the law on the grounds that it was unconstitutional.[53] Arguing for the federal government, Solicitor General James M. Beck claimed that Congress possessed a broad spending power.[54] The Supreme Court upheld the law. In his opinion for the Court, Justice George Sutherland explained that the law did not require the state to accept the funds.[55] As for the question of whether Congress has usurped the powers of the states, the high court held that it was "an abstract question of political power" and not "judicial in character."[56] The justices held that an individual plaintiff in a companion case did not have standing to file suit in federal court contesting the legality of congressional appropriations. Justice Sutherland distinguished the case from suits brought against municipalities by taxpayers on the grounds that the interest in expenditures of a federal taxpayer is "comparatively minute and indeterminable; and the effect upon future taxation, of any payment out of the funds, is so remote, fluctuating and uncertain, that no basis is afforded for an appeal to the preventive powers of a court of equity."[57] As there were already cities with several million people, in which the harm caused by any particular expenditure also seemed small, the difference seemed inconsequential. Of more importance was the fact that, as one historian pointed out, the holding seemed to conflict with *Marbury v. Madison*'s proviso that judicial review must be allowed to go forward even and especially when constitutional questions are involved. "If no one has standing to challenge a federal spending program, there is no way to prevent unconstitutional spending."[58] Once again, the high court had employed a legal doctrine of doubtful relevance to avoid resolving what had become the central legal issue of American federalism. The justices were undoubtedly aware of the consequences of holding the Sheppard Towner Act unconstitutional as beyond the scope of the spending power. The existence and legal authority of entire agencies, bureaus, and even departments would have been immediately subject to question.[59] The federal courts themselves would have been besieged by indignant taxpayers demanding that judges issue orders slicing the federal establishment. Forcing federal judges to review each federal agency and determine which were fit to survive may well have been too much to ask.

In 1921, the Underwood Tariff had been on the books for eight years. The benefits of low tariffs were limited by the war, which severely reduced imports.[60] Manufacturers thrived with the lack of competition during the conflict and "war babies"—industries that sprang up in the absence of foreign competition—demanded an increase in tariffs once it ended, lest they be ruined by foreign competitors. The conflict itself produced a widespread belief that the nation must be self-sufficient in the production of a range of goods, thereby adding momentum to calls for more protection. Wilson vetoed a steep tariff hike just before leaving office in March 1921, but Republicans quickly put together an emergency tariff that became law in May 1921. It imposed steep duties on agricultural products. The law failed to prevent a drop in the prices of the protected commodities.[61]

With farmers bought off, the Republican leadership in each house had little difficulty in pushing through a steep tariff law in 1922—the Fordney-McCumber Tariff.[62] Duties on cheap and medium cotton goods were high enough to bar imports altogether. Ad valorem rates for woolens averaged 50 percent.[63] Raw wool carried an effective rate of 111 percent. Among the "war babies" that received aid were manufacturers of cheap imitation jewelry; they benefited from a 70 percent tariff on the products of their foreign competitors. The rate for aluminum was set at two to five cents a pound; its price thereafter rose from 20 to 28 cents a pound—thus the conclusion of one historian that the rate hike was "primarily a license to overcharge" for domestic manufacturers.[64] John W. Davis, Democratic presidential candidate in 1924—the party's most conservative nominee in 20 years—charged that it netted Andrew Mellon, Secretary of the Treasury as well as an aluminum tycoon, $10 million annually.[65] In raising prices, the Fordney-McCumber Tariff impaired the purchasing power of the American consumer—a problem in a time when the American economy was increasingly built around the ability of citizens to buy the goods being turned out by the leading manufacturing nation of the world. With a high tariff once again providing more tax revenue, the Coolidge administration was able to push through income tax cuts following the 1924 election. The gift tax was abolished and the maximum estate tax dropped from 40 to 20 percent in early 1926.[66]

In the 1922 midterm elections the huge Republican majorities in each House of Congress were severely reduced: the party lost 78 seats in the House and eight in the Senate. The narrow majorities that remained proved useless—a "farm bloc" had emerged to divide the party just as Progressives had divided it during the previous decade, and Republicans found that they did not have a functioning majority in either house in the new Congress. During the summer of 1923, rumors of wrongdoing on the part of Harding administration officials began to emanate from Washington. Harding tried to focus on the impending presidential election with a tour of the West only to suffer a massive heart attack. He died on August 2. His office passed to Calvin Coolidge, a taciturn New Englander. Unwilling to embrace government activism or reverse it, the new president consoled himself by doing as little as possible and saying less. Charles Evans Hughes, Secretary of State from 1921 to 1925, recalled that on multiple occasions when he went to the White House in the afternoon to speak with the president, he found Coolidge relaxing on a couch, smoking a cigar, and reading a newspaper.[67]

The new president had gained national recognition for his role in breaking the Boston police strike of 1919 while he was Governor of Massachusetts. He had been regarded as pro-labor at the time the strike began—he supported maximum hour and minimum wage laws as well as workers' compensation acts. During the summer of 1919, Boston policemen, angry over 12-hour days (six days a week), went on strike. Coolidge called in the state militia to guard city streets and he refused to allow the mayor of Boston to recognize the police union. With telegraph and railroad workers threatening to join in a general strike such as had occurred in Seattle, Coolidge fired the striking police officers.[68] Coolidge's experience with the public employees of Massachusetts would serve him well in the White House as he spent much of his presidency fighting off attempts of various interest groups seeking to gorge themselves at the public trough. In May 1924, Congress sent him a bill increasing the salaries of postal employees. Coolidge refused to sign it; in his veto message he pointed out that postal workers had received pay raises three times in the previous six years. He also noted that the salaries of rural carriers had increased 160 percent since 1907.[69] As the Post Office now employed 280,000 Americans—more workers than the federal government had in 1900—and postal employees had grown accustomed to intimidating politicians, the veto was no small act of courage. Following the Civil War, veterans' organizations allowed two decades to lapse before demanding pensions for those who emerged unscathed from the war; the American Legion began demanding assistance for doughboys almost before they exited the troop ships. After toying with a "farms for veterans" scheme, the Legion moved on to a cash bonus designed to compensate those who served for the difference between what they made in the military ($30 a month) and what they would have earned had they remained at home and held civilian jobs ($10 to $12 a day).[70] Republicans in Congress took up the idea with enthusiasm in 1921. Only Warren Harding's lobbying killed the measure. Congress took it up again in early 1922. The *Nation* was appalled. It believed that the bill—"a vote-catching device for elections next autumn"—would cost $3 billion; it complained that Congress was contemplating new taxes and a bond issue to pay for it.[71] A week later the *Nation* warned that the measure constituted "an entering wedge toward repetition of the shameful history of the Grand Army of the Republic's pension grabbing." The article closed with a note of regret regarding the party of Lincoln. "To dole out the surplus in the Treasury to its backers and its protégés has been the one cardinal principle of the Republican Party ever since it abandoned its Civil War-time ideals."[72]

Congress passed a bill providing a bonus of $50 for each month of service, only to see it vetoed by Harding. The House voted to override the veto but the Senate did not. The effort was renewed in 1924. Three years of lobbying by veterans' organizations paid off; Coolidge refused to go along but Congress passed the bill over his veto in May. The Adjusted Compensation Act provided each veteran with a credit worth $1.25 for each day enlisted persons served overseas ($1 a day for those who remained at army bases in the United States) in excess of 60 days, with the credit not to exceed $625.[73] Each veteran would receive an adjusted service certificate reflecting the present value of what the award would be worth in 20 years. They could borrow up to 25 percent of the certificate's value. The president vetoed another bill that extended the date of the end of the Civil War for the purpose of benefit eligibility from April 13, 1865, to August 20, 1866 (the idea of pensions for those who served during peacetime had not yet occurred to anyone). In his veto message, Coolidge cited the measure's cost ($415 million during its first 10 years), the fact that pensions had been increased as recently as 1920, and the attempt of Congress to rewrite history.[74]

While there were only 100,000 Union army veterans still alive in the early 1920s, the American Legion—composed largely of men who served in World War I—had 700,000 members. It demonstrated its power in helping to defeat several senators and representatives who had voted against the 1922 bonus bill. Thirteen of 17 U.S. senators reelected in 1922 voted for the bonus bill; four who voted to sustain the veto were defeated by pro-bonus candidates.[75] Thus, the single largest stream of money extending from the federal treasury into the pockets of voters, after dwindling for years with the deaths of Union army veterans, once again formed a raging torrent by 1932, when 1.28 million veterans collected benefits.[76]

Despite this growth, veterans lost their place as the leading recipients of federal largesse during the 1920s. They were surpassed by farmers. During the war the income of farmers increased dramatically due to higher demand for foodstuffs, but when the federal government stopped guaranteeing the price of wheat in June 1920, prices dropped through the floor. The problem stemmed in part from the increase in the annual harvest; the 1919 wheat crop was three times the size of the average annual crop in the five years before World War I.[77] The release of agricultural commodities stored by federal officials during the war further depressed prices, triggering the worst agricultural depression in American history. A farm bloc formed in Congress to seek solutions. Composed of approximately 20 senators and 30 representatives, it began by seeking traditional measures, such as increased protection for agricultural commodities.[78] The Tariff Act of May 27, 1921, gave them what they wanted, but it failed to stem the decline in prices.

The farm bloc next turned to the War Finance Corporation, which Congress revived at the end of Wilson's presidency over his veto. The Agricultural Credits Act of August 24, 1921, authorized it to loan up to a billion dollars to banks, livestock companies, and cooperative marketing associations to help them market agricultural commodities.[79] The War Finance Corporation doled out $300 million in loans, enabling co-ops to store crops rather than place them on the market and further depress prices.[80] The Capper-Volstead Act of February 18, 1922, exempted farm cooperatives from antitrust laws and allowed them to enforce their agreements.[81] These organizations were thus encouraged to sell their products at set rates; only the California Fruit Growers Association succeeded in raising the price of products raised by its members.[82] That the public paid higher prices for California fruit was of secondary concern. Congress took up the idea of expanding the credit resources available to farmers in early 1922. When some talked of what they believed the federal government was obligated to do for farmers, Carter Glass of Virginia scoffed: "It has become fashionable when nobody has a legal claim that he can establish against the Government, to talk about moral responsibility." He did not believe that aid for farmers constituted, as some claimed, the beginning of European socialism in America. "This is not even socialism. It is special privilege run mad."[83] The momentum was with the other side. The Federal Intermediate Credit Act of March 4, 1923, established federal intermediate credit banks to provide farmers with loans of intermediate duration, i.e., longer than seasonal loans and shorter than mortgages.[84] The money went to cooperative associations, from which farmers took out loans.[85]

In early 1922, two former members of the War Industries Board, George N. Peek, a farm machinery manufacturer, and Hugh S. Johnson, president of the Moline Plow Company, devised a plan under which American farmers would receive a "protected price" for their crops from the national government that would guarantee them "fair exchange value." It would be based on the ratio of the average price of their crops to the consumer price index during the 10 years prior to World War I. It was hoped that the measure would restore to farmers the purchasing power they had enjoyed before the war. A federal export corporation would purchase commodities at the protected price and then sell them abroad, presumably at a loss. Farmers themselves would make up the difference by paying an equalization fee on their crops. Two Republicans, Senator Charles McNary of Oregon and Congressman Gilbert Haugen of Iowa, devised a bill based on the Peek-Johnson Plan. Among the plan's defects was that the farmers would go broke quickly if they alone had to pay the difference between the guaranteed price and the actual world price. Critics suggested the measure would encourage overproduction, and in turn lower prices even further.[86] McNary and Haugen began pushing their bill in early 1924. They labeled it an emergency measure, perhaps to attract lawmakers conditioned by World War I to accept novelties as legally justified by their alleged necessity. Farmers recalled the prosperity they had enjoyed during the war when the federal government set high prices for their crops and embraced the McNary-Haugen bill.

For a measure that was supported by so many politicians, the bill inspired an extraordinary amount of criticism. The *Chicago Daily Tribune*, now in the hands of one of one of the most reactionary publishers in America, Colonel Robert McCormick, was merciless. In a March 11, 1924, editorial, the *Tribune* charged that the bill was designed "to provide a subsidy to backward farmers, to create many bureaucratic jobs for its administration, to fix prices, to buy American wheat at an arbitrary high price at home and sell it at a lower price in foreign markets." It predicted that the losses "would be shared proportionately by the growers of the farm product involved and, presumably, by the treasury's capital in the commission or corporation [the export corporation]."[87] The *Atlanta Constitution* was not sympathetic either; it claimed the McNary-Haugen bill was tantamount to treating a patient with narcotics instead of attempting to eradicate the disease.[88] Later that fall, the *Atlantic* placed blame for the bill not on farmers themselves but on businesses such as farm implement manufacturers and banks that catered to farmers—they were frustrated with the inability of their customers to pay their debts.[89] It was no accident that the head of a farm implements manufacturer devised the plan; it gave an early indication of how corporate America could be made to see the wisdom of programs that put money in the pockets of consumers.

In the House, Kentucky Democrat David Kincheloe predicted that passage of the law would result in "at least 50,000 extra officeholders appointed, running over the country, meddling in almost every transaction that the farmer makes." He noted that while the export corporation would receive an appropriation of $200 million, it would be authorized to issue up to a billion dollars' worth of bonds. It would be unable to sell them because they were not guaranteed by the federal government. Commodity prices would invariably drop after the export corporation purchased the surplus. "About next December, and from time to time thereafter, this corporation will be coming back to Congress and asking for an appropriation of from $200 to $400 million out of the Treasury, because (it) will be broke and the farmer's market destroyed by that time."[90]

Ira Hersey, Republican of Maine, complained that farmers in northwestern states had been deceived in the midterm elections—they had been called on to send members of "farm-labor blocs" to Washington in the belief that they would obtain "high prices for their farm products, lower freight rates and government relief by government ownership, operation and control."[91] Walter H. Newton of Minnesota predicted that the bill would cause farmers to grow more wheat—thereby placing additional downward pressure on prices.[92] In the Senate Peter Norbeck, a South Dakota Republican, claimed the Adamson Act served as precedent for the bill, as it would give farmers higher income, even as he complained the cost of the Adamson Act to farmers amounted to as much as $2 billion a year in the form of higher railroad rates. He pointed out that other groups, including factory hands, school teachers, and government employees, had demanded and obtained their own wage hikes, producing inflation and increasing the costs borne by farmers. Now it was the farmer's turn.[93] In the spring of 1924, efforts to pass the measure failed due to a lack of support among southerners but proponents of the McNary-Haugen approach vowed to redouble their efforts following the fall election.

While the nation acquiesced in the expansion of federal authority for the benefit of labor, farmers, students, women, and children—albeit via strained constructions of the Constitution—it remained hostile to the exercise of already existing federal powers for the benefit of blacks. Encouraged by the hollow legalese of *Plessy v. Ferguson*, the southern states passed Jim Crow laws at the turn of the century that required separate public facilities for blacks and whites. If there was some truth in W. E. B. DuBois' observation that these measures were designed to compensate poor whites in the South for inadequate schools and labor regulations (by gratifying their racial vanity), that was of little consolation to blacks.[94]

Almost 2,500 blacks were lynched between 1885 and 1900.[95] While the number of victims declined after the turn of the century, the failure to prosecute perpetrators remained a serious problem, especially in the southern states. In 1919 84 blacks were lynched; the last one was a black soldier just returned from Europe who was still dressed in his uniform.[96] The National Association for the Advancement of Colored Persons called for a federal anti-lynching law from the time of its founding in 1909. In 1912 it endorsed a bill modeled on an 1896 Ohio law that imposed criminal penalties on all persons participating in lynch mobs and imposed fines on counties that did not protect blacks.[97] The situation seemed to be precisely that which the equal protection clause was designed to meet—law enforcement officials and courts in southern states were refusing to prosecute persons involved in these heinous crimes, thus denying blacks the equal protection of the laws. Southern members of Congress bitterly opposed an anti-lynching bill proposed in the House in 1918 by Leonidas C. Dyer, a Missouri Republican.[98] The measure would have imposed steep fines on counties that failed to punish those who perpetrated lynching and subjected persons who participate in mob violence to criminal penalties. It also would have made the failure to protect prisoners a federal offense. The bill passed the House in 1922, but southern senators put a stop to its progress in the Senate with a filibuster.

While the Wilson administration segregated federal offices, the Supreme Court provided a ray of hope to blacks in 1915 when it held void the Oklahoma constitution's grandfather clause as a violation of the Fifteenth Amendment. The provision exempted all those who were a direct descendant of a person allowed to vote on January 1, 1866, from a literacy test required for voters.[99] By basing the exemption on a date at which no blacks could vote, the law had the effect of denying the franchise to illiterate blacks while bestowing it on illiterate whites. The case constituted a rare example of the Court's willingness to examine the motives of a legislative body.[100] In 1917 the Supreme Court held void a municipal ordinance requiring that blacks and whites live in separate neighborhoods.[101] If the decision was flawed by its reliance on the amorphous and illegitimate doctrine of freedom of contract (the law was said to violate the right of owners to rent their property to whomever they wished), it nonetheless demonstrated that the high court was at least willing to prevent some forms of public discrimination.

In 1927 the Supreme Court held void a Texas law barring blacks from voting in the state's Democratic primary as a violation of the equal protection clause.[102] Five years later the high court invalidated a Texas statute authorizing the state Democratic Committee to determine the eligibility of persons to vote in the party's primary elections on the grounds that the Committee's actions were discriminatory (blacks were barred from voting). The Court held that the Committee's actions constituted state action impermissible under the equal protection clause of the Fourteenth Amendment as they occurred under the authority of state law.[103] As one historian noted, this analysis could be extended to corporations brought into existence by the states.[104] Two years later, the Court backed away from the revolutionary notion that the activities of state-authorized or incorporated institutions qualified as state action. In *Grovey v. Townsend*, it held that a resolution of a Texas state Democratic Convention limiting the right to participate in Texas state Democratic primaries to whites did not qualify as a state action and was therefore beyond the purview of the Fourteenth and Fifteenth amendments.[105]

Blacks in the South remained outside of the political process for the most part during the 1920s, as the indirect methods of disenfranchisement put in place at the turn of the century such as literacy tests remained in effect. Still, the enactment of the Nineteenth Amendment during the 1920s helped loosen the ossified power structures of the southern states, as it greatly increased the number of persons otherwise qualified to vote who were denied that right by devices such as literacy tests and poll taxes. Republicans made some gains in Virginia, Tennessee, and even Texas in the 1920 election—including the election of seven congressmen from the South—due in part to the votes of black women. White women also helped restore political diversity to the region; for the first time since the days of the Populists, the stranglehold of the Democratic Party over the South's white votes eased. The Republican Party returned the favor by entering into its "lily white" phase that saw it bestow patronage on whites and even Democrats in the South at the expense of blacks.[106]

Discrimination and the availability of jobs in northern factories during World War I caused blacks to leave the South for northern cities. Southern whites were not willing to lose a source of cheap labor and they used every tool at their disposal, including violence, to stop the exodus. The mayor of New Orleans asked the Illinois Central to bar blacks from trains heading north, and southern politicians convinced the U.S. Employment Service to stop helping them move. Blacks nonetheless streamed north in hope of a better life; they did not always find it. When race riots broke out in East St. Louis, Illinois, in 1917, Justice Department officials determined that indictments might be issued pursuant to the Civil Rights Act of 1866 but the Attorney General refused to act. Two years later race riots broke out in cities from Washington to Omaha.[107] In Chicago, where the black population doubled to 125,000 during the war, racial frictions led to an explosion in July 1919. Whites dragged blacks out of street cars and beat them. A full blown riot ensued, resulting in the deaths of 38 persons, including 23 blacks. The city council responded by calling for the complete segregation of the races.[108]

The Ku Klux Klan came back to life after World War I and while its wrath was now directed at Jews and Catholics as well as blacks, the latter still felt most of the heat. While it was still based in the South, the organization proved popular in northern and western states including New York, Maine, Oregon, and California and it boasted of four million members at one point during the 1920s. Texas and Indiana elected Klansmen to the U.S. Senate and governors won office with the assistance of the Klan in Georgia, Alabama, California, and Oregon. While black disenfranchisement in most of the South remained, little help was forthcoming from Washington. Republicans in Congress talked of investigating black disenfranchisement as late as 1927; despite healthy majorities in each house, they failed to act. The party's monopoly of the black vote was now entering its final years, and it was increasingly characterized by cynicism. Republicans renewed their efforts to win white votes in the South, confident that their attempts to appease the dominant race would not cost them the support of blacks.[109] When Herbert Hoover ran for president in 1928, his candidacy was dogged by allegations that while handling relief efforts following the Mississippi River flood of 1927, he allowed black laborers to be herded like cattle and worked to the bone at gunpoint. It was also said that Hoover allowed relief agencies to turn an inordinate share of supplies over to planters, who used their monopoly over foodstuffs and other necessaries to maintain rigid control over blacks.[110]

Republicans nominated Calvin Coolidge for a full term in 1924. The remnants of the Progressive Party nominated Robert M. LaFollette on a platform calling for farm "relief" though laws barring speculation in grain futures and establishing agricultural cooperatives, as well as the reduction of freight rates. The platform also advocated public ownership of railroads and utilities. Progressives proposed to amend the Constitution in order to (1) subject federal judges to elections every 10 years, (2) give Congress the right to reverse rulings of federal judges when they held federal laws invalid, and (3) endow the national government with the power to ban child labor.[111] Progressives refused to add a plank endorsing the Dyer antilynching bill despite being asked to do so by the NAACP. Democrats held their convention at Madison Square Garden New York City. The party required 103 ballots and two-and-a-half weeks to nominate John W. Davis, a Wall Street lawyer, over Al Smith, the Roman Catholic Governor of New York. The convention divided over Smith's religion as well as proposals to denounce the Ku Klux Klan and the League of Nations. When a plank condemning the Klan failed to pass, hooded Klansmen held a huge rally across the Hudson River in New Jersey celebrating their victory. With the party divided, few held out hope of victory in November.

The party of Jefferson and Jackson gave its candidate a platform that spoke the old gospel of states' rights; it held that the states "constitute a bulwark against the centralizing and destructive tendencies of the Republican

Party." The platform also condemned the opposition for seeking "to nationalize the functions and duties of the states." Democrats told the country that they opposed "the extension of bureaucracy, the creation of unnecessary bureaus and federal agencies and the multiplication of offices and officeholders." The platform also called for publicly funded political campaigns and limits on individual contributions to the campaigns of representatives, senators, and presidential candidates. In an indication of the fact that Democrats were aware of the growing power of federal civil servants, the platform endorsed "adequate salaries to provide decent living conditions for postal employees."[112]

Republicans ran on the status quo, ignoring Davis and attacking the Progressive candidate for his party's promise to weaken the federal judiciary. Party officials collected about $4 million in contributions compared to the Democratic take of $800,000.[113] Coolidge won over 15 million votes to 8.4 million for Davis and 5 million for LaFollette. Republicans won the 12 largest cities by a cumulative total of 1.3 million votes.[114] They maintained narrow majorities in each house of Congress. The Progressive Party expired following the election while the movement remained in suspense, its members aware of the futility of maintaining their own organization but doubtful of the prospects for success within the confines of either of the major parties.[115]

JAZZ AGE FEDERALISM

With the death of the Progressive Party as an independent force, the momentum of centralization slowed. It did not go into reverse. The federal government's expenditures had ballooned during the war; they remained high following the return of peace. Before the conflict annual federal expenditures never exceeded a billion dollars; they topped out at $18.5 billion in 1920 before dropping to an average of $3 billion a year in the late 1920s.[116] A variety of interest groups secured places at the public trough while lawmakers proposed initiatives that would not have been thought of 10 years earlier. Federal bureaucrats employed in new agencies learned to enlist the support of members of Congress in maintaining and expanding the budgets of their departments.

It was not long before complaints over centralization began anew. Kentucky Democratic Senator August Stanley blamed Republicans. In a July 4, 1922, speech given before the Society of Tammany in New York City, Stanley offered a witch's brew of vituperation, partisanship, and states' rights. "The Republican Party, born in the throes of sectional hate and fratricidal strife, poisoned in its vitals by the virtue of Federalism, has, during all the years of its evil existence, never ceased to advance with steady and stealthy tread over the whole field of jurisdiction." The prognosis was not good. "From the crushing weight and inordinate expense of an abominable system of endless and irresistible federal interference, there is no escape. Great states are to be stripped of all actual control over their penal, eleemosynary and educational institutions. The citizen is to be left helpless and exposed to the prying interference and vexatious intermeddling of the delator and the spy even in his most intimate domestic relations." The tyranny extended to the newborn. "Babies are to be born by federal aid and suckled under federal supervision. You cannot milk a cow without a federal inspector at your heels. The factory, the mill, the counting house, the office and the home literally swarm with a horde of petty and pestiferous representatives of this paternalistic regime." Federal spending had exploded over the past 10 years, all to pay "this appalling cost of a hundred different commissions, boards and bureaus, employing an innumerable army of deputies, inspectors, supervisors, spies and political parasites." It was about to get worse: Bills were pending in Congress "to regulate, supervise, censor or control the public press, public utilities, the sale of securities, the mining of coal and minerals and the weaving of cloth, horseracing, football, baseball, moving pictures, Sunday amusements, everything in fact from the operation of a railroad to the setting of a hen."[117]

Such comments might be expected from a Democratic border state senator; what was different about the postwar period was that even the staid journals of the northeast detected trouble, perhaps because, with the new income and estate taxes, it was their well-to-do subscribers who were footing the bill. In an August 1923 article in the *North American Review*, Wisconsin Supreme Court Justice Marvin Rosenberry claimed that statutes banning the interstate trafficking of lottery tickets, diseased animals, adulterated food, and impure drugs had produced a sea change in public attitudes toward the central government. "It is impossible to estimate the effect upon the public mind of this constant reiteration of federal power." Rosenberry conceded the need for federal regulation of railroads. Antitrust laws had also proved necessary. Other measures were more questionable: "to the constitutional lawyer perhaps the most startling innovation was the enactment of the Mann Act." Other remarkable innovations included the Federal Reserve, with its power to enlarge the money supply at will, the income tax, which brought people into constant contact with the federal government, and the takeover of the railroad and telegraph systems during World War I—an experiment he viewed as rich with possibilities for the future.[118]

In Rosenberry's view, Americans expected the federal government to take the lead in protecting their well-being and they "no longer question the rights of the federal government or seek to limit its activity." Of the use of federal appropriations to influence state practices, he charged that

Congress "in effect purchases a right to interfere in the local affairs of the states which accept the federal bounty." He acknowledged that Americans often turned to the federal government for protection because it enforced laws more effectively than the states. Rosenberry warned that powers "once exercised by the federal government are seldom if ever voluntarily suspended." He feared centralization would erode state authority and in turn "lessen the people's sense of responsibility."[119]

The *New Republic*, once the flagship journal of the Progressive movement, assessed what it saw as growing sentiment against centralization in January 1925. While in the past the nation's two political parties had altered their view of federal power depending on whether they held the reins, it believed recent objections were more weighty and sincere. The *New Republic* blamed this in part on the disastrous experiment of Prohibition, the futility of which was increasingly apparent, at least in the Northeast. It conceded that many Americans feared that if the process of centralization continued, the nation would be "ruled by a necessarily irresponsible federal bureaucracy which will dry up the sources of local initiative and responsibility." The *New Republic* agreed that the country was too large to be safely governed from Washington alone. It did not endorse a program of retrenchment, though. "The refusal to parallel the increasingly interstate organization of American business by a corresponding increase of federal political control will do nothing to revive American local initiative and sense of responsibility, but its effects will alarm American popular opinion, particularly in the cities, and increase the existing tendency to excitability and violence."[120] A 1925 article in the *Iowa Law Review* applauded the process of centralization; it went so far as to assert that "socially and economically, the states are antiquated political areas."[121]

In a 1925 Memorial Day address at Arlington National Cemetery, President Coolidge addressed concerns over the concentration of power in Washington. He pointed out that the states still conducted the bulk of governmental activity and collected most of the taxes while federal expenditures were being reduced. He acknowledged that people "are given to thinking and speaking more of the national government as 'the government.' They demand more from it than it was ever intended to provide; and yet in the same breath they complain that federal authority is stretching itself over areas which do not concern it." The president blamed this development on the states. "Some have done better and some worse, but as a whole they have not done all they should. So demand has grown up for a greater concentration of powers in the federal government." The remedy in his view was more effective local government. Coolidge bemoaned the growing use of federal grant-in-aid programs. "We may go on yet for a time with the easy assumption that 'if the states will not, the nation must.' But that way lies trouble. When the national treasury contributes half, there is temptation to extravagance by the state." This pattern had already manifested itself with excesses in the construction of roads. Coolidge saw grant-in-aid programs as a means for some states to gouge others via the federal apparatus while neglecting their own duties.[122]

One periodical went so far as to compare Coolidge to Jefferson in his hostility to federal authority.[123] While he limited federal spending, in practice the president was far from being a Jeffersonian. In his annual message of December 6, 1927, Coolidge called for the establishment of a department of education and relief even as he conceded that the maintenance of schools was "strictly a state and local function."[124] Even progressives found it hard to stomach the idea of a department of education. Idaho Senator William E. Borah warned it would be the "nose of the camel under the tent." Why not, he asked, also establish departments devoted to "athletics, hygiene and matrimony?"[125] The bureaus and divisions already concerned with education were startling in their variety: Home Education, Education Extension, Agricultural Education, School and Home Gardening, the Kindergarten Division, Negro Education and Commercial Education. A National Advisory Committee on Education was formed in 1929. It asserted that there were "national responsibilities for education which only the federal government can adequately meet."[126]

In a February 1931 article in the *Atlantic*, Lawrence Sullivan reported that the national government consisted of 10 departments, 134 bureaus and divisions, and 35 independent "establishments" that together employed some 800,000 persons—not including a quarter million Americans in the armed forces. After adding family members of these persons, Sullivan concluded that 2 percent of the population "live directly off the national government"—and that figure didn't include those who received veterans' pensions.[127] In another article later that year, Sullivan counted 15 different federal agencies that administered river-and-harbor projects, and 25 that oversaw construction projects. The captain of an American ship returning to an American port had to deal with "thirteen Federal officials operating in seven different departments." Sullivan claimed that in recent years, a common assumption in both parties held that the federal government spent about a billion dollars more annually than was necessary.[128]

James M. Beck of Pennsylvania had been appointed assistant attorney general by McKinley; he later served as solicitor general before winning election to Congress. While he had once supported a more vigorous exercise of federal authority, by the late 1920s Beck was a bitter critic of the concentration of power in Washington. He turned out several screeds decrying this development during the postwar years. The last, *Our Wonderland Bureaucracy*, examined the federal establishment as it existed in 1932. Beck's verdict was hinted at in the subtitle: *A Study of the Growth of the Bureaucracy in the Federal Government, and Its Destructive Effects upon the Constitution.* Beck decried the various agencies and bureaus devoted to agriculture, as "the Constitution never gave the federal government any power, as such" (though he conceded the commerce clause authorized federal quarantines of diseased cattle). This incursion constituted "a bald and palpable usurpation of the function of the states, maintained for the benefit of one class and largely at the expense of the taxpayers of the industrial states, who have no practical interest in agriculture."[129] Except, of course, when they ate. Beck noted that numerous bureaus established during the war survived, including the Women's Bureau, which began as an emergency measure in 1918. He blamed federal extravagance on the fact that so few Americans paid income taxes—fewer than 400,000 persons paid 97 percent of federal income tax revenues in 1928. When it came to federal spending, "why should the remaining 120,000,000 care?" Federal printing expenses alone ran to $50 million a year by the early 1930s. Much of it went to the publicizing of activities of various agencies. The federal bureaucracy turned out thousands of pamphlets each year on subjects that seemed more than a little afield, i.e., "Self-Help Suits for the Small Boy" and "Vitamins in Relation to Salad Dressing." One brochure provided instructions for making a cat trap. It advised the reader to place a bag over the cat's hat before drowning it in the nearest river, lest it apprehend its impending doom.[130]

Beck noted that federal agencies were acutely aware of the importance of publicity in obtaining ever-increasing appropriations. Classified civil servants including mail carriers had become adept at pressuring members of Congress into increasing their salaries, and lawmakers complied to avoid incurring the wrath of public employee unions. Businesses benefiting from the growth of agencies also lobbied on their behalf, e.g., ship owners sought more money for the U.S. Shipping Board and airplane manufacturers wanted larger subsidies for air mail. The problem was worsened by the failure of Congress to investigate the appropriation requests made by the bureaus. Bills to reduce the power of bureaus or federal agencies invariably met the opposition of those same agencies, as well the hostility of interested parties in the private sector who lobbied on their behalf. [131]

As Beck noted, relatively few Americans paid income taxes. Just over four million persons filed income tax returns for 1928; 37 million persons cast ballots in the presidential election that year.[132] It may have been fortunate that relatively few Americans paid income taxes, as the tax code had already evolved into a monstrosity. The 1913 law establishing the income tax consumed 15 pages of the U.S. Statutes-at-Large; the 1928 Revenue Act required some 92 pages to describe various deductions, credits, methods of calculation, and procedures—and that did not include the voluminous Treasury regulations that had been issued. The verbosity of the tax code stemmed in part from the almost impossible task of treating various elements of the economy equally, but it was already apparent that those involved in the process had resigned themselves to the existence of a body of law to which no two accountants gave identical interpretations.[133] The evils produced by an inscrutable tax code multiplied as the century progressed and more Americans found themselves required to comply with it. It subjected taxpayers to criminal penalties for their failure to comply with a law even tax commissioners did not always comprehend and produced a cottage industry of lawyers and accountants ready to fight any attempt to simplify it lest they lose a lucrative business. Worst of all, its voluminous provisions made a wide variety of industries dependent for their fortunes on the stability of its provisions. A schedule that provided for depreciation over five years might enable a manufacturer to survive, while one that stretched this allowance over 20 years could ensure ruin. It was the tariff fight all over again, on an even larger scale.

Among the Americans who were troubled by the concentration of power in Washington was H. L. Mencken, perhaps the nation's most prominent journalist during the 1920s. Mencken displayed an appreciation for decentralized government, perhaps because his success enabled him to join that limited class of Americans who were asked to pay for the experiment in progress in Washington. Writing in July 1927 regarding Maryland Governor Albert Ritchie's candidacy for the 1928 Democratic presidential nomination, he predicted that the issue of "of states' rights . . . is likely to make a great deal of progress in the years to come," though he conceded that "the time for it is not yet." Americans "are gluttons for punishment. They will stand a great many more doses of federal usurpation before they will revolt at last. Today they complain only of Prohibition: they will have a lot more to complain of before the tale is told."[134]

One area in which federal authority did not advance during the 1920s was disaster relief. Congress first provided aid during the 1790s, when it appropriated money for the benefit of Santo Domingo following a hurricane. The sum was deducted from the debt owed to France, as Santo Domingo was a French possession. Contrary to the assertions of some, it was not viewed at the time as an exercise of a broad spending power. The Freedmen's Bureau and the army aided destitute persons in the South following Appomattox. These acts were viewed as exercises of the war powers of Congress.[135] Three appropriations of 1874 provided aid to victims of floods in the Mississippi Valley—the first such acts that had no relation to any of the enumerated powers.[136] In 1875, Congress authorized the purchase of seeds for distribution to victims of grasshopper plagues in the Plains states.[137] Congress provided approximately $1 million in aid for victims of floods on the Ohio and Mississippi Rivers in 1882 and 1884.[138] Washington did not aid Chicago or Boston following the fires of 1871 and 1872. Tents were provided by the Army following the Galveston hurricane of 1900. In 1900 Congress gave the American Red Cross a federal charter and authorized it to aid the victims of natural disasters as well as wars. It did not provide it with money.[139] The spigot opened a bit following the San Francisco earthquake of 1906. A fire in the aftermath destroyed much of the city, leaving thousands of residents destitute. Congress appropriated $4 million for the secretary of war to use at his discretion for the benefit of victims lacking shelter or sustenance.[140] The Army supervised the distribution of donated relief supplies.[141] Appropriations of 1913, 1914, and 1916 provided aid for victims of floods, tornadoes, and fires in the Carolinas, Tennessee, Florida, Texas, Massachusetts, Alabama, Nebraska, and West Virginia.[142] During the 1920s, the Department of Agriculture provided loans to farmers affected by droughts.[143] As occurred with grant-in-aid measures, the congressional debates that preceded appropriations to aid victims of disasters featured almost no discussion of their legality.

One of the worst disasters in American history occurred in 1927, when the Mississippi River overflowed its banks and placed an area the size of several states under water. The disaster was at least 50 years in coming. The Mississippi River Commission focused on navigability and not flood control; it decided against using spillways or other means to drain excessive water. The construction of numerous levees increased the flow of water down the river and made a disaster inevitable. Horrendous floods occurred along the Mississippi and its tributaries in 1882, 1912, 1913, and 1922. After the 1913 floods killed 2,000 in Ohio, the state built its own reservoir and spillway system. The Mississippi River Commission refused to take the hint; instead it closed off natural spillways such as Cypress Creek in 1921. The river, more hemmed in than ever, rose to dangerous levels with regularity—two feet high levees in New Orleans had been sufficient to stop the flood of 1850; since that time they had to be raised to a height of 20 feet to contain the river.[144]

Heavy rains began in the fall of 1926 and continued through the winter. By April 1927 millions of acres of land along the upper Mississippi and its tributaries such as the Ohio River were underwater, including parts of Pittsburgh and Cincinnati.[145] As the water moved downstream, heavily taxed levees began to give way. At one point a 130-foot high wall of water three-quarters of a mile wide broke through levees and into the delta. The crevasse at Mounds Landing, Mississippi, resulted in flooding of an area 50 miles wide and 100 miles in length that had been occupied by 185,000 persons. The surge reached Yazoo, 40 miles from the river, where floodwaters rose above the tops of houses. In Louisiana, levees in the rural districts were blown up in order to save New Orleans. Overall 27,000 square miles were flooded by up to 30 feet of water, and 1.5 million acres were still under water as of July 27. Some 931,000 lived in the area that had been flooded; deaths in the Mississippi Delta region alone were estimated to number about 1,000.[146] Between floods in the Mississippi River Valley and New England, some 1.5 million Americans were left homeless.[147]

Setting up headquarters in Memphis, Secretary of Commerce Herbert Hoover coordinated the relief efforts of private agencies such as the Red Cross; he also convinced the railroads to transport the dispossessed at no charge. A grant from the Rockefeller Foundation was used to establish medical facilities. The army provided 100,000 blankets to refugees; several federal agencies donated boats used to evacuate victims. The Federal Intermediate Credit Corporation made loans available to farmers in stricken areas. In April 1927, the president assured the country that the federal government was "giving aid as lies within its powers." Coolidge asked Americans to contribute to relief agencies such as the Red Cross; he said nothing regarding additional federal assistance.[148] In early June, Secretary of the Treasury Mellon assured that the needs of persons who remained homeless were being met with funds from private sources.[149] While some claimed that the Red Cross could not be expected to foot the bill, it raised enough money through donations to shelter and feed at least 130,000 Americans—mostly for brief periods—in the aftermath of the flood, when entire counties in the lower Mississippi Valley remained under as much as eight feet of water.[150] The relief camps slowly emptied as summer turned into fall—they had 63,378 inhabitants in June, 17,100 in July, and only 1,927 in September.[151]

Despite the pleas of politicians in the Mississippi Valley and lawmakers in Washington, Coolidge refused to visit afflicted areas—he was not the type to indulge others with empty gestures.[152] Nor would he call Congress into special session to enact a massive river control bill sought by lawmakers from the South and the Midwest. In his annual message of December 1927, the president reported that the national government provided services, equipment, and supplies to flood victims worth about $7 million.[153] Further aid would not be forthcoming. In May 1928, the president and Congress agreed on a bill providing $325 million for flood control measures including spillways; it did not provide aid to victims of the flood.[154] Congress gave Vermont, New Hampshire, and Kentucky $5.2 million to repair or replace roads and bridges wiped out by flooding.[155]

At the time of the flood, the federal government was already seven years into the disastrous experiment known as Prohibition. The Eighteenth Amendment provided, in part, that the "manufacture, sale, or transportation of intoxicating liquors within, the importation thereof into, or the exportation thereof from the United States and all territory subject to the jurisdiction thereof for beverage purposes is hereby prohibited." It gave the states and Congress concurrent power to enforce its terms. Prohibition arose out of the same moral fervor that had once produced Abolitionism; it was also a product of a growing rift between urban and rural America that for a time threatened to replace sectionalism as the great dividing line in American politics. To some extent Prohibition constituted an attempt by rural Protestant America to impose its will on the ethnic Catholics of the cities. In 1928, H. L. Mencken wrote that two-thirds of the Baptist and Methodist newspapers of the South "devote half their space to bawling that anyone who is against Prohibition is against God, and the other half to damning the pope."[156] The hostility of rural America to the cities had a nativist and even a nationalistic quality to it; this attitude manifested itself in the immigration laws of 1921 and 1924 that limited the number of persons from southern and eastern Europe who could enter the United States each year. It was also revealed in the revival of the Ku Klux Klan. Laws against the teaching of evolution and measures compelling children to attend public schools also arose out of the hostility of rural America to immigrants and Catholics. Some allowance must be made for the honest conviction that alcohol ruined lives, that it was a national problem, and that it required a national solution. Many Americans believed in Prohibition. Given this commitment, it remains a mystery as to why Congress was from the start unwilling to properly fund what it must have known would be a monumental undertaking.

Federal and state officials arrested 500,000 persons for violating the Volstead Act—the law implementing the Eighteenth Amendment—and obtained over 300,000 convictions.[157] During June 1925, an average day in Chicago saw U.S. marshals serve 49 writs and make 18 arrests for violations of Prohibition laws.[158] Cases involving alleged violations clogged the federal courts. The burden was so overwhelming—the accused often waited a year before they were tried—that it led to the use of plea bargains on a wide scale in federal courts for the first time.[159] State courts were also overworked, and the efforts of law enforcement officials were often in vain as jury nullification—the refusal to convict even those who guilt was plain—was rampant. The prosecutions did nothing to stem the deluge of liquor that washed over the country. Americans seemed to take pride in violating the Volstead Act; even in the Capitol itself the speaker of the House and his Democratic counterparts engaged in drinking bouts.[160] The distribution of liquor passed from legal entities to criminal organizations, greatly enriching and strengthening them in the process.

Secretary of the Treasury Andrew Mellon resented having the unhappy task of surveying America's drinking habits assigned to his bailiwick; he sought to have the Prohibition Bureau transferred to the Justice

Department. Employees of the Bureau conducted investigations while U.S. marshals made the necessary arrests. Investigations required searches of businesses, homes, warehouses, and hotels. Wiretaps were obtained without warrants. The Supreme Court upheld the legality of the practice in 1928.[161] As Chief Justice Taft explained, "there was no seizure. The evidence was secured by the use of the sense of hearing and that only. There was no entry of the houses or offices of the defendants."[162] For the suggestion that the Fourth Amendment's ban on unreasonable searches barred warrantless wiretaps, Taft had no sympathy. "The language of the Amendment cannot be extended and expanded to include telegraph wires reaching to the whole world from the defendant's house or office. The intervening wires are not part of his house or office any more than are the highways along which they are stretched."[163] In his dissent, Justice Brandeis inaugurated the hoary practice of pretending that provisions of the Bill of Rights when combined bestowed rights that could not be reasonably extracted from any of its individual parts. In his view, the Fourth and Fifth Amendments "sought to protect Americans in their beliefs, their thoughts, their emotions and their sensations. They conferred, as against the government, the right to be let alone—the most comprehensive of rights and the right most valued by civilized men."[164] This approach was pregnant with mischief—if adopted it would endow judges with the power to reverse any conviction that arose out of evidence obtained through the observation of activities that took place in or around a defendant's home.

The Eighteenth Amendment authorized the states to supplement federal legislation with their own statutes enforcing its terms and all but Maryland did so. Like Congress, they refused to provide their law enforcement establishments with the resources necessary to make Prohibition effective. New York State repealed its prohibition law in 1923. When the president issued an executive order in 1926 authorizing the Treasury Department to appoint state law enforcement personnel prohibition officers of the Treasury Department, protests were intense. The Senate Judiciary Committee concluded the practice did not violate the Constitution in part because participation was voluntary. Federal employees were themselves deputized by states during the 1920s; they also enforced state game and hunting laws.[165] By the end of the 1920s, the Volstead Act was being publicly flouted across the North and politicians such as Jimmy Walker of New York City—the "nightclub mayor"—rose to prominence through their willingness to frequent illegal drinking establishments.[166] Advocates of Prohibition looked at the unwillingness of states in the northeast to enforce it and charged they were engaging in a latter-day version of nullification. Following his election to the presidency, Herbert Hoover transferred the Prohibition Bureau to the Justice Department and placed it within the Civil Service. By 1932, the country had lost patience with the experiment. The Twenty-First Amendment, which repealed the Eighteenth, became part of the Constitution in December 1933.

The failure of the federal government to make Prohibition effective obscured a more fundamental change during the 1920s that saw it play an increasingly prominent role in law enforcement. By 1930, many federal agencies had their own law officers, including the Customs Service and the Narcotics Bureau, the alcohol tax unit, the intelligence unit of the Bureau of Internal Revenue, the Interstate Commerce Commission, and even the Veterans' Administration.[167] There were nearly 10,000 by 1932.[168] The Justice Department first obtained an investigatory capacity via an 1871 statute that provided the attorney general with funds ($50,000) to be used to detect and prosecute crimes against the United States.[169] The idea of detectives in the Justice Department remained unpopular, and for many years it hired outside agents, such as those provided by the Pinkerton Agency, even as other bureaus employed their own detectives. The practice was terminated in 1892 when Congress barred the Justice Department from using private detectives; thereafter it used employees of other departments, such as Secret Service personnel employed by the Treasury Department. In 1907, the Justice Department began to collect criminal records to be provided to state officials on request. A Bureau of Investigation was finally established in the Justice Department in 1908 after Congress barred it from using Secret Service agents.[170] The new Bureau remained inadequately funded and understaffed until J. Edgar Hoover was appointed director in 1924. Hoover turned the Bureau of Investigation into a formidable agency known for its professionalism. The FBI investigated the Cincinnati Police Department for alleged violations of the Volstead Act. Hoover had to deny requests to investigate 72 police departments across the country due to a lack of authority. Even at that point the Bureau of Investigation agents lacked the power to make arrests. When an FBI agent was killed in a Chicago garage in 1925, the accused murderer had to be charged under state law as there was no federal statute prohibiting the killing of federal agents. During the early 1930s, Congress gave agents authority to make arrests and carry weapons; killing an agent was made a federal crime. When J. Edgar Hoover opposed attempts to add the Bureau of Investigation to the Civil Service—he wanted promotions based on merit instead of seniority—his resistance constituted an indictment of the Civil Service and not the Director.[171]

A larger federal law enforcement apparatus became imperative during the 1920s—or so it was thought—as automobiles enabled criminals to move easily across state lines. In 1925 the Supreme Court upheld a 1919 law barring the interstate transportation of stolen cars as an appropriate exercise of the commerce clause "police power" of Congress without a dissenting vote.[172] In his opinion for the Court, Chief Justice Taft explained that Congress may pass laws preventing the use of interstate commerce for immoral or illegal purposes.[173] The inadequate police forces of the states also seemed to warrant an expanded federal role in law enforcement. State police departments had only recently been inaugurated, and state governments exercised little control over district attorneys. Half the country was said to live in areas where the only law enforcement officer was an elected county sheriff; even those counties that had deputy sheriffs saw them leave office when the sheriff lost an election.[174] The problem was greatly exacerbated during the 1920s when liquor smugglers or "bootleggers" purchased police officers and state judges by the dozen. The public began to associate federal law enforcement agencies with efficiency in contrast to their allegedly corrupt and inept counterparts at the state level.

In an August 1931 article in the *New York Times*, Columbia University professor Raymond Moley lauded this development. He believed it had much to do with the success of federal agencies in destroying various criminal enterprises: income tax laws had been used to bring down Al Capone in Chicago, alien laws enabled officials to deport organized crime figures, and antitrust laws had been deployed against conspiracies to fix the prices of consumer goods. Customs and mail fraud statutes as well as laws prohibiting the interstate transportation of stolen automobiles had also been applied. The income tax had proven an especially potent law enforcement weapon as it imposed an unhappy choice on criminals. "Either they must account for their illegal income and thus expose it or they must violate the law by omitting it." The relative incorruptibility and superior skill of federal judges made prosecutions in federal court easier, as did the fact that the witnesses, at least in income tax cases, were usually revenue officers who were not easily susceptible to intimidation or bribery. In contrast, urban political organizations and governments, including law enforcement entities, were often linked to organized crime. Moley thought the experiment should be continued and expanded. "Theoretically, then, there is almost no limit to the extent to which an active federalism could proceed against the suppression of crimes against property."[175] In June 1932 Congress enacted a federal anti-kidnapping law following the kidnapping and murder of Charles Lindbergh's son. The statute gave the FBI preeminent investigatory power when the victim was taken across state lines.[176]

The declining reputation of the state governments received ample confirmation in a series of articles that ran in the *Nation* between 1922 and 1925. Discrimination, corruption, and all manner of exploitation seemed rife. In Miami, no blacks except bellboys, porters, and others hotel employees were allowed out of the black section of the city after 9:00 p.m. "Abuse of the negro" remained the "master key to political office" in Florida.[177] In Mississippi, five-year-olds were still "chopping cotton" Many of the black districts lacked schools. During World War I, some in Vicksburg decided everyone should work to aid the war effort; four persons tarred and feathered a pregnant black woman who refused to do so. Two years after the incident, the perpetrators were tried and two of them sentenced to prison but they did not serve any time. Illiteracy was common, and Mississippi's roads, which remained unpaved, were impassable after downpours.[178]

Montana also presented a bleak picture. It remained under the control of the Anaconda Mining Company, whose executives appeared on the eve of elections and legislative votes to distribute the funds necessary to maintain the company's hold on the state. "Money is poured out like water; and men fall by the hundred before the temptations of the bribe-giver or the promise of future preferment, and the fear of the consequences if they do not yield."[179] Nevada was dominated by livestock interests who were greatly aided by federal land policies—the federal government owned 90 percent of the land in the state. Cattlemen bought property along rivers and streams and used adjacent federal lands for grazing at no charge.[180] Rhode Island saw its child labor rates increase while they dropped in the rest of the country. Almost a fifth of the children of Woonsocket were working—the highest percentage in any city in the United States. Legislation aimed at reducing the work week in mills to 48 hours failed due to the threats of the owners to move their mills to the South.[181] In Connecticut, electoral corruption remained the plague it had been in much of the rest of the country at the end of the nineteenth century. Republicans were said to be the "usual purchasers."[182] Delaware had fallen under the rule of the DuPont family, which was said to have controlled the state Republican Party since 1906. All three of the state's daily newspapers were owned by the DuPonts.[183] The federal government could hardly have been expected to intervene in states merely because they were dominated by powerful interests or trailed the rest of the nation in their treatment of minorities or the downtrodden. Still, the corruption of legislatures and political parties by corporate interests explained why Americans looked to the federal government for relief.

DUE PROCESS, INCORPORATION, AND THE REGULATION OF SPEECH

The federal government itself contributed to the impotence of the states. When legislatures managed to overcome entrenched interests and enact needed reforms, they faced the prospect of having their work reversed by the Supreme Court. During the 1920s the justices embraced a view of the

Fourteenth Amendment's due process clause that made the high court a parody of its Gilded Age predecessor—though even the late-nineteenth-century Supreme Court was more respectful of the right of legislatures to regulate labor relations and commercial activity. In 1923 the justices threatened to resuscitate *Lochner v. New York* when they held void a Washington, DC, statute establishing a minimum wage for women as a violation of the Fifth Amendment's due process clause and the right to contract for one's labor as one saw fit.[184] The opinion was marked by an awkward exchange over the question of whether minimum-wage laws for women contributed to the preservation of their morals.[185] All this was necessary because the doctrine of freedom of contract constituted little more than a license used by the high court to invalidate economic legislation it found unreasonable. In 1924 the Court saw fit to hold void a Minnesota law regulating the size of broad loaves—requiring a minimum-sized loaf was acceptable; imposing a maximum limit was not.[186] The dissent of Justice Brandeis was stocked with copious footnotes explaining the problems of weighing and classifying bread loaves—he had no choice given that the test for constitutionality of the law was its reasonableness.[187] From there the court's decisions grew more absurd; a law barring the resale of theater tickets for more than 25 percent above face value was declared to conflict with the Fourteenth Amendment; so were statutes regulating gasoline prices and rates charged by employment agencies—these businesses were not affected with a public interest, and to limit the ability of persons therein to earn a profit was to violate their due process rights bestowed by the Fourteenth Amendment.[188] As Justice Brandeis pointed out in his dissent in *New State Ice Company v. Liebmann*, the public/private dichotomy was a recent invention and lacked any basis in either American or English statutory law.[189] The high court also continued to invalidate rates imposed by the legislatures or state commissions on railroads and utilities as violations of due process or as impermissible regulations of interstate commerce. The nomination of Charles Evans Hughes for chief justice met widespread opposition due to his role as an attorney in obtaining several of these rulings from the high court. His nomination was approved in the Senate by a 52–26 margin in February 1930; 18 senators didn't vote.[190]

By one count, the Supreme Court held state laws void on due process grounds in only 7 percent of the occasions upon which said violations were alleged in cases brought before it between 1913 and 1920 (7 out of 97). During the following seven years, it held state laws void on due process grounds in more than 28 percent of the cases in which such violations were alleged (15 of 53). A contemporary review made the best of what was a muddled and confusing body of law; it acknowledged that the high court had applied a series of related but confusing tests with inconsistent results in determining whether state laws violated the Fourteenth Amendment, i.e., whether they served legitimate ends, had a legitimate relationship to those ends, whether they exceeded the permissible sphere of legislatures, constituted an acceptable exercise of the police power, or whether rights the Court deemed fundamental had been violated. The author referred the reader to common law innovations of judges in the field of torts in defense of judges examining the public policy ramifications of their decisions—as if there was not an enormous difference between the incremental development of the common law and federal judges misreading constitutional provisions to wield a veto power over state legislation.[191]

In an October 1924 article in the *New Republic*, future Supreme Court justice Felix Frankfurter called for the repeal of the due process clauses in the Fifth and Fourteenth Amendments due to the mischief that spurious interpretations of them had produced.[192] Six years later, he suggested that the Supreme Court's assumption of the power to invalidate state economic regulations might well constitute the greatest change thus far in the nation's constitutional system. "The termination of slavery and the participation of the negro in the free life of the nation mark political changes of stupendous meaning. But even more important consequences, perhaps, flow from the new subjection of the states to national control through the effectual veto power exercised by the Supreme Court over state legislation. The vague words of the Fourteenth Amendment furnish the excuse for this immense power."[193] The Court's assumption of a "veto power" over the "social-economic legislation of the states, thus exercised through the due process clause, is the most vulnerable aspect of undue centralization. It is at once the most destructive and the least responsible: the most destructive, because judicial nullification on grounds of constitutionality stops experimentation at it source, and bars increase to the fund of social knowledge by scientific tests of trial and error; the least responsible, because it so often turns on the fortuitous circumstances which determine a majority decision and shelters the fallible judgment of individual justices, in matters of fact and opinion not peculiarly within the special competence of judges, behind the impersonal dooms of the Constitution."[194]

A whole new field for judicial creativity was opened by the discovery that the Fourteenth Amendment extended at least a portion of the federal Bill of Rights to the states. The traditional view was embraced as late as 1916. A lawsuit involving the federal Employer's Liability Act had been tried before a jury in Minnesota state court that was allowed to arrive at a less than unanimous verdict. The appellant claimed the lack of unanimity violated his right to a jury trial provided by the Seventh Amendment. In his opinion for the Supreme Court, Chief Justice White repeated what had been the prevailing view for half a century: "The first ten amendments, including of course the seventh, are not concerned with state action and deal only with federal action." Thus, "the Seventh Amendment does not, anymore than the other first ten amendments, apply in state court."[195]

The route taken by the Supreme Court in this endeavor was a circuitous one. The justices expanded the meaning of the word *liberty* contained in the due process clause of the Fourteenth Amendment beyond liberty of contract to noncommercial activities. As early as 1907, Justice Holmes stated in his opinion for the majority in *Patterson v. Colorado* that the Court would "leave undecided the question whether there is to be found in the Fourteenth Amendment a prohibition similar to that in the First."[196] Many would have been surprised to learn that it was a question. In his dissent, Justice John Harlan took the bait; he thought the privileges of free speech and a free press "constitute essential parts of every man's liberty, and are protected against violation by that clause of the Fourteenth Amendment forbidding a state to deprive any person of his liberty without due process of law."[197] In *Meyer v. Nebraska* (1923), the Supreme Court held that the Fourteenth Amendment's due process clause rendered void a Nebraska law barring the teaching of any language other than English in the public schools.[198] In his opinion for the majority, Justice James McReynolds held that the liberty protected by the due process clause of the Fourteenth Amendment includes the "right of the individual to contract, to engage in any of the common occupations of life, to acquire useful knowledge, to marry, establish a home and bring up children, to worship God according to the dictates of his own conscience, and generally to enjoy those privileges long recognized at common law as essential to the orderly pursuit of happiness by free men."[199] A hundred judges might have given a hundred different answers to the question of what privileges the common law viewed as "essential to the orderly pursuit of happiness by free men." It is doubtful that many would have included the right to have one's children taught a foreign language among this class of privileges, but seven of the nine justices held that it did. As one historian said of the high court's use of the word "liberty" in the due process clause, "once torn from its historical moorings (it) may as well embrace freedom of any kind."[200] Such things were perhaps inevitable when the justices used the Constitution to develop a sort of constitutional common law and paid more attention to prior cases in evaluating new ones than the plain text and history of the charter.

The high court continued to expand its role as a sort of privy council charged with controlling errant and immature colonies two years later in *Pierce v. Society of Sisters*, when it held void an Oregon law requiring all children to attend public schools.[201] Justice McReynolds suggested the law impaired the liberty of parents to raise their children as they wish. "As often heretofore pointed out, rights guaranteed by the Constitution may not be abridged by legislation that has no reasonable relation to some purpose within the competency of the state."[202] The law was ridiculous and even tyrannical to be sure, but the decision raised the question as to what statute might not be deemed by any group of five lawyers to be lacking in reasonableness.

In *Gitlow v. New York*, the Supreme Court upheld a conviction for violating a New York law against criminal anarchy (advocating the violent overthrow of the government).[203] Benjamin Gitlow had published a document in which he asserted that it was "necessary to destroy the parliamentary state." He claimed, rather hopefully, that "strikes are developing which verge on revolutionary action, and in which the suggestion of proletarian dictatorship is apparent."[204] In his opinion for the majority, Justice Edward T. Sanford announced that the New York law was constitutional.[205] Of more significance was his assertion that the Fourteenth Amendment incorporated rights also contained in the First Amendment. "For present purposes we may and do assume that freedom of speech and of the press—which are protected by the First Amendment from abridgment by Congress—are among the fundamental personal rights and 'liberties' protected by the due process clause of the Fourteenth Amendment from impairment by the states."[206] As it was originally understood, the clause did no such thing.[207]

In *Near v. Minnesota* (1931) the Supreme Court held void a statute as violating the freedom of the press protected by the Fourteenth Amendment.[208] The law declared "malicious, scandalous and defamatory" periodicals to be public nuisances subject to injunctions prohibiting further publication. In his dissent, Justice Pierce Butler pointed out that the First Amendment had been understood as barring only prior restraints on publication, such as had been exercised by the crown when it withheld licenses to prevent the publishing of attacks on its policies.[209] The decision has been celebrated as a victory for the cause of a free press. It extinguished a statute that was overly broad and abusive, but it also inaugurated a trend that would see the high court effectively deprive the states of the power to protect persons in public life against defamatory libel. Common law protections against defamation dated from the thirteenth century. Removal of them may well have discouraged participation in public life, thereby diminishing freedom of expression instead of protecting it.[210]

In 1926, Charles Warren predicted that the Supreme Court would eventually hold that the entirety of the Bill of Rights applied to the states.[211] Despite the fact that 60 years went by after the Fourteenth Amendment was ratified before the Supreme Court embraced the incorporation doctrine, some scholars tried to demonstrate that it had been understood at the time it was ratified as extending the Bill of Rights to the states. When the matter was debated in Congress, two lawmakers, Representative John Bingham of

Ohio and Senator Jacob Howard of Michigan, claimed section one would extend the Bill of Rights to the states.[212] In contrast, dozens of representatives and senators treated the amendment as merely providing a constitutional basis for the Civil Rights Act of 1866.[213] The debate that followed the amendment's submission to the states did not see advocates of ratification claim that it would extend the Bill of Rights to the states.[214] Instead they also suggested it would secure the rights protected by the Civil Rights Act of 1866. Newspapers of the period contain hundreds of accounts of the ratification debate; they are almost complete devoid of any mention of the Bill of Rights. Some later pointed to the fact that newspapers reprinted the speeches of Senator Howard and John Bingham as evidence that the country realized Congress intended to apply the Fourteenth Amendment to the states.[215] As newspapers routinely printed excerpts of congressional speeches, there was nothing particularly notable about the fact that the comments of these gentlemen appeared in print—so did the speeches of other lawmakers who defined Section 1 differently.

Some have cited the almost complete lack of any discussion regarding the Bill of Rights itself as evidence of the country's acquiescence in the view of Howard and Bingham, on the theory that silence implies consent.[216] That a nation still teeming with politicians and lawyers dedicated to protecting the prerogatives of the states would have embraced such a revolutionary extension of federal authority without protest is, of course, absurd.[217] Democrats deployed every possible argument against the amendment; they did not suggest that it extended the Bill of Rights to the states. Instead they warned it would result in the enfranchisement of blacks. A survey of the ratification debate in Illinois, Ohio, and Pennsylvania reveals no mention of the Bill of Rights in the speeches of the amendment's backers.[218] Advocates of ratification in the southern states did not suggest it incorporated the Bill of Rights either.[219] If it is incumbent on Congress to explain the meaning of a proposed amendment—especially one expanding federal authority—when it sends it to the states for ratification, the almost complete absence of any acknowledgment that the states would be required to comply with the Bill of Rights seems fatal. The failure of the members of legislatures to acknowledge the possibility of subjecting the states to the federal Bill of Rights when they met to consider ratifying the Fourteenth Amendment—many of the state constitutions contained provisions in conflict with its provisions—makes it clear that the states did not believe they were subjecting themselves to the terms of the first 10 amendments in accepting the Fourteenth.[220]

The text of the Amendment itself condemns the incorporation doctrine as nothing in it gives any indication of this purpose. It did not explicitly extend the Bill of Rights to the states or even mention it. In 1869 the Supreme Court heard a litigant claim for the first time that the Bill of

Rights applied to the states; it rejected the argument without even considering the possibility that the Fourteenth Amendment incorporated it.[221] Six years later in his opinion for the high court in *U.S. v. Cruikshank*, Chief Justice Waite turned aside the claim that the Second Amendment right to bear arms of several black men had been violated by Louisiana state officials: "this is one of the amendments that has no other effect than to restrict the powers of the national government." [222]

The debate was reminiscent of the discussion regarding the general welfare clause and the question of whether the Constitution was understood at the time of its ratification as containing a broad spending power. Although a handful of persons claimed the general welfare clause bestowed a broad spending power while the Constitution was being considered by state ratifying conventions (almost all in private correspondence), most did not detect a broad spending power. Advocates of the Constitution such as James Madison denied the general welfare clause bestowed broad powers of any kind.[223] It was therefore a simple matter for strict constructionists to demonstrate that the states did not act in the belief that they were bestowing a broad spending power on the federal government when they ratified the Constitution.[224] Eighty years later, the people of the states and their legislatures did not act in the belief that the Fourteenth Amendment required that state laws and constitutions conform to the Bill of Rights when they ratified it. That some of the drafters thought the amendment would extend the Bill of Rights to the states cannot be disputed. Still, the historical record is almost completely devoid of any indication they or anyone else communicated this view to the public during the ratification debate and displaced the prevailing belief that Section 1's privileges and immunities clause merely provided a constitutional basis for the Civil Rights Act of 1866.

An interesting postscript to the Supreme Court's conversion of itself into a defender of civil liberties occurred in the failure of the federal judiciary to keep the other branches of the national government from violating the First Amendment. In 1927, Congress imposed an exacting regulatory framework on the growing radio industry. It seemed a situation appropriate for federal action under the commerce clause, as the assignment of radio frequencies by 48 states would have produced chaos. The Federal Radio Act of 1927 established a Radio Commission to regulate radio stations; it required each one to obtain a license before broadcasting.[225] Section 11 authorized the Commission to deny a license to applicants if it determined that granting one would not serve the public interest, convenience, or necessity. Such a broad power seemed to authorize the board to censor speech, but Section 29 provided that "nothing in this act shall be understood or construed to give the licensing authority the power of censorship over the radio communications or signals transmitted by any radio station." It also stipulated that "no regulation or condition shall be promulgated or fixed by the licensing authority which shall interfere with the right of free speech by means of radio communications."

Within five years of its formation, the Federal Radio Commission appeared to violate both Section 29 and the First Amendment when it refused to renew the license of the Trinity Methodist Church on the grounds that it had broadcast vicious attacks on the Catholic Church. Trinity Methodist appealed the commission's ruling. The U.S. Court of Appeals in Washington upheld the decision.[226] The Court's opinion noted that the radio station allowed the Reverend Dr. Robert Pierce Shuler to speak over the radio regarding contempt proceedings against him underway in California. He charged judges with committing immoral acts and labeled a union hall in Los Angeles a "gambling and bootlegging joint." Jews were also targeted by the Reverend. The Court of Appeals suggested the First Amendment had not been violated because Shuler was free to continue his diatribes in a forum other than the public airways. As his comments were not in the public interest, his license need not be renewed.[227] Just as questionable was the Radio Commission's denial of a broadcast license to the Chicago Federation of Labor on the grounds that only a portion of the public would have listened to its radio station—thus failing one of the statutory criteria for granting a license (comparative popularity).[228] In the view of one critic, the discretion vested in the Commission to deny licenses was too broad. In his view, it "clearly enables the Commission, by its exercise of the licensing power, to curb free speaking. The constitutional guarantee of freedom of speech . . . connotes the immunity of publication from previous restraint or subsequent punishment to the extent that those restrictions are not socially justified. If renewal of license be refused because a station has broadcast speeches which the Commission finds inimical to the public interest, the equivalent of a subsequent penalty is imposed."[229]

The statute granting the Radio Commission authority to deny, suspend, or revoke radio licenses depending on the content of speech of licensees or the popularity of applicants constituted a clear violation of the First Amendment. Federal officials had to exercise some authority over the content of radio communications if, for example, obscene or defamatory speech was to be kept off the airways. Yet the power to withhold licenses over speech that it believed was not in the public interest vested in the Radio Commission a power to monitor political speech and invited the censoring of unpopular ideas. Whether the federal executive branch, with its century old tradition of using offices for partisan ends, could be trusted with such a vast responsibility seemed doubtful. Just as appalling was the federal judiciary's acquiescence in the Radio Commission's revocation of a license over speech it deemed contrary to the public interest. It occurred at the same time the Supreme Court had assumed a power to force states to comply with the First Amendment, thereby presenting the spectacle of federal judges refusing to apply the First Amendment to the federal government—as the Constitution required—even as they applied it to the states, which the Constitution did not authorize. The desire to remove the speck from the eyes of one's neighbor rather than one's own was as old as humanity, but rarely in American history had it been displayed with such impunity by government officials. The excesses of the Radio Commission did not elude the watchful eyes of the opposition; in 1928 Democrats included a plank in their platform holding that "government supervision must secure to all the people the advantage of radio communications and likewise guarantee the right of free speech."[230]

Even more appalling than the censorship of groups seeking to communicate their ideas Replace to via radio was the insistence of the Post Office and Customs Bureau on determining what Americans could read. During the 1920s, customs officials barred the importation of books by authors including Balzac, Rabelais, Ovid, and Voltaire on the specious grounds that they violated tariff laws barring the importation of obscene materials (each tariff law since 1842 had included a provision barring the importation of obscene materials, and an act of 1872 barred obscenity from the mails). Erich Remarque's *All Quiet on the Western Front* had to be edited before it was made available to American readers. An August 1928 conference of Customs Bureau and Post Office lawyers devised a list of over 700 books they viewed as obscene that would be barred from the mails and could not be imported.[231] When Random House decided to publish an unedited version of James Joyce's *Ulysses*, the Treasury Department filed suit. In late 1933 federal district judge John Woolsey held that the book was not obscene and that it could be distributed in the United States.[232]

Congress had to regulate radio communications and it alone had authority to keep the mails and the "stream of commerce" free of materials deemed injurious to the public. It was also appropriate for Congress to use its commerce power to protect Americans from more mundane hazards such as pollution, and it had been making efforts in this area since the 1890 Rivers and Harbor Act barred the dumping of debris in navigable rivers and streams (though the goal of the measure was the protection of navigation).[233] The abject purchase of many state legislatures by industrial and mining interests warranted a federal presence in this area. There were limits, though; unless federal lands or navigable streams were involved, there was no way for Congress to act. Nevertheless attempts were made by Congress to protect the environment and wildlife, occasionally in ways that did not appear connected to any of its enumerated powers. The Lacey Act of May 25, 1900, prohibited the transfer across state lines of wildlife killed in violation of state laws.[234] The Oil Pollution Act of June 7, 1924, barred the discharge of oil into the navigable waters of the United States.[235] The Northern Pacific Halibut Act of 1924 prohibited catching halibut in the territorial waters of the United States between mid-November and mid-February.[236] The Weeks-McLean Migratory Bird Act of March 4, 1913, asserted federal custody over all migratory bird species and prohibited their destruction except in accordance with its provisions.[237] Edward S. Corwin made a heroic attempt at connecting the statute with the commerce clause in 1916. He maintained that because the clause authorized Congress to maintain navigable streams, the maintenance of which depends on intact forests at their headwaters and the forests depended on bird life, it could regulate the hunting of birds.[238] Two federal courts held the Migratory Bird Act void.[239] In one case, a federal judge explained that birds belonged to the states and not to the federal government.[240] Reducing the question to a matter of title might not have been appropriate; yet if birds failed to recognize the claim of ownership and left states without regret, the same was true of the country.

The federal government made another attempt to protect migratory birds in 1916, when the United States and Great Britain entered into a treaty limiting the duration of the hunting season. A law enforcing the treaty went into effect on March 3, 1918, and the law as well as the treaty were reviewed in a 1920 Supreme Court case.[241] The question of whether the federal government could use the treaty power to regulate matters otherwise beyond the province of Congress had vexed lawmakers since the 1790s. It did not vex the Supreme Court. It upheld the treaty and the law putting it into effect. In his opinion for the high court, Justice Holmes avoided defining the treaty power by pretending the national government was not one of delegated powers. Instead it might do anything under the treaty power that was not explicitly prohibited. "The treaty in question does not contravene any prohibitory words to be found in the Constitution. The only question is whether it is forbidden by some invisible radiation from the general terms of the Tenth Amendment. We must consider what this country has become in deciding what that Amendment has reserved."[242] Holmes spared the reader a lecture on what "the country had become" and limited himself to explaining that birds move across state lines—therefore the matter could not be left to the legislatures.[243] These animals constituted a "national interest of very nearly the first magnitude" and Holmes did not believe the Constitution required the government to sit by "while a food supply is cut off and the protectors of our forests and our crops are destroyed."[244] The possibility that the treaty power might be used to convert a limited government into an omnipotent one was thus born anew.

While the discovery of a limitless treaty power promised a future pregnant with mischief, another judicial fiction reached its zenith during the 1920s.

In *Swift v. Tyson* (1842), Justice Joseph Story misread Section 34 of the Judiciary Act of 1789, thereby removing from federal courts the obligation to follow state case law when adjudicating cases brought before them under their diversity jurisdiction. In Story's view, judicial opinions are "only evidence of what the laws are."[245] The practical consequence in *Swift* was that the high court was able to apply general common law principles regarding commercial paper to the dispute before it; the justices thereby avoided the obligation to follow the reasoning of New York State cases on the subject that would have produced a different result. Thereafter the Supreme Court was able to mold a sort of "commercial common law" that assured businesses across the country need not fear being victimized by varying state court precedents and opinions. Critics of the *Swift* decision remained relatively quiet before the Civil War, as the doctrine did not have practical consequences for most litigants. Its potential for abuse was revealed by century's end, as the Supreme Court used its ability to ignore state court decisions to build up a federal common law on a variety of subjects. Retrograde applications of tort law were embraced for the benefit of employers. The fellow-servant rule shielded employers from liability for injuries to employees that resulted from the negligence of their coworkers. Federal courts continued to apply this doctrine even after state courts had begun modifying it to assure the victims of industrial accidents at least some compensation for injuries that often left them unable to work. In 1893 the Supreme Court ordered a new trial in a case involving an employee of the Baltimore & Ohio Railroad who had been injured by the negligence of another employee. In doing so it reversed a ruling of the Ohio Supreme Court, which had upheld a judgment for the Plaintiff following a trial. In his opinion for the majority, Justice Brewer explained that the duties of a railroad to its employees are a matter of "general" and not local law. While the Ohio courts applied Ohio law—under which employers were liable for all injuries of their employees—the Supreme Court applied "general law," which in its view provided that liability could be imposed on employers only for injuries that occurred while employees were acting at their direction at the moment of the injury.[246] In a withering dissent, Justice Field insisted that the judgment of the trial court was consistent with the "settled law of Ohio." In his view, federal courts cannot "disregard the decisions of the state courts in matters which are subject to state regulation" and labor relations fell within this category. As for the fiction perpetrated 50 years before by Justice Story, Field pointed out that "the law of the state(s) on many subjects is found only in the decisions of its courts."[247]

By the 1920s, frustration with the federal judiciary's insistence on the right to develop its own common law—and the use of that power to aid corporate America at the expense of employees and consumers—led some to call for abolishing its diversity jurisdiction.[248] In 1928, the Supreme Court resolved a Kentucky contract dispute by looking at the "general law" instead of Kentucky state court cases. Under Kentucky law the contract, which gave the Brown & Yellow Taxicab Company the exclusive right to service the Louisville & Nashville Railroad's Bowling Green depot, was void as monopolistic. Federal common law, on the other hand, did not condemn the measure. The high court left it in place. Justice Holmes issued a sharp dissent. He pointed out that in truth there was really no such thing as a general common law that federal courts might embrace; it existed only in the states, and then only when the legislatures had adopted it via statute. Holmes insisted that Story had been in error in claiming the 1789 Judiciary Act did not embrace state court opinions.[249] The Supreme Court finally reversed *Swift v. Tyson* in 1938 when it held that state court decisions constituted part of the laws of the states.[250]

FARMERS AND REPUBLICANS

Even as the rest of America enjoyed a boom during the 1920s a depression gripped rural America. In 1926, Charles McNary and Frank Haugen reintroduced their bill that would have guaranteed farmers a minimum price for their crops. It had been modified to meet objections over its provisions for dumping American crops abroad, but it still provided for a two-price system along with an equalization fee. The bill made McNary so popular that he was asked to campaign for other members of Congress in the 1926 elections. Secretary of the Treasury Andrew Mellon warned that if the bill was enacted it would result in American consumers "paying a bonus to the producers of five major agricultural products."[251] Mellon himself was receiving a "bonus" in the form of an aluminum tariff that enabled him and other manufacturers to raise their prices, but that fact did not alter the validity of his criticism.

Proponents of the McNary-Haugen bill found themselves asking Congress to defy the law of supply and demand as well as the Constitution. Representative Lester Dickinson of Iowa denied that artificially high prices would cause farmers to grow more crops, thereby worsening the glut. "The matter of acreage depends largely upon conditions outside of the price regulations. Take a good farmer. If he is getting a dollar for his corn and he finds that he needs only a certain amount to carry him along on his farm, he is very apt to put the other acreage in grass, where he does not have to work so hard or hire a man, and in that way he will not have overproduction." Dickinson claimed the McNary-Haugen bill would do nothing more than "give farmers the same power to withhold surplus supply of these five products that the U.S. Steel Corporation and other large industrial groups have in their products. It may withhold products from the market or sell in foreign markets at lower prices for the purpose of maintaining fair and stable domestic prices. Why should not cotton farmers, wheat farmers, corn farmers, rice farmers, and hog producers be given a practical means to exercise the same rights and the same powers as the numerous corporations composing U.S. Steel?"[252]

Walter Newton remained unable to see the wisdom of the bill. Speaking on February 4, 1927, the Minneapolis congressman conceded that the purchasing power of farmers had declined; he wanted to see it improve but he insisted that the measure would only worsen the problem: "This bill will stimulate overproduction. That is one of the causes of the farmer's present trouble. All recognize this and the difficulties in controlling production in an industry as individualistic as that of the farmer. Why will this bill stimulate overproduction? The obvious purpose is to increase the domestic price. That is in itself an inducement for the farmer to plant more. There is always an increased acreage put to wheat following a year of high prices." Newton claimed this was precisely what occurred following an increase in wheat prices during 1924—the amount of land devoted to that crop was increased by 10 percent, or five million acres.[253]

Newton predicted that the revolving fund set aside under the plan "will not last long" and that the program would require the raising of additional money. Although the plan provided at present for the board to purchase wheat at a set price, eventually the board be would forced to impose prices. (Under the McNary-Haugen bill, farmers could sell to entities other than the Farm Board if they chose to do so.) In the meantime processors would import Canadian wheat (No. 3 Manitoba Northern) rather than purchase Minnesota wheat (No. 1 Dark Northern) at artificially inflated prices, as it would be cheaper, even with a 42 percent tariff. The Farm Board would end up stuck with wheat it could not sell.[254] The House passed the bill. When it reached the Senate, Carter Glass dismissed claims that the Federal Reserve Act provided a precedent for the measure when he pointed out that it did not provide a huge subsidy for banks—the system was established at a cost of less than $50,000. Capital was supplied by member banks, and in one year alone they paid $62 million to the treasury. McNary-Haugen on the other hand "affords a continuing subsidy to a restricted circle of farmers at the expense of all the people. It taxes more farmers than it pretends to aid." Worse still, "the money of the American taxpayer is to be used for the purpose of compelling the very man who puts the money into the Federal Treasury to pay more for his bread and meat and clothing."[255] The Senate refused to pass the bill. Congress settled for the establishment of a Division of Cooperative Marketing and gave it $250,000 to assist agricultural cooperatives.[256] A sharp drop in cotton prices, from 29 cents to 18 cents a pound (the harvest increased sharply in 1925), caused southern farmers to see the wisdom of selling their crop at prices set by the federal government. About 60 percent of southern members of Congress supported the McNary-Haugen bill when it came up for a vote again in early 1927, thereby enabling both houses to pass it.[257] A measure appropriating $250 million for the purchase of agricultural commodities went to the desk of the president. Coolidge vetoed the bill on February 25, 1927.

In his veto message, the president suggested that the key to the farm problem was crop diversification, yet the bill "put a premium on one crop farming." Government price-fixing would, he believed, have "no justice and no end." The measure would enable one group of farmers to profit at the expense of other farmers as well as the rest of the population. The bill also flew "in the face of economic law as well established as any law of nature." Higher prices would only encourage farmers to grow more crops. The measure would also produce increased food prices for consumers. What was needed was reduced production, and that would result only from lower prices.[258] The president also believed the measure to be unconstitutional; instead of saying why he referred the reader to an opinion of John Sargent, the attorney general. Sargent conceded that the Constitution allowed for the delegation of legislative authority when "a controlling rule is fixed by the legislative body." While the rule had been applied liberally, there was no way it could be stretched enough to encompass the proposed commission—it would have authority to set prices as it saw fit. Congress had established no legislative guidelines for it to follow in performing that task. Sargent then moved on to the bill's most fundamental defect—none of the enumerated powers authorized it. The commerce clause had been cited in support of the measure, but he did not buy it. In Sargent's view, legislation under the commerce clause had been limited to carrying out its original purpose, "which was to prevent undue discriminations against or burdens or restraints on interstate commerce."[259]

Farm leaders were furious; one critic called the veto a "repudiation" of the platform on which Coolidge ran in 1924.[260] The race for the 1928 Republican nomination was born in the intra-party dispute over the McNary-Haugen bill—Congress passed it again in the spring of 1928 and the president again vetoed it. Until Coolidge announced that he would not seek reelection, some thought the anger of farmers over his vetoes might result in his being denied the Republican nomination. Secretary of Commerce Herbert Hoover had been angling for the presidency since 1920. He helped draft the lengthy veto message of 1927 and also spoke against McNary-Haugen, thereby earning the enmity of farmers despite his work in setting up agricultural cooperatives. The commerce secretary's pet program for farmers, a farm board that would help cooperatives market agricultural surpluses, was considered inadequate. An engineer by trade, Hoover earned fame for his work in coordinating relief efforts benefiting Belgium, Russia, and other European countries following World War I. He served as vice-chairman of the Second Industrial Conference of 1919, which recommended laws limiting the work week to 40 hours, a minimum wage, a ban on child labor, and equal pay for both sexes, as well as shop committees that would bargain with management on behalf of employees.[261]

After failing to obtain the Republican nomination for president in 1920, Hoover served as secretary of commerce under Harding and Coolidge. In that position he sought to manage the president, the rest of the executive branch, and the American economy. His preferred approach was "coordination" within various industries; he organized an endless series of industry committees and trade councils. In 1921, Hoover oversaw discussion among federal, state, and local authorities regarding the feasibility of increased funding for public works projects to ease the effects of economic downturns. Two years later he successfully pressed the leading steel manufacturers to reduce the workday in their industry from 12 to 8 hours, largely by browbeating them in the press.[262] Hoover's relief work made him the star of American politics for a time after the war; his fame was declining when the Mississippi Flood of 1927 occurred. While overseeing flood relief efforts, he had his staff prepare stories and editorials regarding the efforts of the secretary of commerce in aiding Americans left helpless by the catastrophe.[263]

Hoover's chief rival was Frank Lowden, former governor of Illinois. In December 1926, the *Atlanta Constitution* called Lowden the "most formidable contender" for the 1928 nomination due to his support for McNary-Haugen.[264] When a group of rural newspapers organized a straw poll in 29 states during the spring of 1927, Lowden came in second to the president, who had not yet announced his decision to forego another term.[265] While the conservative element in the Republican Party was strong enough that it probably would have checked Governor Lowden without further assistance, federal officeholders did everything they could to aid Hoover when state party nominating conventions met. This development did not stem from the president's support for Hoover. Coolidge grew to dislike his secretary of commerce; later he complained that the publicity-grasping engineer had "offered him unsolicited advice for years, all of it bad."[266] Federal civil servants arrived at the simple calculation that Hoover had the best chance to win and ensure they retained their posts. With the number of federal civil servants now over half a million, their wishes could not be ignored—though the arrival of primaries deprived state party conventions of their former importance in many states.[267] Federal civil servants still managed to flood nominating conventions in states where they survived. In September 1927, the *Chicago Daily Tribune* reported that federal officeholders had arrived "in force" at the New York State Republican convention in Rochester. The "federal crowd" was said to be "talking Hoover persistently."[268] Lowden never really had a chance and Hoover was nominated on the first ballot when Republicans met at Kansas City in early June, though farmers gathered outside of Convention Hall to protest the party's decision.[269] A minority plank endorsing McNary-Haugen was rejected by the delegates.

Al Smith, governor of New York, won the Democratic presidential nomination with ease over Governor Albert Ritchie of Maryland. The platform promised "farm relief" and held that federal action was needed for "the control and orderly handling of agricultural surpluses, in order that the price of the surplus may not determine the price of the whole crop." Americans could be forgiven if they did not realize the two could be separated. In an indication of the party's changing priorities, the platform noted that extensive preparations for war were made in peacetime but that there had been precious little planning for a domestic calamity such as large scale unemployment. It called for increased spending on public projects during downturns. In a bid for the civil servant vote, the platform demanded a "living wage" for federal employees.[270]

The Democratic candidate carried the burden of a New York accent; his exotic twang sounded almost foreign to Americans just getting used to hearing the voices of people in distant parts of the country on their radios. His religion—he was a Roman Catholic—was a far more serious problem. Questions were raised as to whether a Catholic could pursue the best interests of the United States. Another difficulty for Smith stemmed from his call for an end to Prohibition. Assistant Attorney General Mabel Walker Willebrandt told a gathering of Methodist ministers Ohio to exhort their congregations to vote against Smith and preserve the Eighteenth Amendment.[271] The greatest obstacle to Smith was the fact that the nation was doing well. Real per capita income increased from $522 in 1921 to $716 in 1929—an increase of over 40 percent.[272] Wages of industrial workers increased by 26 percent between 1919 and 1929. Stimulated by the burgeoning automobile industry, the suburbs exploded, along with the construction industry.[273] Americans enjoyed more creature comforts than ever before, including cars, radios, refrigerators, and movies.

Among the elements of the population that did not participate in the new prosperity were farmers, and both candidates were expected to provide more details as to how they would resolve the farm crisis. Governor Smith addressed the issue on September 18 in Omaha. He charged that farmers had to buy in a protected market and sell in an unprotected market; yet he acknowledged that more protection for their crops would provide only limited aid, as they did not face foreign competition in the American marketplace. Nor were more inland waterways the answer, though they were supported by both parties (as a sop to farmers annoyed with the railroads). Voluntary methods such as cooperatives and stabilization corporations would not solve the problem, even with government aid. None of these things could work in Smith's view unless "coupled with the control of the exportable surplus with the cost of lifting it out of the domestic market assessed back on the crop benefited." Having thrown his listeners a bone, the candidate retreated to what would prove a favorite for twentieth-century politicians: he would turn the problem over to a commission.[274] While speaking in Newark on October 31, Smith complained that the Republican Congress had failed to enact the suggestions of the 1921 Commission on Unemployment. There had been 1.8 million unemployed the previous winter, and lots purchased in the cities for new federal buildings remained empty when the unemployed could have been put to work.[275]

Herbert Hoover began his campaign with an August 11 speech at Stanford Stadium. Sixty thousand watched while another 30 million heard it broadcast over the radio. The candidate was pleased to announce that poverty was disappearing—apparently the poor would not always be with us: "We in America today are nearer to the final triumph over poverty than ever before in the history of any land." He promised policies designed to ensure jobs for all. His administration would also seek to establish "for our farmers an income equal to those of other occupations." Hoover went on to declare his opposition to repeal of the Eighteenth Amendment—instead he called for more "efficient enforcement of the laws." He promised a limit to the use of labor injunctions and endorsed collective bargaining. His administration would also seek ways to limit the effect of economic downturns.[276] In a St. Louis speech of November 2, Hoover spoke of his proposal to establish a federal farm board that would assist farmers in marketing, establishing warehouse facilities, and eliminating waste in the distribution of their crops. He called for the establishment of "farmer-owned and farmer-controlled stabilization corporations which will protect the farmer from depressions and the demoralization of summer and periodic surpluses. It is proposed that this board should have placed at its disposal such resources as are necessary to make it effective."[277] Hoover proposed to go even further than the McNary-Haugen bill in securing a place for farmers at the federal trough. Instead of merely allowing them to tax themselves for the purpose of funding crop purchases, the Republican candidate would obligate the federal government itself to subsidize entities charged with buying crops until prices reached a level satisfactory to farmers.

Many saw Hoover as more progressive than Smith, in part due to the New York governor's history of opposition to women's suffrage and past statements that seemed to reveal a hostility to federal authority.[278] For those disturbed by the prospect of increased federal spending, this state of affairs did not make Hoover more appealing. H. L. Mencken spoke for this group when he complained that the secretary of commerce "is immensely liberal with other people's money."[279] Organized labor split between the two candidates; John L. Lewis of the United Mine Workers and William Green of the American Federal of Labor gave the appearance of favoring Hoover, though they did not endorse him.[280] Hoover won in a rout. His huge majority in the Electoral College included the votes of five southern states—an indication of how strong Prohibition sentiment and anti-Catholic feeling ran in that part of the country. Democrats fared better in the North; they won the cities after losing them in 1924.[281] Republicans won majorities in both Houses of Congress.

FEDERALISM AND THE GREAT DEPRESSION

The first year of the Hoover administration saw White House conferences on subjects that until recently were not viewed as within the federal sphere, including housing and children.[282] A second housing conference in 1931 recommended the establishment of a federal housing agency and annual grants to the states for the clearing of slums.[283] At Hoover's request, Maine Governor Ralph Brewster outlined a proposal to establish a $3 billion reserve for public works to be used in times of economic distress at a governors' conference in late 1928.[284] When the proposal received a cool reception, the new president discarded it.

In 1929, the booming stock market began to wobble. Trouble was a long time coming. Just as federal officials had taken the easy route in managing the Mississippi River—hemming it in and increasing the volume of water moving down the river while refusing to build spillways and reservoirs—the Federal Reserve had produced a highly volatile economy through artificial stimulation. It allowed the amount of credit available to increase from $45.3 billion in 1921 to $73 billion in 1929 (mainly be easing credit requirements), even as the amount of money in circulation decreased slightly. The Federal Reserve banks reduced interest rates below their natural levels to appease Wall Street and stimulate the economy.[285] Having decided to act as the nation's central banker, it was perhaps inevitable that the federal government would allow the matter of interest rates to be driven by political considerations. Over-expansion of the nation's industrial capacity was one result: American manufacturers produced more goods than consumers could buy. Easy credit stimulated demand for a time, and the stocks of industrial concerns traded at values that far exceeded their actual worth. While the Gross National Product grew by 59 percent during the 1920s, the Dow Jones Average went up by 400 percent. Even after it became plain that stocks were overvalued, the Federal Reserve itself continued buy government securities on the open market (thereby inflating the money supply) and district reserve banks loaned money to their members so they could advance cash to brokers and others in the stock market. Brokers loaned the money to their customers when they allowed them to buy stocks on margin—customers paid as little as 10 percent of a stock's market price. Between late 1927 and October 1929, the quantity of money loaned to brokers and others in the stock market almost doubled. The Federal Reserve banks waited until too late in the boom to increase discount rates—early 1928—and then moved too slowly, in part out of fear of a popular backlash such as occurred when they raised rates from 4 percent to 7 percent between November 1919 and June 1920.[286] During 1929, Federal Reserve officials twice warned the country that too much money was being devoted to speculation, but they did not allow the New York Federal Reserve Bank to raise the discount rate until August—the first hike in over a year.[287]

The end finally came, or began, on October 21, 1929, when stocks fell sharply and the first margin calls occurred. Three days later on October 24 another steep drop hit the market, followed by "Black Tuesday," October 29, when the sharpest drop yet took place. By mid-November, the Dow Jones index had dropped to 224 from a peak of 452. As it had been at only 245 the previous December, there seemed little reason to expect anything beyond a temporary dislocation.[288] While less than 3 percent of Americans owned stocks, the effects of the crash reached every corner of the nation as companies shorn of much of their former value cut back, and well-to-do Americans sold their investments and reduced their spending. As layoffs began, Secretary of the Treasury Andrew Mellon advised the president to allow matters to take their natural course—ailing companies should be allowed to cut spending and payrolls, and imperiled debtors should be allowed to default. Hoover would have none of it; he was convinced the federal government could manage, spend, and cajole the nation out of the downturn. He seems to have believed that manufacturing concerns and banks could be convinced to do together—maintain wages and large payrolls and issue loans—what they were not willing to do individually. In late 1929, Hoover met with the executives representing industry, construction, and utilities; under intense pressure from the president, they agreed to refrain from cutting wages or laying off workers. During the next two years Hoover applied considerable pressure on large industrial concerns to maintain wages and payrolls. While industry leaders tried to comply with the president's wishes, declining demand for goods and services and falling prices eventually forced them to acknowledge reality and reduce their expenses. The president also lobbied governors and mayors to spend more money on public works. He convinced Congress to increase the 10-year appropriation for the construction of federal buildings and it complied in March 1930.[289]

Even as Congress appropriated more money for construction projects, state spending on construction declined due to sharply reduced revenues (several state constitutions barred deficit spending). As federal spending was still only 3 percent of the Gross National Product (as of 1929), the additional money did little to prop up demand. The state and local governments spent an amount equal to about 15 percent of the gross national product (and employed five times as many people as the federal government). The disparity in construction spending was about the same—in 1932 Congress spent $318 million on construction projects; state and local spending totaled $1.56 billion.[290] Due to the growth of state and local government spending during the first three decades of the century, federal spending actually comprised a lower percentage of total government expenditures in 1932 (32.4%) than it had in 1902 (34%).[291]

By the spring of 1930 there were four million unemployed Americans and breadlines appeared in the cities for the first time since 1921.[292] In Washington lawmakers convinced themselves that the worst was over, in part because federal revenues remained high—they would produce a surplus for the fiscal year ending June 30. Congress busied itself with yet another tariff rate hike despite the impending surplus. The Smoot-Hawley Tariff was born in the special session of 1929 called to aid farmers; a bill to raise rates for the benefit of agriculture gave way to an across-the-board rate hike. Western agricultural interests lost faith in the measure after the administration and Republican leaders refused to include export debentures or other measures aiding farmers.[293] Imported shoes now came with a 20 percent tax and woolens were subject to a 60 percent tax. Ad valorem rates increased from an average of 33 percent under the Fordney-McCumber Tariff of 1922 to 40 percent.[294] Twenty-five countries imposed retaliatory tariffs within two years.[295] While international trade had started to drop before the law's enactment, it accelerated the freefall. With their incomes curtailed by the loss of the American market, foreign nations reduced their purchases of American goods. Exports dropped by almost 80 percent by 1932, thereby worsening the depression.[296] With the United States manufacturing far more goods than it could consume, the nation was highly dependent on exports, and the tariff hike constituted a severe body blow to the economy. With the exception of the Kansas-Nebraska Act, the Smoot-Hawley Tariff may well constitute the most disastrous piece of legislation in American history. Its effects were magnified when the Federal Reserve banks made one of the worst mistakes in their history—they attempted to preserve the gold standard by raising interest rates (from 1.5 to 3.5%) and reducing the money supply.[297]

Farm state legislators sought a program of export debentures—script that would be issued to producers of six agricultural commodities that could be used to pay tariff duties. It was expected that farmers would sell the debentures to merchants who would use them to pay tariff duties. The plan failed due to the president's opposition. Farmers had to settle for the Agricultural Marketing Act of June 15, 1929.[298] The law constituted the most significant expansion of the pecuniary relationship between the federal government and the American people in the nation's history. It proved an unmitigated disaster. To "promote the effective merchandising of agricultural commodities in interstate and foreign commerce, and to place agriculture on a basis of economic equality with other industries," the act established a Federal Farm Board. It authorized the Board to form stabilization corporations and loan money to agricultural cooperatives for the purpose of keeping surpluses off the market when prices were low. Section 6 authorized future appropriations of $500 million as a revolving fund for loans to cooperatives and for the purchase of commodities on the open market. While the measure was still pending, Missouri Democrat Clarence Cannon was impudent enough to ask "what could be more uneconomical or unconstitutional than reaching into the Treasury of the United States and taking $500 million of the people's money, contributed by every taxpayer, and using it for the individual benefit of one class or industry?"[299] The president called it "the most important measure ever passed by Congress in aid of a single industry"[300] The law's enactment was widely viewed as a win for moderation as the debenture plan was now dead. Perhaps realizing it was something else altogether, the *Atlanta Constitution* defended the Act as having saved the country from dependency on foreign nations for foodstuffs. The "stabilization of agriculture," whatever its cost, "must be borne and charged to the account of the 'first line of defense' of the nation's life."[301]

Supporters of the measure saw the direct purchase of commodities by the stabilization corporations as a tool that would be used only rarely—the law's goals would instead be achieved under normal circumstances through cooperative associations. A decline in prices following the stock market crash and the ineffectiveness of the cooperatives in helping farmers keep their crops off of the market led farmers to demand that the Farm Board authorize mass purchases of their crops. For a time the Farm Board focused on advancing loans to cooperatives and in turn farmers so that they would not have to dump their harvests on the market. When wheat prices continued to fall, the Board authorized stabilization corporations to buy it on the open market, first at a price set by the board and then at market prices.[302] Similar entities were formed for the purpose of buying cotton and wool. The Farm Board dared to recommend voluntary reductions in the amount of land devoted to certain crops. One critic suggested it would "pretty near have to kill off twenty percent of the farmers" to adequately reduce the wheat acreage.[303] Market forces would likely have secured the same result had they been allowed to operate—if wheat prices dropped low enough they would drive people out of farming altogether—but Congress was no longer of a mind to allow the economy to operate free of interference. The Farm Board sent experts to the upper Mississippi Valley to convince wheat farmers to grow other crops such as flax, barley, alfalfa, and sweet clover. The *Nation* noted that on the same day in December 1930 Congress voted to give the board another $150 million to buy wheat, the price of a bushel at the Chicago Board of Trade dropped to its lowest level since 1901. The editors were appalled. "To subsidize farmers to grow an unprofitable crop without any possibility of restricting production is a suicidal arrangement for farmers and Treasury alike; yet that seems to be the Farm Board's wheat policy."[304] Even as the Grain Stabilization Corporation stored 60 million bushels from the previous year, officials obtained authority to purchase more. It did have some success in temporarily propping up prices but at an enormous cost—by June 1931, the government of the United States had spent $169 million and accumulated 257 million bushels of wheat.[305] At that point the Board began to liquidate its holdings, thereby worsening a glut that developed when farmers responded to the government's generosity by growing more wheat.[306] The program did accomplish one end long sought by farmers. Speculation in wheat futures came to a halt for a time as private parties stopped purchasing them and the wheat pit at the Chicago Board of Trade was turned over to corn traders.[307]

Similar futility characterized the farm board's approach to cotton. It dropped from 14 cents a pound in 1930 to nine cents in 1931 and six cents in 1932 as the Farm Board authorized the purchase of more of it.[308] During the summer of 1931, federal officials asked southern governors to request that farmers discard every third row of cotton still growing; they might just as well have asked wage earners to stop working on Mondays. Louisiana went so far as to enact a law prohibiting the planting of cotton in 1932 but the plan was contingent on other southern states taking the same step and none did.[309] In December 1932, Senator John Bankhead of Alabama conceded that Congress could not impose quotas on farmers "directly" but he thought it should limit the amount of agricultural commodities that could be introduced into interstate commerce by each state, with farmers subject to individual limits—if they exceeded it, they would have to carry the surplus. Bankhead proposed to limit the next cotton harvest to just half of that of 1932.[310] Some called for Congress to simply pay farmers to refrain from using all of their acreage. The necessary precedent seemed available; four years earlier in 1928 Congress appropriated $5 million to compensate farmers who were subject to state programs targeting the spread of pink bollworm that barred the growth of cotton in certain areas.[311] Massachusetts Democratic Representative William P. Connery thought restraints on production via the commerce power could be exercised for the benefit of labor as well as farmers. In January 1933 he proposed a bill barring from interstate commerce products made in factories operating more than six hours or day or five days a week.[312] The proposals of Bankhead and Connery confirmed fears expressed a quarter of a century earlier at the time of the child labor bill—that Congress would move beyond barring what were generally viewed as evils and use the commerce power to warp the national marketplace for the purpose of enriching important constituencies.

Even as farmers found their way into the U.S. treasury, the economy that sustained it fell into a stupor. While some thought the downturn had eased in the first half of 1930, the economy dropped like a stone in the second half of the year—the gross national product fell 12.6 percent off of its 1929 level.[313] Democratic lawmakers began pressing for measures designed aid the growing ranks of unemployed. With Democratic politicians such as Franklin Delano Roosevelt and Al Smith blaming Hoover for what increasingly looked like a depression, Democrats gained over 50 seats in the House in the midterm elections. Although the parties appeared to be tied in the number of House seats each won immediately following the election, the deaths of several congressmen during the next 13 months allowed Democrats to organize the House in the 72nd Congress when it met in December 1931.

Following the election a deluge of bank failures overtook the country and the failure to establish federal deposit insurance began to have disastrous consequences. By 1917, 14 states had established deposit insurance in some form.[314] While some of the systems were excellent, the failure to establish a nationwide plan left millions of Americans susceptible to ruin and posed a mortal risk to the economy. In 1929, 659 banks failed, a figure that was, incredibly, within normal limits. The pace picked up in late 1930, and 600 banks closed during the final two months of the year. Some of those who were able to withdraw funds deposited them in postal savings banks, as they were guaranteed against loss. On December 11, the Bank of United States in New York City failed, depriving 400,000 depositors of their savings—the largest single bank failure thus far in the nation's history. The leading banks sat quietly as the disaster unfolded, confident that the Federal Reserve would play the same role J. P. Morgan's consortium had in 1907 and provide cash infusions to stricken institutions. It didn't.[315] A plague of bank failures hit the South as the region struggled under the weight of a crippling drought. (Congress appropriated $45 million for loans to affected farmers in December 1930.[316]) Between 1929 and the end of 1933, 9,000 banks failed, resulting in losses to depositors of $1.3 billion.[317] The problem stemmed in part from the expansion of credit—total mortgage debt had tripled during the 1920s. This development followed Herbert Hoover's success in convincing Congress to authorize national banks to devote more funds to home mortgage loans (resulting in passage of the McFadden Act of 1927).[318] The *Wall Street Journal* quoted one observer who thought the law would enable national banks to pour another $300 million into mortgage loans.[319] The commerce secretary foreshadowed later advocates of home ownership in his view of the widespread incidence of renting as vaguely exploitative and as indicative of some sort of national failure.[320] After the downturn began and banks stopped making loans, many homeowners found they could not refinance their loans—as they had to repeatedly under the short-term mortgages that were standard during that period—and a wave of defaults followed. As the banks suffered under multiple waves of defaults on mortgages, one after another failed. Mortgage defaults played a far larger role in ruining the banking industry than losses on loans to persons speculating in the stock market. The wave of bank failures served as the critical ingredient in turning a stock market bust into the worst depression in the nation's history.

The overexpansion of other forms of credit also created difficulties. During the 1920s, Americans began purchasing everything from phonographs to refrigerators to clothes on credit.[321] As layoffs soared, installment payments were not forthcoming. The broadening of access to credit undoubtedly made the bounty of industrial civilization available to Americans at an earlier period in their lives than otherwise would have been possible, yet it also constituted a development pregnant with mischief. Corporate America and its agents in the marketing and advertising industries would spend the rest of the century making war on thrift—among the most important traits in any population that expects to maintain a republican government. It would lead to a world in which Americans spent their paychecks quickly, saved nothing, and rendered themselves defenseless in the event of economic downturns—with a future that promised them little beyond serving as wards of the state and as prey for demagogues.

With widespread bank failures, millions of Americans who had depended on their savings were now left to the generosity of family members and what public relief was available. In October 1930 President Hoover established an Emergency Committee for Employment; two months later he asked Congress for $150 million for public works. A conference of economists at Princeton concluded that a much larger sum ought to be spent, and that the debt incurred would inflict no harm on the economy.[322]

Senator Robert Wagner, Democrat of New York, thought the president's proposal inadequate. In a speech of December 11, 1930, Wagner complained that federal public works expenditures grew by almost $50 million in 1929 but by only $4 million in 1930. The time had come to act on a scale appropriate to the emergency. "No employer of labor is as favorably situated as the federal government to contribute to stability. It is the largest single employer of labor in the world. It has no competitors. It is not concerned with profits. It is in a position not only to act itself so as to affirmatively contribute to the regularity of employment but to coordinate actions by others."[323] In a radio address of October 1931, Hoover claimed increased federal expenditures for federal public works were supporting almost 700,000 families.[324] The effectiveness of this spending was limited by the Davis-Bacon Act March 1931, which required that federal public works projects pay prevailing wages—in effect it required that wage levels at each project must be at least equal to those enjoyed by local union workers in the same field.[325] The measure stemmed from union complaints over competition from small construction firms whose employees had not organized. In requiring the payment of prevailing wages, the law removed the incentive to hire construction firms that relied on nonunion labor and offered cheaper rates. The Davis-Bacon Act increased the income of those fortunate enough to obtain public works jobs, but it made projects more expensive and reduced the number of persons who benefited from them. It also fell hard on southern construction firms that relied heavily on black nonunion, unskilled laborers who were paid considerably less than union construction workers. The goal of employing as many persons as possible was sacrificed to the need to appease influential labor interests—an unfortunate step that would be repeated often in coming years. In an effort to ensure that Americans held what jobs existed, during 1931 Secretary of Labor William Doak cooperated with local officials in deporting aliens who had violated immigration laws by becoming public charges. Illegal aliens were also identified and expelled.

In late 1930, Senator Wagner of New York proposed a bill to provide federal unemployment insurance. Realizing it had no hope of immediate passage, the New York senator justified the proposal on the grounds that the public would require convincing over an extended period if such a revolutionary measure was ever to become law.[326] In a November 1931 article in the *Atlantic*, Sidney Hillman, head of the Amalgamated Clothing Workers of America, estimated that if a compulsory national system of unemployment insurance had been set up in 1925, with employees contributing 1.5 percent of their salaries and employers contributing 3 percent of their payroll costs, the system could have paid out benefits totaling $3 billion in 1930 (to five million persons) and 1931 (to six million persons) and it would still have a reserve of $2 billion remaining at the end of 1931. These payments would have increased consumer spending and helped stimulate the economy.[327]

For the moment, grants to the states for relief seemed more feasible, at least in political terms, than federal unemployment insurance. In late 1930, Massachusetts Senator David Walsh proposed a bill with that end in mind. Farm state lawmakers objected. Indiana Republican James Watson supported a bill to relieve victims of drought; he did not believe that widespread want existed in urban areas. (The drought itself produced food riots in cities from Missouri to California in early 1931.) He noted that the drought bill authorized the secretary of agriculture to extend loans only when he thought it appropriate. Senator Robert M. LaFollette Jr. of Wisconsin was incredulous over Watson's dismissal of hardship in the cities. He read letters from persons around the country on the floor of the Senate; one claimed 20,000 unemployed persons in Pittsburgh depended on the municipal government, and that its resources had reached the point of exhaustion. Another letter claimed the relief fund of Reading, Pennsylvania, would be gone in six months.[328] If, LaFollette continued, there had been an earthquake "there would be no question about the federal government promptly and generously discharging its responsibility, but because these millions of unemployed and their dependents are the victims of an economic earthquake, caused by bankruptcy in leadership of American industry, finance and government, an attempt is made to discredit any appropriation for their relief by the federal government by calling it a dole. . . . No one raised that cry when Herbert Hoover asked for one hundred million to relieve and feed the stricken in Europe; no one called it a dole when we appropriated twenty-five million . . . to assist the starving in Russia."[329] LaFollette proceeded to cite statutes providing relief to victims of flooding and plagues, the earliest of which dated from the 1870s. Daniel Hastings of Delaware asked LaFollette if Congress had ever spent money as "pure charity for people who are suffering from hunger?" LaFollette refused to answer; instead he asked why the cause of the deprivation mattered.[330]

Guy Goff, Republican of West Virginia, insisted that until the states have demonstrated they cannot handle the problem, Congress "has no jurisdiction and no prerogative to enter the field and usurp or exercise the state sovereignty of any of the states of the Union." LaFollette did not buy it. "Does the Senator from West Virginia think that the citizens of Wheeling would rise up and stand on their states' rights if the federal government offered to assist them 50–50 as provided in the bill introduced by the Senator from Massachusetts [Mr. Walsh] in helping to meet a situation which they did not themselves create?" Goff later conceded that he did not believe anything in the Constitution barred Congress from "making donations" if it saw fit to do so.[331] The sponsor of the bill to provide matching grants, Senator David Walsh of Massachusetts, inserted an article he wrote for the December 15, 1930, *Washington Evening Star* into the Congressional Record. It hinted at what Walsh saw as the legal justification for federal intervention. Defining an emergency as an "unforeseen occurrence or condition calling for immediate action," the article stated that wars produce emergencies, as do natural disasters. So had the economic downturn. "Who can doubt that the sudden denial, whatever may be the causes, to millions of human beings of the necessities of life through unemployment is an emergency of an extraordinary character? In many respects it is the most destructive, distressing, and dangerous of all emergencies, because it creates a state of unrest, uncertainty, worry—in brief, a state of mind that invites the acceptance of dangerous social, political and economic theories that may threaten free institutions."[332] Due to the opposition of the president and the Republican majority in the House, the session expired without Congress providing grants to the states for relief.

As with many challenges facing American governments in the twentieth century, the problem of relief was greatly exacerbated by the ineffectual response of the state governments. While the nations of Europe had long provided unemployment insurance, the American states had just begun to address that need. The reluctance of the states to aid the unemployed stemmed in part from fears that imposing the necessary payroll taxes on employers would cause them to move to other states as well as a misplaced sense of economy. It was not until 1931 that New York established the first state program to assist the unemployed; it was followed quickly by New Jersey, Pennsylvania, Rhode Island, Ohio, Wisconsin, and Illinois. Total state spending on unemployment relief went from approximately $500,000 in 1931 to $100 million in 1932.[333] Wisconsin established the first state-level unemployment insurance program in 1932.[334]

While farm state and urban politicians fought over places at the federal trough, neither had the degree of access enjoyed by veterans' organizations. Following the override of Coolidge's 1924 bonus bill veto, Congress revised the statutes devoted to veterans' benefits (the "veterans code") four times in six years as a way of surreptitiously increasing benefits. A bill providing a "final settlement" to Spanish-American War veterans became law in 1920 only to be followed by another act increasing benefits in 1930. With more generous benefits, the number of Spanish American War pensioners jumped, from 30,000 in 1920 to 235,000 in 1930.[335] Veterans' organizations lobbied Congress to provide pensions for World War I veterans even though the life insurance policies given to them in 1921 had been designed as a substitute. The Emergency Adjusted Compensation Act of 1931 increased the portion of the certificates issued under the 1924 Adjusted Compensation

Act that could be used as collateral for loans by 3.5 million veterans from 25 to 50 percent. Congress acted despite the fact that as Hoover noted, the 1924 law was passed in part on the understanding that veterans' organizations would not come back to Washington seeking to increase the percentage of the certificates that could be used as collateral.[336]

In the spring of 1932 impoverished veterans appealed for another round of payments. World War I veterans, many of whom were unemployed, wanted the entirety of the bonus they were scheduled to receive in 1945 under the 1924 Adjusted Compensation Act. In an episode reminiscent of Coxey's army of 1894 that traveled to Washington to demand public works jobs, many decided to go to the capital. A "bonus army" of 15,000 veterans and their families made camp on the flats across the Anacostia River from Washington, DC, in June 1932. The House passed a bill giving veterans what they wanted, but it died in the Senate. The president became understandably nervous over the presence of a band of desperate men within rioting distance of the White House, and he went along with a bill to provide the capital's visitors with enough money to return home. Most departed; the few that remained became restless. When the municipal police tried to clear Pennsylvania Avenue and adjacent buildings of veterans on July 26, a fight broke out and two bystanders were killed. Army troops were sent to clear the flats. They used tear gas to disperse the stragglers and torched the shacks occupied by the veterans and their families.

If the demand of farmers that the federal government guarantee their incomes rang hollow and the attempts of veterans' organizations to secure increases in benefits every few years seemed manipulative, there was no denying that the economy suffered from a lack of demand. American consumers—the driving force of the economy—would not be able to push it forward unless they were provided with jobs or unemployment compensation. Public works employment and other forms of relief multiplied the risks of public plunder and electoral corruption tenfold, but there seemed to be no alternative. If the states could not fund these projects themselves, federal assistance would have to be provided. The consequences of involving the federal government in relief were demonstrated by a new generation of demagogues that made William Jennings Bryan a virtuous Jeffersonian in comparison. The most notorious of those who rose upon their ability to exploit the sufferings of the poor was Huey Long of Louisiana. During the 1920s, Long had been something of a progressive; he sought free textbooks for school children as well as more funds for state hospitals and road construction. The state bosses supported many of these efforts because they expanded their opportunities to enrich themselves at the public trough. Once elected, governor Long secured a more equitable tax system by forcing oil companies to pay taxes.[337]

Following his election to the U.S. Senate, Long looked for issues that would help him earn the favor of a larger audience; widespread joblessness and deprivation fit the bill. In a speech of March 18, 1932, he blamed the paralysis of industry and labor on the "handful of men in the United States (who) own all the money in this country. That is the only reason for present deplorable conditions."[338] Three days later he spoke of what he and many others saw as the solution to the problem: the redistribution of income from the wealthy to the poor. "Let us have it understood that it is our object and that it is our purpose to bring the fruits of this land, the wealth of this land, to be enjoyed by 120,000,000 people; that there will be no surplus of food with people starving; that there will be no overproduction of clothes with people naked; that there will be no empty houses with people sleeping on park benches and walking the roads; that there will be no idleness of factories because people have not the money with which to buy the products those factories make—but that we will distribute the wealth, the products, the fruit, the fortunes of this land not only to support the government but to provide . . . a chance to live and a chance to grow to the people of the United States." As Long sat down, applause echoed from the gallery.[339] The speech instantly made him one of the leading progressives of the Senate. The Louisiana senator endorsed Arkansas Senator Hattie Caraway's proposal to limit incomes to a maximum of a million dollars—earnings above that threshold would be confiscated via income taxes.[340] Even Theodore Roosevelt had talked of using the tax code to limit income disparities, but Long's rhetoric separated him from anything uttered thus far by mainstream politicians. While temporary aid for the unemployed was needed to restart the economy, the redistribution of income as a permanent policy would create a risk of electoral corruption on a massive scale that would have made the veterans' pension excesses of the previous 60 years look like child's play. It also would have deprived voters of their role as supervisors of the national government. The northern electorate had stared down three proslavery administrations in Washington to prevent the expansion of slavery in the territories during the 1840s and 1850s. Would American voters be able to check the next administration that attempted to impose immoral policies on the nation if many of them were dependents of the national government?

In the fall of 1931, the administration began a campaign to convince Americans to contribute to private relief agencies. When the 72nd Congress met in December, the first Democratic majority in the House in 12 years embraced more aggressive measures. As unemployment had risen above 15 percent, there was only mild resistance. Congress and the president agreed on a bill to establish the Reconstruction Finance Corporation and give it $500 million. It received authority to loan money to banks and other credit institutions, as well as farm cooperatives for the benefit of "agriculture, commerce and industry."[341] The measure was in large part an attempt to save faltering banks; it followed the formation of a pool of financial institutions (the National Credit Corporation) that did not succeed when its members refused to contribute more than nominal sums.[342] Modeled on the War Finance Corporation, the RFC proceeded to lend money to banks, trusts, railroads, insurance companies, and agricultural entities. Having secured a place at the federal trough, the financial industry looked askance upon those interests that remained out in the cold. When a bill authorizing the RFC to loan money to cities was debated in early 1932, the *Wall Street Journal* opposed it as it would only reward municipal governments for profligate spending. Profligate lending, on the other hand, ought to be rewarded—though the *Journal* believed the conditions imposed on banks seeking aid were too stringent.[343] The first Glass-Steagall Act was also intended to aid banks; it added government bonds to the types of assets—gold and commercial paper—that national banks could use as collateral for loans from the federal reserve banks. This provision relieved banks from need to deposit ever larger quantities of gold that had been necessitated by a decline in the amount of commercial paper available.[344]

Congress spent much of the first half of 1932 dithering over a bill to slow the plague of mortgage disclosures. The measure that became law in July—the Federal Home Loan Act—allowed banks and other mortgage lenders to use mortgages as security with which they could obtain loans at 12 home loans banks set up by the act.[345] (The Federal Reserve Act had barred national banks from obtaining loans from the Federal Reserve on the security of mortgages they held.) Senator James Couzens, Republican of Michigan and a former banker, wondered how home loan banks could assist persons whose lack of employment left them unable to pay their mortgages. As the country's ills stemmed in part from an excess of credit, he doubted that more credit was what Americans needed.[346] After raising $134 million through a stock issue in September, the home loan banks began operating in mid-October, and hopes were high that they would be able to "thaw" the frozen mortgage market.[347] During his reelection campaign, the president boasted that the law constituted "the greatest act yet undertaken by any government at any time on behalf of the thousands of owners of small homes."[348] One real estate executive thought the Home Loan Act inadequate; he called for the establishment of a federal mortgage loan company that would issue mortgages itself.[349] In August 1932 the comptroller of the currency ordered the national banks to suspend foreclosures. The Home Loan Board asked the state governments to issue the same order to state banks.[350] While the organization of a national network of banks devoted to home loans was no more novel than one dedicated to farmers, the pressure brought on banks to avoid foreclosures often only delayed the inevitable. It also put additional financial pressure on banks at a time when many were already facing failure.

In late 1931, politicians around the country again demanded that Congress provide grants to the states for the purpose of aiding the unemployed. For a time state officials had assured the administration that local governments were adequately funding relief; after they were besieged by cities and counties for help even as state tax revenues dwindled, they turned to Washington. Governor Gifford Pinchot of Pennsylvania thought Congress should act because state government expenditures were still derived largely from the pockets of the poor and the middle class.[351] Federal revenue, on the other hand, was provided largely by the income tax, which was paid by the wealthy. This fact explains in part why southern and western lawmakers increasingly favored federal aid—the share of income taxes paid by residents of their states was relatively modest. In January 1932, Senators Robert M. LaFollette Jr. and Edward Costigan, a Colorado Democrat, proposed a massive grant-in-aid bill giving the states $375 million, to be used to fund relief and construction programs. Others favored a substitute bill devised by Hugo Black of Alabama and David Walsh of Massachusetts that would have loaned the states $375 million for the same purposes instead of giving them the money outright. It dispensed with the massive federal oversight machinery provided for by the LaFollette-Costigan bill.[352] The two sides cobbled together a compromise measure known as the Wagner bill that spring. The *Chicago Daily Tribune* was appalled. “If poor relief is not the function of the states and the localities, it is difficult to believe that there is such a thing as local responsibility for anything in the United States.” It complained that the states that pay the most money to the federal government in taxes and received the least back were the same states that had the largest populations needing relief (the urban states). Yet Wagner’s relief bill, focusing as it did on road-building projects, would cause even more money to be diverted from the urban states with impoverished populations to small rural, western states that already received a huge windfall from the federal government.[353] The *Tribune’s* objections were valid but action was necessary—the newspaper’s home state of Illinois, despite being among the wealthiest in the country, had nearly reached the limits of its resources. Eighteen million dollars obtained by the state through a bond issue had nearly been exhausted by July 1932, and a Cook County bond issue failed due to a lack of bids—the RFC had to take the bonds as collateral for loans. By that fall, all of the relief being provided to Chicago families originated in the federal treasury.[354] In April 1932, Senator Wagner cited a report indicating that the municipal governments in Cleveland and Los Angeles would run out of relief funds by May; they would be followed by Detroit and New York City in June and San Francisco in July.[355]

The Wagner bill reached the president's desk on July 9 only to be vetoed. A reworked bill won the president's signature on July 21, 1932. The Emergency Relief and Reconstruction Act authorized the Reconstruction Finance Corporation to loan the states up to $300 million for self-liquidating public works projects and housing for families with low incomes. Said loans could also be used by the states "in furnishing relief and work relief to needy and distressed people and relieving the hardship resulting from unemployment."[356] The RFC was also authorized to loan money to corporations engaged in the improvement of public works and roads—with the proviso that 30 hours constituted the maximum anyone employed on said projects could work in a single week. Governors had to demonstrate that their states lacked the resources needed to meet actual needs. The sums loaned to states were to be deducted from future highway grants. The RFC loaned only $30 million to the states during the rest of 1932; a lesser amount went to public works.[357] The disbursal of money was slowed by the high interest rates charged by the RFC as well as bureaucratic hurdles (states had to establish their own relief administrations to qualify for loans).[358] Pennsylvania asked for $45 million. The RFC conducted an investigation and concluded the state should draw on its own resources first. After the legislature appropriated $12 million for relief, the RFC relented and authorized a loan of $2.5 million.[359] Despite such difficulties the measure was revolutionary: "it proclaimed the federal government's willingness at long last to accept a share in the provision of material aid to the unemployed."[360] The utility of the RFC and the Emergency Reconstruction Act in priming the pump was undermined by the 1932 Revenue Act.[361] The law stemmed from both the drain of gold out of the country and a massive hike in spending—the federal budget grew from $4.2 billion in 1930 to $5.5 billion in 1931, producing a deficit of $2.2 billion. The law raised the maximum income tax rate from 25 to 63 percent, the greatest hike ever in peacetime. The estate tax was raised to 45 percent. In paying vastly higher taxes, the public had less money to purchase goods and services, and demand was severely impaired.

Perhaps the most revolutionary of all proposals to expand the pecuniary relationship between Americans and their national government made in Congress during the Hoover administration was the call to establish federally funded old age pensions. Thus far, 17 states had established old age pension systems.[362] Four lawmakers proposed measures for that purpose in late 1931. Congressman David Glover of Arkansas discussed his pension bill in a speech of January 1932. He claimed that old age pensions were needed because the elderly were being driven out of the workforce by the fast pace of the twentieth-century economy. While some states were already providing pensions to the aged, most of the states were too poor to fund their own systems. The elderly were just as deserving of the generosity of the nation as veterans; as Glover put it, "the pioneer of this country who has helped to build the nation is as valiant as a soldier as has ever fought in the trenches." Under his bill, states would have to match the grants provided by the federal government and devise bureaucracies to administer the system. Glover explained that his bill would limit payments to the needy—those worth less than $500. He proposed to provide a stipend of a $1 day to those elderly persons of limited means who possessed "good moral character."[363] He did not state how the federal government would determine which citizens met that test. In March 1932, the House Labor Committee reported favorably on another measure, the Dill-Connery bill, which would have provided matching federal grants to the states for old age pensions. William Connery, a Massachusetts Democrat in the House and one of the sponsors of the measure, suggested that if Congress could spend $2 billion to aid the banks, it could also provide assistance to the aged. Abraham Epstein of the American Association for Old Age Security told a Senate committee that a federal system of old age pensions would cost no more than $44 million a year.[364] Lawmakers thus proposed to multiply the demagoguery, manipulation, and expense that had characterized veterans' pensions during the previous six decades by a factor of 10 or more; as the political history of twentieth-century America would demonstrate, the elderly proved far more willing than veterans to allow their dependence on federal payments to dictate their votes, and the enterprise proved far more expensive for their fellow citizens.

The unprecedented foray of Congress into the business of putting money into the pockets of as many Americans as possible inspired a lacerating article in the August 1932 *Atlantic*. Clinton W. Gilbert charged that "Congress is the greatest vote-buying organization in the world. The individual members and their friends do not, of course, make a practice of directly corrupting the electorate by handing out two dollar bills on election day. They buy the votes out of the public treasury, with appropriations. The proposed cash payment of $2.4 billion to the veterans chiefly interests the members as a means of purchasing the good will of that powerful minority." Gilbert blamed the high income taxes imposed by the Revenue Act of 1932 on lawmakers from the South and West who had determined that the wealthier parts of the country ought to shoulder more of the tax burden. Despite the deficit, a proposal to cut the wages of federal workers died in Congress out of "fear of the organized federal employees."[365] Gilbert's criticism revealed one aspect of a conflict that would face federal policymakers for the rest of the twentieth century. Aware of the danger of corruption, waste, and manipulation inherent in a system that placed the impoverished of every state on the public payroll, they also faced the task of propping up demand in an economy that needed it in order to survive. The federal government surely exceeded the limits of its powers in funding relief—as those powers were originally understood—but such excesses were necessary if radicalism was to be checked and if the economy was to be resuscitated.

In mid-1932 unemployment reached a quarter of the workforce. Only one-fourth of the jobless were on relief. Two million idle Americans wandered the country looking for work.[366] The upper Midwest saw farmers forcibly prevent their colleagues from taking crops to market in a futile attempt to maintain "farm strikes" and increase crop prices. As the 1932 presidential campaign began, most observers gave the president little hope of obtaining reelection. The favorite for the Democratic nomination was Franklin Delano Roosevelt, the 50-year-old governor of New York and a distant cousin of Theodore Roosevelt. Elected governor in 1928 by only 25,000 votes, he won reelection easily in 1930. He was the first governor to push through a state-level relief program, the Temporary Emergency Relief Administration. He also arranged for the state to provide jobs at conservation projects. The state income tax was increased by half to pay for relief. Roosevelt gave his first radio speech in April 1932. In promising to "stand up for the forgotten man at the bottom of the economic pyramid," he revealed the animated baritone voice that would make him one of the star politicians of the radio age.[367]

Not everyone was convinced. Roosevelt won the early primaries, but he suffered painful upset losses in Massachusetts (to Al Smith) and in California (to House Speaker John Nance Garner of Texas). His unwillingness to take a position on Prohibition almost proved fatal; it was not until the eve of the party convention that he announced his support for repeal of the Eighteenth Amendment. At the Democratic Convention in Chicago, Roosevelt found himself in a deadlock with Garner. The New York governor had the lead but could not obtain the required two-thirds majority. On the third ballot Roosevelt forces appeared ready to crack until Huey Long firmed up the Arkansas and Mississippi delegations—he threatened to campaign against Senator Pat Harrison of Mississippi and Congressman Joe Robinson of Arkansas.[368] The logjam finally broke when Joseph P. Kennedy and James Farley convinced William Randolph Hearst to switch the California delegation to Roosevelt. FDR won the nomination on the fourth ballot. After a white-knuckle flight from New York, the nominee addressed the delegates at Chicago Stadium. Roosevelt criticized "Washington" for claiming that there were no destitute persons in the country and for insisting that even if they exist, their condition was a matter for the states. He promised to seek trade agreements with other countries and repeal of the Agricultural

Marketing Act of 1929 that compelled "the federal government to go into the market to purchase, sell and speculate" in cotton, wheat, and corn. "Americans," he announced, are "looking to us here for guidance and more equitable opportunity to share in the distribution of national wealth." Roosevelt closed by promising a "new deal for the American people."[369]

The Democratic platform was full of contradictions. It called for reducing government expenditures and a balanced budget while endorsing federal loans to the states for unemployment relief, as it was "impossible" for the states to provide for the needy. The workday ought to be reduced to increase employment. Democrats embraced "effective control of crop surpluses" even as they condemned the "extravagance" of the Farm Board. The platform endorsed unemployment and old age insurance "under state laws." Utilities, holding companies, and securities exchanges ought to be subject to federal regulation. The convention overwhelmingly rejected a plank endorsing federal insurance of bank deposits; instead the platform called for "a more rigid supervision of national banks for the protection of depositors and the prevention of the use of their money in speculation to the detriment of local credits."[370]

Republicans renominated the president; in their platform they promised to authorize the Reconstruction Finance Corporation to make more loans. Additional money would be extended to the Farm Board and to the states for relief purposes. They also announced their support for an amendment that would allow states to legalize the sale of liquor.[371] Republicans took to the fall campaign with a listlessness that was understandable—the party was heading for a disaster and everyone knew it. The two candidates differed little on the issues. FDR wanted the federal government to build and operate power-generating dams; Hoover thought the one dam owned by the national government (Muscle Shoals) should be sold and that Washington should stay out of the electricity business. The Democratic candidate temporized on the tariff. He called for cuts but when Republicans began to make headway on the issue, Roosevelt assured that tariffs on farm products would remain. At one point the New York governor called for cutting federal expenditures 25 percent.[372] FDR played both sides on the issue of centralization in order to placate the states' rights wing of his party; he attacked Hoover for his belief that "we ought to center control of everything in Washington as rapidly as possible."[373] Governor Ritchie of Maryland assured that Democrats would put a stop to federal usurpation of the rights of the states and terminate government competition with private enterprise.[374]

In a September speech at Topeka, Roosevelt seemed to embrace the domestic allotment plan that was gaining support among farm interests when he called for the "planned use of farmland." Under the latest version of the plan, the federal government would set a price for key agricultural commodities based on their cost of production and determine the maximum amount that each farmer could grow; excess crops would not receive the fixed price. Farmers would also be paid to reduce their acreage. Said payments would be financed by an excise tax on their crops. Excise taxes could not possibly pay for such an endeavor—general revenues would have to be used—but that did not stop Roosevelt from charging that the Farm Board had squandered "hundreds of millions" of dollars. He also called for the refinancing of farm mortgages.[375]

In a speech at Albany in mid-October, FDR endorsed the expansion of public works projects. He noted that New York state had taken up the task of aiding the poor when the task proved beyond the capacity of counties. "Where the state is unable successfully to fulfill the obligation which lies upon it, it then becomes the positive duty of the federal government to step in and help." He complained that it took the Hoover administration almost three years to "recognize this principle."[376] In a radio address of November 1, Democratic Senator of Carter Glass blamed Republicans for the nation's difficulties. The easy money policies of the 1920s had fueled speculation and contrary to the assertion of Treasury Secretary Ogden Mills, who claimed the failure of European banks caused the depression, 10 million were already unemployed when those institutions defaulted. The Reconstruction Finance Corporation stood idle until prodded into making loans by Congress. Glass conceded that the Wagner Act (the Emergency Relief Act) was "utterly extraordinary and unorthodox." He blamed the bonus bill episode on "sordid Republican politics." Glass refuted Hoover's charge that Democrats would impose federal deposit insurance, saying that a plank embracing it had been rejected overwhelmingly at the Democratic convention.[377]

Hoover emphasized that oldest of Republican shibboleths in the final weeks of the campaign, warning that the protective tariff was in danger.[378] At Indianapolis on October 28 he pointed out that American wages remained the highest in the world and noted that the federal government provided for increased construction work during the winters of 1930 and 1931. Hoover blamed the Democratic House for not passing the home loan bill in time to prevent numerous foreclosures.[379] In a Halloween speech at Madison Square Garden, Hoover charged that Democratic policies would result in a massive expansion of the federal bureaucracy and repeated his opposition to the idea of the national government going into the "power business."[380]

The result was as expected: Hoover won only six states, all in the northeast. The reversal in Congress was shattering: Democrats won 60 seats in the Senate and three-quarters of the seats in the House. The *New Republic* listed the items the country could expect from the incoming administration and a Democratic Congress: public works programs, relief for the unemployed—federal where state relief was inadequate, compulsory unemployment insurance, a voluntary allotment plan for farmers including payments in exchange for crop reductions, and regulation of the stock market, holding companies and utilities, as well as industrial planning.[381] If Republicans winced when they encountered such predictions, they could not have been shocked. Some of the most important Democratic initiatives had precedents in laws and programs devised by Republicans. Federally funded public works programs and unemployment relief had been initiated under Hoover, albeit in the form of grants to the states under the Emergency Relief and Reconstruction Act. Compulsory unemployment insurance would constitute a novel departure, though it had already been proposed in Congress—as had old age pensions. A voluntary allotment plan for farmers had a strong precedent in the Agricultural Marketing Act of 1929—if Congress could pay farmers for their crops, surely it could pay farmers to refrain from growing them. Regulation of the capital markets took precedent not only from the supervision of national banks but also from the laws applicable to the issuance of securities by railroads.

During the four-month interim between Roosevelt's election and the inauguration, Hoover spent weeks trying to cajole his successor into promising that he would not try to spend his way out of the depression or inflate the currency. While the president concentrated his energies on bullying Roosevelt, a new round of bank failures set in—by March 22 states had passed laws requiring banks to close to prevent more.[382] The economy was not only in freefall; certain sectors of it appeared to be dead. With state treasuries all but empty and the electorate gripped by fear, events had set the stage for the federal government to exploit the precedents set during the past 70 years and establish its omnipotence once and for all.

NOTES

INTRODUCTION

1. See, for example, James Madison, *The Federalist* #46, Clinton Rossiter, ed., *Federalist Papers* (New York: Penguin Books, 1961), 294.

2. Brian Balogh, *A Government Out of Sight: The Mystery of National Authority in Nineteenth Century America* (New York: Cambridge University Press, 2009); Richard Franklin Bensel, *Yankee Leviathan: The Origins of Central State Authority in America* (New York: Cambridge University Press, 1990); Kimberley S. Johnson, *Governing the American State: Congress and the New Federalism, 1877–1929* (Princeton, NJ: Princeton University Press, 2007).

3. Johnson, *Governing the American State*, 12.

CHAPTER 1

1. James D. Richardson, ed., *Compilation of the Messages and Papers of the Presidents*, 1897–1917, 20 vols. (New York: Bureau of National Literature, 1917), 7:3214–15. The 1795 law authorized the president to call forth the state militias in the event of combinations too powerful to be suppressed by normal legal processes. Statutes at Large of the United States, 1789–1936, 49 vols. (Boston: Little & Brown, 1845–1936), 1 (1789): 424.

2. *Messages and Papers of the Presidents*, 7:3215–16 (South Carolina, Georgia, Alabama, Florida, Mississippi, Louisiana, Texas); Ibid., 3216 (Virginia and North Carolina).

3. Ibid., 3216–17.

4. James M. McPherson, *Battle Cry of Freedom: The Civil War Era* (New York: Oxford University Press, 1988), 293.

5. Fred Shannon, *The Organization and Administration of the Union Army*, 2 vols. (Cleveland, OH: The Arthur Clark Company), 1:45.

6. "A Question of Sovereignty," *New York Times*, June 23, 1862, 4; *Digest of the Official Opinions of the Attorneys General of the United States, 1789–1974*, 42 vols. (Washington, DC: Government Printing Office, 1885–1982), 10:279–84. Article I, Section 8 gave Congress authority to "provide for organizing, arming, and disciplining the Militia, and for governing such Part of them as may be employed in the Service of the United States, reserving to the States respectively, the Appointment of the Officers, and the Authority of training the Militia according to the discipline prescribed by Congress."

7. Phillip Shaw Paludan, *A People's Contest: The Union and Civil War, 1861–1865* (New York: Harper & Row, 1988), 18–19.

8. Shannon, *The Organization and Administration of the Union Army*, 1:46.

9. Ibid., 48, 35, 23.

10. C. K. Yearley, *The Money Machines: The Breakdown and Reform of Governmental and Party Finances in the North, 1860–1920* (Albany, NY: State University of New York Press, 1970), 138.

11. Harry J. Carman, David M. Ellis, James A. Frost, and Harold C. Syrett, *A History of New York State* (Ithaca, NY: Cornell University Press, 1967), 352.

12. John Niven, *Connecticut for the Union: The Role of the State in the Civil War* (New Haven, CT: Yale University Press, 1965), 94–95.

13. Shannon, *Organization and Administration of the Union Army*, 1:110–11.

14. Allan Nevins, *The War for the Union*, 4 vols. (New York: Charles Scribner's Sons, 1959–1971), *Volume 1: The Improvised War, 1861–62*, 348.

15. Mark Wilson, *The Business of Civil War: Military Mobilization and the State, 1861–1865* (Baltimore: Johns Hopkins University Press, 2006), 23–30.

16. Ben Perley Poore, *Perley's Reminiscences*, 2 vols. (Philadelphia: Hubbard Brothers, 1886) 2:80.

17. "Washington as a Camp," *Atlantic Monthly*, July 1861, 105–18 at 108.

18. Poore, *Perley's Reminiscences*, 2:76–77.

19. *U.S. Statutes at Large* 12 (July 27, 1861): 279.

20. Margaret Leech, *Reveille in Washington* (New York: Harper & Brothers, 1941), 71, 80–84.

21. Carl Sandburg, *Abraham Lincoln: The War Years*, 4 vols. (New York: Harcourt, Brace & Co., 1936–39), 1:231.

22. James G. Randall, *Constitutional Problems under Lincoln* (Champaign, IL: University of Illinois Press, 1964), 231, 233.

23. Sandburg, *The War Years*, 1:231, 233.

24. *U.S. Statutes at Large* 12 (1861): 255.

25. Ibid., 12 (1861) 292 (tax law); 12 (1861) 259 (treasury notes); 12 (1861) 268 (volunteers); 12 (1861) 281 (authority to call out the army and navy); 12 (1861) 256–57 (prohibition of trade with the southern states); *Messages and Papers of the Presidents*, 7: 3238–39.

26. Ibid., 12 (1861): 326.

27. Ibid., 12 (1861): 319.

28. See the comments of Senator James A. McDougall of California at U.S. Congress, *Congressional Globe*, 46 vols. (Washington, DC: Blair & Rives, 1834–73) 37th Cong., 2d Sess. Vol. 32, Part 2 (March 4, 1862): S 66.

29. Quoted in Sandburg, *The War Years*, 1:330.

30. Samuel Eliot Morison, *The Oxford History of the American People* (New York: Oxford University Press, 1964), 658.

31. Leonard White, *The Republican Era, 1869–1901: A Study in Administrative History* (New York: Macmillan Company, 1958), 58; John Steele Gordon, *An Empire of Wealth: The Epic History of American Economic Power* (New York: HarperCollins, 2004), 192.

32. *The Prize Cases*, 67 U.S. 635 (1863).

33. Ibid. at 666–68. The 1795 act authorized use of the militia to defeat combinations too powerful to be suppressed by normal legal processes; the 1807 act authorized the use of the land and naval forces for that purpose. *U.S. Statutes at Large* 1 (February 28, 1795): 424; Ibid., 2 (March 3, 1807): 443. A blockade was necessary even though it conferred belligerent status on the Confederacy because only it would enable the United States to detain neutral ships under international law. An embargo, such as that proclaimed by Jefferson in 1807, would not.

34. McPherson, *Battle Cry of Freedom*, 623–24.

35. *Messages and Papers of the Presidents*, 7:3219.

36. Ibid. (July 2, 1861), 3220.

37. Ibid., 3226.

38. Randall, *Constitutional Problems under Lincoln*, 162.

39. Quoted in Sandburg, *The War Years*, 1:279–80.

40. *The Federal Cases: Comprising Cases Argued and Decided in the Circuit and District Courts of the United States from the Earliest Times to the Beginning of the Federal Reporter*, 30 vols. (St. Paul, Minnesota: West Publishing Co., 1894–97), *Ex parte Merryman*, 17 Fed. Cases 144, 148 (1861).

41. Ibid., at 148–49.

42. Daniel Farber, *Lincoln's Constitution* (Chicago: University of Chicago Press, 2003), 188–90.

43. *Opinions of the Attorneys General*, 10: 74–92, 82–84, 90.

44. Ibid., 82–83.

45. See Randall, *Constitutional Problems under Lincoln*, 125–27.

46. *Congressional Globe* 37th Cong., 1st Sess. Vol. 31 Appendix (July 19, 1861): S 14–17.

47. Ibid., 37th Cong., 2d Sess. Vol. 32, Part 3 (May 2, 1862): S 1920–21.

48. Ibid., 37th Cong., 3rd Sess. Vol. 33 Part 2 (February 19, 1863): S 1093.

49. Ibid., 1092.

50. *U.S. Statutes at Large* 12 (March 3, 1863): 755.

51. Randall, *Constitutional Problems under Lincoln*, 166–67.

52. *Messages and Papers of the Presidents*, 7:3371–72.

53. Randall, *Constitutional Problems under Lincoln*, 152, 156. The actual figure may have been much higher. See Mark E. Neely, *The Fate of Liberty: Abraham Lincoln and Civil Liberties* (New York: Oxford University Press, 1992), 130.

54. Quoted in Sandburg, *The War Years*, 1:331.

55. Randall, *Constitutional Problems under Lincoln*, 149–50.

56. Leech, *Reveille in Washington*, 143.

57. *Messages and Papers of the Presidents* (February 14, 1862, Executive Order Number 1), 7:3305–7.

58. Allan Nevins, *The War for the Union, Volume 2: War Becomes Revolution, 1862–63*, 316.

59. McPherson, *Battle Cry of Freedom*, 622.

60. Winston Groom, *Vicksburg 1863* (New York: Alfred A. Knopf, 2009), 197.

61. Sandburg, *The War Years*, 1:331.

62. Randall, *Constitutional Problems under Lincoln*, 492–93.

63. "General Burnside's Department," *New York Times*, June 4, 1863, 8.

64. "Suppressing Newspapers," *Chicago Daily Tribune*, June 22, 1863, 2.

65. *Messages and Papers of the Presidents*, 7:3438.

66. Nevins, *War for the Union*, 2:316; Allan Nevins, *The War for the Union Volume 4: The Organized War to Victory, 1864–65*, 128.

67. Leech, *Reveille in Washington*, 275.

68. McPherson, *Battle Cry of Freedom*, 596–97.

69. *Ex parte Vallandigham*, 68 U.S. 243 (1863) at 251–53.

70. Nevins, *War for the Union*, 2:454–55.

71. *Congressional Globe*, 38th Cong., 1st Sess. Vol. 34, Part 3 (April 29, 1864): H 1972–73.

72. Nevins, *War for the Union*, 2:6–8.

73. *Messages and Papers of the Presidents*, 7:3255.

74. Ibid., 3269–70.

75. *U.S. Statutes at Large* 12 (1862): 617.

76. David P. Currie, "The Civil War Congress," *University of Chicago Law Review* 73, no. 4 (Autumn 2006): 1152–53.

77. Nevins, *War for the Union*, 2:114.

78. *Messages and Papers of the Presidents*, 7:3337–38.

79. Randall, *Constitutional Problems under Lincoln*, 366.

80. Allan Nevins, *The War for the Union, Volume Three: The Organized War, 1863–64*, 424.

81. Leech, *Reveille at Washington*, 246–47.

82. *U.S. Statutes at Large* 12 (1862): 376.

83. Nevins, *War for the Union*, 2:93.

84. Leech, *Reveille in Washington*, 245–46.

85. *U.S. Statutes at Large* 13 (June 28, 1864): 200.

86. *Messages and Papers of the Presidents* (Proclamation of May 19, 1862) 7: 3292–93.

87. *U.S. Statutes at Large* 12 (1862): 432.

88. 60 U.S. 393 (1857).

89. Speech of June 26, 1857, at Springfield, Illinois; Roy Basler, ed., *The Collected Works of Abraham Lincoln*, 8 vols. (New Brunswick, NJ: Rutgers University Press, 1953–55), 2:398–410.

90. *Messages and Papers of the Presidents*, 7:3297–99.

91. The second Confiscation Act provided for the confiscation of all property of persons serving in the Confederate or state governments in the South as well as in the Confederate Army. *U.S. Statutes at Large* 12 (July 17, 1862): 589. After he signed the measure, the president sent Congress an unused draft veto message. In it he suggested the bill ought to have transferred ownership of slaves of persons supporting the rebellion to the national government as a penalty for treason. The national government could then free them as a matter of policy, as had Kentucky when slaves of persons without heirs passed to it by escheat. Message to Congress of July 17, 1862. John T. Woolley and Gerhard Peters, *The American Presidency Project* [online]. Santa Barbara, CA. Available from http://www.presidency.ucsb.edu/ws/?pid=69771.

92. U.S. Congress, *Register of Debates*, 14 vols. (Washington, DC: Gales & Seaton, 1825–1837) 24th Cong., 1st Sess. Vol. 12, Part 2 (May 25, 1836): H 4047; Randall, *Constitutional Problems under Lincoln*, 345–47.

93. Nevins, *War for the Union*, 3:452.

94. *Messages and Papers of the Presidents*, 7:3358–60.

95. Nevins, *War for the Union*, 3:377.

96. Ibid., 418, 433–41.

97. "The President's Proclamation," *New York Times*, January 1, 1863, 4.

98. Benjamin R. Curtis, *Executive Power*, Cambridge, Massachusetts 1862, 13–15.

99. Nevins, *War for the Union*, 2:238–39.

100. Quoted in Sandburg, *The War Years*, 1:567.

101. *Congressional Globe* 37th Cong., 3rd Sess. Vol. 33, Part 2 (February 23, 1863): H 1230.

102. Quoted in Sandburg, *The War Years*, 2:472.

103. See the comments of Benjamin F. Thomas of Massachusetts, *Congressional Globe* 37th Cong., 3rd Sess. Vol. 33, Part 2 (February 25, 1863) H: 1289.

104. Ibid. (February 28, 1863): H 1363.

105. *U.S. Statutes at Large* 12 (1862): 597.

106. *Messages and Papers of the Presidents*, 7:3321–22.

107. Shannon, *Organization and Administration of the Union Army*, 1:285–86.

108. 12 Stat 731.

109. Shannon, *Organization and Administration of the Union Army*, 2: 106–7.

110. "Federal Authority and State Rights," *New York Times*, March 21, 1863, 4.

111. "What Is the Militia," Ibid., October 4, 1863, 4.

112. McPherson, *Battle Cry of Freedom*, 601–2.

113. Nevins, *War for the Union*, 2:466.

114. Sandburg, *The War Years*, 2:444.

115. *Messages and Papers of the Presidents*, 7:3371–72; Neely, *The Fate of Liberty*, 70–73.

116. Edwin G. Burrows, Mike Wallace, *Gotham: A History of New York City to 1898* (New York: Oxford University Press, 1999), 888–96.

117. *U.S. Statutes at Large* 12 (March 2, 1861): 178.

118. Heather Cox Richardson, *The Greatest Nation on Earth: Republican Economic Policies during the Civil War* (Cambridge, MA: Harvard University Press, 1997), 105–8.

119. *U.S. Statutes at Large* 12 (1861): 292; Richardson, *Greatest Nation on Earth*, 111–15.

120. *U.S. Statutes at Large* 12 (1862): 543; F.W. Taussig, *The Tariff History of the United States* 7th ed. (New York: G.P. Putnam's Sons, 1930), 162–67.

121. Nevins, *War for the Union*, 2:371.

122. *U.S. Statutes at Large* 13 (1864): 202; Taussig, *Tariff History of the United States*, 167.

123. Nevins, *The War for the Union*, 2:509.

124. See the comments of Representative Justin Morrill at *Congressional Globe*, 38th Cong., 1st Sess. Vol. 34 Part 3 (June 2, 1864): H 2674–75.

125. Ibid., 38th Cong., 1st Sess. Vol. Part 2 (April 25, 1864): H 1858.

126. Ibid., Vol. 34 Part 3 (June 2, 1864) H: 2677–80.

127. Johnson, *Governing the American State: Congress and the New Federalism*, 65.

128. W. Elliot Brownlee, *Federal Taxation in America: A Short History* (New York: Cambridge University Press, 1996), 31.

129. McPherson, *Battle Cry of Freedom*, 447n38.

130. Richardson, *Greatest Nation on Earth*, 42–52.

131. *Briscoe v. Bank of Kentucky*, 36 U.S. 257 (1837).

132. Richardson, *Greatest Nation on Earth*, 36, 44.

133. Bray Hammond, *Sovereignty & an Empty Purse* (Princeton, NJ: Princeton University Press, 1970), 162, 204–5.

134. See the comments of John W. Crisfield of Maryland in the House of Representatives of February 5, 1862. *Congressional Globe*, 37th Cong., 2nd Sess. Vol. 32 Part 4 Appendix: H 47–49.

135. Ibid., Vol. 32 Part 1 (February 5, 1862): H 662.

136. Ibid. (February 6, 1862): H 679.

137. Ibid., Vol. 32 Part 4 Appendix (February 12, 1862): H 53.

138. Paludan, *The People's Contest*, 110.

139. *U.S. Statutes at Large* 12 (February 25, 1862): 345.

140. Nevins, *War for the Union*, 2:168, 211–13.

141. McPherson, *Battle Cry of Freedom*, 447.

142. *U.S. Statutes at Large* 12 (March 3, 1863): 709.

143. Henry Steele Commager, Samuel Eliot Morison, *The Growth of the American Republic* 2 vols., 5th ed. (New York: Oxford University Press, 1962), 1:749.

144. *Hepburn v. Griswold*, 75 U.S. 603 (1870).

145. Ibid. at 621–22.

146. Charles Warren, *The Supreme Court in United States History*, 2 vols. (Boston: Little, Brown & Company, 1937) 1:515–20.

147. *The Legal Tender Cases*, 79 U.S. 457 (1871).

148. Ibid. at 537.

149. Ibid. at 541.
150. Ibid. at 544–45.
151. *Juillard v. Greenman* 110 U.S. 421 (1884).
152. Ibid. at 448.
153. *Hammond, Sovereignty & an Empty Purse*, 290–92, 311, 327.
154. James Blaine, *Twenty Years of Congress*, 2 vols. (Norwich, CT: Henry Bill 1884), 1:473.
155. *Congressional Globe*, 37th Cong., 3rd Sess. Vol. 33 Part 1 (February 11, 1863): S 869–74.
156. *The Debates and Proceedings in the Congress of the United States, 1789–1824*, 42 vols. (Washington, DC: Gales & Seaton, 1834–1856), (hereafter *Annals of Congress*), 11th Cong., 3rd Sess. (February 15, 1811): H 211.
157. Currie, "The Civil War Congress," 1163–74.
158. *Richardson, Greatest Nation on Earth*, 53, 91–92.
159. *U.S. Statutes at Large* 12 (February 25, 1863): 665.
160. Richardson, *Greatest Nation on Earth*, 91–92.
161. *U.S. Statutes at Large*, 13 (June 3, 1864): 99.
162. Niven, *Connecticut for the Union*, 423.
163. Paludan, *The People's Contest*, 124–26.
164. Richardson, *Greatest Nation on Earth*, 54–62.
165. *U.S. Statutes at Large* 12 (February 25, 1863): 665, 670.
166. Ibid., 13 (1865): 484.
167. *Congressional Globe* 38th Cong., 1st Sess. Vol. 34 Part 3 (May 1, 1864): S 2592.
168. Ibid., 38th Cong., 2nd Sess. Vol. 35 Part 2 (March 1, 1865): S 1239–40.
169. Ibid., 37th Cong., 3rd Sess. Vol. 33 Part 2 Appendix (January 8, 1863): S 51.
170. Ibid., 38th Cong., 1st Sess. Vol. 34, Part 3 (May 30, 1864): S 2563.
171. 75 U.S. 533, 548–49 (1869).
172. *U.S. Statutes at Large* 12 (1861): 292, 309.
173. Brownlee, *Federal Taxation*, 49.
174. *U.S. Statutes at Large* 13 (March 2, 1865): 478–79 (maximum rate raised to 10 percent); 12 (July 1, 1862): 474–75 (deduction allowed for state and local taxes); 12 (March 3, 1863): 713, 723 (deduction for rental expenses added).
175. Joseph A. Hill, "The Civil War Income Tax," *The Quarterly Journal of Economics*, 8, no. 4 (July 1894): 434.
176. Ibid., 438.
177. *U.S. Statutes at Large* 12 (1862): 432, 485–88.
178. Ibid., 457–79.
179. Nevins, *War for the Union*, 2:509.
180. Adam Gifford, "Whiskey Margarine and Newspapers: A Tale of Three Taxes," in *Choice: The Predatory Policies of Fiscal Discrimination*, ed. William F. Shughart II (Oakland, CA: The Independent Institute, 1997), 63.
181. "The Tax Law," *Harper's Weekly*, September 27, 1862, 610.
182. *Congressional Globe*, 37th Cong., 2nd Sess. Vol. 32 Part 4 Appendix (May 30, 1862): S 229–32.

183. "Sales and Licenses," *Chicago Daily Tribune*, July 24, 1865, 2.

184. Nevins, *War for the Union*, 3:151.

185. *Congressional Globe*, 37th Cong., 2nd Sess. Vol. 32 Part 3 (June 4, 1862): S 2550.

186. Ibid., 37th Cong., 2nd Sess. Vol. 32 Part 4 Appendix (May 30, 1862): S 229.

187. Ibid., 230–31.

188. *U.S. Statutes at Large* 12 (March 3, 1863): 713, 727 (section 25).

189. "Law Intelligence," *Chicago Daily Tribune*, October 7, 1862, 4.

190. As David Currie wrote, the Madisonian view of the spending power "had been the prevailing interpretation before the (Civil) War." Currie, "The Civil War Congress," 1153.

191. *U.S. Statutes at Large* 1 (August 7, 1789): 53.

192. *U.S. Statutes at Large* 5 (September 4, 1841): 453.

193. *Congressional Globe*, 37th Cong., 2nd Sess. Vol. 32 Part 3 (May 21, 1862): S 2248; Ibid. (May 20, 1862): S 2432.

194. McPherson, *Battle Cry of Freedom*, 451.

195. *U.S. Statutes at Large* 12 (July 2, 1862): 503.

196. Roger L. Williams, *The Origins of Federal Support for Higher Education: George W. Atherton and the Land Grant College Movement* (University Park, PA: The Pennsylvania State University Press, 1991), 40–41.

197. Nevins, *War for the Union*, 2:208.

198. *U.S. Statutes at Large* 12 (May 15, 1862): 387. See also the comments of Senator John P. Hale of New Hampshire, *Congressional Globe*, 32nd Cong., 2nd Sess. Vol. 32 Part 3 (May 8, 1862): S 2014

199. Nevins, *War for the Union*, 3:263.

200. *U.S. Statutes at Large* 12 (1862): 392.

201. Richard Hofstadter, *The Age of Reform: From Bryan to F.D.R.* (New York: Alfred A. Knopf, 1966), 55.

202. Paludan, *The People's Contest*, 135.

203. A law of September 20, 1850, gave a right of way through public lands of 100 feet on each side of lines extending through Illinois, Mississippi, and Alabama as well as alternate sections in rows of six on each side of the lines to these states, with proceeds from the sale of said lands to aid the construction of railroads along said lines. The railroads thereby constructed would be "public highways for the use of the government of the United States, free from toll or other charge upon the transportation of any property or troops of the United States." *U.S. Statutes at Large* 9 (1850): 466.

204. Allan Nevins, *Ordeal of the Union*, 2 vols. (New York: Charles Scribner's Sons, 1947), *Volume 2: A House Dividing 1852–1857*, 202.

205. *U.S. Statutes at Large* 12 (1862): 489.

206. In an 1888 opinion, Justice Joseph Bradley cited the commerce, postal, and war powers in support of the constitutionality of federal aid for the construction of a transcontinental railroad. He explained that the "power to construct, or to authorize individuals or corporations to construct, national highways and bridges from state to state, is essential to the complete control and regulation of

interstate commerce." *California v. Central Pacific R.R.*, 127 U.S. 1, 39. This interpretation was in conflict with the view of antebellum Democrats such as James Polk. In an 1846 veto message explaining his rejection of a river-and-harbors bill, he insisted that the commerce clause "confers no creative powers." *Messages and Papers of the Presidents*, 5:2475.

207. Currie, "The Civil War Congress," 1145–46; see also *Congressional Globe*, 37th Cong., 2nd Sess. Vol. 32, Part 2 (amendment and comments of Thaddeus Stevens), (April 30, 1862): H 1889–90.

208. A law of 1826 authorized the secretary of the treasury to purchase up to a thousand shares of the Louisville and Portland Canal Company. *U.S. Statutes at Large* 4 (May 12, 1826): 162.

209. *U.S. Statutes at Large* 12 (1863): 806.

210. Nevins, *War for the Union*, 3:327.

211. Nevins, *War for the Union*, 2:482–98.

212. McPherson, *Battle Cry of Freedom*, 817.

213. *U.S. Statutes at Large* 12 (March 2, 1863): 696–97; see also Wilson, *The Business of Civil War*, 182–89.

214. Niven, *Connecticut for the Union*, 436.

215. Wilson, *The Business of Civil War*, 93–99.

216. Paludan, *A People's Contest*, 196.

217. Bensel, *Yankee Leviathan: The Origins of Central State Authority in America*, 248, 265–74.

218. Ibid., 345.

219. McPherson, *Battle Cry of Freedom*, 817.

220. Nevins, *War for the Union*, 3:279.

221. Ibid., 461.

222. *U.S. Statutes at Large* 12 (January 31, 1862): 334.

223. Nevins, *War for the Union*, 2:300–301, 460–62.

224. Hermon King Murphey, "The Northern Railroads and the Civil War," *The Mississippi Valley Historical Review* 5, no. 3 (December 1918): 332.

225. Bensel, *Yankee Leviathan*, 151.

226. Nevins, *War for the Union*, 3:299–300, 459.

227. Bruce Tap, *Over Lincoln's Shoulder: The Committee on the Conduct of the War* (Lawrence, KS: University Press of Kansas, 1998), 67.

228. Kenneth C. Martis, *Historical Atlas of Political Parties in the United States Congress, 1789–1989* (New York: Macmillan, 1989), 117.

229. Nevins, *War for the Union*, 2:391–92.

230. Sandburg, *The War Years*, 3:632.

231. McPherson, *Battle Cry of Freedom*, 742–43.

232. Quoted in Nevins, *War for the Union*, 4:105.

233. Donald Bruce Johnson, Kirk H. Porter, comp., *National Party Platforms, 1840–1956* (Champaign, IL: The University of Illinois, 1956), 35.

234. Nevins, *War for the Union*, 3:95.

235. "The Popular Tide," *Chicago Daily Tribune*, September 21, 1864, 2.

236. "Important and Interesting Interview," Ibid., September 2, 1864, 2.

237. "The Presidency," *New York Times*, September 9, 1864, 8.

238. "Read! Read! Read! Startling Utterances of Treason," *Chicago Daily Tribune*, October 30, 1864, 2.

239. *The Diary of Gideon Welles*, 3 vols. Howard K. Beale, ed. (New York: W.W. Norton, 1960) (October 10, 1865), 2:380–81.

240. Quoted in Nevins, *War for the Union*, 4:110–11.

241. Jonathon M. White, "Canvassing the Troops: The Federal Government and the Soldiers' Right to Vote," *Civil War History* 50 (September 2004), 291–317.

242. Sandburg, *The War Years*, 4:275.

243. Leech, *Reveille in Washington*, 352.

244. Nevins, *War for the Union*, 4:139.

245. "The Danger to Property from McClellan's Election," *New York Times*, November 8, 1864, 4.

246. Nevins, *War for the Union*, 4:139.

247. Sandburg, *The War Years*, 3:564–65.

248. Nevins, *War for the Union*, 4:138–39.

249. Dale Baum, *The Civil War Party System: The Case of Massachusetts, 1848–76* (Chapel Hill: University of North Carolina Press, 1984), 95, 97.

250. Sandburg, *The War Years*, 3:568.

251. Allan Nevins, Milton Halsey Thomas, eds. *The Diary of George Templeton Strong*, 3 vols. (New York: Macmillan, 1952) (November 9, 1864), 3:511.

252. *U.S. Statutes at Large* 13 (Joint Resolution Number Twelve, February 8, 1865): 567–68.

253. Nevins, *War for the Union*, 4:329, 336.

254. Eric Foner, *Reconstruction: America's Unfinished Revolution* (New York: Harper & Row, 1988), 125.

255. Ibid., 23.

256. Albert Castel, *The Presidency of Andrew Johnson* (Lawrence, KS: The Regents Press of Kansas, 1979), 11.

257. Ibid., 38.

258. Woodrow Wilson, "The Reconstruction of the Southern States," *Atlantic Monthly*, January 1901, 11–14.

259. Currie, "The Civil War Congress," 1226.

260. Quoted in Allan Nevins, *Hamilton Fish: The Inner History of the Grant Administration*, 2 vols. (New York: Frederick Ungar Publishing Company, 1957), 1:227.

261. Paludan, *A People's Contest*, 224.

262. D. W. Meinig, *Continental America, 1800–67* (New Haven: Yale University Press, 1993), 513.

CHAPTER 2

1. Sandburg, *The War Years*, 1:656; *Diary of Gideon Welles* (December 29, 1862), 1:208–9. For the opinion of Attorney General Edward Bates, see *Opinions of the Attorneys General*, 10:426–35.

2. *U.S. Statutes at Large* 12 (December 31, 1862): 633–34; see also Randall, *Constitutional Problems under Lincoln*, 458–66.

3. William C. Harris, *With Charity for All: Lincoln and the Restoration of the Union* (Lexington, KY: University of Kentucky Press, 1997), 233–46.

4. *Congressional Globe*, 38th Cong., 2nd Sess. Vol. 35 Part 2 (February 25, 1865): S 1093–94.

5. Martis, *Historical Atlas of Political Parties*, 115, 117.

6. William B. Hesseltine, *Lincoln's Plan of Reconstruction* (Tuscaloosa, AL: Confederate Publishing Co., 1960), 56–62.

7. *Congressional Globe*, 37th Cong., 3rd Sess. Vol. 33 Part 1 (January 8, 1863): H 239.

8. Ibid.

9. Ibid., 243.

10. Charles Sumner, "Our Domestic Relations, or How to Treat the Rebel States," *Atlantic Monthly*, October 1863, 507–21.

11. Ibid., 521–26.

12. *Messages and Papers of the Presidents* (December 8, 1863), 7:3414–16.

13. *Congressional Globe*, 38th Cong., 1st Sess. Vol. 34 Part 1 (January 5, 1864): S 97–98.

14. Ibid., Vol. 34, Part 2 (March 30, 1864): H 1354–57.

15. Ibid., 38th Cong., 1st Sess. Vol. 34 Part 4 Appendix (March 22, 1864): H 83. In 1849, Chief Justice Taney held that it "rests with Congress to decide what government is the established one in a state. For as the United States guarantees to each state a republican government, Congress must necessarily decide what government is the established one in a state. For as the United States guarantees to each state a republican government, Congress must necessarily decide what government is established in the state before it can determine whether it is republican or not. And when the senators and representatives of a state are admitted into the councils of the Union, the authority of the government under which they are appointed, as well as its republican character, is recognized by the proper constitutional authority." *Luther v. Borden*, 48 U.S. 1, 42 (1849).

16. Ibid., 38th Cong., 1st Sess. Vol. 34 Part 2 (April 19, 1864): H 1737–38.

17. The text of the bill may be found at *U.S. Statutes at Large* 13 (July 8, 1864): 744.

18. *Congressional Globe*, 38th Cong., 1st Sess. Vol. 34, Part 3 (June 13, 1864): S 2899.

19. *Messages and Papers of the Presidents*, 7:3423–24.

20. Quoted in Sandburg, *The War Years*, 3:138.

21. Niven, *Connecticut for the Union*, 290–91.

22. Harris, *With Charity for All*, 263–64.

23. *The Collected Works of Abraham Lincoln*, 8:399–405.

24. Quoted Sandburg, *The War Years*, 4:266.

25. Blaine, *Twenty Years of Congress*, 2:13–14.

26. Attorney General James Speed justified military trials for the assassins on the grounds that in conspiring to kill the commander in chief, they violated the laws of war. *Opinions of the Attorneys General*, 11:297–317.

27. *Messages and Papers of the Presidents*, 7:3508–10.

28. Ibid., 3510–12.

29. *Diary of Gideon Welles* (April 16, 1865), 2:291.

30. Edwin Percy Whipple, "Reconstruction and Negro Suffrage," *Atlantic Monthly*, August 1865, 241–45.

31. Castel, *The Presidency of Andrew Johnson*, 44, 49–51.

32. "Reorganization," *Harper's Weekly*, July 1, 1865, 402.

33. "The Public Safety," Ibid., July 8, 1865, 418.

34. "Legal Fictions," *The Nation*, October 12, 1865, 455–56.

35. Baum, *The Civil War Party System*, 104.

36. Foner, *Reconstruction*, 216.

37. *Acts of the General Assembly of Alabama, 1865–66* (Montgomery, AL: Stokes & Co., 1866), Act No. 112 (December 15, 1865): 119; *Acts Passed by the General Assembly at the Extra Session Held & Beginning at the City of New Orleans on November 23, 1865* (New Orleans, LA: J.O. Nixon, 1866) Act No. 12 (December 20, 1865): 16–20.

38. *The Statutes at Large of South Carolina*, 1861–66, 15 vols. (Columbia: SC: Republican Printing Co., 1875), (December 21, 1865), 13:269.

39. George F. Hoar, *Autobiography of Seventy Years*, 2 vols. (New York: Charles Scribner's Sons, 1903), 1:256.

40. "Southern Indiscretion," *The Nation*, November 23, 1865, 646–47.

41. Henry Winter Davis, letter to the editor, *The Nation*, November 30, 1865, 680–81.

42. Foner, *Reconstruction*, 28.

43. Paul Johnson, *A History of the American People* (New York: HarperCollins, 1997), 503.

44. *Diary of Gideon Welles* (December 8, 1865), 2:393

45. *Messages and Papers of the Presidents*, 8:3554–55.

46. Martis, *Historical Atlas of Political Parties*, 119.

47. *Congressional Globe*, 39th Cong., 1st Sess. Vol. 36 Part 1 (December 4, 1865): H 3–4; Robert V. Remini, *The House: The History of the House of Representatives* (Washington, DC: Library of Congress, 2006), 192–93.

48. *Congressional Globe*, 39th Cong., 1st Sess., Vol. 36 Part 1 (December 18, 1865): H 72–74.

49. Ibid., December 21, 1865, 120–25. See also *Prize Cases*, 67 U.S. 635, 668–70.

50. *Congressional Globe*, 39th Cong., 1st Sess. Vol. 36 Part 5 Appendix (January 19, 1866): H 49.

51. The "power to suppress rebellion includes authority to maintain the peace in areas regained from the insurgents . . . this power continues after actual hostilities are concluded." Currie, "The Reconstruction Congress," *University of Chicago Law Review* 75, no. 1 (Winter 2008): 412.

52. *U.S. Statutes at Large* 13 (March 3, 1865): 507.

53. Foner, Reconstruction, 159–62.

54. Walter L. Fleming, "Forty Acres and a Mule," *North American Review*, May 1906, 734.

55. Currie, "Reconstruction Congress," 391.

56. *Congressional Globe*, 38th Cong., 2nd Sess. Vol. 35 Part 2 (February 22, 1865): S 985.

57. *Messages and Papers of the Presidents* (February 19, 1866), 8:3596–3601.

58. Quoted in Claude G. Bowers, *The Tragic Era: The Revolution after Lincoln* (Cambridge, MA: Houghton Mifflin Company, 1929), 104.

59. *U.S. Statutes at Large* 14 (July 16, 1866): 173. The law described its purpose as helping freedmen make the freedom conferred by state laws, the Emancipation Proclamation, and the Thirteenth Amendment "available to them and beneficial to the republic."

60. Morison, *The Oxford History of the American People*, 711.

61. *U.S. Statutes at Large* 15 (Joint Resolution Number 28, March 30, 1867): 28; 15 (Joint Resolution Number 29, March 30, 1867): 28; 15 Stat (Joint Resolution Number Seven, January 31, 1868): 246.

62. Morison, *Oxford History of the American People*, 713.

63. Foner, *Reconstruction*, 148–51, 165–67.

64. "The Work of the Freedman's Bureau," *Springfield Daily Republican* (Springfield, Massachusetts), November 21, 1871, 5.

65. *The Diary of Gideon Welles* (March 21, 1866), 2:460–61.

66. *U.S. Statutes at Large* 14 (April 9, 1866): 27. In his opinion for the majority in *Dred Scott v. Sandford*, Chief Justice Taney held that blacks were not citizens of the United States, as they were not recognized as such at the time of the Constitution's ratification. He based this conclusion on this the existence of numerous state laws in effect during the 1780s that discriminated against blacks. 60 U.S. 393, 404–22 (1857). As Justice Benjamin Curtis pointed out in his dissent, at the time of the Constitution's ratification, several states bestowed citizenship on all free, native-born inhabitants; blacks in those states thereby became citizens of the United States automatically with the ratification of the Constitution. Ibid. at 572–83. In an opinion of November 29, 1862, Attorney General Edwin Bates held that Taney's assertions regarding the citizenship of blacks were dictum—extraneous comments on issues not necessary to the resolution of the case and therefore not binding law—and that all free persons born in the United States are citizens (he expressly refused to take a position on whether slaves are citizens). There was, he insisted, no historical support for the position that inhabitants of a country who happen to be members of a particular ethnic group are not citizens. *Opinions of the Attorneys General*, 10:382–413.

67. Article IV, Section 2 protects certain rights enjoyed by Americans while they are in states other than their own. In *Corfield v. Coryell*, Justice Washington suggested that these rights included, at a minimum, "the right of a citizen of one state to pass through, or to reside in any other state, for purposes of trade, agriculture, professional pursuits, or otherwise; to claim the benefit of the writ of habeas corpus; to institute and maintain actions of any kind in the courts of the state; to take, hold and dispose of property, either real or personal; and an exemption from higher taxes or impositions than are paid by the other citizens of the state." *Corfield v. Coryell*, 6 Fed. Cas. 546 (1823). See also David R. Upham, "Corfield v.

Coryell and the Privileges and Immunities of American Citizenship," *Texas Law Review* 83, no. 5 (April 2005): 1530.

68. Harold Hyman, *A More Perfect Union: The Impact of the Civil War and Reconstruction on the Constitution* (New York: Alfred A. Knopf, 1973), 240–56.

69. *Congressional Globe*, 39th Cong., 1st Sess. Vol. 36 Part 2: S 1755–61.

70. Ibid., 39th Cong., 2nd Sess. Vol. 37 Part 3 Appendix (April 6, 1866): S 182–84.

71. *Diary of Gideon Welles* (March 26, 1866) 2:463–64; Ibid. (April 10, 1866), 2:479.

72. *Messages and Papers of the Presidents*, 8:3603–11.

73. William S. McFeely, *Grant: A Biography* (New York: W.W. Norton & Company 1981), 259.

74. *Messages and Papers of the Presidents*, 8:362, 3632.

75. *Diary of Gideon Welles* (August 17, 1866), 2:579.

76. Foner, *Reconstruction*, 262–63.

77. Ibid., 251.

78. *Congressional Globe*, 39th Cong., 1st Sess. Vol. 36 Part 1 (December 5, 1865): H 10.

79. Ibid. (December 6, 1865): H 14.

80. Foner, *Reconstruction*, 252.

81. "The explanation most prominently proffered in Congress . . . was that the amendment would remove lingering doubts as to the constitutionality of the Civil Rights Act and protect it against possible repeal." David Currie, "The Reconstruction Congress," 406.

82. *Congressional Globe*, 39th Cong., 1st Sess. Vol. 36 Part 3 (May 9, 1866): H 2502.

83. Castel, *The Presidency of Andrew Johnson*, 74–75.

84. David Currie suggested that the equal protection clause was intended to provide a constitutional basis for Section 1 of the Civil Rights Act of 1866's provision affording nonwhites "the full and equal benefit of all laws and proceedings for the security of persons and property, as is enjoyed by white citizens." Currie, "The Reconstruction Congress," 403.

85. *Congressional Globe*, 39th Cong., 1st Sess. Vol. 36 Part 3 (May 8, 1866): H 2459.

86. Ibid. (May 8, 1866): 2462.

87. Ibid., 2467.

88. "Close of the Session of Congress—the General Result," *New York Times*, July 30, 1866, 4.

89. "The Objections to the Amendment," *Chicago Daily Tribune*, October 16, 1866, 2.

90. "How to Amend the Amendment," Ibid., May 5, 1866, 2.

91. "Great Speech of Senator Trumbull," Ibid., August 31, 1866, 2.

92. "Speech of Emery A. Storrs," Ibid., September 22, 1866, 2.

93. Castel, *The Presidency of Andrew Johnson*, 86.

94. Bowers, *The Tragic Era*, 136.

95. Blaine, *Twenty Years of Congress*, 2:239.
96. Bowers, *The Tragic Era*, 142–43.
97. *The Diary of Gideon Welles* (December 12, 1866), 2:640–41.
98. *Ex parte Milligan*, 71 U.S. 2, 121–22.
99. Ibid. at 122–23.
100. Ibid. at 126–27.
101. Ibid. at 140–42.
102. Warren, *The Supreme Court in United States History*, 1:448–49.
103. "The Milligan Decision," *Springfield Daily Republican*, January 2, 1867, 4.
104. "The Milligan Case-False Alarms," Ibid., January 10, 1867, 2.
105. *Congressional Globe*, 39th Cong., 2nd Sess. Vol. 37 Part 1: S 15.
106. *Diary of Gideon Welles* (December 24, 1866), 2:644–46.
107. *Congressional Globe*, 39th Cong., 2nd Sess. Vol. 37, Part 1 (January 3, 1867): S 251–52.
108. "The True Radical Plan," *Springfield Daily Republican*, January 4, 1867, 2.
109. Diary of Gideon Welles (January 8, 1867), 3:9–12.
110. Ibid. (January 19, 1867), 27.
111. *Congressional Globe*, 39th Cong. 2nd Sess. Vol. 37 Part 3 Appendix (January 21, 1867): H 63–64.
112. Ibid. (January 28, 1867): H 79.
113. Ibid. (February 7, 1867): H 85.
114. Ibid. (February 7, 1867): H 94–95.
115. Ibid. (February 9, 1867): H 103.
116. "Military Rule and Reconstruction," *Springfield Daily Republican*, February 22, 1867, 2.
117. "The Military Bill as Passed," *Baltimore Sun*, February 22, 1867, 2.
118. *U.S. Statutes at Large* 14 (March 2, 1867): 428.
119. *Messages and Papers of the Presidents*, 8:3696–3709.
120. David P. Currie, *The Constitution in the Supreme Court: The First Hundred Years, 1789–1888* (Chicago: University of Chicago Press, 1985), 297.
121. "The President and the Reconstruction Bill," *New York Times*, March 4, 1867, 4.
122. Samuel S. Cox, *Three Decades of Federal Legislation* (Providence, RI: Reid Publishers 1886), 377–79.
123. "Let the Constitution Slide," *Springfield Daily Republican*, March 23, 1867, 4.
124. *Mississippi v. Johnson*, 71 U.S. 475 at 501 (1867).
125. *Georgia v. Stanton*, 73 U.S. 50, 77 (1868).
126. *U.S. Statutes at Large* 14 (March 2, 1867): 430.
127. See the comments of James Madison in the House of Representatives, *Annals of Congress*, 1st Cong., 1st Sess. (June 16, 1789): H 480–81.
128. *Congressional Globe*, 39th Cong., 2nd Sess. Vol. 37 Part 3 Appendix (February 7, 1867): H 87.
129. *Messages and Papers of the Presidents*, 8:3690–96; see also *Ex parte Hennen*, 38 U.S. 230 at 257–60 (1839).

130. *U.S. Statutes at Large* 14 (1867): 485–87.

131. For the veto message, see *Messages and Papers of the Presidents*, 8:3279–83.

132. *U.S. Statutes at Large* 15 (March 23, 1867): 2.

133. "Maryland—Her Relations to the Union and Her Duties to Herself," *Baltimore Sun*, March 25, 1867, 2.

134. "The Maryland Radical Minority Movement," Ibid., March 27, 1867, 2; see also Jean H. Baker, *The Politics of Continuity: Maryland Political Parties from 1858 to 1870* (Baltimore: Johns Hopkins University Press, 1973), 175–79.

135. *U.S. Statutes at Large* 14 (February 5, 1867): 385.

136. Ibid., 15 (March 27, 1868): 44.

137. *Ex parte McCardle*, 74 U.S. 506, 514 (1869).

138. Castel, *The Presidency of Andrew Johnson*, 128–30.

139. *U.S. Statutes at Large* 15 (1867): 14.

140. *Messages and Papers of the Presidents* (July 19, 1867), 8:3734–43.

141. Castel, *The Presidency of Andrew Johnson*, 132–37.

142. James Rhodes, *History of the United States from the Compromise of 1850 to the End of the Roosevelt Administration*, 9 vols. (New York: Macmillan, 1928), 6:187–93.

143. *U.S. Statutes at Large* 15 (June 22, 1868): 72; Ibid., 15 (June 25, 1868): 74.

144. For the veto messages see *Messages and Papers of the Presidents*, 8:3846–49.

145. Foner, *Reconstruction*, 318–20, 283, 291, 305, 348–49.

146. Ibid., 365, 371, 375, 355.

147. Hoar, *Autobiography of Seventy Years*, 2:60.

148. Rhodes, *History of the United States from the Compromise of 1850*, 6:204.

149. Castel, *The Presidency of Andrew Johnson*, 146.

150. Bowers, *The Tragic Era*, 300–304.

151. Foner, *Reconstruction*, 381, 386.

152. Nevins, *Inner History of the Grant Administration*, 2:744.

153. *Springfield Daily Republican*, December 25, 1871, 4.

154. Commager, Morison, *Growth of the American Republic*, 5th ed., 2:43.

155. *Concise Dictionary of American History*, ed. Wayne Andrews (New York: Charles Scribner's Sons, 1962), 817–18. In defaulting on their bonds, the states were thought by many to have violated the contract clause of the Constitution. In 1890 the Supreme Court held that the federal courts lacked jurisdiction to hear a lawsuit brought against Louisiana by a citizen of the state seeking to force it to pay interest on bonds it had issued. *Hans v. Louisiana*, 134 U.S. 1.

156. Foner, *Reconstruction*, 334.

157. Ibid., 172–73.

158. *Preliminary Proceedings in the House of Representatives and the Senate, Together with the Eleven Articles of Impeachment and the Whole of the Proceedings in the Court of Impeachment* (Philadelphia: T.B. Peterson & Brothers, 1868) (hereafter *Impeachment Proceedings*), 19–20.

159. Castel, *Presidency of Andrew Johnson*, 186.

160. *Impeachment Proceedings*, 101–5.

161. Currie, "The Reconstruction Congress," 451.

162. Castel, *The Presidency of Andrew Johnson*, 187–88.

163. Foner, *Reconstruction*, 336.

164. Rhodes, *History of the United States from the Compromise of 1850*, 6: 260–61.

165. James E. Bond, *No Easy Walk to Freedom: Reconstruction and the Ratification of the Fourteenth Amendment*, (Westport, CT: Praeger 1997), 37, 56–58, 80–81, 104, 124–25, 149.

166. Joseph B. James, *The Ratification of the Fourteenth Amendment* (Atlanta, GA: Mercer University Press, 1984), 223.

167. *Messages and Papers of the Presidents*, 8:3854–55.

168. Castel, *The Presidency of Andrew Johnson*, 200.

169. Rhodes, *History of the United States from the Compromise of 1850*, 6: 273–74.

170. *Diary of Gideon Welles* (October 16, 1868), 3:456.

171. *National Party Platforms*, 37–38.

172. Ibid., 39.

173. Quoted in Foner, *Reconstruction*, 340.

174. Georges Clemenceau, *American Reconstruction, 1865–70*, ed. Fernand Baldensperger (New York: Lincoln Longmans Green & Company, 1928) (October 6, 1868), 249–50.

175. Foner, *Reconstruction*, 341.

176. Rhodes, *History of the United States from the Compromise of 1850*, 6:190–91.

177. Foner, *Reconstruction*, 342.

178. "Governor Seymour," *New York Times*, October 24, 1868, 3.

179. *U.S. Statutes at Large* 15 (1868): 257.

180. McFeely, *Grant*, 284.

181. Charles Fairman, *Reconstruction and Reunion, 1864–88* (New York: Macmillan, 1971), 1267–69.

182. Jack Beatty, *Age of Betrayal: The Triumph of Money in America, 1865–1900* (New York: Alfred A. Knopf, 2007), 131.

183. *Congressional Globe*, 40th Cong., 3rd Sess. Vol. 40, Part 2 (February 17, 1869): S 1307.

184. *U.S. Statutes at Large* 16 (April 10, 1869): 40–41.

185. Rhodes, *History of the United States from the Compromise of 1850*, 6:347.

186. *U.S. Statutes at Large* 16 (December 22, 1869): 60.

187. "A Ruinous Victory," *Atlanta Constitution*, December 28, 1869, 1.

188. Quoted in Rhodes, *History of the United States from the Compromise of 1850*, 6:400–402.

189. *U.S. Statutes at Large* 16 (July 15, 1870): 363.

190. Ibid., 16 (1870): 62.

191. Bowers, *The Tragic Era*, 208.

192. Foner, *Reconstruction*, 413.

193. *U.S. Statutes at Large* 17 (May 22, 1872): 142.

194. *Ex parte Rodriguez*, 39 Texas 705 (1873).

195. Ben H. Procter, *Not Without Honor: The Life of John H. Reagan* (Austin: University of Texas Press, 1962), 200–204.

196. Foner, *Reconstruction*, 552.

197. Bowers, *The Tragic Era*, 392–93.

198. Foner, *Reconstruction*, 561–62.

199. Ibid., 551.

200. *Bowers*, 442–46.

201. Foner, *Reconstruction*, 414–16, 548.

202. Ibid., 422–23.

203. Ibid., 588–93.

204. Charles Lane, *The Day Freedom Died: The Colfax Massacre, the Supreme Court and the Betrayal of Reconstruction* (New York: Henry Holt 2008), 100–109, 266.

205. Homer Cummings and Carl McFarland, *Federal Justice: Chapters in the History of Justice and the Federal Executive* (New York: The Macmillan Company, 1937), 234.

206. Beatty, *Age of Betrayal*, 128.

207. Joint Select Committee, *Report of the Joint Select Committee on the Condition of Affairs in the Late Insurrectionary States*, 42nd Congress, 2nd Sess., H. Rep. 22, Part 1 (February 19, 1872), 18.

208. Ibid., 22.

209. Foner, *Reconstruction*, 442.

210. *U.S. Statutes at Large* 16 (1870): 140.

211. *Congressional Globe*, 41st Cong., 2nd Sess. Vol. 42 Part 7 Appendix (May 27, 1870): H 397–401.

212. Ibid. (May 27, 1870): S 416.

213. Ibid. (May 20, 1870): S 468–73.

214. *U.S. Statutes at Large* 16 (1871): 433. The Naturalization Act imposed heavy penalties for naturalization frauds (Republicans suspected they were losing elections due to the manipulation of immigrants) and authorized federal judges to appoint persons to oversee the casting of ballots and the counting of votes in congressional elections on the request of two citizens in cities of 20,000 or more. Marshals could appoint as many special deputies as were needed to maintain order. *U.S. Statutes at Large* 16 (July 14, 1870): 254. The act was of limited utility in part because some states allowed un-naturalized immigrants to vote. The law constituted an exercise of the power of Congress to regulate elections for the U.S. House of Representatives as well as its power to enact laws regarding naturalization.

215. *Congressional Globe*, 41st Cong., 3rd Sess. Vol. 43, Part 3 41:3 Appendix (February 15, 1871): H 127.

216. *U.S. Statutes at Large* 17 (1872): 347–48.

217. Burrows, Wallace, *Gotham*, 927.

218. Quoted in the *Congressional Globe*, 41st Cong., 3rd Sess. Vol. 43 Part 3 Appendix (February 15, 1871): H 130.

219. William Gillette, *Retreat from Reconstruction, 1869–1879* (Baton Rouge, Louisiana: Louisiana State University Press 1979), 48–49.

220. Ibid., 13.

221. *Messages and Papers of the Presidents*, 9:4081–82.

222. Quoted in Rhodes, *History of the United States from the Compromise of 1850*, 6:375.

223. Foner, *Reconstruction*, 456.

224. *Congressional Globe*, 42nd Cong., 1st Sess. Vol. 44 Part 2 Appendix (April 4, 1871): H 183–84.

225. Ibid. (April 6, 1871): H 181–82.

226. Frederick S. Calhoun, *The Lawmen: U.S. Marshals and Their Deputies, 1789–1989* (Washington, DC: The Smithsonian Institute Press, 1991), 112.

227. Cummings, *Federal Justice*, 237.

228. Ibid., 273, 234–40.

229. Foner, *Reconstruction*, 459.

230. Cummings, *Federal Justice*, 236.

231. "The Lynching of Three Negroes," *Springfield Daily Republican*, November 22, 1871, 2.

232. "A New Phase of the Klu Klux Question," Ibid., December 8, 1871, 4.

233. "The President and the South," Ibid.

234. Foner, *Reconstruction*, 500–501.

235. "Mr. Greeley's Constitutionalism," *Atlanta Constitution*, September 14, 1872, 1.

236. "The Cause Greeley Represents," Ibid., October 15, 1872, 2.

237. Gillette, *Retreat from Reconstruction*, 66–67.

238. Rhodes, *History of the United States from the Compromise of 1850*, 6:187.

239. Nevins, *The Inner History of the Grant Administration*, 2:733–34, 749–51.

240. See John Palmer, *The Story of an Earnest Life* (Cincinnati, OH: Robert Clark, 1901), 354–77; Andrew L. Slap, "The Strong Arm of the Military Power of the United States," *Civil War History* 47, no. 2 (June 2001): 146–63.

241. Special message of February 8, 1875, John T. Woolley and Gerhard Peters, *The American Presidency Project* [online]. Santa Barbara, CA. Available from http://www.presidency.ucsb.edu/ws/?pid=70449. See also Nevins, *The Inner History of the Grant Administration*, 2:757–60.

242. Gillette, *Retreat from Reconstruction*, 192–202, 240–41, 256–58.

243. Martis, *Historical Atlas of Political Parties in the United States Congress*, 129.

244. For a discussion of the school clause and the civil rights bill, see *Congressional Record*, 156 vols. (Washington, DC: Government Printing Office 1873–Present) 43rd Cong., 2nd Sess. Vol. 3 Part 2 (February 4, 1875): H 996–1011.

245. *U.S. Statutes at Large* 18 (March 1, 1875): 335.

246. Gillette, *Retreat from Reconstruction*, 273–79.

247. Ibid., 18 (March 3, 1875): 470.

248. *Congressional Record*, 43rd Cong., 2nd Sess. Vol. 3 Part 2 (February 4, 1875): H 979.

249. "The Civil Rights Bill," *Atlanta Constitution*, March 6, 1875, 3; "That Civil Rights Affair," Ibid., March 7, 1875, 3.

250. *Congressional Record*, 43rd Cong., 2nd Sess. Vol. 3 Part 3 Appendix (February 26, 1875): S 103–05; 83 U.S 36 at 79–80 (1873).

251. *Congressional Record*, 43rd Cong., 2nd Sess. Vol. 3 Part 2 (February 27, 1875): S 1861–63.

252. Warren, *The Supreme Court in United States History*, 1:421, 485–86.

253. *The Slaughterhouse Cases*, 83 U.S. 36, 79–80 (1873).

254. Ibid. at 62.

255. Ibid. at 72–74.

256. Ibid. at 74.

257. Ibid. at 77.

258. Ibid.

259. Ibid. at 79–80. See also *Crandall v. Nevada*, 73 U.S. 35, 44 (1868).

260. Ibid. at 100–101. Article IV, Section 2 prohibited states from impairing the privileges and immunities of citizens other states while within their borders; with passage of the Fourteenth Amendment, the states "were to be forbidden to deny to *any* citizens, including their own" equal privileges and immunities. Currie, "The Reconstruction Congress," 407.

261. Raoul Berger, *Government by Judiciary: The Transformation of the Fourteenth Amendment* (Cambridge: Harvard University Press 1977, Second Edition, Indianapolis: Liberty Fund, 1997), 64–65.

262. 83 U.S. at 96.

263. Warren, *The Supreme Court in United States History*, 1:539–43.

264. *U.S. v. Reese*, 92 U.S. 214, 221–22 (1876).

265. Ibid. at 219–20.

266. Warren, *The Supreme Court in United States History*, 1:607–8.

267. *U.S. v. Cruikshank*, 92 U.S. 542, 555 (1876).

268. *U.S. v. Harris*, 106 U.S. 629 (1883).

269. Ibid. at 639–40.

270. David Currie, *The Constitution in the Supreme Court: The Second Century, 1888–1986* (Chicago: University of Chicago Press, 1990), 397.

271. *The Civil Rights Cases*, 109 U.S. 3 (1883).

272. Ibid. at 13.

273. Ibid. at 19.

274. Ibid. at 58–59.

275. Ibid. at 52–58.

276. "A Righteous and Welcome Decision," *Atlanta Constitution*, October 16, 1883, 4.

277. *Strauder v. West Virginia*, 100 U.S. 303 (1880).

278. *Ex parte Siebold*, 100 U.S. 371, 387–89 (1880).

279. "Notes at Washington," *Springfield Daily Republican*, December 22, 1874, 4.

280. White, *The Republicans*, 373.

281. Nevins, *Inner History of the Grant Administration*, 2:790–817.

282. "Letter from Governor Tilden," *Atlanta Constitution*, October 25, 1876, 1.

283. *National Party Platforms*, 53.

284. Ari Hoogenboom, *The Presidency of Rutherford B. Hayes* (Lawrence, KS: University of Kansas Press, 1988), 18.

285. Nevins, *Inner History of the Grant Administration*, 2:840.

286. Quoted in Bowers, *The Tragic Era*, 491.

287. Nevins, *Inner History of the Grant Administration*, 2:840–41.

288. Irwin Unger, *The Greenback Era: A Social and Political History of American Finance, 1865–79* (Princeton, NJ: Princeton University Press, 1964), 316.

289. *Messages and Papers of the Presidents* (October 17, 1876), 9:4350–51.

290. McFeely, *Grant*, 439.

291. Hoogenboom, *The Presidency of Rutherford B. Hayes*, 22–23.

292. Rhodes, *History of the United States from the Compromise of 1850*, 7:287, 291.

293. Hoogenboom, *Presidency of Rutherford B. Hayes*, 25–31.

294. *U.S. Statutes at Large* 19 (1877): 227.

295. *Electoral Count of 1877: Proceedings of the Electoral Commission and of the Two Houses of Congress in Joint Meeting Relative to the Count of Electoral Votes Cast December 6, 1876 for the Presidential Term Commencing March 4, 1877* (Washington, DC: Government Printing Office, 1877), 1021.

296. Bowers, *The Tragic Era*, 535.

297. "The Count and the High Court," *Atlanta Constitution*, February 6, 1877, 2.

298. Hoogenboom, *The Presidency of Rutherford B. Hayes*, 42–43.

299. Bensel, *Yankee Leviathan*, 367–72.

CHAPTER 3

1. Mark Wahlgren Summers, *Party Games: Getting, Keeping and Using Power in Gilded Age Politics* (Chapel Hill, NC: The University of North Carolina Press, 2004), 126–31.

2. Baum, *The Civil War Party System*, 208.

3. Burrows, Wallace, *Gotham*, 1021.

4. *Concise Dictionary of American History*, 710.

5. Foner, *Reconstruction*, 513–15.

6. Hoogenboom, *The Presidency of Rutherford B. Hayes*, 79.

7. "The Army and the Militia," *New York Times*, June 11, 1878, 4.

8. "The Baltimore & Ohio Strike," *Springfield Daily Republican*, July 19, 1877, 5.

9. John A. Garraty, *The New Commonwealth, 1877–1890* (New York: Harper & Row, 1968), 159.

10. William E. Forbath, "The Shaping of the American Labor Movement," *Harvard Law Review* 102, no. 6 (April 1989): 1156.

11. Hoogenboom, *The Presidency of Rutherford B. Hayes*, 89–90.

12. Rhodes, *History of the United States from the Compromise of 1850*, 8:35–49.

13. Foner, *Reconstruction*, 584–86.

14. T. Harry William, ed., *Hayes: The Diary of a President, 1875–1881* editor (New York: David McKay, 1964) (July 27, 1877), 90.

15. Hoogenboom, *The Presidency of Rutherford B. Hayes*, 86–90.

16. Gerald G. Eggert, *Railroad Labor Disputes: The Beginnings of Federal Strike Policy* (Ann Arbor, MI: The University of Michigan Press, 1967), 30–32, 49–50.

17. "The President on His Policy: An Interesting Interview with a Georgia Democrat," *Springfield Daily Republican*, March 29, 1877, 8.

18. Hoogenboom, *The Presidency of Rutherford B. Hayes*, 63–68.

19. Garraty, *The New Commonwealth*, 26.

20. *U.S. Statutes at Large* 20 (June 18, 1878): 152.

21. "Army and Navy Affairs," *New York Times*, October 6, 1878, 2.

22. *Congressional Record*, 47th Cong., 1st Sess. Vol. 13 Part 4 (May 1, 1882): S 3457–58.

23. Gary Felicetti, John Luce, "The Posse Comitatus Act: Liberation from Lawyers," *Parameters, The Army War College Quarterly* 34, no. 3 (Autumn 2004): 100–101.

24. Hoogenboom, *The Presidency of Rutherford B. Hayes*, 72–73.

25. For the veto messages see *Messages and Papers of the Presidents*, 9:4475, 4484, 4488, 4493, 4497.

26. *Hayes: Diary of a President* (March 30, 1879), 208.

27. Ibid. (April 7, 1879) 215, (April 6, 1879) 214.

28. Hoogenboom, *Presidency of Rutherford B. Hayes*, 77.

29. For the veto message of June 15, 1880, see *Messages and Papers of the Presidents*, 9:45444–50.

30. *U. S. Statutes at Large* 28 (February 8, 1894): 36.

31. Hoogenboom, *The Presidency of Rutherford B. Hayes*, 195.

32. Hoar, *Autobiography of Seventy Years*, 1:399–404.

33. Thomas Platt, *The Autobiography of Thomas Platt* (New York: B.W. Dodge, 1910), 125.

34. *Lemmon v. New York*, 20 N.Y. 562 (1860).

35. Justin D. Doenecke, *The Presidencies of James A. Garfield and Chester A. Arthur* (Lawrence, KS: The Regents Press of Kansas, 1981), 21, 27.

36. Stanley P. Hirshson, *Farewell to the Bloody Shirt: Northern Republicans and the Southern Negro, 1877–93* (Bloomington, IN: Indiana University Press 1962), 79.

37. *National Party Platforms*, 62.

38. "The Blunders of the Campaign," *Boston Globe*, October 10, 1880, 4.

39. Rhodes, *History of the United States from the Compromise of 1850*, 8:131–33.

40. "The Tariff Difficulties of the Democrats," *The Nation*, October 14, 1880, 267–68.

41. "The Solid South and the National Treasury," Ibid., October 28, 1880, 300.

42. Quoted in Hoogenboom, *Presidency of Rutherford B. Hayes*, 206.

43. "That Certain Small Use of Money and Services of Officeholders," *The Nation*, November 11, 1880, 338.

44. Hoogenboom, *The Presidency of Rutherford B. Hayes*, 206–7.

45. Summers, *Party Games*, 17.

46. Rhodes, *History of the United States from the Compromise of 1850*, 8:134–36.

47. Platt, *The Autobiography of Thomas Platt*, 145–65.

48. C. Vann Woodward, *Origins of the New South, 1877–1913* (Baton Rouge, LA: Louisiana State University Press, 1951), 98–106.

49. Doenecke, *The Presidencies of James Garfield and Chester Arthur*, 115.

50. Hirshson, *Farewell to the Bloody Shirt*, 105–6.

51. House Select Committee, *Report of Covode Select Committee to Investigate Alleged Corruptions in Government*, 36th Cong., 1st Sess., H. Report 648 (June 16, 1860).

52. Blaine, *Twenty Years of Congress*, 2:650.

53. Hoogenboom, *Presidency of Rutherford B. Hayes*, 104–24.

54. Senate Select Committee, *Report of the Select Committee to Inquire into & Examine the Methods of Business and Work in the Executive Departments of the Government*, 50th Cong., 1st Sess., S. Rep. 507 (March 3, 1888), 2–3.

55. Senate Select Committee, *"Supplement to Report of the Select Committee on Methods of Business and Work in the Executive Departments of the Government,"* 51st Cong., Special Session, S. Rep. 3 (March 28, 1889), 4.

56. Senate Select Committee, *"Report of the Select Committee on Methods of Business and Work in the Executive Departments of the Government,"* 50th Cong., 1st Sess., S. Rep. 507 (March 3, 1888), 8.

57. Senate Committee on Investigation & Retrenchment, *New York Customhouse Investigation*, 42nd Cong., 2nd Sess., S. Rep. 227, 4 vols. (June 4, 1872), 4:119–22.

58. *U.S. Statutes at Large* 12 (February 25, 1863): 665 (section 1).

59. Ibid., 16 (April 5, 1869): 5; Ibid., 24 (March 3, 1887): 500.

60. Hoar, *Autobiography of Seventy Years*, 1:248.

61. Quoted in Doenecke, *The Presidencies of James Garfield and Chester Arthur*, 12.

62. Dorothy Ganfield Fowler, *John Coit Spooner: Defender of Presidents* (New York: University Publishers, 1961), 125.

63. Ellis, *History of New York*, 364.

64. Quoted in Rhodes, *History of the United States from the Compromise of 1850*, 6:414.

65. Quoted in Mark Summers, *The Era of Good Stealings* (New York: Oxford University Press, 1993), 103.

66. *U.S. Statutes at Large 16* (March 3, 1871): 544–45.

67. White, *The Republicans*, 280–84.

68. An order applicable to the New York Customhouse was issued on May 26, 1877; its terms were made applicable to all executive departments on June 22, 1877. *Messages and Papers of the Presidents*, 9:4402–3.

69. "The President's Order," *Harper's Weekly*, July 21, 1877, 558.

70. Blaine, *Twenty Years of Congress*, 2:649–50.

71. Hoogenboom, *The Presidency of Rutherford B. Hayes*, 138–47.

72. Quoted in Ibid., 141.

73. *Messages and Papers of the Presidents* (December 6, 1880), 9:4555–57.

74. Hoogenboom, *The Presidency of Rutherford B. Hayes*, 139.

75. The Boss System and the Maine Election, *The Nation*, September 23, 1880, 214.

76. "The Danger of an Aristocracy of Officeholders," Ibid., December 9, 1880, 404.

77. "Government and his Employees," *New York Times*, December 27, 1880, 4.

78. Doenecke, *The Presidencies of James A. Garfield and Chester A. Arthur*, 40–41.

79. "Civil Service Reform Bills," *Springfield Daily Republican*, January 25, 1882, 4.

80. Summers, *Party Games*, 235.

81. Quoted in Rhodes, *History of the United States from the Compromise of 1850*, 8:163n1.

82. *U.S. Statutes at Large* 22 (1883): 403.

83. *Messages and Papers of the Presidents*, 9:4748–53.

84. Summers, *Party Games*, 235.

85. Ibid., 236.

86. *U.S. v. Perkins*, 116 U.S. 483 (1886), 485; *U.S. Statutes at Large* 22 (August 5, 1882): 284, 286.

87. *Myers v U.S.*, 272 U.S. 52, 117 (1926); *U.S. Statutes at Large* 19 (July 12, 1876): 80. The law divided postmasters into four classes; fourth class postmasters, those with the lowest pay, were the most numerous.

88. Vincent P. De Santis, "President Arthur and the Independent Movements in the South," *Journal of Southern History* 19, no. 3 (August 1953): 354.

89. Doenecke, *The Presidencies of James Garfield and Chester Arthur*, 123.

90. Hoar, *Autobiography of Seventy Years*, 1:377.

91. "Southern Office Holders," *New York Times*, November 25, 1898, 4.

92. *Messages and Papers of the Presidents*, 11:5079–80.

93. Allan Nevins, *Grover Cleveland: A Study in Courage* (New York: Dodd, Meade, 1932), 371.

94. Shelby M. Cullom, *Fifty Years of Public Service* (Chicago: A.C. McClurg, 1911), 260–61.

95. "Civil Service Reform" (Remarks of George William Curtis to the National Civil Service Reform League), *Springfield Daily Republican*, August 4, 1887, 2–3.

96. C. Vann Woodward, *Tom Watson: Agrarian Rebel* (New York: Macmillan, 1938), 253.

97. Horace Samuel Merrill, *Bourbon Democracy of the Middle West, 1865–96* (Baton Rouge, LA: Louisiana State University Press, 1953), 243–44.

98. Nevins, *Grover Cleveland: A Study in Courage*, 251.

99. White, *Republicans*, 30–31.

100. Harold U. Faulkner, *Politics, Reform and Expansion, 1890–1900* (New York: Harper & Brothers, 1959), 96.

101. *Congressional Record*, 52nd Cong., 1st Sess. Vol. 23 Part 5 (May 28, 1892): H 4815.

102. Commager, Morison, *Growth of the American Republic*, 5th ed., 2:324.

103. Faulkner, Politics, *Reform and Expansion*, 264.

104. "The Civil Service Rules," *New York Times*, August 4, 1897, 1.

105. White, *The Republicans*, 338.

106. Yearley, *The Money Machines*, 265.

107. Culver H. Smith, *Press, Politics and Patronage: The American Government's Use of Newspapers, 1789–1875* (Athens, Georgia: University of Georgia Press, 1977), 233–35.

108. Paul Van Riper, *History of the United States Civil Service* (Evanston, IL: Row, Peterson, 1958), 48.

109. Smith, *Press, Politics and Patronage*, 234–35.

110. Foner, *Reconstruction*, 350.

111. Mark W. Summers, *The Press Gang: Newspapers and Politics, 1865–78* (Chapel Hill, NC: The University of North Carolina Press, 1994), 212.

112. Summers, *Party Games*, 88.

113. Summers, *The Press Gang*, 48, 35, 174.

114. *U.S. Statutes at Large* 17 (1872): 66. See also Smith, *Press, Politics and Patronage*, 237–43.

115. Diary of a President (April 11, 1880), 273; see also Hoogenboom, *Presidency of Rutherford B. Hayes*, 111.

116. *Springfield Daily Republican*, February 26, 1890, 4.

117. Taussig, *Tariff History of the United States*, 167.

118. Clemenceau, *American Reconstruction* (January 5, 1867), 76.

119. Quoted in *Springfield Daily Republican*, December 15, 1874, 4.

120. If the benefit of protection for the North—promoting industry—is weighed against the loss of income in the South and West, the result "would probably be slightly negative or, at best, nothing at all." Richard Franklin Bensel, *The Political Economy of American Industrialization, 1877–1900* (New York: Cambridge University Press 2000), 465.

121. *Congressional Globe*, 39th Cong., 2nd Sess. Vol. 37 Part 3 Appendix (February 27, 1867): H 129–31.

122. Beatty, *Age of Betrayal*, 200.

123. *U.S. Statutes at Large* 14 (1867): 559; Taussig, *Tariff History of the United States*, 198–205, 218.

124. *U.S. Statutes at Large*, 16 (1870): 256; Taussig, *Tariff History of the United States*, 179, 223, 226.

125. "New England Changing Front," *Springfield Daily Republican*, October 17, 1871, 4.

126. *U.S. Statutes at Large* 17 (June 6, 1872): 230; see also Foner, *Reconstruction*, 504.

127. *U.S. Statutes at Large* 18 (1875): 339; see also Taussig, *Tariff History of the United States*, 190.

128. "The Tariff Debate," *Springfield Daily Republican*, April 3, 1882, 4.

129. Rhodes, *History of the United States Since the Compromise of 1850*, 8:175–77.

130. *U.S. Statutes at Large* 22 (1883): 488; see also Doenecke, *The Presidencies of James Garfield and Chester Arthur*, 170.

131. *Congressional Record*, 47th Cong., 2nd Sess. Vol. 14 Part 3 (February 7, 1883): S 2187–89.

132. Bensel, *Yankee Leviathan*, 344.

133. *U.S. Statutes at Large* 16 (1870): 223.

134. John M. Barry *Rising Tide: The Great Mississippi Flood of 1927 and How It Changed America* (New York: Simon & Schuster, 1997), 40, 61, 67.

135. Arthur DeWitt Frank, *The Development of the Federal Program of Flood Control on the Mississippi River* (New York: Columbia University Press, 1930), 42.

136. *U.S. Statutes at Large* 21 (1879): 37.

137. "The Week," *The Nation*, April 27, 1882, 347–48.

138. Editorial, *New York Times*, April 22, 1882, 4.

139. *U.S. Statutes at Large* 22 (1882): 208.

140. Frank, *Development of the Federal Program of Flood Control on the Mississippi River*, 45–47, 140–43.

141. A law of March 1, 1917, appropriated $45 million for flood control along the Mississippi and Sacramento Rivers. *U.S. Statutes at Large* 39 (1917): 948.

142. Mark Twain, *Life on the Mississippi* (1883; repr., New York: Bantam Books, 1981), 137–38.

143. Barry, *Rising Tide*, 89.

144. "The River and Harbor Fraud," *New York Times*, August 5, 1879, 4.

145. "Miles Ross's Plunder," Ibid., July 31, 1882, 5.

146. Summers, *Party Games*, 156.

147. *Congressional Record*, 49th Cong., 2nd Sess. Vol. 18 Part 3 Appendix (January 15, 1887), 135.

148. James Bryce, *The American Commonwealth*, 2 vols. (New York: Macmillan, 1910), 1:179, 183.

149. *Messages and Papers of the Presidents*, 10:4707–9.

150. *U.S. Statutes at Large* 22 (August 2, 1882): 191.

151. "A Timely Veto," *New York Times*, August 2, 1882, 4.

152. *San Francisco Bulletin* quoted in *Springfield Daily Republican*, December 15, 1874, 4.

153. "The Week," *The Nation*, August 10, 1882, 101.

154. Nevins, *War for the Union*, 3:281.

155. Theda Skocpol, "America's First Social Security System: The Expansion of Benefits for Civil War Veterans," *Political Science Quarterly* 108, no. 1 (Spring 1993): 85–116 at 90.

156. *U.S. Statutes at Large* 12 (1862): 566.

157. Fourth annual message of Ulysses S. Grant, December 2, 1872, *Messages and Papers of the Presidents*, 10:4156.

158. Summers, *The Era of Good Stealings*, 105.

159. *Congressional Record*, 51st Cong., 1st Sess. Vol. 21 Part 8 (August 1, 1890): H 8037–42.

160. White, *The Republicans*, 213–17.

161. Nevins, *The Inner History of the Grant Administration*, 2:760–61.

162. *U.S. Statutes at Large* 17 (1873): 572.

163. Ibid., 20 (1879): 265.

164. Rhodes, *History of the United States from the Compromise of 1850*, 8:295.

165. *Congressional Record*, 45th Congress, 3rd Sess. Vol. 8 Part 1: S 390.

166. "The Week," *The Nation*, February 20, 1879, 127.

167. "Correspondence: The Arrears of Pensions Bill Again," Ibid., February 27, 1879, 148.

168. *U.S. Statutes at Large* 20 (March 3, 1879): 470.

169. *National Party Platforms*, 74.

170. Rhodes, *History of the United States from the Compromise of 1850*, 8:295–96.

171. Fish, *The Inner History of the Grant Administration*, 2:326–27.

172. Skocpol, "The Expansion of Benefits for Civil War Veterans," 109.

173. Nevins, *War for the Union*, 3:230–31.

174. Unger, *The Greenback Era*, 101, 120.

175. Rhodes, *History of the United States from the Compromise of 1850*, 6:223–25.

176. Castel, *The Presidency of Andrew Johnson*, 118–19; see also Unger, *The Greenback Era*, 79–85.

177. Rhodes, *History of the United States from the Compromise of 1850*, 6:160–61.

178. *U.S. Statutes at Large* 16 (March 18, 1869): 1.

179. Nevins, *The Inner History of the Grant Administration*, 2:696.

180. Unger, *The Greenback Era*, 224, 234–43. For the text of the veto, see *Messages and Papers of the Presidents*, 9:4222–25.

181. Unger, *The Greenback Era*, 252–63.

182. *U.S. Statutes at Large* 18 (1875): 296.

183. Unger, *The Greenback Era*, 401–6, 277–86.

184. *Republican Campaign Textbook of 1884* (New York: Republican National Committee, 1884), 127.

185. *U.S. Statutes at Large* 17 (February 12, 1873): 427.

186. Unger, *The Greenback Era*, 338, 345.

187. *U.S. Statutes at Large* 20 (February 28, 1878): 25.

188. Rhodes, *History of the United States from the Compromise of 1850*, 8:258.

189. Unger, *The Greenback Era*, 393–94.

190. *U.S. Statutes at Large* 12 (May 15, 1862): 387.

191. Ibid., 19 (March 3, 1877): 356.

192. A 1905 law gave the secretary of agriculture $190,000 "to meet the emergency caused by the ravages of the Mexican cotton boll-weevil." Ibid., 33 (March 3, 1905): 883.

193. Richard L. Watson, *The Development of National Power, The United States 1900–1919* (Boston: Houghton Mifflin 1976), 24.

194. White, *The Republicans*, 237–42.

195. *U.S. Statutes at Large* 23 (May 29, 1884): 31.

196. *U.S. Statutes at Large* 24 (March 3, 1887): 499.

197. *Congressional Record*, 49th Cong., 2nd Sess. Vol. 18 Part 2 (January 27, 1887): H 1107.

198. Ibid., 1108–9.

199. A. Hunter Dupree, *Science in the Federal Government: A History of Policies and Activities to 1940* (Cambridge, MA: The Belknap Press, 1957), 165.

200. *U.S. Statutes at Large* 12 (July 2, 1862): 503.

201. *U.S. Statutes at Large* 24 (March 2, 1887): 440.

202. Garraty, *The New Commonwealth*, 65.

203. *U.S. Statutes at Large* 28 (August 8, 1894): 271.

204. Ibid., 26 (August 30, 1890): 417.

205. Williams, *The Origins of Federal Support for Higher Education*, 155, 208, 214.

206. *U.S. Statutes at Large* 31 (May 17, 1900): 179.

207. *Congressional Globe*, 39th Cong., 2nd Sess. Vol. 37 Part 3 (February 26, 1867): H 1843.

208. *U.S. Statutes at Large* 14 (1867): 434.

209. Ibid., 15 (1868): 106. It was renamed the Bureau of Education in the early 1870s.

210. Hoar, *Autobiography of Seventy Years* I, 264.

211. Ibid., 265.

212. *U.S. Statutes at Large* 12 (July 1, 1862): 501; Howard R. Lamar, *The New Encyclopedia of the American West* (New Haven, CT: Yale University Press, 1998), "Edmunds Act," 331.

213. *U.S. Statutes at Large* 22 (March 22, 1882): 30; Ibid., 24 (March 3, 1887): 635; see also Lamar, *The New Encyclopedia of the American West*, "Edmunds Act," 331.

214. *U.S. Statutes at Large* 12 (1862): 489.

215. Ibid., 13 (July 2, 1864): 356; Richardson, *Greatest Nation on Earth*, 188, 202–6.

216. Carter Goodrich, *Government Promotion of Canals and Railroads 1800–1890* (New York: Columbia University Press, 1960), 192.

217. Johnson, *History of the American People*, 534.

218. Bensel, *The Political Economy of American Industrialization*, 293.

219. *U.S. Statutes at Large* 19 (1877): 377.

220. *Concise Dictionary of American History*, 494.

221. *U.S. Statutes at Large* 28 (August 18, 1894): 422.

222. Faulkner, *Politics, Reform and Expansion*, 66–67.

223. *Congressional Record*, 51st Cong., 1st Sess. Vol. 21 Part 11 Appendix (April 2, 1890): H 73.

224. *U.S. Statutes at Large* 32 Stat (June 17, 1902): 388.

225. "The President and Irrigation," *New York Times*, September 5, 1906, 8.

226. "Irrigation," *Wall Street Journal*, May 28, 1904, 2.

227. Donald J. Pisani, "Federal Reclamation and the American West in the Twentieth Century," *Agricultural History* 77, no. 3 (Summer 2003): 396–99.

228. Richard J. Orsi, *Sunset Limited: The Southern Pacific Railroad and the Development of the American West, 1950–1930* (Berkeley: University of California, 2005), 238–41, 266–67.

229. *U.S. Statutes at Large* 20 (March 3, 1879): 379.

230. Henry Steele Commager, William E. Leuchtenberg, Samuel Eliot Morison, *The Growth of the American Republic*, 7th ed., 2 vols. (New York: Oxford University Press, 1980), 2:19, 20, 28, 29.

231. Cummings, MacFarland, *Federal Justice*, 250–52, 270.

232. Henry Steele Commager, Leuchtenberg, Morison, *Growth of the American Republic*, 7th ed., 2:6.

233. Heather Cox Richardson, *West from Appomattox: The Reconstruction of America after the Civil War* (New Haven: Yale University Press, 2007), 76–77.

234. *Concise Dictionary of American History*, 60.

235. Wilcomb E. Washburn, *The Indian in America* (New York: Harper & Row, 1975), 205.

236. Andrew R. Graybill, *Policing the Great Plains: Rangers, Mounties and the North American Frontier, 1875–1910* (Omaha, NE: University of Nebraska Press, 2007), 37–49.

237. *U.S. Statutes at Large* 16 (March 3, 1871): 566.

238. See *Johnson v. McIntosh*, 21 U.S. 543 (1823) and *Cherokee Nation v. Georgia*, 30 U.S. 1 (1831).

239. 112 U.S. 94; *U.S. Statutes at Large* 43 (June 2, 1924): 253.

240. *U.S. Statutes at Large* 23 (March 3, 1885): 385; *U.S. v. Kagama*, 118 U.S. 375, 379 (1886).

241. *U.S. Statutes at Large* 24 (February 8, 1887): 388.

242. Commager, Leuchtenberg, Morison, *Growth of the American Republic*, 7th ed., 2:9.

243. Washburn, *The Indian in America*, 231, 247.

244. *U.S. Statutes at Large* 12 (July 27, 1861) 328; Ibid., 15 (March 12, 1867): 19.

245. *Congressional Record*, 44th Cong., 1st Sess. Vol. 4, Part 6 Appendix (January 20, 1876): H 3.

246. Ibid. (January 25, 1876): H 5–6.

247. Ibid. (January 20, 1876): H 12.

248. Ibid., 44th Cong., 1st Sess. Vol. 4 Part 1 (January 25, 1876): H 629–30. In 1836, Congress funded an expedition led by Charles Wilkes that explored the seas adjacent to Antarctica (1838–42). *U.S. Statutes at Large* 5 (May 14, 1836): 36. In 1870, Congress provided funds for the Polaris expedition to the North Pole. Ibid., 16 (July 12, 1870): 251.

249. *U.S. Statutes at Large* 19 (1876): 3.

250. In his 1833 work, *Commentaries on the Constitution of the United States*, U.S. Supreme Court Justice Joseph Story offered what was probably the most-cited argument in favor of a broad spending power via the general welfare clause to be issued during the nineteenth century. Story asserted that the Articles of Confederation government exercised broad powers under the wording of a similar clause; he also cited several comments made in the state ratifying conventions in support of a broad spending power. The Confederation did not act under the view that it possessed a broad spending power, and an examination of the speeches cited by Story reveals they do not support his claim. In addition, as Story himself

acknowledged, by a margin of 10 states to one, the Constitutional Convention voted down a clause that would have explicitly authorized Congress to collect taxes for the payment of debts incurred by the Articles of Confederation "and for the defraying of expences that shall be incurred for the common defence and general welfare." See Joseph Story, *Commentaries on the Constitution*, 3 vols. (Boston: Hilliard Gray, 1833) 3:366–99 (sections 902–28); Max Farrand, ed., *The Records of the Federal Convention of 1787* (New Haven, CT: Yale University Press, 1937) (August 25, 1787), 2: 414.

251. In a speech of January 1824, Henry Clay dismissed the president's claim that general welfare clause bestowed a broad spending power. "There is no specific grant in the Constitution of a power of appropriation." *Annals of Congress*, 18th Cong., 1st Sess. Vol. 41: S 1027. In a speech in the Senate of June 19, 1854, William Seward dismissed President Pierce's claim that Republicans saw the general welfare clause as bestowing a broad power of appropriation. "No member of Congress had advocated that principle since this bill was inaugurated, half a dozen years ago. The principle is obsolete, if it ever had advocates. No statesmen has advocated it, in or out of Congress, for a period of forty years." *Congressional Globe*, 33rd Cong., 1st Sess. Vol. 23 Appendix: S 959–60.

252. Currie, "The Civil War Congress," 1153. See also Peter Zavodnyik, *The Age of Strict Construction* (Washington, DC: The Catholic University of America Press), 128–44, 176–77, 205–10, 299–311.

253. *Concise Dictionary of American History*, 754.

254. Thomas J. Schlereth, *Victorian America: Transformations in Everyday Life, 1876–1915* (New York: HarperCollins, 1991), 179.

255. *Congressional Record*, 52nd Cong., 1st Sess. Vol. 23 Part 5 (May 28, 1892): H 4803.

256. Ibid., 4815.

257. Egbert T. Bush, "A Rural View of Free Delivery," *North American Review*, March 1906, 381–90.

258. *Congressional Globe*, 41st Cong., 2nd Sess. Vol. 42 Part 7 Appendix (December 22, 1869): H 1–6.

259. An act of 1843 appropriated $30,000 for the construction of a telegraph line. *U.S. Statutes at Large* 5 (March 3, 1843): 643.

260. *U.S. Statutes at Large* 12 (June 16, 1860): 41.

261. Harry James Brown and Frederick D. Williams, eds., *The Diary of James Garfield* 4 vols. (East Lansing, MI: Michigan State University Press, 1967) (December 23, 1872) 2: 128.

262. Ibid. (May 27, 1874), 327.

263. *Springfield Daily Republican*, December 2, 1887, 5.

264. "In Favor of a Postal Telegraph," Ibid., March 19, 1890, 5.

265. *Messages and Papers of the Presidents* (annual message of December 1, 1873) 9:4204.

266. Gordon, *An Empire of Wealth*, 223.

267. "Postal Savings Banks," *Harper's Weekly*, April 10, 1886, 227.

268. *Springfield Daily Republican*, January 10, 1882, "Something Better Than Postal Savings Banks," 4.

269. *National Party Platforms*, 144–49, 159.

270. *U.S. Statutes at Large* 36 (June 25, 1910): 814.

271. Ibid., 5 (August 30, 1842): 566–67.

272. Ibid., 13 (March 3, 1865): 507.

273. Ibid., 17 (June 8, 1872): 302.

274. Ibid., 17 (March 3, 1873): 598.

275. Burrows, Wallace, *Gotham*, 1013–16.

276. Hoogenboom, *The Presidency of Rutherford B. Hayes*, 125.

277. Burrows, Wallace, *Gotham*, 1063.

278. *U.S. Statutes at Large* 29 (February 8, 1897): 512.

279. *Messages and Papers of the Presidents*, 12:5515–16.

280. *U.S. Statutes at Large* 26 (1890): 465.

281. *In re Rapier*, 143 U.S. 110, 134 (1892).

282. *U.S. Statutes at Large* 20 (1878): 37.

283. Senate Committee on Epidemics, *Preventing the Introduction of Contagious Diseases into the United States*, 45th Cong., 3rd Sess., S. Rep. 734 (February 7, 1879), 3. See also Edwin Maxey, "Federal Quarantine Laws," *Political Science Quarterly* 23, no. 4 (December 1908): 628–29.

284. *Messages and Papers of the Presidents* (December 2, 1878), 9:4444–45.

285. *Congressional Record*, 45th Cong., 3rd Sess. Vol. 8, Part 3 Appendix (March 1, 1879): 232.

286. "Inviting the Pestilence," *New York Times*, March 3, 1879, 4.

287. *U.S. Statutes at Large* 20 (1879): 484.

288. "A State's Rights Distinction," *Chicago Daily Tribune*, April 14, 1879, 4.

289. *U.S. Statutes at Large* 21 (1879): 5–6.

290. Senate Committee on Epidemic Diseases, *Report on Amending an act entitled to prevent the introduction of contagious diseases into the U.S.*, 47th Cong., 1st Sess., S. Rep. 415 (April 18, 1882), 2–6.

291. W. G. Smillie, "The National Board of Health, 1879–1883," *American Journal of Public Health and the Nation's Health* 33, no. 8 (August 1943): 925–30.

292. *U.S. Statutes at Large* 25 (Joint Resolution 48, October 12, 1888): 631.

293. Ibid., 26 (March 27, 1890): 31.

294. Dupree, *Science in the Federal Government*, 264–66; *U.S. Statutes at Large* 26 (March 3, 1891): 1085. During the Civil War, Congress established the U.S. Emigrant Office in New York City for the purpose of protecting the newly arrived from fraud. *U.S. Statutes at Large* 13 (July 4, 1864): 385–86.

295. *U.S. Statutes at Large*, 27 (February 15, 1893): 449.

296. Walter Wymann, "The Present Organization and Work for the Protection of Public Health in the United States," *Public Health Reports* 25, no. 38 (September 23, 1910): 1303–13.

297. *U.S. Statutes at Large* 37 (August 14, 1912): 309.

298. Johnson, *Governing the American State*, 89.

299. *Congressional Record*, 49th Cong., 1st Sess. Vol. 17 Part 7 (July 20, 1886): S 7186–88.

300. Ibid., Vol. 17 Part 8 Appendix (May 26, 1886): H 147.

301. "The Oleomargarine Bill," *Chicago Daily Tribune*, July 21, 1886, 4.

302. *U.S. Statutes at Large* 24 (August 2, 1886): 209.

303. The text of the bill can be found at *Congressional Record*, 51st Cong., 1st Sess. Vol. 21, Part 3 (March 21, 1890): S 2462.

304. Ibid., 52nd Cong., 1st Sess. Vol. 23 Part 6 Appendix (June 6, 1892): H 442–43.

305. Ibid., 51st Cong., 1st Sess. Vol. 21 Part 11 Appendix (August 21, 1890): H 589–90.

306. *McCray v. U.S.*, 195 U.S. 27 (1904).

307. Ibid. at 55–58.

308. Ibid. at 62–63.

309. "Politicians and State Rights," *The Nation*, June 26, 1879, 430–31.

310. "The Strong Government Idea," *Atlantic Monthly*, February 1880, 273–77 at 273–74.

311. Ibid., 274.

312. Ibid., 275.

313. Ibid., 276–77.

314. Ibid., 277.

315. David Dudley Field, "Centralization in the Federal Government," *North American Review*, May 1881, 409–13. On July 24, 1866, Congress enacted a law authorizing telegraph companies to extend lines along postal routes, military roads, through federal lands, and across the navigable waters of the United States. The law also authorized the United States to purchase said lines after five years had elapsed following the law's enactment. 14 Stat 221. In 1878 the Supreme Court invalidated a Florida law granting a monopoly on telegraphic communication within the state as conflicting with the above-mentioned federal law. *Pensacola Tel. Co. v. Western Union Telegraph Co.*, 96 U.S. 1 (1878).

316. Field, *Centralization in the Federal Government*, 414.

317. Ibid., 418.

318. "State Rights Under the New Order," *Springfield Daily Republican*, July 21, 1887, 4.

319. Ibid.

320. Cox, *Three Decades of Federal Legislation*, 680.

321. *National Party Platforms*, 77.

322. Hoar, *Autobiography of Seventy Years*, 2:175.

323. Cooley's treatise on the limits of state authority grew thicker with age as it catalogued more cases limiting the police power of the states; published in 1868, 15 years later it was already in its fifth edition. Thomas M. Cooley, *A Treatise on the Constitutional Limitations Which Rest Upon the Legislative Powers of the States* (Boston: Little, Brown, 1868). For a southern point-of-view of the federal system during the Gilded Age, see John Randolph Tucker, *The Constitution of the United States: A Critical Discussion of its Genesis, Development and*

Interpretation (Chicago: Callaghan, 1899). For a survey of constitutional law treatises of the postwar period and their treatment of federalism, see Charles E. Larsen, "Nationalism and State's Rights in Commentaries on the Constitution after the Civil War," *The American Journal of Legal History* 3, no. 4 (October 1959): 360–69.

324. Bryce, *The American Commonwealth*, 2: 903.

325. Ibid., 904; Ibid., 1:405.

326. Ibid., 2:905–6.

327. Ibid. 1:387.

328. Ibid., 391.

329. Ibid., 403–5.

330. Commager, Morison, *Growth of the American Republic*, 5th ed., 2:194–95.

331. Schlereth, *Victorian America*, 29.

332. Burrows, Wallace, *Gotham*, 1062.

333. Beatty, *Age of Betrayal*, 347.

334. Foner, *Reconstruction*, 481.

335. Burrows, Wallace, *Gotham*, 1110.

336. Summers, *Party Games*, 189.

337. *U.S. Statutes at Large* 15 (June 25, 1868): 77.

338. Ibid., 25 Stat (May 24, 1888): 157.

339. Ibid., 27 (August 1, 1892): 340.

340. *Congressional Globe*, 42nd Cong., 2nd Sess. Vol. 45 Part 1 (December 13, 1871): H 102.

341. *U.S. Statutes at Large* 23 (June 27, 1884): 60.

342. Garraty, *The New Commonwealth*, 135.

343. Richardson, *The Greatest Nation on Earth*, 150.

344. Alyn Brodsky, *Grover Cleveland: A Study in Character* (New York: Truman Talley Books/St. Martin's Press, 2000), 167.

345. *U.S. Statutes at Large* 25 (October 1, 1888): 500.

346. *Congressional Record*, 49th Cong., 1st Sess. Vol. 17 Part 8 Appendix: H 39–40.

347. Foner, *Reconstruction*, 469–70.

348. Commager, Morison, *Growth of the American Republic*, 5th ed., 2:114.

349. Yearley, *The Money Machines*, 150.

350. Foner, *Reconstruction*, 486.

351. Commager, Leuchtenberg, Morison, *Growth of the American Republic*, 7th ed., 2:29.

352. Summers, *Party Games*, 167.

353. William Allen White, *The Autobiography of William Allen White* (New York: Macmillan, 1946), 350–51.

354. Ibid., 150.

355. Quoted in White, *The Republicans*, 383.

356. Summers, *The Era of Good Stealings*, 4.

357. Burrows, Wallace, *Gotham*, 1109.

358. "Tammany Hall and the People of New York," *Harper's Weekly*, October 24, 1891, 814.

359. Yearley, *The Money Machines* 148, 5–6, 18–29, 145.

360. Albert L. Sturm, "The Development of American State Constitutions," *Publius* 12, no. 1 (Winter 1982): 67.

361. Beatty, *The Age of Betrayal*, 215.

362. Summers, *Party Games*, 98–102.

363. Burrows, Wallace, *Gotham*, 1033.

364. "Notes and Comment," *Springfield Daily Republican*, November 5, 1890, 4.

365. Hoar, *Autobiography of Seventy Years*, 1:305.

366. "Magnificent Mistakes," *Harper's Weekly*, December 12, 1874, 1014.

367. Woodward, *Origins of the New South*, 177, 107.

368. Ibid., 30–31, 39–43.

369. Ibid., 35–47.

370. Commager, Leuchtenberg, Morison, *Growth of the American Republic*, 7th ed., 2:132.

371. Foner, *Reconstruction*, 134, 173–74.

372. Woodward, *Origins of the New South*, 125, 132.

373. Richard M. Abrams, *Conservatism in a Progressive Era: Massachusetts Politics, 1900–1912* (Cambridge, MA: Harvard University Press, 1964), 74.

374. Woodward, *Origins of the New South*, 307.

375. Hirshson, *Farewell to the Bloody Shirt*, 63–71.

376. Foner, *Reconstruction*, 590.

377. *Congressional Record*, 51st Cong., 2nd Sess. Vol. 22 Part 1 (December 20, 1890): S 713–28.

378. *Williams v. Mississippi*, 170 U.S. 213 (1898).

379. Ibid. at 222–25.

380. Woodward, *Origins of the New South*, 321–23.

381. Loren P. Beth, *The Development of the American Constitution, 1877–1917* (New York: Harper & Row, 1971), 114–15.

382. Alexander Keyssar, *The Right to Vote: The Contested History of Democracy in the United States* (New York: Basic Books, 2000), 112.

383. *Guinn v. U.S.*, 238 U.S. 347 (1915).

384. Charles A. Lofgren, *The Plessy Case: A Legal-Historical Interpretation* (New York: Oxford University Press, 1987), 20–22.

385. Woodward, *Origins of the New South*, 351–55.

386. Susan B. Carter, ed., *Historical Statistics of the United States: Earliest Times to the Present Millennial*, 5 vols. (New York: Cambridge University Press, 2006) 3:209.

387. Commager, Leuchtenberg, Morison, *Growth of the American Republic*, 7th ed., 2:140.

388. Richardson, *West from Appomattox*, 158.

389. John D. Hicks, *The Populist Revolt: A History of the Farmers' Alliance and the People's Party* (University of Minnesota Press, 1931, repr., Omaha, NE: University of Nebraska Press, 1961), 10–32, 84, 210.

390. Ibid., 104–10.

391. Faulkner, *Politics, Reform and Expansion*, 113–14.

392. Woodward, *Origins of the New South*, 277.

393. Martis, *Historical Atlas of Political Parties in the United States Congress*, 149.

394. *Congressional Record*, 52nd Cong., 1st Sess. Vol. 23 Part 8 Appendix (August 5, 1892): H 610–11.

395. Ibid., 611–12.

396. "State Help and Self Help," *Springfield Daily Republican*, May 30, 1890, 4.

397. *Congressional Record*, 52nd Cong., 1st Sess. Vol. 23 Part 5 (May 28, 1892): H 4812–13.

398. Ibid., 4813–14.

399. Ibid., 4815.

400. House Committee on Ways and Means, *System of Subtreasuries*, 52nd Cong., 1st Sess., H. Rep. 2143 (August 5, 1892), 1–7.

401. *Concise Dictionary of American History*, 410.

402. *Cooley v. Board of Wardens*, 53 U.S. 299 (1851).

403. *Steamship Co. v. Portwardens*, 73 U.S. 31 (1867).

404. Ibid. at 34.

405. Currie, *Constitution in the Supreme Court*, 1:333–34.

406. *The Daniel Ball*, 77 U.S. 557 (1871).

407. Ibid. at 558–60.

408. *Cooley*, 77 U.S. at 563–66.

409. *Munn v. Illinois*, 94 U.S. 113 (1877).

410. Companion cases include *Chicago, Burlington & Quincy R.R. v. Iowa*, 94 U.S. 155 (1877) and *Peik v. Chicago & Northwestern R.R.*, 94 U.S. 164 (1877).

411. *Munn*, 94 U.S. at 135.

412. Ibid. at 125.

413. Ibid. at 125–34.

414. Ibid. at 152–53. In 1870 Congress enacted a law establishing a maximum interest rate of 10 percent in Washington, DC. *U.S. Statutes at Large* 16 (April 22, 1870): 91.

415. *Peik v. Chicago & Northwestern RR.*, 94 U.S. 164.

416. Ibid. at 177.

417. "The Granger Decision," *Springfield Daily Republican*, March 13, 1877, 4. See *Dartmouth College v. Woodward*, 17 U.S. 518 (1819).

418. Currie, *The Constitution in the Supreme Court*, 1:373.

419. "Parliament exercised power over trade and commerce in statutes prohibiting forestalling, regrating and engrossing . . . as well as acts . . . fixing the prices of every conceivable article of commerce. At the time of the American Revolution, at least eight of thirteen colonies passed price fixing statutes equally extensive in scope." Breck P. McAllister, "Lord Hale and Business Affected with a Public Interest," *Harvard Law Review* 41, no. 5 (March 1930): 766–67.

420. *Wabash, St. Louis and Pacific Railway Company v. Illinois*, 118 U.S. 557, 572.

421. Warren, *The Supreme Court in United States History*, 2:634.
422. *Hall v. DeCuir*, 95 U.S. 485 (1878).
423. Ibid. at 489–90.
424. Rhodes *History of the United States from the Compromise of 1850*, 8:162–66.
425. James B. Murphy, *L.Q.C. Lamar: Pragmatic Patriot* (Baton Rouge, LA: Louisiana State University Press, 1973), 192–96, 262.
426. Willie D. Halsell, "The Appointment of L.Q.C. Lamar to the Supreme Court," *Mississippi Valley Historical Review* 28, no. 3 (December 1941): 399–403.
427. "Considering Lamar," *The Atlanta Constitution*, January 11, 1888, 1.
428. Halsell, "The Appointment of L.Q.C. Lamar to the Supreme Court," 405–12.
429. *Bowman v. Chicago & Northwestern R.R.*, 125 U.S. 465 (1888).
430. *Leisy v. Hardin*, 135 U.S. 100 (1890).
431. Ibid. at 109–10.
432. Ibid. at 119.
433. Ibid. at 125.
434. Ibid. at 128–29.
435. Ibid. at 148.
436. Ibid. at 157–58.
437. *Springfield Daily Republican*, July 7, 1890, 4.
438. Edward Stanwood, "Fretting about the Constitution," *North American Review*, July 1890, 122–24.
439. *U.S. Statutes at Large* 26 (1890) 313.
440. Ibid., 37 (1913) 699.
441. See, for example, the July 1, 1870, statute authorizing the building of a bridge across the Arkansas River at Little Rock, Arkansas. *U.S. Statutes at Large* 16 (1870): 185.
442. Ibid., 16 (February 28, 1871): 440.
443. The relevant provisions of the charter of the Camden & Amboy are quoted in the *Congressional Globe*, 39th Cong., 1st Sess. Vol. 36 Part 1 (January 15, 1866): S 227.
444. For an account of the dispute see Charles Merriam Knapp, *New Jersey Politics during the Period of the Civil War and Reconstruction* (W.F. Humphrey: Geneva, New York, 1924), 109–15.
445. Hermon King Murphey, "The Northern Railroads and the Civil War," *Mississippi Valley Historical Review* 5, vol. 3 (December 1918): 326–27.
446. *Congressional Globe*, 38th Cong., 2nd Sess. Vol. 35 Part 2 Appendix (February 22 & 23, 1865): S 84.
447. *Congressional Globe*, 39th Cong., 1st Sess. Vol. 36 Part 1 (January 15, 1866): S 227–28.
448. *Diary of James Garfield*, 1:48.
449. Ibid., 1:51–60.
450. Charles Fairman, "Mr. Justice Bradley's Appointment to the Supreme Court and the Legal Tender Cases," *Harvard Law Review* 54, no. 6 (April 1941): 984–85.
451. *U.S. Statutes at Large* 14 (1866): 66.

452. *Opinions of the Attorneys General*, 12:337–47. An act of July 1, 1864, authorizing the construction of a telegraph line from the west coast through Canada to Russia (it was not built) provided that rates charged on said line would not exceed "the average usual rates in Europe and America for the same service." *U.S. Statutes at Large* 13 (1864): 340–41.

453. House Committee on Roads and Canals, *Regulation and Control of Railroads*, 40th Cong., 2nd sess., H. Rep. 57 (June 9, 1868), 1–5.

454. Ibid., 6.

455. Ibid., 7.

456. Ibid., 8–16.

457. "Congress and the Railroads," *New York Times*, June 20, 1868, 4.

458. *Congressional Record*, 43rd Cong., 1st Sess. Vol. 2 Part 6 Appendix (March 3 & 4, 1874): H 75–83.

459. In January 1788, Madison wrote that a "very material object of this power was the relief of the States which import and export through other States, from the improper contributions levied on them by the latter" (*The Federalist* # 42).

460. See Randy Barnett, "The Original Meaning of the Commerce Clause," *University of Chicago Law Review* 68, no. 1 (Winter 2001): 116–25; and Calvin H. Johnson, "The Panda's Thumb: The Modest and Mercantilist Meaning of the Commerce Clause," *William & Mary Bill of Rights Journal* 13, no. 1 (October 2004): 1–59.

461. Procter, *The Life of John H. Reagan*, 210–12.

462. *Congressional Record*, 45th Cong., 2nd Sess. Vol. 7 Part 4 (May 2, 1878): H 3097.

463. Ibid. (May 11, 1878): H 3393–94. See *The Federalist*, #22, #42.

464. Ibid., 3396.

465. "Congress and Interstate Commerce," *The Nation*, January 30, 1879, 79.

466. Procter, *The Life of John H. Reagan*, 224–34.

467. Ibid., 253–56.

468. Gabriel Kolko, *Railroads and Regulation, 1877–1916* (Princeton, NJ: Princeton University Press, 1965), 30, 35–41.

469. James W. Ely, *Railroads and American Law* (Lawrence, KS: University Press of Kansas, 2001), 90.

470. *U.S. Statutes at Large* 24 (1887): 379.

471. Ibid.

472. *Councill v. Western & Atlantic R.R.*, 1 I.C.C. 339, 346–47 (1887). The Commission ordered the Western & Atlantic to improve its "colored" cars so that they were equal in quality to those afforded whites.

473. Ely, *Railroads and American Law*, 139.

474. Kolko, *Railroads and Regulation*, 55.

475. *I.C.C. v. Cincinnati, New Orleans and Texas Pacific Railway*, 167 U.S. 479 (1897).

476. Ibid. at 505–6.

477. Ibid. at 509–10.

478. Cullom, *Fifty Years of Public Service*, 327–28. For rulings limiting the authority of the I.C.C., see Ely, *Railroads and American Law*, 93–96.

479. *Congressional Record*, 49th Cong., 1st Sess. Vol. 17 Part 8 Appendix (March 31, 1886): S 60–61.

480. *U.S. Statutes at Large* 25 (1888): 501.

481. Hoar, *Autobiography of Seventy Years*, 2:363.

482. Johnson, *History of the American People*, 601.

483. *Springfield Daily Republican*, January 17, 1888, 4.

484. *Congressional Record*, 51st Cong., 1st Sess. Vol. 21 Part 3 (March 25, 1890): S 2604; Vol. 21 Part 7 (June 30, 1890): S 6737.

485. Ibid. Vol. 21 Part 3 (March 21, 1890): S 2461–62.

486. Ibid. (March 24, 1890): S 2569.

487. Ibid. (March 25, 1890): S 2609.

488. Ibid.: S 2614.

489. Ibid. Vol. 21 Part 2 (February 27, 1890): S 1768–70, quoting Veazie v. Moor, 55 U.S. 568, 575 (1853).

490. Ibid. Vol. 21 Part 3 (April 2, 1890): S 2901.

491. *U.S. Statutes at Large* 26 (July 2, 1890): 209.

492. Hoar, *Autobiography of Seventy Years*, 2:364.

493. William Letwin, "The First Decade of the Sherman Act: Early Administration," *Yale Law Journal* 68, no. 3 (January 1959): 466–81.

494. *U.S. v. E. C. Knight*, 156 U.S. 1 (1895).

495. Ibid. at 12–13.

496. Ibid. at 17.

497. Ibid. at 33–36.

498. Ibid. at 37–38.

499. *Addyston Pipe & Steel Company v. U.S.*, 175 U.S. 211, 234–35 (1899).

500. *Swift & Co. v U.S.*, 196 U.S. 375, 398–99 (1905). See also David Gordon, "Swift & Co. v. United States: The Beef Trust and the Stream of Commerce Doctrine," *The American Journal of Legal History* 28, no. 3 (July 1984): 244–79.

501. Edmund Morris, *Theodore Rex* (New York: Modern Library, 2001), 28.

502. *U.S. v. Trans-Missouri Freight Association*, 166 U.S. 290, 327–28, 340–41 (1897).

503. Ibid. at 343.

504. *Standard Oil Co. v. New Jersey*, 221 U.S. 1, 60 (1911).

505. Hoar, *Autobiography of Seventy Years*, 1:407.

506. Ibid., 408.

507. Rhodes, *History of the United States from the Compromise of the 1850*, 8:208.

508. Beatty, *Age of Betrayal*, 99.

509. *National Party Platforms*, 65–68.

510. Nevins, *Grover Cleveland: A Study in Courage*, 173.

511. Nevins, *Grover Cleveland: A Study in Courage*, 157.

512. "Carl Schurz's Speeches," *Boston Globe*, October 23, 1884, 1.

513. Mark W. Summers, *Rum, Romanism and Rebellion: The Making of the President 1884* (Chapel Hill, NC: University of North Carolina Press, 2000), 169.

514. Nevins, *Grover Cleveland: A Study in Courage*, 326–27.

515. Skocpol, "The Expansion of Benefits for Civil War Veterans," 109–10.
516. Brodsky, Grover Cleveland, 85–86.
517. "Politicians in the Pension Bureau," *The Nation*, February 26, 1885, 172–73.
518. John William Oliver, *History of the Civil War Military Pensions* (Madison, WI: University of Wisconsin, 1917), 111.
519. "Dudley," *Atlanta Constitution*, October 23, 1884, 4.
520. Summers, *The Making of the President* 1884, 299.
521. Martis, *Historical Atlas of Political Parties*, 139.
522. Cox, *Three Decades of Federal Legislation*, 680.
523. *Messages and Papers of the Presidents*, 11:5001.
524. Nevins, *Grover Cleveland: A Study in Courage*, 22–29.
525. Ibid., 330.
526. *Congressional Record*, 49th Cong., 2nd Sess. Vol. 18 Part 3 Appendix (March 2, 1887): H 132.
527. *Messages and Papers of the Presidents*, 11:5134–42.
528. "The Soldier Vote," *The Nation*, February 24, 1887, 159–60.
529. "Pensions," *Harper's Weekly*, December 24, 1887, 934–35.
530. *U.S. Statutes at Large* 15 (March 30, 1867): 28; Ibid., 18 (January 25, 1875): 303; Ibid., 18 (February 10, 1875): 314.
531. "At Washington," *Springfield Daily Republican*, February 3, 1887, 4; *Congressional Record*, 49th Cong., 2nd Sess. Vol. 18 Part 2 49:2 (February 2, 1887): S 267–68.
532. *Messages and Papers of the Presidents*, 11:5142–43.
533. "Dawes and Hoar," *Springfield Daily Republican*, February 18, 1887, 4.
534. "The Week," *The Nation*, February 24, 1887, 153.
535. Nevins, *Grover Cleveland: A Study in Courage*, 368, 378.
536. Joanne Reitano, *The Tariff Question in the Gilded Age: The Great Debate of 1888* (University Park, PA: The Pennsylvania State University Press, 1994), 4–6.
537. Nevins, *Grover Cleveland: A Study in Courage*, 368–78.
538. *Messages and Papers of the Presidents*, 11:5165–75.
539. Reitano, *The Tariff Question*, 8–9.
540. "The Week," *The Nation*, December 8, 1887, 447.
541. Taussig, *The Tariff History of the United States*, 253.
542. "The Week," *The Nation*, December 15, 1887, 467.
543. Reitano, *The Tariff Question*, 20–21.
544. Rhodes, *History of the United States from the Compromise of 1850*, 8:307.
545. Nevins, *Grover Cleveland: A Study in Courage*, 389.
546. *Congressional Record*, 50th Cong., 1st Sess. 50:1, Vol. 19, Part 4: H 3057–63. For the comments of Representative Justin Morrill cited by Mills, see *Congressional Globe*, 38th Cong., 1st Sess. Vol. 34 Part 3 (June 2, 1864): H 2674–75.
547. *Congressional Record*, 50th Cong., 1st Sess. 50:1, Vol. 19, Part 4: H 3302–3.
548. Ibid., 3307–13.
549. Ibid., 3350–53.
550. Ibid., 3357–62.

551. "The Tariff Farce at Washington," *Springfield Daily Republican*, April 30, 1888, 4.

552. *Congressional Record*, 50th Cong., 1st Sess. Vol. 19 Part 4: H 3692–97.

553. Ibid., 62–64.

554. Ibid. Vol. 19 Part 10 Appendix, 181–84.

555. Ibid., 50th Cong., 1st Sess. Vol. 19 Part 5: H 4334–35.

556. Ibid., 4443–51.

557. Nevins, *Cleveland: A Study in Courage*, 393.

558. Skocpol, *The Expansion of Benefits for Civil War Veterans*, 112.

559. Rhodes, *History of the United States from the Compromise of 1850*, 8:297.

560. Commager, Morison, *Growth of the American Republic*, 5th ed., 2:324.

561. *National Party Platforms*, 80–81.

562. Quoted in Garraty, *The New Commonwealth*, 298.

563. Rhodes, *History of the United States from the Compromise of 1850*, 8:320–21.

564. Quoted in Richard Jensen, *The Winning of the Midwest: Social and Political Conflict, 1888–96* (Chicago: University of Chicago Press, 1971), 13–14.

565. Ibid.

566. Nevins, *Grover Cleveland: A Study in Courage*, 418–19, 432–33.

567. Quoted in James A. Kehl, *Boss Rule in the Gilded Age: Matt Quay of Pennsylvania* (Pittsburgh, PA: University of Pittsburg Press, 1981), 105.

568. Summers, *Party Games*, 10.

569. Rhodes, *History of the United States from the Compromise of 1850*, 8:324.

570. Commager, Leuchtenberg, Morison, *Growth of the American Republic*, 7th ed., 2:164.

571. Kehl, *Matt Quay of Pennsylvania*, 110.

572. Quoted in Beatty, *The Age of Betrayal*, 218.

573. Nevins, *Grover Cleveland: A Study in Courage*, 438–39.

574. "Dudley and the Administration," *Springfield Daily Republican*, January 10, 1890, 4.

575. "How Dudley Triumphed," Ibid., January 11, 1890, 4.

576. Commager, Morison, *Growth of the American Republic*, 5th ed., 2:330.

577. *Congressional Record*, 51st Cong., 1st Sess. Vol. 21 Part 11 Appendix (May 9, 1890): H 131–35.

578. Ibid., Part 8 (July 30, 1890): S 7885.

579. Ibid., Vol. 21 Part 9 (August 14, 1890): S 8541–43.

580. *U.S. Statutes at Large* 26 (1890): 567; Taussig, *Tariff History of the United States*, 274–75.

581. Ibid., 583 (Schedule E, Section 231).

582. *Congressional Record*, 51st Cong., 1st Sess. Vol. 21 Part 11 Appendix (September 27, 1890): H 748.

583. "The Socialistic Sugar Bounty," *Harper's Weekly*, April 25, 1896, 410–11.

584. *U.S. v. Realty*, 163 U.S. 427, 438–40 (1896).

585. Quoted in Rhodes, *History of the United States from the Compromise of 1850*, 8:348.

586. Ibid., 109.

587. *Congressional Globe*, 41st Cong., 2nd Sess. Vol. 42 Part 7 Appendix (June 6, 1870): H 478–85.

588. Ibid., 42nd Cong., 2nd Sess. Vol. 45 Part 1 (February 6, 1782): H 850–64. See, for example, the March 1, 1817, act applicable to Mississippi and the March 3, 1845, statute applicable to Florida. *U.S. Statutes at Large* 3 (1817): 348, Ibid., 5 (1845): 788.

589. *Messages and Papers of the Presidents*, 9:4288.

590. Ibid., 4431.

591. *National Party Platforms*, 61.

592. Quoted in Hoogenboom, *The Presidency of Rutherford B. Hayes*, 204–5.

593. "The Week," *The Nation*, September 9, 1880, 179.

594. Allen J. Going, "The South and the Blair Education Bill," *Mississippi Valley Historical Review* 44, no. 2 (September 1957): 269–70.

595. Ibid., 268.

596. *Congressional Record*, 46th Cong., 3rd Sess. Vol. 11 Part 1 (December 17, 1880): S 229.

597. Ibid. (December 16, 1880): S 179.

598. Ibid., 184.

599. Albion Tourgee, "Aaron's Rod in Politics," *North American Review*, February 1881, 139–63. Tourgee would later serve as counsel for Homer Plessy in *Plessy v. Ferguson*, 163 U.S. 537 (1896).

600. The text of the bill may be found at *Congressional Record*, 47th Cong, 1st Sess. Vol. 13 Part 1 (December 20, 1881): S 227.

601. "Government Aid to Schools," *Springfield Daily Republican*, April 1, 1882, 4.

602. The text of the bill may be found *at Congressional Record*, 48th Cong., 1st Sess. Vol. 15 Part 3 (March 28, 1884): S 1999.

603. Republican National Committee, *Republican Campaign Textbook of 1884* (Chapter Eight), 70–84.

604. Going, "The South and the Blair Education Bill," 280.

605. Woodward, *Origins of the New South*, 63–64.

606. Going, "The South and the Blair Education Bill," 282–87.

607. *Congressional Record*, 49th Cong., 1st Sess. Vol. 15 Part 3 (March 28, 1884): S 2368–70.

608. Ibid., 2371.

609. Ibid., 2373.

610. Ibid., Volume 15 Part 6 Appendix (February 14, 1888), 3–4.

611. *Messages and Papers of the Presidents* (December 3, 1889), 12:5489–90.

612. "Public Schools at the South," *Springfield Daily Republican*, January 11, 1888, 2.

613. Quoted in Hirshson, *Farewell to the Bloody Shirt*, 195–96.

614. Ibid.

615. *Congressional Record*, 51st Cong., 1st Sess. Vol. 21 Part 2 (March 3, 1890): S 1865–76.

616. Mark Elliott, *Color-blind Justice: Albion Tourgee and the Quest for Racial Equality from the Civil War to Plessy v. Ferguson* (New York: Oxford University Press, 2006), 244.

617. *Congressional Record*, 51st Cong., 1st Sess. Vol. 21 Part 2 (February 25, 1890): S 1677–88.

618. Ibid., Vol. 21 Part 3 (March 17, 1890): S 2292–97. The cited laws did not provide direct aid: the laws of February 19, 1803, and March 19, 1804, merely allowed importers in Portsmouth, New Hampshire, and Norfolk, Virginia, to provide new bonds after those cities suffered fires. *U.S. Statutes at Large* 2 (1803): 201; Ibid., 2 (1804): 272. An April 5, 1872, act repealed duties on items sent for the relief of Chicago residents following the fire of October 1871. Ibid., 17 (1871): 51. An act of Sept 26, 1888, provided money for the eradication of yellow fever. Ibid., 25 (1888): 630.

619. *Congressional Record*, Vol. 21 Part 3 (March 17, 1890): S 2301–2.

620. Quoted in Going, "The South and the Blair Education Bill," 283.

621. "Defeat of the Blair Bill," *Springfield Daily Republican*, March 21, 1890, 4.

622. "Politics and the Blair Bill," *Id.*, March 22, 1890, 4.

623. Woodward, *Origins of the New South*, 405–6.

624. Rhodes, *History of the United States from the Compromise of 1850*, 8:359.

625. "How the Democrats Steal Votes," *Chicago Daily Tribune*, August 7, 1890, 4.

626. *Messages and Papers of the Presidents*, 12:5491–92.

627. *U.S. Statutes at Large* 5 (June 25, 1842): 491.

628. Ibid., 12 (July 14, 1862): 572.

629. E. Irving Smith, "The Legal Aspects of the Southern Question," *Harvard Law Review* 2, no. 8 (March 15, 1889): 358–76.

630. *Congressional Record*, 51st Cong., 1st Sess. Vol. 21 Part 7: H 6538–50.

631. Hirshson, *Farwell to the Bloody Shirt*, 203.

632. Josephus Daniels, *Tar Heel Editor* (Chapel Hill, NC: The University of North Carolina Press, 1939), 486–87.

633. *Congressional Record*, 51st Cong., 1st Sess. Vol. 21, Part 11 Appendix (June 28, 1890), 563–67.

634. Ibid., Vol. 21 Part 7 (June 26, 1890): H 6548–54.

635. Ibid., 6940–41.

636. "The Lodge Bill and Republican Representatives from the South," *The Springfield Daily Republican*, July 2, 1890, 4.

637. Hirshson, *Farewell to the Bloody Shirt*, 218–22.

638. "The Boycott in Politics," *Harper's Weekly*, August 9, 1890, 614.

639. "Does the Cure Hit the Case?", *Springfield Daily Republican*, June 2, 1890, 4.

640. "To Meet the Force Bill," *Atlanta Constitution*, July 20, 1890, 14.

641. *Congressional Record*, 51st Cong., 2nd Sess. Vol. 22 Part 4 Appendix (December 19, 1890): S 11–14.

642. Between 1877 and 1893, over half of federal appropriations for electoral supervision were spent in New York City. Keyssar, *The Right to Vote*, 166.

643. *Congressional Record*, 51st Cong., 2nd Sess. Vol. 22 Part 1 (December 20, 1890): S 713–28.

644. Hirshson, *Farewell to the Bloody Shirt*, 226–33.

645. *U.S. Statutes at Large* 28 (February 8, 1894): 36.

646. White, *The Republicans*, 76.

647. Donald L. McMurry, "The Bureau of Pensions during the Administration of President Harrison," *Mississippi Valley Historical Review* 13, no. 3 (December 1926): 347–52.

648. *Messages and Papers of the Presidents* (December 3, 1889), 12:5485.

649. Quoted in William Henry Glasson, *History of Military Pension Legislation in the United States* (New York: Columbia University Press 1900), 112–14.

650. *Springfield Daily Republican*, April 1, 1890, 4.

651. *Congressional Record*, 51st Cong., 1st Sess. Vol. 21, Part 11 Appendix (April 7, 1888): H 88.

652. Ibid. (April 30, 1890), 107. Federal spending grew from 3.3 percent to 6.42 percent of the gross national product between 1860 and 1900. *Historical Statistics of the United States*, 5:11.

653. *U.S. Statutes at Large* 26 (1890): 182.

654. Quoted in Commager, Leuchtenberg, Morison, *Growth of the American Republic*, 7th ed., 2:330.

655. Rhodes, *History of the United States from the Compromise of 1850* VIII, 345–46.

656. Beatty, *Age of Betrayal*, 59.

657. "Warning from the Tribune," *New York Tribune* quoted in *Springfield Daily Republican*, July 8, 1890, 4.

658. Rhodes, *History of the American People from the Compromise of 1850*, 8:346.

659. Jensen, *The Winning of the Midwest*, 164.

660. Glasson, *History of Military Pension Legislation*, 117.

661. *Congressional Record*, 53rd Cong., 3rd Sess. Vol. 27 Part 4 Appendix (December 14, 1894): H 236.

662. *Springfield Daily Republican*, July 16, 1890, 4.

663. Rhodes, *History of the United States from the Compromise of 1850*, 8:365–66.

664. *Springfield Daily Republican*, November 11, 1890, 4.

665. Hicks, *The Populist Revolt*, 181.

666. "The Congressional Revolution," *Springfield Daily Republican*, November 6, 1890, 4.

667. Faulkner, *Politics, Reform and Expansion*, 129.

668. "The Re-nomination of the President," *Harper's Weekly*, June 18, 1892, 578.

669. "He Believes the South Was Wrong," *Chicago Daily Tribune*, June 13, 1892, 2.

670. *National Party Platforms*, 93.

671. Faulkner, *Politics, Reform and Expansion*, 122–23.

672. *National Party Platforms*, 87–89.

673. Rhodes, *History of the United States from the Compromise of 1850*, 8:388.

674. Jensen, *The Winning of the Midwest*, 163.

675. John Sherman, *Recollection of Forty Years in the House, Senate and Cabinet*, 2 vols. (Chicago: Werner, 1895), 2: 1188.

676. *U.S. Statutes at Large* 26 (July 14, 1890): 289.

677. The "monetization of silver in fact stimulated the outflow of gold." Richard H. Timberlake Jr., *The Origins of Central Banking in the United States* (Cambridge, MA: Harvard University Press, 1978), 157.

678. John B. Andrews, Elizabeth Brandeis, John R. Commons, H. E. Hoagland, Don D. Lescohier, E. B. Mittleman, Scott Perlman, David J. Saposs, Helen L. Sumner, Phillip Taft, Helen L. Sumner, *History of Labor in the United States*, 4 vols. (New York: MacMillan, 1926–35), 3:219, 170.

679. Faulkner, *Politics, Reform and Expansion*, 164.

680. White, *The Republicans*, 4–5.

681. *Messages and Papers of the Presidents*, 12:5822.

682. "State Rights and State Duties," *Harper's Weekly*, July 21, 1894, 674–75.

683. Eggert, *Railroad Labor Disputes*, 81–90, 125–28.

684. *Springfield Daily Republican*, August 25, 1890, 4.

685. *U.S. v. Workingmen's Amalgamated Council*, 54 Fed. 994, 996 (E.D. La. 1893); Carl Brent Swisher, *American Constitutional Development* (Boston: Houghton Mifflin, 1943), 433–34.

686. "Turned Down," *Los Angeles Times*, May 5, 1894, 1. In the *Federalist* #81, Alexander Hamilton suggested that impeachment would be an appropriate remedy for judicial "encroachments" on the powers of Congress.

687. "Judge Jenkins," *Los Angeles Times*, May 23, 1894, 1.

688. Faulkner, *Politics, Reform and Expansion*, 169–72.

689. Brodsky, *Grover Cleveland*, 335–39.

690. Eggert, *Railroad Labor Disputes*, 160.

691. Letwin, "The First Decade of the Sherman Act," 484–85. An opinion of the attorney general issued in April 1894 claimed that "knowingly and willfully" obstructing passage of trains carrying the mails violated section 5440 of the Revised Statutes—a provision establishing criminal penalties for those who conspired to defraud the United States. It said nothing regarding the Sherman Antitrust Act. *Opinions of the Attorneys General*, 21:9.

692. U.S. Attorney General, *Appendix to the Annual Report of the Attorney General for 1896 Containing the Correspondence Relating to the Action of the Government with Reference to the Interruption by Force of Interstate Commerce, the Carriage of the Mails, etc., in the Year 1894*, 54th Cong., 2nd Sess., H Doc. 9 (November 30, 1896), 62, 66, 71, 73–74.

693. Faulkner, *Politics, Reform and Expansion*, 180–81.

694. Quoted in Nevins, *Grover Cleveland: A Study in Courage*, 626.

695. Both letters were reprinted in "To Hold the Force," *Chicago Daily Tribune*, July 6, 1894," 2.

696. "Breaks Loose Again," Ibid., July 7, 1894, 9.

697. Brodsky, *Grover Cleveland*, 344.

698. *Messages and Papers of the Presidents*, 13:5931–32.

699. David Gray Adler, "The Steel Seizure Case and Inherent Presidential Authority," *Constitutional Commentary* 19 (Spring 2002): 184–85.

700. Brodsky, *Grover Cleveland*, 345.

701. "State Rights and State Duties," *Harper's Weekly*, July 21, 1894, 674–75.

702. U.S. Strike Commission, *Report of the U.S. Strike Commission* 2 vols., 53rd Cong., 3rd Sess., Senate Ex. Doc. 7 (December 10, 1894) 2: 52.

703. Ibid., 52–54.

704. *In Re Debs*, 158 U.S. 564 (1895).

705. Ibid. at 564–70.

706. Ibid. at 580–93.

707. Ibid. at 600.

708. Commager, Morison, *Growth of the American Republic*, 5th ed., 2:244.

709. Henry J. Fletcher, "A National Department of Transportation," *Atlantic Monthly*, July 1895, 119–25.

710. Josephus Daniels, *Editor in Politics* (Chapel Hill, NC: The University of North Carolina Press, 1941), 71.

711. *U.S. Statutes at Large* 28 Stat (August 27, 1894): 508.

712. *Pollock v. Farmers' Loan & Trust Co.*, 158 U.S. 601 (1895). The Supreme Court upheld the Civil War income tax (it was not apportioned among the states) as a valid excise tax in *Springer v. U.S.*, 102 U.S. 586 (1881).

713. 158 U.S. 601 at 637.

714. Milton Friedman and Anna Jacobson Schwartz, *A Monetary History of the United States, 1867–1960* (Princeton, NJ: Princeton University Press, 1963), 91.

715. An 1873 law authorizing the issuing of coins omitted silver coins for use in the domestic trade. *U.S. Statutes at Large* 17 (February 12, 1873): 427.

716. *Congressional Record*, 51st Cong., 1st Sess. Vol. 21 Part 11 Appendix (June 6, 1890): H 342–43. The stock of money grew an average of 6 percent a year from 1879 to 1897 and 7.5 percent a year between 1897 and 1914. Friedman, Schwartz, *Monetary History of the United States*, 91.

717. *Congressional Record*, 51st Cong., 1st Sess. Vol. 21, Part 11 Appendix (June 6, 1890): H 342.

718. Milton Friedman, Schwartz, *A Monetary History of the United States*, 91.

719. Nevins, *Grover Cleveland: A Study in Courage*, 682–84.

720. Festus P. Summers, ed., *The Cabinet Diary of William L. Wilson, 1896–97* (Chapel Hill, NC: University of North Carolina Press, 1957) (May 27, 1896), 91.

721. Paolo E. Coletta, *William Jennings Bryan*, 3 vols. (Lincoln, NE: University of Nebraska Press, 1964), Vol. 1: *Political Evangelist, 1860–1908*, 116–18.

722. Ibid., 51–57, 85, 205–6.

723. "It Looks Like Bland," *Springfield Daily Republican*, July 6, 1896, 6.

724. "Gold Men Thrown Out," *Ibid.*, July 9, 1896, 7.

725. "A Day of Delirium," *Ibid.*, July 10, 1896, 7, 10.

726. Ibid., 10.

727. Daniels, *Editor in Politics*, 164.

728. Ibid.

729. Ibid., 164–66.

730. Coletta, *William Jennings Bryan*, 145.

731. *National Party Platforms*, 98.

732. Ibid., 101.

733. "They Will Accept McKinley," *Springfield Daily Republican*, May 3, 1896, 16.

734. George E. Mowry, *The Era of Theodore Roosevelt and the Birth of Modern America, 1900–1912* (New York: Harper & Row, 1958), 166.

735. Kehl, *Matt Quay of Pennsylvania*, 199.

736. *National Party Platforms*, 108.

737. "McKinley and Business Prosperity," *Springfield Daily Republican*, May 12, 1896, 6.

738. Margaret Leech, *In the Days of McKinley* (New York: Harper & Bros., 1959), 6–16, 36, 48–54.

739. Quoted in Coletta, *William Jennings Bryan*, 194–95.

740. "The Political Horizon II: The Coming Campaign," *Atlantic Monthly*, April 1900, 560–61.

741. Daniels, *Editor in Politics*, 197–98.

742. Brodsky, *Grover Cleveland*, 389.

743. Kenneth Whyte, *The Uncrowned King: The Sensational Rise of William Randolph Hearst* (Berkeley, CA: Counterpoint, 2009), 137, 168, 177.

744. "Mr. Bryan's Stump Tour," *Springfield Daily Republican*, August 31, 1896, 4.

745. Coletta, *William Jennings Bryan*, 1:168–76.

746. H. W. Brands, *The Reckless Decade: America in the 1890's* (New York: St. Martin's Press, 1995), 281.

747. Faulkner, *Politics, Reform and Expansion*, 206.

748. Coletta, *William Jennings Bryan*, 1:182, 169–70.

749. William Jennings Bryan, *The First Battle: A Story of the Campaign of 1896* (Chicago: W.B. Conkey & Sons, 1896), 324–25, 545.

750. "At Faulkner's Home," *Boston Globe*, October 1, 1894, 4; "John Brown's Old Home," Ibid., 4.

751. "An English Financial Expert," *Atlanta Constitution*, September 4, 1896, 4.

752. Leech, *In the Days of McKinley*, 61–62, 81, 83.

753. Jensen, *The Winning of the Midwest*, 288–89.

754. Faulkner, *Politics, Reform and Expansion*, 205.

755. Cullom, *Fifty Years of Public Service*, 274.

756. Leech, *In the Days of McKinley*, 87.

757. "Honorable Thomas B. Reed," *Boston Globe*, October 8, 1896, 4.

758. "Moral Aspects of the Campaign," *Harper's Weekly*, September 12, 1896, 890.

759. White, *Autobiography of William Allen White*, 279–80.

760. Quoted in Ibid. (August 15, 1896, Emporia, Kansas, *Gazette*), 280–84.

761. Leech, *In the Days of McKinley*, 87.

762. Daniels, *Editor in Politics*, 196.
763. Jensen, *The Winning of the Midwest*, 55–56.
764. *The Cabinet Diary of William L. Wilson* (October 29, 1896), 158–59.
765. Burrows, Wallace, *Gotham*, 1205.
766. Coletta, *William Jennings Bryan*, 1:193, 203, 210.
767. Jensen, *The Winning of the Midwest*, 292–95.
768. "The Defeat of Socialism," *Harper's Weekly*, November 14, 1896, 1114–15.
769. "The Political Menace of the Discontented," *Atlantic Monthly*, October 1896, 447–51 at 451.
770. Ibid., 450.
771. *U.S. Statutes at Large* 30 (1897) 151.
772. Taussig, *The Tariff History of the United States*, 333.
773. "Sky-Scraping Tariff Taxes," *The Nation*, April 5, 1906, 275.
774. *U.S. Statutes at Large* 30 (June 1, 1898): 424.
775. *Adair v. U.S*, 108 U.S. 161, 178–79.
776. Ibid., 31 (1900) 45.
777. Coletta, *William Jennings Bryan*, 1:240, 264–65.
778. Ibid., 270.
779. Leech, *In the Days of McKinley*, 557–58, 599.

CHAPTER 4

1. *Munn v. Illinois*, 94 U.S. 113.
2. Edward S. Corwin, "The Doctrine of Due Process of Law before the Civil War," *Harvard Law Review* 24 no. 6 (April 1911): 366–85.
3. Chistopher Wolfe, "The Original Meaning of the Due Process Clause," in *The Bill of Rights: Original Meaning and Current Understanding*, ed. Eugene W. Hickok Jr. (Charlottesville: University of Virginia Press, 1991), 221–22.
4. *Murray v. The Hoboken Land and Improvement Co.*, 59 U.S. 272 (1856).
5. *Dred Scott v. Sandford*, 60 U.S. 393, 446–52.
6. *Munn v. Illinois*, 94 U.S. 113, 125–34.
7. Ibid. at 142.
8. *Davidson v. New Orleans*, 96 U.S. 97, 104 (1878).
9. *In re Jacobs*, 98 N.Y. 98 (1885).
10. *Ritchie v. The People*, 155 Il. 98 (1895).
11. Roscoe Pound, "Liberty of Contract," *Yale Law Journal*, 18, no.7 (May 1909): 472–73.
12. *Chicago, Milwaukee & St. Paul Ry. v. Minnesota*, 134 U.S. 418.
13. Ibid. at 418–41.
14. Ibid. at 457.
15. Ibid. at 458.
16. Ibid. at 459–66.
17. Richard C. Cortner, *The Iron Horse and the Constitution: The Railroads and the Transformation of the Fourteenth Amendment* (Westport, CT: Greenwood Press, 1993), 115–16.

18. *Smyth v. Ames*, 169 U.S. 466 (1898).

19. Ibid. at 526.

20. Ibid. at 546–47.

21. Ibid.

22. *Allgeyer v. Louisiana*, 165 U.S. 578 (1897).

23. Ibid. at 589.

24. *Lochner v. New York*, 198 U.S. 45.

25. Ibid. at 53.

26. Ibid. at 54–56. The Utah law was upheld in *Holden v. Hardy*, 169 U.S. 366 (1898). Justices Brewer and Peckham dissented.

27. *Lochner at* 57–59.

28. Ibid. at 65, 70.

29. Ibid. at 74–75.

30. Ibid. at 76.

31. "The Ten Hour Decision," *New York Times*, April 28, 1905, 8.

32. Rent seeking has been defined as "hiring the coercive power of the state by some private citizens to gain an advantage over others." Gifford, "Whiskey Margarine and Newspapers," *The Predatory Policies of Fiscal Discrimination*, 70.

33. David E. Bernstein, "*Lochner v. New York*: A Centennial Perspective," *Washington University Law Quarterly* 83, no. 5 (2005): 1476–83.

34. "The Police Power and the Ten Hour Bakery Law," *Yale Law Journal* 14, no. 8 (June 1905): 452–54.

35. *Muller v. Oregon*, 208 U.S. 412.

36. Ibid. at 420n1.

37. Ibid. at 422.

38. Charles Warren, "The Progressiveness of the United States Supreme Court," *Columbia Law Review* 13, no. 4 (1913): 309. *Connolly v. Union Sewer Pipe Co.* saw the high court hold void as a violation of the equal protection clause an 1893 Illinois law that exempted agricultural businesses from its provisions banning attempts to fix the price of commodities. 184 U.S. 540, 562–63 (1902).

39. George W. Alger, "The Courts and Legislative Freedom," *Atlantic Monthly*, March 1913, 351.

40. *Osborne v. Bank of the United States*, 22 U.S. 738 (1824).

41. *Hans v. Louisiana*, 134 U.S. 1 (1890).

42. Ibid. at 14–15.

43. *Perkins v. Northern Pacific*, 155 F. 445 (C.C.D. Minn. 1907).

44. *Ex parte Young*, 209 U.S. 123, 145 (1908). See also Cortner, *The Iron Horse and the Constitution*, 146–77.

45. Ibid. at 159–60.

46. Ibid. at 168, 174.

47. Ibid. at 176–78.

48. Ibid. at 182.

49. Ibid. at 203–4.

50. *Hunter v. Wood*, 209 U.S. 205 (1908).

51. *Yick Wo v. Hopkins*, 118 U.S. 356 (1882).

52. Ibid. at 374.
53. Ibid. at 366.
54. *Plessy v. Ferguson*, 163 U.S. 537 (1896).
55. For the briefs filed on behalf of Plessy, see Westlaw documents 1893 WL 10660 and 1896 WL 13990. http://www.westlaw.com/.
56. 1896 WL 13990, 13991. http://www.westlaw.com/.
57. *Plessy v. Ferguson*, 163 U.S. 537, 544.
58. Ibid. at 550–51.
59. Ibid. at 551.
60. Ibid. at 552.
61. Ibid. at 557.
62. Ibid. at 559.
63. "Heated Hot: Supreme Court Decision Is Denounced," *Boston Globe*, May 20, 1896, 6.
64. "No Objection Is Raised by the Negro," *Atlanta Constitution*, May 22, 1896, 4.
65. *Corfield v. Coryell*, 6 Fed. Cases 546 (C.C.E.D. Pa.) 1823.
66. *Crandall v. Nevada*, 73 U.S. 35, 44 (1868).
67. On December 5, 1865, Thaddeus Stevens proposed an amendment to the Constitution: "All national and state laws shall be equally applicable to every citizen, and no discrimination shall be made on account of race and color." *Congressional Globe*, 39th Cong., 1st Sess. Vol. 36 Part 1 (December 5, 1865): H 10.
68. Andrew C. McLaughlin, *A Constitutional History of the United States* (New York: D. Appleton-Century Co., 1935), 727.
69. Theodore Roosevelt spoke to this fear in an October 4, 1906, speech in Harrisburg, Pennsylvania. "Certain judicial decisions . . . have . . . left vacancies, left blanks between the limits of possible state jurisdiction and the limits of actual national jurisdiction over the control of the great business corporations." Theodore Roosevelt, *The Works of Theodore Roosevelt*, ed. Hermann Hagedorn, 20 vols. (New York: Charles Scribner's Sons, 1926–27) 18: 83–84.
70. *U.S. v. Knight*, 156 U.S. 1 (1895).
71. *Champion v. Ames*, 188 U.S. 321 (1903).
72. Ibid. at 344, 354.
73. Ibid. at 356–57.
74. Ibid. at 358–59. *U.S. Statutes at Large* 23 (1884): 31.
75. *Champion* at 359.
76. Ibid., 364–70. In *Paul v. Virginia*, the Supreme Court refused to hold void a statute of Virginia prohibiting insurance companies incorporated in other jurisdictions from doing business in the state unless they deposited bonds with the state worth at least $30,000. Justice Field turned aside the claim that the law constituted an impermissible regulation of interstate commerce; he explained that "issuing a policy of insurance is not an article of commerce." *Paul v. Virginia*, 75 U.S. 168, 183 (1869).
77. *Champion* at 371.

78. Ibid. at 374.

79. "The Lottery Case," *Harvard Law Review* 16, no. 7 (May 1903): 508–9.

80. See Barnett, "The Original Meaning of the Commerce Clause," 139–46.

81. *Adair v. U.S.*, 208 U.S. 161 (1908).

82. Ibid. at 179.

83. Ibid. at 188.

84. White, *Autobiography of William Allen White*, 297–98.

85. Morris, *Theodore Rex*, 133, 151, 159–60.

86. "The Commonwealth and the Coal Operators," *New York Times*, August 23, 1902, 8.

87. "Comment," *Harper's Weekly*, October 25, 1902, 1539–45.

88. "A Legal Solution to the Coal Strike," *New York Times*, October 12, 1902, 3.

89. Mowry, *The Era of Theodore Roosevelt*, 137.

90. Jonathan Grossman, "The Coal Strike of 1902—Turning Point in U.S. Policy," *Monthly Labor Review*, October 1975, 10.

91. "Price of Steam Higher," *New York Times*, October 2, 1902, 3.

92. H. W. Brands, *T.R.: The Last Romantic* (New York: Basic Books), 1997, 453.

93. "Coal Conference Proves a Failure," *New York Times*, October 4, 1902, 1; Morris, *Theodore Rex*, 159–60.

94. "All State Army Sent to Mines," *Chicago Daily Tribune*, October 7, 1902, 1.

95. "Mr. Olney's Views on the Political Situation," *Harper's Weekly*, October 25, 1902, 1546.

96. "Roosevelt Ends Seven Big Years," *Chicago Daily Tribune*, February 28, 1909, 1; Theodore Roosevelt, *The Rough Riders/An Autobiography*, ed. Louis Auchincloss (New York: Macmillan, 1913, repr., New York: Literary Classics of the United States, 2004) (*An Autobiography*), 730.

97. U.S. Anthracite Coal Strike Commission, *Report to the President on the Anthracite Coal Strike of May–October 1902* (Washington, DC: Government Printing Office, 1903).

98. Grossman, *The Coal Strike of 1902*, 10.

99. *The Cabinet Diary of William L. Wilson* (March 12, 1896), 44.

100. "Federal Printers Uneasy," *New York Times*, July 28, 1903, 2.

101. "Evade Open Shop Rule," Ibid., February 19, 1904, 3; Van Riper, *History of the United States Civil Service*, 188n51.

102. *Messages and Papers of the Presidents* (July 13, 1903), 14:6783.

103. Ibid., 6703.

104. Mowry, *The Era of Theodore Roosevelt*, 140.

105. Morris, *Theodore Rex*, 28.

106. *U.S. Statutes at Large* 32 (February 14, 1903): 825.

107. Cummings, Macfarland, *Federal Justice*, 333–35.

108. *U.S. v. Armour & Co.*, 142 F. 808 (N.D.Ill. 1906); "The Week," *The Nation*, March 29, 1906, 251. The 1903 act establishing the Department of Commerce and Labor provided immunity to persons who provided evidence in response to a subpoena issued by the Bureau of Corporations. The self-incrimination clause of the Fifth Amendment was viewed as requiring that

persons providing information to antitrust investigations by federal agencies be exempt from prosecutions relying on evidence contained in the information they provided. See Francis Walker, "The Beef Trust and the U.S. Government," *The Economic Journal*, 16 no. 4 (December 1906): 491–514.

109. *Messages and Papers of the Presidents* (December 3, 1901) 14:6647–49.

110. *Northern Securities Co. v. U.S.*, 193 U.S. 197 (1904).

111. Ibid., 364, 368.

112. Ibid., 400, 408.

113. Ibid., 410–11.

114. Lawrence E. Mitchell, *The Speculation Economy: How Finance Triumphed Over Industry* (San Francisco, CA: Berrett Koehler, 2007), 136.

115. The text of the amendment may be found at *Congressional Record*, 56th Cong., 1st Sess. Vol. 33 Part 7 (May 31, 1900): H 6304.

116. U.S. Industrial Commission, *U.S. Industrial Commission Final Report*, 57th Cong., 1st Sess., H. Doc. 380 (February 10, 1902), 650–62. A law of June 18, 1898, established the Industrial Commission and provided for it to investigate questions regarding labor, agriculture, manufacturing, and business and report to Congress regarding appropriate legislation in these areas. *U.S. Statutes at Large* 30 (1898): 476.

117. *Congressional Record*, 57th Cong., 2nd Sess., Vol. 36 Part 2 (February 7, 1903): H 1894–1909.

118. Ibid., Vol. 36 Part 3 (February 17, 1903): H 1914–15; see also Mitchell, *The Speculation Economy*, 139–57.

119. "Federal Franchises Is President's Plan," *New York Times*, December 22, 1904, 1.

120. "Attitude of Financial Interests," *Wall Street Journal*, December 28, 1904, 1.

121. "Federal License as Rein on Trusts," *Chicago Daily Tribune*, April 6, 1906, 1.

122. Henry Clews, *Fifty Years in Wall Street* (New York: Irving Publishing Company, 1908), 940.

123. Mowry, *The Era of Theodore Roosevelt*, 166, 172.

124. "The President and the Bosses," *The Nation*, January 18, 1906, 46–47.

125. Wayne MacVeagh, "A Great Victory for Honest Politics," *North American Review*, January 1906, 1–18, 8.

126. Morris, *Theodore Rex*, 327.

127. During Grover Cleveland's administration, the Pension Bureau issued an order setting age 75 as evidence of a disability; during the McKinley administration, it issued an order setting age 65 1/2 as evidence of a half disability. Rhodes, *History of the United States from the Compromise of 1850*, 9:297–98n1.

128. "The Pension Inequity," *The Nation*, March 24, 1904, 224.

129. Morris, *Theodore Rex*, 340–42.

130. "The Dissolvent Candidacy," *The Nation*, August 11, 1904, 110.

131. "The Week," Ibid., November 10, 1904, 365.

132. Daniels, *Editor in Politics*, 476.

133. "Standard Oil Gave $100,000," *New York Times*, September 9, 1907, 1.

134. *Messages and Papers of the Presidents*, 15:6975–7012.

135. "Congress and Roosevelt's Hands," *The Nation*, January 18, 1906, 46.

136. *U.S. Statutes at Large* 32 (March 2, 1903): 943; Ibid., 27 (March 2, 1893): 531.

137. Ibid., 32 (February 19, 1903): 847.

138. *Opinions of the Attorneys General*, 25:422–41.

139. *Congressional Record*, 59th Cong., 1st Sess. Vol. 40 Part 1 (December 11, 1905): S 276.

140. Ibid., 277.

141. Ibid., 278.

142. Ibid., Vol. 40 Part 6 (April 26, 1906): S 5887–99.

143. Ibid. (April 27, 1906): S 5946.

144. *U.S. Statutes at Large* 34 (1906): 584.

145. Ibid., 34 (1906): 594–95 (section 20).

146. *Atlantic Coast Line v. Riverside Mills*, 219 U.S. 186 (1911).

147. Ibid. at 203.

148. Kolko, *Railroads and Regulation*, 218.

149. Albro Martin, *Enterprise Declined: Origins of the Decline of American Railroads, 1897–1917* (New York: Columbia University Press, 1971), 32–34, 95, 116–17, 128–35, 263, 284–310.

150. *U.S. Statutes at Large* 34 (July 11, 1906): 232.

151. *The Employers' Liability Cases*, 207 U.S. 463.

152. Ibid. at 502.

153. Ibid. at 497–98.

154. *U.S. Statutes at Large* 35 (April 22, 1908): 65.

155. *The Second Employers' Liability Cases*, 223 U.S. 1 (1912).

156. Ibid. at 51.

157. *U.S. Statutes at Large* 34 (March 4, 1907): 1415.

158. *Baltimore & Ohio R.R. v. I.C.C.*, 221 U.S. 612, 619 (1911).

159. *U.S. Statutes at Large* 26 (March 3, 1891): 1089.

160. *Congressional Record*, 59th Cong., 1st Sess. Vol. 40 Part 10 Appendix (June 22, 1906): H 124–25.

161. Ibid., 128.

162. Ibid., 129.

163. Morris, *Theodore Rex*, 437–38.

164. *U.S. Statutes at Large* 34 (1906): 674.

165. Johnson, *Governing the American State*, 90–95.

166. Ilyse D. Barkan, "Industry Invites Regulation: The Passage of the Pure Food and Drug Act of 1906," *American Journal of Public Health*, 75, no. 1 (January 1985): 18–26.

167. *U.S. Statutes at Large* 34 (June 30, 1906): 768.

168. *Hipolite v. Egg*, 220 U.S. 45, 58.

169. *Chicago, Rock Island & Pacific v. Hardwick Farmers Elevator Co.*, 226 U.S. 426, 433–35 (1913).

170. Steven Gardbaum, "The Breadth v. The Depth of Congress's Commerce Power: The Curious History of Preemption during the *Lochner* Era," in *Federal*

Preemption: State Powers, National Interests, ed. Richard A. Epstein, Michael S. Greve (Washington, DC: The American Enterprise Institute, 2007), 62–64.

171. Ibid., 67–73.

172. Woodward, *Origins of the New South*, 416–19.

173. *Congressional Record*, 59th Cong., 2nd Sess. Vol. 41 Part 2 (January 23, 1907): S 1552–57.

174. Ibid. (January 28, 1907): S 1807–8.

175. Ibid., 1824.

176. Ibid. (January 29, 1907): S 1872.

177. Ibid., 1875.

178. Ibid.

179. Ibid., 1876.

180. Ibid., Vol. 41 Part 5 Appendix (March 2, 1907): H 46–47. See *Swift v. United States*, 196 U.S. 375, 399 (1905).

181. *Paul v. Virginia*, 75 U.S. 168 (1869).

182. James Beck, "The Federal Regulation of Life Insurance," *North American Review*, August 1905, 191–201.

183. *Messages and Papers of the Presidents* (December 3, 1906), 15:7048.

184. Wilbur Larremore, "American Divorce Law," *North American Review*, July 1906, 71, 75.

185. Ibid., 74–75.

186. P. Orman Ray, "The Unconscious Trend Towards Socialism," *The Sewanee Review*, October 1908, 472, 474.

187. Ibid., 474–77.

188. Ibid., 478–80. Congress spent $1.37 billion on the improvement and construction of inland waterways between 1890 and 1931. Paul F. Barrett, Mark H. Rose, Bruce E. Seely, *The Best Transportation System in the World* (Columbus, OH: The Ohio State University Press, 2006), 33.

189. Ray, "The Unconscious Trend Towards Socialism," *The Sewanee Review*, 480.

190. Elihu Root, *Addresses on Government and Citizenship* (Cambridge, MA: Harvard University Press, 1916), 367.

191. Ibid., 368.

192. Ibid.

193. Ibid., 369.

194. Ibid., 370.

195. "The Editor's Diary: Autocracy or Democracy," *North American Review*, December 1906, 1322–25. For an early critique of the notion that the Constitution has the capacity to evolve, see Arthur W. Machen Jr., "The Elasticity of the Constitution," *Harvard Law Review* 14, no. 3 (November 1900): 200–216.

196. *U.S. Statutes at Large* 22 (May 6, 1882): 58.

197. William L. Silber, *When Washington Shut Down Wall Street: The Great Financial Crisis of 1914 and the Origin's of America's Monetary Supremacy* (Princeton, NJ: Princeton University Press, 2007), 48–57.

198. Morris, *Theodore Rex*, 495–501.

199. Coletta, *William Jennings Bryan*, 1:377–78, 358.

200. *National Party Platforms*, 144–49. Between 1900 and 1910, the number of persons employed in the federal civil service increased from 230,755 to 388,708. *Historical Statistics of the United States* 5:127–28.

201. Mowry, *The Era of Theodore Roosevelt*, 227.

202. "Roosevelt Denies Patronage Abuses," *New York Times*, February 10, 1908, 1; "Taft and Postmasterships," Ibid., May 26, 1908, C4.

203. Paolo E. Coletta, *The Presidency of William Howard Taft* (Lawrence, KS: The University Press of Kansas, 1973), 15.

204. *National Party Platforms*, 159–60.

205. Mowry, *The Era of Theodore Roosevelt*, 229.

206. Coletta, *William Jennings Bryan*, 425.

207. Daniels, *Editor in Politics*, 548–50.

208. Coletta, *William Jennings Bryan*, 1:428, 440.

209. Quoted in Ibid., 1: 412, 417.

210. "Taft Replies to Labor Critics," *Chicago Daily Tribune*, October 3, 1908, 4.

211. Republican National Committee, *Republican Campaign Text-Book of 1908* (Philadelphia: Dunlap Printing Company, 1908), 307–17.

212. For Taft's September 28, 1908, speech in St. Paul, Minnesota, on the subject of postal bank deposits, see William Howard Taft, *The Collected Works of William Howard Taft*, ed. David H. Burton, 8 vols. (Athens, OH: Ohio University Press, 2001) Vol. 2: *Political Issues and Outlooks, Speeches Delivered between August 1908 and February 1909*, 107.

213. Ibid. ("A Pledge of Tariff Reform," September 24, 1908, speech in Milwaukee, Wisconsin), 2: 99–106.

214. Mowry, *The Era of Theodore Roosevelt*, 287.

215. "Taft Kansas Trip Biggest Boom Yet," *Chicago Daily Tribune*, October 11, 1908, 4.

216. "President Singed by Abbot's Irony," Ibid., October 7, 1908, 4.

217. Commager, Morison, *Growth of the American Republic*, 7th ed., 2:307.

218. The office of weights and measures was renamed the National Bureau of Standards pursuant to a law of March 3, 1901. *U.S. Statutes at Large* 31 (1901): 1449; Dupree, *Science in the Federal Government*, 271–75.

219. Quoted in Morris, *Theodore Rex*, 444.

220. Elting Morison, ed., *The Letters of Theodore Roosevelt*, 9 vols. (Cambridge, MA: Harvard University Press, 1954), vol. 6: *The Big Stick, 1907–09*, Appendix II, John Blume, "Theodore Roosevelt and The Hepburn Act: Toward an Ordered System of Control," 1558–71.

221. Morison, ed., *The Letters of Theodore Roosevelt, Volume 7: The Days of Armageddon, 1909–1914* (November 2, 1910, letter to Alfred Borden), 152–53.

222. Coletta, *Presidency of William Howard Taft*, 48, 60–70.

223. *U.S. Statutes at Large* 36 (1909): 11; Commager, Leuchtenberg, Morison, *Growth of the American Republic*, 7th ed., 2:323.

224. Taussig, *Tariff History of the United States*, 362–69, 393, 402.

225. Quoted in Coletta, *Presidency of William Howard Taft*, 73.

226. January 7, 1910, Message on Interstate Commerce Law, John T. Woolley and Gerhard Peters, *The American Presidency Project* [online]. Santa Barbara, CA. Available from http://www.presidency.ucsb.edu/ws/?pid=68486.

227. Robert LaFollette complained in 1913 that because of the Taft administration's acquiescence in certain purchases by the New Haven Railroad, one "cannot ship a pound of anything from Massachusetts except on the terms imposed by a single corporation." Robert M. LaFollette, *LaFollette's Autobiography: A Personal Narrative of Political Experience* (Madison, WI, 1913, repr., Madison, WI: University of Wisconsin Press, 1960), 180.

228. Coletta, *Presidency of William Howard Taft*, 154.

229. *U.S. Statutes at Large* 36 (June 18, 1910): 539.

230. Mowry, *The Era of Theodore Roosevelt*, 260.

231. Kolko, *Railroads and Regulation*, 194–200.

232. *U.S. Statutes at Large* 36 (1910) 814.

233. Mowry, *The Era of Theodore Roosevelt*, 262.

234. *U.S. Statutes at Large* 34 (January 26, 1907): 864.

235. Ibid., 36 (1910): 823.

236. Ibid., 37 (1911): 25.

237. *Newberry v. U.S.*, 256 U.S. 232 (1921).

238. Ibid. at 258.

239. Coletta, *Presidency of William Howard Taft*, 117.

240. Quoted in Arthur S. Link, *Woodrow Wilson and the Progressive Era, 1910–1917* (New York: Harper & Brothers, 1954), 17.

241. *Congressional Record*, 62nd Cong., 2nd Sess. Vol. 48 Part 1 (December 11, 1911): S 188.

242. Ibid., 703.

243. Ibid., 704.

244. Ibid., Vol. 48, Part 2: S 1250–54.

245. Ibid., Vol. 48 Part 12 Appendix (April 2, 1912): H 111–13.

246. *U.S. Statutes at Large* 37 (April 9, 1912): 79.

247. Johnson, *Governing the American State*, 139–40.

248. *U.S. Statutes at Large* 36 (1910): 825.

249. David J. Langum, *Crossing Over the Line: Legislating Morality and the Mann Act* (Chicago: University of Chicago, 1994), 4, 23, 38.

250. *U.S. Statutes at Large*, 18 (March 3, 1875): 477; Ibid., 12 (March 24, 1860): 3.

251. *Congressional Record*, 61st Cong., 2nd Sess. Vol. 45 Part 1 (January 11, 1910): H 521.

252. Langum, *Crossing Over the Line*, 43.

253. Hoke v. U.S., 227 U.S. 308 (1913).

254. Ibid. at 321–23.

255. Langum, *Crossing Over the Line*, 4, 11, 68–75, 77–96, 152.

256. Rhodri Jeffreys-Jones, *The F.B.I.: A History* (New Haven, CT: Yale University Press, 2007), 57–65.

257. Langum, *Crossing Over the Line*, 49–58.

258. *U.S. Statutes at Large* 37 (July 31, 1912): 240. See also Dan Streible, “A History of the Boxing Film, 1894–1915: Social Control and Social Reform in the Progressive Era,” *Film History* 3, no. 3 (1989): 235–57.

259. Mark Sullivan, *Our Times*, 6 vols. (New York: Scribner's, 1935), 6: 219–20.

260. *U.S. Statutes at Large* 36 (1910): 370.

261. Ibid., 37 (April 9, 1912): 81.

262. Ibid., 37 (March 4, 1913): 736.

263. Ibid., 34 (February 6, 1907): 879.

264. Skocpol, *The Expansion of Benefits for Civil War Veterans*, 114.

265. *Congressional Record*, 62nd Cong., 2nd Sess. Vol. 45 Part 9 Appendix (December 8, 1911): H 6.

266. Ibid., December 12, 1911: H 13.

267. *U.S. Statutes at Large* 37 (May 11, 1912): 112.

268. “In civil life, persons are employed and paid to perform services, and are not retained or placed upon a retired list or allowed a pension when they are no longer, for any cause, able to perform the services for which they are to be paid. The same rule should be enforced in the departments.” Senate Select Committee, *“Supplement to Report of the Select Committee on Methods of Business and Work in the Executive Departments of the Government,”* 51st Cong., Special Session, S. Rep. 3 (March 28, 1889), 45.

269. *Congressional Record*, 63rd Cong., 1st Sess. Vol. 50 Part 7 Appendix (May 8, 1913): H 125.

270. *U.S. Statutes at Large* 41 (May 22, 1920): 614.

271. Ibid., 37 (1912): 555.

272. Sterling D. Spero, “Collective Bargaining in the Public Service,” *Annals of the American Academy of Political and Social Science* 248 (November 1946): 146–53.

273. Coletta, *Presidency of William Howard Taft*, 33.

274. Commager, Morison, *Growth of the American Republic*, 5th ed., 2:252.

275. “Making Steel and Killing Men,” *Everybody's Magazine*, November 1907. In Arthur Weinberg, Lila Weinberg, eds., *The Muckrakers: The Era in Journalism that Moved America to Reform—The Most Significant Articles of 1902–1912* (New York: Simon & Schuster, 1961), 342–58, 343.

276. Mowry, *The Era of Theodore Roosevelt*, 83–84.

277. Burrows, Wallace, *Gotham*, 1229.

278. Abrams, *Conservatism in a Progressive Era*, 11–18.

279. Mowry, *The Era of Theodore Roosevelt*, 72–78, 81.

280. Ralph A. Rossum, *Federalism, The Supreme Court and the Seventeenth Amendment: The Irony of Constitutional Democracy* (Lanham, MD: Lexington Books, 2001), 183–94.

281. Ibid., 219.

282. Johnson, *History of the American People*, 624.

283. Herbert Croly, *The Promise of American Life* (New York: Macmillan, 1909, repr., Boston: Northeastern University, 1989), 11.

284. Ibid., 172.

285. Ibid., 190.

286. Ibid., 274–75.

287. Ibid., 351.

288. Ibid., 360–61.

289. Ibid., 352–55.

290. Ibid., 70, 377–87.

291. *Works of Theodore Roosevelt*, 19:16–26.

292. Theodore Roosevelt, *The New Nationalism* (New York: The Outlook Company, 1911) (speech of September 17, 1910), 232–34.

293. *Works of Theodore Roosevelt*, 19: 205–6.

294. "Roosevelt Hits Taft Again," *New York Times*, March 21, 1912, 1.

295. *Works of Theodore Roosevelt*, 19:106–8.

296. Paoletta, *Presidency of William Howard Taft*, 234–35.

297. Morison, *Letters of Theodore Roosevelt* (March 16, 1912, letter of Roosevelt to Kohlsaat), 7:526–29n2.

298. "265 Taft Delegates to Roosevelt's 27," *New York Times*, March 31, 1912, 4.

299. "Taft Answers Roosevelt in Boston Speech," *Boston Globe*, April 26, 1912, 8.

300. Link, *Woodrow Wilson and the Progressive Era*, 14–15.

301. James Chace, *1912: Wilson, Roosevelt, Taft & Debs—The Election That Changed the Country* (New York: Simon & Schuster, 2004), 116, 122.

302. LaFollette, *LaFollette's Autobiography*, 282.

303. Quoted in Claude G. Bowers, *Beveridge and the Progressive Era* (Boston: Houghton Mifflin, 1932), 427–29.

304. *National Party Platforms*, 175–82.

305. Ibid., 175–82.

306. Ibid., 189–91.

307. Quoted in Woodward, *Origins of the New South*, 470.

308. Woodrow Wilson, "Constitutional Government in the United States," in *The Papers of Woodrow Wilson*, ed. Arthur Link, 69 vols. (Princeton, NJ: Princeton University Press, 1966–94), 18: 186–87.

309. Ibid., 191–99.

310. Woodward, *Origins of the New South*, 470–72.

311. Chace, *1912*, 143.

312. Link, *Woodrow Wilson and the Progressive Era*, 11.

313. Champ Clark, *My Quarter Century in American Politics*, 2 vols. (New York: Harper & Brothers, 1920), 2:392.

314. Chace, *1912*, 146–55.

315. Clark, *Quarter Century in American Politics*, 2:423–24.

316. Josephus Daniels, *The Wilson Era: Years of Peace, 1910–1917* (Chapel Hill, NC: The University of North Carolina Press, 1944), 59.

317. White, *Autobiography of William Allen White*, 479.

318. "Indianan Named for Vice-President Early Today," *Washington Post*, July 3, 1912, 1.

319. Link, *Woodrow Wilson and the Progressive Era*, 13; Chace, *1912*, 142, 157.

320. "The Vote of Illinois Made Wilson's Nomination Sure," *New York Times*, July 3, 1912, 1; Chace, 1912, 157–58.

321. Link, *Woodrow Wilson and the Progressive Era*, 13.

322. According to one account, possibly apocryphal, Roger Sullivan and Hoosier boss Tom Taggart secured Marshall's place on the ticket at a late night meeting with Wilson aide William F. McCombs in a Baltimore hotel room, with all three men clad in pajamas. Daniels, *Years of Peace*, 550–51.

323. Quoted in Chace, *1912*, 159.

324. Arthur Link, *The Road to the White House* (Princeton, NJ: Princeton University Press, 1947), 464–65.

325. Clark, *Quarter Century in American Politics*, 2:407.

326. Coletta, *Presidency of William Howard Taft*, 240.

327. *National Party Platforms*, 168–75.

328. Chace, *1912*, 51.

329. *Papers of Woodrow Wilson* 25:8–17.

330. Paoletti, *Presidency of William Howard Taft*, 25–26.

331. Taussig, *Tariff History of the United States*, 410–11.

332. *National Party Platforms*, 184–85.

333. "Democrats Show Up Tariff Iniquities," *New York Times*, September 9, 1912, 3.

334. "Wilson Hits Tariff and the Third Party," Ibid., September 10, 1912, 3.

335. *Papers of Woodrow Wilson*, 25:335.

336. "Roosevelt Scorns Wilson's Philosophy," *New York Times*, September 15, 1912, 8.

337. "Roosevelt Pledges Quick Extra Session," Ibid., September 18, 1912, 5.

338. Martis, *Historical Atlas of Political Parties in the United States Congress*, 167.

339. Francis E. Leupp, "The Passing of a Dynasty," *Atlantic Monthly*, March 1913, 306.

340. *U.S. Statutes at Large* 36 (August 5, 1909): 112.

341. *Messages and Papers of the Presidents*, 16:7872.

342. Taussig, *Tariff History of the United States*, 432–33.

343. Link, *Woodrow Wilson and the Progressive Era*, 40–42.

344. *U.S. Statutes at Large* 38 (October 3, 1913): 114.

345. Ibid., 167–68.

346. David M. Kennedy, *Over Here: The First World War and American Society* (New York: Oxford University Press, 1980), 16.

347. In 1930, tariffs produced $587 million in revenues for the federal government, while internal taxes (income, tobacco and alcohol) produced over three billion dollars in revenue. *Historical Statistics of the United States*, 5:84.

348. A. B. Hepburn, "Credit Currency," *North American Review*, December 1906, 1171–78.

349. *U.S. Statutes at Large* 35 (May 30, 1908): 546.

350. Link, *Woodrow Wilson and the Progressive Era*, 44–50.

351. *Congressional Record*, 63rd Cong., 1st Sess. Vol. 50 Part 5 (September 10, 1913): H 4342–47.

352. Ibid., 63rd Cong., 2nd Sess. Vol. 51 Part 1: S 831–36.

353. Link, *Woodrow Wilson and the Progressive Era*, 52–53.

354. See the comments of Carter Glass at *Congressional Record*, 63rd Cong., 2nd Sess. Vol. 51 Part 17 Appendix (December 11, 1913): H 562.

355. *U.S. Statutes at Large* 38 (1913): 251.

356. James Grant, *Money of the Mind: Borrowing and Lending in America from the Civil War to Michael Milken* (New York: Farrar Straus Giroux, 1992), 140–41.

357. Swisher, *American Constitutional Development*, 572.

358. Gordon, *An Empire of Wealth*, 280–81.

359. *U.S. Statutes at Large* 38 (September 26, 1914): 717.

360. Ibid., 38 (October 15, 1914): 730.

361. Swisher, *American Constitutional Development*, 575.

362. Robert Bork, *The Antitrust Paradox: A Policy as War with Itself* (New York: Basic Books, 1978), 48–49.

363. *Loewe v. Lawlor*, 208 U.S. 274 (1908).

364. Link, *Woodrow Wilson and the Progressive Era*, 69.

365. An act of March 1, 1913, authorized the I.C.C. to value all railroad property. *U.S. Statutes at Large* 37 (1913): 701.

366. Ibid., 39 (June 18, 1910): 556.

367. Railroad Securities Commission, *Report of the Railroad Securities Commission*, 62nd Cong., 2nd Sess., H. Doc. 256 (November 1, 1911), 7–12.

368. "Lawyer Calls Owen Bill a Dangerous Measure," *Wall Street Journal*, February 2, 1914, 1.

369. *Congressional Record* 63rd Cong., 2nd Sess. Vol. 51 Part 3 (February 2, 1914): H 2719.

370. "Exchange Men See Flaws in Owen Bill," *New York Times*, January 20, 1914, 14.

371. *Congressional Record*, 63rd Cong., 2nd Sess. Vol. 51 Part 10 (June 2, 1914): H 9684–87.

372. Ibid. (June 15, 1914), 9894–95.

373. "Exchange Men Favor the Rayburn Bill," *New York Times*, May 17, 1914, 11.

374. *Papers of Woodrow Wilson* (letter of May12, 1914), 30: 24. See also Link, *Woodrow Wilson and the Progressive Era*, 58.

375. Link, *Woodrow Wilson and the Progressive Era*, 57–58, 30.

376. *Congressional Record*, 63rd Cong., 2nd Sess. Vol. 17 Part 2 Appendix (February 17, 1914): H 141–43.

377. *U.S. Statutes at Large* 39 (1916): 360.

378. Link, *Woodrow Wilson and the Progressive Era*, 226.

379. "Federal Farm Loan Act Puts Farmer on Equal Footing with other Business Men," *Atlanta Constitution*, July 18, 1916, 8.

380. John D. Hicks, *The Decline of Laissez Faire* (New York: Holt, Rhinehart and Winston, 1951), 365.

381. Myron T. Herrick, "The Federal Farm Loan Act," *Atlantic Monthly*, February 1917, 225.

382. Ibid., 232.

383. *Smith v. Kansas Title & Trust Co.*, 255 U.S. 180 (1921).

384. Ibid. at 208–11.

385. David J. Danelski and Joseph S. Tulchin, eds., *The Autobiographical Notes of Charles Evans Hughes* (Cambridge, MA: Harvard University Press, 1973), 92–93.

386. Clara Eliot, *The Farmer's Campaign for Credit* (New York: D. Appleton & Co., 1927), 72–79.

387. *U.S. Statutes at Large* 39 (August 11, 1916): 486.

388. Ibid., 31 (May 17, 1900): 179.

389. Ibid., 36 (March 1, 1911): 961.

390. Ibid., 38 (May 8, 1914): 372.

391. Gordon, *An Empire of Wealth*, 298.

392. James F. Byrnes, *All in One Lifetime* (New York: Harper & Brothers, 1958), 25.

393. *U.S. Statutes at Large* 27 (March 3, 1893): 734, 737.

394. Johnson, *Governing the American State*, 116–19.

395. *U.S. Statutes at Large* 37 (1912): 551.

396. Schlereth, *Victorian America*, 222.

397. Johnson, *Governing the American State*, 125.

398. Schlereth, *Victorian America*, 25.

399. *Congressional Record*, 63rd Cong., 2nd Sess. Vol. 51 Part 17 Appendix (February 5, 1914): H 107.

400. Byrnes, *All in One Lifetime*, 32.

401. *U.S. Statutes at Large* 39 (1916): 355.

402. John D. Hicks, *Republican Ascendancy, 1921–33* (New York: Harper & Brothers, 1960), 9.

403. *U.S. Statutes at Large* 39 (1917): 929.

404. V.O. Key Jr., *The Administration of Federal Grants to States* (Chicago: Public Administration Service, 1937), 13.

405. *U.S. Statutes at Large* 39 (February 28, 1916): 21.

406. Key, *Administration of Federal Grants*, 15.

407. See, for example, the comments of Simeon Fess, Republican of Ohio, in the House of Representatives regarding grants for vocational education. *Congressional Record*, 64th Cong., 2nd Sess. Vol. 54 Part 6 Appendix (January 2, 1917): H 81–82.

408. Chace, *1912*, 214.

409. Link, *Woodrow Wilson and the Progressive Era*, 65.

410. Kenneth C. O'Reilly, "The Jim Crow Policies of Woodrow Wilson," *The Journal of Blacks in Higher Education* 17 (Autumn 1997): 117–21.

411. Garrison Villard, *Fighting Years: Memoirs of a Liberal Editor* (New York: Harcourt, Brace & Co., 1939) 239.

412. Ibid., 311.

413. Arthur S. Link, "Woodrow Wilson and the Democratic Party," *The Review of Politics* 18, no. 2 (April 1956): 150.

414. Ibid., 154.

415. Swisher, *American Constitutional Development*, 578–79.

416. For a description of what one Congressman saw as the pro-labor measures enacted by the Wilson administration, see the comments of Representative John Adair of Indiana at *Congressional Record*, 63rd Cong., 2nd Sess. Vol. 51, Part 17 Appendix (September 15, 1914): H 1000–1001.

417. *U.S. Statutes at Large* 1 (July 20, 1790): 131.

418. In upholding a law limiting the liability of ship owners to their share of the ownership of vessels, the Supreme Court (Justice Bradley) explained that as jurisdiction over admiralty cases was vested in the federal government, Congress necessarily enjoyed authority to enact laws related to that subject, as the states could no longer do so. *In re Garnett*, 141 U.S. 1, 14 (1891).

419. In the *Legal Tender Cases*, Justice William Strong described laws regarding the working conditions of seamen as exercises of the commerce power. *Legal Tender Cases*, 79 U.S. 457, 537 (1871).

420. *U.S. Statutes at Large* 38 (March 4, 1915): 1164.

421. *Papers of Woodrow Wilson* (letter of January 24, 1914), 29:170 quoted in Link, *Woodrow Wilson and the Progressive Era*, 59.

422. Stephen B. Wood, *Constitutional Politics in the Progressive Era: Child Labor and the Law* (Chicago: University of Chicago Press, 1968), 49–51.

423. Link, *Woodrow Wilson and the Progressive Era*, 59, 227.

424. *U.S. Statutes at Large* 39 (1916) 675.

425. Link, *Woodrow Wilson and the Progressive Era*, 235.

426. *U.S. Statutes at Large* 38 (July 15, 1913): 103.

427. Martin, *Enterprise Declined*, 327–28.

428. "Summary of the News," *The Nation*, August 24, 1916, 163.

429. "The Week," Ibid., 188.

430. *Messages and Papers of the Presidents* (August 29, 1916), 17:8144–49.

431. *Congressional Record*, 64th Cong., 1st Sess. Vol. 53, Part 13 (September 1, 1916): H 13580.

432. Ibid., 13600.

433. Ibid. (September 2, 1916): H 13647.

434. *U.S. Statutes at Large* 39 (1916): 721.

435. "Wilson Greeted by Great Crowds," *Atlanta Constitution*, September 4, 1916, 10.

436. "A National Humiliation," *New York Times*, September 1, 1916, 8.

437. "Stopping the Strike," *Washington Post*, September 1, 1916, quoted in the *Congressional Record*, 64th Cong., 1st Sess. Vol. 53, Part 13 (September 7, 1916) H: 13994.

438. "Legislation by Strike Threats," *Chicago Daily News*, September 1, 1916, quoted in the *Congressional Record*, 64th Cong., 1st Sess. Vol. 53, Part 13 (September 2, 1916): H 13618.

439. "For President: Charles Evans Hughes," *North Atlantic Review*, October 1916, 504.

440. *Wilson v. New*, 243 U.S. 333 (1917).

441. Ibid. at 348.

442. Ibid. at 349.

443. Ibid. at 386–87.

444. Ibid. at 376–81.

445. "No More Strikes Worry Concerns in Interstate Commerce," *Atlanta Constitution*, March 20, 1917, 3; "Railroad Strikes Things of the Past," Ibid., March 21, 1917, 3.

446. Charles Kellogg Burdick, "The Adamson Law Decision," *Cornell Law Quarterly* 2, no. 4 (May 1917): 320–24.

447. Samuel O. Dunn, "Political Phases of Government Ownership," *Atlantic Monthly*, February 1915, 209.

448. Ibid., 211.

449. "Brandeis Unfit, Declares Taft," *Atlanta Constitution*, March 15, 1916, 3.

450. Martin, *Enterprise Declined*, 206–23.

451. Leonard Baker, *Brandeis and Frankfurter: A Dual Biography* (New York: Harper & Row, 1984), 102–21.

452. *National Party Platforms*, 207.

453. "The Week," *The Nation*, August 24, 1916, 164.

454. White, *Autobiography of William Allen White*, 530.

455. *National Party Platforms*, 194–99.

456. Link, *Woodrow Wilson and the Progressive Era*, 229, 239.

457. "Hughes Deals Hard Blows to Wilson Record," *Chicago Daily Tribune*, September 20, 1916, 1.

458. Link, *Woodrow Wilson and the Progressive Era*, 240–43.

459. Ibid., 245–50.

460. White, *Autobiography of William Allen White*, 532.

461. Wilmer T. Stone, "Can America Endure—a Plea for National Centralization," *Sewanee Review*, October 1916, 393–94.

462. Ibid., 398.

463. Stone, "A Plea for National Centralization," 399.

464. Ibid., 403.

465. Ibid.

466. Ibid., 404.

467. Silber, *When Washington Shut Down Wall Street*, 95–115.

468. *U.S. Statutes at Large 38* (September 2, 1914): 711.

469. Martha Derthick, *The National Guard in Politics* (Cambridge, MA: Harvard University Press, 1965), 22–35.

470. George C. Herring Jr., "James Hay and the Preparedness Controversy, 1915–1916," *The Journal of Southern History* 30, no. 4 (November 1964): 394.

471. *U.S. Statutes at Large* 38 (1916): 166.

472. Link, *Woodrow Wilson and the Progressive Era*, 187.

473. *Messages and Papers of the Presidents*, 17:8017–18.

474. *U.S. Statutes at Large* 39 (1916): 728.

475. Kennedy, *Over Here*, 339.

476. Commager, Morison, *Growth of the American Republic*, 5th ed., 2:580–81.

477. *U.S. Statutes at Large* 39 (September 8, 1916): 756.

478. An act of February 24, 1919, imposed a supplemental tax of 65 percent on incomes over a million dollars. *U.S. Statutes at Large* 40 (1919): 1062–64. That levy supplemented but did not replace the income surtax of 13 percent imposed by the September 8, 1916, tax law.

479. Kennedy, *Over Here*, 101–12.

480. *U.S. Statutes at Large* 40 (1918): 506.

481. Carroll H. Wooddy, *The Growth of the Federal Government, 1915–1932* (New York: McGraw-Hill, 1934), 200–202.

482. Kennedy, *Over Here*, 103.

483. Swisher, *American Constitutional Development*, 647.

484. "C.I.C. Expects Cooperation," *Wall Street Journal*, February 9, 1918, 10.

485. Watson, *Development of National Power*, 237–38, 331.

486. "Legislation Wanted to Protect Investors," *Wall Street Journal*, December 27, 1918, 7.

487. "Bill to Deal with Wildcat Securities," Ibid., January 3, 1919, 8; *Congressional Record*, 65th Cong., 3rd Sess. Vol. 57 Part 3 (January 30, 1919): H 2412.

488. John Keegan, *The First World War* (New York: Alfred A. Knopf, 1999), 372.

489. *U.S. Statutes at Large* 40 (May 18, 1917): 76.

490. Kennedy, *Over Here*, 144–50.

491. See the speech of Charles Evans Hughes to the American Bar Association contained in the *Congressional Record*, 65th Cong., 1st Sess. Vol. 55 Part 7 (September 10, 1917) H: 6838.

492. Keegan, *The First World War*, 392.

493. Kennedy, *Over Here*, 127–30.

494. Paul Koistinen, *Mobilizing for War: The Political Economy of American Warfare, 1865–1919* (Lawrence, KS: University Press of Kansas, 1997), 226.

495. Mark Sullivan, *Our Times*, 5:384.

496. Kennedy, *Over Here*, 133–36.

497. Watson, *The Development of National Power*, 287–88.

498. Martin, *Enterprise Denied*, 337.

499. Kennedy, *Over Here*, 252–53.

500. *U.S. Statutes at Large* 39 (1916): 645.

501. Ibid., 40 (March 21, 1918): 451.

502. Link, *Woodrow Wilson and the Progressive Era*, 149–50, 170–72.

503. *U.S. Statutes at Large* 40 (1917): 276.

504. Kennedy, *Over Here*, 117.

505. *Congressional Record*, 65th Cong., 1st Sess. Vol. 55 Part 5 (June 28, 1917): S 4405–7.

506. Ibid., 4413.

507. Sullivan, *Our Times*, 5:421.

508. Commager, Morison, *Growth of the American Republic*, 5th ed., 2:571–72.

509. Merrill Peterson, *The President and the Biographer: Woodrow Wilson and Ray Stannard Baker* (Charlottesville, VA: University of Virginia Press, 2007), 133.

510. Swisher, *American Constitutional Development*, 637–38, 684–85.

511. *U.S. Statutes at Large* 40 (1918): 904.

512. Ibid., 40 (1918): 821.

513. Kennedy, *Over Here*, 261–62.

514. *U.S. Statutes at Large* 34 (February 20, 1907): 898.

515. "What of the Moose?", *Harper's Weekly*, November 28, 1914, 505.

516. Andrews, *History of Labor in the United States*, 3:199–202.

517. "World's Biggest Agency for Jobs," *New York Times*, September 22, 1918, 47.

518. "Work or Fight Order to all on Draft Rolls," Ibid., May 24, 1918, 5; "Will Shift 500,000 to Class 1 in Draft," Ibid., June 18, 1918, 5; "Movie Trade Is Essential," Ibid., July 1, 1918, 12; "Labor Shortage Becoming Acute," Ibid., June 28, 1918, 7; "Baseball Teams Must Go to Work," Ibid., July 20, 1918, 5.

519. Commager, Morison, *Growth of the American Republic*, 5th ed., 2:573.

520. Kennedy, *Over Here*, 55–65.

521. George T. Blakey, *Historians and the Great War: American Propagandists for the Great War* (Louisville, KY: University Press of Kentucky, 1970), 106–11.

522. *U.S. Statutes at Large* 40 (1917): 217.

523. *Congressional Record*, 65th Cong., 1st Sess. Vol. 55 Part 1 (April 18, 1917): S 779.

524. Ibid.

525. *Schenck v. U.S.*, 249 U.S. 17 (1919).

526. Ibid. at 51–52.

527. Swisher, *American Constitutional Development*, 604.

528. Kennedy, *Over Here*, 83.

529. James Harvey Robinson, "The Threatened Eclipse of Free Speech," *Atlantic Monthly*, December 1917, 813–14.

530. *U.S. Statutes at Large* 40 (1918): 553.

531. "Spies and Plotters," *New York Times*, April 28, 1918, 76; Wilson Opposes New Spy Bill," Ibid., April 23, 1918, 6.

532. Commager, Morison, *Growth of the American Republic*, 5th ed., 2:575–76.

533. Swisher, *American Constitutional Development*, 610.

534. Harry N. Scheiber, *The Wilson Administration and Civil Liberties, 1917–1921* (Ithaca, NY: Cornell University Press, 1960), 30–35.

535. Nancy K. Bristow, *Making Men Moral: Social Engineering during the Great War* (New York: New York University Press, 1996), 31–32, 56–65, 98–130.

536. Ann Hagedorn, *Savage Peace: Hope and Fear in America, 1919* (New York: Simon & Schuster, 2007), 323.

537. Kennedy, *Over Here*, 81.

538. Swisher, *American Constitutional Development*, 606–7.

539. Scheiber, *The Wilson Administration and Civil Liberties*, 37–40, 49.

540. Hagedorn, *Savage Peace*, 26, 31–32.

541. Kennedy, *Over Here*, 288–89.

542. Hagedorn, *Savage Peace*, 219–30, 321, 431.

543. Proclamation 1364 of April 6, 1917, John T. Woolley and Gerhard Peters, *The American Presidency Project* [online]. Santa Barbara, CA. Available http://www.presidency.ucsb.edu/ws/?pid=598.

544. Kennedy, *Over Here*, 290. The Alien Act authorized the summary deportation of any alien not yet naturalized. *U.S. Statutes at Large* 40 (April 16, 1918): 531.

545. Cummings, Macfarland, *Federal Justice*, 429.

546. Kennedy, *Over Here*, 291–92.

547. Commager, Morison, *The Growth of the American Republic*, 5th ed., 2:639.

548. Kennedy, *Over Here*, 273.

549. Hagedorn, *Savage Peace*, 381.

550. "To Extend Food Law," *New York Times*, November 1, 1919, 3.

551. Keegan, *The First World War*, 407–19.

552. John M. Barry, *The Great Influenza: The Epic Story of the Deadliest Plague in U.S. History* (New York: Viking Press, 2004), 303–20, 374, 397–98; *U.S. Statutes at Large*, 46 (May 26, 1930): 379.

553. Swisher, *American Constitutional Development*, 677–78.

554. *U.S. Statutes at Large* 41 (1919): 1359.

555. Ibid., 42 (August 25, 1921): 1939.

556. Ely, *Railroads and American Law*, 242–45.

557. Hicks, *The Republican Ascendancy*, 15.

558. *U.S. Statutes at Large* 41 (February 28, 1920): 456.

559. "Strike Makes 50,000 Idle in Pittsburgh," *New York Times*, April 11, 1920, 3; "Copeland Fears Crisis Soon," Ibid., April 13, 1920, 1.

560. "Men Dissatisfied with Rail Award," Ibid., July 20, 1920, 1; "Public Must Pay $600 Million Rise to Rail Workers," Ibid., 1.

561. *Dayton-Goose Creek R.R. v. U.S.*, 263 U.S. 456 (1924).

562. "It is instructive to trace the expansion of the commerce clause in the railroad cases. At each point the Supreme Court seemed aware that there must be some limit to the commerce power, but on virtually every occasion it found the federal legislation at issue not to exceed the limit." Richard A. Epstein, "The Proper Scope of the Commerce Power," *Virginia Law Review* 73, no. 7 (November 1987): 1414–15.

563. "Get Steam Up on Railroads," *Chicago Daily Tribune*, May 8, 1920, 6.

564. Rose, *The Best Transportation System in the World*, 11–13.

565. Ely, *Railroads and American Law*, 258–59; *U.S. Statutes at Large* 44 (May 20, 1926): 577.

566. "Watson-Parker Fallacies," *Wall Street Journal*, May 12, 1926, 1.

567. *Texas & New Orleans R.R. v. Brotherhood of Ry. & S.S. Clerks*, 281 U.S. 548, 570 (1930).

568. "Federal Protection of Collective Bargaining under the Railway Labor Act," *Yale Law Journal* 40, no. 1 (November 1930): 98.

569. *U.S. Statutes at Large* 41 (1921): 1084.

570. Ibid., 41 (June 10, 1920): 1063.

571. Ibid., 45 (December 21, 1928): 1057.

572. *Arizona v. California*, 283 U.S. 423, 454 (1931).

573. Joseph E. Stevens, *Hoover Dam: An American Adventure* (Norman, OK: University of Oklahoma Press 1988), 259–60.

574. *U.S. Statutes at Large* 41 (1920): 988, 991.

575. Wooddy, *Growth of the Federal Government*, 236–39.

576. *U.S. Statutes at Large* 44 (May 20, 1926): 568.

577. In 1917 the Supreme Court all but discarded *Lochner* when it upheld a state law limiting the hours of persons working in flour mills. *Bunting v. State of Oregon*, 243 U.S. 426 (1917).

578. *Coppage v. Kansas*, 236 U.S. 1 (1915).

579. Ibid. at 16–18.

580. *Wilson v. New*, 243 U.S. 332 (1917).

581. *Hammer v. Dagenhart*, 247 U.S. 251 (1918).

582. Ibid. at 270.

583. Ibid. at 271–72.

584. Ibid. at 273–74.

585. Ibid. at 279–80.

586. Alexander M. Bickel, Benno C. Schmidt, *The Judiciary and Responsible Government, 1910–1921* (New York: Macmillan, 1984), 457.

587. *U.S. Statutes at Large* 40 (February 24, 1919): 1138.

588. *Bailey v. Drexel Furniture*, 259 U.S. 20 (1922).

589. Ibid. at 38.

590. Wood, *Constitutional Politics in the Progressive Era*, 273.

591. *Hill v. Wallace*, 259 U.S. 44, 67–69 (1922); *U.S. Statutes at Large* 42 (August 24, 1921): 187.

592. *Hill* at 68.

593. *Board of Trade v. Olsen*, 262 U.S. 1, 32–33 (1923); *U.S. Statutes at Large* 42 (September 21, 1922): 998.

594. Ibid., 36.

595. *U.S. Statutes at Large* 38 (December 17, 1914): 785.

596. *U.S. v Doremus*, 249 U.S. 86 (1919).

597. Ibid. at 94.

598. Ibid. at 95.

599. Kennedy, *Over Here*, 88–92.

600. Swisher, *American Constitutional Development*, 660–61.

CHAPTER 5

1. David Morgan, *Suffragists and Democrats* (East Lansing, MI: Michigan State University Press, 1972), 96, 98, 110; *Congressional Record*, 63rd Cong., 3rd Sess. Vol. 52 Part 2 (January 12, 1915): H 1483–84.

2. *National Party Platforms*, 199, 207.

3. Morgan, *Suffragists and Democrats*, 150–51.

4. The Voight Act was sought by the dairy industry to prevent the sale of a competing product that threatened its profits. As with oleomargarine, the health concerns raised over filled milk proved to be exaggerated. *U.S. Statutes at Large* 42 (March 4, 1923): 1486.

5. George Madden Martin, "American Women and Paternalism," *Atlantic Monthly*, June 1924, 746–47.

6. George Madden Martin, "The American Woman and Representative Government," Ibid., March 1925, 365–66.

7. *U.S. Statutes at Large* 42 (November 23, 1921): 224.

8. Edward R. Schlesinger, M.D., "The Sheppard-Towner Era: A Prototype Case Study in Federal-State Relations," *American Journal of Public Health* 57, no. 6 (June 1967): 1034–40.

9. Lorraine Gates Schuyler, *The Weight of Their Votes: Southern Women and Political Leverage in the 1920's* (Chapel Hill, NC: University of North Carolina Press, 2006), 180, 207–11.

10. *National Party Platforms*, 219.

11. Ibid.

12. Norman Beasley, Rixey Smith, *Carter Glass: A Biography* New York: (Longmans, Green & Co.), 1939, 211.

13. *National Party Platforms*, 230.

14. Quoted in George H. Douglas, *The Golden Age of the Newspaper* (Westport, CT: Greenwood Press, 1999), 203.

15. Villard, Fighting Years, 475.

16. In 1921, Congress spent $5 billion; in 1922 it spent $3.3 billion. *Historical Statistics of the United States Colonial Times to 1870*, 2 vols. (Washington, DC: U.S. Department of Commerce, 1970), 2:1104.

17. *U.S. Statutes at Large* 42 (November 23, 1921): 227; Ibid., 43 (June 2, 1924): 253; David Cannadine, *Mellon: An American Life* (New York: Alfred A. Knopf, 2006), 287–88, 315

18. "Roosevelt Gives Jobless $10,000," *New York Times*, January 27, 1915, 1.

19. "Adopts Program for Quick Relief of Unemployed," Ibid., October 1, 1921, 1; "Harding Appeals for Aid of States on Unemployment," Ibid., October 4, 1921, 1.

20. Andrews, *History of Labor in the United States*, 3:211.

21. Wooddy, *The Growth of the Federal Government*, 373.

22. Joseph G. Rayback, *A History of American Labor* (New York: Macmillan, 1959), 325.

23. Arthur M. Schlesinger Jr., *The Age of Roosevelt*, 3 vols. (Boston: Houghton Mifflin, 1957), Volume 1: *The Crisis of the Old Order, 1919–33*, 65, 84.

24. Hicks, *The Republican Ascendancy*, 14–16.

25. Spero, "Collective Bargaining in the Public Service," 148–49.

26. Colin Davis, *Power at Odds: The 1922 National Railroad Shopmen's Strike* (Champaign, IL: University of Illinois Press, 1998), 97–111, 127–28.

27. Felix Frankfurter, Nathan Greene, *The Labor Injunction* (New York: Macmillan, 1930), 253–63; see also *U.S. v. Railway Employees' Department of American Federation of Labor*, 283 Fed. 479 (N.D. Ill. 1922).

28. Hicks, *The Republican Ascendancy*, 72.
29. *Truax v. Corrigan*, 257 U.S. 312.
30. Ibid. at 328.
31. Ibid. at 333.
32. Ibid. at 348–49.
33. "Does Mr. Taft Want Direct Action?", *The Nation*, January 11, 1922, 32.
34. Swisher, *American Constitutional Development*, 810.
35. *U.S. Statutes at Large* 47 (March 23, 1932): 70.
36. Ibid., 40 (1918): 268.
37. Ibid., 40 (1918): 886.
38. Ibid., 41 (1919): 158.
39. Ibid., 41 (June 2, 1920): 735.
40. *Congressional Record*, 68th Cong., 1st Sess. Vol. 65 Part 8 (May 10, 1924) H: 8292–93.
41. Ibid.
42. *U.S. Statutes at Large* 43 (June 5, 1924): 430.
43. Ibid., 42 (November 9, 1921): 212.
44. Walter Thompson, *Federal Centralization: A Study and Criticism of the Expanding Scope of Congressional Legislation* (New York: Harcourt, Brace & Co., 1923), 88.
45. Johnson, *Governing the American State*, 131–32.
46. Jane Perry Clark, *The Rise of a New Federalism: Federal-State Cooperation in the United States* (New York: Columbia University Press, 1938), 203, 223–25.
47. Joseph F. Zimmerman, *Congressional Preemption: Regulatory Federalism* (New York: State University of New York Press, 2005), 45.
48. *U.S. Statutes at Large* 43 (June 7, 1924): 653.
49. *U.S. Statutes at Large* 46 (March 2, 1931): 1468.
50. Johnson, *Governing the American State*, 148–50, 162.
51. See *Congressional Record*, 67th Cong., 1st Sess. Vol. 61 Part 3 (June 28, 1921): S 3142 (William Kenyon, Republican Senator of Iowa); Ibid., Vol. 61 Part 7 (November 1, 1921) H: 7144–49 (Caleb Layton, Republican Congressman from Delaware); Ibid., Vol. 61 Part 9 Appendix (July 21–22, 1921): S 8759–69 (James Reed, Democratic Senator of Missouri).
52. Ibid., 67th Cong., 2nd Sess. Vol. 62 Part 9 (June 29, 1922): H 9701–6.
53. *Massachusetts v. Mellon*, 262 U.S. 447 (1923).
54. Ibid. at 453–58.
55. Ibid. at 482.
56. Ibid.
57. Ibid. at 487.
58. Currie, *The Constitution in the Supreme Court*, 2:184–85. See *Marbury v. Madison*, 5 U.S. 137, 176–78 (1803).
59. As legal historian Edward S. Corwin wrote in 1923, "any attempt to apply the Madisonian test to national expenditures today would call for a radical revision in the customary annual budget of the government and for a revolution in

national administration." "The Spending Power of Congress—Apropos the Maternity Act," *Harvard Law Review* 36, no.4 (March 1923): 573–75.

60. Taussig, *Tariff History of the United States*, 448–51.

61. Ibid., 451; *U.S. Statutes at Large* 42 (May 27, 1921): 9.

62. *U.S. Statutes at Large* 42 (September 21, 1922): 858.

63. Taussig, *Tariff History of the United States*, 464–67.

64. Hicks, *The Republican Ascendancy*, 59.

65. Ibid.

66. *U.S. Statutes at Large* 44 (February 6, 1926): 21.

67. *Autobiographical Notes of Charles Evans Hughes*, 200.

68. Robert Sobel *Coolidge: An American Enigma* (Washington, DC: Regnery, 1998), 76, 117, 124, 130–47.

69. *Supplement to the Messages and Papers of the Presidents Covering the Term of Warren Harding and the First Term of Calvin Coolidge* (Washington, DC: Bureau of National Literature 1925) (message of June 7, 1924), 9416–19.

70. Kennedy, *Over Here*, 363.

71. *The Nation*, February 22, 1922, 209.

72. "The Bonus Swindle," *The Nation*, March 1, 1922, 209.

73. *U.S. Statutes at Large* 43 (May 19, 1924): 121.

74. *Supplement to the Messages and Papers of the Presidents Covering the Term of Warren Harding and the First Term of Calvin Coolidge* (message of May 3, 1924), 9402–3.

75. Willard Cooper, "The Soldier Vote," *Atlantic Monthly*, September 1924, 387–90.

76. Approximately 999,000 veterans received benefits in 1900, 615,000 in 1918, and 1,278,000 in 1932. *Historical Statistics of the United States*, 5:421–22.

77. Eliot, *The Farmer's Campaign for Credit*, 163.

78. Hicks, *The Republican Ascendancy*, 54.

79. *U.S. Statutes at Large* 42 (August 24, 1921): 181.

80. Wooddy, *The Growth of the Federal Government*, 200–202.

81. *U.S. Statutes at Large* 42 (1922): 388.

82. Hicks, *The Republican Ascendancy*, 194.

83. Quoted in Beasley, Smith, *Carter Glass*, 217.

84. *U.S. Statutes at Large* 42 (1923): 1454.

85. Hicks, *The Republican Ascendancy*, 194–95.

86. John D. Hicks, Theodore Saloutos, *Agricultural Discontent in the Middle West 1900–1939* (Madison, WI: University of Wisconsin, 1951), 380–83.

87. "Shall We Communize the Farms," *Chicago Daily Tribune*, March 11, 1924, 8.

88. "Another Wild Scheme," *Atlanta Constitution*, May 19, 1924, 4.

89. F. E. Haynes, "LaFollette and LaFollettism," *Atlantic Monthly*, October 1924, 543.

90. *Congressional Record*, 68th Cong., 1st Sess. Vol. 65 Part 9 (May 23, 1924): H 9321–22.

91. Ibid., 9359.

92. Ibid., 9365.

93. Ibid., Vol. 65 Part 8 (May 9, 1924): S 8191–92.

94. W. E. B. DuBois, "Georgia Invisible Empire State," *The Nation*, January 21, 1925. Daniel H. Borus, ed., *These United States: Portraits of America from the 1920's* (Ithaca, NY: Cornell University Press, 1992), 98–99.

95. Commager, Morison, *Growth of the American Republic*, 5th ed., 2:451.

96. Hagedorn, *Savage Peace*, 419.

97. Elliott, *Color-Bind Justice*, 237–38.

98. See Dyer's comments on February 28, 1919, in the House of Representatives, *Congressional Record*, 65th Cong., 3rd Sess. Vol. 57 Part 5 (1919), H 4645–46.

99. *Guinn v. U.S.*, 238 U.S. 347 (1915).

100. Currie, *The Constitution in the Supreme Court*, 2:106–7.

101. *Buchanan v. Warley*, 245 U.S. 60 (1917).

102. *Nixon v. Herndon*, 273 U.S. 536 (1927).

103. *Nixon v. Condon*, 286 U.S. 73, 88–89 (1932).

104. Currie, *The Constitution in the Supreme Court*, 2:251.

105. *Grovey v. Townsend*, 295 U.S. 45 (1935).

106. Schuyler, *The Weight of their Votes*, 24–25, 65, 97, 111, 134.

107. Kennedy, *Over Here*, 280–83.

108. Hagedorn, *Savage Peace*, 308–19.

109. Vincent P. de Santis, "Republican Efforts to Crack the Solid South," *The Review of Politics*, 14, no. 2 (April 1952): 261.

110. Barry *Rising Tide*, 319–20, 334.

111. *National Party Platforms*, 254. In June 1924 Congress submitted an amendment to the states that would have given it the power to ban child labor. It was not ratified. *U.S. Statutes at Large* 43 (June 4, 1924): 670.

112. *National Party Platforms*, 248–49.

113. Hicks, *The Republican Ascendancy*, 100.

114. Schlesinger, *The Crisis of the Old Order*, 129.

115. Hicks, *The Republican Ascendancy*, 103.

116. *Historical Statistics of the United States*, 5:92–93.

117. "Stanley Denounces Paternalistic Rule," *New York Times*, July 5, 1922, 4.

118. Marvin P. Rosenberry, "Development of the Federal idea," *North American Review*, August 1923, 150–58.

119. Ibid., 160–67.

120. "The Revival of Antifederalism," *The New Republic*, January 21, 1925, 211–12.

121. John G. Ely, "State Rights," *Iowa Law Bulletin* 10, no. 4 (May 1925): 308.

122. *Supplement to the Messages and Papers of the Presidents Covering the Second Administration of Calvin Coolidge* (New York: Bureau of National Literature 1929), 9501–3.

123. "Coolidge the Jeffersonian," *Outlook*, August 18, 1926, 529–30.

124. *Supplement to the Messages and Papers of the Presidents Covering the Second Administration of Calvin Coolidge*, 9739.

125. Quoted in LeRoy Ashby, *The Spearless Leader: Senator Borah and the Progressive Movement of the 1920's* (Champaign, IL: University of Illinois Press 1972), 67–68.

126. Quoted in Wooddy, *The Growth of the Federal Government*, 432–36.

127. Lawrence Sullivan, "The Great American Bureaucracy," *Atlantic Monthly*, February 1931, 140.

128. Lawrence Sullivan, "Wasting a Billion a Year," Ibid., April 1931, 504. A more recent estimate asserts that the federal government had 395,000 employees in 1915, 854,000 in 1918, 553,000 in 1925, and 467,000 in 1932. Federal spending grew from $572 million in 1902 to $3.76 billion in 1922. *Historical Statistics of the United States*, 5:45, 114.

129. James M. Beck, *Our Wonderland of Bureaucracy: A Study of the Growth of the Bureaucracy in the Federal Government, and its Destructive Effects Upon the Constitution* New York: Macmillan, 1932), 69.

130. Ibid., 78, 84, 90–91.

131. Ibid., 91–93, 200, 205–6.

132. In 1913, 357,598 Americans filed returns, when the income tax was reintroduced. *Historical Statistics of the United States*, 5:112.

133. One review of the 1928 Revenue Act's provisions applicable to tax disputes involving corporations observed that the law "does not operate on the theory that there is in every tax case only one exact and ascertainable figure of income of just so many dollars and cents. On the contrary, it assumes that a taxable income is a determination of many fallible judgments." Roy E. Blakey, "The Revenue Act of 1928," *The American Economic Review* 18, no. 3 (September 1928), 447.

134. Al Smith and His Chances," *Baltimore Evening Sun*, July 5, 1927. Malcolm Moos, ed., *A Carnival of Buncombe: H.L. Mencken* (Baltimore: The Johns Hopkins University Press, 1956), 145.

135. Charles Warren, *Congress as Santa Clause: National Donations and the General Welfare Clause of the Constitution* (Charlottesville, VA: Michie Co., 1932), 77–78.

136. *U.S. Statutes at Large* 18 (April 23, 1874): 34; Ibid., 18 (May 13, 1874): 45; Ibid., 18 (June 23, 1874): 230.

137. Ibid., 18 (January 25, 1875): 303; 18 (February 10, 1875): 314.

138. Ibid., 22 (February 25, 1882): 378; 22 (March 10, 1882): 378; 22 (March 11, 1882): 378; 22 (March 21, 1882): 379; 22 April 1, 1882): 379–80; 23 (February 12, 1884): 267; 23 (February 12, 1884): 268; 23 (March 27, 1884): 269; 23 (June 7, 1884): 273. See also Michelle Landis Dauber, "The Sympathetic State," *Law and History Review* 23, no. 2 (Summer 2005): 1–85.

139. *U.S. Statutes at Large* 31 (June 6, 1900): 277.

140. See *U.S. Statutes at Large* 34 (April 19, 1906) 827; 34 (April 24, 1906): 828; 34 (June 30, 1906): 644.

141. Gordon Thomas and Max Morgan Witts, *The San Francisco Earthquake* (New York: Stein and Day, 1971), 164–65, 271–73.

142. *U.S. Statutes at Large* 38 (October 22, 1913): 211 & 215; 38 (August 1, 1914): 681; 39 (February 15, 1916) 10; 39 (February 15, 1916): 11, 30 (April 11, 1916): 50; 39 (August 3, 1916): 434; 39 (August 24, 1916): 534.

143. Charles Warren, *Congress as Santa Clause*, 114–15.

144. Barry, *Rising Tide*, 90, 156–60, 166–67; see also Frank, *Development of the Federal Program of Flood Control on the Mississippi River*, 115–24.

145. Barry, *Rising Tide*, 187.

146. Ibid., 202–06, 257, 285–86.

147. Sobel, *Coolidge*, 315–17.

148. "President Appeals for Relief Fund," *Atlanta Constitution*, April 23, 1927, 4.

149. Sam W. Small, "Looking and Listening: Is President Coolidge Playing Politics with the Relief Problem?" Ibid., June 2, 1927, 6.

150. "Victims of Flood Relief Still Plea for Aid," *New York Times*, July 3, 1927, E1; "Hoover Flood Plan Asks $200 Million," Ibid., July 21, 1927, 1.

151. Frank, *Development of the Federal Program of Flood Control on the Mississippi River*, 197.

152. Barry, *Rising Tide*, 287.

153. *Supplement to the Messages and Papers of the Presidents Covering the Second Administration of Calvin Coolidge*, 9732–34.

154. *U.S. Statutes at Large* 45 (May 15, 1928): 534. See also Matthew T. Pearcy, "After the Flood: A History of the 1928 Flood Control Act," *Journal of the Illinois State Historical Society* 95, no. 2 (Summer 2002): 172–91.

155. *U.S. Statutes at Large* 45 (May 16, 1928): 570.

156. "Der Wille Zur Macht," September 10, 1928, *Baltimore Evening Sun*. In *Carnival of Buncombe*, 192.

157. *U.S. Statutes at Large* 41 (October 28, 1919): 305; Commager, Morison, *Growth of the American Republic*, 5th ed., 2:632.

158. Calhoun, *U.S. Marshals and Their Deputies*, 243.

159. Michael A. Lerner, *Dry Manhattan: Prohibition in New York City* (Cambridge, MA: Harvard University Press, 2007), 88–90.

160. Remini, *The House*, 290–91, 302.

161. *Olmstead v. United States*, 277 U.S. 438 (1928).

162. Ibid., 464–65.

163. Ibid. Congress directed the justice department to obtain warrants prior to using wiretaps via a law of March 1, 1933. *U.S. Statutes at Large* 47 (1933): 1381.

164. *Olmstead*, 277 U.S. 438, 478.

165. Clark, *The Rise of a New Federalism*, 94–95, 106–8.

166. Lerner, *Prohibition in New York City*, 168–69.

167. Cummings, Macfarland, *Federal Justice*, 370. Congress established the Narcotics Bureau in the Department of the Treasury for the purposing of ensuring that illegal narcotics were not imported. *U.S. Statutes at Large* 46 (June 14, 1930): 585.

168. Albert E. Sawyer, "The Enforcement of National Prohibition," *Annals of the American Academy of Political and Social Science*, 163 (September 1932): 11.

169. *U.S. Statutes at Large* 16 (March 3, 1871): 497; Cummings, Macfarland, *Federal Justice*, 372.

170. Cummings, Macfarland, *Federal Justice*, 373–74, 380.

171. Curt Gentry, J. *Edgar Hoover: The Man and the Secrets* (New York: W.W. Norton & Company, 1991), 146–48, 156.

172. *Brooks v. U.S.*, 267 U.S. 432 (1925); *U.S. Statutes at Large* 41 (October 29, 1919): 324.

173. *Brooks* 267 U.S. at 436–37.

174. Donald C. Stone, "Reorganization for Police Protection," *Law and Contemporary Problems*, 1, no. 4 (October 1934): 454.

175. Raymond Moley, "Stopping the Racket: the Defenses Open to Society," *New York Times*, August 16, 1931, 105.

176. *U.S. Statutes at Large* 47 (June 22, 1932): 326.

177. Clara G. Stillman, "Florida: The Desert and the Rose," *The Nation*, October 31, 1923. In *These United States*, 87–93.

178. Beulah Amidon Ratliff, "Mississippi: Heart of Dixie," *The Nation*, May 17, 1922. In Ibid., 196–204.

179. Arthur Fisher, "Montana: Land of the Copper Collar," *The Nation*, September 19, 1923. In Ibid., 213–19, 214.

180. Anne Martin, "Beautiful Desert of Buried Hopes," *The Nation*, July 26, 1922 In Ibid., 227–35.

181. Robert Cloutman Dexter, "Rhode Island: A Lively Experiment," *The Nation*, February 27, 1924. In Ibid., 319–25.

182. Don C. Seitz, "Connecticut: A Nation in Miniature," *The Nation*, April 18, 1923. In Ibid., 71–78.

183. Arthur Warner, "Delaware: The Ward of a Feudal Family," *The Nation*, September 6, 1922. In Ibid., 79–86.

184. *Adkin's v. Children's Hospital*, 261 U.S. 525, 545–47 (1923).

185. Ibid. at 555–56 (Sutherland), 566–67 (Taft).

186. *Jay Burns Baking Co. v Nebraska*, 264 U.S. 504, 516–17 (1924).

187. Ibid. at 517–34.

188. *Tyson & Brother v Banton*, 273 US 418 (1927) (theatre tickets); *Williams v. Standard Oil*, 278 U.S. 235 (1926) (gasoline); *Ribnik v McBride* 277 U.S. 350 (1928) (employment agencies).

189. *New State Ice Co. v. Liebmann*, 285 U.S. 262 (1932) 280, 305–6 (1932).

190. For the comments of senators who objected to confirming the nomination, see *Congressional Record*, 71st Cong., 2nd Sess. Vol. 72, Part 4 (February 1930): S 3448–49, 3499–505, 3553–591.

191. Ray A. Brown, "Due Process of Law, Police Power, and the Supreme Court," *Harvard Law Review* 40, no. 7 (May 1927): 967.

192. "The Red Terror of Judicial Review," *The New Republic*, October 1, 1924, 110–13.

193. Felix Frankfurter, *The Public and Its Government* (New Haven, CT: Yale University Press, 1930), 43.

194. Ibid., 50–51.

195. *Minneapolis & St. Louis Railway Co. v Bombolis*, 241 U.S. 211, 217 (1916).

196. *Patterson v. Colorado*, 205 U.S. 454, 462 (1907).

197. Ibid. at 465.

198. *Meyer v. Nebraska*, 262 U.S. 390 (1923).

199. Ibid. at 399.

200. Currie, *The Constitution in the Supreme Court*, 2:154.

201. *Pierce v. Society of Sisters*, 268 U.S. 510 (1925).

202. Ibid. at 534–35.

203. *Gitlow v. New York*, 268 U.S. 652 (1925).

204. Ibid. at 657.

205. Ibid. at 670.

206. Ibid. at 666.

207. See Berger, *Government By Judiciary*, 155–75.

208. *Near v. Minnesota*, 283 U.S. 697, 723–24 (1931).

209. Ibid. at 723, 732–38.

210. In his dissent in *Near*, Justice Butler complained that the majority ruling "exposes the peace and good order of every community and the business and private affairs of every individual to constant and protracted false and malicious assaults." Ibid. at 737–38.

211. Charles Warren, "The New Liberty under the Fourteenth Amendment," *Harvard Law Review* 39, no. 4 (January 1926): 431, 445, 459–60.

212. On February 28, 1866, Representative Bingham asserted the amendment would extend the Bill of Rights to the states; On May 23, 1866, Senator Howard suggested the privileges and immunities clause of the amendment would extend the Bill of Rights to the states. See *Congressional Globe*, 39th Cong., 1st Sess. Vol. 36 Part 2: H 1088 (Bingham); Ibid., Vol. 36, Part 3: S 2765 (Howard).

213. "The explanation most prominently proffered in Congress . . . was that the amendment would remove lingering doubts as to the constitutionality of the Civil Rights Act and protect it against possible repeal." David Currie, "The Reconstruction Congress," 406.

214. "The most puzzling anomaly for incorporationists is the failure of proponents of the amendment to make explicit references to the Bill of Rights as a whole during the ratification campaign." Earl M. Maltz, *Civil Rights, the Constitution and Congress* (Lawrence, KS: University Press of Kansas, 1990), 117–18.

215. For a survey of newspapers that quoted or acknowledged the comments of Bingham and Howard, including the *New York Times* and the *Philadelphia Inquirer*, and the argument that this constituted notice to the country that Congress viewed the Fourteenth Amendment as incorporating the Bill of Rights, see Bryan H. Wildenthal, "Nationalizing the Bill of Rights: Revisiting the Original Understanding of the Fourteenth Amendment in 1866-67," *Ohio State Law Journal* 68, no. 6 (Summer 2007): 1509–626, and David T. Hardy, "Original Popular Understanding of the Fourteenth Amendment as Reflected in the Print Media of 1866–68," *Whittier Law Review* 30, no. 4 (Summer 2009): 695–722.

216. See Wildenthal, "Nationalizing the Bill of Rights," 1600–1614.

217. See George C. Thomas III, "The Riddle of the Fourteenth Amendment: A Response to Professor Wildenthal," *Ohio State Law Journal* 68, no. 6 (Summer 2007): 1627–57. "To find fair notice from silence is a bridge too far." Ibid., 1633–34.

218. James E. Bond, "The Original Understanding of the Fourteenth Amendment in Illinois, Ohio and Pennsylvania," *Akron Law Review* 18, no. 3 (Winter 1985): 450.

219. Bond, *No Easy Walk to Freedom*, 21, 24, 56–58, 80–81, 149, 252–54.

220. Charles Fairman, "Does the Fourteenth Amendment Incorporate the Bill of Rights? The Original Understanding," *Stanford Law Review* 2, no. 1 (December 1949): 81–126.

221. *Twitchell v. Pennsylvania*, 74 U.S. 321, 325–27 (1869).

222. *U.S. v. Cruikshank*, 92 U.S. 542, 553 (1876).

223. See the *Federalist* #41.

224. For an exploration of the meaning of the general welfare clause as it was understood at the time of ratification, see Zavodnyik, *The Age of Strict Construction*, 12–35.

225. *U.S. Statutes at Large* 44 (February 23, 1927): 1162.

226. *Trinity Methodist Church v. Federal Radio Commission*, 62 Fed.2d 850 (App.D.C. 1932).

227. Ibid., 852–53.

228. "The Freedom of Radio Speech," *Harvard Law Review* 46, no. 7 (April 1933): 987–93.

229. *National Party Platforms*, 276.

230. *National Party Platforms*, 276.

231. Paul S. Boyer, *Purity in Print: The Vice Society Movement and Censorship in America* (New York: Charles Scribner's Sons, 1968), 208–18.

232. *U.S. v. One Book Called Ulysses*, 5 Supp. 182 (S.D.N.Y. 1933).

233. *U.S. Statutes at Large* 26 (September 19, 1890): 453.

234. Ibid., 31 (1900): 188.

235. Ibid., 43 (1924): 604.

236. Ibid., 43 (June 7, 1924): 648.

237. Ibid., 37 (March 4, 1913): 847.

238. Edwin S. Corwin, "Game Protection and the Constitution," *Michigan Law Review* 14, no. 8 (June 1916): 613–25.

239. *U.S. v. Shauver*, 214 Fed. 154 (Circ. Ct. Ark 1914); *U.S. v. McCullagh*, 221 Fed. 288 (Circ. Ct. Kans 1915).

240. *McCullagh* at 292–93.

241. *Missouri v. Holland*, 252 U.S. 416 (1920).

242. Ibid. at 433–34.

243. Ibid. at 434.

244. Ibid. at 435.

245. *Swift v. Tyson*, 41 U.S. 1, 18 (1842). Section 34 of the Judiciary Act of 1789 provided that "the laws of the several states, except where the Constitution, treaties or statutes of the United States shall otherwise require or provide, shall

be regarded as rules of decisions in trials at common law in courts of the United States in cases where they apply." *U.S. Statutes at Large* 1 (September 1, 1789): 92.

246. *Baltimore & Ohio R.R. v. Baugh*, 149 U.S. 368, 374–88 (1893).

247. Ibid. at 391–400.

248. Edward A. Purcell Jr., *Brandeis and the Progressive Court: Erie, the Judiciary Power, and the Politics of the Federal Courts in Twentieth Century America* (New Haven, CT: Yale University Press, 2000), 52, 80–81.

249. *Black and White Taxicab v. Brown and Yellow Taxicab*, 276 U.S. 518, 532–35 (1928).

250. *Erie R.R. v. Tompkins*, 304 U.S. 64 (1938).

251. Quoted in *Sobel*, Coolidge, 327.

252. *Congressional Record*, 69th Cong., 2nd Sess. Vol. 68, Part 3 (February 5, 1927): H 3044–46.

253. Ibid., 2993.

254. Ibid., 2994–95.

255. Beasley, Smith, *Carter Glass* (June 22, 1926 speech in the Senate), 241–44.

256. *U.S. Statutes at Large* 44 (July 2, 1926): 802.

257. Phillip A. Grant Jr., "Southern Congressmen and Agriculture, 1921–32," Agricultural History, 53, no. 1 (January 1979): 344. *Historical Statistics of the United States*, 3:210.

258. *Supplement to Messages and Papers of the Presidents Covering the Second Administration of Calvin Coolidge*, 9659–62.

259. *Congressional Record* 69th Cong., 2nd Sess. Vol. 68 Part 5 (February 25, 1927): S 4776.

260. "Corn Belt Fires on Coolidge Farm Bill Veto," *Chicago Daily Tribune*, February 26, 1927, 2.

261. Martin L. Fauswold, *The Presidency of Herbert C. Hoover* (Lawrence, KS: University Press of Kansas, 1985), 9–13, 22.

262. Joanne Hoff, *Herbert Hoover: Forgotten Progressive* (Boston: Little, Brown, 1975), 94.

263. Barry, *Rising Tide*, 288.

264. "The Lowden Program," *Atlanta Constitution*, December 15, 1926, 8.

265. "Weathervane," *Time*, June 6, 1927, 9–10.

266. Quoted in Paul Johnson, *Modern Times* (New York: Harper & Row), 229.

267. By one estimate, 502 of 1,089 delegates to the Republican national convention of 1928 were chosen in primaries. Hoff, *Herbert Hoover*, 126.

268. "New York G.O.P. Told Coolidge Is Out of the Race," *Chicago Daily Tribune*, September 30, 1927, 8. According to one estimate, 300 federal officeholders attended the Republican Convention in Chicago in June 1932. "Naked Repeal," *Time*, July 4, 1932, 13.

269. Fauswold, *Presidency of Herbert Hoover*, 23.

270. Ibid., 270–78. The federal government had 395,000 employees in 1911, 854,000 in 1918, 553,000 in 1925, and 467,000 in 1932. *Historical Statistics of the United States*, 5:114.

271. Lerner, *Prohibition in New York City*, 248–49.

272. Johnson, *History of the American People*, 722.

273. Hicks, *Republican Ascendancy*, 110, 115.

274. *Campaign Addresses of Governor Alfred E. Smith, Democratic Candidate for President 1928* (Washington, DC: Democratic National Committee, 1929), 27–42.

275. Ibid., 251–55.

276. *The New Day: Campaign Speeches of Herbert Hoover of 1928* (Stanford, CA: Stanford University Press, 1929), 16, 23, 27, 33–34.

277. Ibid., 195.

278. Fauswold, *Presidency of Herbert Hoover*, 25.

279. "The Show Begins," *Baltimore Evening Sun*, September 3, 1928. In *Carnival of Buncombe*, 187–92, 188.

280. Fauswold, *Presidency of Herbert Hoover*, 27–28.

281. Schlesinger, *The Crisis of the Old Order*, 129.

282. Fauswold, *Presidency of Herbert Hoover*, 59.

283. "Urge $5,500,000,000 for Mass Housing," *New York Times*, December 4, 1931, 4.

284. Udo Sautter, "Government and Unemployment: The Use of Public Works Before the New Deal," *Journal of American History*, 73, no. 1 (June 1986): 73–74.

285. Johnson, *History of the American People*, 727–28.

286. Allan H. Meltzer, *A History of the Federal Reserve*, 2 vols. (Chicago: University of Chicago, 2003), 1:254, 264–65, 401.

287. Paul M. Warburg, *The Federal Reserve System: Its Origin and Growth*, 2 vols. (New York: Macmillan, 1930), 1:501–13.

288. Johnson, *History of the American People*, 735.

289. The measure increased the 10-year appropriation originally authorized by the 1926 Public Buildings Act from $448 million to $568 million. *U.S. Statutes at Large* 46 (March 31, 1930): 136.

290. David M. Kennedy, *Freedom from Fear: The American People in Depression and War, 1929–1945* (New York: Oxford University Press, 1999), 54–56; *Historical Statistics of the United States Colonial Times to 1870*, 2 vols. (Washington, DC: Government Printing Office, 1975), 2:1123; *Historical Statistics of the United States*, 5:43.

291. *Historical Statistics of the United States*, 5:11.

292. Schlesinger, *Crisis of the Old Order*, 167.

293. Taussig, *Tariff History of the United States*, 489–97.

294. *U.S. Statutes at Large* 46 (June 17, 1930): 590.

295. Commager, Morison, *Growth of the American Republic*, 5th ed., 2:636.

296. Gordon, *An Empire of Wealth*, 321.

297. Ibid., 323–24.

298. *U.S. Statutes at Large* 46 (1929): 11.

299. *Congressional Record*, 71st Cong., 1st Sess. Vol. 71 Part 1 (April 18, 1929): H 128.

300. "Hoover Signs the Farm Relief Bill," *New York Times*, June 16, 1929, 1.

301. "Farm Aid Is First Aid," *Atlanta Constitution*, June 15, 1929, 8.

302. Albert U. Romasco, *The Poverty of Abundance: Hoover, the Nation, the Depression* (New York: Oxford University Press, 1965), 111–22.

303. Quoted in Ibid., 419.

304. "Summary of the News," *The Nation*, January 7, 1931, 1–2.

305. Hicks, Saloutos, *Agricultural Discontent in the Middle West*, 420–23; Romasco, *The Poverty of Abundance*, 117.

306. Ibid., 423–24.

307. C.D. Sturtevant, "Opposing the Agricultural Marketing Act," *Annals of the American Academy of Political Science*, 155, no. 1 (May 1931): 65–73.

308. *Historical Statistics of the United States*, 5:210.

309. George Brown Tindall, *The Emergence of the New South, 1913–1945* (Baton Rouge, LA: Louisiana State University Press, 1967), 356–57.

310. *Congressional Record*, 72nd Cong., 2nd Sess. Vol. 76 Part 1 (December 7, 1932): S 104–10.

311. *U.S. Statutes at Large* 45 (May 21, 1928): 688.

312. *Congressional Record*, 72nd Cong., 2nd Sess. Vol. 76 Part 3 (January 31, 1933): H 3052.

313. Cannadine, *Mellon*, 396–99.

314. *Federal Deposit Insurance Corporation, the First Fifty Years: A History of the F.D.I.C.* (Washington, DC: Federal Deposit Insurance Corporation 1984), 3.

315. Kennedy, *Freedom From Fear*, 67, 69.

316. *U.S. Statutes at Large* 46 (Joint Resolution 211, December 20, 1930): 1032.

317. *Federal Deposit Insurance Corporation*, 3.

318. *U.S. Statutes at Large* 44 (February 25, 1927): 1232.

319. "New Bank Bill Aids Real Estate," *Wall Street Journal*, February 28, 1927, 10.

320. In 1923 Hoover declared that "maintaining a high percentage of individual home owners is one of the searching tests that now challenge the people of the United States"; 461 of every 1,000 families owned homes in 1900; in 1920, 456 did. "To Help Homeowners," *New York Times*, September 9, 1923, S8.

321. Arthur Pound, "The Land of Dignified Credit," *Atlantic Monthly*, February 1926, 252–60.

322. Sautter, "Government and Unemployment," 81.

323. *Congressional Record*, 71st Cong., 3rd Sess. Vol. 74 Part 1: S 552–53.

324. Radio Address to the Nation on Unemployment Relief, October 18, 1931, John T. Woolley and Gerhard Peters, *The American Presidency Project* [online]. Santa Barbara, CA. Available at http://www.presidency.ucsb.edu/ws/?pid=23015.

325. *U.S. Statutes at Large* 46 (March 3, 1931): 1494.

326. J. Joseph Huthmacher, *Senator Robert Wagner and the Rise of Urban Liberalism* (New York: Atheneum, 1968), 81–83.

327. Sidney Hillman, "Unemployment Reserves," *Atlantic Monthly*, November 1931, 661.

328. *Congressional Record*, 71st Cong., 3rd Sess. Vol. 74, Part 1 (December 15, 1930): S 696–703.

329. *Congressional Record*, 71st Cong., 3rd Sess. Vol. 74, Part 1 (December 15, 1930): S 703. Congress appropriated $20 million to aid Russia in 1921 and $6 million to aid Japan following a 1925 earthquake. *U.S. Statutes at Large* 42 (December 21, 1921): 351; Ibid., 43 (February 24, 1925): 963.

330. *Congressional Record*, 71st Cong., 3rd Sess. Vol. 74 Part 1 (December 15, 1930): S 708–9.

331. Ibid., 709.

332. Ibid., 710.

333. James T. Patterson, *The States and the New Deal: Federalism in Transition* (Princeton, NJ: Princeton University Press, 1969), 42.

334. Arthur M. Schlesinger, *The Age of Roosevelt vol. 2: The Coming of the New Deal, 1933–35* (Boston: Houghton Mifflin, 1959), 303.

335. "The Veteran Racket," *Atlantic Monthly*, April 1933, 400–401.

336. *U.S. Statutes at Large* 46 (February 26, 1931): 1429; veto message of February 26, 1931, John T. Woolley and Gerhard Peters, *The American Presidency Project* [online]. Santa Barbara, CA. Available at http://www.presidency.ucsb.edu/ws/?pid=22997.

337. T. Harry Williams, *Huey Long* (New York: Alfred A. Knopf, 1969), 247, 260–63, 308.

338. *Congressional Record*, 72nd Cong., 1st Sess. Vol. 75 Part 6 (March 18, 1932): S 6452.

339. Ibid. (March 21, 1932): S 6543–44.

340. Williams, *Huey Long*, 559, 584.

341. *U.S. Statutes at Large* 47 (January 22, 1932): 5.

342. Fauswold, *Presidency of Herbert Hoover*, 153.

343. "No Federal Aid to Cities," *Wall Street Journal*, January 12, 1932, 8; "Banks and the R.F.C.," Ibid., February 8, 1932, 8.

344. *U.S. Statutes at Large* 47 (February 27, 1932): 56; Romasco, *The Poverty of Abundance*, 192–93.

345. *U.S. Statutes at Large* 47 (July 22, 1932): 725; Kennedy, *Freedom from Fear*, 83–84.

346. *Congressional Record*, 72nd Cong., 1st Sess. Vol. 75 Part 13 (July 5, 1932): S 14563–64.

347. "Home Loan Banks Open Doors Today," *New York Times*, October 15, 1932, 2.

348. "First Loan and Repealer," *Time*, December 26, 1932, 6–7.

349. "Easing of Home Mortgage Burden Forecast Under Federal Loan Program," *New York Times*, October 9, 1932, RE 1.

350. "U.S. Orders Halt on Foreclosures," *Wall Street Journal*, August 27, 1932, 1.

351. "Pinchot Urges U.S. to Aid Unemployed," *Atlanta Constitution*, December 1, 1931, 10.

352. Huthmacher, *Wagner*, 89–102.

353. "Poor Relief and the Beggar States," *Chicago Daily Tribune*, June 1, 1932, 12.

354. Andrews, *History of Labor*, 3: 241.

355. *Congressional Record* 72nd Cong., 1st Sess. Vol. 75 Part 8 (April 19, 1932): S 8467–70.

356. *U.S. Statutes at Large* 47 (1932): 709.

357. Schlesinger, *The Crisis of the Old Order*, 241.

358. Sautter, "Government and Unemployment," 83–85.

359. Romasco, *The Poverty of Abundance*, 224–26.

360. Sautter, "Government and Unemployment," 83.

361. *U.S. Statutes at Large*, 47 (June 6, 1932): 169.

362. Patterson, *The New Deal and the States*, 12.

363. *Congressional Record*, 72nd Cong., 1st Sess. Vol. 75 Part 3 (January 28, 1932): H 2919.

364. "Urges Bill to Pension Aged," *New York Times*, March 27, 1932, 18; "Slump Spurs Drive for Grants to Aged," Ibid., March 31, 1932, 23.

365. Clinton W. Gilbert, "The People Against Pork," *Atlantic Monthly*, August 1932, 132–36.

366. Commager, Morison, *Growth of the American Republic*, 5th ed., 2:646–47.

367. Amity Schlaes, *The Forgotten Man: A New History of the Great Depression* (New York: HarperCollins, 2007), 128–29.

368. William, *Huey Long*, 581.

369. "The Roosevelt Week," *Time*, July 11, 1932, 10–11.

370. *National Party Platforms*, 331–32.

371. Ibid., 339–51.

372. Schlesinger, *Crisis of the Old Order*, 433–34.

373. Quoted in Ibid., 434.

374. Ibid.

375. "10,000 Cheer the Nominee," *New York Times*, September 15, 1932, 1; "Roosevelt Steps Left and Right," *The New Republic*, September 28, 1932, 164–65. See also William R. Johnson, "National Farm Organizations and the Reshaping of Agricultural Policy in 1932," *Agricultural History* 37, no. 1 (January 1963): 35–42.

376. "Governor Roosevelt Gives Views on Aiding Jobless," *Chicago Daily Tribune*, October 14, 1932, 1.

377. Beasley, Smith, *Carter Glass*, 471–95.

378. Schlesinger, *Crisis of the Old Order*, 432, 434.

379. *Campaign Speeches of 1932 by President Hoover and ex-President Coolidge* (Garden City, NJ: Doubleday, Doran & Co., 1933), 139–66.

380. Ibid., 167–96.

381. "Roosevelt's Revolution," *The New Republic*, November 9, 1932, 340–41.

382. Hicks, *The Republican Ascendancy*, 277–78.

SELECT BIBLIOGRAPHY

Baker, Jean. *Affairs of Party: The Political Culture of Northern Democrats in the Mid-Nineteenth Century*. Ithaca, NY: Cornell University Press, 1983.

Balogh, Brian. *A Government Out of Sight: The Mystery of National Authority in Nineteenth Century America*. New York: Cambridge University Press, 2009.

Barnett, Randy. "The Original Meaning of the Commerce Clause." *University of Chicago Law Review* 68, no. 1 (Winter 2001): 101–47.

Barry, John M. *Rising Tide: The Great Mississippi Flood of 1927 and How It Changed America*. New York: Simon & Schuster, 1997.

Baum, Dale. *The Civil War Party System: The Case of Massachusetts, 1848–76*. Chapel Hill: University of North Carolina Press, 1984.

Beasley, Norman, and Rixey Smith. *Carter Glass: A Biography*. New York: Longmans, Green, 1939.

Beck, James M. *Our Wonderland of Bureaucracy: A Study of the Growth of the Bureaucracy in the Federal Government, and Its Destructive Effects Upon the Constitution*. New York: Macmillan Company, 1932.

Bensel, Richard Franklin. *Yankee Leviathan: The Origins of Central State Authority in America, 1859–77*. New York: Cambridge University Press, 1990.

Berger, Raoul. *Government by Judiciary: The Transformation of the Fourteenth Amendment*. Cambridge, MA: Harvard University Press, 1977; Indianapolis, IN: Liberty Fund, 1997.

Blaine, James G. *Thirty Years of Congress: From Lincoln to Garfield*. Norwich, CT: Henry Bill, 1886.

Bowers, Claude G. *Beveridge and the Progressive Era*. New York: Houghton Mifflin, 1932.

Bowers, Claude G. *The Tragic Era: The Revolution after Lincoln*. Cambridge, MA: Houghton Mifflin, 1929.

Brands, H. W. *The Reckless Decade: America in the 1890's*. New York: St. Martin's Press, 1995.

Brodsky, Alyn. *Grover Cleveland: A Study in Character*. New York: St. Martin's Press, 2000.

Bryce, James. *The American Commonwealth*. New York: The Macmillan Company, 1910.

Burrows, Edwin G., and Mike Wallace. *Gotham: A History of New York City to 1898*. New York: Oxford University Press, 1999.

Campaign Speeches of 1932 by President Hoover and Ex-President Coolidge. Garden City, NJ: Doubleday, Doran & Company, 1933.

Carter, Susan B. *Historical Statistics of the United States: Earliest Times to the Present*. 5 vols. Millennial Edition, five volumes, New York: Cambridge University Press, 2006.

Castel, Albert. *The Presidency of Andrew Johnson*. Lawrence, KS: The Regents Press of Kansas, 1979.

Chace, James, *1912: Wilson, Roosevelt, Taft & Debs—the Election That Changed the Country*. New York: Simon & Schuster, 2004.

Clark, Champ. *My Quarter Century of American Politics*. New York: Harper & Brothers, 1920.

Coletta, Paolo E. *The Presidency of William Howard Taft*. Lawrence, KS: The University Press of Kansas, 1973.

Coletta, Paolo E. *William Jennings Bryan. Vol. 1: Political Evangelist, 1860–1908*. Lincoln, NE: University of Nebraska Press, 1964.

The Collected Works of William Howard Taft, David H. Burton, General Editor. Athens, OH: Ohio University Press, 2001.

Commager, Henry Steele, and Samuel Eliot Morison. *The Growth of the American Republic*. 5th ed. New York: Oxford University Press, 1962.

Commager, Henry Steele, William E. Leuchtenberg, and Samuel Eliot Morison. *The Growth of the American Republic*. 7th ed. New York: Oxford University Press, 1980.

Corwin, Edward S. "The Spending Power of Congress—Apropros the Maternity Act." *Harvard Law Review* 36, no. 5 (March 1923): 548–75.

Cox, Samuel S. *Three Decades of Federal Legislation*. Providence, RI: Reid, 1886.

Croly, Herbert. *The Promise of American Life*. New York: Macmillan, 1909; Boston: Northeastern University Press, 1989.

Cullom, Shelby H. *Fifty Years of Public Service*. Chicago: A. C. McClurg, 1911.

Cummings, Homer, and Carl McFarland. *Federal Justice: Chapters in the History of Justice and the Federal Executive*. New York: Macmillan, 1937.

Currie, David P. "The Civil War Congress." *University of Chicago Law Review* 73, no. 4 (Fall 2006): 1131–226.

Currie, David P. *The Constitution in the Supreme Court: The First Hundred Years, 1789–1887*. Chicago: University of Chicago Press, 1985.

Currie, David P. *The Constitution in the Supreme Court: The Second Hundred Years, 1888–1986*. Chicago: University of Chicago Press, 1990.

Currie, David P. "The Reconstruction Congress." *University of Chicago Law Review* 75 (Winter 2008): 1, 383–495.

Daniels, Josephus. *Editor in Politics*. Chapel Hill: The University of North Carolina Press, 1941.

Daniels, Josephus. *The Wilson Era: Years of Peace, 1910–1917*. Chapel Hill: The University of North Carolina Press, 1944.

de Santis, Vincent P. "Republican Efforts to 'Crack' the Democratic South." *The Review of Politics* 14, no. 2 (April 1952): 244–64.

Doenecke, Justin M. *The Presidencies of James A. Garfield and Chester A. Arthur*. Lawrence, KS: The University Press of Kansas, 1981.

Dupree, A. Hunter. *Science in the Federal Government: A History of Policies and Activities to 1940*. Cambridge, MA: Harvard University Press, 1957.

Ely, James W., Jr. *Railroads and American Law*. Lawrence, KS: University Press of Kansas, 2001.

Epstein, Richard. "The Proper Scope of the Commerce Power." *Virginia Law Review*, 73, no. 8 (November 1987): 1387–1455.

Farber, Daniel. *Lincoln's Constitution*. Chicago: University of Chicago Press, 2003.

Faulkner, Harold U. *Politics, Reform and Expansion, 1890–1900*. New York: Harper & Brothers, 1959.

Fausold, Martin L. *The Presidency of Herbert C. Hoover*. Lawrence, KS: The University Press of Kansas, 1985.

Foner, Eric. *Reconstruction: America's Unfinished Revolution, 1863–1877*. New York: Harper & Row, 1988.

Fowler, Dorothy Ganfield. *John Coit Spooner: Defender of Presidents*. New York: University Publishers, 1961.

Frankfurter, Felix. *The Commerce Clause under Marshall, Taney and Waite*. Chapel Hill: The University of North Carolina Press, 1937.

Friedman, Milton, and Anna Jacobson Schwartz. *A Monetary History of the United States, 1867–1960*. Princeton, NJ: Princeton University Press, 1963.

Garraty, John M. *The New Commonwealth, 1877–1890*. New York: Harper & Row, 1968.

Gillette, William. *Retreat from Reconstruction, 1869–1879*. Baton Rouge, LA: Louisiana State University Press, 1979.

Glasson, William Henry. *History of Military Pension Legislation of the United States*. New York: The Columbia University Press, 1900.

Going, Allen J. "The South and the Blair Education Bill." *Mississippi Valley Historical Review* 44, no. 2 (September 1957): 267–90.

Hagedorn, Ann. *Savage Peace: Hope and Fear in America, 1919*. New York: Simon & Schuster, 2007.

Hayes, Benjamin. *The Diary of a President, 1875–1881*. Edited by T. Harry Williams. New York: David McKay, 1964.

Hicks, John D. *The Populist Revolt: A History of the Farmers' Alliance and the People's Party*. Minneapolis: University of Minnesota Press, 1931; Lincoln, NE: University of Nebraska Press, 1961.

Hicks, John D. *Republican Ascendancy, 1921–1933*. New York: Harper & Bros., 1960.

Hicks, John D., and Theodore Saloutos. *Agricultural Discontent in the Middle West, 1900–1939*. Madison, WI: University of Wisconsin Press, 1951.

Hirshson, Stanley P. *Farewell to the Bloody Shirt: Northern Republicans and the Southern Negro, 1877–1893*. Bloomington, IN: Indiana University Press, 1962.

Hoar, George F. *Autobiography of Seventy Years*. 2 vols. New York: Charles Scribner's Sons, 1903.

Hofstadter, Richard. *The Age of Reform: From Bryan to F.D.R.* New York: Alfred A. Knopf, 1966.

Hoogenboom, Ari. *The Presidency of Rutherford B. Hayes*. Lawrence, KS: The University Press of Kansas, 1988.

Hoover, Herbert. *The New Day: Campaign Speeches of Herbert Hoover of 1928*. Stanford, CA: Stanford University Press, 1929.

Huthmacher, J. Joseph. *Senator Robert Wagner and the Rise of Urban Liberalism*. New York: Atheneum, 1968.

Johnson, Kimberly S. *Governing the American State: Congress and the New Federalism, 1877–1929*. Princeton, NJ: Princeton University Press, 2007.

Johnson, Paul. *A History of the American People*. New York: Harper Collins, 1997.

Kehl, James H. *Boss Rule in the Gilded Age: Matt Quay of Pennsylvania*. Pittsburgh: University of Pittsburgh Press, 1981.

Kennedy, David M. *Freedom from Fear: The American People in Depression and War, 1929–1945*. New York: Oxford University Press, 1999.

Kennedy, David M. *Over Here: The First World War and American Society*. New York: Oxford University Press, 1980.

Key, V. O., Jr. *The Administration of Federal Grants to States*. Chicago: Public Administration Service, 1937.

Keyssar, Alexander. *The Right to Vote: The Contested History of Democracy in the United States*. New York: Basic Books, 2000.

Kimmel, Lewis H. *Federal Budget and Fiscal Policy, 1789–1958*. Washington, DC: The Brookings Institution, 1959.

Kolko, Gabriel. *Railroads and Regulation, 1877–1916*. Princeton, NJ: Princeton University Press, 1965.

LaFollette, Robert M. *La Follette's Autobiography: A Personal Narrative of Political Experiences*. Madison, WI: The Robert M. La Follette Company, 1913; Madison, WI: The University of Wisconsin Press, 1960.

Leech, Margaret. *In the Days of McKinley*. New York: Harper & Brothers, 1959.

Leech, Margaret. *Reveille in Washington*. New York: Harper & Brothers, 1941.

Link, Arthur S. *The Road to the White House*. Princeton, NJ: Princeton University Press, 1947.

Link, Arthur S. *Woodrow Wilson and the Progressive Era, 1910–1917*. New York: Harper & Brothers, 1954.

Lofgren, Charles A. *The Plessy Case: A Legal-Historical Interpretation*. New York: Oxford University Press, 1987.

Martin, Albro. *Enterprise Declined: Origins of the Decline of American Railroads, 1897–1917*. New York: Columbia University Press, 1971.

Martis, Kenneth. *The Historical Atlas of Political Parties in the United States Congress, 1789–1989*. New York: Macmillan, 1989.

Matz, Earl M. *Civil Rights, Congress and the Constitution*. Lawrence, KS: University Press of Kansas, 1990.

Maxey, Edwin. "Federal Quarantine Laws." *Political Science Quarterly*. 23, no. 4 (December, 1908): 617–36.

McFeely, William S. *Grant: A Biography*. New York: W.W. Norton 1981.

McLaughlin, Andrew C. *A Constitutional History of the United States*. New York: D. Appleton-Century Co., 1935.

McPherson, James *Battle Cry of Freedom: The Civil War Era*. New York: Oxford University Press, 1987.

Merrill, Horace Samuel. *Bourbon Democracy of the Middle West, 1865–96*. Baton Rouge, LA: Louisiana State University Press, 1953.

Mitchell, Lawrence E. *The Speculation Economy: How Finance Triumphed Over Industry*. San Francisco: Berrett Koehler, 2007.

Morison, Samuel Eliot. *The Oxford History of the American People*. New York: Oxford University Press, 1965.

Morris, Edmund. *Theodore Rex*. New York: Random House, 2001.

Mowry, George E. *The Era of Theodore Roosevelt and the Birth of Modern America, 1900–1912*. New York: Harper & Row, 1958.

National Party Platforms 1840–1956. Edited by Donald Bruce Johnson and Kirk H. Porter. Champaign, IL: University of Illinois Press, 1956.

Nevins, Allan. *Grover Cleveland: A Study in Courage*. New York: Dodd, Mead, 1932.

Nevins, Allan. *Hamilton Fish: The Inner History of the Grant Administration*. 2 vols. New York: Frederick Ungar, 1936.

Nevins, Allan. *The War for the Union*. 4 vols. New York: Charles Scribner's Sons, 1959–71.

Patterson, James T. *The States and the New Deal: Federalism in Transition*. Princeton, NJ: Princeton University Press, 1969.

Peterson, Merrill. *The Jefferson Image in the American Mind*. New York: Oxford University Press, 1960.

Pierce, Franklin. *Federal Usurpation*. New York: D. Appleton & Company, 1908.

Pisani, Donald J. "Federal Reclamation and the American West in the Twentieth Century." *Agricultural History* 77, no. 3 (Summer 2003): 391–419.

Procter, Ben H. *Not Without Honor: The Life of John H. Reagan*. Austin, TX: University of Texas Press, 1962.

Randall, James G. *Constitutional Problems under Lincoln*. Champaign, IL: University of Illinois Press, 1951.

Reagan, John H. *Memoirs*. New York: Neale, 1906.

Reitano, Joanne. *The Tariff Question in the Gilded Age: The Great Debate of 1888*. University Park, PA: The Pennsylvania State University Press, 1994.

Rhodes, James Ford. *History of the United States from the Compromise of 1850 to the End of the Roosevelt Administration*. 9 vols. New York: Macmillan, 1928.

Richardson, Heather Cox. *The Greatest Nation on Earth: Republican Economic Policies during the Civil War*. Cambridge, MA: Harvard University Press, 1997.

Richardson, Heather Cox. *West from Appomattox: The Reconstruction of America after the Civil War*. New Haven, CT: Yale University Press, 2007.

Romasco, Albert U. *The Poverty of Abundance: Hoover, the Nation, the Depression*. New York: Oxford University Press, 1965.

Roosevelt, Theodore. *The New Nationalism*. New York: Outlook, 1911.

Roosevelt, Theodore. *The Works of Theodore Roosevelt*. Edited by Hermann Hagedorn, 20 vols. New York: Charles Scribner's Sons, 1926–27.

Roosevelt, Theodore. *The Rough Riders/An Autobiography*. Edited by Louis Auchincloss. New York: Literary Classics of the United States, 2004.

Rossum, Ralph A. *Federalism, the Supreme Court and the Seventeenth Amendment: The Irony of Constitutional Democracy*. Lanham, MD: Lexington Books, 2001.

Sandburg, Carl. *Abraham Lincoln: The War Years*. 4 vols. New York: Harcourt, Brace, 1936–39.

Schlaes, Amity. *The Forgotten Man: A New History of the Great Depression*. New York: HarperCollins, 2007.

Schlereth, Thomas J. *Victorian America: Transformations in Everyday Life, 1876–1915*. New York: HarperCollins, 1991.

Schlesinger, Arthur M., Jr. *The Age of Roosevelt*. 3 vols. Boston: Houghton Mifflin, 1957.

Schuyler, Lorraine Gates. *The Weight of their Votes: Southern Women and Political Leverage in the 1920s*. Chapel Hill: University of North Carolina Press, 2006.

Shannon, Fred Albert. *The Organization and Administration of the Union Army*. Cleveland: Arthur Clark, 1928.

Skocpol, Theda. "America's First Social Security System: The Expansion of Benefits for Civil War Veterans." *Political Science Quarterly*, 108, no. 1 (Spring 1993): 85–116.

Skowronek, Stephen. *Building a New American State: The Expansion of National Administrative Capacities, 1877–1920*. New York: Cambridge University Press, 1982.

Smith, Alfred E. *Campaign Addresses of Governor Alfred E. Smith, Democratic Candidate for President 1928*. Washington, DC: Democratic National Committee, 1929.

Smith, Culver H. *Press, Politics and the Patronage: The American Government's Use of Newspapers, 1789–1875*. Athens, GA: University of Georgia Press, 1977.

Sobel, Robert. *Coolidge: An American Enigma*. Washington, DC: Regnery, 1998.

Spero, Sterling D. "Collective Bargaining in the Public Service." *Annals of the American Academy of Political and Social Science* 248 (November 1946): 146–53.

Stone, Wilmer T. "Can America Endure—a Plea for National Centralization." *The Sewanee Review* 24, no. 4 (October 1916): 393–411.

Summers, Mark W. *The Era of Good Stealings*. New York: Oxford University Press, 1993.

Summers, Mark W. *Party Games: Getting, Keeping and Using Power in Gilded Age Politics*. Chapel Hill: The University of North Carolina Press, 2004.

Summers, Mark W. *The Press Gang: Newspapers and Politics, 1865–78*. Chapel Hill: The University of North Carolina Press, 1994.

Summers, Mark W. *Rum, Romanism and Rebellion: The Making of the President 1884*. Chapel Hill: University of North Carolina Press, 2000.

Swisher, Carl Brent. *American Constitutional Development*. New York: Houghton Mifflin, 1954.

Taussig, F. W. *The Tariff History of the United States*. New York: G. P. Putnam's Sons, 1892, 1930.

These United States: Portraits of America from the 1920's. Edited by Daniel H. Borus. Ithaca, NY: Cornell University Press, 1992.

Thompson, Walter. *Federal Centralization: A Study and Criticism of the Expanding Scope of Congressional Legislation*. New York: Harcourt, Brace, 1923.

Unger, Irwin. *The Greenback Era: A Social and Political History of American Finance, 1865–79*. Princeton, NJ: Princeton University Press, 1964.

Van Riper, Paul. *History of the United States Civil Service*. Evanston, IL: Row, Peterson, 1958.

Villard, Oswald Garrison. *Fighting Years: Memoirs of a Liberal Editor*. New York: Harcourt, Brace and Company, 1939.

Warren, Charles. *Congress as Santa Clause or National Donations and the General Welfare Clause of the Constitution*. Charlottesville, VA: Michie Co., 1932.

Warren, Charles. *The Supreme Court in United States History*. 2 vols. Boston: Little, Brown and Company, 1937.

Washburn, Wilcomb E. *The Indian in America*. New York: Harper & Row, 1975.

Welles, Gideon. *Diary of Gideon Welles*. Edited by Howard K. Beale. 3 vols. New York: W.W. Norton, 1960.

White, Leonard. *The Republican Era, 1869–1901: A Study in Administrative History*. New York: Macmillan, 1958.

White, William Allen, *The Autobiography of William Allen White*. New York: Macmillan, 1946.

Wilson, Mark. *The Business of Civil War: Military Mobilization and the State, 1861–1865*. Baltimore: Johns Hopkins University Press, 2006.

Wilson, Woodrow. *The Papers of Woodrow Wilson*. Edited by Arthur Link. 69 vols. Princeton, NJ: Princeton University Press, 1966–94.

Wooddy, Carroll H. *The Growth of the Federal Government, 1915–1932*. New York: McGraw-Hill, 1934.

Woodward, C. Vann. *Origins of the New South, 1877–1913*. Baton Rouge, LA: Louisiana State University Press, 1951.

Yearley, C. K. *The Money Machines: The Breakdown and Reform of Governmental and Party Finance in the North, 1860–1920*. Albany, NY: State University of New York Press, 1970.

INDEX

About the Author

PETER ZAVODNYIK is a lawyer in private practice in Chicago. Mr. Zavodnyik has written *The Age of Strict Construction: A History of the Growth of Federal Power, 1789–1861* (Washington, DC: The Catholic University of America Press, 2007).